THE HARMONIOUS CIRCLE

THE
HARMONIOUS
CIRCLE

*The Lives and Work of
G. I. Gurdjieff, P. D. Ouspensky,
and Their Followers*

by
James Webb

G. P. Putnam's Sons
New York

Library of Congress Cataloging in Publication Data

Webb, James, date.
   The harmonious circle.

   1. Gurdjieff, Georges Ivanovitch, 1872–
1949. 2. Philosophers—Russia—Biography.
3. Mystics—Russia—Biography. I. Title.
B4249.G84W4 1978   133′.092′4   B 77-16261
ISBN 0-399-11465-3

Printed in the United States of America

Acknowledgments

I am grateful to the following for permission to quote from copyright and unpublished sources:

For permission to quote from the works of G. I. Gurdjieff: Routledge and Kegan Paul Ltd.; Triangle Editions Inc. For permission to quote from the work of P. D. Ouspensky: Routledge and Kegan Paul Ltd.; Hodder and Stoughton Ltd.; Faber and Faber Ltd.; Turnstone Press Ltd.; Mrs. Tanya Nagro; Alfred A. Knopf Inc.; Harcourt Brace Jovanovich Inc. For permission to quote from the work and unpublished letters of A. R. Orage: Mrs. Jessie Orage; Artemis Press Ltd. For permission to quote from the work and unpublished papers of Jean Toomer: Mrs. Marjorie Content Toomer. For permission to quote from the work of Maurice Nicoll; Watkins Publishing. For permission to quote from the work of Rodney Collin: Mrs. Chloe Dickins; Watkins Publishing. For permission to quote from the work of J. G. Bennett: Hodder and Stoughton Ltd.; Turnstone Press Ltd. For permission to quote from the work of Katherine Mansfield: The Society of Authors; Alfred A. Knopf Inc. For permission to quote from the work of John Middleton Murry: The Society of Authors. For permission to quote from the work of Jane Heap and Margaret Anderson: Mr. Michael Currer-Briggs. For permission to quote from the work of Margaret Anderson: Routledge and Kegan Paul Ltd.; Samuel Weiser Inc. For permission to quote from the work of Fritz Peters: Victor Gollancz Ltd.; Samuel Weiser

Inc. For permission to quote from the work of T. S. Eliot: Faber and Faber Ltd.; Harcourt Brace Jovanovich Inc.; New Directions Publishing Corporation, Inc. For permission to quote from the work of Waldo Frank: Mrs. Jean Frank. For permission to quote from a broadcast talk: Mr. J. M. Cohen. For permission to quote from private letters: the late A. S. Neill; Mr. J. B. Priestley. For permission to quote from her work: Mrs. Irmis Barrett Popoff. For permission to quote from the work of Thomas and Olga de Hartmann: Cooper Square Publishers Inc. For permission to quote from the work of Rom Landau and Paul Selver: Allen and Unwin Ltd. For permission to quote from the work of Rowland Kenney: J. M. Dent and Sons Ltd. For permission to quote from the work of Philip Mairet: J.M. Dent and Sons Ltd.; University Books Inc. For permission to quote from the work of William Seabrook: George G. Harrap and Co. Ltd.; A. Watkins Inc. For permission to quote from the work of Paul Selver: Allen and Unwin Ltd. For permission to quote from the work of Boris Mouravieff: Mme. Larissa Mouravieff; Le Centre d'Etudes Chrétiennes Esoteriques. For permission to quote from the work of Michel Random: Editions Denoël. For permission to quote from work by C. Daly King: University Books Inc. For permission to quote from the work of William Welch: George Braziller Inc. For permission to quote from the work of C. E. Bechhofer Roberts: David Higham Associates Ltd. For permission to quote from the work of James Young: Mrs. Marcelle Hasenfratz-Young. For permission to quote from the work of Sir Paul Dukes: A. P. Watt and Son. For permission to quote from the work of Edwin and Willa Muir: The Hogarth Press Ltd. For permission to quote from the work of F. E. Lea: Methuen and Co. Ltd. For permission to quote from the work of Kathryn Hulme: A. M. Heath and Co. Ltd.; Little, Brown and Co.; the Atlantic Monthly Press. For permission to quote from the work of Beryl Pogson: Watkins Publishing. For permission to quote from the work of Mabel Dodge Luhan: Martin Secker and Warburg Ltd. For permission to quote from from the work of T. S. Matthews: Mr. T. S. Matthews; Anthony Blond Ltd. For permission to quote from Roger Shattuck's translation of the work of René Daumal: Watkins Publishing; Pantheon Books/Random House. For permission to quote from the work of Monk Gibbon: Rupert Hart-Davis/ Granada Publishing; Macmillan Publishing Co. Inc. For permission to quote from the work of John Unterecker: Anthony Blond Ltd.; Farrar, Straus and Giroux Inc. For permission to quote from the work of Alan Watts: Jonathan Cape Ltd.; Pantheon Books/Random House. For permission to quote from the work of Joseph Wood Krutch: Harcourt Brace Jovanovich Inc. For permission to quote from the work of Edmund Wilson: Farrar, Straus and Giroux Inc. For permission to quote from the work of J. B. Priestley: William Heinemann Ltd.; A. D. Peters and Co. Ltd.;

Doubleday and Co., Inc. For permission to quote from Brom Weber's edition of the letters of Hart Crane: The University of California Press. For permission to quote from H. P. D. Lee's translation of Plato's *Timaeus:* Penguin Books Ltd. For permission to quote from from David Magarshack's translation of Dostoievsky's *The Brothers Karamazov:* Penguin Books Ltd. For permission to quote from the work of Claude Bragdon: Alfred A. Knopf Inc. I am required to state that *In Search of the Miraculous* is copyright 1949 by Harcourt Brace Jovanovich Inc.

Every effort had been made to communicate with holders of copyright material, but in some cases it has proved impossible to establish contact. The author and publishers apologize to anyone who has been overlooked because of circumstances beyond their control.

Contents

Preface

"You have taken on a large task," warned one well-known author who had known Gurdjieff. "Looking for G. historically must be like looking for the historical Moses." The analogy appeared increasingly apt as my work on this book progressed. For who was Moses? And *what* was Moses? A historical figure or a myth? And if the latter, with what motives did the mythmakers start to weave their glittering fabric? In the case of Moses we even begin with an enigma: the mysterious child abandoned in the bulrushes. In the case of Gurdjieff, the situation is not much different.

A biographer in search of the authentic Gurdjieff begins by suspecting a campaign of mystification—and to some extent he may continue to hold this opinion. Part of the difficulty is that there has never been a book written about Gurdjieff and his followers by someone not personally involved in their activities; and the grinding of axes among the Master's successors has resulted in much of what has been written being—either deliberately or unconsciously—distorted. Ten years ago J. B. Priestley appealed in his *Man and Time* for an assessment by an independent writer. This is the first attempt to provide such a book, and at the same time to tell a fascinating story before the possibilities of telling it are obliterated forever. The book is largely based on unpublished documents and interviews—some with people now dead; it seeks also to place in historical context the extensive and confusing body of literature concerning Gurdjieff, Ouspensky, Orage and their leading followers.

There are peculiar difficulties in the way of the would-be independent critic of Gurdjieff. The geographical obstacles to far-flung research are considerable; but as it was, I ranged from Austria to Tennessee. In Vienna the Keyserlings demonstrated their extraordinary musical instrument, the Chakraphone, until the hairs on the back of my neck rose like the hackles of a dog; in Geneva I was kindly received by Mme. de Stoerneval in her house, which had been the last home of the novelist Robert Musil; in Paris Pierre Schaeffer interrupted a busy life to spend two hours discussing the decadence of modern music and the structure of the universe; whether in London, New York, or Paris, I was helped on my way by a stimulating variety of people.

However, in only a very few cases have I introduced the names of living persons whose role in events has hitherto been unknown. This is largely because the particular problems of gathering information about "the Work" involved threading my way through a labyrinth of "political" complications, some of which were probably real, others, almost certainly manufactured. Some of my informants asked me not to use their names, others did not mind being mentioned, and some actually forbade me to use any information without stating from what source it came. Sometimes it seemed that such requests were part of a particular game which was in progress—and the reader will have to go some way into the book before he understands what is meant. In order to eliminate such uncertainties and to avoid deploying a large cast of peripheral characters, I have reduced most of my informants to anonymity. The reader will have to accept my word that (to take some examples), "a pupil of Ouspensky," "a follower of Orage," or "an inmate of the Prieuré" actually exists, and my judgment of each as a reliable source of information.

Both the subject matter and my sources have placed certain limitations on the book, which it is the duty of a preface to indicate. Some limitations are voluntarily imposed. The music written jointly by Gurdjieff and Thomas de Hartmann and the body of dances and physical exercises known as Gurdjieff's "movements," are not discussed in detail. This is partly for reasons of space, but chiefly because the book is primarily a historical and biographical study concerned with certain aspects of psychology. But—to take the movements as an instance—those limitations make a virtue of necessity. I have read about the movements, talked about them, listened to the music which accompanies them, and inspected notebooks in which the sequence of positions is recorded. I think I have a shrewd idea of what the movements are designed to achieve. But I have not practiced them myself, nor have I seen a live performance or a showing of the films on which they are recorded. This is not for want of trying.

Other limitations imposed on this book come neither from the economics of publishing nor the elusive quality of the subject. They result from a deliberate policy of obstruction on the part of some of Gurdjieff's followers. There can be no real quarrel with this, because these followers are acting in complete good faith, protecting what they see as the integrity of the ideas with which they have been entrusted. There is no reason whatever for someone to cooperate in an undertaking of which he or she may thoroughly disapprove. I have been refused permission to quote from certain unpublished writings, and it is also probable that a large quantity of potentially useful information has been withheld or suppressed.

Gurdjieff's successors have provided a sort of limited cooperation—which in some cases went far beyond the bounds of anything I had a right to expect—but in others seemed like a hand proferred only to turn into a clenched fist. In addition, it was always open to my informants to transform what seemed a straightforward process of research into the kind of ambiguous situation which Gurdjieff excelled in creating. In fact, it eventually became clear that an attempt was being made to ensnare me forcibly in the sort of activities about which I had hoped to write from a detached point of view.

I must admit that this attempt was temporarily successful, and I am certain that it greatly helped me to understand the nature of Gurdjieff's curious discipline. Yet the ethics of the situation continue to puzzle me. At one point I suspected that I had been manipulated into writing the sort of book which the hierarchy wanted written; at another that the attempt to engorge me in the Work was designed to ensure that no book would be written at all. While very much in debt to certain people for the pains taken on my behalf, I must remain skeptical of the good faith of others.

Why all this secrecy? Partly it can be explained by the nature of the Work, which has little interest in coherent explanations, and partly as the consequence of decades of unthinking ridicule. Some followers of Gurdjieff and Ouspensky have uncomfortably thin skins and what must be a uniquely developed ability to see criticism where none is intended. This characteristic can militate against any view of the Work as a serious discipline and makes it impossible to believe in the strict accuracy of assertions made from within the movement. The resulting impression is of a morbid fear of criticism and a tendency to play fast and loose with historical fact. But to leave matters there would not be entirely fair either to Gurdjieff or to the better natures of his followers.

On one level Gurdjieff was a fraud, a liar, a cheat, and a scoundrel. He also possessed compensating qualities of sympathy, compassion, charity, and an eccentric code of honor. He attempted to use the friction generated by his negative qualities to strike fire from the hearts of his disciples; and Gurdjieff's successors have studied their Master's technique. Are they really so insecure as to fear any criticism? Do they in fact wish to canonize Gurdjieff, Ouspensky, Orage, and Nicoll? Or, are such attitudes designed to reproduce the impression that Gurdjieff himself made on those who encountered him?

The historian must separate hard historical fact from evidence of another sort. Individuals "in the Work" are often unreliable sources of historical information. On the other hand, their very equivocation makes it possible to recapture something of the uncertainty which they themselves experienced when they approached the Old Magician. In the last analysis, this may be more useful than any conventional assistance. I have therefore to acknowledge help of an unusual nature, while at the same time, the interests of future writers compel me to register doubts. The reader should be warned that—despite constant vigilance—incidents may have crept into these pages which were intended as fables illustrating particular points, or even as moral allegories directed at the author.

Because of the circumstances that compelled me to choose anonymity for many of my informants, I cannot acknowledge some of my greatest debts; and it would be invidious to name some who helped me while other names were absent. All I can do is offer a general expression of gratitude to at least fifty people, named or unnamed, who corresponded with me, allowed me to interview them, lent me rare or unpublished material, or undertook the thankless task of criticizing my typescript.

Of those debts which can be acknowledged in conventional fashion, I should like to thank the librarians and staffs of the University Library, Cambridge, the British Museum, the London Library, the Warburg Institute, University of London, the Public Record Office, the India Office Library, the Bibliothèque Nationale, Paris, the town library at Fontainebleau, the Bayerische Staatsbibliothek, Munich, the New York Public Library, and the Special Collections Department of the Library, Fisk University, Nashville, Tennessee. For academic (as distinct from Gurdjieffian) assistance, I am grateful to Drs. Phillippe Berchtold and Edmond Stadler (Geneva), Trevor Hall (Leeds), and Michael Weaver (Exeter). I am particularly indebted to Stanley Baron and Frances McFadyen for their patient advice on the reduction of a typescript of over one thousand pages to more manageable proportions.

In the pages which follow, a scholarly reader might object to certain inconsistencies. Transliterations from the Russian do not always follow the same system: it seems unnecessary to complicate matters by transforming P. D. Ouspensky into "P.D. Uspenskii" because this spelling conforms to a system of transliteration in general use. If a person in the story is commonly known by one particular spelling of his name, that should be sufficient reason for using it: one could spell "Gurdjieff" "Gourdjieff," or "Gurdjiev," and a more fashionable transliteration might be "Gurdzhiev." Nor are Russian women's names always accurately rendered: it is clearly unnecessary to call Sophia Grigorievna Ouspensky "Ouspenskaya," which was her real name. The same sort of liberties have been taken with place-names in Russia and the East; in all cases I have preferred spellings used by the followers of Gurdjieff themselves.

London, November 1978

Introduction

The Invisible Man, the Impossible Task

One day in the late 1920s a ferociously driven automobile might have been seen traveling along the Paris-Orléans road. If the driver were keeping to his usual custom, the journey would have been nerve racking in the extreme; and the psasengers would be jolted, bruised, and scared as they read from a manuscript which appeared to recount the unflattering opinions of Beelzebub on the human race. It is reported that one of the captives in the car risked a glance out of the window. He saw that the road which his determined chauffeur was so wantonly traversing was dominated by a gigantic figure of Christ perched on a hilltop. He decided to risk distracting the driver from the task in hand.

"Georgeivanitch, they have put your colleague up there on the hill!"

The driver—no doubt with a number of choice imprecations—loudly demanded when he had ever said that Christ and he were colleagues. The passenger, who was the artist Alexander de Salzmann, provided chapter and verse: it had been in such and such a place—Tiflis, Constantinople, Berlin—on such and such a day. From the driver's seat came only the sound, "Humph!"

Thirty years later the man who had been driving the car was dead, and mingled with the praises of his followers was a countercurrent of violent criticism. Certain rumors became common property: these concerned Gurdjieff's ways with women, his supposed hypnotic power, his alleged

17

responsibility for several deaths in suspicious circumstances. A Catholic writer published what he called a "Ceremony of Execration" instead of an obituary. A writer in a philosophical journal declared that if Gurdjieff were not an avatar he was a *skandalon*—the term the early Church had used for emissaries of the devil. A more rationalist critic in *Nouvelles Littéraires* fought to combat this alarmism.

"He was not the devil," he wrote, "but a false prophet, a pretentious ignoramus."

If Gurdjieff seemed any of these things, it was only to certain people. For Gurdjieff was an invisible man.

In 1922 this strange individual appeared in Western Europe with a band of followers whom he had rescued from the chaos of the Russian Revolution. He established himself in a château in the Forest of Fontainebleau, where he founded something he called "The Institute for Harmonious Development of Man." Writers and intellectuals were attracted by Gurdjieff's ideas and the lectures which his leading follower, P. D. Ouspensky, was giving in London; and Katherine Mansfield died of tuberculosis at Fontainebleau. In 1924 Gurdjieff and his pupils traveled to New York, where they created a sensation, leaving the celebrated editor A. R. Orage behind to preach the gospel. Then, in the middle of the 1930s, Gurdjieff appeared to quarrel with all his oldest followers. He disappeared from sight until after the Second World War, when, in the few years remaining to him, he again became the enigmatic prophet who fascinated the intellectuals of Europe and America. He died in 1949, leaving behind an enormous work published under the title *All and Everything: First Series*, but more usually known as *Beelzebub's Tales to his Grandson*.

P. D. Ouspensky, who died two years earlier in England, left a record of his time with Gurdjieff in his book *In Search of the Miraculous*. Since its appearance in 1949, there has been a spate of literature reminiscing about Gurdjieff, whose character and teaching are perhaps more controversial today than during his lifetime. The body of activity deriving from Gurdjieff, Ouspensky, and Orage has become known as "the Work," and it has spread to every continent and been extraordinarily influential. Neither a church nor a sect nor a school of philosophy, it is extremely difficult to define.

It is also hard to be precise about its originator. However unwillingly, the biographer must recognize that understanding Gurdjieff's "invisibility" is an essential part of understanding the man; worse yet, this invisibility can only become apparent as the story unfolds. Gurdjieff does not present himself as a man with a continuous life like other men. He seems more to be a collection of incidents.

An old man, sitting in the sun on the terrace of a Paris café, or playing host to a horde of strangers in his tiny flat, a flat packed with people and hot as an oven . . . a man of early middle-age with a bristling mustache, wearing an astrakhan hat and an overcoat, entertaining in a Moscow restaurant frequented by prostitutes, or sitting Oriental fashion in a St. Petersburg salon . . . the same man, this time simply clothed in Caucasian dress, leading a party of terrified intellectuals through mountainous country in a state of civil war, his trousers hitched up by a fireman's belt . . . the hollow-cheeked and hollow-eyed guru who enticed the famous to his Institute at Fontainebleau . . . or the fox of the Levant, up to his eyes in shady financial operations, his dress untidy, spattered with food, his environs a gray snowstorm of cigarette ash, a glint of stratagem in his eye . . . a Man of Power, seducer of women and exploiter of men; monstrous, monstrous Mr. Gurdjieff.

These are all snapshots. The fact that they are not arranged in the order in which they were taken makes no difference.

They represent roles through which, occasionally, the man beneath the role was glimpsed.

All the photographs were taken in a certain context, for a particular purpose, directed at definite people. So the theory goes; and how far it is valid will be for the reader to say. But it would be unfair to tell the story of a man who believed that covering his tracks was an integral part of his work, without trying to show how the very act of making him historical denies what he set out to achieve. Unless the inquirer is aware of the concept of "playing a role," he risks misinterpreting the story of Gurdjieff and his followers altogether. For—except in an unusual and specialized context—it is virtually impossible to assess the motives of any particular person at any particular time. The sense of events will be completely distorted if judged by ordinary standards. What was really happening, for example, when Gurdjieff invited a sweet young thing to his Paris flat at midnight? Perhaps it was to gratify his natural appetites—and why not? Perhaps it was to shock a starry-eyed girl out of her illusions. Perhaps it was simply to see what answer he would receive; there were certainly cases when a girl actually slept in Gurdjieff's flat, after being invited to stay the night, and was completely unmolested. And what was her reaction to being left to sleep alone?

Gurdjieff himself described his apprenticeship in the discipline of role playing in a passage quoted by his follower C. S. Nott from an unpublished work called "A Letter to a Dervish":

The sign of a perfected man and his particularity in ordinary life must be that in regard to everything happening outside him, he is able to, and can in every action, perform to perfection externally the part corresponding to the given situation; but at the same time never blend or agree with it. In my youth, I too . . . worked on myself for the purpose of attaining such a blessing . . . and . . . I finally reached a state when nothing from outside could really touch me internally; and so far as acting was concerned, I brought myself to such perfection as was never dreamed of by the learned people of ancient Babylon for the actors on the stage.

The theory of role playing holds that the technique is an aid to detachment. Outwardly one plays the role in which one is cast, inwardly one becomes free from this role: the object is to detach the sensation of "I" from the experiences and reactions of the organism, while at the same time extending one's range by adopting unfamiliar parts. "'I' am not 'it'" is the motto which the role player must always remember—he must, as Gurdjieff said, "*self*-remember"—even when unjustly accused by a ferocious Gurdjieff who snapped at, cursed, and generally hauled one over the coals.

In his book *Meetings with Remarkable Men,* Gurdjieff illustrates this principle with the fable of "Yelov" and "Pogossian." The two men are extremely close, but conceal their affection under assumed roles. If Yelov is offered a delicacy in a house where politeness demands that he accept it, he resists the pressure to conform; and although he is very fond of the sweet offered to him, he takes it home for his friend Pogossian. But he actually gives the tidbit to his friend with a volley of insults—and Pogossian takes the gift, no doubt aware of the difficulties Yelov had suffered in resisting both convention and his own sweet tooth, and devours the offering while insulting his benefactor in turn.

When writers talk about Gurdjieff, the man, they show only a series of disconnected snapshots; when they talk about his ideas, their books degenerate into a series of logoi, or sayings of Gurdjieff. To avoid distortion the snapshots are mounted in albums and their captions are the briefest possible. For to string the pictures together would be to commit the sin of making history—and history, in Ouspensky's favorite phrase, is "the history of crime." History attends only to unimportant things, and the process of historical selection is arbitrary and misleading. However, some men can avoid the history of crime; and because they are superior to the ordinary run of humanity, they vanish from its ken. They have escaped from the trap, and so far as history is concerned become invisible.

Margaret Anderson, the founder of *The Little Review,* has published an entire book called *The Unknowable Gurdjieff,* partly with the object of proving how a book can never be written about the Master. The American novelist Jean Toomer recorded his uncertainties in some manuscript notes made after more than fifteen years of contact with Gurdjieff. "I do not know G.," he wrote. "I have never known G. I never will." Gurdjieff's invisibility was most complete for those who knew him personally, and the historical observer has a direct advantage over his immediate associates. But for the historian too, Gurdjieff's doctrine of role playing produces a peculiar result. If there is a hidden meaning in every ordinary-seeming event, the story itself soon appears to have a significance independent of its component incidents. The Work assumes the aspect of a living organism, and the various external events which form its history appear to be deliberately created for the benefit of the chronicler. The pattern of discipleship and schism, loyalties and hatreds, takes on the appearance of having been arranged: the actors seem to weave a web of collusion even when they are apparently at daggers drawn.

It is a vast symbol: a glyph etched in history. The glyph is composed not of pen strokes on paper or chisel marks in stone, but of the lives of men and women and their interaction. The long upstroke here indicates Gurdjieff's quest in Central Asia; that convergence of two lines—the last conversation of Orage and Katherine Mansfield; the cross-hatching there stands for countless hirsute Peters and Magdalenes pursuing the reality of that *fons et origo* of the magic influences: Gurdjieff.

It is as if the biographer becomes a scribe occupying a small cell somewhere in the library of Alexandria. It is several hundred years after the birth of Christ, and before him the scribe has set out the interpretation of Christ's teaching made by Origen. This, too, finds a covert meaning in events, records echoes from the harmonies of the universe. The scribe knows the dangers seen in this interpretation by members of Origen's own religion, and he is a skeptical scribe, trained in the schools of Greek rationalism, aware that around him in this city of Alexandria—in this library in particular—there are learned men discussing Buddhism, the Cabala, and texts attributed to Thrice-Great Hermes. This accumulated pressure surrounds the scribe in the corridors of the library, the streets of the great city, and the lecture rooms of the philosophers. He resists it. It is there to be resisted.

Yet, the legend which the wretched Origen has suggested to him is an obsessively interesting one, and he returns to his room to study the codices. He must concede that the aspiration shown by the prophet and his followers is extraordinary. Their goals are, to say the least, uncommon in any century. They want to awaken poor dozing Everyman from his stupor, blow a trumpet in his ear and persuade him to share their struggles, with a view to acquiring a permanent identity which he does not in fact possess, to maintaining perfect control over his largely automatic actions, and by a series of difficult exercises—physical, emotional, and intellectual—to inherit eternal life.

PART 1

"And I beheld the Man . . ."

I saw the Man.

His figure reached from earth to heaven and was clad in a purple mantle. He stood deep in foliage and flowers and his head, on which was the head-band of an initiate, seemed to disappear mysteriously in infinity.

Before him on a cube-shaped altar were four symbols of magic—the sceptre, the cup, the sword and the pentacle.

His right hand pointed to heaven, his left to earth. Under his mantle he wore a white tunic girded with a serpent swallowing its tail.

His face was luminous and serene, and when his eyes met mine, I felt that he saw the most intimate recesses of my soul. I saw myself reflected in him as in a mirror and in his eyes I seemed to look upon myself.

And I heard a voice saying:

—"Look, this is the Great Magician!"

—P. D. OUSPENSKY, *The Symbolism of the Tarot* (St. Petersburg, 1913)

1

The Seeker for Truth

Georgei Ivanovitch Gurdjieff was born . . . and here all pretensions to accuracy stop. He was born; we can insist on that, and it is even fairly certain that he was born in the town of Alexandropol (now Leninakan) on the frontier between Russia and Turkey. But the precise birth date and even Gurdjieff's real name remain debatable, and they are only the first of the difficulties which confront the biographer. Evidence about the career of Gurdjieff is at all stages subject to special qualifications which the story alone can make clear. The man himself delighted in giving countenance to the most absurd tales about his past. This complicates in a peculiar fashion any attempt to reconstruct the story of his life until he appeared in Moscow about the year 1913.

Georgei Ivanovitch Gurdjieff is said to have been born either in 1872 or 1877. Both dates have their supporters, although some writers suggest that he was born in 1886, and the American journalist William Seabrook favored the year 1873. Gurdjieff himself was fond of claiming a life of Methuselahan proportions. Once on a trip to the United States it was discovered that there had been confusion over the details on his passport. Consternation reigned among immigration officials and Gurdjieff's aides. The passport gave his date of birth as sometime in the far distant future. "No mistake," said the veteran of every conceivable traveling difficulty. "No mistake—you go arrange." And somehow things were disentangled. The biographer himself must "go arrange," and opt for the year 1874, for reasons which will become clear in the next chapter.

The day which Gurdjieff himself celebrated as his birthday and which his followers still honor in his memory is January 13. By the Old Style calendar used in Russia until the Revolution, this represents New Year's Day; and as Gurdjieff declared that he had been born precisely at midnight, this may be taken as a purely symbolic birthday. Yet to state bluntly that this extraordinary man was *not* born at midnight, on January 1 Old Style, may well be an unjustified reaction from those who accept the date and derive from it some supernatural significance. People *are* born at midnight: it is even a likely hour for a child to arrive in the world. The double coincidence of hour and date would not be the strangest thing about Georgei Ivanovitch Gurdjieff.

There is also a problem with his name. Gurdjieff was the son of a Greek father and an Armenian mother. Although he spoke both Greek and Armenian, the latter was the language of the Gurdjieff household. Gurd*jieff* is the Russian form of the name which in Armenian society would be rendered Gurd*jian*. Such an alteration was the rule for Asiatic Russians who had dealings with European Russia. William Seabrook states bluntly that Gurdjieff was born "George S. Georgiades," and it is probable that "Georgiades" was the original Greek name of Gurdjieff's father, who altered it to "Gurdjian" when he found himself moving in circles in which Armenian was the lingua franca.

The country where Gurdjieff grew up was an almost unbelievable patchwork of races and religions. In classical times over seventy languages were spoken in Caucasia, and fifty are still in use. In Gurdjieff's childhood, Georgians, Armenians, and Azerbaijans rubbed shoulders with Greeks, Turks, and Persians; further north the high mountains of the Caucasus concealed pockets of puzzling tribes like the Khevsurs and Ossets who had no known genetic affiliations. There were the Russian masters of the area, Kurds wandering up from the south, Tartars, Cossacks from the north, and in the extreme northeast, Kalmuck Mongols in the provinces of Astrakhan and Stavropol on the coast of the Caspian Sea. The circumstances of Gurdjieff's birth, writes the French critic Manuel Rainord, "make one believe in a sort of geographical vocation."

The southern Caucasus was a frontier area in perpetual dispute between Turkey, Russia, and Persia. War and rapine had resulted in frequent migrations of peoples between the aggressor nations. The smaller races— Armenians and Kurds particularly—were always in danger of persecution from one or another of their enemies. The Caucasus range itself had traditionally formed a refuge for the disinherited; and the security of its inaccessible valleys was a further reason why the lands between the Black

Sea and the Caspian Sea gave the appearance almost of an experiment in the confusion of humankind. Gurdjieff clearly derived immense pleasure and stimulation from the diversity of people he encountered in his childhood. The gusto of some of the tales in *Meetings with Remarkable Men* and the stage directions for his "ballet" *The Struggle of the Magicians* bear witness to his delight in the variety—*yet sameness in that variety*—of human beings.

Gurdjieff's family were themselves a product of this cosmopolitan situation. His father came from a family of Greeks from Asia Minor which had been slowly migrating eastward ever since the Turkish capture of Byzantium. According to Gurdjieff, they had first settled in central Turkey, then moved north to the east coast of the Black Sea, and next to Georgia. Shortly before the Russo-Turkish War of 1877–78, Gurdjieff's father left his brothers in Georgia and moved to the Armenian town of Alexandropol, where Gurdjieff was born. After this move, he suffered a financial disaster; and from being a rich grazier, he was forced to turn to manual labor to support his family. His efforts as a carpenter met with little success and his prospects appeared better in Kars, a frontier town which the Russians had taken from the Turks in 1877. The Gurdjieff family moved yet again.

It was in Kars that Georgei Ivanovitch Gurdjieff grew up. The family remained very poor, and there were three sisters and Gurdjieff's brother Dmitri to be fed. The severity of their living conditions is shown by a story Dmitri Gurdjieff used to tell of a time when the two boys were rivals in love. It was not that they were rivals for the same girl, but if they both wanted to go out on the same evening, there was only a single pair of shoes between them. Gurdjieff's experience of extreme poverty undoubtedly affected him throughout his life and made him impatient with dreamers, dropouts, and those who wanted to discard their worldly obligations. "Very important have piece of paper in life," he would say, advising a young man to go away and pass his exams; or, "I also am business-man."

Apart from a few stray rumors, our only sources for Gurdjieff's early life are his own writings, which present great problems when they are treated as biographical material. Certain episodes are illuminated by the privately published manuscripts known as the *Third Series*. Gurdjieff's pamphlet, *Herald of Coming Good* (1933), gives a rather confusing outline of his development up to the time when he appeared in Russia. The gargantuan *Beelzebub's Tales to his Grandson* (1949) can be combed for biographical details; but because of the deliberately obscure method of narration and the quite unbelievable fantasies put in the mouth of Gurdjieff's benevolent and wise old Beelzebub, it is dangerous to take any statement as illustrating a real event. It is obvious, however, that there are autobiographical passages in *Beelzebub's Tales*, and its huge, irritating, and delightful bulk provides many more general indications of where Gurdjieff traveled and what he saw. The chief source for the events of Gurdjieff's early life is the so-called autobiography, *Meetings with Remarkable Men* (1963).

Meetings with Remarkable Men is Gurdjieff's account of his education and his wanderings, first in his native Caucasus, and later in Central Asia with a band of explorers he calls "the Seekers for Truth." The book was partly designed, he warned, to satisfy the merely inquisitive by providing answers to the recurring questions which most frequently made inroads on his time. In addition, it was meant to serve as material to prepare for an understanding of his system. He claimed that it was also designed to give a picture of his own life; but in what style this was painted he did not say. And although the prose is clear, racy, and uncluttered by the Oriental complexities of *Beelzebub's Tales to his Grandson*, the book is similarly laden with symbols and allegorical stories.

The narrative is in the time-honored form used by Marcus Aurelius. "From so-and-so I learned such-and-such, from such-a-one I learned something else." Gurdjieff arranges his material in chapters which are known by the names of the "remarkable men" they portray; but beside the important personages are other characters, the subjects of tales-within-tales or the mouthpieces of sermons designed to illustrate particular points. The reader hears of Gurdjieff's boyhood friend, "Sarkis Pogossian," whose mechanical abilities eventually won him a trading ship in the South Seas, or "Abraham Yelov," the Assyrian bookdealer of Tiflis, who accompanied Gurdjieff in philosophical inquiries and eventually emigrated from Soviet Russia to the United States. Lesser characters are "Mme. Vitvitskaya," whose interests in music and vibration enable Gurdjieff to suggest the unusual way of considering sound which was so important to his system, and "Father Giovanni," an Italian missionary whom the narrator meets in Kafiristan and who serves as his sponsor to the "World Brotherhood" and its remarkable monastery.

Most of these characters probably had no historical existence. There may never have been a Yelov or a Mme. Vitvitskaya. But throughout the brightly colored adventure story and through the fumes of armagnac which Gurdjieff proclaimed he had drunk in heroic quantities while writing the book, comes an undeniable sense of authenticity. The characters may be imaginary or composites, but a rich supply of autobiographical experience from Gurdjieff's undoubtedly adventurous past went into their making.

The reader soon becomes able to distinguish the different styles employed by Gurdjieff for the most obvious levels of *Meetings with Remarkable Men*. The account of his life and of his "remarkable" acquaintances is written in a straightforward fashion. Into the mouths of the characters are inserted more oratorical declamations, rather in the manner of Beelzebub, which should be taken like the pronouncements of that oracular personage. There are passages of deliberately "literary" compositions such as the melodramatic introduction to Mme. Vitvitskaya as a victim of the white slave trade; and sharp doses of the deliberately absurd to keep the critical faculties alert. Also there are short fables or parables, which lend themselves to interpretation—and like all parables, to endless dispute about the meaning intended.

It is dangerous to label any particular passage in the book as allegorical, for what seems obvious allegory often has a basis in fact. An example of this can be found in the chapter called "Prince Yuri Lubovedsky," in which the members of the Seekers for Truth call a conference in the Gobi Desert to discuss the best method of crossing the sand with the resources at their disposal. A plan of what seems transparent symbolism is unfolded. It is discovered that because the sand is of "purely vegetable origin," the sheep belonging to the expedition can be kept going for longer by mixing a certain proportion of sand with their food. The difficulty of extending their food supply is thus overcome. But what about the sandstorms so common in the desert? One of the Seekers for Truth discovers that with a ladder he can see over the sandstorms and suggests that the party equip themselves with stilts. A final expert ties the whole plan together. By fastening their stilts between the sheep, they can form panniers to carry baggage and even themselves, thus conserving their energy. "We were all so astounded," writes Gurdjieff, "that all of a sudden it seemed to us that the difficulties of crossing the Gobi had been intentionally exaggerated, and even the impossibility of it suggested expressly for the traveller."

Of course, the obvious allegory is probably the point of the episode. It demonstrates certain principles of the Gurdjieff Method. There must be *sheep* in his work, because the *travelers* need *food*. They also need to see above appearances. The poor sheep—who are only sheep anyway and can never transcend the obvious like the stilt walkers—can carry the stilts, and the men as well, who can use the time to "learn all the languages we shall need in future expeditions." If you like, it is an allegory about the uses to which sheep can be put by an intending goat. Why set it in the Gobi Desert, except to play mystery man? But what is really astonishing is the essential realism of the allegory, which is apparent only if the inquirer has experienced sandstorms which *do* in fact often stop at a short height above the ground. Stilts would be a theoretical although impractical way of seeing over the top. But sheep as baggage animals? That is surely carrying implausibility too far. Not according to Captain H.H.P. Deasy whose *In Tibet and Chinese Turkestan* was published in 1901. "The best beasts of burden for Tibet," he writes, "are undoubtedly the sheep of the country or of Ladak. If in good condition at starting, and in charge of a man who knows

his business, they will carry loads of about 22 lbs. for a long time. . . ."
Carrying a man is an obvious impossibility, but by this time the inquirer is
wondering about that sand . . . *could* it in fact be composed of vegetable
matter?

He would be wise to wonder no further. Gurdjieff's statements are
neither one thing nor the other—indeed, that is precisely what they are:
neither-one-thing-nor-the-other—and confusion alone can result from following a too literal or a too skeptical approach. On one occasion Gurdjieff
was embarked on some traveler's tale of Egypt when his follower P. D.
Ouspensky confronted him with a man who was able to denounce his
"recollections" as bogus. On the other hand, his knowledge of Central Asia
frequently proves extensive. Underneath the conceptual juggling one thing
is clear: It is generally more likely than not that Gurdjieff had been where
he said he had been, although no one can ever be certain exactly where his
inventiveness runs away with the facts.

Within this all but overwhelming jungle of allegory and symbolism lies
the central metaphor of *Meetings with Remarkable Men:* the metaphor of
the persons of the book.

For from whatever materials Gurdjieff constructed his characters—people
like his father or "Lubovedsky" whom he had actually met, personifications of
one aspect of his work like "Vitvitskaya," composites of several influences
which had in truth operated in his life, or spokesmen for various schools of
thought he. had met in the East—their place in the structure of the tale is
determined by their effect on the Gurdjieff who is telling the story, the
"Gurdjieff" whom the author wished to present to his readers. The characters
are introduced in some sense as his teachers, and perhaps certain of them
actually were. But the most instructive way of reading *Meetings with
Remarkable Men* from a historical point of view is to treat each character as if
he were an aspect of Gurdjieff himself. Gurdjieff taught that every man is
composed of countless little "I's," hundreds of small and demanding egos
whose competing claims deny man any individuality. On the one hand the
characters represent the various "I's" of Gurdjieff which directed his pilgrim's
progress. On the other hand they are expository, and symbolic. In Rainord's
interpretation, "'My Father' is, if you like, the goal of existence, 'Father Borah'
the destiny of the male and female together, 'Bogachevsky' objective morality,
'Pogossian' the necessity of work, 'Abraham Yelov' the operation of thought,
'Prince Yuri Lubovedsky,' the summons to leave our darkness." The lessons
they teach and the indications they offer as to where Gurdjieff drew his
material are the things of most value.

Gurdjieff begins by acknowledging the debt he owed to his father. Ivan
Gurdjieff was a traditional poet and storyteller of the type his son calls

ashokh, who was in demand at the competitions where the peoples of the Caucasus met to judge the quality of their bards. As an *ashokh* he was the repository of much traditional lore. Gurdjieff remembers how one night he heard his father repeat one verse of the legend of Gilgamesh so often that its words were imprinted on his memory. Then just before the First World War, Gurdjieff relates, he read in a magazine about the discovery in the ruins of Babylon of ancient tablets engraved with the story of Gilgamesh. The particular stanza which his father had repeated was printed in almost the same form as Gurdjieff remembered it. As a boy he was thus under the influence—all the more powerful for being unperceived—of traditions which had survived virtually unchanged for millennia.

Gurdjieff's father had a friend in "Dean Borsh" of the Kars Military Cathedral. According to *Meetings with Remarkable Men,* it was the Dean who superintended the young Gurdjieff's education. The boy was at first sent to the Greek school in Kars, and then to the Russian municipal school. He attracted the attention of the Dean because he sang in the Cathedral choir—and a fine voice as a child may have inspired his lifelong interest in music. On Dean Borsh's advice, Gurdjieff was taken away from the municipal school and educated at home by a series of tutors. It was decided that he was to be both a priest and a physician. "I myself, however, was drawn towards quite another way of life," records Gurdjieff. "Having from my early childhood an inclination for making all sorts of things, I dreamed of technical specialization."

In other words he became a convinced Westernizer, and developed the interest in mechanical gadgets which lasted all his life. In Gurdjieff's childhood, the wonders of Western science were just beginning to penetrate the Caucasus. By 1870 the main towns were linked by telegraph and two years later, the railway was completed between Poti on the Black Sea and Tiflis, the capital of Transcaucasia. The railway was an important factor in Gurdjieff's youth. In *Meetings with Remarkable Men* he tells of how he once worked as a stoker in the Tiflis station yard, and in *Beelzebub's Tales* there is the story of the "extremely sympathetic Karapet of Tiflis" who had the task of blowing the steam whistle which woke the Tiflis railway workers and also most of the town. Gurdjieff also claims to have acted as assistant to the engineer surveying the proposed railway route between Tiflis and Kars: apparently a most profitable venture. He writes—in his most gleeful impersonation of the Levantine shark—that he extracted a great deal of money from villages along the route by promising to have the railway track laid nearby.

His fascination with mechanics continued to provide Gurdjieff with a source of income. In his essay, "The Material Question," he describes how for a bet he started a "Universal Travelling Workshop" which "makes, alters and repairs everything" in the country between the Caspian and the Aral Sea. The traveling workshop probably has an allegorical significance, but the description of the extraordinary objects which were handed in for repair shows the relish of Gurdjieff the handyman: "an apparatus for plucking out grey hairs, a machine for stoning cherries for jam, a grinder for grinding copper sulphate to sprinkle on the sweat zones of the body, a special iron for ironing wigs. . . ." Yet it seems that, despite his unconcealed joy in his first automobile, and the perpetual enchantment which small gadgets gave him, Gurdjieff's early Westernizing ideas later became a source of regret. His scathing comments on the aping of European civilization by the people of the Transcaspian region would hardly reflect that his brother opened the first cinema in Tiflis or that Ouspensky's first view of his leader in his native Caucasus was of Gurdjieff setting up a dynamo for his brother. "These newly-rich people," he writes, "according to the inherency of all upstarts, imitated everything 'cultured' and 'fashionable'—in the given case every-thing European. But, drawing all their information about this culture and fashion only from Russian papers and magazines compiled by persons themselves ignorant in these matters, they presented to the impartial observer a comical and at the same time sad caricature."

In later life Gurdjieff denounced European civilization in the strongest terms as causing the destruction of religious feeling and partriarchal society. But he never renounced the machine. "Man is a machine" was the beginning of his teaching, and although he may have chosen mechanical analogies only for facility in introducing his ideas to the mechanized West, he used the framework of Victorian science with a certain conviction. Beelzebub tells his grandson: "Objective Science says that 'everything without exception in the Universe is material.'" When the Universal Traveling Workshop became the Institute for the Harmonious Develop-ment of Man, its director would tell his pupils: "You are spoiled automobiles. You must be repaired."

The tension between East and West which was felt by so many peoples as the colonial powers reached the limits of their expansion was experienced by Gurdjieff as an existential problem. Unusual circumstances of birth and upbringing enabled him to sense the dilemma in an unusual fashion. His solution was bound to be extraordinary.

In *Meetings with Remarkable Men*, he describes how his eyes were gradually opened to the existence of happenings for which the impressive knowledge of the West had no explanation. He was bewildered by a séance during which the "spirits" rapped out messages, and further amazed when a wandering *ashokh* made predictions about him which were fulfilled. Then he witnessed the spectacle of a boy imprisoned by a circle drawn on the ground. The boy was a Yezidje—a member of a heterodox religious sect inhabiting the Caucasus—and apparently he was powerless to leave the circle unless released by a Yezidje priest. From what Ouspensky says, the Yezidjes did exercise a fascination over Gurdjieff, who claimed to have experimented on the phenomenon of the imprisoning circle during his later investigations into hypnotism;* and it is possible that in all his tales of the supernatural, only the incident of the Yezidje boy has any basis in fact. What we are to understand is that, despite the captivating effect of Western science, Gurdjieff found himself demanding explanations which the educated men around him could not supply. The boy Gurdjieff became disillusioned with the accepted partial versions of the truth and, conceiving that truth existed, set out to find it. The result was "what modern psychologists might term an 'irresistible Mania'":

This mania began to impose itself upon my being at the time of my youth when I was on the point of attaining responsible age and consisted in what I would now term an "irrepressible striving" to understand clearly the precise significance in general, of the life process on earth of all the outward forms of breathing creatures, and, in particular, of the aim of human life in the light of this interpretation.

What does it all mean? What is humanity? Is there a purpose to life? Who am I? Such questions occur to most people at certain times in their lives, usually to be shrugged off as irrelevant to the business of living. But there are always some individuals for whom life seems impossible without a clear understanding of its significance; for whom meaning is the fuel without which life itself flickers out. Sometimes—most often in late adolescence or at a time of personal crisis—the lack of a definite rationale can induce an anguished condition which impels the sufferer to seek explanations. The search for meaning may eventually lead a person to a teacher of the sort which Gurdjieff later became, and as an adolescent Gurdjieff too was at the mercy of the sort of anxiety which drove those who became his pupils. In fact, he seems to have experienced the meaninglessness of life with a peculiar intensity, and his "irresistible mania" led him to dash hither and thither, from one supposed authority to the next.

His search turned from the pundits of materialist science to the recognized experts on spiritual matters:

Having become extremely interested in supernatural phenomena I had plunged into books and also applied to men of science for

*This phenomenon is not unknown in occult literature. The Irish poet and mystic A. E. (George Russell) was immobilized in a similar way by his guru, the American Theosophist James Morgan Pryse.

explanations of these phenomena. But failing to find answers that satisfied me . . . I began to seek them in religion. I visited various monasteries and went to see men about whose piety I had heard, read the Holy Scriptures and the Lives of the Saints, and was even for three months an acolyte of the famous Father Yevlampios in the monastery of Sanaïne; and I also made pilgrimages to most of the holy places of the many different faiths in Transcaucasia.

The racial mixture of the Caucasus resulted in the jumbling together of every conceivable form of religion. There were the relatively established churches of Oriental Christianity: Greek, Russian, and Armenian. There were Nestorian and Assyrian Christians, the Manichean Yezidjes, and eclectic peoples like the Ossets, who were part Christian, part Mohammedan, part pagan. Even in the north of the Caucasus, around Vladikavkaz, Mohammedans could be found; and to the northeast, the Buddhist Kalmucks wandered on the steppes of Stavropol and Astrakhan. Countless sects from the bewildering variety of Russian dissenters inhabited secluded valleys. There were colonies of Doukhobors, Molokans, and European Protestants. In the south could be found all the different shades of Islam. According to one missionary, writing in 1896, some of the nominally Christian tribes of the mountains were "really polytheists, and worship, besides what they call the Christ-God, a god of war, and gods or 'angels' of the earth, the oak, the mountain and so forth."

Even the Christian churches with which Gurdjieff came in contact were the result of an agelong mingling of doctrines, and derived ultimately from traditions quite different from those which formed Western Christianity. Heresy and dissent flourished in secret. For example, after the Russo-Turkish War of 1828–29, a number of Turkish Armenians fled to the territories which Russia had recently conquered. In 1837 their bishop warned the Synod of the Orthodox Armenian Church in Echmiadzin that some of these families were really Paulicians, and a great scandal developed. The migration of peoples sometimes considerably altered their religious practices. As late as 1920 Sir Harry Luke, the British Commissioner in Tiflis, recorded in his diary that he had received a deputation of Greeks who had emigrated eastward like Gurdjieff's ancestors. "They were accompanied by their *papas*," wrote Luke, "who told me that he celebrated the liturgy in Greek but preached (when he had occasion to do so) in Georgian."

It is possible to analyze Gurdjieff's teaching and to point to features which might have come from the various religious traditions of the Caucasus. Some indications of his sources will be given at the end of this book. All that is important at this stage is that he had access to Greek,

Russian, and Armenian churches by the simple facts of his birth and upbringing. "Father Yevlampios" has disappeared in the mists of time, but the monastery of Sanaïne or Sanahin is a celebrated foundation dating from the tenth century and situated just south of Tiflis. If the idea of Gurdjieff's educators was to bring him up as a priest and a physician, it may be wondered how far along the path of the seminarian he traveled. He told his groups in Russia that his teaching might be called "esoteric Christianity," and several of the characters in the early pages of *Meetings with Remarkable Men* are priests or novices. Gurdjieff's admission that he had been acolyte to Father Yevlampios permits speculation that he proceeded some way along the road to the priesthood before becoming disillusioned.

In his account of the Gurdjieff family home in 1917, Ouspensky mentions a photograph which was kept in the house. It showed Gurdjieff "when he was quite young, dressed in a black frock coat with his curly hair brushed straight back." This "determined with undoubted accuracy," Ouspensky writes, "what his profession was at the time the portrait was made—though Gurdjieff never spoke of it. This discovery gave me many interesting ideas. But since it was my own personal discovery I shall keep it to myself." There are few occupations which are readily indentifiable from a photograph, and Ouspensky later told his pupils that in this portrait Gurdjieff was wearing "a high hat." Just possibly this might mean the white conical hat worn by the Mevlevi dervishes, but probably it refers to the familiar black headgear of the Orthodox priesthood.

If Gurdjieff had been a "spoiled" priest this would explain his dislike of the religious professionals who in his view had usurped the name of priest. But the evidence is not conclusive, and all that can safely be said is that Gurdjieff made a thorough investigation of the exotic territory of Transcaucasian religion. He tells of miraculous cures brought about by icons; of a service to honor a particularly venerated icon which caused rain to fall in the middle of a drought; of his own pilgrimage to the Armenian holy city, Echmiadzin, southeast of Kars and Alexandropol, when he took his baggage "in the wagon of the Molokan sect." "But in my stay at Echmiadzin," he writes, "I did not find what I was looking for and, having spent enough time to realize that I could not find it there, I went away with a feeling of deep inner disillusionment." This is Gurdjieff's general comment on the relationship between the organized religions of his youth and the knowledge of which he was in search. His questioning mind turned in other directions.

Gurdjieff was by no means the only seeker for hidden truth caught in the friction between old and new. Throughout all Western Europe, the last quarter of the nineteenth century witnessed an increasingly frantic search for security. This resulted in the creation of a number of new religions and a burgeoning interest in the supernatural, magic, and the occult. Partly as a reaction against the menacing changes in society and the destruction of treasured beliefs, partly also as a protest against the extensive claims of materialist science, the occult revival was a powerful intellectual force. It penetrated Russia, where the half-Oriental religious conventions of Orthodoxy easily absorbed it, and the gloriously diverse ideas of the Orthodox priesthood found in the occult more grist to their mill. At the same time, the conditions of disatisfaction and anxiety which attracted Western Europeans to mysticism and magic, turned Russians to their own luxuriant spirituality. From the point of view of Gurdjieff's search two occult groups are important. The first is the Theosophical Society, which was founded in New York in 1875 by the redoubtable Russian Helena Petrovna Blavatsky and the American Colonel H. S. Olcott. The Theosophical Society transferred its base to Adyar, near Madras in India, and became extraordinarily influential among the seekers for truth of Europe and America. Although H. P. Blavatsky's books and her Society were banned in Russia, small groups of Theosophists continued to meet. They were supplied with literature by travelers abroad; and the earliest and most dedicated of these Theosophical colporteurs was a Mme. Nina de Gernet, one of whose ports of call was a circle of Theosophists in Vladikavkaz, the capital of the central Caucasus. It is certain that Gurdjieff had read Theosophical literature. He afterward said that it had cost him an immense amount of labor to track down the erroneous statements in Mme. Blavatsky's *The Secret Doctrine*, and delighted to tell a completely mythical story of how its author had fallen in love with him. It is not unlikely that Gurdjieff, realising he would not find the answers he sought in orthodox religion, came across Theosophical works which had traveled to Russia through Vladikavkaz.

Another mystical group which may have had some connection with Gurdjieff originated in Tiflis itself. This was centered around Pavel Alexandrovitch Florensky (b. 1882), an eccentric genius whose mother, like Gurdjieff's, was Armenian. With his friends A. V. Elchaninov (b. 1881), V. F. Ern (b. 1881), and the child prodigy V. P. Sventitsky, Florensky moved to Moscow and entered the priesthood. This group absorbed the influences of the occult revival and incorporated what in the West would have been called occultism with Orthodox theology. They began to publish—most notably Florensky's *The Pillar and Foundation of Truth* (1914) and Sventitsky's book on the hermits of the Caucasus (1913)—about the time that Gurdjieff appeared in Moscow. The Florensky circle were all younger than Gurdjieff and it may be reading too much into the situation to see a direct connection in their Tiflis origins. But the ideas of contemporary occultism which influenced them were also current in Gurdjieff's milieu, and in *Meetings with Remarkable Men*, he indicates the increasingly occult tone of his search for meaning in the chapters on "Captain Pogossian" and "Abram Yelov"—both of whom the story places among his Tiflis friends.

"Abram Yelov" is introduced as a polyglot Assyrian bookdealer. Books must have become increasingly important to Gurdjieff in the pursuit of his "irresistible mania": whether books on religious questions, books on the supernatural—in *Beelzebub's Tales* he mentions one called *Dreams and Witchcraft* which "Karapet of Tiflis" acquired—or books on hypnotism, a subject with whose literature he claimed a specialist's familiarity. Science and the more easily accessible forms of religion had failed him; but here was the enormous and daily increasing library of occult texts, whose authors all dropped tantalizing hints that they possessed the explanation of the universe which the priests and the scientists had failed to grasp. Gurdjieff succumbed to the same influences as many of his less remarkable contemporaries and immersed himself in occult literature.

His reading made him familiar with the occultists' most cherished idea: that there had existed from time immemorial an esoteric Tradition of secret knowledge, transmitted from initiate to initiate down through the centuries. Gurdjieff later gave the unwieldy name of "legominism" to what he considered a true or valid item of Traditional wisdom, but from his incessant abuse of "occultists," it is clear that he soon became disillusioned with those who claimed to be the contemporary guardians of esoteric wisdom. In *Beelzebub's Tales* he calls them "criminal gangs" and refers to the "great initiates" they venerate as men who pass through "fire-water-copper-pipes-and-even-through-all-the-roulette-halls-of-Monte-Carlo."

But disillusionment with the occult did not mean that Gurdjieff abandoned all hopes of finding a secretly proved explanation of the universe. He decided that if truth were accessible, the esoteric Tradition must have degenerated over the ages. In *Meetings with Remarkable Men,* he claims that he and his friend "Sarkis Pogossian" decided to reconstruct what they could of its original form:

> Pogossian and I had come to the definite conclusion that there really was "a certain something" which people formerly knew, but that now this knowledge was quite forgotten. We had lost all hope of finding any guiding clue to this knowledge in contemporary exact science, in contemporary books or from people in general, and so we directed all our attention to ancient literature.

The earliest writings of humanity might hold the key to knowledge which had existed before the rot set in. Other seekers for wisdom had made similar deductions, but Gurdjieff was uniquely placed to proceed from theory to practice. If the knowledge he sought was not to be found in books which were readily available or even in the spiritual labyrinth of the Caucasus, he would travel further afield in search of it.

Meetings with Remarkable Men gives examples of this search. One episode begins when he and "Pogossian" settle down with a collection of rare books in the ruins of the ancient Armenian town of Ani, near Alexandropol. They vary their diet of study with amateur excavation in the ruins. Here they find a collection of old letters from one monk to another, in which a society known as the "Sarmoun Brotherhood" is mentioned. Gurdjieff and Posgossian have already stumbled on references to this society, "a famous esoteric school which, according to tradition, was founded in Babylon as far back as 2500 B.C." They decide that traditions stemming from this school will be preserved among the Assyrian Christians, and set off on a journey in search of its surviving tradition. On their way the pair stay at the house of an Armenian priest, who proves to have in his possession "a map of pre-sand Egypt." This discovery so excites Gurdjieff that he burgles the priest's locked chest and copies the map. With this in his possession, he decides at once to embark on a journey to Egypt.

The story reads like a boy's treasure-hunting adventure, and it gives only general indications of what Gurdjieff wanted to convey. He sought for traces of Traditional knowledge in ancient literature, in inaccessible manuscripts, in recent archaeological discoveries. The association of secret wisdom with the Assyrian Christians whom Gurdjieff calls "Aissors" is probably to be taken more seriously. "Abram Yelov" was an "Aissor," and Gurdjieff mentions his contacts among members of this widely scattered group on more than one occasion. There would have been logical reasons for Gurdjieff to look for knowledge among the Aissors, and these will be discussed in connection with his doctrine. What he meant by his tale of the "map of pre-sand Egypt" is a matter for guesswork. Most probably it signifies some guide to the state of human consciousness before it became perverted; but the expression might simply have been chosen to conform to the expectations of a mystery-loving audience.

In *Herald of Coming Good*, Gurdjieff writes that despite all his searching, he was unable to throw light on the questions which interested him until the year 1892. In the prospectus issued to mark the opening of his Institute for the Harmonious Development of Man at Fontainebleau, he places the foundation of the society of the Seekers for Truth in 1895. Between these dates it can be inferred that Gurdjieff's search took on a more ambitious aspect; and perhaps his tale of dashing off to Egypt with an esoteric map in his pocket indicates that he extended his travels beyond the relatively local expeditions he had previously made. That Gurdjieff suddenly vanished from his home and was lost to the sight of his family is confirmed by P. L. Travers: "While he was still a very young man, Gurdjieff, true to his role, 'disappeared'—as Odysseus must have seemed to disappear from his local world of Ithaca—into that cauldron of history, tradition and ideas that we know as the Middle East."

Gurdjieff is usually thought to have first left home about the age of sixteen; but recently his follower J. G. Bennett published a story which suggests that his wanderings began even earlier. Gurdjieff told a Miss Anna Durco (whom he met as a child in 1934) that he had run away with the gypsies who passed through Kars each spring on their way to trade horses. At the age of eleven his friendships with the gypsy boys developed into a protracted period of truancy with a tribe of nomads from the Carpathians. As he later told the story, Gurdjieff made it seem that he was more intrigued by the legends of hidden wisdom attached to the gypsies than by their romantic way of life. It would be too much to expect a child of eleven to have any interest in philosophical matters; but there is nothing against believing that the young Gurdjieff was enthralled by the more romantic aspects of gypsy lore. His precocious appetite for adventure is confirmed by William Seabrook's impression that he "ran away to sea at an early age."

He was ridden by a particularly merciless daemon. From childhood, he writes, he had "an 'irresistible urge' to do things not as others do them." So "if all the other children slid down the hill head first, I tried to do it, and moreover, each time better and better, as the children then called it, 'backside-first.'" The deliberate contrariness of the child was reflected in the obstinacy of the youth and the matured philosophy of the man, whose entire rationale ran cross-grained to his surroundings. To this natural mulishness was added a sense of urgency which must have had some basis in the facts of his early life. One story in *Meetings with Remarkable Men* suggests an explanation. He and his schoolfellow "Peter Karpenko" fell in love with the same girl. They decided to spend a day on the local artillery range while firing was in progress, and let the gunners settle their differences for them. Both survived their harrowing experience to become fast friends. In early manhood Gurdjieff was no stranger to the chances of sudden death, and a number of narrow escapes may have been partly responsible for his later conviction that the only way of saving mankind would be to implant in each human being the consciousness of his own mortality.

We know further that this young man once commiserated with a group of ladies from the literary world with the words: "I too was once sick for art." In Europe and the United States he was surrounded by Bohemians and "artistic" people; and he was reported in 1919 to be on familiar terms with the Georgian poets and artists of the day. If he associated with any particular group of artists during his early life, we know nothing of it, although his chosen art would beyond all doubt have been the theater. Yet, even if Gurdjieff were really "sick" for art, his sickness was subordinated to the demanding irritation of his "itching-itch," the pursuit of meaning. At some time or another he concluded that the knowledge he sought existed not only in the form of secrets handed down among "genuine initiates," but in works of art constructed according to a definite purpose by the ancient guardians of the esoteric Tradition. The feeling that the wonders of the ancient world *meant* something, were actually capable of revealing to man secrets known to their makers, was common among nineteenth-century occultists influenced by Blavatsky; and Gurdjieff was not immune to this sort of speculation. But he went further, and his view of the role of art was more extensive. In *Beelzebub's Tales* he describes an imaginary club called "The-Adherents-of-Legominism" dedicated to passing on wisdom by artistic means. The members of this club are supposed to have decided that they should construct their works of art—be they paintings, statues, or dances— on the basis of the universal "Law of Sevenfoldness," one of the laws on which Gurdjieff based his cosmology. Into works made according to this system of relation and proportion, the artists would introduce "intentional inexactitudes" or deliberate departures from the canon. These were intended to point the message which the work of "objective art" was designed to convey.

Perhaps we are to imagine Gurdjieff inspecting the wonders of the world in the light of his own later teaching about art as a transmitter of legominism. In this spirit he once described his discovery of a "strange figure" in the desert at the foot of the Hindu Kush—perhaps one of the famous Buddhas of Bamian. "At first," he told Ouspensky, "it produced upon us simply the impression of being a curiosity. But after a while we began to *feel* that this figure contained many things, a big, complete and complex system of cosmology. And slowly, step by step, we began to decipher this system. It was in the body of the figure, in its legs, in its arms, in its head, in its eyes, in its ears: everywhere. In the whole statue there was nothing accidental, nothing without meaning. And gradually we understood the aim of the people who built this statue. We began to feel their thoughts, their feelings. Some of us thought that we saw their faces, heard their voices. . . ."

Where did Gurdjieff travel in his search for the knowledge which so obsessed him? Three times he made unheralded appearances in the centers of European civilization, and each time the tale was vague yet apparently circumstantial. To Ouspensky in Moscow he spoke of "Tibetan monasteries, the Chitral, Mount Athos; Sufi schools in Persia, in Bokhara, and eastern Turkestan; he mentioned dervishes of various orders; but all of them in a very indefinite way." Cecil Sharp, the editor of the London *New Statesman*, located the area of Gurdjieff's search in "that little-known region which lies between Eastern Persia and Tibet." William Seabrook, who knew Gurdjieff in New York, wrote that he "spent many years in Outer Mongolia and Tibet, where he is said to have been at one time a Tibetan monk, and to have absorbed the mystical practices and teachings of the Sufis, Yogis, Melewi, Rufiah, and Persian dervishes. I can testify of my own knowledge," concluded Seabrook, "that Gurdjieff knows more about dervish mysticism and magic than any man I have ever met outside a dervish monastery."

All the rumors concerning the source of his knowledge point to Central Asia; and of course, to its most inaccessible parts. Sometimes it seems that every mystical philosopher has claimed to have been in Tibet. The origin of the Tibetan obsession lies in Mme. Blavatsky's invention of the "Tibetan Mahatmas" who watched over the Theosophical Society. But in Gurdjieff's case the legend is almost certainly based on fact. The stories of his travels almost always contain circumstantial evidence—like the idea of using sheep as baggage animals—which supports their accuracy. His teaching certainly incorporated elements from Tibetan Buddhism, and many of his earliest followers were convinced that he had been in Tibet. C. S. Nott even tells us that Gurdjieff had himself been made collector of revenues for the Dalai Lama; and other disciples remember that Gurdjieff's establishment in France was sometimes visited by inscrutable guests from Central Asia.

Gurdjieff first became known in the West as a "teacher of dancing"; and the names of the places where his dances are said to have originated provide further evidence that he had been where he claimed to have been. There are several helpful indications in the program of dances and movements which Gurdjieff presented at Christmas 1923 in Paris. On the one hand places are mentioned which are easily identifiable, like the city of Mazar-i-Sharif in northern Afghanistan, or Yangi Hissar, a sizeable town south of Kashgar in Central Asia. Then there are more general references to Chinese Turkestan and Kafiristan which cannot be checked. Lastly, there are names difficult to find on any map, but which provide the best evidence of all that Gurdjieff was in Central Asia. We learn of the "monks of Matchna," at the monastery of "Kisil-Djan" at the "Oasis of Keril" [Chinese Turkestan]; the monastery of "Souxari" near "Outchan-Su in Kashgaria," the medical temple of "Sari" in Tibet, and "the Sanctuary of Houdankr, Lotko country in the Chitral." It may be possible to find these locations on unusually detailed maps, and it is certainly possible that Gurdjieff's dances did not come from the sources he indicated—although, he also specifies other out-of-the-way places like Sessi Madane in Transcaucasia which do exist. But what is peculiarly interesting in the references to "Kisil-Djan," "Outchan-Su," "Sari," and "Houdankr," is that although they resist identification, in each case the etymology of the name is consistent with the language of the area in which they are supposed to be. The conclusion is inevitable either that Gurdjieff had been there, as he said, or that he was closely associated with men who had traveled in those regions.

Gurdjieff told Ouspensky that his journeys in the East had been undertaken in the company of "all sorts of specialists." Some were working, he said, some had since died, others were "in seclusion." After Ouspensky arrived in London in 1921, Cecil Sharp published in the *New Statesman* some further information on the Seekers for Truth which was probably derived from Ouspensky himself, or from pupils at Fontainebleau like Sharp's wife.

> The movement originated some thirty years ago in an expedition organised by Mr. Gurdjieff—then very young—and two Russian savants, with the object of discovering what, if possible, lay behind the fabled "wisdom of the East." Five years were spent in gathering and training a band of about thirty investigators, mostly Russians, who between them might claim to know all that Europe knew of science and art. They then set out . . . and . . . separated, each to seek entry into some "school" where esoteric knowledge might be found. . . . After several years a few of them returned and organised a second expedition. Some of the members of both expeditions are still in Central Asia and will probably never return. Others including Mr. Gurdjieff, after spending the best part of twenty years in various Eastern schools, came back to Europe and are now engaged in working upon the masses of material that they brought with them, while maintaining communication with those who have remained behind.

The prospectus for Gurdjieff's Institute at Fontainebleau—which contains a quantity of false, not to say fraudulent information—talks of a company of "doctors, archaeologists, priests, painters, etc., etc., with the aim of mutual assistance in research into so-called *supernatural* phenomena which interested each one from a particular point of view." Gurdjieff frequently told outrageous lies, even when it was clear that the listener had no thought of believing him: Thus, to an American doctor and pupil whom he knew to be familiar with his personal circumstances, he announced blandly that in France he had "two hundred pupils—all *docteurs*." The picture of a sort of combined Society for Psychical Research and Royal Central Asian Society is certainly exaggerated. But on balance it is probable that Gurdjieff did have some collaborators in his quest, even if they were only traveling companions or chance acquaintances.

There is an outside possibility that a regular group did form for certain expeditions; in *Meetings with Remarkable Men* Gurdjieff mentions an expedition of 1898 in the Gobi Desert and another of 1900 in the Pamirs. The "savants" to whom Sharp refers may have been the characters portrayed as "Prince Lubovedsky" and "Professor Skridlov." In two different places Gurdjieff talks of meeting two Russian savants beside the Pyramids, and although such a meeting might represent only a continued "quest for the inexplicable," the repetition of this incident may indicate a real experience. On each occasion one of the figures is said to have been "Skridlov," the Professor of Archaeology. In *Beelzebub's Tales* the other is unnamed; but in *Meetings with Remarkable Men*, the second Russian is named as "Prince Lubovedsky," "my elder comrade and closest friend." There is a strong tradition that Gurdjieff's aristocratic patron was a real person, and Ouspensky thought that he had met the archaeologist. But it is safest to regard the Seekers for Truth as a body in which Gurdjieff's friends would be included but which comprehends all those in pursuit of eternal things; just as the World Brotherhood which the group is said to have contacted, is composed of all those practicing the right methods to spiritual attainment:

Among the adepts of this monastery there were former Christians, Jews, Mohammedans, Buddhists, Lamaists, and even one Shamanist. All were united by God the Truth.

All the brethren of this monastery lived together in such amity that, in spite of the specific traits and properties of the representatives of the different religions, Professor Skridlov and I could never tell to which religion this or that brother had formerly belonged.

Where then did Gurdjieff travel? He mentions Turkey, Athos, Crete, Jerusalem, and Egypt, where he was a tourist guide at the Pyramids. According to *Meetings with Remarkable Men* he went as far south as Ethiopia, and at the end of his life he professed an undying affection for that part of the world. He claimed to have penetrated Mecca and Medina, but was disappointed in the holy places of Islam. He considered the center of "real" knowledge preserved in Islamic form to be in Central Asia, near Bokhara, Merv, and Samarkand, and above all, *Meetings with Remarkable Men* is filled with the gusto of the Central Asian khanates approached up the River Oxus.

The next chapter will show that Gurdjieff visited India, Tibet, and China; he claimed also to have taken part in a journey through Siberia; and at a later period of his life he spent much time in Turkestan and the lands around Kashgar. It seems that he probably knew sufficient languages for his purpose. Greek, Armenian, Tadjik, and Turkish he would have known from early youth. He is supposed also to have spoken Arabic and Italian—the common languages of the Mediterranean at the turn of the century—and he probably picked up some French and English. His claims to fluency in eighteen different languages should be taken with a pinch of salt, but these claims were probably more nearly true than false.

What Gurdjieff brought back from his journeys will be considered separately. Apart from various Sufi orders and monasteries both Christian and Buddhist, he mentions that he was a member of a society of Persians which met at Baku to study magic, and also that he was at one time a practitioner of yoga. However, some of his energies may well have been absorbed by less esoteric studies.

In the Middle East, the years of Gurdjieff's search were those of the most romantic period of archaeology. By 1890 archaeological exploration of Assyria—Gurdjieff's personal interest—had reached a peak. Gurdjieff speaks of a journey to Thebes with "Professor Skridlov" which continued via the Red Sea to Babylon, where he left his friend "to continue his excavations." The exciting discoveries of contemporary archaeologists, among them Flinder Petrie, undoubtedly spurred on his search for the knowledge which he believed had been buried by the generations.

In Central Asia the great age of Russian exploration had been inaugurated by N. M. Prjevalsky's expedition through Mongolia in 1870. In 1888, on his fifth journey, Prjevalsky died; but in the early 1890s his successor, P. K. Kozlov, mounted expeditions in Turkestan and in the later part of the 1890s in Mongolia and the middle Gobi. Non-Russian explorers like Sven Hedin and Aurel Stein entered the field, and Central Asia became the favorite area for adventurous scholars. When Gurdjieff talks of an expedition into the Gobi Desert to find a city rumored to be buried beneath the sands, he may well be dealing in symbols; but such rumors did draw archaeologists to the Gobi, and reports of sand-buried cities came from Sven Hedin himself. The disinterring of ancient knowledge and the uncovering of the true nature of man are undoubtedly intended, but the symbolism is prompted by the conditions surrounding Gurdjieff's personal quest.

Gurdjieff might have been able to satisfy his interest in ancient civilizations and gain access to distant and inaccessible lands by joining scientific expeditions in Central Asia; and a gift for languages would have been highly prized. The idea helps to explain how a young man from a penniless family was able to make ends meet in unfamiliar country. If we discount the idea of financial backing from the Seekers for Truth, Gurdjieff's initial forays into Central Asia require some plausible grounding. A possibility which provides a more convincing explanation of his early mobility is that from an early age he was an agent of the Russian secret service.

This possibility has been responsible for certain portrayals of Gurdjieff as a Black Magician straight from the pages of Dennis Wheatley. Louis Pauwels, editor of the anthology *Monsieur Gurdjieff*, mixes the occult and politics into an impossible conspiracy involving both Hitler and Stalin. Stalin and Gurdjieff, says Pauwels, "were at school together," and J. G. Bennett claims to have heard Gurdjieff endorse this tale himself. It is certainly true that the young Joseph Dzhugashvili—who became Joseph Stalin—was a lodger with the Gurdjieff family at some time during his career at Tiflis Theological Seminary from 1894 to 1899; and that he left owing them a substantial sum of money. It has been said by Stalin's enemies that he acted at one time as an agent for the Tsarist authorities, and possibly some confused thinking led to the connection with Gurdjieff being distorted. What is interesting is that the charges against Stalin originate in the well-known habit of the Tsarist Intelligence Service of offering a suspect the choice of serving with them as an alternative to punishment.

A story about Gurdjieff which used to circulate in London émigré circles was that he had been imprisoned for evading military service. The source was Prince Mikail Sumbatov, who in the early 1890s was Commissioner for Special Duties attached to the Governor of Kars; and it is totally in keeping with our knowledge of Gurdjieff that he should have tried to dodge the draft. There is not a shred of evidence to support the speculation, but it is tempting to wonder whether he was offered the sort of choice which the authorities held out to others. Even if this possibility is discounted, some sort of government backing best explains Gurdjieff's confusing statement in *Herald of Coming Good* about the great advantages his "peculiar conditions" of life gave him over the ordinary man. The pronouncement otherwise reads like a symptom of paranoia, and it does not have the same ring as the deliberately boastful passage about its author's endowment with "the highest degrees of comprehension attainable by man," which precedes it.

> I had, in accordance with the peculiar conditions of my life, the possibility of gaining access to the so-called "holy-of-holies" of nearly all hermetic organisations such as religious, philosophical, occult, political and mystic societies, congregations, parties, unions, etc., which were inaccessible to the ordinary man . . .

There is only one sort of job which secures rapid entrance into all organizations, whether political, religious, or intellectual, and that is the task of the agent who can rely on the contacts built up by his organization to establish his good faith.

In *Meetings with Remarkable Men* Gurdjieff describes how he and his friend "Pogossian" had themselves appointed the agents of an "Armenian

Committee" in order to finance their travels in search of knowledge. This Armenian Committee was presumably connected with the Armenian Social Revolutionary Party known as the Dashnaktsutiun, which was established in Tiflis in 1890 and adopted a political program two years later. Gurdjieff places his expedition with Pogossian in a year of militant Armenian nationalism when the hero "Andronik" (alias Ozanian) first began to attract attention. Although it is impossible to identify the year exactly, if there is any historical basis for this episode, it probably occurred in the early 1890s. It was not the last of Gurdjieff's ventures into politics.

In the *Third Series* Gurdjieff relates that three times in his life he was seriously wounded by stray bullets. The first time was in Crete in the year 1896, "the year before the Graeco-Turkish war." It may have been the year before war actually broke out between the two nations, but it was the year of the Greek rebellion against the Turks which provoked the war. Gurdjieff was evidently involved with the revolutionaries, as he was transported out of the island by certain Greeks who were strangers to him and brought to Jerusalem to recover from his wound. We may ascribe Gurdjieff's involvement in this political squabble solely to his Greek ancestry and the exhortations of "true patriots" of the sort he describes elsewhere in connection with the Cretan uprising; but this seems most unlikely. Russia had an interest in the war, as for various reasons it opposed the union of Crete with Greece. While Gurdjieff may simply have been using political occasions for his private ends, a career associated with both Greek and Armenian nationalism simply invites speculation.

Besides being the great age of archaeology and exploration, the last quarter of the nineteenth century was the high point of the expansion of Imperial Russia. The capture of Kars shortly before the Gurdjieff family moved there was the culmination of the Russian drive south; but the empire builders even had their eyes on Africa. Ideas of founding an Abyssinian colony were combined with a suggestion that the Abyssinian Church be brought into a union with Russian Orthodoxy. The head of the Abyssinian Church decided that Russia ought to take not only the Abyssinian Church under her protection, but also the related Coptic and Armenian Churches. This resulted in a series of embassies exchanged between St. Petersburg and the Emperor Menelik; and the Russian delegations usually comprised both military and ecclesiastical personnel. At the Fashoda incident in July 1898, a Russian colonel commanded the Abyssinian army in support of the French challenge to Britain. In the context of this peculiar military-ecclesiastical situation, Gurdjieff's supposed visit to Abyssinia takes on a very different coloring.

The chief area of Russian expansion, however, was Central Asia. Russian occupation of the khanates at the head of the Oxus had been followed by a steady push into the sparsely populated areas of Kashgar and Turkestan. In this context, Gurdjieff makes one quite remarkable admission about his travels in Central Asia. "Of course," he writes, "for journeys taken on behalf of some government or other for a certain political aim and for which large sums are allocated, . . . one might hire as many porters as one wishes to pack and unpack everything." This is an almost explicit statement that he did undertake political missions in Central Asia, and it fits very neatly with the most persistent rumors about his work on behalf of Russian Intelligence.

In 1892—the year which Gurdjieff himself selects as a watershed in his activities—he would have turned eighteen. This coincides too closely with the advent of military age to avoid reemphasis in the light of the rumor about his evasion of military service. From this year onward, Gurdjieff's activities must all lie under suspicion of being associated with political intrigue; and his involvement with the Cretan revolt at the age of twenty-two may have been the exploit of an already seasoned campaigner. This means that his own version of his early years is probably misleading in countless nonphilosophical ways, and only when evidence is available from other sources can anything be said for certain. The trail, which begins when we take for granted Gurdjieff's career in espionage, does lead to such evidence; and this provides the date of birth which has been assumed in this chapter, as well as other personal details. It was in Tibet—that most obvious of places from which a bogus mystic might flaunt his credentials, and therefore a fitting port of call for a man who later delighted to impersonate the charlatan—that Gurdjieff broke cover. The invisible man appears in the annals of the history of crime.

2

The Great Game

By 1900 the regions through which the Seekers for Truth are supposed to have traveled had become areas of anxious concern to Imperial Russia and the British Raj. The remoteness of those mountainous frontier lands which spoke to Theosophists of divine wisdom meant sleepless nights for English and Russian empire builders alike. In Afghanistan and Tibet, agents recruited by either side collected intelligence or attempted to win over the inhabitants to the cause of Delhi or St. Petersburg. As well as being the age of the great explorers, the turn of the century was the high point in the clandestine battle for India which became known to the British as the Great Game. Exploration was easily used as a cover for activities of another sort. For example, a geologist supposedly named "Bogdanovitch," who was a member of Prjevalsky's last expedition, was widely rumored to be in reality Colonel Alexei Nikolaievitch Orlov of the Russian General Staff.

Officials of the Government of India kept a watchful eye on the states of the Himalaya and the Pamirs. The picture of undercover rivalry given by Rudyard Kipling's *Kim* is not far from the truth. In response to the Russian overtures to Tibet, the British in India sent out agents known as "pandits"—like Kipling's "fearful man" Huree Babu—of whom the most famous was Sarat Chandra Das who actually spent several weeks in Lhasa. *Kim* was published in 1901 when the Game had been in progress for some time. Two years later, the expedition of Colonel Younghusband set out from

India for Tibet. The small British force entered Lhasa in 1904, after the Dalai Lama had fled north into the Gobi Desert with a mysterious figure known to British Intelligence as "the Lama Dordjieff." This Dordjieff was believed to be the main Russian agent in Tibet, and his great influence on the Dalai Lama had been used by Lord Curzon to persuade a reluctant government to agree to Younghusband's expedition in the first place. One of the most intriguing rumors to attach themselves to Gurdjieff is that he and Dordjieff were the same man.

Stories that Gurdjieff had been vaguely connected with the Tsarist Intelligence Service in Tibet began to circulate soon after his arrival in Europe. J. G. Bennett, who met him while serving as an officer in British Intelligence in Constantinople in 1920, has recorded that his first information about Gurdjieff came in a file from the Government of India warning him about Gurdjieff's shady past. On one of the visits which Gurdjieff made to London early in 1922, he was interviewed by a police or security organization and accused of having been a Tsarist agent. Gurdjieff, of course, denied the charge, but it is possible that this old score was behind the failure of his eminent supporters to secure him a permit of residence in Britain and their subsequent difficulties in persuading the French authorities to let him stay in France. The legend that Gurdjieff was the Lama Dordjieff was widely believed by his Western disciples.

The evidence which made the idea of Gurdjieff-Dordjieff widely known was published by Rom Landau in 1935 in a book called *God Is My Adventure*, a bestselling survey of contemporary spiritual leaders. Landau's source was the writer Achmed Abdullah, who met Gurdjieff at a New York luncheon given by John O'Hara Cosgrave, a former editor of the *New York World* and a follower of Gurdjieff's disciple, Orage. Abdullah was astounded to find that the famous guru had been one of his opposite numbers in Tibet in 1903. "I was convinced that he was Lama Dordjieff," he wrote to Rom Landau. "I told him so—and he winked. We spoke in Tadjik." Claude Bragdon, another writer who witnessed this incident, recorded that "Gurdjieff, through Orage, acknowledged that he had been in Lhasa, saying that his political activities had been but a cloak to his religious interests: he was there studying Buddhist theology, he explained."

"Achmed Abdullah" was the pseudonym used by a writer and adventurer who would never reveal his true name. His autobiography was published the year before *God Is My Adventure*, and it is as colorful and romantic as any of his novels. Abdullah (1881–1945) was the son of a Russian father and an Afghan mother. His great-uncle was Abdur Rahman, and he had a brother who was a Cossack colonel. He was in Tibet as a regular officer with the Younghusband Expedition and implies that he had also operated in Central Asia in other capacities. A man of many talents, he contrived to obtain a Turkish commission in the Balkan War of 1912–13 on the orders of the Indian Army. His romances come out of the same stable as the more novelistic passages in *Meetings with Remarkable Men*. To play the Great Game evidently demanded imagination as well as courage.

It is possible that Gurdjieff had made some prior arrangement with Achmed Abdullah. In some respects they were birds of a feather, used to the subtleties of Oriental intrigue and exaggeration. But the story has many marks of authenticity. Abdullah knew much more about the Lama Dordjieff than was common property in the 1930s, and he had certainly been in the right place at the right time. Although he was mistaken, his story is the first real clue to finding Gurdjieff's trail. In the Great Game, smoke rarely occurred without fire, and Abdullah gave a circumstantial picture of Gurdjieff-Dordjieff. "He spoke Russian, Tibetan, Tartar, Tadjik, Chinese, Greek, strongly accented French and rather fantastic English. As to his age—well—I would say ageless. A great man who, though he dabbled in Russian imperialistic politics, did so—I have an idea—more or less in the spirit of jest." He concluded with a verdict on Gurdjieff which has become famous. "I am a fairly wise man. But I wish I knew the things which Gurdjieff had forgotten."

What romantic could resist the vision of the master of both spiritual and temporal things which Abdullah conjured up? Gurdjieff's reputation as a political maestro had reached epic proportions. Louis Pauwels even records rumors that he was in Tibet "in 1903, and again in 1905, 1906, 1907 and 1908" together with Professor Karl Haushofer, the mentor of Rudolph Hess. Pauwels and his collaborator Jacques Bergier devote a long section of their bestselling *The Dawn of Magic* (1960) to arguing the existence of an occult plot involving Gurdjieff, Haushofer, and certain eccentrics who presided over the birth of the Nazi Party. Various aberrations taken from nineteenth-century Theosophy are used to manufacture a sinister center of diabolism located in Tibet and to create a new picture of Gurdjieff as the agent of the "King of Fear," in Shamballa, whose mystical mission was to destroy the intellectuals of the West . . . .

Unfortunately, this theory will not do, although the idea even passed—in a dignified, academic form—into a scholarly work by K. M. Pannikar, *Asia and Western Dominance* (1953). The occult ravings apart, it was very soon after the publication of *Monsieur Gurdjieff* that Alexandra David-Neel, who had spent several years in Tibet and had adopted a Tibetan lama as her son, published an article directly denying that Gurdjieff and Dordjieff had anything in common. She attributed the confusion to the similarity of the two names and published a photograph of Dordjieff to prove that by no stretch of the imagination could one face develop into the other. Gurdjieff himself told his pupils that he had once been given a Tibetan pass by an official who mistook the initial syllable of his name and described him as

"Dordjieff." Somewhere among files long since vanished may lie a clue to a mistake which resulted in British Intelligence organizations confusing—as Achmed Abdullah himself may have confused—the master and the pupil.

A case based solely on the available documents of the Great Game could leave the impression that there was no doubt about the matter; however, the evidence also includes a collection of photographs which is particularly perplexing. Some could well be pictures of the young Gurdjieff, others apparently could not, and at least one photograph has obviously been tampered with before publication. Although all are supposed to show the same man, there must be considerable doubt whether they in fact do so. This presents a peculiar problem. It is stretching coincidence too far to argue that another adventurer, resembling Gurdjieff in many particulars, was in the same area at the same time. On the other hand, a case which accepted all the photographs at their face value could not stand. There seem to be good reasons for suggesting that some of the photographs have been confused or made to lie for subterranean purposes; but a reader might plausibly retort that this belief was the result of an *idée fixe* on the author's part. The only solution seems to be to describe the inquiry step by step and to leave the verdict open.

It is, first of all, certain that any traveler, however innocent, who ventured into so sensitive an area would be investigated and his name pass into the files of the Great Game at Delhi, Simla, and Whitehall. By his own admission Gurdjieff was in Tibet while these files were open. Then, there are significant resemblances between the sacred dances of Tibet and Gurdjieff's own. Next, halfway through the thicket of *Beelzebub's Tales to his Grandson*, the reader stumbles across an outburst directed specifically at the Younghusband Expedition. The genial exasperation of Beelzebub with human folly is directed at denouncing the way mankind infallibly overturns the social organizations created by the great religious teachers. Things were going quite well in Tibet, says Beelzebub, owing chiefly to its isolation; and a part of the teaching of "Saint Lama" was actually applied in daily life. The result was rejoicing among certain cosmic authorities that some aims of the founder of Lamaism might actually be achieved.

> But your favourites did not allow even this to happen, but by their "military expedition" or Anglo-Tibetan war, without so much as a thought, knocked this possibility soundly on the head.
>
> About this "military expedition" I will tell you a little later.
>
> And I shall tell you about it chiefly because I myself happened by chance to be an eyewitness of all those lamentable events.

This passage about Tibet also occurs in a typescript version of *Beelzebub's Tales* which dates from before Achmed Abdullah's letter to Rom Landau.

With these various indications it was almost certain that a thorough search would reveal something. To anyone familiar with *Meetings with Remarkable Men* and the identifiable style of Gurdjieffian cunning, it will not come as a surprise that the first clue to a possible *nom de guerre* adopted by Gurdjieff had to do with *phonographs* and led to the discovery of a highly suspicious character coming from the general area of the Caucasus, using an unnecessary number of false names and carrying to Dordjieff and the Dalai Lama a strange assortment of baggage, which included a phonograph and its blank wax rolls for recording. Two rumors current among the followers of Gurdjieff and Ouspensky provide some confirmation of the identification which follows. The first is that Gurdjieff's mistrust of the British resulted from their having interned him in India. The second—for which the source is P. D. Ouspensky—is that Gurdjieff had a wife and children "elsewhere." (This latter piece of gossip accounts for the fact that the woman later known as Gurdjieff's "wife" never took the name of "Gurdjieff" but always remained "Madame Ostrowsky.") Both conditions are fulfilled by the man who called himself Ovshe or Ushe Narzunoff, although the existence of his family is bound up with the perplexing question of the photographs. Even if Ushe Narzunoff were not the same person as G. I. Gurdjieff, it is hard to believe that his activities were not related to Gurdjieff's own exploits in "those for me extremely memorable places," the mountains of Tibet.

The Government of India first took notice of Narzunoff in March 1900. It is not clear whether this was as the result of definite information or simply because of a security-conscious attitude toward Russian travelers. Narzunoff's suspicious contacts were later disclosed by the Reverend Graham Sandberg, the Anglican chaplain at Darjeeling. Sandberg was the author of a Tibetan grammar and an expert on Tibetan affairs; on behalf of the Government of India and the Great Game, he kept his ear very close to the ground. He connected Narzunoff with the Lama Dordjieff and with an equally mysterious Tibetan called Badmaieff who was closely linked to the Tsar of Russia. Before Narzunoff landed in India, the word had already been passed that he should not be allowed to cross the frontier to Tibet.

On March 6, 1900, there arrived in Calcutta from Marseilles aboard the S.S. *Dupleix* a man bearing a passport issued by General Nipi Khoraki, the Governor of Stavropol, dated September 29, 1899. This described him as "Ovshe Moutchkindoff Norzunoff"—the name was at other times spelled Narzunoff, Norzanaff and Norzanong—but when Narzunoff registered at the Continental Hotel, Calcutta, it was under the name of Myanoheid Hopityant, who was described as belonging to "the Post and Telegraph Department, Sangata, Stavropolsk Government." He had a letter of introduction to the French consul from a professor in Paris—this was probably a M. Joseph Deniker of whom there will be more to say. But as he spoke only Mongolian and Russian, the French consul sent him to a Mr. Branson, the Accountant-General for Bengal, who knew the latter language and could be expected to help him on his way. Narzunoff told Branson that he had once before been through Calcutta to Tibet via Darjeeling and that he now intended proceeding again to Tibet with a case of presents for the Dalai Lama. He explained that the presents were from himself in gratitude for previous kind treatment and as an offering to the head of the Buddhist Church. On March 10, Narzunoff left Calcutta for Darjeeling—in a considerable panic, as it later appeared—and on the way, stayed at Ghoom with a lama from Bhutan named Serap Gyatsho. On March 12, the traveler was interviewed at Ghoom by the Darjeeling Police. Under questioning, he proved undeniably shifty, although some trouble probably arose merely because of language difficulties.

At his first interview in March Narzunoff—unaccountably dressed as a Chinese—told the following story. In January of the previous year "he had passed through the Darjeeling district on his way to Peking, where he purchased some 9,000 rupees' worth of goods for trading purposes, and returned with them by a French steamer to Calcutta, left the goods in the Calcutta Custom House, and proceeded to Ghoom enroute to Yatung, where he intended remaining until he received remittances from his agents in Tibet and Mongolia; he averred that he was a trader pure and simple, and disowned the names of Norzunoff and Myanoheid Hopityant, stating that he had never made use of them." His real name, he said, was Obishak, and he was evidently trying to give the impression that he was a merchant, concerned chiefly with the trade between Tibet and China. But on March 27, he changed his tune and admitted that he had come from Paris and had also visited St. Petersburg and Berlin. A week later he confused his story yet again by muddling the ships on which he had traveled. He was detained at Ghoom until the end of August.

Meanwhile the Calcutta Customs had investigated the baggage which Narzunoff had left behind in bond. His personal effects included a telescope, two phonographs, a camera, and *"one rifle"*—this last officially italicized. The weapon, a .45 caliber sporting rifle sighted up to 450 yards, was confiscated, and Narzunoff was allowed to take away his personal luggage. But he was also in charge of thirty-one cases which he had imported as cargo and which evidently caused the customs officials a certain amount of perplexity. A single case contained some spirit lamps, a quantity of coral, photographic film, and silk. The remaining thirty held 590 metal bowls together with apparatus for suspending them, and their use was a matter for guesswork. At some time during Narzunoff's detention, his agents, Thomas Cook and Son, took these cases in charge and apparently delivered them to several lamas, including "a Tsanite Khamba (who is believed to be no other than Dordjieff)" whom Narzunoff had summoned from Lhasa. The friendly lamas failed to persuade the Darjeeling Police to allow Narzunoff into Tibet, and for five months he had to await the pleasure of the Queen-Empress. He applied to the Deputy Commissioner of Police at Darjeeling for the subsistence allowance which the Bengal Government had ordered be provided for him, but refused to accept the meager stipend of one rupee a day which he was offered.

While Narzunoff was cooling his heels at Ghoom, the Darjeeling Police took detailed notes about him. The description circulated was of a man, "height about 5 feet 10 inches, broad and well built, head now shaved, Mongolian features, slight moustache twisted down Chinese fashion, medium complexion." He gave his age as twenty-six. This appears to have been correct, as the wily Police Commissioner discovered a photograph given by Narzunoff to a Mongolian lama during the period of his detention, on the back of which was written: "In kind remembrance to the Mongolian Lama Yarphel from Ovisha Muchknoff Norsunoff, 26th July 1900, on the 26th year of his age." Not much reliance can be placed on a single preposition, "on," which has had to survive translation from Narzunoff's inscription and probable mauling by Anglo-Indian English, otherwise we might think that this revealed Gurdjieff's exact birth date. The photograph was reproduced and circulated by the Darjeeling Deputy Commissioner, who was later able to identify Narzunoff—looking most un-Mongolian—from this print.

For Narzunoff was officially declared persona non grata. On August 2, 1900, the Government of India decided to deport him to Russia "on the ground that it was undesirable that a Mongolian or quasi-Russian adventurer with several aliases should trade with Tibet through British India, and that though Norzanoff's goods seemed to be harmless, his intentions might be the reverse." He left India for Odessa on August 31, in the very ship which had brought him. In a final examination before his departure, Narzunoff disclosed three of the four names which enable a reconstruction of his affiliations in the Great Game. Besides his passport and a letter of introduction from the General Secretary of the Paris Geographical Society, he carried a letter from Prince Ukhtomsky, the editor of the newspaper, *Riga Viedomosti*. Ukhtomsky described Narzunoff as a *zaissan* or noble of the Kalmuck Buddhists, and declared that he was a member of the Imperial Russian Geographical Society who was "undertaking a journey to Tibet both on a religious pilgrimage and in the interests of science and commerce." Narzunoff seems to have decided to make a clean breast of his concerns to the Calcutta Police; he was, he said, "travelling at the expense of a very rich

Lama of Chinese Mongolia who lives in Urga, about 350 miles south of Irkutsk." The name of this lama was "Akchwan Darjilicoff"—whom the British authorities at once identified with Dordjieff. Dordjieff had visited London and Paris and wished to make presents to the lamas in Tibet of "special utensils"—the mysterious bowls—which he had failed to obtain in St. Petersburg and so ordered from "J. Denmiker and Cie., 8 Rue Buffon, Paris." Narzunoff was acting as courier on Dordjieff's behalf.

A fourth name must be added to the names "Ukhtomsky," "Dordjieff" and "Deniker" before the full tally of Narzunoff's sponsors is complete. This name is that of the strange character Shamzaran Badmaieff, who appears frequently in the archives of the Great Game and whom the suspicious British considered to be Narzunoff's spymaster. The concerns of Gurdjieff paralleled those of Badmaieff in many respects, and this similarity of interests is another good argument for assuming Gurdjieff and Narzunoff to be the same person. To make the relationship of these unfamilar characters intelligible, their history must be reconstructed.

The common interest of the group was in Russian expansion in Central Asia. Both Badmaieff and Dordjieff were Buryat Mongols from Russian territory around Lake Baikal. The Buryats assumed great importance in the Russian plans to penetrate Tibet, because their Buddhist faith allowed them access to the Forbidden City of Lhasa, whereas Europeans were turned back at the Tibetan border. As the political importance of Russian Buddhists increased, the Buryats themselves developed a degree of self-consciousness. Their intellectuals came to St. Petersburg and Moscow for education and a printed literature sprang up. Such happenings were associated with the activities of Dordjieff and Badmaieff, both of whom were concerned with developments that were political as well as cultural.

The long arm of the Russian Government stretched across Central Asia with the building of the Trans-Siberian Railway. The first stone of the sector inland from Vladivostok was laid in 1891 by Nicholas II when as Tsarevitch he traveled round the world. By 1898 the line was open with the exception of the section around Lake Baikal—about which Badmaieff had strong views—and a stretch along the Amur river. Eighteen ninety-eight is the year in which Ushe Narzunoff steps into recorded history.

Shamzaran Badmaieff (1851–1919) was educated at Irkutsk and St. Petersburg University, where he studied Chinese-Mongolian languages. He became converted from Buddhism to Orthodox Christianity and changed his name to Peter Alexandrovitch, at a ceremony where the Tsar Alexander III acted as godfather. From this time on, Badmaieff enjoyed a relationship of extraordinary favor with Alexander and his son Nicholas II, both of whom leaned heavily on his advice on Eastern questions. In 1875 Badmaieff left his lecturing job at the University and held a post in the Civil Service until 1893.

His value to Nicholas II was not simply that of a political advisor. He practised "Tibetan medicine" in an apothecary's shop which became a resort of fashionable St. Petersburg. On the birth of the hemophiliac Tsarevitch, Nicholas and his wife Alexandra found a new use for the mysterious Badmaieff and his medicines. Even the advent of Rasputin—with whom Badmaieff was on excellent terms—never weakened his position at court, although outside the circle of the Tsar and the Tsaritsa, he made many enemies. It was rumored that the patients at his clinic had political information recorded on their files, and his name was often coupled with those of Rasputin and the other gurus who attempted to establish a hold over the credulous Imperial couple. But Badmaieff stood head and shoulders above the crowd of magi and holy fools who clamored round the steps to the throne. This was simply because of his very obvious abilities. In 1917 he was arrested by the Bolsheviks on his way to join monarchist sympathizers in Finland; and in jail he made a deep impression even on his sceptical captors.

Agwan Dordjieff (d. 1938) was another remarkable Buryat, very close in age to Badmaieff. He was born about 1850 at Cherniskaia in the Russian province of Verknie-Udinsk, and educated successively at Gandan (the lamaic college at Urga in Mongolia) and at the huge monastery of Drepung, a few miles northwest of Lhasa. Here he acquired the degree of Tsanit Khanpo, which is roughly translated as Professor (or Abbot) of Metaphysical Theology. His career blossomed when he became tutor to the thirteenth Dalai Lama. It seems likely that it was Dordjieff's care which prevented the early death by poison or unexplained accident which had been the fate of so many of his pupil's predecessors, and when the Dalai Lama attained his majority, Dordjieff's vigilance was rewarded. He was given the title of "Work-Washing Abbot," a post which carried the duty of censing the Dalai Lama's chambers with perfumed water. Thus he was still closely attached to the person of the Dalai Lama after his period of tutorship was over. The British Secret Service, who saw him as a rich and powerful gray eminence, were not inaccurate in their assumptions. According to the German explorer Wilhelm Filchner, Dordjieff became a Russian agent in 1885, two years after the fourth expedition of Prjevalsky in which he took part.

Dordjieff's influence extended outside the borders of Tibet and over the hundreds of thousands of Russian Buddhists—the Buryats of Central Asia and the Kalmucks of the region round Astrakhan at the head of the Caspian Sea. The Dalai Lama appointed him as the agent who traveled through these areas preaching, distributing "life pills" and collecting tribute for the exchequer. Dordjieff's particular concern was to establish institutes of higher education in the various Kalmuck districts where these were lacking, and in 1906, a declaration supporting this plan was issued by the Russian Department of Foreign Creeds. Not content with establishing schools for his own faith, Dordjieff executed an audacious coup by building a Buddhist temple in St. Petersburg itself. When this project became public about 1911, a scandal of ferocious proportions broke out as the clergy of Holy Russia fulminated against the incursion of heathendom, and the plan was completed only with the support of powerful sympathizers. One of these was Prince Ukhtomsky of the Department of Foreign Creeds.

Dordjieff was a man of exceptional abilities. Apart from his political and religious activity, he found time to adapt the Tibetan alphabet to Buryat needs. He was a member of the Imperial Russian Geographical Society and contributed notes to its publications. He spoke French as well as Asian languages and traveled through Western Europe where he held Buddhist services in Paris, Vienna, and Rome and visited the Vatican. After the Russian Revolution, he was exiled to Leningrad where he spent most of his time in the temple he had built, until his arrest and imprisonment a year before his death in 1938. The picture of the Master of Heaven and Earth has—it must be admitted—a basis in reality.

The Government of India was perfectly correct in assuming that Dordjieff intended them no good. Although it is not clear whether he and Badmaieff agreed completely on the destiny of Central Asia, it was certainly in the interests of both to cooperate in attaching Tibet securely to the Russian sphere of influence. The Tibetans—or at least those of Dordjieff's party, which included the Dalai Lama himself—were apprehensive of the vast British power which had already established itself in Kashmir and was tangling with the Russians in Afghanistan. Dordjieff began diplomatic moves to encourage the Russians to act as a counterforce, while Badmaieff made propaganda on the Tsar's behalf. Their campaign is best approached through the figure of Prince Esper Esperovitch Ukhtomsky, who was a good friend to both of them.

Ukhtomsky was an Orientalist and came of a family with interests in Central Asia. He made an extensive collection of objects and manuscripts relating to the Buddhism of Mongolia and Tibet, most of which he housed in Irkutsk, and this deep interest in Buddhism led him to enter the Department of Foreign Creeds (which controlled non-Christian religions within the Empire). Besides being editor of the *Riga Viedomosti*, he was a director of the Russo-Chinese Bank. Most significantly, Ukhtomsky was of the extremely mystical temperament common to the Russian intelligentsia of the turn of the century, and claimed—in a catalogue of his Tibetan and Mongolian collection published outside Russia—that he had been a practicing Buddhist since the age of fifteen.

In 1890 and 1891 Nicholas II, while still Tsarevitch, undertook the journey around the world during which he opened construction on the Trans-Siberian Railway. Ukhtomsky was seconded from the Department of Foreign Creeds to act as recorder to the expedition. In his huge and lavish account of the journey, the chronicler betrays his expansionist sentiments at every opportunity. Russia was more Oriental than Western, he insisted, and emphasized the "inner" kinship of Indian and Russian peasants. The reason for all this fellow feeling was crystal clear. "We are, and must be," declared Ukhtomsky, "supported by the idea of an ever-possible advance of the irresistible North over the Hindu Kush."

It may have been because of the personal sympathies of this mystical imperialist or because of the natural inclination of Nicholas that the party visited the headquarters of the Theosophical Society at Adyar on February 7, 1891. Ukhtomsky knew all about Mme. Blavatsky, "our talented countrywoman," and translated her colleague Colonel Olcott's Buddhist catechism into Mongolian. His description of the Theosophical Society is significant. "At the insistence of H. P. Blavatsky, a Russian lady who knew and had seen much, the idea sprang up of the possibility, and even the necessity, of founding a society of theosophists, of *searchers for the truth**† in the broadest sense of the word, for the purpose of enlisting adepts of all creeds and races, of penetrating deeper into the most secret doctrines of oriental religions, of drawing Asiatics into true spiritual communion with educated foreigners in the West, of keeping up secret relations with different high priests, ascetics, magicians, and so on."

Ukhtomsky saw support for his ideas of Russian expansion in the "readiness of the Indians to group themselves under the banner of this strange *northern* woman." He argued that Mme. Blavatsky had been forced to leave India by "the suspiciousness of the English." Although this may simply represent a protest by the Theosophical Prince against unkind rejection of Mme. Blavatsky's very dubious "miracles," it raises the specter of the notorious accusations that the foundress of Theosophy was in India as a Russian spy. These accusations came not only from paranoid colonial officials, but also from one of the lady's own countrymen, and there is some evidence that Badmaieff himself was in contact with Mme. Blavatsky. The combination of an occult quest and intelligence work was not as improbable as it may sound, and if Mme. Blavatsky or Gurdjieff became mixed up in

* My italics.

such activities, they would by no means have been the only seekers for truth who were also spies.

The campaign of Russian expansion in which Badmaieff, Dordjieff, and Ukhtomsky played a part was the same as that in which Ushe Narzunoff became swept up. Some documents from Badmaieff's own archives enable us partially to reconstruct its progress.

In April 1894, Badmaieff began what he referred to as his "real activities," building up Russian influence in Central Asia. He kept in touch with Dordjieff and Ukhtomsky, and all three shared a brand of mystical imperialism. Dordjieff had visions of a pan-Mongol state under Russian protection. In his efforts to bring this about, he made use of the Mongolian belief in the coming of the Kingdom of Shamballa ("source-of-all-luck"), traditionally said to be situated in the north and therefore, to be equated with Russia. In 1896 Ukhtomsky was writing that the Mongols saw the Tsar as an incarnate Buddha. "The Tibetans," he hinted, "who keep up very near relations with our Buryats, are gradually but deeply imbibing identical ideas." As the campaign among the Mongols gathered momentum, Badmaieff began to trumpet success. "My arrival on the frontier," he announced to Nicholas II on January 15, 1897, "has shaken the whole of the Buddhist world . . . Buryats, Mongols and especially lamas . . . were always repeating that the time had come to extend the frontiers of the White Tsar in the east . . . ."

Not long afterward Prince Ukhtomsky turned up in Ceylon. On April 23, he met the President of the Theosophical Society, Colonel Olcott, at Colombo, and the pair went joyriding in an outrigger canoe. The Prince told Olcott that he was on his way to China with presents for the Emperor and a message from the Tsar, and invited him to join him on the return trip which he intended to make via the lamasaries of Mongolia.

Dordjieff's role at this stage of the Great Game is equivocal. It seems most likely that he was not the direct agent of Russia like Ukhtomsky or Badmaieff, but that he found it convenient to cooperate with their schemes to ensure the continued independence of Tibet. But as time wore on, Badmaieff increased his pressure on the Tsar to support a policy of direct annexation. "Am I," he inquired, "merely to organise trade, in order to widen our commercial-political influence in the East for further needs, or am I to prepare the ground for a final annexation . . . systematically occupying important points with the help of Buryats and Mongols?" His recommendation was quite open. "Tibet, being the highest plateau in Asia, dominating the Asian continent, should obviously be in Russian hands. With Tibet in her power, Russia will certainly be able to force England to be more compliant."

From London, Lord Curzon was pursuing a similar policy with regard to the Government of India. He too argued that Tibet was a key point dominating Central Asia and that his own government must beware of the machinations of the rival empire. It has been the fashion to write off such suspicions as proceeding from the imagination of an ambitious imperialist, but evidence shows that his intelligence service was correct in pointing the finger at Dordjieff and Badmaieff. In fact, the vigilance of the British simply resulted in driving Tibet further into the embrace of the White Tsar; and Dordjieff's anxious search for a protector provided the final lever which Curzon was able to use to persuade his own government to intervene.

Dordjieff made his first visit to St. Petersburg in 1898. Younghusband later heard a rumor that he had made contact with the Tsar and Tsaritsa through Rasputin, but Badmaieff is the more obvious channel. In 1900 Dordjieff was presented to the Tsar, and in the following year, he returned to Russia at the head of a mission from Tibet. The Mission of 1901 became a red rag to the British. Russia had obviously stolen a march on Britain and a military expedition was the only answer.

The Younghusband Expedition crossed the Tibetan frontier in July 1903. Two years had elapsed since the Dordjieff Mission to St. Petersburg. During this time reports kept reaching the Government of India of renewed Russian activity in Central Asia, and when the British expedition finally reached Lhasa, rumors came back that Dordjieff had established an arsenal there and was manufacturing rifles. But before the arrival of the British, he and the Dalai Lama had vanished into the Gobi Desert. They are supposed to have arrived at the monastery of Gandan in November 1904. After this point the attention of the Russian agents in Central Asia was diverted by the Russo-Japanese War; and Badmaieff and Ukhtomsky redirected their energies to ensuring that the Buddhist tribes remained loyal to the Tsarist régime.

"Ushe Narzunoff" was in the thick of the plotting and counterplotting which surrounded Dordjieff's mission to St. Petersburg in 1901. His exploits should be seen against the general background of Russian espionage in Central Asia and the specific efforts of Badmaieff to recruit likely candidates for his intelligence network. "I am training young men in two capitals—Peking and Petersburg—for further activities," Badmaieff informed the Tsar; and if Gurdjieff had wanted to penetrate Tibet, the context in which he could most easily have done so was in that of this operation. In 1924 Wilhelm Filchner published the memoirs of one of Badmaieff's "young men," the Buryat Tserempil, who claimed to have been recruited by Dordjieff at an early age. Tserempil was trained in the Indian Section of the Russian General Staff for "exploration and intelligence work" and sent on missions to Calcutta and Peshawar. It is significant that at the exact time when Narzunoff fell foul of the British authorities, Tserempil was also engaged in a mission through India, and like Narzunoff, he went disguised as a Chinese. Tserempil's identity was created for him by the Russian Colonel Orlov, who had given him his orders in St. Petersburg where he maintained a suite in the Hotel Europe under his cover name of Bogdanovitch. His more immediate controller was known as "Professor Stungevitch," and worked from a base in the Pamirs. According to Tserempil, the Professor was the head of the Indian Section of Russian Intelligence; and it is worth recalling here Gurdjieff's friendship with another professor, the archaeologist "Skridlov."

We possess the reports on Ushe Narzunoff which reached the Foreign Office in London; and also his own side of the story, which was edited by the French scholar Joseph Deniker. By the time this version of events was made public, Narzunoff had been exposed by the Government of India. He had been detained for a long period, and his physical appearance had been noted in minute detail by the Police Commissioner at Darjeeling. Narzunoff knew that his description had been taken down, and he mentions this fact in his diaries. For undercover work, he had become a decided risk, and it is quite possible that the reminiscences which he allowed Joseph Deniker to publish were designed to repair his damaged cover story and distract attention from the nonreligious activities of his master, Dordjieff.

Joseph Deniker (1852–1918) was of French origin but born in Astrakhan. He studied chemistry in Moscow and St. Petersburg, became interested in anthropology, and moved to Paris where he obtained his doctorate and was appointed librarian of the Museum of Natural History. Apart from his work on scientific bibliography, he published a series of books on racial characteristics, most notably *Races and Peoples of the World* (1900). Because of his upbringing, he spoke Russian, and made a speciality of Buddhism and Oriental languages. This resulted in his becoming the chief means of communication between the Russian experts on Central Asia and the Western world: Deniker would translate articles appearing in the Russian scientific press into French and was in constant correspondence with V. V. Grigoriev, the Secretary-General of the Imperial Russian Geographical Society. He knew Prince Ukhtomsky, and his interest in Buddhism led to his introduction to Agwan Dordjieff through the distinguished Orientalist, Sylvain Lévi. Deniker remained in touch with Dordjieff and did him many favors. When the *Times* correspondent with the Younghusband Expedition published his account of the sinister role attributed to Dordjieff, Deniker criticized this as "much exaggerated."

In 1898 Dordjieff made his first visit to St. Petersburg and passed on to Paris where he met Joseph Deniker. On June 27, the Tsanit Khanpo celebrated a Tibetan ceremony in the Musée Guimet with Dr. Deniker acting as interpreter. On this visit Dordjieff was asked in the interests of science to record some prayers on a phonograph—the old-fashioned kind with wax cylinders. He became enthusiastic and bought a machine with many cylinders, saying that for purposes unspecified this magnificent invention could be of great use. On a second visit to Paris, Dordjieff entrusted Deniker with a most unusual commission. The Tibetan priest was in search of steel, begging bowls for his monks, but these had by custom to be made from a single piece of metal. An experiment with a German company had failed, as welding had been used on the bowls, and it was Deniker's task to find a firm which would cast large numbers of vessels in accordance with lamaistic precepts. Ushe Narzunoff arrived in Paris in 1900 to fetch these bowls, which formed the mysterious cargo that so puzzled the Indian Customs.

This was the beginning of his acquaintance with Deniker, which culminated when Deniker published the narrative of his expeditions to Lhasa, based partly on Narzunoff's diaries and partly on conversations which took place in Paris in 1902, in the magazine Le Tour du Monde for 1904. Narzunoff may then have been collecting the special lightweight tse-boum—a ritual object—which Dr. Deniker was having made by French craftsmen for the Dalai Lama. His presence in Paris in 1902 shows without any doubt that his journeys in central Asia did not end with the last journey he described to Joseph Deniker, that of 1901. It may well have been that he wished to establish his bona fides by releasing an explanation of his ill-fated journey with the begging bowls. While a brief account might indeed have allayed some suspicions, the quantity of detail published by Deniker provides countless reasons for considering that Narzunoff was not what he seemed. His story simply will not stand up. By the time it appeared in the press, the Government of India had more information connecting Narzunoff with Dordjieff and the operations of Russian Intelligence. And the reminiscences published by Joseph Deniker are packed with details which point to the conclusion that this suspicious customer—half pilgrim, half adventurer—was Gurdjieff himself.

The question of the photographs which Deniker published—and of others which he did not publish—will be considered separately. For the moment we shall concentrate on the diary and conversations which Deniker edited, and which he introduced with the remark that Agwan Dordjieff was "to some extent the sponsor of Narzunoff's journeys." Deniker's conversations with Narzunoff had been conducted in Russian—in which language Narzunoff's diaries were written—with a few Kalmuck expressions thrown in which Deniker recognized from his childhood acquaintance with the language.

Ushe Narzunoff began with the story of his upbringing as a Kalmuck squire in the province of Stavropol, his education in a Cossack school and his nomadic life with his family on the steppes. He claimed to have met Dordjieff on one of his preaching trips among the Kalmucks. By his own account Narzunoff was a pious young man who was disgusted by the drunkenness of his fellows; and Dordjieff had "advised him to make a pilgrimage to Lhasa." In the light of his later activities it is quite clear that Dordjieff's interest in Narzunoff was much more than that of a general religious duty, and that the education Narzunoff possessed was more extensive than that of a Cossack school. However they came together, Narzunoff and his protector left Russia in August 1898, and traveled on the Trans-Siberian Railway as far as Verknie-Udinsk on Lake Baikal. From there they continued to Urga, and on October 5, Narzunoff was dispatched to Lhasa with a letter and gifts for the Dalai Lama from Dordjieff.

Narzunoff's journey toward the Gobi Desert was not always by the obvious route. He called at several secluded monasteries, including the convent of Youndoun-beissin-kure—which, he emphasized to Deniker, was not to be found on any maps of Mongolia—apparently in order to watch the ceremony known as "tsam." This service was accompanied by mime and dancing, for which the lamas don masks representing terrifying deities who appear to them in the state of dream or ecstasy called "xan-tohi" in Tibetan. Narzunoff, therefore, displayed an interest in sacred dances very shortly after beginning his expedition. He proceeded by camel across the Gobi and on the south side of the desert fell in with a party of Mongols who offered to guide him into Tibet. Narzunoff's account of his adventure with these guides makes it quite certain that he was not what he seemed, and was European to boot:

On the way I told my guides that I was a Mongol, a Chinese subject, and that I was going to Lhasa on a pilgrimage. Nonetheless, towards the end of the journey, my guides discovered my secret, and for two reasons: 1. In order to conceal the fact that I was a Russian subject, knowing how to read Russian, I also took notes in the diary of my journey in Kalmuck. But, because Kalmuck writing is slightly different to Eastern Mongol script, my companions noticed it . . . 2. To keep warm I was wearing under my furs a jacket of European cut, [and] as I undressed during a halt the Mongols noticed my jacket. No doubt because of all this when we arrived in their native country, the Mongols began to say that I was a Russian subject, that I was wearing Russian clothes and was keeping a travel-diary. In consequence, they refused to lead me to the agreed place . . .

Why was a devout Kalmuck traveling under the protection of a Buryat dignitary wearing Western clothes? The inquirer might be forgiven for doubting whether the differences between Kalmuck and Buryat script were as great as those between any form of script and the Russian in which Narzunoff was undoubtedly keeping his diary—only this can explain the obtrusive "also" in the extract quoted above. The "also" is directed either at Deniker, the recorder of the conversation, or by Deniker at his audience. Besides the Russian—"which you see here, my dear Dr. Deniker," or "which I have before me, my dear readers"—Narzunoff was "also" keeping his diary in Kalmuck. He must have let his tongue run away with him in the memory of his narrow escape. According to Narzunoff he managed to bribe his companions, and their goodwill was secured when he burned his jacket before their eyes.

Without further mishap he crossed into Tibet and reached Lhasa, where he stayed a little over a month. He had an audience with the Dalai Lama, to whom he presented the gifts and letters he was carrying. The splendid ceremonial of the reception—Narzunoff claims that he passed through an escort of a hundred men—seems a little lavish for the private emissary of the Dalai Lama's old tutor, and it is possible that Narzunoff's embassy was on behalf of others. He was entertained and rewarded with money. In his account of the episode, Narzunoff twice refers to Dordjieff as "my master"—no doubt in the sense of "spiritual master"—and this expression does seem to indicate the nature of the relationship between them.

Narzunoff's description of Lhasa is packed with observations on Tibet and its customs. He left the holy city in April 1899, and in May arrived at Darjeeling where he hired a Chinese-speaking Mongol to act as his guide to Peking. Narzunoff was made extremely nervous by his guide's calm announcement that most others would have poisoned him for the money he carried, and had to submit to being grossly overcharged for all the services his companion performed. In Peking he escaped from his guide's clutches and made his way through Mongolia to Urga, which he reached at the end of July.

According to Narzunoff, he arrived back in his native steppes in August. Let us say that he traveled to the general area of the Caucasus. The passport which the Governor of Stavropol issued to him was dated September 29, so it is possible that further journeys were contemplated immediately. We know nothing of Narzunoff until his departure for Paris in January 1900, in the capacity of Dordjieff's messenger boy. He also had a commission from the Russian Geographical Society to take photographs of Lhasa. On his arrival on January 25, Joseph Deniker took him to a meeting of the Paris Geographical Society and introduced him to the secretary. Deniker's son, M. Georges Deniker, who as a boy of fifteen, met Ushe Narzunoff on this occasion, remembers that he was gadget-crazy; he bought electric lamps, a camera, a tie pin which lit up, and, of course, a phonograph and its cylinders.

The love of mechanical marvels was something which Gurdjieff never lost; even the touch of the illuminating tie pin seems characteristic. But it is the phonographs which seem to say most clearly, "Here is Gurdjieff!" The phonograph pervades his writings. For example, in *Meetings with Remarkable Men,* he recalls how he was forced to leave in Moscow "a few hundred" of the songs his father sang, "recorded on phonograph rolls." Almost certainly he intended to use this new invention for collecting traditional music in Asia. In *Beelzebub's Tales,* Gurdjieff gives a fatuous account of his birth in which an Edison phonograph is one of the actors; in *Meetings with Remarkable Men,* he describes how he once achieved a striking commercial success by recording popular songs and bawdy stories on the blank rolls of "an Edison phonograph" and renting out ear-phones in the bazaars. Whether this story is true is neither here nor there—there is a possible moral attached—but it shows the impact the phonograph made on Gurdjieff's mind. It even found its way into his teaching as one of his mechanical analogies. By the time *Beelzebub's Tales* was written, phonographs with rolls had given place to those with disks, and Gurdjieff used the comparison—at least as early as 1919—to describe the registration of sense impressions on the three apparatuses which he said were responsible for preserving past experiences. "They consist in adaptations recalling clean wax phonograph disks; on these 'disks' or, as they might otherwise be called, 'reels,' all the impressions received begin to be recorded from the first days after the appearance of a man in the world, and even before, during the period of his formation in his mother's womb."

At the beginning of March 1900, Narzunoff disembarked in Calcutta with his cargo of begging bowls. His story goes that he learned from a Russian-speaking contact that he would be prevented from reaching Tibet. "Moved by the emotion of fear," as he puts it, he donned his Chinese disguise and left for Darjeeling with the object of sending word to Tibet. He was detained by the authorities in Darjeeling, near which place he stayed with a Mongolian lama. In May three Tibetans arrived with a certificate that he was an innocent Buddhist pilgrim, and he felt free to take photographs without being clapped in prison. In August he was sent under armed escort to Calcutta where he was imprisoned for a week and then informed that he was to be deported. Meanwhile his efforts to dispatch the begging bowls to Tibet were frustrated at every turn. He had managed to send three cases in charge of a trusted emissary, but the man died en route and his wife refused to surrender the goods. In Calcutta he suffered agonies because the remaining twenty-eight cases had been reclaimed from the Customs by a "powerful and unknown" man during his detention in Darjeeling. The difficulty arose from the translation through several languages of the name of the powerful man—"Koukanssen," who proved to be Narzunoff's agent, Thomas Cook and Son, whose capable services not only whisked the begging bowls off to Lhasa, but forced the recalcitrant widow to disgorge her cache of loot.

At his own request, the "*quasi*-Russian adventurer" was shipped off to Odessa rather than Paris or Peking. He arrived in Russia on October 3, 1900. The Government of India received information through Graham Sandberg that Dordjieff himself had passed through India and traveled separately to Odessa, where he and Narzunoff met Badmaieff and all three proceeded to Livadia in the Crimea. On October 15, the *Journal de St. Petersbourg* announced the Tsar's reception of Dordjieff at Livadia. Somewhat naturally, the diaries of Ushe Narzunoff make no mention of this association with royalty and instead offer a version which reeks of implausibility. "As soon as I arrived back in my encampments," he writes— one wonders who was looking after the stock all this time—"I had no further thought than to return again to Tibet. By a happy combination of circumstances, the Tsanit Khanpo Agwan Dordjieff was in Siberia, in the Transbaikalia, his native land, and on the point of leaving for Lhasa. All that was necessary to make my master decide to wait for me in Urga were several exchanges of telegrams." Such a coincidence and Narzunoff's hearing about it are manifestly impossible, and the gallant teller of tales was unlucky in the informants of the Government of India. To rephrase the narrative in what was most probably its real sequence: Narzunoff accompanied Dordjieff from Livadia to Urga, which they left with six companions on January 5, 1901.

This was a remarkable journey by any standards. If Narzunoff is to be believed, they arrived in Lhasa on February 28, having crossed the Gobi in a record time of two months, twenty-four days. If we allow for some exaggeration, it was still a vastly quick time ("not for forest am I specialist, but for sand," said Gurdjieff later) and there must have been some urgency. The reception of Dordjieff by the Tsar and his contact with Badmaieff could have provided the immediate causes. The necessity for speed was almost certainly because the plans of Dordjieff and Badmaieff now called for the open reception by the Tsar of a Tibetan mission. Having decided on this irrevocable course, no doubt it was best to consult the Dalai Lama and send the mission on its way before the English somehow circumvented the plan. Dordjieff and Narzunoff spent only a month in Lhasa before setting off again on their travels.

During this time Narzunoff was once more presented to the Dalai Lama who inquired how the British had treated him in captivity. He was rewarded for his privations by the gift of a ceremonial tiger skin. Once a man had been allowed to sit on such a seat of honor in the presence of the Dalai Lama, his name was inscribed in a register and from then on the privilege was his by right. During his stay, Narzunoff could at last make use of the camera which Grigoriev of the Imperial Russian Geographical Society had given him, although he was forced to be circumspect because of the Tibetan ban on photography. He managed to photograph some of the principal buildings in Lhasa and on excursions outside the town he took several more pictures. One of these trips took him to the Drepung, with its two thousand monks; another to the monastery of Sera with its surrounding hermitages and a third to Galdan which preserved the largest collection of relics of Tsong Kapa, the founder of the Yellow Hat sect of Buddhist lamas.

On his way back from this last expedition, Narzunoff saw and photographed a remarkable local custom—of which, as Gurdjieff, he makes particular note. This was the spectacle of pilgrims measuring their length round the perimeter of Lhasa. "They let themselves fall full-length, get up and prostrate themselves again," writes Narzunoff, "having placed their feet on the spot which they had earlier touched with their head. In this manner they go round the town in two or three days." A more extreme form of devotion was practiced by those who followed the same procedure—but measured the distance they could advance by the length of their faces. In *Beelzebub's Tales* Gurdjieff inserts a completely isolated paragraph commenting on the practice, and one of the dances which he taught his pupils was based on this uncomfortable maneuver—only it was said to be a Christian custom, native to the Caucasus.

On March 28, Narzunoff left Lhasa for Tashi-Lumpo where he was presented to the Panchen Lama. At first his account is given in the first person, as if he was the sole or principal traveler, but it soon appears that Dordjieff was one of the party. Because of the mountainous terrain, horses were out of the question and Narzunoff was forced to walk. In contrast, Dordjieff behaved as a true Mongol, and hired a sherpa to carry him on his back into Nepal. It was an incongruous start to the famous Dordjieff Mission which so annoyed the British. In Nepal they spent five days, Narzunoff told Deniker, "disguised as pilgrims." From the King of Nepal they obtained permits to visit the holy places of Buddhism in the south and, armed with these documents, they succeeded in entering India. Between the Nepalese frontier and the Indian border they survived three customs inspections. Narzunoff had hidden half his photographic film in a box taped to his thigh, and the other half in a jar of flour. His Russian passport was in the sole of his boot. On May 10, the party reached the railhead where they had to submit to an interrogation about their purpose in visiting India. This inquisition, they were told, was because of the efforts of a certain Russian agent to penetrate Tibet the previous year. "My life," records a nervous Narzunoff, "was hanging by very thin threads."

The mission was allowed their tickets to Bombay and proceeded from Bombay to Colombo where they embarked on the Russian steamer *Tambof,* which reached Odessa on June 12. The *St. Petersburg Gazette* announced the arrival of Dordjieff with an official embassy and carried an article by Badmaieff describing "Owshe Norsinof" as Dordjieff's "secretary and translator." According to Narzunoff's journal, Dordjieff and he parted company at Odessa—presumably to allow the homesick Narzunoff to return to his encampments. Unfortunately for this story, the Deputy Commissioner at Darjeeling had obtained the photograph Narzunoff had given to his Mongolian friend during his detention. From this he identified him in a picture of a landau containing members of the Dordjieff Mission in St. Petersburg, published in *The Graphic*. Ushe Narzunoff is bare headed, and in formal dress with a medal on his chest.

Wise after the event, the Deputy Commissioner plodded on his investigations. He suborned a Tibetan guide called Pat-ma-wang-cha, who had acted as courier to the mission from Katmandu to Bombay, and discovered evidence which proved to his satisfaction that the four allegedly Mongolian members of the Dordjieff party had in fact been Russians. The reasons which he gave for these suspicions were as follows:

1. They were not able to understand Tibetan, or to make themselves understood to Tibetans, which they would have been if they had been Mongolians.
2. One of them had a curious watch, which he showed to the Lama of the Buddhist Chorten at Katmandu, and which he informed him had been bought in Russia, and was worth Rs 300. The lama also told him that they were really "u-ru-su" Russians.
3. They ate meat largely whenever they could get it.
4. One of them (the youngest) knew English, as he was always able to read the railway tickets and detect when they were overcharged. The youngest of these "Mongolian lamas," when they got to Bombay, procured a suit of European clothes from somewhere, and shaved himself, and went on board the ship as a European.

There is something about that youngest lama—undoubtedly Narzunoff—which rings warning bells. A Gurdjieffian cunning, the Sly Man himself, the adept—how would one learn better except on the professional stage—of *acting in life*, of playing a role . . . ?

After July 1901, when Dordjieff was officially presented to the Tsar, he and his associates were fixed in the official mind as the opposition. Francis Younghusband was convinced by rumors which reached him that the outcome of the mission was a proposal to send Badmaieff to Tibet, and in February 1902, reports from the pandit Sarat Chandra Das told him of a "so-called Mongolian Mission," with a Russian at its head, which had been received in Lhasa. Suspicion continued to mount until the British military expedition of July 1903.

Like Dordjieff, Narzunoff came into the open after the reception of the mission from Tibet. In October 1901, Joseph Deniker published his photograph of the Potala at Lhasa. It was the first photograph of Lhasa to be published and narrowly missed being the first taken. In 1902 Narzunoff visited Deniker in Paris, where he volunteered the information which the scholar published in two articles, one in the American magazine the *Century* in August 1903, and another the following year, in *Le Tour du Monde*. In the autumn of 1903, the Imperial Russian Geographical Society published a selection of Narzunoff's photographs together with descriptions of those by the Buryat professor Tsybikov, another of Badmaieff's agents.

None of the photographs of Narzunoff himself was published until after the British had reached Lhasa, by which time the news value of the story was immense. And although Deniker had the notes of his conversations with Narzunoff since 1902, he published nothing based on them until after the Younghusband Expedition. The evidence seems overwhelming that Narzunoff was, among other things, a Russian agent; and the appearance of his self-portrait as an innocent pilgrim and traveler was astutely timed to coincide with anti-British feeling after the flight of the Dalai Lama.

There is one further point which is relevant to Ushe Narzunoff and G. I. Gurdjieff. In November 1904, a large collection of Orientalia was sold in a Paris auction room. One part of this sale was devoted entirely to Tibetan items: over one thousand lots of statues, pictures, and manuscripts. For this Tibetan sale, Joseph Deniker and a colleague of his at the Musée Guimet wrote the catalogue. Deniker hinted that the collection might have been formed in Peking. But it was sold under the name of "Collection G. . . ."

"The business I preferred above all others," writes Gurdjieff in his essay, "The Material Question," "which never required my specially devoting to it any definite time or needed any fixed place of residence, and which moreover was very profitable was the trade in carpets and antiques of all kinds." Badmaieff's agent Tsybikov returned from Lhasa in 1901 with a huge collection of manuscripts, and if Gurdjieff was in Tibet at the time of the Younghusband Expedition in 1903–04, it would have been quite feasible for him to withdraw from the country after the disruption caused by the British invasion and to realize his assets. It is also possible—if Gurdjieff was Narzunoff—that he may have acted as an intermediary for the sale of the "Collection G . . . ," and that his principal was the antique collector, Ukhtomsky.

On this evidence alone, it would be hard to believe that Ushe Narzunoff was not Gurdjieff. If Gurdjieff had wanted to penetrate Tibet, he would have had to go as a Buddhist, and to disguise himself as a Kalmuck was the obvious choice. Stavropol, where Narzunoff's passport was issued, is a town in the north of the Caucasus, and it is as near Gurdjieff's home in the Caucasus proper as a Kalmuck might have been expected to come— Astrakhan would have been a more likely province to issue a passport to a Kalmuck. Narzunoff was exactly the right age, and his birthday in 1874 even falls directly between the two dates most favored for Gurdjieff—1872 and 1877. He was the right build and height; and if it is thought that the Indian police's description of his "Mongolian" features puts him out of court, it should be emphasized that they later changed their minds about his Mongolian nationality, and that both Ouspensky in 1915 and Carl Bech-hofer Roberts in 1919 remarked on Gurdjieff's "oriental" appearance.

These considerations are important, because the latest photograph of Ushe Narzunoff was taken in 1908, and almost a decade separates it from the first known photograph of Gurdjieff in his role as teacher. In ten years a man can change greatly, irrespective of any considerations of fraud. Some features—in particular the size of the feet and the long, sensitive fingers— are very Gurdjieffian; others, including the more fleshy appearance of the whole head in some of the photographs, seem to rule out the identification altogether. The photographs, however, are so disparate as to suggest either that their subject was a master of disguise or that some very funny business was going on.

The first photograph of Narzunoff published by Joseph Deniker was supposedly taken in 1898. This is a formal portrait, showing a young man with a rosary or chaplet in one hand and the other holding a book on a table. Even in the badly defined face Gurdjieff's most prominent characteristics can be seen: the protruding chin, the distinctively shaped—and undisguisa-ble—ears, the small flat triangular patch at the bridge of the nose. It is fairly clear that this picture has been doctored. The real depth of the eye sockets—note the shadow above the right eye—may have been disguised by highlighting the eyelids to produce a more "Mongolian" effect. The hair is quite obviously painted in. No human being of whatever nationality ever had hair which could lie in the way Narzunoff's hair is supposed to lie in the photograph. Two strokes of a paint brush would produce a similar effect. The reason for this tampering? Perhaps a shaven head, indicating that Narzunoff had already impersonated a Mongolian lama, or Gurdjieff's own naturally curly hair which was totally un-Mongolian.

Further photographs were published by Joseph Deniker in *Le Tour du Monde*. A small portrait with a shaven head shows ears and brow ridge approximating Gurdjieff's, but it is quite unlike another portrait of Narzunoff in Chinese dress, said to have been taken in Peking. Either Narzunoff was trying to look "Chinese" or this is a picture of a different person. It may be that this is further evidence of shiftiness on Narzunoff's part, as Deniker preserved, but did not publish, another photograph of his friend in the same Chinese costume which he identified specifically as having been taken in St. Petersburg. Neither in these "Chinese" pictures nor in another published in the *Century Magazine* (and supposed to show Narzunoff and his guides in the Himalayas) is there any possibility of making out Gurdjieff's face in that of the man said to be Narzunoff. On the other hand, it cannot be said for certain that these Oriental pictures show the same man as appears in the full-length portrait or the small portrait with the shaven head. The suspicion begins to germinate that perhaps this embarrassment of portrait studies was designed purposely in order to confuse.

This impression is not dispelled by a collection of portraits of himself, his wife, and his children sent by Narzunoff to Deniker and never published. There is one of his eldest son, Daidan or Datsun, dressed in a sailor suit and holding a chaplet, said to have been taken in Moscow in 1904. Another shows Daidan, aged twelve, his younger brother Dordje, aged eight, and their lama "educator" in Verknie-Udinsk by Lake Baikal. It is undated, but might be a year or so earlier than the photograph of the elder son taken in 1904. On the back of the Verknie-Udinsk photograph, Narzunoff scribbled a petition to Deniker to be "as good a friend" to his children as he had been to himself. In view of Deniker's earlier role as the editor of Narzunoff's misleading memoirs, it might not be over cynical to read a double meaning into this request. On the other hand, it might be the polite gesture of thanks which it appears to be.

Additional difficulties are presented by a photograph of Narzunoff and his wife taken in Verknie-Udinsk on November 6, 1908. Narzunoff has larger and more cosmopolitan mustache than in his earlier photographs, and a physiognomy considerably different from the Asiatic type of the lady beside him. At first sight there is little in the face to suggest Gurdjieff, although it is possible to point to a number of resemblances to Gurdjieff's face in later life. There are the strong lines etched from the corners of the nose to the mouth, the beginnings of the dimple which was to mark Gurdjieff's chin, and—most telling of all—the eyes. First, they are not Mongolian eyes which conceal the tear-duct under the skin at the corner; and second, they show the squint in the left eye which becomes increasingly obvious in Gurdjieff's later photographs. The direct studio lighting might have been arranged to flatten out Narzunoff's face, and a bone structure similar to Gurdjieff's can be detected by a study of the shadow contours along the nose and around the top of the eyes. On the other hand, the general appearance of the face is not that of Gurdjieff—nor of the "Narzunoff" of the shaven-headed portrait or the figure with the rosary. This Narzunoff does seem to resemble the pictures of the "Narzunoff" in Chinese dress. Is this evidence of a similarly effective disguise, or were two or more men photographed in the Narzunoff identity?

We do not possess the photograph which would settle the matter. This is the portrait which Narzunoff gave the lama Yarphel at Ghoom in 1900, and which presumably showed him as he was, with no possibility of deception. However, the *Graphic* photograph of the Dordjieff mission is almost as good, because the Deputy Commissioner of Police at Darjeeling was able to identify Narzunoff as one of the party by comparison with the Yarphel photograph in his possession. This is the only photograph of Narzunoff taken without the benefit of studio conditions and the cosmetic accessories of the photographer's art. It is the only photograph which does not emanate from Narzunoff himself, through Deniker. It is the only photograph which can be said with reasonable certainty to show the historical Narzunoff who was in trouble in British India in 1900. And of all the photographs it is the one which most resembles Gurdjieff.

In *Meetings with Remarkable Men* Gurdjieff describes how he and "Pogossian" disguised themselves as "Caucasian Tartars," and in another place how he and "Skridlov" spent an extensive period of preparation for an attempt to impersonate a Persian dervish and a Sayyid. These explicit admissions that Gurdjieff had adopted exotic disguises must be coupled with his enthusiasm for the trick of the actor's trade. Disguises are to be expected from Gurdjieff; but some of the photographs of Narzunoff do seem to exceed all acceptable limits of the idea of disguise. The theory that some of the photographs were planted and others doctored to cover the tracks of a leading Tsarist agent is more likely. But such an argument is open to the powerful criticism that it can be used to explain away as concocted any inconvenient item of evidence. It must be admitted that if this theory were held dogmatically, it would be extremely dangerous. However, the same reasons which made it necessary to examine the possibility that Gurdjieff was Narzunoff also mean that the idea of deliberate falsification must be kept seriously in mind. We need not accept it, but we are compelled not to dismiss it out of hand.

Although further comparison between Gurdjieff and Narzunoff must be categorized as suggestive speculation only, a number of other points of contact should not be ignored. For example, there are the apparently troublesome photographs from Verknie-Udinsk, showing the wife, the lama "educator," and the boys Daidan and Dordje. Gurdjieff's Beelzebub has two sons called Tooilan and Tooloof, whose "educator" is mentioned with special affection. According to J. G. Bennett, Gurdjieff later claimed that his eldest son became the abbot of a Buddhist monastery at a precociously early age, so that it is quite natural to find the twelve-year-old Daidan already wearing the robes of a novice monk.

It is significant that the younger child is called Dordje. In Tibetan Buddhism, the *dordje* is the symbol of the lightning, of power flowing from heaven to earth, and thus of the fully realized man, the agent of heaven. The expression also has a ritual significance, and the *dordje* itself is often referred to as the "lamaic sceptre": a metal object gripped in the fist, with the projecting ends becoming first bulbous, then tapering to a point. This is the concrete symbol of power descending from heaven, and is also said to be the symbol of *method*. A story told by Maurice Nicoll, one of Gurdjieff's leading followers, relates that once, in a New York hotel, when Gurdjieff thought he was quite alone, he was overheard repeating to himself: "I am *dordje* . . . I am *dordje* . . ." Presumably he meant to affirm his function as the lightning flash between heaven and earth, and the incident is one small piece of evidence among many which demonstrate Gurdjieff's debt to Tibetan Buddhism.

This indebtedness is clear from *Beelzebub's Tales;* and it may well be the greatest single debt Gurdjieff owed to any existing system. If the young seeker for truth had become interested in Buddhism in his native Caucasus, the nearest large communities of Buddhists would have been the Russian Kalmucks. It is not beyond the bounds of belief that his investigations led him across the path of Agwan Dordjieff and Prince Ukhtomsky. If Gurdjieff had wanted to study Tibetan Buddhism at the source, he could have had no better tutor than Dordjieff, a Tsanit Khanpo at the right hand of the Dalai Lama. Prince Esper Ukhtomsky, with a personal and long-standing commitment to Buddhist practice, and his belief in the "necessity" of a brotherhood of seekers for the truth, would also have been able to further the young man's quest. Ukhtomsky is the most likely original of the character "Prince Lubovedsky" in *Meetings with Remarkable Men*. Like that prince, Ukhtomsky had occult and Oriental interests; and when "Ushe Narzunoff" was searched in India, he had a letter of introduction from Ukhtomsky in his pocket.

It was never really possible to consider Gurdjieff an adventurer pure and simple, and as "Ushe Narzunoff," he is even more difficult to discount as a fraud. Clearly he was engaged in work on behalf of Russian Intelligence, and even received a medal for it if the *Graphic*'s picture of the Dordjieff Mission is any guide. But this in no way excludes a more earnest side to his career. The imperialism of Ukhtomsky and Badmaieff was of a distinctly mystical nature, and who is to say where Gurdjieff's intelligence activities stopped and his spiritual quest began? Stories which he told during the 1930s hint that for a time he became the Buddhist monk which his shaven head perpetually suggested. The evidence implies that with Dordjieff as his spiritual director, Gurdjieff combined politics with his personal search. To see him as a Russian Kim might not be far from the truth—and Kim also had his lama.

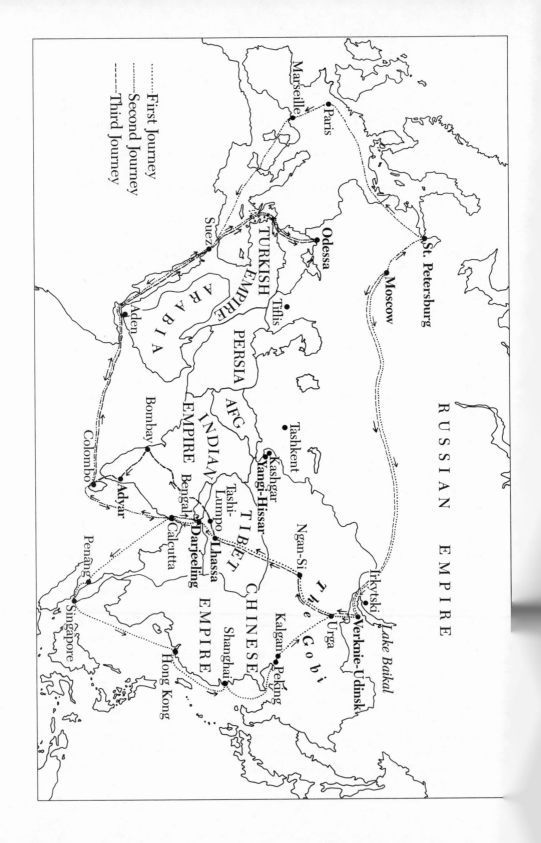

First Journey
Second Journey
Third Journey

Marseille
Paris
St. Petersburg
Moscow
Odessa
Suez
Tiflis
TURKISH EMPIRE
ARABIA
Aden
PERSIA
AFG
Tashkent
Kashgar
Yangi-Hissar
BOmbay
INDIAN EMPIRE
Colombo
Adyar
Bengal
Calcutta
Darjeeling
Tashi-Lumpo
Lhassa
TIBET
Ngan-Si
Penang
Singapore
Hong Kong
CHINESE EMPIRE
Shanghai
Kalgan
Peking
The Gobi
Urga
Verknie-Udinsk
Irkytski
Lake Baikal

RUSSIAN EMPIRE

3

The Professional Hypnotist

As "Ushe Narzunoff," Gurdjieff would have been intimately concerned with Tibet, at least until 1904. According to extracts from the *Third Series* quoted by J. G. Bennett, it was in Tibet that he was accidentally wounded for the second time. This happened in 1902, and Gurdjieff was taken by friends to convalesce at the edge of the Gobi Desert near Yangi Hissar. We know little about his movements for the next two years. Like the Buryat agent Tserempil, he might have joined the party of Dordjieff and the Dalai Lama as they withdrew northward into the Gobi. Certainly, by the end of 1904—about the time when the "Collection G . . . ." went on sale in Paris— Gurdjieff was back in the Caucasus, where he had his contretemps with the third stray bullet. On this occasion the disaster took place at Chiatur, on the southern slopes of the Caucasus between Tiflis and the Black Sea. When he had recovered, Gurdjieff wandered back through the Transcaspian toward Central Asia and returned to the place near Yangi Hissar to which he had been brought two years before.

Apparently it was here, on the southeastern fringes of the desert, that he reached his conclusions about the important role played by hypnotism in human affairs. This train of thought was directly associated with the turbulent nature of his career to date. Bennett suggests that the skirmish in which Gurdjieff was hit for the third time was connected with the social unrest which culminated in the abortive Russian revolution of 1905. He argues that Gurdjieff had penetrated the revolutionary movement on behalf of the authorities, and was possibly even acting as a double agent. Although he may have spied for the Tsarist Government, Gurdjieff's political sympathies were later known to be at the opposite end of the spectrum to those of his more aristocratic Russian pupils, and the boy from the deprived background could have played the part of a social revolutionary with some conviction. But by Gurdjieff's own account, the chief result of his close acquaintance with political intrigue was to surfeit him with rhetoric and fill him with horror at the ease with which ordinary people allowed themselves to be led by the nose. Partly in reaction against the violence he had seen and partly as a result of conversations with "various revolutionists" he had met in Italy, Switzerland, and the Caucasus, Gurdjieff decided that he "must discover, at all costs, some manner or means for destroying in people the predilection for suggestibility which causes them to fall easily under the influence of 'mass-hypnosis.'"

Hypnotism had come increasingly to occupy the forefront of his thoughts. His quest for meaning had halted before the blank conclusion that no existing knowledge could help him. The sole remaining possibility was the discovery of something new, not in the sense of "lost wisdom," but new facts about the nature of man, resulting from a pioneering analysis of the psyche. He decided that "the answers for which I was looking . . . can only be found, if they are at all accessible to man, in the sphere of 'man's subconscious-mentation.'" In search of a key to the subconscious mind, he began to collect all the data he could on Asiatic theories of hypnotism.

In Bennett's view, this reorientation was the result of an important change in Gurdjieff's psychological attitude. No longer was he seeking knowledge or power for himself, but he was proposing to liberate humanity from the illusions under which it labored. This is true so far as it goes, and perhaps Gurdjieff's decision does represent a newfound altruism. But his conclusions bore the same relation to his search for wisdom as the chicken to the egg. They also—given Gurdjieff's unusual tenacity—represented the only possible outcome.

In *Herald of Coming Good* there is a skeleton chronology which covers the half-dozen years following 1904; but the wording is so ambiguous that little can be made of it, and the whole sequence of events may well be spurious. Gurdjieff claims that for two years he stayed in a Central Asian monastery, occupied in a theoretical study of hypnotism. He then decided to carry his investigations into the sphere of practical experiment. "I began to give myself out to be a 'healer' of all kinds of vices and to apply the results of my theoretical studies to them, affording them at the same time real relief." For the next few years he was experimenting with actual purpose in order to explain the psychological questions which interested him personally, and to discover a satisfactory way of freeing people from their liability to suggestion. The experimental nature of his activities created certain moral problems, and in *Herald of Coming Good* Gurdjieff was concerned to justify himself:

> To make use of people, who display a special interest in an Institute founded by me, for purely personal ends would surely strike those around me as a manifestation of "egotism," but at the same time the people, who had anything to do with such an Institute . . . could in this way alone, profit by the result of knowledge amassed by me due to exceptional circumstances of my life and which had regard to nearly all the aspects of reality and objective truth, and thus use them for their own benefit.

If the idea of establishing an Institute had crossed Gurdjieff's mind by the late 1900s, that prospect must have been distant. For the moment he confined himself to observation and experiment. The passage in *Beelzebub's Tales* which describes his activities as a "healer" is one of those in which the character Beelzebub represents Gurdjieff himself. He became, says Gurdjieff, a "professional hypnotist" in the towns of Chinese Turkestan.

Turkestan is the area which extends roughly from the Aral Sea eastward into China. East or Chinese Turkestan corresponds to the present-day Chinese province of Sinkiang, which separates Mongolia from Tibet. At the westernmost end lies the city of Kashgar, and the central area is occupied entirely by the desert of the Takla-Makan. To the south are the Himalayas and north of the desert, the Mongolian Altai. It is even now a very isolated part of the world, with the few communities pinned to river valleys and oases. It was even more isolated when Gurdjieff lived there. In 1905 the American traveler, Oscar Terry Crosby, found only "half a dozen Russian telegraph engineers, two small garrisons in Russian Turkestan, one small garrison in Chinese Turkestan," in the 200 miles between Osh and Kashgar.

In fact, Gurdjieff simply used the area as a base. In Beelzebub's words, he "also travelled a good deal, visiting almost all the continents, and during these travels I encountered beings of most, as they say, 'peoples.' During these travels of mine I remained nowhere for long excepting in certain independent countries on the Continent Asia called 'China,' 'India,' 'Tibet' and, of course, also that lately largest half-Asiatic, half-European community called 'Russia.'" J. G. Bennett's friend, the Turkish Prince Sabaheddin, told him that he had met Gurdjieff in 1908 when he was returning from Europe to Asia. It is quite possible that Gurdjieff visited America as well as Europe, and no doubt he kept up his contacts with Agwan Dordjieff, Shamzaran Badmaieff, and Esper Ukhtomsky. The photograph of "Ushe Narzunoff" and his Chinese wife was taken by a photographer named Kosarev in Verknie-Udinsk—Dordjieff's Mongolian headquarters and the chief Russian garrison town for the area—on November 6, 1908.

If Gurdjieff's travels were as Beelzebub describes them—in India, Tibet, and China—it is possible that he continued to work for the Tsarist Intelligence Service. In "The Material Question" he represents himself as a businessman specializing in the antique trade, but able to turn his hand to a multitude of other projects.

> I engaged in the most varied enterprises, sometimes very big ones. For instance: I carried out private and government contracts for the supply and construction of railways and roads; I opened a number of stores, restaurants and cinemas and sold them when I got them going well. I organised various rural enterprises and the driving of cattle into Russia from several countries, chiefly from Kashgar; I participated in oil-wells and fisheries; and sometimes I carried on several of these enterprises simultaneously.

Gurdjieff always refers with the greatest affection to Turkestan, "concerning which place there are and will be preserved in my common presence the data then fixed for pleasant memories." Perhaps his pleasant memories were of family life with the lady of the photograph. Whether or not he still acted as a secret agent, his government connections cannot have hindered his business activities—which would have harmonized nicely with Badmaieff's economic war—although those to which he refers in "The Material Question" are said to have taken place as a concentrated effort to raise a large sum of money before he left for Moscow. For once, he was probably in easy circumstances, and able to devote time to his occupation as a "physician-hypnotist."

Like some of his European contemporaries—Freud and Jung among them—he was trying to use hypnosis to break through man's "normal waking consciousness" to the subconscious mind, "which ought in my opinion," Gurdjieff wrote, "to be the real human consciousness." He saw the appalling situation of humanity as caused by the division of human consciousness into waking consciousness and subconsciousness. Human beings, thought Gurdjieff, had largely lost the capacity for faith, hope, and love, but buried in their subconscious was what he called "Objective-Conscience." This was for Gurdjieff the characteristic which alone distinguished man from lower creatures. To Ouspensky he explained that the idea of "conscience" was equivalent in the realm of the emotions to the idea of consciousness in that of thought. "*Conscience* is a state in which a man *feels all at once* everything that he in general feels or can feel." It became the basic aim of Gurdjieff's Method to prod this conscience into operation.

If a man whose entire inner world is composed of contradictions were suddenly to feel all these contradictions simultaneously within himself, if he were to feel all at once that he loves everything he hates and hates everything he loves; that he lies when he tells the truth and that he tells the truth when he lies; and if he could feel the horror of it all, this would be the state which is called "conscience."

Man, Gurdjieff taught, has developed mechanisms called "buffers" to prevent his ever entering such an intolerable state of contradictions. They keep him in the state of "normal waking consciousness" and suppress conscience altogether.

In Gurdjieff's view, the normal waking consciousness operates under continuous hypnotic influence, noticeable only in particularly intensified cases. Man is almost always *asleep*. This is because in adolescence, when his consciousness divides into two—and the "real" part of this consciousness becomes the *sub*conscious—the human being is subject to great pressure from his parents and teachers to adopt the state of consciousness "normal" for man; that is, to fall asleep. At the same time, so Gurdjieff declared, an alteration in the blood circulation results in a new tempo of circulation developing for the normal waking consciousness as well as that which corresponds to the functioning of the subconscious or real consciousness. He claimed to have invented a new method of hypnosis—an advance on the method by which the subject is hypnotized by staring at a bright object— which consisted in altering the tempo of the blood circulation "by means of a certain hindering of the movement of the blood in certain blood vessels." The result was that although the circulation continued at the normal mechanical tempo, he could evoke the properties of the buried sub- conscious as well.

Only the story of Gurdjieff's relations with his pupils can explain what his new form of hypnosis in fact was, or how he went about breaking down man's normal waking consciousness and encouraging the growth of con- science instead. As for the circulation of the blood, his uncompromising materialism naturally extended to explanations of hypnosis. He approved wholeheartedly of Mesmer and the early theorists of animal magnetism, and poured scorn on James Braid, Charcot, and other specialists who denied the material basis of hypnotic phenomena. Medically speaking, this may be ridiculous, but Gurdjieff never claimed to be an orthodox doctor.

According to Beelzebub, he chose to adopt the disguise of a "healer" in order to further his psychological researches. He had observed that people speak frankly only to doctors and priests, and he had no desire to restrict his liberty by impersonating a holy man. Although he joined the medical profession in a spirit of experiment, he acquired considerable skill at his new calling. In Chinese Turkestan the chief disabilities which came within his province were opium addiction and the chewing of hashish. When, in about 1910–11, he transferred his activities to Russian Turkestan, he concentrated on the equivalent Russian vice: addiction to vodka. "This maleficent means," explains the sagacious Beelzebub to his grandson, "is obtained there chiefly from the surplanetary formation they call the 'potato.'"

Gurdjieff's skill as a hypnotist was to stand him in good stead when he was forced to earn money in the West; and it was probably in Turkestan that he acquired his knowledge of the effect of drugs on human beings. His later use of alcohol is well known, and the nature and composition of opium remained one of his interests up to the time when he was writing *Beelzebub's Tales*. Western medicine was for Gurdjieff an object of contempt. He afterward identified only three useful drugs from the whole pharmacopoeia—opium, castor oil, and a substance obtained from a certain tree.

There are several reasons for linking Badmaieff with Gurdjieff's activities as a "physician-hypnotist." For someone interested in non-European medicine, the Badmaieff dispensary would have been a natural port of call in St. Petersburg, particularly if that someone were associated with Dordjieff. In *Meetings with Remarkable Men*, Gurdjieff introduces his friend "Soloviev" as a patient whom he cures of alcoholism in Central Asia. Soloviev was "an authority on what is called eastern medicine in general, and on Tibetan medicine in particular, and he was also the world's greatest specialist in the knowledge of the action of opium and hashish on the psyche and organism of man." He probably never existed, but the list of his specialities is significant: "Eastern and Tibetan medicine, opium and hashish." As far as is known, Shamzaran Badmaieff was the greatest expert on such subjects in the Western world.

Badmaieff had consolidated his position at the Russian court with a prescription which cured the Tsar's stomach complaint—this was said to be a mixture of henbane and hashish. The ill will stimulated by his privileged position gave rise to an absurd legend that he, Rasputin, and the Tsaritsa's confidante, Anna Virubova, were trying to poison the Tsarevitch with "a yellow powder." A memorandum of Badmaieff's survives, dated October 9, 1912, which recommends treatment for the sick child. "Europe has no treatment against internal or external blows," he wrote, "except ice, iodine, and massage. . . . If you succeed in persuading them to try my medicine, please ask them to give no other medicine, either internally or externally, this includes ice. As food, only oatmeal, bouillon and milk." The remedies themselves were enclosed in small envelopes. There were "boiled Dabsen-Tan, against knocks," a stomach medicine for constipation, and a preparation called "Gabir-Nirnga," a specific against high fever.

Badmaieff was therefore still closely in touch with the court about the time that Gurdjieff returned to Russia, and it is likely that Gurdjieff was in contact with him throughout his career as a hypnotizing doctor. Gurdjieff describes a visit which Beelzebub pays to Russia in his capacity as a "physician-hypnotist," which is supposed to have taken place well before the First World War. The incentive is given by an elderly Russian, who invites him to St. Petersburg to help in the unending war against alcoholism. The Russian explains that he is the head of a foundation to combat the problem, and hopes that the specialist Beelzebub will join, to help consolidate the organization. Beelzebub accepts the invitation.

One of his motives is that he has already decided "to set up in one or another of their great inhabited spots a 'something' of the kind they call there a 'chemical laboratory'"—with Gurdjieff, "chemistry" always meant his special brand of alchemistry—"in which I intended, by means previously decided beforehand to proceed with special experiments on several deeply concealed aspects of their ever the same strange psyche." This is very much what he said in plainer language in *Herald of Coming Good*. Making allowances for the fact that Gurdjieff may here be fusing two or more visits to the Russian capital to provide background for Beelzebub's caustic remarks about the folly of Russians and of humanity in general, his story is not unbelievable. Beelzebub travels to St. Petersburg with the elderly Russian but finds himself left much to his own devices. He decides to use his free time to try to secure a permit for his projected "laboratory," but becomes lost in the impenetrable jungle of Russian bureaucracy. Eventually, Beelzebub balks at undergoing an examination by a doctor—which would, of course, reveal his tail. This is a stock metaphor in Gurdjieff for a tricky situation in which he would be forced to reveal his real purposes unwillingly. Beelzebub accordingly abandons his "foolish hustlings around."

During his stay in St. Petersburg he has also been giving his elderly acquaintance various suggestions on running the foundation. At first these are accepted and put into practice, but when the news leaks that Beelzebub is the source of such proposals—"some foreign doctor or other, not even a European"—a serious dispute arises. Without a laboratory of his own, and unable to use the foundation for his experiments "on the psyche of the terrestrial beings *en masse*," Beelzebub decides to go elsewhere. However, news of his work on alcoholism reaches the Tsar, and Beelzebub is first subjected to a long ceremonial presentation which leaves him quite blank as to what the Tsar even looked like.

Gurdjieff had probably been presented to the Tsar as a member of the

Dordjieff Mission of 1901, but it is quite possible that the idea of a foundation to combat alcoholism had Imperial approval. Pavlov's colleague, V. M. Bekhterev (1857–1927) had long been interested in using hypnotic techniques for this very purpose, and in 1912–13 he published a number of pamphlets on the problems of alcoholism. According to Bennett, Gurdjieff later told his pupils that he had met Nicholas II several times and had been "in direct contact with Rasputin." Neither of these claims is improbable, if he had had the patronage of Badmaieff; and their likelihood is reinforced by the fact that Gurdjieff had now decided to extend his activities into the world of the occult.

In *Herald of Coming Good* he explains the reasoning behind this change of direction. He had convinced himself that the solution to the problems which interested him must be sought in the conditions of man's waking consciousness as well as in the subconscious mind. In other words, he wanted to study the mechanisms which kept humanity in a state of sleep. The result was a decision to appoint himself a "professor-instructor" of the so-called occult sciences.

Gurdjieff had without doubt become familiar with most aspects— including the trickery—of supposedly supernatural phenomena. In *Beelzebub's Tales* he refers to a time when he had been a "professional Indian Fakir," and in *Meetings with Remarkable Men*, the character "Ekim Bey," whose life "was arranged down to the smallest detail like my own," stands partly as a personification of Gurdjieff as the "great maestro of the supernatural." According to *Herald of Coming Good*, Gurdjieff worked for over two years in his role as occultist—and again he was experimenting. During the "so-called 'manipulations' in the realm of the beyond" which he demonstrated to members of one occult society, he writes, "I began to observe and study various manifestations in the waking state of the psyche of these trained and freely moving Guinea-Pigs, allotted to me by Destiny for my experiments. . . ."

He realized that Europe was suffering from an epidemic of occultism. As he put it: "At that time there was among men a widely prevalent and specific psychosis which, as has been long established, attains periodically a high degree and is manifested by people giving themselves up to various 'woeful' ideas in those spheres of quasi-human knowledge . . . which today are called 'occultism,' 'theosophism,' 'spiritualism,' etc." Gurdjieff had read widely in the literature of such cults, and he knew the language of contemporary occultism like the back of his hand. When he discovered that his ideas were particularly attractive to "such people as were already in the highest degree 'possessed' of the before-mentioned 'specific-psychosis,'" he altered his tactics accordingly.

When Gurdjieff returned to Russia, the occult fever had reached heights unknown in the West. Popular churchmen, like Father John of Kronstadt, attracted the huge followings associated with Indian gurus. Saintly hermits like Ambrose of the Optina monastery played confessor to an endless chain of pilgrims. At court the influence of Orthodox holy men had been replaced, first by that of the French occultists "Papus" (Dr. Gérard Encausse) and his spiritual master "Monsieur Philippe," then by the predominance of Rasputin. In polite society spiritualism and legend were interminable topics of conversation. The intelligentsia pounced eagerly on Theosophical and occult literature imported from the West, confounded it with philosophy and a dash of aesthetics, and created an intoxicating potpourri of intellectual superstitions. The hysterical atmosphere was intensified by anxiety generated by social discontent. On the outbreak of the 1917 Revolution, the *skoptsy*, a bizarre cult of self-castrators, are thought to have numbered one hundred thousand. There is little more telling evidence of the way the wind blew.

Gurdjieff appeared as a man of mystery in an atmosphere of mystery. Although he inevitably came into contact with occultists of many descriptions, he remained invisible. His origins, his ideas, and his motives were hidden in the deepest doubt.

In *Herald of Coming Good* Gurdjieff describes how he at first contented himself with establishing an ascendency over several existing occult societies. However, he explains, he was unable to find a large enough selection of human types for his psychological observations, and so established occult groups of his own "in three different cities." Still he failed to attract a sufficiently broad cross section of humanity. He therefore realized all his assets with a view to founding an organization of his own, and moved to Russia. In *Herald of Coming Good* he dates his arrival in 1911, and in various prospectuses issued to advertise his Institute for the Harmonious Development of Man, states that his first Russian headquarters was Tashkent. In the strange document known as *Glimpses of Truth*, written at his instigation in the winter of 1914, Gurdjieff is said to have come to Russia "two or three years ago" and at first to have lived in St. Petersburg (in an alternative unpublished translation, the time span is extended to three or four years).

The approximate date of his move was therefore 1910–11, and this is suggestive, both because it coincides with Dordjieff's plan for a St. Petersburg temple, and because these years were a time of great crisis in the affairs of Tibet.

In 1910 the Chinese invaded the country and the Dalai Lama fled to the protection of the British in India. This choice of protection was forced on him—he was cut off from Russian territory by the invading army—but it was still a defeat for the pro-Russian party. In India he issued a statement declaring that Dordjieff was "a purely spiritual advisor." When a Russian professor who had been on the committee of the St. Petersburg Buddhist temple approached the Dalai Lama with a letter of introduction from Dordjieff, his request for help in reaching Tibet was refused on the grounds of his obligation to the British. In June 1912, Dordjieff himself applied to the British agent in Tibet for permission to travel to Russia through India, and when this was denied, had to make his way circumspectly through Mongolia. This journey was probably to announce the formal secession of Tibet from China which Dordjieff reported next year to St. Petersburg and Paris.*

It is difficult not to link Gurdjieff's abrupt transition to Muscovy with the Tibetan policy of Dordjieff and Badmaieff. His withdrawal to Tashkent— from Chinese territory to Russian Turkestan—coincides with the invasion of Tibet. In *Glimpses of Truth* his initial stay in St. Petersburg is said to have lasted from 1910–11 to 1914, during which period he devoted "his efforts and his knowledge to some work of his own." This "work of his own" may have been connected less with Gurdjieff's unfathomable "work on himself" than with Tibetan diplomacy. It is possibly significant that according to *Glimpses of Truth*, Gurdjieff moved to Moscow in 1914, by which time events in Western Europe had begun to outweigh in diplomatic importance those in Central Asia.

One account, which seems to describe Gurdjieff—on a mysterious errand, accompanied by a "slant-eyed" friend—in St. Petersburg during the winter and early spring of 1913–14, is contained in the autobiography of Sir Paul Dukes (1889–1967). Dukes received his knighthood for intelligence work in Russia after the Revolution, and later became a regular dining companion of Ouspensky. Before the outbreak of the First World War, Dukes was a music student at the St. Petersburg Conservatoire, where the pianist Anna Essipova introduced him to the works of H. P. Blavatsky. He continued his education in occult matters through Spiritualist séances organized by Sidney Gibbes, the English tutor to the Imperial family. Then, through his occult contacts, he met a professional hypnotist and healer known as "Lev Levovitch" or "the Lion," a man who was said to have served many years in the army in Central Asia, and to have once been

---

*Some time in 1913 Joseph Deniker had to organize an interview with Philippe Berthelot at the Quai d'Orsay. For this Dordjieff insisted on wearing European clothes. The only garments which could be found in time included a tweed sport jacket, violently patterned in red and brown checks. M. Georges Deniker was astounded to see his friend wearing this eye-catching creation on the railway platform at Verknie-Udinsk in the first week of August 1914. They traveled together as far as St. Petersburg, where the train arrived on August 15—thus locating Dordjieff fairly accurately at the outbreak of war.

pronounced medically dead. He was supposed to have been brought back to life by a Siberian shaman who sent him into the world with a healing mission. Through Lev Levovitch, Dukes met the man who he called "Prince Ozay." The resemblance between Gurdjieff and Ozay is marked, and that between the picture of Gurdjieff given by *Glimpses of Truth* and Dukes's own account of his meeting even more so.

Paul Dukes spent the summer of 1913 on an estate in Tula, where he decided to practice hypnotism on the villagers. On his return to St. Petersburg, he got in touch with Lev Levovitch, with whom he discussed his experiments. Levovitch approved and took him to see the man he called Prince Ozay in a house at the bottom of a small street "not far from the Nicolas station." The manner of their arrival was unusual. They first entered "a very plain apartment" but passed through this to another adjoining apartment, which was "larger and more sumptuous. There was a marked Oriental touch in its decorations. The walls of the hall were adorned with carpets, wrought-iron lamps with coloured glass hung from the ceiling. . . . The room, fairly large, was draped with curtains and other hangings, with lamps to match." The "Oriental" room matches the description given by Ouspensky of Gurdjieff's room in Moscow; it also matches the description of the dacha near Moscow given by the authors of *Glimpses of Truth*. The lamps, when compared with the glittering decorations made by Gurdjieff for his flat in Paris, are suggestive. And the circumspect entrance through a virtually empty apartment hints at a possible connection with the melodramatic trappings of the Great Game.

Ozay's appearance is similar to that of Gurdjieff as he is described in *Glimpses of Truth*. In both cases, the stranger discovers a man sitting cross-legged on a low divan with coffee beside him on a table. The Gurdjieff of *Glimpses of Truth* is alone and smoking a nargileh, while the Ozay of Paul Dukes is playing chess with a man with slanting eyes. Ozay is "wearing a patterned silk dressing-gown and a turban" and is "dark, thickset, with a short, bushy black beard." Later Dukes sees that he is "about medium height, sturdily built." Gurdjieff wore a beard for some time in the 1930s.

Dukes's first encounter with Ozay has the tone of Gurdjieff's jocularity. He is invited to sit down and play chess with his host.

"Take off your shoes if you would be more comfortable," said my host. I did so, and was ashamed to find I had a hole in my sock. I tried to hide it when I doubled my feet under me, but to my embarrassment he pointed at it, smiled, and said: "You believe in ventilation! Good thing—nothing like fresh air! . . . Black or white?" and he held out his closed hands with two pawns in them. When I had picked white I noticed that the other hand had held a white pawn too.

There are other aspects of Ozay which remind the reader of Gurdjieff. He drinks his own powerful brew, and on "a kind of guitar" plays Dukes's "plaintive oriental tunes, sometimes humming, sometimes singing softly in a rich baritone." Dukes used to visit him at night—always accompanied by Lev Levovitch—and stay until three in the morning. Ozay had a stock of ribald stories and could rarely be induced to tell Dukes anything in a straightforward manner—he was "provokingly evasive." His visitor had to probe and endure before Ozay could be induced to answer his questions.

The two topics on which Dukes records Ozay's pronouncements were closely linked. The first concerned the nature of prayer and the meaning of the Christian Scriptures. For Ozay prayer—with which he coupled fasting—was a physiological exercise. Dukes had made use of the English Lord's Prayer as a "magical" charm to impress the simple Russian peasants. "Very int-er-esting," remarked Ozay, and demonstrated how the English Lord's Prayer had been designed as a breathing exercise to be said uninterruptedly on a single bass note. You had to pay attention to the regulation of the breath, to the words of the prayer, and to the sound, to derive the full benefit from the exercise. The function of prayer was to attune "the body—or the soul, if you prefer that metaphor." "You are a musical instrument, as a piano is," said Ozay, "and you need to be kept in tune. That's where fasting and other exercises come in; you can't possibly reflect finer vibrations when your body—or soul if you prefer—is loaded with a lot of food gurgling in the stomach, or while the blood makes a din chasing about veins and arteries." To Dukes this opened up new horizons, new visions of *meaning* to be found in the Christian Scriptures. The Bible became a book of personal instruction, to be decoded, "beginning first of all with the training of the physical body to become a fit temple of the spirit." Fasting and breath control were part of this "esoteric Christianity"—Dukes uses the same phrase as Gurdjieff—as was compulsory celibacy at certain stages of the training. "But," Ozay warned, "the fanatic who becomes a permanent celibate is like a musician who spends his life doing one exercise."

God, is achieved not through activity but through cessation of activity. Cessation to the utmost limit of diet, breath and sex. These are the three pillars on which prayer is built. Each has to be trained and disciplined by restraint—there is no other way because they are all runaway horses. Only when the ground is cleared can true building commence. Only from that point can you begin to act consciously.

During the chaos of the Revolution, Paul Dukes lost touch with the mysterious Prince Ozay and never saw him again. Was he Gurdjieff? It seems difficult to believe that there were two such teachers in the same area at the same time. Ozay spoke English better than he spoke Russian, which in his mouth was markedly accented. To his slant-eyed friend, the Prince spoke a language Dukes could not identify. He claimed to have been "in many churches in England and America." Dukes "had reason to think that my strange host was, nominally at least, a Moslem or a Parsee," but he acquired very little definite information. Ozay was "very learned and much travelled" and Dukes knew nothing of his formal profession, although he "at one time suspected" that the Prince was "visiting the Russian capital on some religious errand." If we choose to regard Gurdjieff as resident in St. Petersburg at Easter 1913, this is confirmed by *Glimpses of Truth*. It is also significant that Ozay was associated with the professional hypnotist and healer Lev Levovitch, whose argument about charging high fees for his cures by suggestion was exactly that used by Gurdjieff to justify a high admission charge to his groups. People do not value something, he explained, unless they are made to pay for it.

It is tempting to construct a chain of events linking Badmaieff, Paul Dukes, Lev Levovitch, Gurdjieff, and any other practitioners of unorthodox medicine in St. Petersburg. Gurdjieff probably did move in the occult society of the capital, and through Badmaieff he may well have met Rasputin and the Tsar. But it is doubtful whether he had anything to do with the complex web of plot and counterplot which surrounded the Russian throne. Such intrigues were not foreign to his nature, but the vision of Gurdjieff as a Rasputin *manqué*—the description was already in use when Carl Bechofer Roberts met him in Tiflis in 1919—belongs to the sort of mythologizing which delights in seeing him as the occult advisor to the Tsar, the Dalai Lama, and Adolf Hitler. The name-calling might have nothing more behind it than the mere fact of Gurdjieff's presence in St. Petersburg during the Indian summer of the autocracy, with whose mystical interests he was associated.

According to *Glimpses of Truth* Gurdjieff moved to Moscow in 1914 and took a country house nearby where he could work undisturbed. The very existence of this house is said to have remained unknown to most of his associates. "Maintaining in his work a certain rhythm understood only by himself, he sometimes leaves it and comes to town, and again returns to his work after a certain time." This house is the setting for the conversation recorded in *Glimpses of Truth*, a document which in its printed form is some forty pages long. It purports to tell the story of its author's meeting with Gurdjieff; but according to Ouspensky, the idea of the story belonged to Gurdjieff himself, and it was actually written by two members of Gurdjieff's Moscow group. Ouspensky remarks that the original version was "evidently written by a man with no literary experience." He himself edited and rewrote a copy which Gurdjieff gave him, and it seems probable that the published version of *Glimpses of Truth* is also the work of several hands. Ouspensky's translation is dated "Moscow, December 1914." On the last page are the words "end of first chapter," but we should beware of assuming that it was actually intended to carry the story further. When Ouspensky first heard it read, he criticized it for lack of clarity—he had found it interesting, but exactly what was this doctrine which the story expounded? He was immediately told by Gurdjieff's pupils that he had "missed the most important part of it."

The story begins with the imaginary narrator's search for wisdom, which he sees as having been guided by an external providence whose workings appear coherent only to himself. The narrator discovers occultism and becomes immersed in it, until suddenly he loses his occult contacts. He embarks on a course of personal investigation, and makes friends among people with similar interests. Eventually, his particularly close companion in this search seems to be growing away from him, and the narrator becomes angry at his apparent lack of friendliness. A point of crisis comes when the seeker finds in the paper a notice of a ballet called, "The Struggle of the Magicians," written by one G. I. Gurdjieff, "an orientalist well known in Moscow." He determines to run Gurdjieff to ground, but his faithless friend attempts to dissuade him. Eventually this friend, A., admits that he knows Gurdjieff and departs without promising anything, leaving the author of the story in a state of nervous expectation.

Next day he is telephoned by A. and told curtly to be at a certain railway station at a certain time. He arrives early—A. arrives late, bearing two huge and mysterious trunks—and they entrain for the country house which Gurdjieff has taken for the winter. On the way the narrator learns that A. had discussed bringing him to Gurdjieff earlier, but was told that it was not yet time. The pair drive by sledge to the large two-story house where the Master awaits them; and they have to carry the heavy trunks. The actual introduction to Gurdjieff takes place in circumstances which suggest Freemasonic ritual: the two visitors enter a room in complete darkness, and only when A. sweeps aside a heavy tapestry does the figure of Gurdjieff appear, smoking his nargileh, seated cross-legged on a divan in a brightly lit room. Gurdjieff's "oriental origin" is at once obvious, and his eyes immediately impress the new arrival—"not so much the eyes themselves as the look with which he met me. It was a look given to one whom one has known long and well." The impact made by the man was intensified by that of the room in which he sat.

"There was no area not covered, either by carpets or hangings of some sort," writes the fictitious author. Carpets and tapestries cover the walls so as to obscure the windows and doors. The ceiling is hung with a mosaic of colored shawls and from its center is suspended a brass lamp. A piano is piled with old embroidered silks so as to be scarcely recognizable; and the Dutch stove is similarly draped. A single carpet covers the floor and the seating is low and Oriental. Three collections of objects decorate the walls: one of strange musical instruments, another of Oriental weaponry, a third of carved pipes. In one corner is a particularly splendid combination of colored silks, in the middle of which hangs an icon of St. George; below the icon on a series of shelves stand several ivory stautettes. Those named are Christ, Buddha, Moses, and Mohammed. In this exotic setting a night-long conversation takes place between Gurdjieff and his visitor, with A. occasionally acting as an intermediary. "He served," says the narrator, "as a sort of transmitter between G. and myself." At the beginning of their talk, Gurdjieff speaks haltingly, in poor Russian, often turning to A. for the completion of a sentence or a thought. But as the conversation becomes increasingly rarefied, Gurdjieff is represented as relying on A. less and less. "His speech flowed more freely and naturally, the necessary words seemed to come of themselves, and I could have sworn that by the end of the conversation, he was speaking the clearest, unaccented Russian. . . ."

In this contrived description of an imaginary meeting, much of Gurd-jieff's technique is already obvious. The difficulties created by A., the abruptness of the appointment, the heavy trunks—which may have contained priceless antiques, scientific instruments or lumps of stone—are all of a piece with Gurdjieff's later tactics. The deliberate theatricality of the room in which the guest is received corresponds to that of Gurdjieff's Moscow apartment, where the unusual decoration helped to create the "special atmosphere" described by Ouspensky. Gurdjieff used often to employ a third party—sometimes as a straightforward interpreter—in his teaching conversations. This device served to familiarize his listeners with his ideas, as well as being a valuable exercise for the intermediary and a means of gauging the pitch of his discourse by watching how his "transmitting station" conveyed his meaning to an audience which he knew better than Gurdjieff himself. The gradual perfection of Gurdjieff's Russian could mean one of several things, but it was a phenomenon also noticed by pupils who spoke French or English.

The conversation which forms the body of the chapter contains little which does not appear in a more expanded form in Ouspensky's *In Search of the Miraculous*. Gurdjieff talks of the unity of all things descending into plurality; he describes the Law of Seven and the Law of Three on which his cosmology is based—and which will shortly be outlined; he analyzes the Ray of Creation which Ouspensky describes. But the fragmentary character of the description bears out Ouspenky's criticism: it is difficult to discover the real nature of the doctrine which the protagonists are discussing, and it is certain that the story would not make sense if the reader were unfamiliar with the outline given in *In Search of the Miraculous*. From the clamor of Gurdjieff's pupils it seems that this must have been deliberate. *Glimpses of Truth* was written for a particular purpose: to give *glimpses* only of the majestic building whose outlines the conversation had allowed the narrator to grasp. This may have been in order to encourage a reader to find out more for himself, or simply to tantalize him. Gurdjieff asked Ouspensky whether the story could be published in a newspaper, and in the tale itself, the narrator asks if the ideas he has heard cannot be made more widely known. Gurdjieff answers that the previous summer he and his friends decided to try to disseminate their ideas through the press, but that the outbreak of war prevented the attempt from being properly made.

Glimpses of Truth, with its rubric "end of first chapter," may therefore have been an abortive attempt to gain publicity for Gurdjieff's ideas. Alternatively, it may simply have been a sketch which was intended for a particular use at a particular time. For it is quite clear that Gurdjieff—ever experimenting, perhaps balked in his attempts to establish his work under a "scientific" umbrella in St. Petersburg—was fishing. *Glimpses of Truth* is bait, and with the realization of this fact, many of Gurdjieff's later activities take on a new aspect; as of brightly colored floats dotting the surface of a murky river.

Gurdjieff was trailing his coat. If he were "Ozay," he discussed music with the young musician, Paul Dukes. He talked of "the miraculous" to Ouspensky. With others, he discussed dancing—or love. Many a hard-headed "dollar-holder" heard from him the smirking remark of the greasy Levantine: "I, too, am businessman." Some of his later attacks on particular professions—doctors, writers, artists—can be pinned down to the fact that he was surrounded by such people, and in order to lead them into the maze of his ideas, he had first to engage their interest by showing where the particular questions in which they were interested impinged on the view of the world which he designed that they approach for themselves. Once well in and engaged in the cosmic machine, their props were knocked from under them. They must then learn to swim in good earnest.

In *Glimpses of Truth* Gurdjieff emphasizes that occultism is not necessary as a jumping-off point. It was a warning he repeated later to his pupils in Europe. But faced by his imaginary visitor, embarked on an occult quest, he began their talk with the formula from the Emerald Tablet of Hermes: "As above, so below." "At the same time I must say that there is no need to use occultism as the base from which to approach the understanding of truth," Gurdjieff is made to say. "Truth speaks for itself in whatever form it is manifested. . . . Well, I repeat, I begin with the occult formula because I am speaking to *you*." During the discussion Gurdjieff applies his complicated cosmic laws to the principles of modern science. The narrator asks him whether an uneducated man could understand his ideas. Gurdjieff replies that an uneducated shepherd might acquire, in the course of one day's profound meditation, what it would take a scientist many years to discover. "The material you refer to was quoted only because I spoke to you. . . . Forms may be very different."

So they proved to be. Gurdjieff advises his questioner, when he asks about the occult idea of initiation, to forget it altogether. "All your researches in this area were good exercises for your mind; therein lies their great value, but only there."

Glimpses of Truth is surprisingly frank about Gurdjieff's reasons for acting in what was often an incomprehensible way. It would have been open to any reader to put two and two together from the description of his remarkable room, with its "delicate scent that mingled agreeably with an aroma of tobacco," the riot of colored silk, and the hangings which so shut out the everyday world that the character A. can remark, when he opens the curtains on broad daylight, "As you can see, time does not exist here." All the cards are on the table, but not face up. It is the task of the reader or the listener to discover their denominations.

One critic thinks that *Glimpses of Truth* gives a "melodramatic picture of a sort of stage superman," and there is undoubtedly something over-produced about the Gurdjieff whom the story presents. If he really does possess such fundamental knowledge, the reader is inclined to ask, why all the obvious stage management, why the cat and mouse tactics with the pathetically eager narrator? An important problem is raised by the rather dubious first impression which Gurdjieff made on many people who afterward became his devoted disciples.

In *Herald of Coming Good,* Gurdjieff says that twenty-one years earlier—that is, in 1912—he took an oath to live for that period "in some ways an artificial life, modelled upon a programme which had been previously planned in accordance with certain definite principles." The "artificial life" had to do with a renunciation of the skill he had developed as a hypnotist. In 1933 he spoke to the American author Jean Toomer of the oath he had taken. "I tell you something secret," he said, "only for yourself. Twenty-one years ago I vowed never to use hypnotism to effect my aims. Recent circumstances have made me struggle with myself to keep my vow . . . I do not want to break it." The reasons he gives for embarking on this program in *Herald of Coming Good* are, first, that he recognized that he was what would now be called a charismatic figure; and second, that he wanted his pupils, at all costs, to display their personal initiative, which might be stifled if he employed his full personal magnetism and strength of character. J. G. Bennett connects this decision with the Sufi doctrine of "the path of Malamat" or "blame-taking," in which the aspirant to spiritual development acts in such a way as to attract to himself calumny and the ill opinion of his fellowmen. There is evidence that Gurdjieff's artificial life was indeed governed by some such plan; although the idea can clearly be used to excuse every slip he made.

The vaguely fraudulent impression induced by *Glimpses of Truth* may therefore be one result of the tactics which Gurdjieff deliberately adopted in 1912. But to what end was such deviousness directed? Gurdjieff had been a seeker for esoteric knowledge, a student of the unconscious mind, a "physician-hypnotist," a professional occultist—intermittently, a secret agent and dealer in Orientalia—and apparently by 1912, at the start of his "teaching" proper, he was something else again. We may disbelieve in the story of his oath—it is always wise to be chary of accepting Gurdjieff's every statement—but at first sight it is difficult to see what, if anything, he intended by his teaching. The narrator of *Glimpses of Truth* is given hints about the "Great Knowledge" which Gurdjieff possesses and is told that in a year's time he will understand more than is at present possible for him to know. Meanwhile, although he has the sensation of having lifted the outer veil of the mysteries, he has no idea at all of what the inner tabernacles hold.

What was the aim of Gurdjieff's teaching? asked one of his Russian pupils. Ouspensky recorded the answer:

"I certainly have an aim of my own," said G., "but you must permit me to keep silent about it. At the present moment my aim cannot have any meaning for you, because it is important that you should define your own aim. *The teaching by itself cannot pursue any definite aim*. It can only show the best way for men to attain whatever aims they may have."

The men and women who came to Gurdjieff in Russia were desperately uncertain, scared of the future, plagued by myths and expectations of the miraculous. That is, they were as men and women have always been in every land and every generation—although the place and the time generated particular problems. Gurdjieff entered a historical situation in which the normal hopes and fears of mankind were given an unnatural intensity, and his teaching was therefore experienced by his Russian followers with particular vividness. When everything seemed lost, Gurdjieff appeared as the guide and mentor: the Man Who Knows.

They beheld the Great Magician.

Each pupil experienced Gurdjieff in a different way, and differing reasons brought people to him. He appears to have begun his first Moscow circle through a series of personal contacts. One of his childhood friends was a cousin named Dmitri Merkouroff, who by 1914 was a successful sculptor in Moscow. Through Merkouroff, Gurdjieff met Vladimir Pohl, a musician who was close to him during the pre-Revolutionary period. Pohl in his turn introduced him to P. D. Ouspensky. Ouspensky is the most significant figure after Gurdjieff in the history of the Work, and the meeting of the two men proved to be the beginning of many developments. In itself, the occasion was just one more encounter between a man who was anxious to learn and another who had something to teach. But in a historical—even scriptural—perspective, the event was momentous.

Ouspensky recorded the progress of his relationship with Gurdjieff in his book *In Search of the Miraculous,* and from the date of their meeting in the spring of 1915, Gurdjieff appears to become a fact of history. But, paradoxically, it is just when the uncertainties seem on the point of resolution that all becomes most uncertain. The invisible man gives hostages to fortune in every one of his roles, and it must be remembered that he *is* playing a role. Any of his actions—from the amazingly benevolent to the unutterably obscene—may be "acting." The multicolored cloak of the Master, iridescent in the sun's rays, takes on the whole procession of the spectrum, and vanishing through infrared becomes—invisible again.

4

Life Against Life

"One life ends and another begins. One time ends and another begins. Death is really a return to the beginning."

Pyötr Demianovitch Ouspensky was born in Moscow on March 5, 1878, Old Style. His father was an officer in the Survey Service, and a talented spare-time mathematician whose particular hobby was the fashionable topic of the fourth dimension. Although Demian Ouspensky died when his son was quite young and all his writings were lost, he passed on his mathematical enthusiasms. The manner in which Pyötr Ouspensky was to apply such ideas had little to do with academic mathematics; and a mistake made by the translators of his first book to appear in English has meant that he is still represented as a severe figure who escaped by accident from the established academies to found his own Stoa. Ouspensky was an artist rather than a scholar—potentially a good one, as is shown by his novel, *Strange Life of Ivan Osokin*—and he became instead a romantic philosopher. He was very much a child of his time and place.

His parents had shared artistic interests: Ouspensky's mother was herself a painter and an amateur of French and Russian literature. Ouspensky grew up in the atmosphere of the Russian intelligentsia, and his earliest memories were of his mother's parents' house, which was a center of artistic society. His maternal grandfather was an artist who had turned from specializing in portraiture to painting for churches, a branch of art which in

Holy Russia had a peculiar importance and its own mystique. His grandfather died in 1882, and his grandmother became the chief influence on the young Ouspensky. She was clearly a remarkable and intelligent woman: Ouspensky would later recall the pleasure she had given him and his younger sister with her stories of old Moscow days. Her house on Pimenovskaya Street was frequented by all sorts and classes of people. Ouspensky remarks that it was "in many ways a very old-fashioned house, and in other ways very much ahead of its time"; it may not be reading too much into this to see the house as connected with the movement in Russian art which was resurrecting traditional styles and folk motifs so as to make them the essence of the contemporary. The art of the icon played a leading part in this revival, and as a church painter Ouspensky's grandfather may have been associated with the fashion.

Ouspensky's brief accounts of his early life are vivid and evocative. When his *A New Model of the Universe* was published in 1931, reviewers were quick to note the excellence of the passages which described his own adventures. But because of the nature of his work, Ouspensky must always seem to suffer at the hands of a biographer; for much of what he wrote or said on any topic was based on a rigorous analysis of his own failings. To criticize Ouspensky is often merely to echo his own self-criticism and to honor a sometimes enviable degree of self-knowledge.

There is a particular difficulty in treating the stray personal references in his writings as evidence of a documentary sort. Ouspensky revised his early publications several times, and the screen of his later psychological ideas— whether those he learned from Gurdjieff or those of his own later development—interposes between the recorded experience and the reader. For example, his account of dreaming was begun in 1905, revised several times in accordance with his changing ideas and published in 1931 as an adjunct to a body of thought to which Ouspensky then referred as a "system." In some cases it is possible to trace the development of his thinking, but in others the dividing line between reportage and hindsight is not so clearly marked. Although this need not affect an assessment of his ideas, it limits the scope of a biographer.

At about the age of five, Ouspensky learned to read. A year or so later he discovered Lermontov's *A Hero of Our Time* and Turgenev's *Notes from a Sportsman's Album*. In a household of Russian "intelligents" there was nothing odd in such books being available to a six-year-old, and Ouspensky's precociousness in taking to the classics at such an early age was the beginning of a largely self-conducted education. The "enormous impression" produced by these two books was a lasting influence on the boy. *A Hero of Our Time*, with its protagonist the very type of the disillusioned romantic, its exotic Caucasian background, and its occasional hints of the numinous, had made the book a cult among youth. Turgenev's gentle tales of country life directed the attention of the literary world toward the realities of peasant existence. Both books would have formed part of the required reading of the generation to which Ouspensky's parents belonged; and they stood in the naturalistic tradition which was then fashionable. Ouspensky was to make a name for himself on the crest of the Symbolist wave which overwhelmed such standards; but, as his only novel shows, he never lost the gifts of precise observation and a romantic attitude to nature which characterized his early masters in literature. Soon after his literary explorations had begun, he discovered poetry and painting, started to draw, and developed a lasting enthusiasm for engravings and old prints like those which hung on the walls of the house at Pimenovskaya Street.

Two peculiar features about Ouspensky's earlier years were directly connected with his later interests. The first was his extraordinarily vivid memory of childhood. He later maintained that he could remember several incidents which had happened before he was two years old. "From the age of three," he wrote, "I remember myself quite clearly." Among such memories was Moscow of the early 1880s, and an old town called Zvenigorod, thirty miles west of Moscow on the Moscow River. "I remember the river there, boats with a smell of tar, hills covered with forests, the old monastery, etc. I remember the exhibition of 1882 in Moscow, and the coronation of Alexander III, chiefly the illuminations." The unusual clarity of his early memories later became connected in Ouspensky's mind with the frequent sense of *déjà vu* which he had experienced as a child. "With me," he wrote, "these sensations . . . began when I was about six years old. After eleven they became much rarer. One of them, extraordinary for its vividness and persistence, occurred when I was nineteen. The same sensations, but without a clearly pronounced feeling of repetition, began still earlier, from very early childhood, and were particularly vivid during the years when the sensations of repetition appeared, that is, from six to eleven; and they also came later from time to time in various conditions."

During childhood Ouspensky shared these experiences with his younger sister, to whom he was very close. Later he described to his pupils how they used to sit at their nursery window and make accurate predictions of events which took place in the street below. The children concealed their ability from the grown-up members of the family, because—as Ouspensky's sister contemptuously remarked—"They don't understand anything."

The sensation of "I have been here before" was to prove the greatest single impulse in Ouspensky's life, and it is one of the pervading themes of the novel, *Strange Life of Ivan Osokin*, which he drafted in 1905. The novel deals with the schooldays and *Wanderjahre* of Ivan Osokin, and the impression that it is strictly "autobiographical" should be qualified. *Ivan Osokin* was written to illustrate the theme of eternal recurrence, and the incidents are shaded according to the author's didactic purpose. Ouspensky later said that he was "never such a fool as Osokin" and that many of the events of the novel were borrowed from the lives of his acquaintances. Despite these qualifications and despite the fact that the English edition of *Ivan Osokin* was considerably rewritten before publication, there is much of purely biographical value in the novel. Ouspensky admitted that the heroine, Zinaida, was a real person, and, like Ivan Osokin, Ouspensky was expelled from school. This last fact dominated his early life.

The Second Moscow Gymnasium at which Ouspensky (and his alter ego Osokin) studied was a school arranged on the standard Russian government pattern based on the classical curriculum. Ouspensky loathed the school routine, and *Ivan Osokin* is redolent of the atmosphere of petty regulations, boredom and ink-stained squalor which the boarders at the Gymnasium had to endure. He hated Latin and Greek and found the work as irksome as the discipline. In the novel the only classes in which Osokin avoids disgrace are the French lessons, because his French is already far beyond the abilities of his contemporaries. He finds solace in a series of "fantastic dreams which, in the past, were responsible for many unprepared lessons and for many bad marks. The dreams are called 'Travels in Oceanis.' They are his best method of running away from reality." These daydreams take Osokin on adventurous Pacific voyages inspired by Captain Marryat, and they are evidently based on Ouspensky's own boyhood dreams of travel and the sea.

Ouspensky's main purpose in his account of Osokin's daydreams was to show the delusory effects of the imagination. But his description of the "Travels in Oceanis" demonstrates another aspect of his fantasy-life which he noticed in his studies of dreaming some years later. "There was in me an artist, sometimes very naive, sometimes very subtle, who worked at these dreams and created them out of the material which I possessed but could never use in full measure while awake."

But he was "never such a fool as Osokin," and as the pupils were left very much to themselves, he continued surreptitiously to educate himself along his own lines. At the age of twelve, he became interested in scientific subjects: first it was natural history and biology, then physics. In the Introduction to *A New Model of the Universe,* he evokes the memory of a preparation class in 1890 or 1891. Instead of the prescribed Latin grammar he is reading a physics textbook, overwhelmed with wonder at the magnificence of the idea of levers—the phenomena which the principle explains, and the very class of lever strike him as a revelation of the unity of things. He falls foul of the German proctor, who confiscates his book. "I hear round me ironical whispers and comments that Ouspensky reads physics. But I don't care. I shall have the 'Physics' again tomorrow; and the tall German is all made up of large and small levers!"

Private studies did not compensate for public disgrace. His character, Ivan Osokin retreats from reality and—almost deliberately, Ouspensky hints—breaks a succession of rules. The authorities are more and more annoyed at his conduct, and eventually, a harmless practical joke during the visit of an inspector of schools results in Osokin's expulsion. Like Osokin's, Ouspensky's career in formal education ended about the age of fourteen or fifteen. Osokin's greatest emotion in the novel is remorse for the pain which his expulsion has inflicted on his mother. He immediately promises to work hard under a tutor in order to pass into university even more quickly than he would have done from school, and the university is the great goal which Osokin promises himself. Ouspensky never obtained a university degree, and it is possible to see in some of his work—in the length of his published books, in the ambitious nature of his ideas, and in the later structure of his own activities—a pressure for some compensating achievement.

An important consequence of Ouspensky's expulsion from the Gymnasium found its way into his later teaching. This was his insistence on the necessity of submitting to the discipline of a school. The word "school," shorn of its article in the Russian manner, is still part of the jargon of his followers, and Ouspensky's search for an "esoteric school" became one of his greatest drives. The discipline which he imposed on his pupils he learned from Gurdjieff, but the insistence on *rules* was his own. "A man is unable *to keep watch* on the *whole of himself*, that is, on all his different sides," Gurdjieff told him. "Only school can do this, school methods, school discipline—a man is much too lazy, he will do a great deal without the proper intensity, or he will do nothing at all while thinking that he is doing something; he will work with intensity on something that does not need intensity and will let those moments pass by when intensity is imperative. Then he spares himself; he is afraid of doing anything unpleasant. He will never attain the necessary intensity by himself. If you have observed yourselves in a proper way you will agree with this." Gurdjieff certainly meant the statement to be taken generally, but the emphasis given to the idea by Ouspensky was entirely personal.

Another result of his expulsion from school was that Ouspensky's education continued along its eclectic and self-willed course. From this fact came aspects of his character both attractive and forbidding. His occasional arrogance and dictatorial manner—although no doubt sometimes assumed—are very much part of the self-educated philosopher. On the other hand, from his lack of orthodox schooling came a breadth of interests and a wide culture which belong to the polymath and not to the academic specialist. Ouspensky enrolled as a "free listener" at Moscow University, a status which allowed him to attend what lectures he pleased without working for a formal degree. He may also have studied with a tutor for a time after leaving school; but it is impossible to distinguish any set course of instruction. In 1894, at the age of sixteen, he discovered Nietzsche. Two years later he started to write. He studied biology, mathematics and psychology "very intensely." In mathematics he became "enormously excited" by theories of the fourth dimension, and in psychology his chief interest was a topic which had intrigued him from the age of thirteen—the study of dreams.

In all these avenues of inquiry, Ouspensky's attitude was that of the rebel. "I was very anarchistically inclined at that time," he wrote. "I particularly distrusted all forms of academic science and took a firm decision never to pass any examinations and never to take any degrees." This has the savor of sour grapes, and it is a common attitude to find among adepts of the occult arts. But it is also the sort of attitude which can lead a man to see beneath appearances—always assuming that there is something to see. At the end of the nineteenth century, scientific materialism had begun to appear as constricting a series of dogmas as the religions it had displaced. The epidemic of occultism arose as a form of overreaction to this fact. A less hysterical attitude was displayed by many farsighted men; for indeed if science had remained crudely mechanistic, had failed to develop concepts like relativity and the uncertainty principle, there were, by definition, limits to the expansion of knowledge. Ouspensky was dissatisfied with the stagnant state of affairs. "I felt that there was a dead wall everywhere, even in mathematics, and I used to say at that time that professors were killing science in the same way as priests were killing religion." He saw his treasured idea of the fourth dimension trampled beneath scientific feet. Instead of the liberating possibilities he sensed in the concept, it was turned into an academic game. At the same time, he did not yet dare to abandon the materialist standpoint and remained for the time being an orthodox rationalist.

In 1896 Ouspensky undertook what he calls "my first independent travels." He had already visited Paris with his family for the Exposition of 1888, and his newfound independence probably related to his mother's death. Between 1896 and 1905 there is little known with certainty about his movements. The early part of this period was taken up with studies and traveling. He later told Rom Landau that he attended lectures at various Russian and European universities, but it is impossible to find out which. He knew Paris well, and his fluent French would have made it easy for him to form—like a character in *Ivan Osokin*—part of Georges Sorel's audience at the Sorbonne. He also explored the wilder parts of Russia, visiting the remote monasteries of the far north, and once described to Maurice Nicoll how he had managed to repay the Circassian villages through which he traveled for their ruinously generous hospitality. The technique was to admire a small object of no value, whereupon the host would be bound under his code of honor to give it to you. The guest then insisted that his host accept a gift in exchange; and Ouspensky carried a number of cheap revolvers with which to reimburse his benefactors.

About 1900, soon after he was twenty-one, Ouspensky's long-standing interest in dreams led him to make a series of observations. He had already devoured most of the psychological literature on the subject, so he began by attempting to write down his dreams on waking. "I said to myself that if I could *know in sleep that I was asleep* I should find the possibility of continuing the dreams, or of going behind them and perhaps finding their cause." He very soon found that his attempts to record dreams produced distortion and alteration of the dream experience itself. This led to the discovery of a method of observing dreams in what Ouspensky called a "half-dream state," which was brought about by deliberate effort either just before falling asleep or after awakening. His observations convinced Ouspensky that in the majority of cases—what he called "simple dreams"— a dream was the product of associations—either physical associations resulting from the position of the dreamer's body, or psychical associations resulting from unconscious preoccupations.

He found occasional examples of dreams which seemed to have almost boundless significance for the dreamer; but the most interesting conclusion he reached—and which was to be of great importance in preparing him for the ideas of Gurdjieff—was the conviction that dreams continue in waking life. Therefore, he could afterward say, there was little justification for making a sharp difference between being asleep and being awake. To the state of sleep was added what was called "the waking state" but which should really be known as "sleep plus waking state."

How long this scholar-gypsy life lasted is uncertain. Ouspensky was attracted by journalism and by 1905 it had become his profession. His job gave him the chance to travel to Europe and the East Coast of the United States, journeys which may have taken place at any time up to 1912. America provides the setting for an unsuccessful story called "The Inventor," which tells the reader little about its author apart from his distaste for the cruder forms of capitalism.

During the political troubles which culminated in the revolution of 1905, Ouspensky wrote the original version of *Ivan Osokin*, entitled *The Wheel of Fortune*, which was published ten years later under the title *Kinema-drama*. Only general ideas can be gleaned from the novel about what he had been doing, but *Ivan Osokin* does provide flesh to cover the bare bones of ten years of studies and journalism. It reveals the man Ouspensky—the charming, romantic, convivial artist—who became hidden by the teacher's severity and the façade of serious intellectualism built up by his inner compulsions.

The charming Tanechka idyll and the military episode in *Ivan Osokin* have little to associate them with what we know of Ouspensky from other sources, but like all Osokin's disasters, these involve a woman. Susceptibility is part of his Achilles heel—as Gurdjieff would have said, his *Chief Feature*—but it is an attractive susceptibility stemming from an incorrigibly romantic attitude to life. He feels the experience of his night with Tanechka as magic, as a poetic truth naturally apprehended. It has nothing to do with the physical explanation of the act of love. By the time Ouspensky came to write *Tertium Organum* (1912), his early lyricism had abated not at all. If anything, it had increased, and the chapter on "Occultism and Love" occupies a key place in that book.

Ouspensky had great trouble with this chapter, and the concern he showed for it demonstrates the importance he attached to the subject. Between the first Russian edition of 1912 and the second of 1916, the section was considerably revised and expanded; and it was the only chapter to be significantly altered in the second English edition of 1922. Even in his final version, Ouspensky retained the same poetic association between love and the world of nature as he had implied in the Tanechka passages of *Ivan Osokin*. "In the springtime with the first awakening of love's emotions the birds begin *to sing* and *build nests*," he writes. Perhaps, he suggests, bird song is not just the means of attracting a mate—as scientists would have us believe—but "the principal function" of a species, necessary for some unrecognized natural harmony. In the 1916 version of *Tertium Organum*, revised with no reference to Gurdjieff's ideas, Ouspensky declares explicitly that the hidden purposes of love provide the key to the mysteries:

It is difficult to understand all this and to make it seem rational. But by seeking to understand these mysterious purposes and by departing from mundane interpretations, man, without even being conscious of it at first unites himself with *the higher purposes* and finds that thread which in the end of all ends will lead him out of the labyrinth of earthly contradictions.

The Ouspensky of 1905 found his consolations in the mysteries of love. He had not completely broken from the materialism of the age when he completed the first draft of *Ivan Osokin*, but the romantic vision of love had evidently come to replace his schoolboy fantasy life as the "magical" element in his world. The chivalrous attitude to women which this evoked persisted till the end of Ouspensky's life, and became part of his basic outlook. Ivan Osokin sees women as "more interesting" than men. The later Ouspensky was to see them as belonging to a higher caste altogether, and the courtesy which he showed his women followers is at one with this attitude. In the days when the word "normal" meant *super*human in the language of his groups, love remained an example of glorious normality; and when two of his pupils announced their engagement, he wrote to them of his pleasure at hearing of something really normal in a perverted age.

Connected with the hints of something *more* which the young Ouspensky found in sex were the promptings of other things felt by the artist in him. Toward the end of *Ivan Osokin,* the hero and Zinaida discuss literature. Osokin writes poems, about which he is very sensitive. He prefers those of one line only, for then the reader must experience the rest of the poem in himself. Zinaida's friends cannot understand this, and are scathing about Osokin's "impressions from beyond." Between such conventional attitudes and those of Osokin's creator, there was an ever-widening gulf; for the notion of the complete autonomy of the poem itself and the idea of poetry coming from "beyond" betray the influence of Symbolist theories to which Ouspensky was exposed at the time he wrote *Ivan Osokin.*

The various occult and religious groups which sprang up in turn of the century Russia were closely linked with the Symbolist movement in literature. Just as mystics and magicians traveled from Paris to hawk their wares in the incense-filled gloom of Slavic piety, artistic fashions were imported from the cultural capital of the world. Paris of the 1880s and 1890s had reacted against naturalism in art and materialism in philosophy; and the occult doctrines of the magi directly influenced artistic practice. In particular, the idea of the symbol as a link between the dimly apprehended magical universe and the world of everyday found a place in the new antinaturalist literature. The Russian intelligentsia eagerly adopted such concepts. Their flight into mysticism was encouraged by an exclusion from their natural part in the social agitation which culminated in the revolution of 1905—during which Ouspensky wrote his novel—and it forms part of a luxuriant crop of near-mystical literature, much of which simply obeyed the fashionable forms, but some of which indicated a real religious striving.

The high priest of the Russian intelligentsia was Vladimir Sergeivitch Soloviev (1853–1900) who contrived to fuse Symbolist occultism with Russian piety and make the resulting mixture intellectually palatable. He predicted the coming of the "God-man"—man perfected by his own efforts toward divinity. After his death there was a mushroom growth of societies with names like "The Circle of Seekers of Christian Enlightenment" and "The Religious-Philosophic Society in Memory of Vladimir Soloviev." It became difficult to distinguish the poets from philosophers, and philosophers from priests. The most famous literary names include: Andrei Bely, Konstantin Balmont, Valery Bryusov, Vyacheslav Ivanov, and Alexander Blok. Halfway between the writers and the occultists proper came unconventional philosophers like Dmitri Merezhkovsky, Nicholas Berdyaev, and V. V. Rozanov. They represent a tradition of thought which is almost completely forgotten in the West, and a closer acquaintance with their work makes Ouspensky's ideas a little less extraordinary than they seemed when he first became known outside Russia.

The idea of eternal recurrence on which the book is based is taken chiefly from Nietzsche; and all over Europe at the turn of the century Nietzsche had become inextricably entangled with the occult and Symbolist literature. Indeed, the Russian Decadence began with Nietzsche, when in 1890 Nikolai Minsky published a Zarathustra-like thesis on the liberty of the individual. But it was characteristic of Ouspensky's approach to intellectual fashions that, whereas other intellectuals hailed Nietzsche as a liberator from the prison of bourgeois morality, he was fascinated by the theory of eternal recurrence, which even some ardent Nietzscheans preferred to regard as an aberration. The thought that time repeats itself in identical cycles is to be found in antiquity. Nietzsche probably took it from Pythagoras and Heraclitus, and Ouspensky himself unearthed it in the Alexandrian Fathers. Ouspensky's description of its implications is found in *A New Model of the Universe*.

This means that if a man was born in 1877 and died in 1912, then, having died, he finds himself again in 1877 and must live the same life all over again. In dying, in completing the circle of life, he enters the same life from the other end. He is born again in the same town, in the same street, of the same parents, in the same year and on the same day. He will have the same brothers and sisters, the same uncles and aunts, the same toys, the same kittens, the same friends, the same women. He will make the same mistakes, laugh and cry in the same way, rejoice and suffer in the same way. And when the time comes he will die in exactly the same way as he did before, and again at the moment of his death it will be as though all the clocks were put back to 7.35 A.M. on the 2nd September 1877, and from this moment started again with their usual movement.

To Nietzsche the problem posed by recurrence was simple. He accepted it in his capacity as Superman. "Who can *desire* the recurrence of life?" he asked, and answered: "The great, strong, happy man, whose life is so valuable in his estimation that a repetition and continually a repetition will be a pleasant thought to him. To everyone else, to everything miserable, misbegotten, which only looks upon its own life with dissatisfaction and repugnance, the thought must be frightful."

Ouspensky's use of the idea was anything but a slavish copying of Nietzsche. Later he was to transform the Nietzschean idea of the Superman in a similar fashion. For Nietzsche, "the great, strong, happy man" with the successful will to power might reconcile himself to eternity repeating and repeating in endless cycles, "the worm Ourobouros who eateth his own tail." But Ivan Osokin lives his life again in an atmosphere of regret for missed opportunities. His final crushing disappointment in the love affair with Zinaida ends with him contemplating suicide. His life lived over again has the same results: and the more hopeful ending of the later English version did not form part of The Wheel of Fortune. Ouspensky later used to tell his pupils that Robert Louis Stevenson had taught him as much as Nietzsche about recurrence, and Stevenson's view of the coils of time is pessimistic. The haunting "Song of the Morrow"—published posthumously in Stevenson's Fables of 1896—is a recurring theme in Ivan Osokin. It would have been natural reading for a young romantic—and Stevenson's tale of the King of Duntrine's daughter, who had "hair like the spun gold and . . . eyes like pools in a river," ends with the princess as an ancient crone warning her younger self that she has "no thought for the morrow and no power upon the hour, after the manner of simple men." Writing, as he did, at a time of civil and personal chaos, Ouspensky's life seemed not at all worth repeating, and eternal recurrence can only have presented itself as an assurance of eternal damnation.

For in 1905 he was evidently in a very depressed state. His affair with the original of Zinaida had ended unhappily, and if his financial circumstances were anything like Osokin's, he was very pressed for money. Poverty and refusal to take a secure job are two of the reasons which Osokin gives for the collapse of his affair. "I'm a stranger and an outsider," he complains, "and it's the same everywhere." In the middle of great political upheavals, which ended in armed revolution in Moscow and led the Tsar at last to grant a constitution, Ouspensky's disillusionment with politics was complete. Strange Life of Ivan Osokin is full of denunciations of the futility of the "comrades," whose cabals confront Osokin in Switzerland, Paris, and Moscow. He does not believe in revolution, although he shares the "almost obligatory" antigovernment attitude of the intelligentsia. He sees other possibilities "if only those in official positions would not be so childishly selfish and stupid." Ouspensky later described his dilemma in propria persona: "I mistrusted and disliked all kinds of socialism even more than industrialism or militarism. . . . But when I became interested in journalism I could work only on 'left' papers because 'right' papers did not smell good. It was one of the complexities of Russian life."

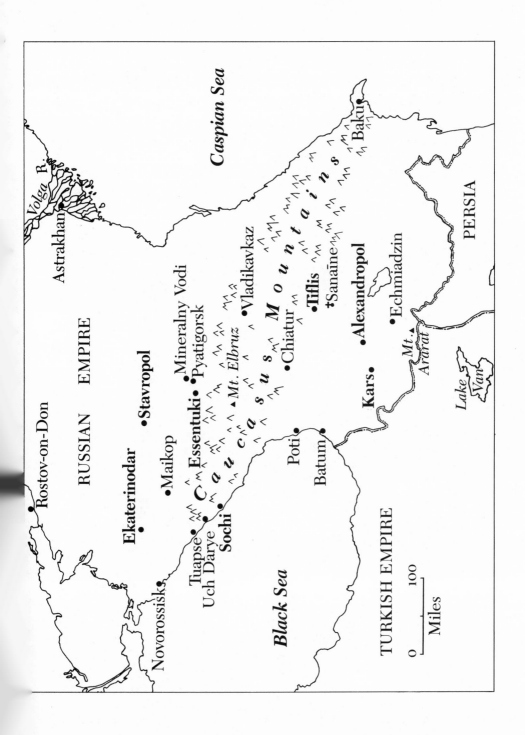

Caspian Sea

Volga R.

Astrakhan•

RUSSIAN   EMPIRE

Rostov-on-Don

•Ekaterinodar

•Stavropol

•Maikop

Mineralny Vodi

•Essentuki   •Pyatigorsk

•Mt. Elbruz

Caucasus   Mountains

•Vladikavkaz

Tuapse

Uch Darye

Sochi•

Novorossisk•

•Chiatur

•Tiflis

†Sanaine

•Alexandropol

•Echmiadzin

Poti•

Batum•

Kars•

Mt.▲
Ararat

Lake
Van

PERSIA

Baku•

Black Sea

TURKISH EMPIRE

0   100

Miles

0

The 1905 revolution led to a personal tragedy. His beloved younger sister had joined an extreme left-wing organization and was imprisoned for revolutionary activities in the Boutirsky prison in Moscow, where in 1908, she died.

Disillusioned with orthodox science, with politics, both established and revolutionary, recovering from an unhappy love affair, Ouspensky may have had little to sustain him: but the innate romantic is not easily cast down. His real search began in the autumn of 1907; and before following him on this new chapter of his existence, we must try to see more of the man behind the questing spirit.

Physically, the young man of 1905 was a more fragile version of his later short and thickset self. A heavy jaw emphasized the dogmatic or domineering side of his nature, a facet which was to alienate several people who met him. A severe mouth, largish nose, and receding hair made up the rest of a not extraordinary face which, apart from the high Slav cheekbones, might have been Teutonic. The most noticeable aspect of his appearance was the pince-nez which his very short sight invariably demanded, and in later years he usually carried about with him a whole armory of glasses and binoculars. Thie fascination with precision instruments—in the case of optical glasses, of necessity—extended to weapons. The story of his carrying cheap revolvers with him through the Caucasus may show that the interest in guns which he demonstrated in England took root early, and in India he carried both camera and revolver.

Ouspensky's romanticism expressed itself in a love of nature. His description of Ivan Osokin's ride in the country is the detailed observation of a keen horseman, and Ouspensky in the saddle was a common sight in later life. But cats were his chief love, and he noticed them wherever he went. In *Tertium Organum* he made several points about the difference in consciousness between man and animals which were based on his observation of cats. In his letters from the Caucasus in the midst of revolution, he had time to observe a dead cat. The ending of *Ivan Osokin* refers to two obscurely significant cats. Ouspensky brought a cat with him to England or acquired one very soon after his arrival, and toward the end of his life, he could scarcely be separated from his pets, which came to his meetings. He said that they had astral bodies, and might benefit from instruction. On his last strange journeys his cats accompanied him.

J. G. Bennett records a tradition that in the Ouspensky family the names Peter and Damian had passed alternately from father to son. The Damians were supposed to be world-rejecting ascetics and the Peters to enter with zest into the joys of life. Ouspensky thought that both Peter and Damian had influenced his character. The conflict between the ascetic side of his nature and the part which made him a heavy drinker and a connoisseur of food was a battle he never resolved. A powerful ascetic drive lay behind his spiritual quest and his intellectual rejection of the material world; but it was the bon viveur who told Maurice Nicoll that he thought he had been born with the noise of a tavern in his blood. For all his feelings of "not belonging," the young Ouspensky most certainly tried to enjoy himself. Several scenes in *Ivan Osokin* are set at parties, and when Carl Bechhofer Roberts ran across Ouspensky in the wreck of the White Armies in 1919, he made a record of an evening they spent together during which his companion reminisced about his early Moscow days. The circumstances were something out of the ordinary—all those concerned were probably tired and very hungry, and had been celebrating their acquisition of coal with "vodka" made from raw spirit. Ouspensky remembered another occasion on which the miraculous effects of improvised spirits had been noticeable.

"It was when I was a young man in Moscow," he was saying, "and my cousin once gave a party. We brewed the vodka together. It was a marvellous brew. There was one man there, the sort of type one sees only in Russia; a young man with long hair, a long beard, long moustaches, and a sad, far-away look in his eyes. Well, after he had one glass of our vodka, he got straight up from his chair and walked out of the house and into the nearest hairdressers. There he made them run the clippers over his head, and shave him, and he came out as bare of hair as an egg, and went straight home to bed. That shows you what good vodka can do!"

The conversation changed tack, by way of a story of Ouspensky's and the intervention of another member of the party. Then Ouspensky returned to his theme of the gay life of Moscow:

"Don't interrupt me," said Ouspensky. "I was remarking that every policeman in Moscow in the old days knew me by my Christian name, because, unlike most people, when I was drunk, I always tried to compose quarrels and not to start them. Besides, I used to give them big tips. And all the porters at the restaurants used to know me, and when there was a row on, they used to telephone me to come round and stop it. One night I remember I got home with the left sleeve of my overcoat missing. How I lost it, and where, I have never discovered, although I have given the matter very careful thought. Indeed, I once thought of writing a book about it."

This subject would have suited his quirkish turn of mind, and the literary world in which he moved might have received it well. The combination of roistering and spiritual search was a pattern familiar in Symbolist Russia, and indeed, the conflict between the Peter and the Damian was a typically Russian struggle. Like many romantics, Ouspensky retained an inner puritanism as part of his romantic attitude. This showed itself in a refusal to be taken in by the cheap and shoddy, and developed into an inability to compromise. It was a temperament not uncommon among the Russian intellectuals. The mystical bent of the intelligentsia has already been noted, but there was another consequence of their alienation which is relevant to Ouspensky. Harold Williams, who was for a long period *The Times*'s correspondent in Russia and married an "intelligent," put his finger on the spot: "The life of the intelligents was simple, but not ascetic. Many members drank to excess, and there were some who drank themselves to death in search of a refuge from the terrible depression that hung constantly over the Russian educated man, and made the life of the intelligentsia essentially a sad one."

Ouspensky's personal situation increased the sense of hopelessness induced by his milieu. His friend Boris Mouravieff once summed up Ouspensky's state of inner weakness. "Charming—although subject to fits of temper, kind, very skilful in argument, he was not a strong man . . . Full of ideas, tender-hearted, a talented writer, he was not protected internally by the valuable armouring of the scientific method. Everything in him was unanchored, and so open to outside influences. And he was very isolated in life, which did not spare him disappointments." Criticism of his own vulnerability is a strong theme in *Ivan Osokin*, and it agrees with Gurdjieff's estimate of Ouspensky's character: "Very nice man to drink vodka with, but weak man."

But this weakness accounts for the nature of much of his work, and in his work it becomes a source of strength. Ouspensky was more of an original thinker than most of Gurdjieff's followers, but he always needed material on which to operate, whether it was eternal recurrence, the Superman, occultism, or the fourth dimension. All these ideas received twists at his hands which made them seem completely original, but they did not proceed from him in the first place. They were "outside influences" like those to which Mouravieff refers, and Ouspensky's treatment of his material always had more the flavor of art than of philosophy. His most striking ideas are flashes of inspiration, which he emphasizes by italics in his text; his completed structures have the autonomy of works of art rather than the balance of reasoned argument. In this lies both his value and the secret of his success. As the subjective artist, he responded to preoccupations or waves of feeling which were in the air and drew out of the ideas he used implications which their originators did not know they possessed.

The Ouspensky of 1905 was the typical outsider figure of his time and place. At the beginning of this novel, Osokin bewails his lack of prospects and his social isolation, and toward the end of *Ivan Osokin*, Zinaida and her lover discuss the responsibilities of women. Osokin argues the Ouspenskian theory that woman must be extremely fastidious in her choice of a mate, because she bears the responsibility for natural selection. "Woman," he says, "does not demand enough from man *for his own sake*." Can she not "demand a great deal for herself?" asks Zinaida. "That is quite another question," says Osokin. "That is *life*. I was never interested in this."

What Ouspensky means by *life* is explained in a much later work, *A New Model of the Universe*. For this gray existence—"deeply-rooted petrified routine life"—he uses the Russian word *byt*. *Byt* refers to life in external forms, or to firmly established circumstances. Ouspensky tells us that one may speak of "peasants' *byt*, merchants' *byt*, country landowners' *byt*"; also of a "*byt* actor" in a play. For people of *byt* "there can be in their lives nothing unexpected, nothing accidental, no adventures." Such monotony seemed unbearable to the young Ouspensky. The horror of a featureless existence would have been redoubled in the mind of a man who had just discovered eternal recurrence by the prospect of that life repeating . . . and repeating and repeating. . . . *The trap was closing in*.

He continued to feel that sexual experience held the key to a better world, and preserved a dogged faith in a life other than this *life* which appalled him and from which he was separated by such a distance. He was confronted with the irritating fatalism of the people of *byt*, "in some cases passing into a kind of ironical contempt for people who are restless, seeking for something, striving after something." So Ouspensky rejected *life* and set out to discover a larger and fuller life. Vague hints of a magical universe *beyond* resolved themselves into a specific quest. An undirected striving became a search for the miraculous.

In the autumn of 1907, Ouspensky discovered the Theosophists and their literature. Life in the newspaper office where he worked began to resemble his days at the Second Moscow Gymnasium.

The editorial office of the Moscow daily paper *The Morning*. I have just received the foreign papers, and I have to write an article on the forthcoming Hague Conference. French, German, English, Italian papers. . . . I have to make a survey of all these words and opinions, pretending to take them seriously, and then, just as seriously to write something on my own account. But what can I say? It is all so tedious. . . .

Pushing aside the papers I open a drawer in my desk. The whole desk is crammed with books with strange titles, *The Occult World, Life*

After Death, Atlantis and Lemuria, Dogme et Rituel de la Haute Magie, Le Temple de Satan, The Sincere Narrations of a Pilgrim and the like. These books and I have been inseparable for a whole month. . . .

I open one of the books at random, feeling that my article will not be written today. Well, it can go to the devil! Humanity will lose nothing if there is one article the less on the Hague Conference.

His clandestine library consisted of recognized occult classics: works by A. P. Sinnett (the journalist who first published H. P. Blavatsky), Rudolph Steiner (originally a member of the Theosophical Society), Eliphas Lévi (the French reviver of magic), Stanislas de Gauita (the doyen of the Paris Rosicrucians), as well as a Spiritualist text, and the inevitable work of Orthodox piety. The autumn of 1907 was a time of great Theosophical activity in Russia. Although the Society itself was still officially banned, two regular groups with their own publishing house had been founded in 1905, and in November 1908, Theosophy at last became tolerated officially. At the same time, the revolution of 1905 had sent numbers of the intelligentsia scuttling across the frontier to Paris where, in the following year, they attended lectures by the rapidly rising star, Rudolph Steiner. Steiner's mistress, Marie von Sivers, was a Baltic Russian and through her Steiner's influence was transmitted to the Russian intelligentsia. A number of conversions resulted, among them, the poet Andrei Bely. Ouspensky's Theosophical contacts came about as the intelligentsia swung even more directly to occultism in the aftermath of the abortive revolution.

Suddenly the shades of the prison house lightened. Ouspensky began to see more clearly that there was a way out of the trap, a way, what was more, that asserted the real value of the poetic and mysterious world of which he had only preserved the hope. In a rush, he abandoned the materialist view of life. "For so long I have held myself in," he wrote, "have denied myself all dreams about things that could not be held within these bounds."

Meaning poured itself out upon him from so many unnoticed portions of the universe. Fairy tales and superstitions began to disclose their proper significance. The natural world became animate to his perception. The traditions of Russian Orthodoxy again acquired the aspect of comprehensible truth. "And the greatest mystery and the greatest miracle was that the thought became possible that death may not exist . . ." It is clear from *Ivan Osokin* that Ouspensky was deeply affected by the death of his mother, and who knows of what other friends he may not have been thinking? There might be a life beyond, within, or through the life of *byt*—it was the impulse toward this realization which made his occult books important to

him and not the "very naive" speculations which they advanced. He must at
some time have investigated various spiritualistic and occult groups in
Moscow and St. Petersburg and rejected what he found; for his writings are
littered with denunciations of the "subjective" nature of spiritualistic
phenomena. Later he claimed that he had "at once" seen that the weak side
of Theosophical literature was that "it had no continuation." Presumably
this means that it had taken on dogmatic form, and could therefore not
continue to provide the life-giving impulse which it had originally delivered.

Although at first he did swallow some of the more fantastic flights of
fancy, Ouspensky sucked out the yolk from his Theosophical reading. He
learned that there was a way to study religion as a body of knowledge which
meant something. Like Gurdjieff, he discovered the idea of the esoteric
Tradition of secret wisdom. This all pointed onward to the life beyond life of
which Ouspensky had intimations. He decided that if consciousness could
be proved to exist apart from the body, this would open the way to proving
many other things. In default of such a demonstration, he returned to his
early studies of the fourth dimension. If—he suddenly saw—the fourth
dimension was considered from a psychological point of view rather than
from the standpoint of mathematics, it could provide a justification for the
universe beyond the material universe, a door into the life beyond life.
Before, he had shied away from the idea; now he plunged into fresh
researches which linked the fourth dimension with esotericism.

He resolved to write a book which would tell the world of the
connections he had discovered, but this was hardly begun when he gave up
in despair. "I cannot make myself write about the limitless possibilities of
knowledge when for myself I already see the limit. The old methods are no
good; some other methods are necessary." The question had become: "how
to go beyond?" The answer lay in the going—a journey into the self, and a
search for present-day custodians of the esoteric Tradition in lands where
the occultists thought they might be found.

In 1908 he made an expedition through the Middle East with a friend
called Sherbakov. In Constantinople he visited the Mevlevi dervishes in
Pera and was mystified by their whirling. What was the secret of the dance,
and what was the nature of the intense mental effort which seemed to
accompany it? He visited other dervish *tekkes*, including that of the Rifa'i or
"howling" dervishes in Scutari, and passed on through Smyrna and Greece
to Egypt. He sat before the Sphinx and experienced his own transitoriness
in the face of its impassive endurance of the centuries. "I felt that it
represented 'Humanity,' or the 'human race' or 'Man' in general—that
being with the body of a nightingale and the face of a superman." By the

Sphinx and the dervishes he was intrigued but not enlightened, and he returned to Russia feeling that there were secrets which had eluded all but the probing edges of his consciousness.

Some time during this trip in the winter of 1908, he had an intimation of the expanded consciousness which his later experiments were to induce. It happened on a steamer in the sea of Marmora:

> A wave would run at the ship, raised as if desiring to hurl its crest upon it, rushing up with a howl. The steamer heeled, shuddered, and slowly straightened back; then from afar a new wave came running. I watched this play of the waves with the ship, and felt them draw me to themselves. It was not that desire to jump down which one feels in mountains but something infinitely more subtle. The waves were drawing my soul to themselves. And suddenly I felt it went to them. It lasted an instant, perhaps less than an instant, but I entered into the waves and with them rushed with a howl at the ship. And in that instant *I became all*. The waves—they were myself: the far violet mountains, the wind, the clouds hurrying from the north, the great steamship, heeling and rushing irresistibly forward—all were myself. . . .
>
> It was an instant of unusual freedom, joy and expansion. A second— and the spell of charm disappeared.

In early 1909 Ouspensky left Moscow for St. Petersburg. He was now reading intensively in occult and mystical literature, and by 1911, when he began to write *The Symbolism of the Tarot* and *Tertium Organum,* he had a thorough knowledge of Theosophy and the French magical revival. He had investigated seventeenth-century mysticism in the shape of Jacob Boehme and his pupil Gichtel, had delved into the mysteries of Neo-Platonism and Alexandrian Christianity, and rediscovered the mystical traditions of Russian Orthodoxy and the monks of Athos. This reading must have influenced the results of the experiments which he carried out in 1910 and 1911, but Ouspensky himself found nothing for which he was prepared in the beyond he was so earnestly seeking. Instead, he was "carried far beyond the limits of the known and possible." His experiments consisted of an attempt to alter the state of normal consciousness by means of yogic and magical methods. He does not say so explicitly, but it is obvious from the nature of his experiences and from his interest in narcotics that a chief agent was some sort of drug. This was almost certainly hashish, although he may also have used nitrous oxide.

Ouspensky's mystical experiments remain extremely valuable for anyone interested in the borderlands of psychology. It is possible to disagree with the classification he made at the outset and still discover suggestive material. He divided the phenomena in which he was interested into "objective magic," "subjective magic," and "mysticism." By objective magic he meant the class of directly magical phenomena which science broadly speaking denied: the ability to influence things or people at a distance, through time, or beyond the grave; and the "mental phenomena" of the psychic researcher: clairvoyance, telepathy and the whole apparatus of Theosophical seership which included seeing the aura and thought forms. Subjective magic comprised the matter of self-hypnosis, hallucinations, and dreams taken as reality. Mysticism, he thought, was always subjective, and associated with the intensified emotional states provoked by religious practices. The main object which he set himself was to see whether objective magic had any real existence apart from the phenomena of subjective magic or mysticism.

He achieved results much more quickly than he expected. But in his first contact with the *unknown*, he encountered an unexpected difficulty. The unknown—*was* unknown. No familiar categories could be applied to it, no everyday language could describe it. In the beyond, all phenomena were linked with other phenomena, every aspect of the unfamiliar explained and was explained by some other facet of the great whole. The experimenter began to see why accounts of mystical experience had seemed to him so flat and contrived; the beyond was no place for words, and if words were used to try to convey something of the experience, they would be in the jargon to which the writer was accustomed: Theosophist, philosopher, or man of religion, each would use the language of his inheritance. In this observation, as in his accounts of alterations in the time sense and the difficulty in communicating with others, Ouspensky's reports tally with those of much later investigators. He was years ahead of his time, and the clarity of mind which he subsequently brought to bear on his experiences might profitably have been taken as an example by later experimenters.

The first result of his experiments was to give Ouspensky a sense of the duality of himself: he found he was able to observe his own reactions. Under favorable circumstances, this state heralded his entrance into a world "entirely new and entirely unknown to me, which had nothing in common with the world in which we live." This universe might be described as "a world of mathematical relations" in which there was no division between subject and object, observer, and observed.

Passage to this ultimate apprehension was not immediate or assured. Ouspensky distinguished between several states of drug-induced consciousness. There was a transitional state, of which he became very wary, especially after the voices which spoke to him during this stage started to haunt his ordinary life. He found he could ask the voices questions like those asked of spirit mediums at séances, and occasionally discovered clairvoyant effects. Often his experiments stopped here; but sometimes he passed to a "second threshold" which led to the universe of mathematical relations. This contained the answer to all questions and was in a perpetual state of flux. In this world, concepts could only be expressed by hiero-glyphs, what Jacob Boehme had called "the signatures of things," and Ouspensky came to regard it as the source of all real phenomena. A great part was played beyond the second threshold by the activity of the number 3, which appeared as the creative agitation of the universe. The universe itself was "like some great trefoil." No merely verbal expression, wrote Ouspensky (once more exasperated at the deficiencies of language), could give any accurate idea of what he saw.

Another result of his experiments was to wean him from Theosophical literature. Later he decided that at the time he had probably been more under Theosophical influence than he imagined. He was astonished to find that the astral world described by occultists did not exist at all. Neither could he induce any effects of "objective magic." The states which his drugs created were beyond his control, and thought was a poor instrument with which to grasp the profound realities he sensed beyond the second threshold. Deep insights recorded in another state of consciousness vanished in the ambiguities of memoranda like "Think in other categories" which merely tantalized his normal self. One new concept did emerge from the period of experiment: the vision of Linga Sharira, the Long Body of man. Ouspensky came upon this insight while thinking of a relative who had died. Suddenly he saw that human life must be considered as a whole, and that a human being *was* his life extended in time: that it was a wrong definition of man which saw him as a creature bounded by the three dimensions which confined his physical body. To describe the phenomenon "man," the whole extent of his life must be taken into account, which meant adding a fourth dimension . . . of Time.

He was illuminated. His everyday experience was partial and mistaken; he had been failing to *make the right connections*. Walking down the Nevsky Prospekt, he was suddenly transfixed by "an ordinary cab-horse." "Looking at the horse's face I understood all that could be known about a horse. All the traits of horse nature, all of which a horse is capable, all that it can do, all that it cannot do, all this was expressed in the lines and features of the horse's face." Next, a dog revealed itself to him in the same manner. Animals began to seem fragments of larger beings—the "great horse," the "great dog"—and in amazement, Ouspensky applied his revelation to humanity: "I understood then that we also are atoms of a great being, 'the great man.'"

However, barriers still raised themselves before him. His vague belief in a life better than that of ordinary men had led him to occultism: now he passed through occultism to a direct apprehension of the world beyond. He had experienced things for himself. But although he now knew of the existence of what he was coming to call "the miraculous"—"the *real* world that lies behind the wavering mirage of the visible world"—he lacked exact conclusions. How was he to link the world of human affairs with that other level which created and subsumed it?

During the period 1909–12, he continued his journalistic work, probably as a freelance. He gave public lectures on occult and mystical subjects, and successfully published the results of his investigations. He was evidently much in contact with the mystically inclined intelligentsia. From 1909 began his intimacy with A. L. Volinsky, and it is possible that one of the reasons for Ouspensky's leaving the more orthodox atmosphere of Moscow for the exotic air of St. Petersburg was that in the capital, the new occultism associated with the Symbolists was more accessible. In *Tertium Organum* he mentions meeting M. V. Lodizhensky, the editor of an anthology called *Superconsciousness* of which Ouspensky made much use. Lodizhensky had visited Leo Tolstoy at Yasnaya Polyana and discovered coincidences between Tolstoy's thought and the religious experience of Orthodox mystics. Ouspensky tried to interest Tolstoy in his own experiments and may have made use of this connection. Another investigator of unorthodox religion whom he met was V. A. Daniloff, whose influence may have led him to include some doubtful passages about the perception of animals in *Tertium Organum*. And about the same time he exchanged the more conventional atmosphere of "holy Moscow" for what Madame Blavatsky liked to call "mystic Petersburg." Soon he was a member of the St. Petersburg Theosophical Society and had begun to move in the literary and artistic circles which made their headquarters in the famous St. Petersburg cabaret, The Stray Dog.

The Stray Dog had become an institution in St. Petersburg's Bohemia. It was the scene of impassioned dialogue, impromptu poetry readings, and what would now be called "happenings" of all sorts. Here Andrei Bely, Alexander Blok, or Anna Akhmatova might be heard reading their poems, and here the *femmes fatales* of the Progressive world held court among their admirers. Here after the theaters had closed, the actors, singers, and musicians would join the literati. Here, as Ouspensky fondly remembered, "nothing wrong could happen," and he looked back on his period of sociability, carousing, and impassioned exchange of ideas as a golden age. The Stray Dog was his university, where he talked all night, drank champagne, and met some of the writers who had already made their names. Among these were Valery Bryussov and A. L. Volynsky, the latter of whom had a claim to be considered the founder of the Symbolist movement in Russia. After 1909 Ouspensky became a regular partner in discussions with Volynsky ("whose opinions," he writes, "I valued very much") and his decisive turn toward mysticism undoubtedly took place under the influence of the occult fashions so much in vogue among the coteries who inhabited The Stray Dog.

His new contacts may have provided the stimulus to a period of intense literary activity. Apart from some unpublished writings of dreams and his early work on the Fourth Dimension, all the more solid writings which Ouspensky afterward republished in *A New Model of the Universe* were begun during the years 1911 and 1912. These include *The Symbolism of the Tarot, Superman, What is Yoga?* and a work called *The Inner Circle*, the ideas of which are incorporated in the chapters of *A New Model of the Universe* called "Esotericism and Modern Thought" and "Christianity and the New Testament." This burst of activity strove to communicate Ouspensky's breakthrough into the world of the beyond. All the accumulated reading of a life spent in hard and unorthodox study was pressed into the service of the new revelation. The topics were very much those to which he had tried to give literary form before his expedition of 1908, and they compose a body of ideas which he almost took for granted while writing the book *Tertium Organum* which made his name.

Ouspensky took over the idea of esotericism from Theosophical and occult literature. That is to say, he believed in a Tradition of hidden knowledge preserved by an "inner circle" of humanity, which concealed itself from the main body of mankind, either, as the Theosophists said, by living in remote areas like Tibet, or by adopting obscure ways of life. Ouspensky expanded this idea of the inner circle until the esoteric succession became responsible for the major achievements of mankind. It was "the brain, or rather the immortal soul, of humanity, where all the attainments, all the results, all the achievements, of all cultures and all civilisations are preserved." Behind the outward show of established religions there was always the esoteric religion: for example, the teaching of Christ was esoteric and exclusive, intended for those who were seeking salvation—the road to which was known by the inner circle.

So much was purely occult thinking; but Ouspensky allied Nietzsche's concept of the Superman to the esoteric point of view. Humanity, he felt, was only a transitional stage; and the evolution of consciousness led toward the Superman state. This necessarily implied an increasing interest in things inexplicable and occult: a broadening of the mental spectrum as man realized the inadequacies of his existing knowledge. Ouspensky compared the ascent to Superman with the progress of a candidate through the various initiations of the Greek mysteries—the archetypal esoteric religions. The coupling of Nietzsche to ideas of the spiritual evolution of man was not entirely new. Many Theosophists made use of Nietzsche, and the notion of a coming Superman consciousness had been powerfully elaborated by A. R. Orage in England some five years earlier.

The early passion that the fourth dimension had inspired in Ouspensky returned with renewed force as a rational justification for the beyond. Even here, he was not really original; he was following a line of argument pioneered in England by C. H. Hinton and E. A. Abbott: but unlike them, Ouspensky took the fourth dimension as Time, duration. Because this idea is central to *Tertium Organum* there is little point in discussing it separately; but among his less systematic writings on the subject, there is a passage which demonstrates Ouspensky's uncritical acceptance of Hinton's arguments, and which shows how he proceeded from the mere possibility of a fourth dimension to arguing its necessity:

> If the fourth dimension exists, one of two things is possible. Either we ourselves possess the fourth dimension, i.e., are beings of four dimensions, or we possess only three dimensions and in that case do not exist at all.
>
> If the fourth dimension exists while we possess only three, it means that we have no real existence, that we exist only in somebody's imagination and that all our thoughts, feelings and experiences take place in the mind of some other higher being, who visualizes us. We are but products of his mind and the whole of his universe is but an artificial world created by his fantasy.
>
> If we do not want to agree with this we must recognise ourselves as beings of four dimensions.

This argument is neat, and it has a superficial charm, but why, in the name of the beyond itself? Why, if we do not possess the fourth dimension do we not exist at all? Why, if we only exist in the mind of a fourth-dimensional somebody, do we have no "real" existence? To what does that "real" refer? In this passage Ouspensky was doing little more than summarizing Hinton, and his personal assumptions remain hidden. The fourth dimension had the attractiveness of seeming to "prove" his intuitions scientifically, and this probably meant a great deal to the self-taught philosopher. Under the stimulus of his mystical experiences and with the background of occult theory which his reading had given him, Ouspensky set out to resolve his personal equation. Being a clear writer, a man with heart, and in a condition of near ecstasy while he did so, he produced a remarkable solution.

5

The Search for the Miraculous

A story told by Boris Mouravieff epitomizes the world into which Ouspensky let himself with the key of *Tertium Organum*. The incident took place in the 1920s at the Paris home of Baroness Olga Rausch de Traubenberg, who was helping to translate Ouspensky's account of his years with Gurdjieff.

> When leaving the table, the son of the baroness, a little boy of twelve, came up, with his album and asked us to write something in it. He gave me his album first, I wrote this: *"Whatever happens to you in life, never lose sight of the fact that twice two is four."* I passed the album to Ouspensky. He wrote underneath my sentence: *"Whatever happens to you in life, never lose sight of the fact that twice two never make four. . . ."*
>
> He smiled and shot me a malicious glance. Alec read what we had written, showed the album to his mother, . . . who knew Ouspensky extremely well, lightly shrugged her shoulders, looked at each of us in turn and said: "Well!—in your mottoes I can recognise both of you perfectly."

Tertium Organum is a work of revelation. It was written in 1911, while Ouspensky was engaged in his experiments in changing consciousness, and his direct apprehension of the world beyond was incorporated in the book. He has been criticized for his choice of a title: *Tertium Organum, the Third Canon of Thought*, because it seemed that he was placing his work on a level higher than the *Organon* of Aristotle and the Novum Organum of Francis Bacon—the first two canons of thought which the third canon supplements. This is a misunderstanding, which Ouspensky did his best to dispel in a letter published in G. R. S. Mead's magazine, *The Quest*, ten years after the book was written. "By my title," he wrote, "I simply intended to say that a much deeper and larger understanding of the possibilities of *logic* had existed far earlier than the narrow frames given us by Aristotle and Bacon, in which almost all subsequent thought has been confined leaving that which could not be there included as illogical." The Russian word, which was eventually translated as "canon," means "weapon" or "instrument," and Ouspensky's book was intended to show how habitual patterns of thought—particularly those created by the development of materialist science—have imprisoned thought itself. In his view, human consciousness had voluntarily limited the territory in which it could exercise itself—when beyond its cramped backyard was an entire countryside in which to rove and the prospect of the noumenal world beyond the hills.

According to Ouspensky, positivist philosophy denied the existence of certain facts—facts like those he was personally experiencing. The need was for a new system of logic, in which he declared that *"Science must come to mysticism."* His starting point was Kant's proposition about how man perceives the world; that "the things which we intuit are not in themselves the same as our representation of them in intuition." What do we know, and how do we know it? The uncertainties implicit in the idea that our perception of the world cannot be said to correspond to things as they are allows infinite scope for discussing the possibilities of how things are in fact.

It was here that the fourth dimension came in. Ouspensky took his stand on the theories of C. H. Hinton, an Englishman whose *Scientific Romances* (1884–1904) provided H. G. Wells with the idea of the time machine. Ouspensky's own *Ivan Osokin* may have been inspired by Hinton's stories based on the idea of recurrence; and it was Hinton's fate to provide material for others to work on. His books *A New Era of Thought* (1888) and *The Fourth Dimension* (1904) argued that man apprehended reality by means of space. "Space is the instrument of the mind." Hinton postulated a fourth dimension of all apparently three-dimensional objects, claiming that it was merely the structure of the human mind which prevented man from perceiving the fourth dimension. He even declared that it was possible to educate the senses into making out a four-dimensional cube—the tesseract—by means of complicated stacks of ordinary cubes with their surfaces specially colored. Exercises with Hinton's cubes became popular in Theosophical circles.

Ouspensky's experiments had given him the vision of the Long Body of man. He now used this insight to argue that the fourth dimension was Time. A point in motion becomes a line, a line in motion becomes the two-dimensional plane surface, and a plane surface in motion creates a cube of three dimensions. Man in motion—not walking from one place to another in three-dimensional space, but man moving through life, through his personal time—is a being of four dimensions: in his Long Body. Ouspensky thought that his experiments had induced the experience of higher space. Higher dimensions could be apprehended, but they must not be thought of as geometrical dimensions. If space, as Hinton argued, were an instrument of the mind, two different forms of space—three- and four-dimensional—were two differing modes of consciousness, "two methods of receptivity of one and the same unique world of a space which is unique." Here the illumination which had flashed across Ouspensky's mind and had so puzzled him took on its full significance: "think in other categories." "It is necessary to understand," he wrote, "that all objects known to us exist not only in those categories in which they are perceived by us, but in an infinite number of others in which we do not and cannot sense them. And we must learn first *to think* things in other categories, and then so far as we are able, to imagine them therein. Only after doing this can we possibly develop the faculty to apprehend them in higher space—and to sense 'higher' space itself."

The problem therefore remained the development of higher forms of consciousness. Proceeding by analogy, Ouspensky considered how worlds of higher dimensions would appear to beings of one and two dimensions only. This was a line of argument deriving from the celebrated book, *Flatland*, published in 1884 by Dr. E. A. Abbott, a famous preacher and the headmaster of the City of London School, who had himself been inspired by Hinton. Abbott described, for example, how a square—a being of two dimensions—was visited by a sphere—a being of three dimensions—who appeared to the perception of the flatlander to be a circle. Ouspensky applied this analogy to the differences he found between animal and human consciousness. He decided that the space sense of an animal might be two- or even one-dimensional, and concluded that if the existence of lower space senses than the human could be demonstrated it must follow that a higher consciousness was also possible. Ouspensky now brought into his argument support from mathematics and occultism. On the one hand, Einstein and Minkovski were called in to reinforce the idea of the relevance of the fourth dimension to human consciousness; and on the other, H. P. Blavatsky and lesser Theosophists testified in Ouspensky's favor about the nature of the world beyond appearances.

On this foundation, Ouspensky erected a vision of the world as a gigantic hieroglyph which must be decoded. This was very much the concept of the Symbolists, but Ouspensky's interpretation of the symbols was based on his own mystical experiments. He repeated the Platonic myth of the cave; and maintained that in art, and particularly in sex, there were hints of the sunlit world beyond the cavern. He analyzed the various habits of thought and language which trapped man in a three-dimensional universe, and discussed the possibility of higher consciousness as described in Hindu literature. His own experience combined with his wide reading to convince Ouspensky that the nature of the real world was known to the mystics. The attainment of higher consciousness might be described as "unity with the all." He printed long extracts from Orthodox and Theosophical anthologies of mysticism, and made great use of the works of William James and the American Transcendentalist Dr. R. M. Bucke's *Cosmic Consciousness* (1905). He was particularly concerned to point out the complete illogicality of mystical experiences. "They are super-logical, i.e., *Tertium Organum*, WHICH IS THE KEY TO MYSTICAL EXPERIENCE, is applicable to them in all its entirety."

In one important way Ouspensky differed from the Theosophical authors whose books he so freely used. They were mostly content to see the evolution of humanity toward higher consciousness as a process occupying millennia. Ouspensky mistrusted the theory of evolution and had the urgency of his own experience to impel a devotion to Nietzsche. "The future belongs not to man, but *to superman*, who is already born and lives among us. A higher race is rapidly emerging among humanity, and it is emerging by reason of its quite remarkable understanding of the world and of life."

Tertium Organum is an extraordinary book, giving the impression of having been written at white heat. Many devotees of Ouspensky still find it the best piece of work he ever did, and it was certainly the book which made his reputation. It is lucidly written and, in the best sense of the word, "liberating." Ouspensky's central theme of the artificial limitations imposed by accepted categories on human consciousness is important and convincing; and whether his analogies with higher dimensions of space are in any sense more than analogies does not matter at all.

Neither does it matter that in at least two places, his argument is very shaky indeed. His section on the mathematics of infinite magnitudes does not stand up to scrutiny. And the chapters in which he tries to argue about the differences between animal and human consciousness could be demolished completely. Such criticisms begin to matter only if every word

Ouspensky wrote is taken as holy writ. By the time that he published *A New Model of the Universe* in 1931, there were already distressing tendencies in this direction, and Ouspensky's own habit of regarding his personal truths as universally valid—we have noticed this in his remarks on the fourth dimension—no doubt encouraged the trend. Ouspensky is always least impressive where he is trying to be most "scientific." He *proved* nothing—indeed he always insisted that his argument was incapable of proof—but he indicated astonishing possibilities. As a presentation of the idea that man must try to expand his consciousness, *Tertium Organum* remains triumphantly successful.

Ouspensky did not claim great originality; rather, he claimed to have rephrased a truth known to all men of "cosmic consciousness" from time immemorial. "In the world's literature there exist books, usually little known," he wrote, "which accidentally or by design may happen to be assembled on one shelf in one library. These, taken together, will yield so clear and complete a picture of human existence, its path and its goal, that there will be no further doubts about the destiny of humanity. . . ." The experience of the beyond had been a catalyst. The various authors whom he had been so avidly studying seemed to unite their voices, and Ouspensky *saw connections*. "Books are appearing which it is impossible to refer to any accepted library classification, which it is impossible to 'enroll' in any faculty. These books are the forerunners of a new literature which will break down all fences built in the region of thought . . ." His accumulated experience broke, reordered itself, and reformed into *meaning*. The fact that his sources were familiar reading to the mystically inclined intelligentsia of Europe meant that his book would itself have something of the effect on its readers that Ouspensky's private experiences had had on him. The vortex in which swirled Nietzsche, occultism, and a dissatisfaction with the scientific pundits might resolve itself for a reader, as it had for the author, and the buyers of *Tertium Organum* themselves would perceive the connections which Ouspensky had found in a flash of enlightenment. Not only had Ouspensky achieved the reformation of experience which is the mark of all good literature, but he had eliminated from his sources the more crazy occult vaporings: had cracked the code and translated the aspirations of the occultists into ordinary speech.

It is this factor of clarity and reinterpretation which distinguishes *Tertium Organum* from similar productions of the Russian mystical intelligentsia. But even in the second edition of 1916, from which the first English translation was made, *Tertium Organum* remains very much the book of a Russian intellectual. For example, there are the inevitable quotations from Vladimir Soloviev, who began the whole religious revival; and Ouspensky's thoughts on "Occultism and Love" are heavily influenced by Vasily Rozanov, that satyrlike prophet of the cosmic orgasm. Originally the book also contained a lengthy refutation of the sexual ideas of the eccentric Polish guru Wincenty Lutoslawski, which was later excised. Ouspensky concluded *Tertium Organum* with a quotation from Revelations in which an angel proclaims that "there shall be time no longer." He had found the passage in a book by the poet Alexander Dobrolyubov, a hero of the mystical Russian intelligentsia, who after his expulsion from Moscow University had set off to wander round Russia with his body encased in iron hoops, like certain Orthodox holy men. For all the inspiration of *Tertium Organum*, it was part of a recognizable tradition, and its arguments become more, not less impressive, when allowance is made for the particular pressures of time and place.

In 1912 the book was published, and the next year Ouspensky succeeded in persuading three of the newspapers for which he worked to finance a journalistic trip to India. A journey to the East had become increasingly important for him, for the results of his mystical experiments were neither complete enough nor permanent. He noted "the helplessness that I feel in the face of the wall behind which I can look for a moment, but never long enough to account to myself for what I see." He vacillated uneasily between the feeling that he must delay no longer in making experiments with fasting or meditational techniques, and the idea that he should abandon further attempts at occult practice until he knew what he was doing. Despite the tremendous power behind the revelation of *Tertium Organum*, he had been forced to end the book on a note of interrogation. "The meaning of life is in eternal search. *And only in that search* can we find something truly new." His own search reverted to the pursuit of hidden wisdom.

Occult literature made him think that he might find *men who knew* among the Hindu yogis or the Sufis of Islam. "The question of *school* and of a method acquires for me a predominant significance, though it is still not clear and connected with too many fantasies and ideas based on very doubtful theories," he wrote later. "But one thing I see clearly, that alone, by myself, I can do nothing." He needed help.

Ouspensky is quite open about the "fantasies" in which he indulged when he set off to the East. The trouble was that the third weapon of thought was a two-edged sword. It could cleave a passage through the cobwebs of materialism; but just because *Tertium Organum* so satisfactorily destroyed accepted logic, it opened the way to a state of mind where anything was possible. "Let us remember," Ouspensky had written, "that the *world of causes* is the world of the marvellous; that what appears simple to us can never be real. The *real* appears to us as the marvellous." He left for India in the hopes of penetrating to the real world—the life beyond life. He said he was going to the East "in search of the miraculous."

I could not explain it clearly, but it seemed to me that even the beginning of contact with a school may have a *miraculous nature*. I imagined, for example, the possibility of making contact with schools of the distant past, with schools of Pythagoras, with schools of Egypt, with the schools of those who built Notre Dame, and so on. It seemed to me that the barriers of time and space should disappear on making such a contact. The idea of schools in itself was fantastic and nothing seemed to me too fantastic in relation to this idea.

Despite the discouragement of clever men in St. Petersburg who scoffed at the idea of the mysterious East, Ouspensky set off on his occult quest. The universe of the miraculous was only a hairsbreadth away, and anywhere he might find the rent in the fabric which kept him from it. He had planned to go with his friend and traveling companion, Sherbakov, but Sherbakov died just before he set out. On the journey, Ouspensky twice heard his voice speak to him.

He was thrown back on his Theosophical contacts. From Russia he traveled to London where he met A. R. Orage, the editor of the influential magazine, the *New Age;* and possibly he also met Mme. Blavatsky's old secretary, G. R. S. Mead. It was probably in connection with Ouspensky's visit to London that Mme. A. L. Pogossky—who kept a shop in Bond Street which sold Russian arts and crafts and was prominent in Russian Theosophy—made an English translation of his book, *The Symbolism of the Tarot*. This was published in English in St. Petersburg in 1913 and introduced in Ouspensky's name to the English-speaking public. From London the seeker continued to Paris, where he reflected on the esoteric schools of masons who he believed had built Notre Dame. Next, he went to Genoa, where an active branch of the Theosophical Society was headed by the German-Italian botanist, Professor Ottone Penzig. From Genoa he took ship for Cairo where he stayed for three weeks and visited the Pyramids almost daily. Then to Ceylon, where his quest proper began.

He arrived in the East, if anything, more elated than when he had set out, for his journey appeared to provide confirmation of his new beliefs. In *Tertium Organum* he had proclaimed: "On earth there are living two different species of men. The possibility of the appearance or development of cosmic consciousness is the distinguishing mark of one of these species—numerically small. In the other, infinitely more numerous, cosmic consciousness does not appear, and can never appear." The embryo Supermen were already able to recognize one another and might soon assume their responsibilties: "a new race CONSCIOUS OF ITSELF . . . will judge the old races."

As he traveled through Europe among his Theosophical friends, Ouspensky discovered all around him hints that his prophecy was coming true. The European intelligentsia—particularly of a Theosophical sort—formed the nucleus of a new order:

St. Petersburg, London, Paris, Genoa, Cairo, Colombo, Galle, Madras, Benares, Calcutta, were connected by invisible threads of common hopes and common expectation. And the more people I met, the more this side of my journey took hold of me. It was as though there grew out of it some secret society, having no name, no form, no conventional laws, but closely connected by community of ideas and language. I often thought of what I myself had written in *Tertium Organum* about people of a "new Race." And it seemed to me that I had not been far from the truth, and that there is actually carried on the process of the formation, if not of a new race, at least of some new category of men, for whom there exist different values than for other people.

In Ceylon he stayed at a hotel on the seashore near Colombo, and traveled throughout the island. He visited *bhikkus* and made inquiries into Buddhism, convinced that behind what seemed to him an "arid and materialistic" theory of liberation from suffering, there lay an esoteric Buddhism concerned with the methods of attaining enlightenment. He was less concerned with doctrine than with the world of the miraculous. a subject which official Buddhism had apparently made taboo. The intellectualism of his Buddhist acquaintances irritated him beyond measure. Where was the miraculous, the center of all religions? He sensed that nevertheless there was something *there, something, overshadowing; there the gap in the curtain, the intrusion of the miracle into the world. . . .*

And then he found it.

In a small temple near Colombo there was an image of the Buddha with sapphire eyes. It seemed that the image was not locally considered remarkable, and it was not mentioned in any of the guidebooks. Ouspensky was led to it only after lengthy circumambulations around the sights more favored by tourists, and his garrulous guide eventually left him alone before the shrine. "A second or two passed, and I understood that I was in the presence of a miracle. . . . The Buddha *saw* me, saw in me that which I could not see myself, all that was hidden in the most secret recesses of my soul. And under his gaze, which as it were passed me by, I began to see all this myself." It was like the picture of the Great Magician he had drawn in his pen portraits of the Tarot cards: *"I saw myself reflected in him as in a mirror and in his eyes I seemed to look upon myself."* The gaze of the sapphire eyes ordered and calmed the inner disquiet of the beholder, conferred enlightenment and understanding. The learned *bikkhus* were irrelevant to his quest. The miraculous was *there . . . there . . .* and *there,* if only the trick could be learned of breaking out from this heavy *matter* which so imprisoned and oppressed the soul.

From Ceylon the traveler went on to Madras and stayed for six weeks at Adyar, the headquarters of the Theosophical Society. This was a traditional place of pilgrimage for Westerners in search of enlightenment. In 1913 the birds of passage numbered, besides Ouspensky, the Baltic Count Keyserling on the journey around the world which he recorded in his *Travel Diary of a Philosopher;* Carl Bechhofer Roberts, who was in search of Mahatmas and was warned by a Brahman visitor to Adyar against the moral corruption of his hosts; and the enigmatic figure of Boris Soloviev, who later married the daughter of Rasputin and played a dubious role in the murder of Tsar Nicholas II and his family at Ekaterinburg. J. G. Bennett records Ouspensky's story of the pecking order at Adyar: on the ground floor of the headquarters building were the hangers-on and those Theosophically of no account; above them lived the pillars of the Society's funds and organization; on the top floor was the esoteric group—to which Ouspensky was at once admitted.

His stay does not seem to have impressed him, although he was not yet quite weaned from Theosophical ideas. A book just published when he arrived at Adyar, Johann van Manen's *Some Occult Experiences,* found a place in the second edition of *Tertium Organum;* and soon after he left Adyar, he met the Theosophist Bhagavan Das at Benares and discovered striking similarities to his own thought in Das's book, *The Science of Peace.* Ouspensky preserved till the end of his life a respect for the earliest Theosophical literature, but his verdict on later Theosophy—in particular his scathing comments on Bishop Leadbeater's technicolored descriptions of the astral world—have the flavor of a man condemning the illusions of his youth. His ideas of the miraculous were changing, and his contact with some of the more futile aspects of Indian Theosophy was probably one of the reasons for this change. "Beginning with a bold, revolutionary search for the wondrous," he wrote shortly after, "theosophy soon started to fall away from that and to stop at some 'found' truths which it gradually converted into indisputable dogmas."

His own search for men in possession of esoteric knowledge continued. He visited many of the established gurus, the followers of Ramakrishna among them. By all of these he was dissatisfied. "Schools" perhaps they were, but not what he was looking for. Later, on his way back from India, he analyzed his feelings. The frankly devotional schools were useless, for he could have found many such religious "ways" in Russia. There were schools based on yogic exercises, about which he already knew something, but these he mistrusted because they depended on the creation of trance states. This smacked to him of spiritualism, and suggested possibilities of self-deception. He met "nice people" connected with schools like the Ramakrishna Vedantists, but did not feel they possessed "real knowledge." There remained rumors of schools with which he could not make personal contact; schools which appeared to have real knowledge, but which made extraordinary demands on the pupil. If he had submitted himself to such a school, he would have had to stay in India and make a clean break with his former life. This he did not want to do.

Then the miraculous intruded again.

At the beginning of the rainy season in the summer of 1914, Ouspensky left Bombay for Agra and Delhi. A visit by moonlight to the Taj Mahal continued his pilgrimage to those holy and enigmatic places where he might decode the hieroglyph of the world. The point about the hieroglyph—the point about the whole Symbolist approach—was that one never knew exactly when the numinous would reveal its overshadowing presence. The cab horse on the Nevsky, or the Buddha with the sapphire eyes; the mundane and the sublime might equally reveal universal truths. "A grain of sand can become a system of the astral world," one Russian Symbolist had written, and Ouspensky's vision of the new consciousness which he saw developing was greatly influenced by this attitude. In *The Symbolism of the Tarot*, he tried to describe the shift in perception, the apprehension of *meanings*, that slantwise, squinting vision which suddenly becomes clarity itself. "Symbolism cannot be learned as one learns to build bridges or speak a foreign language," he wrote, "and for the interpretation of symbols a special cast of mind is necessary; in addition to knowledge, special faculties, the power of creative thought and a developed imagination are required." The Tarot, like nature itself, contained 'all potential meanings.' Meanings suddenly composed themselves out of this fabric and the very existence of the Taj Mahal.

As Ouspensky sat and gazed at the luminous shape of the great building, the scent of jasmine in his nostrils and the cries of peacocks in his ears, he had only a brief warning—a sense of two worlds existing concurrently—before the miraculous broke through. In a flash of insight, he solved the riddle of the Taj Mahal. He experienced "the wonderful joy of liberation, as if I had come out into the light from some deep underground passage."

The Taj Mahal represented the secret of death. From where he sat, he saw the small light burning within the building above the tomb of the Empress Mumtaz-i-Mahal. This tiny glow, so feeble and so transitory, was the petty life of man on earth. The graceful, shining edifice which enclosed it represented eternal life, which was the same thing as saying "the soul." Suddenly there was revealed to Ouspensky the hidden meaning of the Sufi builders of the mausoleum—he was surrounded by the soul of the Empress, which merged with creation just as the Taj Mahal itself, enclosing the Empress's body, seemed to flow into the sky and the surrounding gardens. Ouspensky understood that the soul of man was not contained in his physical body, but that "the body lives and moves in the soul." The insight was so important to him and seemed so profound that he afterward felt incapable of giving it adequate expression.

The rest of his nocturnal visit confirmed the impression that the Taj Mahal was a Sufi allegory. He marveled at its workmanship and rejoiced at the way in which the architecture returned countless echoes of the shout of "Allah!" repeating "for ever, the name of God." The next day he visited the gardens again, and saw in the spectacle of all sorts and conditions of men mingling around the tomb part of the grand symbolism of its designers who had wished to demonstrate the unity of all things. "As above, so below."

Toward the end of 1914, Ouspensky returned to Ceylon by ship from Madras. He expected to find out whether his newspapers wanted him to return to Russia or to continue his journey to the Far East and America. Also, his search for the custodians of esoteric knowledge seemed on the point of bearing fruit, and he hoped to find in Colombo an acquaintance who had offered to introduce him to "certain Yogis." Instead, he was met on landing by the news of the outbreak of the First World War, and all his plans were disrupted.

The war meant that Ouspensky could not continue his search and had to postpone other journeys he had planned in Russian Central Asia and the Middle East. On his return trip, during which he spent several weeks on London, he found himself infected by the war fever. "Everything I had thought about the results of my search was thrown into confusion by the wild absurdity of the war and by all the emotions which filled the air, conversation and newspapers, and which, against my will, often affected me." But when at last he reached St. Petersburg through Norway, Sweden, and Finland, his old associations revived. He again felt that his search for the miraculous was more important than the hysterias of politicians, and the war began to assume a particular significance in the universe of four-dimensional logic. In the first place, it explained to Ouspensky why he had felt it necessary to hurry in his search for the miraculous. At the same time the reality of war, death, and destruction provided an ominous reminder of the necessity of hurry in the future "and that it was impossible to believe in 'life' which led nowhere."

There was an even more sinister significance which Ouspensky described in a story. "The Benevolent Devil," published in the early days of the war. The story uses his Indian travels as a background, and begins with the narrator's encounter with the devil in the cave temples of Ellora. In a manner which C. S. Lewis was to popularize in *The Screwtape Letters*, the devil describes the various shifts to which his infernal brethren are put to keep mankind from attaining knowledge of the real world beyond the world of matter. "The kingdom of matter is eternal!" shouts the devil, and he explains how certain magical, transcendental or religious ideas constitute the chief danger to diabolic domination of mankind. As an illustration of his methods, he takes the case of a young Englishman called Leslie White, whom the narrator of the story has met in Ceylon. Ouspensky—who loathed Englishmen of the type he imagined to be the Kipling variety and indeed he seems sometimes never to have understood the English at all— describes Leslie White as a type most uncommon in India: one who fraternizes with the Indians, and is fascinated by Buddhism; but he has attached to him a personal devil, whose task is to distract his mind from his transcendental interests. Whenever Leslie White determines to meditate or to study Buddhism, the devil suggests he go sailing, or attend a social engagement or most particularly—and there may be something of self-analysis here—that he eat a large Indian meal.

Unfortunately for his devil, Leslie White may fall by the wayside, but he always picks himself up again, and at the end of the devil's tale is not only living on a meager diet but has made contact with other seekers like himself. The existence of large numbers of such people aggravates the devil, and he leaves the narrator of the story hinting that he will be forced to use "special methods" against them. What these methods are is revealed at the end of the story, when the narrator is in London and sees Leslie White march past in the street at the head of a Scottish regiment. " 'What has Leslie retained from Yoga, from Buddhism?' I asked myself. Now he must think, feel, and live like a Roman legionnaire, whose duty is to defend the Eternal City from barbarians. An entirely different world, another psychology. Now all these refinements of thought seem an unnecessary luxury. Probably he has already forgotten about them, or will soon forget."

"The Benevolent Devil" expresses its author's bitter disappointment that the select band he had imagined capable of cosmic consciousness was to be dispersed and its possibilities shattered by the brute nature of war. At the end of the story Ouspensky's self breaks in: "What chance had they now of recognising each other? . . . I now felt the possibility for any kind of mutual understanding had been shattered for some time ahead."

As for the devil, who appears both in this story and in "The Inventor," which was published with it in an edition of 1916, he is of course no fundamentalist creation. Ouspensky makes it clear, both in the story and in his pen portrait of the card, "The Devil" in the Tarot pack, that his "devil" is created by man himself. "I am the Evil which men say is the cause of all evil," says the Tarot Devil, "and which they invented as an excuse for all the evil that they do. They call me the Prince of Falsehood, and truly I am the Prince of Lies, because *I am the most monstrous creation of human lies.*" In "The Benevolent Devil," Leslie White disappears from his tormentor's vision when he is immersed in higher things, dreaming romantically of a girl, or even reading with full absorption. "To get away from reality means to get away from the devil."

For Ouspensky's search for a life beyond life had led him to deny the existence of *byt* altogether. In the prologue to the story, the narrator dreads a sleepless night which will give him the sensation he calls "immersion in matter." Ouspensky's occult reading had led him to a Gnostic viewpoint from which he proclaimed that man must free himself from "Great Matter," and in the 1916 *Tertium Organum*, the world of matter is equated with the "unreal" world of three-dimensional consciousness which prevents knowledge of infinity beyond. "To feel this infinity it is necessary to understand the unreality of everything material and factual, and the reality of fantasy and the world of the imagination. *The material world does not exist.*"

The Great War represented the victory of the devil in man, and the immersion of European civilization in Great Matter. The imperatives of survival would prevent the birth of the new race which Ouspensky had so confidently expected. The war—"the great European war in the possibility of which I had not wanted to believe, and the reality of which I did not for a long time wish to acknowledge"—was evidently a blow which he took almost personally. At the same time his year in India had rid him of many of the illusions with which he had started out.

No longer did he indulge in fantasies of contact with esoteric schools "on another plane." He saw that these were mere daydreams, and although he was more than ever convinced that there was something to be found in the East, he saw that his search must be directed toward schools whose masters were flesh and blood. Neither had he discovered "facts"—concrete evidence of the miraculous—which would give substance to the legendary miracles of Hind. He had hoped to see mass hypnosis exercised by practitioners of the Indian rope trick, but had found only some uninteresting conjurers in Ceylon. At Benares on the Ganges, he had met a fakir who for a single rupee lay on his bed of nails and allowed himself to be photographed; but Ouspensky found nothing in the "dull, bored and indifferent expression" of the man to indicate that he practiced his painful art as a form of religious asceticism.

Yet the search for the miraculous remained his motive passion. It now proceeded with slightly different premises, but Ouspensky was still in pursuit of what he called "facts." He had as inalienable possessions the facts he had already discovered. His mystical experiences, the inquisition of the Buddha with the sapphire eyes, and the revelation of the Taj Mahal, were after all more important than the lunacies of politicians. And if the war had broken the links which held together the chain of the new race, it had also given a powerful impulse to the traditional aspirations of Holy Russia. Ouspensky's quest suddenly become relevant to many others who took the war "as a gigantic *memento mori*."

He had confirmation of this soon after his return. For six weeks he worked in Moscow for one of the newspapers which had sent him abroad. Then he went to St. Petersburg where, in February and March 1915, he gave lectures on his travels in the hall of the Town Duma. The titles of these lectures were, "In Search of the Miraculous," and "The Problems of Death." At each lecture, his audience numbered over a thousand. He was besieged by letters and callers, and "I felt," he wrote, "that on the basis of a 'search for the miraculous' it would be possible to unite together a very large number of people who were no longer able to swallow the customary forms of lying and living in lying."

6

The Inner and the Outer Revolutions

Soon after Easter 1915, Ouspensky traveled to Moscow to repeat his success as a lecturer. As a result, he met Pohl and Merkouroff, who told him of a mysterious Caucasian Greek who directed an "occult" group in Moscow. In his new critical attitude toward the occult, Ouspensky was not impressed by the rather Theosophical miracles of which they told him: these seemed "all sorts of self-suggested wonders." He only agreed to meet Gurdjieff after Merkouroff's "persistent efforts."

This is important, because it shows that Gurdjieff was out to catch Ouspensky. If so, he was far from the only disciple whom Gurdjieff deliberately ensnared. *Glimpses of the Truth* represents Gurdjieff as urging his friend "P"—perhaps Pohl—to draw the narrator out on esoteric subjects, in order to discover whether they had any real meaning for him. Some eighteen months after Ouspensky had met him, Gurdjieff was quite explicit about the composer, Thomas de Hartmann. "He has to be entangled," he told his follower, Dr. Stoerneval, in de Hartmann's hearing. "Entangle him, Doctor!" It is clear that Gurdjieff was keeping watch for people who could be of use to him, and he may have marked Ouspensky down as early as 1912. He later said—although the remark may have been intended for Ouspensky alone—that when the newspapers had reported Ouspensky's departure for the East, he had given his pupils the task of reading his books and determining from them the nature of their author and what he would be able to find in India.

Ouspensky's doubts were dissipated by his first meeting with Gurdjieff. They were replaced by other doubts, of a quite novel sort. Gurdjieff answered his questions precisely and neither stumbled nor prevaricated. But there were some strange inconsistencies. Ouspensky's description of this first encounter is probably the most famous portrait of Gurdjieff:

> We arrived at a small café in a noisy though not central street. I saw a man of an oriental type, no longer young, with a black mustache and piercing eyes, who astonished me first of all because he seemed to be disguised and completely out of keeping with the place and its atmosphere. I was still full of impressions of the East. And this man with the face of an Indian raja or an Arab sheik whom I at once seemed to see in a white burnoose or a gilded turban, seated here in this little café, where small dealers and commission agents met together, in a black overcoat with a velvet collar and a black bowler hat, produced the strange, unexpected, and almost alarming impression of a man poorly disguised, the sight of whom embarrasses you because you see he is not what he pretends to be and yet you have to speak and behave as though you did not see it. He spoke Russian incorrectly with a strong Caucasian accent; and this accent with which we are accustomed to associate anything apart from philosophical ideas, strengthened still further the strangeness and the unexpectedness of this impression.

They talked of Ouspensky's travels and his interest in narcotics. Then they went together to a meeting of Gurdjieff's pupils, which was to take place, Ouspensky gathered, in an apartment which had caused Gurdjieff great expense, as was only fitting for an undertaking in which many "professors" and "artists" were concerned. Gurdjieff refused to say precisely who among the intelligentsia were intrigued by his work; and it emerged that the meeting was to be held in the sort of barely furnished flat Ouspensky recognized as probably belonging to a municipal schoolteacher, with an audience drawn from the poverty-stricken lesser intellectuals. He was read the story, *Glimpses of Truth,* and noticed a reference to *The Struggle of the Magicians,* which he too had seen advertised in the press. About the actual work which went on in the group he could learn little. Gurdjieff had said that it was something to do with chemistry, and the schoolteacher types talked indefinitely of "work on oneself." Despite the absence of the professors and artists, and despite Gurdjieff's refusal to identify the "famous dancers" who would appear in his ballet, Ouspensky was fascinated by the evening. He had the conviction that he must at all costs arrange to meet Gurdjieff again. He was *caught*.

> I felt myself very strange—a long reading which I very little under-stood, people who did not answer my questions. G. himself with his unusual manners and his influence on his people, which I all the time felt produced in me an unexpected desire to laugh, to shout, to sing, as though I had escaped from school or from some strange detention.

For the next week he continued to meet Gurdjieff in the same shabby café. He rapidly came to see that Gurdjieff deliberately created unfavorable conditions for such conversations, and that over ideas which Ouspensky felt to be profoundly true would take pains to spread a gloss of apparent shiftiness. For example, they were talking about money. Gurdjieff said that his fee for a year's work was a thousand roubles. To Ouspensky this seemed a large sum for someone who did not have private means. Gurdjieff replied that he could not have many pupils and ought not to spend his own money on "the work." People who could not provide such a sum, he said, were probably weak in life and therefore might be weak in the work. Knowledge was not valued unless it was paid for. Ouspensky assented to all these propositions, yet with a sense that Gurdjieff was overacting a part. "I was surprised at G.'s apparent desire to *convince* me of something in connection with the question of money *when I needed no convincing*."

When the week was past, Ouspensky returned to St. Petersburg where he had to prepare books for the press, including a new edition of *Tertium Organum* and his *Occult Tales*. Gurdjieff had let him know that he sometimes traveled to St. Petersburg and would contact Ouspensky if he did come. The war went badly, and Ouspensky buried himself in his work, consoling himself that if necessary, he could always go to Gurdjieff. Then in the autumn of 1915 he was telephoned by Gurdjieff, who was on one of his periodic visits from Moscow. From this renewal of contact with the man who had almost imperceptibly become his Master, sprang the "St. Petersburg group," a group whose activities during the next eighteen months are chronicled by Ouspensky. The internal revolution which he records was paralleled with an extraordinary exactness by the events of the outer world.

It was Ouspensky who was chiefly responsible for creating Gurdjieff's following in St. Petersburg. In 1937 he told his pupils that there had been an explicit understanding that he should screen prospective recruits. By his own account it was largely through his material support that the groups could exist at all, and his new prestige as author and lecturer made him an ideal channel through which people infected by war weariness and *ennui* could pass to Gurdjieff. An account of this period has recently been published which bears out the impression that Gurdjieff was using Ouspensky as his second-in-command and front man.

This account is by Anna Butkovsky, who had become Ouspensky's close companion even before his journey to India. She had met him at a meeting of the St. Petersburg Theosophical Society, and soon found herself at the center of the group of mystically inclined intellectuals who met at The Stray Dog. She accompanied Ouspensky and Volynsky on their nocturnal sorties through St. Petersburg, during which Ouspensky would enlarge on the theme of the "search for the miraculous," a topic to which he returned in daylight in Phillipoff's Café on the Nevsky Prospekt, not far from his own apartments. After Ouspensky's meeting with Gurdjieff, Anna Butkovsky found herself rapidly introduced to this intriguing figure whom Ouspensky believed might lead them both to what he had failed to find in India. Around the pair of them and their teacher a group began to form, which met to listen to Gurdjieff in Phillipoff's Café.

First there were Ouspensky and Anna Butkovsky, the "favorite pupils," although neither of them exempt from the Master's stinging rebukes. Then Anthony Charkovsky, an engineer in his fifties, and a younger engineer named Andrei Z——. Next there was Dr. Leonid Stoerneval, a Finnish specialist in mental illness who may have arrived in Gurdjieff's circle independent of Ouspensky. Stoerneval had interests in hypnotism which may have resulted in some earlier contact with Gurdjieff, for whom he harbored an almost fanatical devotion, "almost slave-like," his wife reports. He was second only to Ouspensky in drumming up recruits. An elderly patient of his made up the sixth of the Phillipoff's group which Gurdjieff seems to have regarded as his inner circle. Meetings were held in Stoerneval's house, in the homes of his patients, and occasionally in the Finnish *dacha* of one particularly well-off lady, a Madame Maximovitch. By January 1916, thirty to forty people had gathered, and Gurdjieff began to visit St. Petersburg regularly, sometimes with pupils from his Moscow groups.

Among Gurdjieff's pupils at this time, two important figures remain puzzling. One of these is the lady who became Mme. Ouspensky—Sophia Grigorievna. Very little is known about her. She was born in 1874 and was twice married. The first marriage was to a student when she was sixteen, and the second was to a mining engineer with whom she traveled to remote areas of Russia. She had a son who was killed comparatively early in life, and a daughter old enough to provide Ouspensky with a step-grandchild in 1919. Ouspensky brought her to Gurdjieff's teaching and she was always known in the West as "Mme. Ouspensky"; but it is doubtful that the pair were ever legally married. It is rumored that Gurdjieff advised Ouspensky strongly against a marriage; and a fiction may have been propagated in order to secure certain rights or privileges for "Mme. Ouspensky" and her daughter during the chaos of civil war and emigration. The situation was generally known and accepted by their pupils in the 1920s; and the couple's relationship became increasingly one of convenience.

The other mysterious figure is the woman who was always known as Gurdjieff's "wife," although she kept her own name of Ostrowsky. Her early life is a complete blank. J. G. Bennett claims that she was "a noble Polish lady from the Imperial court," and the "Polish" at least is true if not the "noble." There may be some reference to Mme. Ostrowsky in Gurdjieff's portrait of the Polish "Mme. Vitvitskaya" in *Meetings with Remarkable Men*. Vitvitskaya was a reformed prostitute and the de Hartmanns hint that Mme. Ostrowsky had a mixed and unhappy past. A legend used to circulate among Gurdjieff's disciples that she kept her own name because she wished to be considered as an ordinary pupil, rather than Gurdjieff's wife; but other reasons spring to mind if we accept that Gurdjieff probably still had a wife living somewhere in Central Asia. And far from being an ordinary pupil, Mme. Ostrowsky always occupied a privileged position in the Work and later often took leading roles in Gurdjieff's dances.

At first Gurdjieff's methods caused confusion in St. Petersburg. He liked to spring meetings on his pupils at short notice. He would change his plans without warning; for example, he might announce his imminent departure, then spend the whole day seeing pupils in cafés and decide at the last possible moment to hold a meeting. ". . . He considered that only by overcoming difficulties, however irrelevant and accidental, could people value his ideas," wrote Ouspensky. The confusion was increased by the *acting* which Ouspensky and his friends noticed in Gurdjieff. He would play, for example, the part of a simple carpet seller, telling his pupils that during his Eastern travels he had acquired a collection of carpets which could be disposed of most advantageously in St. Petersburg—but other people said that he bought the carpets in Moscow and transported them to St. Petersburg to sell. Or he presided over huge dinners which earned him the reputation of a bon viveur—although Ouspensky noticed that he ate little himself, and it was obvious to all his pupils that this was "acting."

Occasionally his tactics seemed brazenly perverse. The American art critic, Carl Zigrosser, has recorded a story of Gurdjieff at this period which Ouspensky told Orage. Ouspensky had arranged a lecture for Gurdjieff before the Moscow Geographical Society. Gurdjieff lectured on the Gobi Desert with great authority and to great effect. Then he described how he had once discovered a valley whose sides were so steep that no one could reach the bottom. The valley floor was covered with diamonds, said

Gurdjieff, and the local inhabitants trained vultures to fly down to retrieve lumps of meat which they flung down in the hopes that the diamonds would become embedded in them. His learned audience was thrown into consternation—some suspecting simple fraud, others perhaps recognizing the tale from the *Arabian Nights* which Gurdjieff had repeated. The lecture turned into a fiasco. Gurdjieff explained to Ouspensky that he had seen that the valuable information which he had given the scholars was going unappreciated, so he decided to cast doubts on the whole substance of his talk.

A lesson for the academics? Or a lesson for Ouspensky, the intellectual, jealous of his standing with his fellows?

Under this unsettling tuition, the St. Petersburg group felt their way into the dense texture of Gurdjieff's ideas. Ouspensky recorded their struggles in *In Search of the Miraculous*.

The peculiar nature of *In Search of the Miraculous* has never been fully defined. It is a book which is both extraordinarily honest and extraordinarily deceptive. Just before his death Gurdjieff was persuaded by his pupils to read Ouspensky's manuscript, and it is said that he pronounced blessings on his former disciple whom for years he had publicly vilified. The book is generally agreed to be an extremely scrupulous piece of reporting, and it can be approached as an accurate picture of what Gurdjieff taught in Russia in 1915–18. *In Search of the Miraculous* refers as much to Ouspensky as to Gurdjieff. When the book was first published in 1950, a reviewer in *The Times Literary Supplement* remarked that "this seems one of the rare cases where the commentator proves almost more important than the subject of his observations." We have what is one aspect of a unique example of the process of "self-observation" which plays such a large part in Gurdjieff's ideas. Gurdjieff mirrors Ouspensky, and Ouspensky reflects Gurdjieff. The Gurdjieff represented is called into being by his pupil: a Gurdjieff whose teaching was angled toward the mystical Russian intelligentsia and—from the point of view of the only record we possess—at Ouspensky in particular.

The intensely personal nature of the record is emphasized by its title. Ouspensky always referred to his manuscript about his years with Gurdjieff as *Fragments of an Unknown Teaching*, and this is the subtitle of the published book. But the full title is very significant. Ouspensky had published two series of sketches describing his Eastern travels as *In Search of the Miraculous*: volumes I and II. To use the same title for his record of Gurdjieff's teaching is to place it where it belongs, in the historical sequence of Ouspensky's own search. This may seem a pedantic point, but it is important. "I even thought," says Ouspensky of the members of Gurdjieff's Moscow group, "that it was very strange to meet them on the way to the miraculous." In his first conversations with Gurdjieff, Ouspensky spoke to him of his plans for returning to the Orient. "'It is good to go for a rest, for a holiday,' said G., 'but it is not worth while going there for what you want. All that can be found here.'" Ouspensky's record of what followed is the record of his passage through the fire of Gurdjieff's purgative system. He embarked on this adventure as the logical continuation of his quest for suitable "schools" in the East.

Because *In Search of the Miraculous* seems to be the clearest existing account of Gurdjieff's teaching, it is widely read, and some of the results have been very odd. The hieratic-religious tone which provided the background to Gurdjieff's talks belongs entirely to the Russian phase of his activity and is directed to the people among whom he was working. It belongs particularly to Ouspensky, whose personal preoccupations naturally influenced the questions he asked Gurdjieff and the items of Gurdjieff's conversation he snapped up. And the book is packed with references to topics of quite transitory interest. How many readers will now recognize the reason for the talks on a universal language which have been found so significant? This almost certainly began with a reference to the artificial language, Esperanto, devised by L. L. Zamenhof (1859–1917). Zamenhof's inspiration came from the linguistic chaos of his birthplace on the Polish-Russian frontier, and from about 1905, universal languages were matters of concern to the intelligentsia of all the Russias. Gurdjieff's skill immediately turned a topical question into a study of universals. There already existed three universal languages, he replied. They related to levels of being and understanding.

With questions of being and understanding, we move into the territory of Gurdjieff's ideas themselves. They were released piecemeal, in a manner deliberately self-contradictory or misleading, and had to be fitted together by his pupils, and even completed by the pupils' investigations. This, together with Gurdjieff's ability never to seem the same person twice, gave rise to numerous disputes and misunderstandings. But despite the tantalizing, crabwise approach, the body of ideas which Gurdjieff gradually revealed presented a strange coherence. The group in St. Petersburg began to talk of "the System." It comprised a cosmology, a psychology, ideas of evolution and the structure of matter—it seemed in a puzzling world to explain everything, and yet to lead to a point at which thought itself was annulled, and explanations became unnecessary. Step by step the pupils approached what the Gurdjieff of *Glimpses of Truth* calls "the abyss which can never be bridged by ordinary human reason."

Gurdjieff was the Man Who Knows, and in *In Search of the Miraculous*, Ouspensky never quite conveys the intensity of a relationship with such a superbeing. However, what he taught Ouspensky during 1916 and 1917 went something as follows:

Man is asleep. He must wake up.

Nothing he thinks or feels or senses is conscious. He is hypnotized, like the sheep whom an Eastern wizard once mesmerized into believing that their procession to the slaughterhouse was both inevitable and good. Man is a machine.

The universe also is a machine. Everything happens. No one can *do* anything. They are *done to* as the forces which move the universe operate in them and the world around them. *It* hails, *it* snows; in the same way *"it* laughs in me."* Over such processes man thinks he has control. He has none. The Great War now in progress: an example of sleep, the hypnotic state in which we are lived rather than live our lives. Such disasters are inevitable in a world of *mad machines*.

WAKE UP

You do not realise your own situation. You are in prison. All you can wish for, if you are a sensible man, is to escape. But how escape? It is necessary to tunnel under a wall. One man can do nothing. But let us suppose there are ten or twenty men—if they work in turn and if one covers another they can complete the tunnel and escape.

Furthermore no one can escape from prison without the help of those *who have escaped before*.

Under the direction of a Man Who Knows, it is possible to escape from prison. A group must be formed which obeys certain rules. Its members can help each other to fathom the working of their machines. They must keep secret what they learn because of the impossibility of transmitting accurately what is said in such groups: this silence is in itself a useful exercise because of the tendency of the human machine to jabber automatically of what most interests it. They must tell the teacher of the group the whole truth, and this is difficult, because the human machine has a horrifying compulsion to lie. Although the teacher of the group cannot be deceived, he can deceive his pupils as much as he wants. It is for their own good.

In order to wake up, members of a group under a teacher must "work on themselves." This "work" includes several basic exercises. At first, a man must observe himself, study the working of the human machine. Then he must try to "remember himself," be conscious of his own being. He must work on what Gurdjieff called "considering," which takes two forms. Internal considering is being concerned or guided by what other people think of us, and is to be avoided. External considering is to be cultivated and involves taking other people's feelings into account, not expressing what Ouspensky called "negative emotions." This exercise was an exercise for the emotions, and work on the emotions—as the most dormant part of unconscious man—formed an important part of Gurdjieff's teaching. There are other exercises for the other centers.

Centers? The structure of the human machine can be diagrammatically represented. Man, Gurdjieff began by saying, has three centers governing his activity: an intellectual center, an emotional center, and a moving center. These are located separately in the body and exist independently of each other. Later Gurdjieff was to refer to man as a "three-brained being." It was part of work on oneself to harmonize the functioning of these hopelessly discordant centers. It became apparent that the description of three centers was one of convenience, for Gurdjieff eventually defined seven. The "moving centre," together with the "instinctive centre" and the "sex centre" form the "centres of the lower story." Above the "intellectual" and "emotional" centers are the "higher intellectual" and "higher emotional" centers, which represent functions present and perfectly developed in man, but which he does not know how to use. They can be used only by higher sorts of man.

There are seven numbers of man. Man number one has his center of gravity in the moving center, man number two in the emotional center, and man number three in the intellectual center. These are the men we know. Man number four results from work in groups. He has begun to balance his centers and has a permanent center of gravity in his attachment to the work of self-development. Men numbers one, two and three have no such permanent element in their being: all they consist of is a hundred little "I's," each with its different demands, likes and dislikes. At any moment "Webb" or "Ivanov" or "Ouspensky" can alter into "Petrov" or a stranger called, say, E. Hamilton Jones. Ordinarily, we "identify" with whichever imaginary "I" happens to be dominant. Men below man number four have no "I"; just a multitude of conflicting tiny selves. But man number four knows where he is going, and in man number five, the permanent attributes are becoming crystallized, for he has attained unity. Man number six is a less perfected form of man number seven, "who has reached the full development possible to man and who possesses everything a man can possess, that is, will, consciousness, permanent and unchangeable 'I,' individuality, immortality, and many other properties, which in our blindness and ignorance, we ascribe to ourselves."

The seven numbers of man represent a functioning of one of the two fundamental cosmic laws. These are the Law of Three and the Law of Seven. They operate both in the structure of the human machine and in the greater machine of the universe. The Law of Three is the working of the universe which creates all phenomena of whatever order. "Every phenomenon, on whatever scale and in whatever world it may take place, is the result of the combination or meeting of three different and opposing forces." In relation to each other, these are expressed as active, passive and neutralizing forces, which Gurdjieff would later term "Holy Affirming, Holy Denying, and Holy Reconciling." In a man who wants to work on himself, said Gurdjieff, the Law of Three would manifest itself in the following fashion: his desire to work for a higher level of being forms the active force; his habitual inertia and mechanicalness, the passively resisting second force; and the reconciling aspect of the triad might be provided by *new knowledge* showing him the pressing need for such work and resolving the stalemate between his good intentions and his innate laziness.

In the great machine of the universe, the Law of Three "is a property of the real world." The Absolute, from which all creation emanates, is composed of three forces—which give rise to such concepts as the Christian idea of the Trinity. The will of the Absolute creates worlds of a second order; and by the creative action of triads of active, passive, and reconciling forces, passes into worlds of different orders far removed from their sources. As the will of the Absolute is diffused further and further along what Gurdjieff called the Ray of Creation, the number of mechanical laws to which created worlds are subject increases. The expression "world" meant for Gurdjieff something like "sphere of being," "plane of matter," or "intensity of vibration." The second fundamental cosmic law is the Law of the Octave or the Law of Seven. This governs the *development* of processes—for example, the course of a man's life. It determines that there shall be seven worlds along the octave of the Ray of Creation. Directly from the Absolute comes a degree of matter containing all created worlds leading to a less refined stage comprising "all suns" which gives place to the order of things existing in all planetary worlds. The Earth comes next to last on the Ray of Creation: it is a very bad place in the universe—very heavy matter—subject to a huge number of mechanical laws. This is why a correspondingly intense effort has to be made by man to overcome his mechanicalness.

Everything which happens to a man in his ordinary life as part of this machine is produced by the *law of accident*. Only by submitting to influences which come as it were from "outside" the mechanism and are transmitted through esoteric channels, can man hope to free himself from the "accidents" which are produced by the automatic working of the machine.

WAKE UP

Organic life on earth, of which man is a part, has a particular cosmic task to perform. To describe this operation of the Law of Seven, Gurdjieff used the metaphor of the musical octave. This requires that there be two intervals in the orderly progression of created worlds: for such intervals occur in the musical octave at the stages where the rate of increase of vibrations becomes retarded. In an ascending octave these intervals occur between the notes *mi* and *fa* and between *si* and *do*. On the descending octave of the Ray of Creation, human life helps to fill the second interval. The cosmic function of humanity is *to transmit and transform energies across this interval*. The proud creature man is a thing with a lowly purpose. There is nothing he can do about it, except to choose between cooperating consciously with the process of transforming energies, thereby acquiring something for himself, and performing his unavoidable function in a way which will satisfy the cosmic machine but profit him nothing.

The status of organisms in the universe can be determined by the classification of the substance on which they feed. Man feeds on three sorts of food: the ordinary food that he eats, the air he breathes, and his impressions. From these foods he manufactures other substances, which in turn can serve as food for organisms which exist on different orders of substance. By work on himself he has the possibility of manufacturing substances of a higher classification, of transforming coarse matter into fine. This process is what the alchemists called transmutation; it was the "chemistry" of which Ouspensky had heard. If from the outside it could be said that work on oneself gives the possibility of attaining higher consciousness, of becoming man number four, it is Gurdjieff's cosmology that explains this inner alchemy and provides the reason why. By work on himself man can not only perform his cosmic function but manufacture the substances necessary for immortality.

Man has no soul—he must get up and *make* one.

Otherwise he goes to feed the moon.

The moon is the last and most mechanical world on Gurdjieff's Ray of Creation. It is a degree of matter in which vibrations have almost ceased. It corresponds to inert mineral life on earth. It is "matter without the Holy Ghost." This is the destiny of automatic man.

The process of transmutation, of manufacturing the substances necessary to give man immortality within the limits of his capacity as an organism, is connected with the acquisition of "higher bodies." There are four bodies possible for the "three-brained being." Three are the carnal or physical body, the natural body of emotions and desires, and the spiritual body of mental functionings. Work on oneself is necessary to produce even the natural and the spiritual bodies. The natural body grows out of the physical body and the spiritual body out of the natural body. If a man has accomplished the transformations of substances necessary to acquire a spiritual body, he can proceed to the acquisition of a fourth body, the divine body of consciousness, will, and a real "I." Gurdjieff followed the *Upanishads* and Plato in comparing the four bodies to a carriage (the physical body), the horse (feelings and desires), the driver (the mind), and the master of horse, carriage and driver (the real "I"). The fourth body is composed of substances much finer than the others and is thus subject to fewer mechanical laws. Man begins to acquire higher bodies by transmuting the finest substance manufactured automatically by his organism. This is "the substance with which sex works." Much later Gurdjieff made it clear that this is sperm itself, rather than some imperceptible corollary. Abuse of sex makes it impossible to begin transmutation.

Something has gone wrong with the functioning of the human organism and has prevented man's orderly evolution to higher states. The "line of knowledge" has outstripped the "line of being." What man actually *is* has been left behind by what he thinks he *knows*. In fact, he even knows very little, because "objective knowledge" is possible only for a man of higher consciousness. This division between the line of knowledge and the line of being corresponds to the division in the psyche between false personality and essence. False personality is what a man thinks he is, and his essence is what he is in fact. Personality is an illusion, maintained by sleep and what Gurdjieff called "buffers," which are mechanisms acquired in order to soften the impact of rare glimpses of the truth. Underneath are all the conflicting "I's" of man and an essence—the core and basis of what he is— which may have stopped growing in infancy. Whereas personality is subject to the law of accident, a man's essence is always of a particular and definable *type*, subject to the law of fate, which can at least be allowed for and predicted. A beginning can be made toward liberating oneself from false personality by struggling not to "identify" too closely with momentary preoccupations; a man must learn to "play a role." Eventually, he may discover his "Chief Feature": the most important of the automatisms, which hold him in bondage.

This complex and closely connected body of ideas was summed up in a symbol Gurdjieff called the enneagram. This is based on a circle whose circumference is divided by nine points, connected by lines to give a six-sided figure and a triangle. The enneagram contains and symbolizes the whole universe and Gurdjieff's explanation of it, including the Laws of Three and Seven and the relationship of all substances to one another. In this symbol Gurdjieff altered his musical analogy by an arbitrary redisposition of the intervals in the octave. If the enneagram is taken as a diagram of possible human evolution, it shows how something is needed to help a man across these intervals. This can be provided only by "shocks" administered by a Man Who Knows.

•   •   •

Gurdjieff's ideas made an extraordinary impact on his pupils. Those who were interested in occultism were confronted by an apparently occult system which seemed to contradict almost every known body of occult ideas. Gurdjieff did relate his teaching to known mystical philosophies, but always in a way which emphasized the differences between what he taught and the object of comparison. For example, the term "Kundalini" is found in much Theosophical literature as the name for a force latent in man which must be awakened. Gurdjieff used the expression to stand for the imagination, the power of fantasy which keeps man asleep and prevents him from participating in the real world. Later, in *Beelzebub's Tales*, he connected this with his doctrine of "buffers" and invented a word, "Kundabuffer," to signify the same hypnotic influence. So much for the romantic dreams of believers in occult tradition. As for the source of his ideas, he would refer vaguely to the researches of the Seekers for Truth. His teaching was "completely self-supporting . . . and it has been completely unknown up to the present time." Once Gurdjieff said that it could be called "esoteric Christianity," but chiefly he preferred the phrase, "The Fourth Way," or "The Way of the Sly Man." The Sly Man, the cunning man—and has not one of his followers compared Gurdjieff to Odysseus?—used every possible trick to keep himself awake. The man of the Fourth Way avoided the pitfalls of imbalanced development which gaped for the followers of the other three "ways"—the intellectual way of the yogi, the emotional way of the monk, the physical way of the fakir. He was harmoniously developed with all his centers in phase.

If, on the other hand, a pupil was a refugee from positivistic science, Gurdjieff's ideas set the virtues of materialism against the materialists themselves. One example is the process of the transformation of energies which Gurdjieff expressed in terms of forces he named after the chemical elements. "Carbon," "oxygen," and "nitrogen" stood for the active, passive, and neutralizing forces which combined to produce the "hydrogen," the phenomenon or grade of matter in the universe. Each of the "elements"—including the "hydrogen"—had a numerical cipher attached to indicate its position in the scale of the density of matter. In theory, therefore, the designation "hydrogen 24" enabled the student to place a form of matter or energy—for Gurdjieff made no distinction between them—in its cosmic relationship with all other substances; and Ouspensky worked out complicated mathematical tables to elaborate the hints he was given of this already complex cosmology.

Ouspensky's record naturally emphasized the topics which most interested him, and among these were several of his old hobbyhorses. One was eternal recurrence, and he at last succeeded—after some six months—in extracting from his teacher a qualified endorsement of the idea (later Gurdjieff himself used the concept in an unpublished lecture, "On Symbols"). Ouspensky's questions about art provided Gurdjieff's teaching on "objective" art. A question about the relation of men to the sources of esoteric knowledge gave Ouspensky the chance to expand Gurdjieff's quite straightforward answer into a beautiful diagram with men numbered like geometrical points. And, when Gurdjieff elaborated his doctrine of the different worlds on the Ray of Creation into a vision of cosmoses arranged in an ascending hierarchy of dimensions, he actually asked his pupil to expand the material from his own point of view. This greatly excited Ouspensky, who at once saw correspondences between Gurdjieff's teaching and the more advanced speculations on multidimensionality which he had been pursuing since *Tertium Organum*.

We can identify the precise time when Ouspensky passed from fascination with Gurdjieff's ideas to a deeper commitment to the practical activity proposed. About a quarter of the way through *In Search of the Miraculous* he records a conversation about personal objectives. What, asked Gurdjieff, did each member of the group really want? Ouspensky's aim had, of course, to do with his fourth dimension, Time. He was convinced that it was possible to know the future and claimed success in practical prediction. This obsession with the future course of events led to resentment at the indignity of a life which might at any second be abruptly ended. It was futile to begin a project without any certainty that it could be completed. Ouspensky told Gurdjieff that at all costs he wanted *"to know the future."*

Gurdjieff's response shows how his angling worked. He replied that the future would be exactly the same as the past—for what was the use of knowing the future if a man could not call himself his own master? Before trying anything so ambitious as knowledge of the future, a man must pay attention to his own machine.

The beginning of the road was self-observation. Gurdjieff asked his pupils what was the most important thing they noticed when they tried to observe themselves. He appeared dissatisfied with the answers given by the group, and he declared that the most important result of self-observation was the realization that one cannot *remember oneself*. Ouspensky's experience seemed at first to confirm this, but with increasing practice, he found that for short periods he did succeed in attaining the condition of "self-remembering." He describes one walk through St. Petersburg which he took with the firm resolution at all costs to "remember himself." He began by finding the life around him too distracting, and to prevent his attention from wandering, he took to the sidestreets. With greater success he became bolder and turned into the Nevsky Prospekt in order to test his abilities against the crowds. He decided to order some cigarettes—and as he writes, "Two hours later I *woke up* . . . far away." In between "forgetting himself" and again emerging into the state of "self-remembering," he had telephoned, written letters, and conducted himself quite properly as a normal—that is, a sleeping—man.

What is this state of self-remembering which is so difficult to attain and hold? Ouspensky thought of it as a double-headed arrow indicating that attention was directed both at an object and on oneself—*but man has no "I"!* One of the achievements of *In Search of the Miraculous* is that it manages to lay stress on this central aspect of Gurdjieff's teaching without being specific about the non-existent "self" which we are supposed to "remember." The double-headed arrow, yes; but what is this curious and vivid state it induces for that—*"instant in and out of time?"* "I have striven at it for over a quarter of a century," writes Henri Tracol, "and I admit, I feel myself as unable to define it in a way which fully satisfies me as on the first day." However, Maurice Nicoll has provided a preliminary description:

> . . . all real Self-Remembering is simply forgetting yourself, your ordinary self, your ordinary negative "I's," your ordinary forms of internal considering, and all the rest of it, and feeling certain that some further state of yourself exists above all this personal uproar that takes place all day long in each one of you, with which you keep on identifying, and when the Work says that we have Real "I" above us you must understand that this act, so to speak, of separating from False Personality, deliberately at some moment every day, is designed to make it possible for us to come in contact with the first traces of Real "I" which is already there and which is our real goal.

Henri Tracol has tried to describe his own experience. This is what the exercise of self-remembering feels like to perform:

> My attention is no longer the same, its power accumulates, its penetration and its freedom make it both larger and more alive. It mobilises in me latent forces, kept until this time in a dormant state. It activates an alteration in the force and the regulation of certain functions, releasing in this way a chain-reaction, through which in the self-same moment there is intensified the global perception I have of myself, a perception which is located far above the plane of perception proper and whose taste could not be confused with any other.
>
> This general activity coincides with the appearance of the intensest

feeling of renewal, a sensation of opening and belonging to the external as much as the internal world, inasmuch as in me they are united.

Ouspensky began to see the practice of self-remembering as the central point of Gurdjieff's teaching, and tried unsuccessfully to transfer some of his enthusiasm to his literary friends. His experiments had proved to his own satisfaction that although mankind did indeed exist as a society of sleepwalkers, *there was a way out*. He may not have realized it at the time, but his attitude had altered considerably since he first met Gurdjieff. "I did not even wish for any changes in myself," he writes about his setting out for India. But now his efforts were concentrated on "waking up." The watchword of Gurdjieff's pupils had become "work on oneself," and soon their efforts were referred to simply as "the Work." Only one thing seems definite about this elusive activity. It involves *change*.

Ouspensky was still in search of the miraculous, but the miraculous had altered its complexion. It had come to be associated with "waking up"; and as 1916 wore on, he and his companions found that Gurdjieff applied more and more pressure on them as he extended their activities. He now spent most of his time in St. Petersburg and began to arrange expeditions into the country. Ouspensky came to realize that during these adventures and picnics, Gurdjieff was observing his pupils in roles which they did not adopt during a formal meeting.

By now Ouspensky's relationship with Gurdjieff's Moscow group had become much closer. At first he had seen them as hopelessly artificial or "playing a part which had been learned beforehand." Now he thought that he knew why this had seemed to be so, and why they had originally refused to answer his questions about the nature of the Work. "I understand now," he wrote, "that these questions could not be answered." "One must *learn* in order to begin to understand this." And with this annoying piece of mystification, all the keys are in our hands.

Ouspensky began a series of experiments in fasting and the exercise of repetitive prayer known to the Orthodox Church as "prayer of the mind," which had helped him in his attempts at self-remembering. He was keyed to a very high emotional pitch when, in August 1916, he arrived to stay at a Finnish dacha—probably the one belonging to Madame Maximovitch. The events of the few days he spent in Finland were in many ways the strangest of his time with Gurdjieff. Ouspensky was reminded of his first meeting with his Master, when he had asked Gurdjieff about *"facts."* He had in mind facts of a "miraculous" nature, the sort of miracles which he had gone to India to find. Gurdjieff had promised that there would be *facts*. But now Ouspensky's ideas were different, and the word "facts," with its significant stressing, related like the miraculous to self-remembering and waking up.

Ouspensky describes what happened with many protests that his experiences are incommunicable—the sort of riders which had always annoyed him in reading the mystics. He emphasizes that he arrived in Finland in an excitable condition, which was aggravated by Gurdjieff's shock tactics. Gurdjieff was particularly harsh to the group and put Ouspensky severely out of countenance by repeating some unfavorable gossip Ouspensky had told him in confidence about Dr. Stoerneval. Then at about ten o'clock in the evening, Gurdjieff took Ouspensky apart with Stoerneval and the mathematician A. A. Zaharoff, and began to demonstrate certain movements of a type which became important later in his teaching. Ouspensky says that Gurdjieff neither hypnotized him "by any of the known methods" nor did he give him a drug. But he began to hear his teacher's thoughts.

At first this took the form of Ouspensky detecting "thoughts" directed specifically at him from among the general instructions Gurdjieff was giving to all three men. Then Gurdjieff's voice started asking questions from a position somewhere inside Ouspensky's chest; and to the astonishment of the other pupils, he began responding vocally to an interrogation which they could not hear. Gurdjieff's questions caused Ouspensky a great deal of agitation. He does not say what they were, but merely that they concerned "certain conditions which I had either to accept or *leave the work*." After half an hour's conversation, Ouspensky reacted to a particular barb from Gurdjieff by rushing outside into the forest. For some time he walked about "wholly in the power of the most extraordinary thoughts and feelings." From this tumult he emerged with the conviction that all Gurdjieff's criticisms of him were correct. At this point he makes his first important statement on the results he obtained from his "miracle." "But I had found something else. I knew that he would not believe me and that he would laugh at me if I showed him this other thing. But for myself it was indubitable, and what happened later showed I was right."

The miracle continued. In bed that night Ouspensky resumed mental contact with his teacher. Gurdjieff broke off communication when something he asked Ouspensky set the pupil trembling with fear. The next morning the apparently telepathic conversation continued. For the three days more that the group stayed in Finland, Ouspensky felt himself "in an unusual emotional state all the time, which sometimes began to be burdensome." In exasperation he asked Gurdjieff how this condition could be made to disappear. Gurdjieff replied that now he had what he wanted; he was no longer asleep. Ouspensky did not think that this was quite accurate. "I undoubtedly 'slept' at some moments."

The miracle did not come to an end with the stay in Finland. After Gurdjieff left St. Petersburg for Moscow, Ouspensky "conversed" telepathically with him while receiving a visual image of Gurdjieff in the train. And, for the next three weeks as he walked around St. Petersburg, he was continually conscious that everyone around him was asleep.

Ouspensky's "miracle" can be explained in a number of ways. The most important fact is that, as a result of the episode, he observed a change taking place in himself. Because he felt that the personal nature of his conversations with Gurdjieff precluded publication, it is impossible to be specific. But he came to conclusions which in the light of later events appear as a statement of principle:

> The first thing I could record was the weakening in me of that extreme individualism which up to that time had been the fundamental feature in my attitude to life. I began to see people more, to feel my community with them more. And the second thing was that somewhere very deep down inside me I understood the esoteric principle of the impossibility of violence, that is, the uselessness of violent means to attain no matter what. I saw with undoubted clarity, and never afterwards did I wholly lose this feeling, that violent means and methods *in anything whatever* would unfailingly produce negative results, that is to say, results opposed to those aims for which they were applied. What I arrived at was like Tolstoi's non-resistance in appearance but it was not at all non-resistance because I had reached it not from an ethical but from a practical point of view; not from the standpoint of what is *better* or what is *worse* but from the standpoint of what is more effective and expedient.

It was after the intrusion of the miraculous into the Finnish dacha—that is, during the autumn and winter of 1916—that Gurdjieff began greatly to expand his cosmology. Then he left the St. Petersburg group largely to their own devices. The progress of the war and the social discontents arising from it had begun to penetrate even their charmed circle. By November 1916, external circumstances—what Ouspensky called "events"—could no longer be ignored; one result was that many new recruits arrived in the group. Ouspensky admits that the sense of imminent disaster which engulfed his friends added to their concern with Gurdjieff's ideas. For the System explained everything. Gurdjieff taught that war was the result of man not producing certain energies—in other words, becoming conscious—and that instead, nature was forced to obtain such energies from the expenditure of human life. His pupils began to compare the System to Noah's Ark. The Bible story appeared as a parable signifying the way in which men could be saved from the world of "events" by esoteric knowledge. "We could not imagine," Ouspensky writes, "how we could live

without it and find out our way in the labyrinth of all existing contradictions."

In the 1950s one reviewer of *In Search of the Miraculous* remarked that
in no other book about the years 1914–19 was there so little reference to the
Russian Revolution. Of course, Ouspensky and his friends took note of
political developments, but the history of crime was what they were trying
to escape. By diminishing personally, they were to become invisible, veiled
by their detachment from the outer world. They were growing small like
Alice in Wonderland, and the Ark in which they drifted on the ocean of
"events" was a raft on the Sea of Tears.

One of the new recruits to Gurdjieff's teaching in the gloomy time just
before the Revolution was Thomas Alexandrovich de Hartmann. De
Hartmann, born in 1886, had already achieved some fame as a composer. In
1906 his ballet *Beauty and the Beast* had been performed in St. Petersburg.
In 1907 another ballet, *The Pink Flower*, was performed at the Opera, in
the presence of the Tsar, with Pavlova, Fokine, and Nijinsky in the cast.

From 1908 to 1911, de Hartmann lived in Munich where he studied
conducting. He believed with Beethoven that "music is a higher revelation
than philosophy and science" and he too embarked on the search for Higher
Powers. He says nothing about the early years of his quest, except that he
"came in contact with many 'ways' and met many exceptional people, but
they never seemed to be what I was looking for." The direction of his search
can only be intimated. In Munich, he frequented the Kandinsky circle,
which was seriously concerned with Anthroposophy. In Russia, he was a
friend of Scriabin, the most Messianic of all the Russian composers, and
studied piano under the Theosophist Essipova, who introduced Paul Dukes
to *The Secret Doctrine*.

The de Hartmanns were members of the Russian aristocracy. Thomas
was the great-nephew of Eduard von Hartmann, the author of *The
Philosophy of the Unconscious;* and he was released from military service to
devote his time to music after a personal meeting with the Tsar. His wife,
Olga Arcadievna de Schumaker, was the daughter of a senior government
official. The couple were living at Tsarskoye Selo when de Hartmann's
search led him to a member of Gurdjieff's St. Petersburg group: A. A.
Zaharoff.

In the autumn of 1916 Zaharoff told de Hartmann that he had at last
found a teacher. The composer was skeptical, having already met his fair
share of quacks. But Zaharoff intrigued him by refusing to reveal his
teacher's name and telling him of the thousand roubles entry fee to the
Work. Although the sum was large, de Hartmann could have paid it, and
eventually that December he was given an appointment to meet Gurdjieff.
The composer had been recalled to the colors, and the meeting was

arranged at a restaurant on the corner of the Nevsky Prospekt in which no Guard's officer would dare to be seen. When Zaharoff appeared, he led poor de Hartmann to an even more disreputable spot, a second-floor café frequented by prostitutes, where discovery would have meant forfeiting his commission. Gurdjieff arrived with Dr. Stoerneval and another man who was possibly Merkouroff. He presented a seedy appearance, with his filthy detachable shirt cuffs, his Caucasian features, and his offensive remarks. At one point Gurdjieff looked round the café and shocked the composer by observing: "There are usually more whores here."

Like Ouspensky, de Hartmann was impressed by Gurdjieff, almost despite himself. And he had never seen such *eyes*. . . . He stuck to his guns and asked to be admitted to Gurdjieff's Work. But when he offered his thousand roubles, Gurdjieff refused them, saying that although he had no need of help at the moment, the time would come when de Hartmann would be glad to hand over all his worldy goods.

The composer had met his Master at the very last minute. Gurdjieff was no longer to be often in St. Petersburg, and the demands of the war were soon to disrupt the little group of disciples. Even Ouspensky had been called up, and spent four months in the Guards Sappers before being discharged because of weak eyesight. In February 1917, Gurdjieff paid his last visit to St. Petersburg, and soon afterward de Hartmann left for the front. With him went his wife, who had met Gurdjieff on only one occasion, but that single encounter and a reading of *Glimpses of Truth* had decided her to follow her husband to Gurdjieff as soon as circumstances allowed.

Gurdjieff left for Moscow by train for the last time—and to some of his pupils, he seemed to be transfigured in the window of his railway carriage. In the same carriage a celebrated journalist was traveling. This man assumed that Gurdjieff was of the same type as the war profiteers and Caucasian oil magnates who filled the coach. Gurdjieff encouraged his companion in this belief, but disquieted him by the cynical amusement with which he surveyed the hubbub of the money-makers. Was Gurdjieff also not anxious for his profits, asked the journalist?

> He smiled in a particularly calm way and answered gravely: "We profit from everything. Nothing can stop us. War or no war, it's all the same to us. We always profit."
> "What do you deal in, then?"
> "In Solar energy."

On March 8 and 9 strikers crossed the Neva into St. Petersburg. The Government reacted in panic. A general strike was called and three hundred thousand took to the streets. On March 11, the first casualties took place, and the next day desertions from the army began. On March 15, the Tsar abdicated in favor of the Grand Duke Michael. Next day the Grand Duke also resigned the throne.

Ouspensky read the news of the abdication on a flyer and felt that Russian history had ended. About a week later he called the leading members of the group to Dr. Stoerneval's house and proposed that they emigrate. There was no sense in staying in a country where they could not *work*. Since most of his companions disagreed, matters went no further. Soon afterward, a postcard arrived from Gurdjieff which said that he was going to Alexandropol in the Caucasus. He asked Ouspensky to continue the work of the group and promised to return by Easter. The card had been written before the Revolution took place, and it was plain that Gurdjieff knew nothing of events. What were they to do?

A week after Easter a telegram came announcing Gurdjieff's arrival in May.

On April 16, Lenin arrived at the Finland Station.

At last, in early June, Ouspensky had a second telegram from Alexandropol. It read: "If you want to rest, come here to me."

Ouspensky set off for the Caucasus through a country still dazed and unsure of what was happening. His train took two days longer than usual to reach Alexandropol because he had to run the gauntlet of drunken deserters and drumhead courts-martial. He arrived to find Gurdjieff assembling a dynamo for his brother.

He liked Alexandropol. Despite the taint of provincialism, which had made the more snobbish of Gurdjieff's Muscovite followers look doubtfully at him, Caucasia was an area of romance. To Ouspensky particularly, as a devotee of Lermontov's *Hero of Our Time*, the Caucasus would have carried all the associations of adventure. The main mountain range is about 750 miles long and at its broadest, over 100 miles wide. The highest peak, Mount Elbruz, is over 18,000 feet high. There are glaciers, forests, rain, snow, and appalling transport difficulties. The inhabitants represent an opposite pole to European townspeople. And here, the torments of Lermontov's hero in the countryside with its frivolous watering places provided a fine precedent for the spiritual battles which developed under Gurdjieff's direction. The romantic associations of the Caucasus may partly explain the special atmosphere of Gurdjieff's work there, which the participants remembered.

After a fortnight in Alexandropol both Ouspensky and Gurdjieff set off for St. Petersburg, but on the way Gurdjieff changed his plans and Ouspensky went on alone. He had instructions not to stay long, but merely to gather any other pupils who wanted to come from Moscow and the capital. Ouspensky had tried to persuade Gurdjieff to emigrate, but without success. In Alexandropol he had had the impression that his Master was waiting for something, and it might have been that Gurdjieff was still listening to the grapevine leading through his intelligence contacts. He told Ouspensky that what appeared to be unfavorable circumstances would in the end prove to have worked to their advantage; and instead of leaving for Europe, he took a house on the outskirts of Essentuki, a spa district in the central Caucasus northeast of Mount Elbruz and quite near the main railway line running north and south.

For six weeks Gurdjieff worked with his pupils in this small rented house. He explained that the Work demanded *"super-efforts."* These meant forcing oneself to make exertions beyond what was strictly necessary; for example, chopping wood in half the time normally required, or persuading the body to face unpleasant conditions when there was really no need. This super-effort would connect a particular center with an almost unlimited source of energy, which Gurdjieff described as a "Great Accumulator." The Work was beginning to take on an increasingly practical aspect; for one thing, the pupils did all the household chores. Gurdjieff showed them exercises for removing muscular tension and introduced them to another exercise for which he became famous. This was the "Stop." When the teacher called "stop," the pupils had to freeze in the position in which they found themselves, no matter how uncomfortable or dangerous. This provided an opportunity to study one's machine which would otherwise not occur. An engineer, who occasionally performed the function of pupil-teacher and whom Ouspensky simply calls P., was caught with a hot glass of tea in his hand. Zaharoff heard the order just after inhaling a cigarette and endured what he described as the most unpleasant experience of his life.

Physical exercises of an entirely new pattern were introduced. Ouspensky has described one.

> A man sits on the ground with knees bent and holding his arms, with the palms of the hands close together, between his feet. Then he has to lift one leg and during this time count: *om, om, om, om, om, om, om, om* up to the tenth *om* and nine times *om*, seven times *om* and so on down to one then again twice *om*, three times *om*, and so on, and at the same time "sense" his left ear and his right eye. Then separate the thumb and "sense" his left ear and so on, and so on.

The order of the movements had to be remembered and coordinated with the counting; and both activities taken by themselves were quite difficult enough. Gurdjieff would complicate the affair with a breathing exercise; not content with this, he introduced a fast during which he exercised his pupils mercilessly. And these, he said, were only the preparatory exercises.

More people arrived. Thomas de Hartmann managed to procure a pass to leave St. Petersburg for Rostov on Don on the pretext of working at military inventions. He and his wife went nowhere near Rostov, but headed straight for Essentuki. The morning after they left St. Petersburg, soldiers called at the home of Mme. de Hartmann's parents to arrest her husband. The de Hartmanns arrived in Essentuki on August 28 and were pitchforked into the extraordinary conditions under which the colony existed. They were so far from appreciating the sort of life they were to experience at the hands of those twin agents of havoc, Gurdjieff and the Revolution, that they brought their chambermaid.

Olga de Hartmann's first glimpse of the assembled disciples reminded her of a scene from Gorky's *Underworld*. She and her husband were introduced to the "Stop" exercise, and also to Gurdjieff's talent for driving his followers to desperation. No sooner had the couple arrived than Gurdjieff began talking of giving up all work and going to Persia. To earn the money to do this, he proposed to break stones on the roads. He seemed to feel that the main obstacle to the de Hartmanns' following him was that after a day of stone-breaking the women must wash their husbands' feet. Now Zaharoff's feet would smell awful, and while there were some women who could wash feet with equanimity, what about Olga de Hartmann who could not do without a chambermaid . . . ?

Gurdjieff's talk of abandoning work discouraged some of the pupils who were still not fully committed. Ouspensky himself was becoming confused by his teacher's erratic changes of mood. Gurdjieff announced his departure for Persia, but in fact left with Zaharoff and Mme. Ostrowsky to stay at Tuapse on the Black Sea coast. Ouspensky followed them there and then decided to pay a visit to St. Petersburg before the winter.

The de Hartmanns stayed with Gurdjieff. One Sunday afternoon they set out with Zaharoff, Gurdjieff, and his wife to walk in the direction of Sochi, further down the coast, taking their luggage in a cart. Gurdjieff decided on a short cut over the mountains. The expedition walked until 2 A.M., and Thomas de Hartmann was deprived of sleep because he was selected for guard duty. Next day he was awarded the privilege of riding in the cart; and he soon discovered why. If he had been walking, it would have been comparatively easy to stay awake, but on top of the pile of luggage, there was the constant temptation to fall asleep—which meant the certainty of tumbling to the ground. At the end of the second day they were allowed two days' rest, but soon the caravan was on its way again. Olga de Hartmann had started out in a pair of fashionable shoes and finished the trip with bare and bleeding feet. The five members of the expedition halted fifteen miles from Sochi at a village called Uch Darye, where Gurdjieff had rented a house. Almost at once de Hartmann collapsed with typhoid, and during his delirium, a letter arrived informing him of the confiscation of his estates.

Ever afterward Thomas de Hartmann was to attribute his recovery to Gurdjieff. It was Gurdjieff who soothed him and prescribed placebos; it was Gurdjieff who removed him to a hospital. When he first became delirious, Gurdjieff had been left alone with him and was discovered by Olga de Hartmann with "his face as white as his suit." "I have no more fear for his head," were his first words, and the implication is that the Master had done something—Tibetan medicine? Hypnotism? Magic?—which had slackened the grip of the illness.

At Uch Darye, the crisis among Gurdjieff's pupils was greater than that caused by the sickness of a single man. Ouspensky arrived to find even the devoted Zaharoff discouraged. The mathematician had seen him off to St. Petersburg with exhortations not to become trapped in the capital. He himself had burned his boats, he said. But now something had happened— Ouspensky suggests that whatever happened, happened as the result of a quarrel between Gurdjieff and his neighbors which Zaharoff had over-heard—and Gurdjieff was behaving in a manner which practically forced Zaharoff to leave. Ouspensky considered that this would be pure idiocy on his part, "I would not have sent a dog to St. Petersburg at that time." But Zaharoff left.

Dr. Stoerneval and his wife had arrived, after receiving a telegram: "Realise everything you can and come at once." Mme. Stoerneval was reluctant to leave her family and the relative comforts of St. Petersburg, even at that late juncture, but eventually her husband's arguments prevailed. Dr. Stoerneval managed to withdraw his bank deposits, and the couple left St. Petersburg two weeks before the Revolution broke out.

Early on the morning of October 25, Bolshevik forces went into action in St. Petersburg; and in the evening, the transfer of power to the Soviets was proclaimed. It was an event which could not fail to have repercussions even on a small band of seekers for truth on the shores of the Black Sea. In the Caucasus the political situation was becoming very confused. In addition to the Soviet-inspired "Trans-Caucasian Commissariat," the White forces had to contend with Caucasian separatists—Georgians, Armenians, and Azer-baijanis—who were not content with establishing claims to their resur-rected nations, but vied incessantly with one another. In the south, the Turks, who were still at war with Russia, occupied Batum. The issue was further complicated by troops of the Allied Powers which were attempting to help the anti-Bolshevik elements and at the same time, prevent the Turks from advancing further into Russia.

At first Gurdjieff moved his household from Uch Darye to another village near Tuapse, lest the colony should be cut off from supplies. Then in December, a rumor was heard that a Caucasian army was moving up the shores of the Black Sea. Gurdjieff decided to return to Essentuki and begin work again. On February 12, a circular letter was sent out over Ouspensky's name to the Moscow and St. Petersburg groups, and in March about forty people collected in Essentuki, including once more Zaharoff.

The life of the colony at Essentuki was a foretaste of what Gurdjieff created on a larger scale at Fontainebleau. His followers rose early. They were allowed a pound of bread a day and had tea in the morning and the evening. At lunch they ate soup, meat, and vegetables out of communal dishes. Gurdjieff never ceased to make difficulties. He changed the arrangement of the rooms in the house, moved the furniture around, and discountenanced members of the Moscow group who were new to this phase of his work. For some time he had been carrying with him a quantity of silk thread; he now decided that this must be sold to obtain funds. De Hartmann was asked to provide sheets of the special paper he kept for his compositions—it had become so rare that Prokofieff had traveled from Kislovodsk for the gift of a quire—which were promptly torn up to make spools on which the silk was wound. The composer was then sent to Kislovodsk to sell the silk. He had many acquaintances in the town, and in acute embarrassment crept off to discharge his obligation under cover of darkness. His attempts were successful—until, on entering yet another shop, he encountered Gurdjieff who called a halt to de Hartmann's salutary lesson in extent of his class pride.

Gurdjieff elaborated the difficult movements he had begun to teach. At one stage the members of the group were taught an alphabetic code expressed through the positions of the body. Then they were forbidden to communicate in any other way. Once Gurdjieff ordained a fast, and moved men and women on to separate floors of the house. There came a time when the women were asked to give Gurdjieff all their jewelry. Olga de Hartmann cried all night, and, completely drained of any affection for her family jewels, delivered them to her Master. Gurdjieff scarcely acknowledged the gift—but as she was leaving, he called her back and returned her property. On the other hand, someone to whom Mme. de Hartmann later told her story blithely surrendered a valuable item to Gurdjieff and never received it back. With such devices Gurdjieff played on his pupils' lives like an artist on an instrument. In the evenings, he talked to them in his own carpet-hung room and occasionally prescribed individual exercises. In the mornings, he sat to watch how his pupils took the announcements of the often unpleasant activities for the day which he posted on the notice board.

The difficulty in trying to describe what was going on at Essentuki is almost insurmountable at this stage. Not only is the Man Who Knows impossible to know himself, but the Work itself is invisible. The story of Olga de Hartmann and her jewels seems a trite morality, and in certain respects it was. But it undoubtedly had its place in the context of the total situation at Essentuki and in the context of Mme. de Hartmann's private situation. What the experience *meant*, what meaning there was in it for her, is the only thing which matters—and there is no way of following up a series of such developments because the necessary frankness would rarely be forthcoming. All the historical observer can do is to concentrate on various points in the Work in a way which may gradually build up a picture of what the process may be.

There is a similar difficulty in discussing Gurdjieff's "movements" and "sacred dances." We can gather from Ouspensky that the immensely difficult movements which required the coordination of separate and wildly complicated tasks for head, heart and hands, must have been connected with the idea of developing the activities of intellect, emotions, and the physical body into one harmonious union. No doubt the pupil would acquire more conscious control of his organism. But was this the sole or even the chief purpose of the exercises? Almost certainly not. Some of Gurdjieff's movements—like the music which he later dictated to Thomas de Hartmann—were given not as if completed for a particular purpose, but almost as problems to be worked out. The principles would be outlined and the skeleton had to be clothed. What then was the object; what were they all doing in the middle of a civil war pretending to be characters from Gorky or Lermontov or Dostoievsky? The spell of Gurdjieff does not explain the intensity of the experiences through which some of his pupils passed, and until the experiences of other followers provide data for comparison, there is no way of conveying the nature of what was actually in progress. Beneath the pupils' accounts runs another level of events at which they may not even hint. This is probably not because their experiences are in any real sense incommunicable, but because a full confession might well be too painful—and would have no chance of conveying the depth of personal meaning which a particular event contained.

Even those activities which were recorded during the time at Essentuki soon became overwhelmed by the demands of survival. In *Meetings with Remarkable Men*, Gurdjieff describes what must have been one of the most tragic events in his whole life. This was the unexpected arrival of nearly thirty of his relations who had fled from Alexandropol to avoid being massacred by the advancing Turks. His father did not escape and was killed by the invading army. Gurdjieff was already supporting a colony of destitute aristocrats and intellectuals, and the appearance of his emaciated family increased still further his material responsibilities.

• • •

During the summer of 1918 the political situation in the spa area around Essentuki gradually deteriorated. Life grew increasingly difficult for the bands of refugees from central Russia. There was no news from the capital and conditions of simple hardship gave way to those of civil war.

Internal conditions were changing also, perhaps as a result of the two months' period of intensive work under Gurdjieff. New perspectives may have been opening up as the results of self-observation and discipline created new meanings—and destroyed old ones.

The destruction of old meanings may have had many different results. It all depended on the person, his aims and attitude toward the process by which he had been forced to discard the meanings which animated him before. Our sole witness for the changes of the summer of 1918 is Ouspensky but, as he himself was a leading figure and the events of which we are certain took place almost entirely inside him, he is the best possible witness we could have. And it should be noted that Ouspensky thought that most of the group which had worked with Gurdjieff for any length of time were experiencing similar processes.

Ouspensky's account of his break with Gurdjieff is extraordinarily important. It was not his only statement on his reasons for parting with his teacher—and the parting was not yet final. His later pronouncements and their significance must wait until the glyph has unfolded a little further and there is more material for assessing the possibilities; but it may begin to appear that *In Search of the Miraculous* is a remarkably subtle book, and that beneath the surface discussions of Gurdjieff's doctrine is concealed another layer of information which may more truly be said to form its subject matter.

"For a whole year," Ouspensky wrote, "something had been accumulating, and I gradually began to see that there were many things I could not understand and that *I had to go*."

> . . . I had for some time begun to separate G. and the *ideas*. I had no doubts about the *ideas*. On the contrary, the more I thought of them, the deeper I entered into them, the more I began to value them and realise their significance. But I began very strongly to doubt that it was possible for me, or even for the majority of our company, to continue to work under G.'s leadership. I do not in the least mean that I found any of G.'s actions or methods wrong or that they failed to respond to what I expected. . . . All work consists in doing what the leader indicates, understanding in conformance with his opinions even those things that he does not say plainly, helping him in *everything* that he does. There can be no other attitude towards the work. And G. himself

said several times that a most important thing in the work was *to remember that one came to learn* and to take no other role upon oneself.

At the same time this does not at all mean that a man has no choice or that he is obliged to follow something which does not respond to what he is seeking.

Gurdjieff himself had admitted that all teachers worked through their different specialities; but what, Ouspensky wondered, if these activities were quite alien to a pupil? He compared his situation to that in which he would have found himself had he discovered that Gurdjieff had all the time been leading him toward a religious attitude—the way of the monk. Then, he would have felt fully justified in leaving the Work. This would not have been because of any prejudice against the ethics of the monastery, which might well be superior to his own; but they were not his ethics, and the way of the monk was not his way. "I had nothing to say against G.'s methods," he writes, "except that they did not suit me." What was the cause of this disillusionment?

Ouspensky says nothing further in *In Search of the Miraculous*—which was completed twenty years before his death. He states bluntly that Gurdjieff was leading him in a different direction from the one he had at first seemed to indicate. But whatever he thought about Gurdjieff's intentions, he does not say; he disguises his suspicions with the metaphor of the monastery walls closing about him. Whether this is the whole truth is another matter, and the inquirer may well decide that further investigation makes this doubtful; for *In Search of the Miraculous* is a book whose clarity is deceptive.

What is clear is that Ouspensky decided after a great struggle to leave Gurdjieff and begin work independently. He left the community and went to live by himself. Although he maintained friendly relations with Gurdjieff, he returned to work on the material which he had begun to arrange in 1911 and which was later published under the title of *A New Model of the Universe*. The working title of this book was "The Wisdom of the Gods"—a translation of the term "theosophy"—and Ouspensky's reversion to his former concerns is typical of the effect of Gurdjieff's teaching on many of his pupils. Ouspensky was still in search of the miraculous, and still believed that through it lay his way.

As the political situation grew even more dangerous, it became clear that the only prudent course was to leave Essentuki. The town had a Bolshevik government, and Gurdjieff had camouflaged his activities under the Soviet-sounding title of an "International Idealistic Society." Cossacks of the White forces began to raid the railway and eventually to attack the town itself. Refugees started to make for Novorossisk across the mountains on the Black

Sea coast. But Ouspensky hung on, although he had already decided to head for London where he had originally planned to publish his "Wisdom of the Gods." He waited until Gurdjieff himself left Essentuki. "In this respect," he wrote, "I had a strange kind of feeling. I wanted to wait until the end; to do everything that depended upon me so that afterwards I could tell myself that I had not let a single possibility escape me. It was very difficult for me to reject the idea of working with G."

Events made the break for him. Gurdjieff himself was worried by the threatening conditions which surrounded his group, and particularly by the danger for his pupils of military age. The Bolsheviks, the White Army, and partisans of every description were conscripting all the ablebodied men they could find, and if the war were moving nearer to Essentuki, they must then be moved out of the combat zone as soon as possible. According to Gurdjieff's account in *Meetings with Remarkable Men*, he then decided to make the escape of his party the occasion for an expedition. He wanted to find certain prehistoric dolmens in which he was interested, and applied to the Essentuki Soviet for permission to mount an archaeological expedition in the mountains. The expedition was to have a secondary aim in searching for gold. Ouspensky told Gurdjieff that, for washing the gold, alcohol would be necessary in large quantities. The higher Soviet in Pyatigorsk was so impressed by Gurdjieff's application that they not only provided equipment for the expedition in the shape of tents and tools, but the alcohol as well. Gurdjieff's efficiency and his choice of cover for his escape argue great familiarity with the ways and means of organizing "scientific" expeditions.

By infiltrating the Soviet passport office, Gurdjieff secured passes for the colony. He gave lessons in finding one's way by the stars and in movement by night. It was apparent that the trial at hand was not merely one of physical endurance and good fortune. The journey would be both internal and external, a mountaineering expedition which was allegorical, yet in desperate earnest. For the de Hartmanns, who had the opportunity to emigrate in comfort under the protection of powerful friends, the coming privations presented real difficulties, especially as Olga de Hartmann was exhausted by the earlier austerities. The rules which Gurdjieff laid down were ferocious. Absolute obedience was demanded. Infringements of the code would be punishable by death. And Gurdjieff placed a large revolver on the table.

The de Hartmanns already knew something of his methods. But they had been with their teacher for a very short time compared to some of the other pupils whom Ouspensky watched leave with forebodings. He clearly expected that those who had worked with Gurdjieff for the same length of time as he himself had would discover identical problems; and to a large extent, he was right. But his hesitations cost him dearly. Gurdjieff's party left at the beginning of August 1918. Ouspensky decided to go to Novorossisk. A week after Gurdjieff's departure, raiding Cossacks cut the railway line. The civil war enclosed Essentuki, and Ouspensky was trapped with the ten or so pupils of Gurdjieff who had remained behind. "I must confess I felt very silly," he writes ruefully. "I had not gone abroad when it was possible in order to work with G. and the final outcome was that I had parted from G. and stopped with the bolsheviks."

History had overtaken him. Like his character, "Leslie White," he was trapped in the battle for survival. "'Events' gave little time," he wrote, "for philosophical speculations." While Gurdjieff was riding the wave, Ouspensky seemed to be temporarily engulfed. This may have been a blessing in disguise, or it may have been the curse it appeared to be. It depends on what interpretation is given to his break with Gurdjieff. The parting from a Man Who Knows, even if the pupil's ideas are changed out of all recognition by his period of learning, may be a painful process. Ouspensky had concluded that Gurdjieff was not the Master for whom he had hoped. He had partially withdrawn the meaning he had projected into the relationship, but it was the physical separation which began to make his choice for him. The outer revolution gave the axis of his inner life another half-turn.

7

The Traveling Circus

Gurdjieff and his expedition started in two groups from Essentuki and the nearby town of Pyatigorsk. They traveled in two railway cars which he had somehow inveigled from the Soviet authorities. After two days, they reached the town of Maikop, at the edge of the mountains on a branch line southwest of the main railway from the Caucasus to Tsaritsyn (Volgagrad) and central Russia. The town was the center of a pitched battle between Red and White forces, and all their official papers from the Bolsheviks were useless. Gurdjieff had originally intended to continue by rail from Maikop to the coastal region near Tuapse, and meant to begin his expedition proper with a line of march roughly parallel to the sea in a southerly direction. But "events" made such a plan unfeasible, and for a time, the company halted in an abandoned farm near Maikop.

They tumbled into an unexpected idyll, for the farm even included a swimming place in the White River, and they were able to relax sufficiently to ignore the bullets whistling overhead.

However, Gurdjieff devised means—even in Arcadia—of creating friction among his followers. The expedition was divided into small parties, each of which had a member responsible for buying and preparing food for the others. Then Thomas de Hartmann was ordered to leave his group of four and to eat with Gurdjieff's own circle. Olga de Hartmann was left to cook first for two other men, and then for just one, whom she did not particularly like. Finally she was left to eat alone. The day was filled with farm work, which provided many opportunities for Gurdjieff's ingenious brand of needling. De Hartmann writes of the appointment of a lady to supervise the grooming of the horses, whose duties did not extend to helping with the work. "And so, when we were scrubbing away with all our might, this lady would appear and say: 'Here you have not scrubbed enough,' or 'a little more there.' This was calculated to irritate us but we would not show our annoyance. Besides, life at the moment was so wonderful that it was impossible to be angry."

The battle for Maikop ended with a temporary victory for the White forces, and Gurdjieff's party left their oasis for the hills. The day after their departure Maikop was recaptured by the Bolsheviks. They had escaped through the last possible gap in the net which had trapped Ouspensky. For a few days their route lay through populated farmlands before striking up into the mountains on a southwesterly course which would take them through sparsely settled highlands and down to the town of Sochi on the Black Sea.

The journey became adventurous. Every so often they had to show their papers—whether these were White Russians or Bolshevik depended on which side of his moustache Gurdjieff twirled. In "The Material Question," Gurdjieff reproduces a certificate which entitled him to carry a revolver. On one side it was signed by the officials of the Essentuki Soviet, and on the other by a White general in Maikop. Gurdjieff himself marveled at the ease with which he managed to extricate his party from the various difficult situations into which they stumbled: "It was not due entirely to my well-developed ability to discern and play upon the slightest changes in the weaknesses of the psyche of people in a psychosis of this kind." But to followers like the de Hartmanns, who hung upon the Master's every word, their good fortune seemed nothing short of "inspired guidance."

Although the direct influence of the war was left beneath them, the party encountered danger from the flotsam and jetsam cast up by the conflict in the hills. They met a monk, fleeing from the Bolsheviks, whose community had established itself in a cave with as much of its church furniture as could be salvaged. Once, a group which included the de Hartmanns was ambushed by bandits with whom Mme. de Hartmann coped resourcefully, even inducing them to sign a piece of paper stating that they had taken all useful possessions. The climb through the mountains with their baggage carried on their backs taught a degree of practicality, even to a collection of city intellectuals. Toward the end of the grueling journey they did find a dolmen. Gurdjieff announced that dolmens might once have been road signs to places of initiation, and asked a party of hunters encountered by the expedition whether they knew of other monuments in the area. The answer was negative; so Gurdjieff embarked on an experiment. He made some calculations, and set off through the woods in a precise direction. Sure enough, another dolmen was found, and a third where Gurdjieff indicated.

At length the scientific expedition emerged on the Black Sea coast at Sochi, well outside the battle zone. They had a celebratory dinner in a good hotel; and Thomas de Hartmann, who had finished the trek with his feet all but useless through septicaemia, had his visions of uninterrupted slumber shattered by a command from Gurdjieff to rise at six o'clock and feed the horses.

The storm which had been gathering now broke. "In Sochi," writes Ouspensky, "the greater part of the company, as I had foreseen, parted company with G." Gurdjieff's own version of events is that "certain members of the expedition, during what might be called our 'Way of Golgotha,' were not equal to the situation, but manifested properties not corresponding at all to the high aim we had in view; I decided to part with them . . ." The de Hartmanns say nothing of the cause of this rupture. "Mr. Gurdjieff suddenly announced that the expedition was finished. He advised us to make plans for the future as he had no more money to support any of us." The result was that only Gurdjieff, Mme. Ostrowsky, the de Hartmanns, the Stoernevals, and possibly one or two others remained in Sochi. Members of Gurdjieff's former Moscow group left for Kiev or returned to Essentuki, which had been retaken by the White forces. Among the defectors were P., the engineer, and Zaharoff. The former left for Maikop, where he became the director of a state school. Zaharoff went to Kiev, but later moved to Rostov-on-Don.

What was the meaning of this dispersal? Was it that Gurdjieff was simply tired of his pupils? Or had they ceased to understand and therefore could not be taught? Perhaps it was a test which the majority of the pupils failed by demonstrating that they placed a low valuation on the Work. But perhaps the pupils who left were the ones who understood? Those who remained were, as Ouspensky said, still "young in the work," with the exception of Dr. Stoerneval, and they may still have had a lot to learn. Possibly Gurdjieff had separated the sheep from the goats deliberately; possibly his conduct was really insupportable for one reason or another, or it may be that the money had indeed run out and circumstances dictated a policy of *sauve qui peut*. The problem is the same as that of Ouspensky's breach with Gurdjieff, and must await a resolution.

In the middle of January 1919, Gurdjieff's diminished company embarked at Sochi for the Georgian port of Poti and so arrived in Tiflis.

The autumn and winter of 1918–19 which Ouspensky passed in Bolshevik-occupied Essentuki were seasons of great difficulty. "For me and my family," he wrote, "things turned out comparatively favourably. Only two people out of four got ill with typhoid. No one died. Not once were we robbed. And all the time I had work and earned money." He does not say that he was supporting Sophia Grigorievna, her daughter Mme. Sventitsky, and Mme. Sventitsky's two children, a heroic endeavor which earned him the undying gratitude of his adopted daughter. He became a house porter and then a teacher at a state gymnasium. When he discovered that the Bolsheviks had requisitioned all the books in the town, he cowed the local Commissar, who "was a simple man and began to be almost frightened of me when I told him that I had written books of my own." Ouspensky had himself made librarian and established a library in the school where he had previously taught. His idea was to preserve the books until better days when they could be returned to their owners. He fortified himself behind a large notice reading ESSENTUKI SOVIET LIBRARY and spent his time reading his collection. One night in January 1919, the Cossacks recaptured Essentuki for the White Army. The librarian was galvanized into activity. "I ran round to the school in spite of the firing and tore down the word 'Soviet' for fear the Cossacks came and destroyed everything, and so it read simply 'ESSENTUKI LIBRARY.' And next day I started to hand back the books to their owners."

Despite this temporary liberation, Ouspensky was not able finally to leave Essentuki until June 1919. At this point, the Volunteer Army of General Denikin was still engaged in the advance it had begun in May, and conditions in south Russia were temporarily brighter. Ouspensky based himself in Ekaterinodar—a city he came heartily to loathe—and through the intervention of Orage in London made contact with Major F. S. Pinder, the head of the British Economic Mission to Denikin's forces. Pinder took Ouspensky on to his staff, even though he had to pay his salary out of his own pocket. Ouspensky's duties consisted chiefly of writing press summaries for the British Mission. He moved to Ekaterinodar from Rostov-on-Don, and from Ekaterinodar to Novorossisk and back again, a weary pilgrimage up and down the railway line as the fighting swayed to and fro. Either through Major Pinder or via his own lines of communication, Ouspensky was by now in fairly regular contact with Orage, who published in the *New Age* a series of his "Letters from Russia." The first is dated from Ekaterinodar, on July 25, 1919, and is the *cri-de-coeur* of a man who has lost hope in the state of the external world:

It is now two years since I last saw THE NEW AGE, and I do not know what is being said and thought and written in England and what you know. I can only guess. During this period we here have lived through so many marvels that I honestly pity everybody who has not been here, everybody who is living in the old way, everybody who is ignorant of what we now know. You do not even know the significance of the words, "living in the old way." You have not the necessary perspective; you cannot get away from yourselves and look at yourselves from another point of view. But we have done so long ago. To understand what "living in the old way" means, you would need to be here, and to hear people saying, and yourself too, from time to time, "Shall we ever live again in the old way?" . . . For you this phrase is written in a quite unintelligible language—do not try to understand it! You will surely begin to think that it is something to do with the re-establishment of the old régime or the oppression of the working classes, and so on. But in actual fact it means something very simple. It means, for example: when shall we be able to buy shoe-leather again, or shaving-soap, or a box of matches?

Ouspensky was deeply marked by the experience of the political revolution. His insistence on the chasm between his own hard-won understanding and the knowledge of the West where conditions were so totally different, is not merely a literary affectation. The influence of his time with Gurdjieff is clearly evident in the way he tried to explain why the inexperienced can never appreciate the nature of the history of crime. "We know too much to be able to speak to you on equal terms. We know the true relation of history and words to facts. We know what such words as 'civilisation' and 'culture' mean; we know what 'revolution' means, and 'a Socialist State,' and 'winter' and 'bread,' and 'stove,' and 'soap,' and many, many more of the same kind." The view of history which he elaborated was of a huge biological machine. "Nations" and "States" were "big two-dimensional creatures" which existed in an unreal world of "politics" and "economics." "We know now that the whole life of individual men and women is a struggle against these big creatures. We are able to understand without difficulty that a Nation is a creature standing on a far lower stage of development than individual men and women; it is about on the level of the zoophytes, slowly moving in one direction or the other and consuming one another."

In Ouspensky's mind the System which had served him and his companions as a sheet anchor through the storms they had weathered, could explain many of the dementing facts of life in a civil war. He denied "preparing to set out an esoteric philosophy," but promptly proposed an examination of the "life of the great forces" in contemporary Russia. "We observe primarily," he commented, "that everything in it acts according to one general rule, which I may call the Law of Opposite Aims and Results. In other words everything leads to results that are contrary to what people intend to bring about and towards which they strive." This is nothing else but Gurdjieff's Law of Otherwise—and in the life of the Great Forces, speaking synchronistically, the Enantiodromia of C. G. Jung—and Ouspensky applied it with substantial effect to show that such factors were the real arbiters of history, not the will of impotent man. Supporters of the Great War had not meant to overthrow the monarchy, reformers intended nothing so little as Kerensky's *fainéance*, the liberals did not mean to encourage Bolshevism. All the independent states which had sprung up since 1917 were in theory an attractive idea, and no doubt they did not mean to foster crime and speculation, but. . . .

On his journey from Mineralny Vodi to Rostov and Novorossisk, Ouspensky had passed through "four States, each with different laws, different prices, different sorts of police, united only by a single common quality, namely, that without bribes . . . you cannot go far." Inflation was the chief source of hardship, particularly for brainworkers, who did not rank as "workers" in the new society and whose wages therefore did not keep pace with rising prices. In Ekaterinodar, supposedly the cheapest place in Russia, the price of bread had doubled in a fortnight. Ouspensky anticipated the disbelief of his English audience.

> You will ask how it is possible to live under such conditions. And this is the most occult aspect of the whole question.
>
> I will answer for myself: I personally am still alive only because my boots and my trousers and other articles of clothing—all "old campaigners"—are still holding together. When they end their existence I shall evidently end mine.

By the time of his second letter of September 18, Ouspensky had obtained copies of old English newspapers and was more than ever convinced of the utter incomprehension of the world outside Russia. In this letter, in a third dated September 25, and in two undated letters from Ekaterinodar which the *New Age* published in December, he set about trying to bridge the gap, although with no illusions as to any possible effect. He did not believe, he wrote, that a single voice could have any effect on politics. Anyway, he was no politician. And events had long since passed the point at which anything could be done. "At present, while I am writing this, a fire is breaking out and spreading over Italy. The reason for this, as well as for many other things that will happen in Europe, lies in the fact that when peace was made no decision was taken about extinguishing the fire in Russia."

The fire was, of course, the Bolshevik menace, and Bolshevism was a menace, Ouspensky believed, particularly because the West in general did not understand—as Russia had earlier not understood—its real nature. He rightly guessed that an influential body of Western opinion was laboring in the grip of an illusion which the Russian intelligentsia had lost in the autumn of 1917. This was the confusion of Bolshevism with "a socialistic and revolutionary movement." "Persons inclined to abstract thinking," wrote Ouspensky, "persist in seeing in Bolshevism not what it actually is, but what it ought to be according to their theoretical deductions." He proceeded to enlighten his readers on the history of Russian socialism, and put forward the sweeping condemnation of Bolshevism which he incorporated in his *A New Model of the Universe*. He had begun work on the revised version of this book the year before his "Letters from Russia" appeared in the *New Age*, and in it, there is much of the bitterness of this period of famine and despair.

In the *New Age* Ouspensky defined Bolshevism as "the dictatorship of the criminal elements." He proposed a new term for Soviet rule to denote its criminal nature, "something like 'kakourgocracy' or 'paranomocracy.'" The weakness of the intelligentsia and its belief that Bolshevism was a real reforming movement had allowed this unnatural phenomenon to come to power. As soon as the Bolsheviks attained a dominant position, they began to attack the intelligentsia, who alone could have penetrated and reformed the movement from within. Ouspensky described with horror how doctors could not prevent the spread of infection because their actions were dictated by Soviets of medical orderlies; how the press had been virtually supplanted by Soviet news sheets; how "science, art, literature were put under suspicion and were handed over to the watchful control of illiterate bodies of workmen." The good of the proletariat excluded the good of anybody else, and ended by preventing any good at all. Ordinary writing paper cost three pounds ten shillings for twenty-seven sheets, all around were cholera, typhoid, and starvation, and Ouspensky's thoughts were already turning in the direction of the Laws of Manu. Although he published nothing on the subject until 1929, the edition he used appeared in St. Petersburg in 1913, and *A New Model of the Universe* cites several precepts of the legendary Hindu lawgiver which have a definite application to Ouspensky's view of Russia during the Civil War:

Verse 31. Chapter I.
    For the prosperity of the worlds he created from his mouth, his arms, his thighs and his feet the Brahmin, the Kshatriya, the Vaisya and the Sudra.

Verse 22. Chapter VIII.
    A kingdom peopled mostly by Sudras, filled with godless men and deprived of twice-born inhabitants, will soon wholly perish, stricken by hunger and disease.

The "Letters from Russia" expressed the desperation of the times, and Ouspensky was not wholly free from the more panic-stricken speculations which led some White Russians to the delusion of conspiracy-theory politics. He saw a devilish German plot behind the Communist successes in China. He made strange and desperate statements like the one about Mrs. Pankhurst: "The personal staff of the advocates of Bolshevism is also a peculiar thing. It consists in its greater part of neurasthenics. . . . The Bolshevik literature was brought over to England by Mrs. Pankhurst. There are names that always mean a lot." And more sinister still—although in all fairness to Ouspensky it should be said that he appears never to have been an anti-Semite—was the reference to "the right to live," "i.e., a written certificate authorising you to reside in any particular place—a measure which used to be applied before to Jews—[which] is now a rule for everybody. I do not know whom we have to thank for such a brilliant solution of the problem of personal rights, but facts remain facts."

The scars caused by the desolation of 1919 never completely healed, and the essentially gentle Ouspensky preserved a hatred for Bolshevism which was all but fanatical. As he wrote his letters to Orage in London, things were going from bad to worse. Allied aid was being withdrawn, and Caucasian partisans were making life difficult for the White forces, which were eventually reduced to about eight thousand men against the sixty-thousand-strong Red Army. Corruption, neglect, debauchery and drunkenness sapped the officers. At the beginning of winter, General Wrangel informed Denikin that his army had ceased to exist as a fighting unit. About the same time, Ouspensky described the White headquarters at the filthy and disease-ridden town of Ekaterinodar as "the most God-forsaken place one can imagine."

The year since Ouspensky had parted from Gurdjieff had produced internal as well as external changes. In Ekaterinodar he decided that he had "acquired a *strange confidence,* one which I could not define in one word." This was a confidence in the complete insignificance of "the self which we usually know." Behind this petty creature of the imagination, Ouspensky felt the presence of "another *I*" which would be able to surmount the appalling disasters which some of his friends had had to face. Two years previously, he wrote, Gurdjieff had asked him whether he could not feel a "new I" inside him, and he had been forced to answer no. Now he did feel the presence of this "I" and knew that it existed definitely as the result of his work with Gurdjieff, not because of greater experience of life. In ordinary circumstances, the customary domination of all the irritating small "I's" went on; but given a big challenge, Ouspensky felt that his new individuality would be able to meet it. A definite result had been attained.

In the midst of the squalor and the sickness, Ouspensky gathered around him a small group and gave a series of lectures on Gurdjieff's System and "the things from ordinary life which lead up to it." He discovered an amount of interest which set him thinking. The ideas "obviously answered the needs of people who wanted to understand what was taking place both in them and around them." The engineer P. came to see him in Ekaterinodar, and Ouspensky tried to improve his "negative frame of mind" by emphasizing the distinction which he himself now made between Gurdjieff and the ideas. Gurdjieff had tried to persuade P. to join him in Tiflis; but, like Ouspensky, the engineer resisted Gurdjieff's attempts to lure him back into the fold. Ouspensky's own reasons for refusing to go to Tiflis were partly the huge material obstacles and partly the "very real" difficulties which had confronted him in Essentuki. "My decision to leave G. had cost me very dear and I could not give it up so easily, the more so as all his motives were to be seen."

By the time winter had begun in earnest, the only considerations which meant anything were those of survival. The Volunteer Army was disintegrating. In December, Wrangel began his long retreat on Rostov-on-Don, in which over 200,000 people died. As the military headquarters moved to Rostov, Pinder's Economic Mission moved too, taking with it Ouspensky. In Rostov he met several former members of the St. Petersburg group and also A. A. Zaharoff, who was completely disillusioned with the Work. The two friends shared quarters in the overcrowded city, and Ouspensky's conversations with Zaharoff seemed to lift the mathematician out of his depression. Once again Zaharoff's feelings altered, but he was apparently unable to follow Ouspensky in distinguishing the Work from the person of its teacher. He began making plans to get through to Gurdjieff in Tiflis.

The pair of them were living in a barn near Rostov when they were visited for two weeks around Christmas by Carl Bechhofer Roberts (1894–1949), a talented and irrepressibly cheerful writer connected with Orage's New Age. He had met Ouspensky in India, possibly at Adyar, and again in St. Petersburg at the outbreak of the war. Bechhofer Roberts had translated some of Ouspensky's articles for the New Age, and was surveying the situation as a freelance journalist. He received a rude awakening into the rigors of life in a country at civil war:

Ouspensky showed me his possessions. They consisted of the clothes he was wearing (principally a rather ragged frock-coat, a remnant of former fortunes), a couple of extra shirts and pairs of socks, one blanket, a shabby overcoat, an extra pair of boots, a tin of coffee, a razor, a file and whetstone, and a towel. He assured me that he considered himself exceptionally fortunate to have so much left. On the next day we transferred our belongings to a new dwelling he had discovered for us. This consisted of two small rooms over a kind of barn . . .

While staying there, Bechhofer Roberts managed to obtain a quantity of coal, and the three celebrated with vodka, manufactured by Ouspensky—much to Zaharoff's dismay—from some neat spirit he had found in the barn, adulterated with orange peel. A hilarious conversation ensued during which Ouspensky told stories of his youth in Moscow. Bechhofer Roberts introduced an unwelcome note of sobriety into the proceedings by wondering where they would all be in a month's time. Both Russians turned on the English journalist, and told him that the uncertainty of the times made it impossible to guess. A month later, Bechhofer Roberts entered in his diary the answer to his question: "I am at Novorossisk, writing this. Ouspensky is, I believe, at Ekaterinodar, trying to get his wife away to the comparative safety of the seashore. I do not know if I shall ever see him again, or where. Zaharov died three days ago of small-pox, contracted at Rostov at the very time when we were living with him. And the Bolsheviks are at Rostov."

The year which ended so disastrously for Ouspensky in the north Caucasus had begun quite favorably for Gurdjieff in the south. By the end of 1918, the Turks had withdrawn from Georgia, and the collapse of Germany led to the evacuation of German troops in the Transcaucasus. The small nations of Georgia, Armenia, and Azerbaijan noisily obtained their independence. When Gurdjieff and his little party arrived in Tiflis in January 1919, the population of the Georgian capital—already a melting pot of races—had long been augmented by streams of refugees from the fighting. Bechhofer Roberts reached the town fifteen months later, and observed that it had "become a centre for what was left of Russian society. One found the strangest people there. Poets and painters from Petrograd and Moscow, philosophers, theosophists, dancers, singers, actors and actresses. Paul Yashvili, the leader of the younger Georgian poets, was once moved, after a hearty meal, to climb on a chair in the Café International, in the chief boulevard of Tiflis, and declare, in a loud voice, that 'Not Paris, but Tiflis, is the centre of the world's culture.'"

Olga and Thomas de Hartmann were two of the additions to the cultural life of Tiflis. Olga had a trained voice and began to sing in the Opera, while her husband became Professor of Composition at the Conservatoire. Their connection with the theater resulted in a meeting which was to have considerable consequence for the spread of Gurdjieff's ideas. The scene painter for the first operatic production in which Thomas de Hartmann took part was an artist called Alexander de Salzmann, whom de Hartmann had met in Munich, and whose wife Jeanne was a teacher of Dalcroze Eurythmics.

Alexander de Salzmann was born in Georgia in 1874. His family was of Baltic origin and his father had been a Councillor of State. The son's youth was eventful and is said to have included a kidnapping by brigands; but as de Salzmann's joker-like temperament rivaled Gurdjieff's in the practice of making fictitious claims about his personal history, we should beware of taking every such story literally. Another trait he shared with his Master-to-be was versatility; the French writer Michel Random described him as "enthusiastic about everything . . . as interested in Chinese script and calligraphy as in Sanskrit, as in studies in rhythm and music, as in canons of proportion and investigations into the Golden Number." Carl Zigrosser remembers him at the end of the 1920s:

> His face with its weather-beaten skin, sunken cheeks and gaps and stumps of teeth, was not easily forgotten. He told me that he had lost his teeth through a fall from a cliff in the Caucasus Mountains when he was chief forest ranger to some Russian Grand Duke. Fortunately he fell into a tree and saved his life. In spite of his artistic sophistication, there was something wild and savage in him, a breath of his native Caucasus perhaps, in his taste in food, in the primitiveness of his personal wants. His method of shaving was simplicity itself: he took a dry razor and scraped his face. Even this was a concession . . .

After studying in Tiflis and Moscow, de Salzmann left Russia for Munich where he worked for many years as an artist and became friendly with Rilke and Kandinsky. De Salzmann became a member of the *Jugendstil* group, and contributed copiously to the periodicals *Jugend* and *Simplicissimus*. In its early numbers, *Jugend* rarely carried fewer than eight of his drawings or paintings a year. De Salzmann used an extraordinary variety of styles which embraced a mannered Art Nouveau, grotesquerie, caricature, and a superbly blatant posterlike technique. By late 1909 his output in *Jugend* had fallen off considerably, and in 1911 he left Munich for Hellerau near Dresden, where Emile Jaques-Dalcroze (1865–1950) had founded an institute for teaching his system of Eurythmics. At Hellerau, de Salzmann developed another of his many talents. He was in charge of lighting the extremely advanced theater designed by the architect Tessenow, and invented for the purpose, a unique system of diffused lighting which captivated, among others, Paul Claudel.

One friend of Claudel thought that the playwright had been bewitched by de Salzmann, and to Jaques-Dalcroze he seemed "a real artist!" He was something of an enfant terrible. Conceiving a dislike for Hegener, the

German translator of Claudel's play, *L'Annonce faite à Marie*, de Salzmann proposed a walk in the forest to resolve a dispute about the production. There he had tied Hegener to a tree and returned to direct rehearsals to his own satisfaction. At Hellerau he met his wife, Jeanne Allemand, who was a pupil of Jaques-Dalcroze and, like him, from Geneva. In 1914 the couple left Germany for Moscow, where de Salzmann's system of lighting was in use, and by 1919 the fortunes of war had brought them back to Alexander de Salzmann's birthplace.

Some time after he and de Hartmann renewed their acquaintance at the Tiflis Opera, a conversation took place between them and their wives about the necessity of a spiritual director. This resulted in the de Salzmanns' introduction to Gurdjieff, who was impressed. "He is a very fine man," he is reported to have said, "and she—is intelligent."

Jeanne de Salzmann, who was only twenty-two or twenty-three, was schooled by the Dalcroze Method and very much in love with Art. In her attempts to write, she began to find that all her ideas seemed to derive from what she had read elsewhere; that when honed down, there was only a scrap which originated in her personal inspiration. She examined the works of the great masters to see where their secret lay. But the great composers and the great writers turned out on inspection to be in their degree as derivative as herself. Why had man so little he could call his own? Her disillusion with the human creative powers which she had idolized became acute—and suddenly here was Gurdjieff, a teacher who could explain exactly why man could *do nothing* of himself.

For a decade longer a few torches would glimmer on the shrine of the great god Art. But the days of his worship were numbered, and the bubble containing the first fine enthusiasms of the turn of the century, when artists became mystics and strove for the Absolute, had been pricked by the First World War. The visionary time had passed, and the visionaries were growing tired. Life had so definitely triumphed over art—and to prove the horrors of this vile dominion, Rheims Cathedral lay in rubble and the Cloth Hall at Ypres was burned—that it became increasingly difficult to believe in the new world which the new art had hoped to inaugurate. The alternatives appeared to be either an immersion in "events" or a withdrawal from them; and to those of a quietist disposition, Gurdjieff's teaching had a direct appeal. As Gurdjieff himself wrote, "among the inhabitants of Tiflis, many people had been deeply affected by the change in their conditions of life and felt the need to turn to other values." Some version of Jeanne de Salzmann's problem was to strike many intellectuals after the War, and events in Tiflis foreshadowed Gurdjieff's future success.

Gurdjieff arrived one day in Mme. de Salzmann's class to watch her pupils pursue the search for rhythmical beauty according to the system of

Dalcroze. He was invited to demonstrate his "sacred dances" and the movements he had taught at Essentuki. Gurdjieff lined the girls up and made them practice military turns, which he said were an essential preliminary to any work on "Sacred Gymnastics." Curiously, the class took to it, and Gurdjieff's movements formed a part of the Dalcroze pupils' next public demonstration. Then Gurdjieff decided that there must be a second performance, which was to consist entirely of his movements with no Dalcroze at all. Rubbing salt in the wound, he directed Mme. de Salzmann to tell her pupils that they would all be paid. To the Dalcroze students this was the last straw, and about two-thirds walked out, but somehow, enough were persuaded to take part. "With those who are left," Gurdjieff announced, "we're going to be able to work."

During the summer of 1919, the de Hartmanns traveled and gave concerts. Gurdjieff returned to his favorite trade as a carpet dealer. His brother Dmitri arrived from the north with the news that most of the valuables which the group had left hidden in their house at Essentuki had been discovered and either destroyed or dispersed. Olga de Hartmann was sent on a hair-raising solo journey to recover what she could. The expedition was doubly frightening because—regardless of the high probability that she would not return—she had never before even walked unaccompanied in the street. She went, fortified by a box containing a pill which Gurdjieff said was to be taken in case of grave necessity, and soon returned to Tiflis having managed to salvage two of Gurdjieff's carpets and a few personal possessions. She realized that neither the carpets nor her own effects were important: "They were just a pretext to have me thrown alone into life, to see how I could manage in conditions far more difficult than anyone, even Mr. Gurdjieff, could imagine in advance."

In the autumn of 1919, Gurdjieff's small group—the Stoernevals, the de Hartmanns and the de Salzmanns—gathered in Tiflis. Gurdjieff's carpet business had apparently prospered so well that he could now afford to give a more permanent form to his activities. Newly independent Georgia was intensely chauvinistic, and well disposed to offer support for vaguely cultural movements which were assumed to confer status. Gurdjieff directed his pupils to puzzle out a name which would describe his proposed establishment. "Afterwards it was clear to me," writes Thomas de Hartmann, "that Mr. Gurdjieff had decided on this name some time earlier, but . . . he forced us to look for it, pushed us, tried to bring us closer to the main thought, till this word emerged. Finally, we had the name. . . . It was: the Institute for the Harmonious Development of Man."

Gurdjieff sent a prospectus for his Institute to Ouspensky in the north Caucasus. This made his former disciple "very thoughtful indeed." On its cover, Gurdjieff's face was encircled by the enneagram. The prospectus stated that Gurdjieff's system was "already in operation in a whole series of large cities such as Bombay, Alexandria, Kabul, New York, Chicago, Christiana, Stockholm, Moscow, Essentuki, and in all departments and homes of the true international and laboring fraternities." The subjects studied were said to be "gymnastics of all kinds (rhythmical, medicinal and others). Exercises for the development of will, memory, attention, hearing, thinking, emotion, instinct, and so on." Ouspensky found attached to the prospectus a list of specialist teachers, which included his own name, as well as those of P. the engineer, and Joukoff, another disaffected pupil. None of the three had any intention of going to Tiflis at all. Ouspensky himself resisted Gurdjieff's invitation to join him. "I realised, of course, that it meant that G. was obviously obliged to give some sort of outward form to his work . . . I also realised that behind this outward form stood the same thing as before and that *this* could not change. I was doubtful only of my own ability to adapt myself . . ."

Ouspensky had already made his separation between the man Gurdjieff and his ideas. Now he made another between the form and the content of Gurdjieff's teaching. He considered the idea of the Institute for the Harmonious Development of Man to be of merely incidental significance. And despite all his misgivings about the eventual outcome of Gurdjieff's altered tactics, he was prepared to overcome them for the sake of a—still obscure—common cause. He was "confident," he writes, "that I should soon have to meet G. again."

In Tiflis, the house where Gurdjieff and his immediate followers were living rapidly became too small for the crowd of pupils who wanted to take part in the movements, so Gurdjieff extracted a promise from the Georgian authorities to provide a building for his work. The fulfilment of this undertaking was perpetually delayed—until de Salzmann published a cartoon of Gurdjieff and his followers cast upon the streets. The result was a sizable house with a hall for the movements.

A piano—deliberately not a good one—was acquired for de Hartmann to play. The members of the Institute were set to making furniture to seat sixty people. Every evening the movements took place. A pattern was emerging, which grew familiar in the days of Gurdjieff's Institute at the château du Prieuré. Later Carl Bechhofer Roberts even thought that "to one who like myself knew the baby institute at Tiflis, there is little new about Fontainebleau." As Ouspensky saw, Gurdjieff seemed now to be basing his efforts on "art"—although he might well have added the category of manual labor.

The theatrical connections of the de Hartmanns and the de Salzmanns dictated another outward form of activity. Gurdjieff was given a room in the Tiflis Opera, and he announced that they would begin work on his ballet *The Struggle of the Magicians*, which had been advertised in St. Petersburg. He began to dictate the scenario, and his followers started work on the staging. De Salzmann designed a stage set, and de Hartmann wrote the music for the first act. For the second act, Gurdjieff began to whistle music which de Hartmann took down. It was clear that there was no real prospect of staging the ballet, as the income of the Institute could not even have financed costumes. What then was the point? Work. The Institute itself, the movements, the project for the ballet: everything was intended to provide a matrix for "work on oneself." The ethic is embodied in de Hartmann's story of how Gurdjieff made a dummy supposedly for use in *The Struggle of the Magicians*. At one point in that magical battle, the scenario calls for the dummy to glow with light and fade. Gurdjieff contrived the effect with a rheostat he had made himself; but the morning after having demonstrated his ingenuity, he was discovered by Mme. de Hartmann smashing the dummy with an axe. "We have made it," he told her, "so we do not need it any more."

Christmas 1919 was celebrated in humble style by Gurdjieff and his followers. The Institute failed to cover its expenses, and no one had any time left from Gurdjieff's strenuous program to earn money. Meanwhile, even in Tiflis, which had at first seemed a sanctuary, conditions of life were unsettled. The Georgian government was expert at nothing but maladministration and linguistic confusion. In 1919 it had issued banknotes in denominations between 50 kopecks and 500 roubles. By the beginning of 1921, the face value of currency was anything up to 100,000 roubles. When in the spring of 1920 Gurdjieff let his Institute dissolve, it was clear that if he were to continue his work, it would have to be abroad.

Before his activities moved into a new phase, he was visied by Carl Bechhofer Roberts, who had escaped from Rostov-on-Don a week before it feel to the Red Army on January 11. He passed through Ekaterinodar and requisitioned a room for Ouspensky and his family if they succeeded in leaving Rostov. He covered the melancholy retreat of the White forces to Ekaterinodar and Novorossisk on the coast, observing with horror the corruption and chaos of the emigration, the bribery which alone secured a passage by regular steamer, the incompetence with which the official embarkation was administered. "However," he noted, "a lot of decent people did get away, Ouspensky and his family (rescued with difficulty from a suburb of Ekaterinodar) among them." Ouspensky was more fortunate then his benefactor, Major Pinder, who had been captured by the Red Army in Rostov and condemned to death. The sentence was, however, never executed, and in the spring of 1920 Pinder was able to visit Gurdjieff. Around April, Bechhofer Roberts reached Tiflis also. He carried a letter of introduction from Ouspensky to the man from whom the writer had not yet quite been able to escape.

Bechhofer frequented Bohemian circles which he entered through the friendship of the Georgian poet, Paolo Yashvili. One afternoon he found himself sitting at a café with Yashvili and a collection of poets, sculptors and èmigré politicians; with them was "a curious individual named Georgei Ivanovitch Gurdjieff."

He had a circle in Moscow in the old days, and many members of it had followed him to the Caucasus in 1917 and wandered about with him ever since. He was still surrounded by this entourage of philosophers, doctors, poets and dancers. He was not exploiting them; on the contrary, several of them were living on his diminishing means. And by them all he was esteemed, almost worshipped, as a guide to the eternal mysteries of the universe. . . . He was a man of striking appearance. Short, dark and swarthy, with penetrating and clever eyes; no one could be in his company for many minutes without being impressed by the force of his personality. One did not need to believe him to be infallible, but there was no denying his extraordinary all-round intelligence.

Bechhofer had been afraid that Gurdjieff would "talk theosophy" to him, but was relieved to find that his new acquaintance was content to show him around Tiflis. Together they went to "many obscure restaurants, Georgian and Persian, where we ate appetising food in sometimes unappetising surroundings." Gurdjieff's gastronomic expertise summoned up "unaccustomed and piquant dishes" for his English guest, and Bechhofer was treated to a luxurious hour or two in a bathhouse run by a "tall, bearded Persian" where the guests lay in stone basins of sulphurous water and were soaped and massaged by the attendant.

In the evenings Bechhofer sometimes dropped in at the Institute for the Harmonious Development of Man to watch rehearsals for *The Struggle of the Magicians*. Gurdjieff was quite open about the provenance of his ballet.

The dances, he declared, were based on movements and gestures which had been handed down by traditions and paintings in Tibetan monasteries, where he had been. The music, also, was of mysterious tradition. He himself could not play a note, and knew nothing of composition; but the academician who interpreted his ideas assured me that he had learned more of the theory of music from Georgei Ivanovitch than in any of the schools. The decorations and costumes were also the work of Georgei Ivanovitch; he had even painted and sewn them himself.

Although Bechhofer later called one of Gurdjieff's Tiflis lectures "a vapid and half-hearted affair," this was not really changing his tune; for the

Gurdjieff he had met and accompanied to restaurants and the baths was not the teacher but the Greek Armenian enjoying the pleasures of his native land. Bechhofer had been sadly disillusioned by his experiences with Indian Mahatmas, and Paul Selver of the *New Age* circle described him as invincibly prejudiced "against all forms of higher thought." The Gurdjieff he found in Tiflis was the *homme sensuel*.

But was this any more the "real" Gurdjieff than the puritanical Master whom other witnesses describe? The only other outside report of Gurdjieff in Tiflis in 1919 is a hazy reference contained in an attack by the Catholic Roger Bezault who claims to have information from an acquaintance who knew Gurdjieff in this period. "In Armenian circles themselves," Bezault writes, "Signor Gurdjian [sic] did not rejoice, on the moral plane at least, in an enviable reputation." What this implies is a matter for guesswork; yet if there is any substance in the allegation, it is merely another example of the equivocal appearance which Gurdjieff displayed to the outside world. What, anyway, was morality? He had explained to Ouspensky in St. Petersburg that in his view morality was a relative affair, except for a man who was "working on himself." Then moral questions resolved themselves according to whether or not an event helped him in his struggles.

The values of the Work were the only admissible standards. What served the aims of the Work was good, what hindered, evil. The individual disciple had to decide how he should react to Gurdjieff's apparently capricious or cruel conduct. The single assumption required of him was that he should remember that, in all cases, the Master acted for his benefit. So how do we take Bechhofer's report that when he left Tiflis, Gurdjieff was growing "weary" of his pupils and looked forward to a journey to Europe or to the East without them? Is this another case of the going to Persia with which he had frightened the de Hartmanns? The task of the pupil, as Thomas de Hartmann understood it, was to stick to Gurdjieff whatever the cost, making use of the unpleasant parts of the experience for "work." But this did not mean that it was always clear when to obey or when to disobey the Teacher's command. In the spring of 1920, Gurdjieff suddenly began to act toward de Hartmann in a hypercritical and imperious fashion, and ordered him to abandon the work with the Moscow Art Theatre which had become his livelihood. De Hartmann decided that he could not possibly give up his only source of income—that the test here was of his ability to make a logical decision for himself, not of whether he could obey his Master's every word. He continued his association with the Theatre, whose personnel Gurdjieff affected to despise, and at a concert de Hartmann gave in Tiflis, he was not surprised to see Gurdjieff in the audience and to hear his favorable verdict—although the entire staff of the Moscow Art Theatre was present.

The increasing difficulties of life around him again forced Gurdjieff to move. Georgia was not attacked by the Bolsheviks until the beginning of 1921, but the perpetual misgovernment of the country and the incessant squabbling with the neighboring—and equally bellicose—countries of Armenia and Azerbaijan, had ruined economic life and made physical survival problematic. Distributing his capital among his followers in the form of carpets, Gurdjieff set off for the Black Sea port of Batum. For a second time, it was an expedition on foot; and as always, Gurdjieff made use of the hazards of the route to drive his points home. For example: there were four horses which the men usually handled. Once there appeared a large cleft in the ground, one particularly difficult to negotiate while leading an animal. A horse was taken from its male keeper and given to Mme. de Stoerneval—who had just given birth to a son in Tiflis and was in any case not greatly taken with the Work—to lead around or over the obstacle under Gurdjieff's gaze.

When the traveling circus reached Batum, about thirty people took ship for Constantinople, where they arrived in June 1920. Almost immediately, Gurdjieff and his companions were again in desperate straits; for the precious carpets which were to serve instead of worthless Georgian currency as negotiable funds had almost all been confiscated en route by one of the many makeshift armies which roamed the Caucasian states.

Constantinople was not the easiest of cities for a refugee. About the time of Gurdjieff's arrival, the British General Harrington was reporting to Winston Churchill in London that "the streets of Constantinople are crowded with Russians—all without money." The crowds which concentrated on the former Russian embassy were "literally starving." The flow of emigrants had been in progress since the defeat of General Wrangel at the beginning of 1920, and among those who had been some months in Constantinople was Ouspensky. He was living with his family in one of the refugee camps on the Princes Isles in the Bosphorus, supporting himself by tutoring in mathematics and teaching English to Russian exiles. He had also started a series of lectures on Gurdjieff's ideas at the Russky Mayak, or White Russian Club, in Pera, the European quarter of Constantinople. Not for the last time, Gurdjieff found a group of people prepared by Ouspensky to cooperate in his designs.

Once more Gurdjieff threw himself into commercial undertakings. He mentions the sale of a ship and a deal in caviar. He also returned to his activities as a "physician-hypnotist" which involved him in an improbable relationship with a Turkish pasha who was determined that his son should become a champion wrestler. The de Hartmanns began to earn money by giving concerts. In the intervals wrested from the struggle for existence, Gurdjieff attended to the group which Ouspensky had formed and—in obedience to his resolve to forget "all former difficulties"—had made over to his Master on his arrival from Batum.

Ouspensky devoted himself to helping Gurdjieff prepare to open an Institute in Constantinople. The relationship was interesting and satisfying for him, but it continued with mounting unease; and there is some evidence that Gurdjieff already enjoyed a generally sinister reputation in émigré society. Boris Mouravieff met him at this period and observed one of the schemes he devised for making money for his Institute. This was to associate with it a celebrated clairvoyant who was married to a Russian diplomat. "From the first contacts," claims Mouravieff, "she refused peremptorily to have anything to do with him." Mouravieff implies that some darkly occult motive lay behind the lady's refusal to cooperate, but says no more about why Gurdjieff seemed to be making his bow in the role of Black Magician.

He clearly intended to continue the pattern begun in Tiflis. In the months before his Constantinople Institute opened in the autumn of 1920, work resumed on the scenario of *The Struggle of the Magicians*, and once more Ouspensky and the others were made to rack their brains in the service of the Master's intentions. Ouspensky has described how they spent a whole night translating a dervish song for the ballet. "This translation took the form of G. recalling the Persian verses, sometimes repeating them to himself in a quiet voice, and then translating them for me into Russian. After a quarter of an hour, let us say, when I had completely disappeared beneath forms, symbols and assimilations, he said: 'There now, make *one line* out of that.'"

The composition which resulted contains a statement of the Laws of Seven and Three, together with an affirmation of the sacredness of all points of view. It is twenty-two lines long, and to this day it remains unfinished. In the ballet the dervish sings this hymn to the fountain of his gnosis in the hubbub of an Eastern marketplace, and a stage direction breaks in where Gurdjieff and Ouspensky were unable to cudgel their brains any further to conceal the missing ending in the brouhaha round a quack doctor.

The ballet itself is not really a ballet, but more of a symbolic play with Gurdjieff's movements and music. From one point of view, it is the purest melodrama; but from another, *The Struggle of the Magicians* has a certain beauty irrespective of its effectiveness in stage terms. The first act takes place in a crowded Oriental town, where the rich and satiated noble Gaffar falls in love with the heroine Zeinab. In the second act it appears that Zeinab is the pupil of a White Magician whose pupils study the cosmoses— the "worlds" of Gurdjieff—and whose symbol is the enneagram. His pupils perform Gurdjieff's movements. In the third act Gaffar's infatuation reaches a point where he is persuaded to call in a Black Magician to overcome the stubbornness of Zeinab. Next, the audience is shown the cave of the Black Magician, whose pupils are ugly and deformed and who dance in a frenzied and uncontrolled fashion. The Black Magician casts a spell on Zeinab compelling her to submit to Gaffar, but in the last act, the White Magician magically destroys his evil counterpart and forces Gaffar and Zeinab to come to him. They arrive like zombies and are aroused by the Magician. A great reconciliation takes place with a final benediction from the White Magician and a prayer to the Creator to help men to avoid involuntary actions.

In Gurdjieff's terminology there is no "magic" in the sense of leaping the bounds of natural law. But someone who has overcome mechanicalness and can *do* consciously—is a real magician. "Black Magic" Gurdjieff defined as "a falsification, an imitation of the outward appearance of 'doing.'" In this way the Black Magician and his pupils are the hollow replicas of the White. The White and Black schools also represent the struggle between the forces of mechanicalness and the will to be. What has happened to Zeinab when she succumbs to the spell of the Black Magician is that she has fallen back into the machine state and is reacting automatically. Gurdjieff intended that the same pupils should dance the parts of the pupils of both White and Black Magicians. Although Ouspensky possessed a text, his followers rarely performed the play because Mme. Ouspensky disapproved of the movements of the Black Magician's school. On the other hand, Gurdjieff himself once seriously frightened at least one American pupil by forcing her to perform the depraved antics of the Black *corps de ballet*.

Despite the stimulus which Ouspensky derived from working with Gurdjieff again, his doubts about their association were rekindled. "Gradually," he records, "the same difficulties arose before me as in Essentuki," and so as not to hinder Gurdjieff, he returned to the Prince's Isles. Although he had withdrawn from all active cooperation, he continued to see Gurdjieff, and they went together to visit the Mevlevi dervishes. Gurdjieff explained that the whirling dance was an exercise based on counting, like the movements he had started to teach at Essentuki.

After giving Gurdjieff a couple of months to establish himself, Ouspensky resumed his lectures in the Russky Mayak, where his audience soon reached such proportions that he needed a larger room. Through another émigré—an aristocratic Tolstoyan—Ouspensky approached an English lady named Mrs. Winifred Beaumont for the use of her drawing room. A young British officer called John G. Bennett was at that time living with Mrs. Beaumont, whom he later married. Ouspensky's meetings sounded to him like "pandemonium."

Bennett's name will recur in the story of Gurdjieff and Ouspensky. He was born in 1897 and, after service in the First World War, found himself by 1921 head of a section of British Intelligence in Constantinople and in the thick of international intrigue. The account of the period which he gives in his autobiography, *Witness* (1962), must have been discreetly glossed over, for later, he admitted that his first introduction to the name Gurdjieff came in a notification from the Government of India that a notorious Russian agent was on his way. His original version was that he had been invited to meet a mysterious occultist and explorer by a Theosophically inclined friend, the Turkish Prince Sabaheddin. The young intelligence officer had recently become interested in hypnotism and was preoccupied with theories of a *fifth* dimension, both topics admirably suited to Gurdjieff's unusual point of view. Gurdjieff explained various hypnotic phenomena as control exercised over the finer substances in nature, and endorsed Bennett's guess that his fifth dimension was the dimension of free will. Such free will could only be attained in this present life, he continued, and if Bennett wanted to attain this higher state he must start to work for it now. However, it is more than likely that a professional interest in the former Tsarist agent preceded Bennett's intellectual absorption in his philosophy.

At all events, he attended a session of the Institute in Pera. He watched the pupils, dressed in white with colored sashes, perform movements, including the one known as "The Initiation of a Priestess." Then Gurdjieff gave the "Stop" exercise in an impressive and dramatic form:

> Everyone lined up at the back of the room while Hartmann played a series of chords. Gurdjieff shouted an order in Russian and all the dancers jumped in the air and rushed at full speed towards the spectators. Suddenly Gurdjieff in a loud voice shouted "Stop!" and everyone froze in his tracks. Most of the dancers, being carried by the momentum of their rush, fell and rolled over and over on the floor. As they came to rest they became rigid like people in a cataleptic trance. There was a long silence.

Another visitor to the Institute in Pera was the German writer, Alphons Paquet, who recorded his impressions in his book, *Delphische Wanderungen*. Paquet (1881–1944) is not well known outside Germany. He was a Quaker and a poet in the tradition of Whitman. In the years before 1921, he had published several books on Russia and the Revolution, and was now on an expedition through Turkey and the Balkans in an effort to escape the "atmosphere of pessimism and occultism" in Germany, and in the hope of recovering some inspiration from the clarity of classical Greece. Strolling up the hill at Pera one day, he noticed the signboard of the Institute for the Harmonious Development of Man. While peering at this intriguing

comehither, he was accosted by a voice speaking with the broadest of
Munich accents. It was Alexander de Salzmann, whom he had known in
Munich before the war. That evening Paquet was introduced to the
Institute.

It was in the ground floor of a maze-like house swarming with Russians.
I got to know the Director of the school, a Caucasian who in the course
of journeys lasting several years in the mountainous lands of Central
Asia, visited monasteries and learned the rituals, dances and knowledge of the monks. This man maintained that the home of wonders was
not India. He talked of the Pamir highlands, of which the West
scarcely knows the names, and of whose marvels the explorers will
never tire of telling. I watched the dances, which his pupils practised
in this shabby, black-and-white-tiled hall; there were scarcely several
dozen men and women. . . . In the curriculum of this Institute there
were lectures from the traditions of Asian schools on religious myths,
on rhythm, on the Law of the Octave, on the science of numbers and
everything that has to do with the Cabala and the magical arts. Here
one learned an interpretation of the remarkable stone monuments
known as dolmens which stretch in an enormous belt from the central
parts of Asia through the Caucasus, South Russia and Poland, over the
northern moors to Scandinavia and England; which can be found in
Brittany, in the Pyrenees, and North Africa, and end their pattern in
Egypt; the secret symbols of an enlightened race from Bactrian and
Atlantean prehistory—forgotten by astronomy and geology. . . .

The Pera Institute did not last very long. Once more political conditions
looked threatening. As Gurdjieff wrote, "The wiseacring of the Young Turks
began to have a peculiar smell," and the ringmaster had seen his show
stopped too often to commit himself prematurely. At the beginning of the
summer of 1921, Gurdjieff closed the Institute. His best-qualified pupils
were placed in charge of groups in Asiatic coastal districts. Gurdjieff himself
began planning to move to Germany, which seemed to him, "owing to its
central position and cultural level," to provide the most hopeful field for his
activities. Undoubtedly the connections of the de Salzmanns influenced this
choice, and judging from his later remarks about the Depression in the
United States, Gurdjieff may well have picked on Germany because of the
prevailing conditions of material hardship.

He tried to persuade Ouspensky to come, but Ouspensky—probably
with the conventional White Russian prejudice against the Germans—had
no wish to join him, and in June had a stroke of luck which made it possible
for him to act independently. Out of the blue there arrived a check for

royalties for an American translation of *Tertium Organum*, made without his knowledge while Russia had been cut off during the Civil War. Ouspensky replied to his unknown publisher, one Claude Bragdon, thanking him for the translation, but protesting that *Tertium Organum* was "to a certain extent my weakness." He asked whether Bragdon could help him and his family to reach England or the United States. This was beyond the American's powers, but a second stroke of luck was in store. On May 14, 1921, Bragdon, in Washington, received a cable from Viscountess Rothermere, the wife of the powerful English press baron. It read: TERTIUM ORGANUM INTERESTS ME PASSIONATELY. DESIRE VERY MUCH TO MEET YOU IF POSSIBLE. LEAVING ENGLAND END OF MONTH. Lady Rothermere followed up her enthusiasm with a visit to Ouspensky's publisher, which resulted in a cable of 100 pounds to Ouspensky in Constantinople and another of Lady Rothermere's telegrams to the author of the book which so engrossed her. This one read: DEEPLY IMPRESSED BY YOUR BOOK TERTIUM ORGANUM WISH MEET YOU NEW YORK OR LONDON WILL PAY ALL EXPENSES.

There remained the problem of visas. These were hard to secure for refugees, and eventually J. G. Bennett used his authority to obtain the necessary permits. He was unable to perform the same service for Gurdjieff, who was probably still dogged by his reputation as a spy. Not until August were Ouspensky's papers at last in order; and by that time, Gurdjieff had reached Germany.

Gurdjieff's party arrived in Berlin in the early summer of 1921. It included the de Salzmanns, the de Hartmanns, and Mme. Ouspensky with her daughter and grandchildren. The Stoernevals had been sent home to Finland to sell their property, and rejoined Gurdjieff somewhat later in Berlin. A large hall was hired in the suburb of Schmargendorf as a temporary headquarters, and Gurdjieff started to travel through Germany to inspect various possible sites for establishing an Institute. The period which the traveling circus spent in Berlin lasted until June 1922 and seems to have been something of a hiatus in the development of Gurdjieff's activities. Thomas de Hartmann was "sure that when we arrived in Berlin even Mr. Gurdjieff did not know what would occur there and in which directions we would have to turn our efforts."

Gurdjieff's activities in the latter half of 1921 dissolve into the shadows of general statements. There are some stray pieces of evidence which suggest that Gurdjieff's ideas did filter through to German mystical circles. In a draft of his *Third Series*, written in the mid-1930s, Gurdjieff talks of a group of followers in Bavaria; nothing else is known for certain of these followers.

Gurdjieff's party arrived in Berlin as one small group of refugees in the immense exodus from Soviet Russia. The capitals of the Russian emigration were initially Berlin and Paris, and to a lesser extent Munich and Sofia. The

Russians brought with them the mystical traditions of their homeland and a hatred of Bolshevism which was often couched in terms of religious fanaticism. All too often this was coupled with a paranoid distaste for Jews, who were seen as the representatives of the new materialist society which had overturned Holy Russia. It is well known that the notorious anti-Semitic forgery, *The Protocols of the Learned Elders of Zion*, was brought from Russia in the baggage of White officers. Defeated Germany—as Alphons Paquet observed—was itself riddled with occultism of every description, and also inclined to manufacture conspiracy-theories which blamed the Jews for the evils attending the defeat of the Fatherland. Disgruntled émigré politicians of the Russian right wing found a ready hearing in Germany; and Munich in the early 1920s saw a notable instance of this combination when Alfred Rosenberg and other refugees from the Revolution gathered around the circles—including Sebottendorff's Thule Bund—which preached a mystical nationalism. So much is perfectly true.*

It is therefore well within the bounds of possibility that Gurdjieff's ideas did interest some Germans whose eyes were fixed on what they imagined to be spiritual values. It is even possible that his ideas penetrated to the Nazi hierarchy. Hitler, Himmler, and Hess were all mystics of one or another description—Rudolf Hess was a devotee of Rudolf Steiner—and among Alfred Rosenberg's contacts in the Russian emigration, there were doubt-less several who had heard of Gurdjieff. I have examined in detail much of the evidence relating to Nazism and the occult and found no support for the idea that Gurdjieff had any direct contact with any of the more prominent Nazis. There is, however, one consistent rumor which is far removed from notions of an occult conspiracy and is even fairly likely. This is that Alfred Rosenberg attempted to practice the ideas of Gurdjieff.

I have myself talked to a former Nazi party member who once lived in the same house as Rosenberg and who confirmed that Rosenberg was interested in the ideas of Gurdjieff with the words, "that was his private study." More than this he did not know. However, there is a further piece of evidence contained in an attack on Rudolf Steiner by Gregor Schwartz-Bostunitch. Schwartz-Bostunitch was an émigré who had been born Grigori Bostunitch in Kiev in 1883. In Russia he published articles on Rasputin and Freemasonry, and, after the Revolution, fled to Germany where he decided that he was an Aryan, changed his name to Schwartz-Bostunitch, and soon became the chief Nazi propagandist against occultism, Anthroposophy, Freemasonry, and the Jews. A talent for personal survival led him to switch allegiance from Rosenberg to Himmler, and he ended his career as an SS *Standartenführer*. He was beyond doubt lunatic, and had more than

* For a discussion of Russian and German occultism and their conjunction after the First World War, see my *The Occult Establishment* (La Salle, Illinois: Open Court, 1976).

dabbled in the cults like Anthroposophy which he later attacked. In his pamphlet, *Doktor Steiner ein Schwindler wie keiner* (1930), he claims that "my first Teacher in esoteric matters—that was in the Caucasus in 1917–18—warned me against Steiner." Possibly there were other esoteric teachers in the Caucasus in 1917, but it seems probable that Bostunitch is referring to Gurdjieff, who roundly condemned all "theosophism," "anthroposophism," and other occultisms as teachings which helped to deprive man of the small percentage of genuine humanity he had contrived to retain.

If this is so, there is a strong possibility that the ideas of Gurdjieff were brought to Rosenberg either by Bostunitch himself, or by similar characters in the underworld of the Russian emigration. Rosenberg might, of course, have made contact with the ideas in Russia, or through his first wife, Hilda Leesmann, who was herself a dancer and a pupil of Jules d'Undine, a friend of Dalcroze. It is probable that Rosenberg did belong to Gurdjieff's elusive Bavarian group, but there is nothing to show that he made contact with the ideas when Gurdjieff was touring Germany in 1921—he might not have become interested until Gurdjieff's German visits began in the late 1920s. And, it is doubtful whether any other of the Nazi leaders—with the possible exception of Hess—would have had the impulse or the application to attend to Gurdjieff. The activities of Gurdjieff remain in the unmapped hinterland of the Russian emigration—where almost anything might have happened.

In later years Gurdjieff was always extremely sensitive about offending the police. His circumspection extended to the most scrupulous observation of the rules governing the amount of fuel in automobiles entering Paris, and it is unlikely that an émigré in a precarious position and with a dubious past would risk being deported by associating with subversive politicians. Gurdjieff's chief German contacts were probably with the circles of artists and intellectuals who were attracted to his ideas like moths to a candle, and the single episode of which we know anything before the spring of 1922 reveals him in just such a situation.

His quest for a permanent home led him to the Dalcroze Institute at Hellerau near Dresden, where the de Salzmanns had worked before the war. The choice of the lavishly equipped buildings of the Dalcroze Institute must have been prompted by the de Salzmann connection, but Hellerau would anyway have been an ideal site for attracting attention to his ideas. The little town preserved some of the atmosphere of the days of hope before the war; but the prophet Dalcroze had departed, and the colony of Progressives was left without a leader.

Jaques-Dalcroze's system of "Rhythmische Gymnastik"—anglicized "Eurythmics"—is designed to develop a sense of rhythm in children by training them to express a musical line with their limbs. Upton Sinclair called it "music made visible" and described how "with your arms you kept the time; a set of movements for three-part time, another for four, and so on. With your feet and body you indicated the duration of notes. . . . You would learn to analyze and reproduce complicated musical structures; expressing the rhythms of a three-part canon by singing one part, acting another with the arms, and a third with the feet." At Hellerau—notably in the performance of Gluck's *Orphée* which Sinclair describes in his novel *World's End*—Dalcroze achieved not only a reeducation of his pupils, but impressive artistic effects.

In this atmosphere Jeanne de Salzmann had worked as a rhythmician and Alexander de Salzmann achieved his extraordinary lighting effects. But the dynamic quality of the prewar colony—it seems to have been scarcely less ecstatic than that other center of the Progressives on Monte Verita at Ascona—was not of this world. Upton Sinclair's *World's End* incorporates a telling parable of the Dalcroze Institute's isolation from everyday reality. On a plain below Hellerau, Sinclair writes, was "an exercise ground of the German army." The drilling and maneuvering which took place daily were ignored by the devotees of Dalcroze as irrelevant to the Utopia "of cultivated and gracious aesthetes in which they were preparing to pass their days." But field-gray and cannon triumphed over Greek tunics and the symphony orchestra. At the outbreak of war in August, the Hellerau Institute was turned into a hospital. Next month, Jaques-Dalcroze signed a petition organized by Geneva intellectuals against the German bombardment of Rheims Cathedral. For his part, he decided not to return to Germany; and on theirs, the German critics, who had once showered him with praises, became rather scathing about the work of a man they regarded as a turncoat.

For some time the Dalcroze buildings lay derelict, until they were leased to three separate establishments: a less ambitious Dalcroze school, a German high school run by Karl Baer, and a school run on Progressive lines by A. S. Neill, the founder of Summerhill. The poet Edwin Muir arrived to teach there in March 1922, soon after Gurdjieff's appearance. He found a climate of "new ideas" and an expectation of a "new life" which was to result from "the simple exercise of freedom."

Hellerau itself had turned from being a craftsman's Utopia into a refuge for what would now be called radical chic: "government officials from Dresden and faddists of all kinds had settled in the place." In the vacuum left by the absence of Dalcroze, all sorts of prophets made their appearance. Muir remembered how, sitting one evening in a garden, "I saw a tall handsome man in flowing robes, a fillet round his head, passing majestically with a beautiful subservient young woman on either side. I never saw him again, and hardly know whether he was a visiting prophet or an apparition."

If Gurdjieff had succeeded in establishing himself at Hellerau, he might easily have swept the board of such trumpery magi and given a new conception of "freedom" and "unfreedom" to the Progressive educators— he would in fact have attacked the people who were to show most interest in his ideas from within one of their own most hallowed citadels. The coup was evidently worth taking trouble over. "Finding this house and its installations more or less suitable for the founding and further development of the headquarters of the Institute," Gurdjieff wrote, "I resolved to acquire the complete establishment." What then took place has remained shrouded in Ouspensky's hints of "strange events . . . which ended in legal proceedings." The sole traceable witness of the affair is the late A. S. Neill:

> There was a big Krach [row] but in German which I hardly knew then. Karl Baer and a few others and I made a Vertrag [agreement] with the owner of the Dalcroze Anstalt I think for five years occupation. Then G. came along and told the owner, Harold Dohrn, that he wanted the building. Dohrn agreed to give it to him in spite of our lease. We said we would fight it by law, and Harold then came round to our side. The story went that G. took him to law in Dresden and in court Dohrn said G. had hypnotised him, saying that his, G.'s work was of greater importance than ours. G. lost the case.

The legal records are not available, but the facts are not in dispute. Against a legally binding agreement, Dohrn was persuaded to lease his property to Gurdjieff, and when he came to himself, he claimed he had been hypnotized. Dohrn might have been trying to find an excuse for conduct which he had belatedly realized was indefensible; but in view of Gurdjieff's known skill as a hypnotist, it seems likely that he was telling the truth. If so, this obliges us to look again at Gurdjieff's repeated declarations about the oath he had taken to refrain from using his hypnotic powers. Either he was lying when he described this oath to his pupils, or he was lying when he gave them to understand that he had kept it. In *Glimpses of Truth* he is represented as warning his pupils to take nothing on trust; and it was an injunction which might usefully have been taken to heart by some of the Westerners who gravitated into his orbit.

Gurdjieff's stay at Hellerau was not entirely without results. He failed to acquire his building, but he captured some of its inmates. Some of Dalcroze's best rhythmicians were still at Hellerau, and several, including Jessmin Howarth and Rosemary Lillard, were so impressed by Gurdjieff's movements that they abandoned Eurythmics to follow the new Master. At Hellerau, there were few signs of the far-reaching changes once dreamed of by Dalcroze—who had hoped to induce in each rhythmician a clear perception of "what he really is." Gurdjieff would have found it child's play to adapt the occult vision of self-mastery which had served in Russia to a less superstitious setting, and present his System as a method of attaining the goals which Eurythmics had failed to reach.

Some hints of the magician's aura, the habit of a master of novices, increasingly the subfusc of the psychologist—all these accoutrements belonged to the "Gurdjieff" who materialized in Europe in 1922. But his outer garments were those of the teacher of dancing, and the successful conversion of the Dalcroze rhythmicians probably decided him on this disguise. The terms in which his teaching was described in the prospectus for the Institute at Fontainebleau—and therefore the way in which his English and American pupils first perceived the Master—owed a lot to the brief adventure of Hellerau.

The variety of Gurdjieff's changing forms and the subtle differences in the way his teaching was presented leave the inquirer confused as to the consistency of his methods. The strange dynamic of the man never alters, but presents itself at different periods as a mission to the occultists, a mission to the intellectuals—and now, at his entrance to Western Europe, as a mission to the Progressives, with Gurdjieff as a *Meister des Urseins* who will return humanity to the state of grace before the Fall. He is playing quite a number of roles at any one moment: the big role of the Teacher, the small immediate role which is designed to produce a particular effect on a particular pupil, and a generalized role to ensure a relationship of *meaning* with the whole milieu in which he chances to be operating. The confusing side effects of this method were not ignored by Gurdjieff, who could make use of them to enhance his mystique. As he says at the end of the first chapter of *Beelzebub's Tales*, "with a signature there must be no joking" and so halts the pen about to set his name on paper. Then being "very, very careful," he writes not a name but a number of descriptions.

> He who in childhood was called "Tatakh"; in early youth "Darky;" later the "Black Greek"; in middle age, the "Tiger of Turkestan"; and now, not just anybody, but the genuine "Monsieur" or "Mister" Gurdjieff, or the nephew of "Prince Mukransky," or finally simply a "Teacher of Dancing."

But despite the fluidity which his changes of role allowed him, Gurdjieff's progress through the world as a teacher *accumulated form*. In Russia his role as magus had been conveniently broken by the Revolution, and it is Ouspensky's writings which have preserved a record of this act of the play. When he detached most of his pupils from him after the expedition across the Caucasus, when Bechhofer Roberts found him apparently weary of his disciples in Tiflis, could this have meant exactly what it seems to mean? Was Gurdjieff in fact trying to divest himself of the pupils who, as it were, had played a role in one production and would be mere extras or impossible to cast in the next? To Ouspensky the program of the Tiflis Institute had seemed to "caricature" Gurdjieff's work; but his understanding of that work had been influenced by his director's previous production. Although no doubt similar truths are hinted at in *The Tempest* and *Peter Gynt*, there are critics who respond more readily to Shakespeare than to Ibsen. No one will object if they announce this fact; only if they claim that Ibsen ought always to have written like Shakespeare.

On the other hand, a successful theatrical director can have his failures, and may indeed lose his touch altogether.

Historical circumstances ensured that when Gurdjieff made his appearance in Western Europe, the earlier forms of his work still hung like a ghostly chrysalis about him. He had not succeeded in ridding himself of all his pupils and most probably only wished to dispense with the minor characters. Gurdjieff's Method demands that the teacher have assistants; and most of his general staff had already collected. Dr. Stoerneval was still with him from the early days in St. Petersburg, the de Hartmanns from Essentuki, the de Salzmanns from Tiflis. But there were others—less close to the Master and sometimes less capable of understanding his intentions— who remembered the earlier stages of Gurdjieff's work with which they had been connected. And so, there inevitably grew up around the invisible Master a cocoon of visible form—not merely the form in which he happened at any given time to be working, but the form in Time, the Long Body of the Work, the oeuvre of all past productions.

His search for a suitable framework for his activities had halted for the moment at the Tiflis conception of an "Institute." Institutes—like that of Dalcroze—were very much the fashion. Gurdjieff's Institute was at first taken at its face value by his English converts—although it bore a puzzling complexion. His public entry to Western Europe was as mysterious an affair as his arrival in Moscow, and the long period waiting in the wings in Germany was forgotten. His past was as unknown to his English pupils as it had been to the Russians; the myth of Gurdjieff had not yet had time to grow, and the glyph was only just beginning to elaborate itself. Once more, for his pupils, he was the invisible man, although to conceal his "tail"—the Long Body of his Work—he needed the agility of a Beelzebub.

PART | 2

Beelzebub and his Grandchildren

These ordinary three-brained beings, who acquire information about every kind of genuine cosmic fact exclusively only thanks to their being-Partkdolg-duty, are more competent than the Angels or Cherubim with their prepared Being, who though perfected in Reason to high gradations, yet as regards practical confrontation may appear to be only such Individuals as our always respected Mullah Nassr Eddin defines in the following words:

Never will he understand the sufferings of another who has not experienced them himself though he may have divine Reason and the nature of a genuine Devil.

—*Beelzebub's Tales to his Grandson*
(my italics)

When I die you will find Gurdjieff written on my heart? Yes? No?

—MS note (undated) of *Jean Toomer*

1

The Maestro of the Musical Glasses

Gurdjieff's initial success in the West was not brought about by the impact of the man himself nor by the forbidding intellect of Ouspensky, but by the personal magnetism of A. R. Orage. The pleasure and the intellectual stimulus Orage gave his friends denote a character of an unusual sort; however, this surface charm is the most difficult aspect of his personality, for it makes him singularly elusive. Like Gurdjieff or Ouspensky, he was the type of man who acquires disciples, but unlike them, he made his disciples his friends. They were sometimes blind to his faults, many of which arose from the facility with which he charmed his listeners, and despite the chorus of praise which arose after his death, his career was never smooth.

Orage was a seducer. Himself seduced by an apparently endless series of causes and intellectual fashions, he seduced these causes to an Oragean purpose. He made disciples not only in esoteric matters but in literature, politics and economics, with theories which were never his own, but all of which he animated. He was an editor of genius, because he possessed, in the words of the Freudian pioneer, Dr. David Eder, "the gift of returning another's halting, half-expressed ideas with a force, a completeness that made one receive it as a word from Heaven."

Orage is remembered in Europe as the editor of the weekly paper, the *New Age*, in which he published—often for the first time—such writers as

195

Ezra Pound, Richard Aldington, John Middleton Murry, and Herbert Read. Its contributors liked to consider it "the paper for those who write the others," and the giants of the literary establishment like Shaw, Wells, and Chesterton were as content to write for it without payment as were the pygmy hopefuls. Of the editor, T. S. Eliot said that he was "the best literary critic of that time in London," and despite the limited circulation of the *New Age* and the equally limited circle of contributors, Orage undoubtedly exercised an important influence on English letters in the early years of this century.

In America a different and more restricted impression of Orage remains. He is thought of as a guru pure and simple, one of the esoteric pantheon: thus in a list of psychedelic beatitudes, Timothy Leary thanks "William Blake and A. R. Orage for Alan Watts." Critics of Orage tend to praise the editor and condemn the guru. "How could he have fallen for such mumbo-jumbo?" asks John Gross in his *The Rise and Fall of the Man of Letters*. "The thought of him spreading the word of Gurdjieff among rich discontented New Yorkers is a profoundly depressing one. And what is the point of having the finest critical intelligence of the day if you devote it to expounding the cosmology of *All and Everything?*" Such a verdict makes the mistake of assuming that Orage's interest in the "mystical" could be separated from his other concerns. It was a mistake not made by those who knew him, even if, like Ezra Pound, they did not share his preoccupations. "I had no interest in Orage's mysticism and am unqualified to define it," he wrote in T. S. Eliot's *Criterion* after the death of Orage. "I was thankful he had it simply because it kept him in action. . . ."

Alfred Richard Orage was born in 1873 in the Yorkshire village of Dacre near Bradford. He was the last of four children, and his father died at the age of forty, only a year and a half after the boy was born. The family was left in difficult circumstances, as William Orage had lost his farm in Cambridgeshire and gambled or drunk away his money before moving to Yorkshire to become a schoolmaster. The youngest son may have inherited from his father some of the famous charm together with the freebooting qualities observed by Shaw when he described Orage as a "desperado of genius." But the most obvious influence on Orage's character was the experience of his childhood poverty in the Cambridgeshire village of Fenstanton where the family returned soon after the father's death.

The Orages of Fenstanton liked to suppose themselves of Huguenot origin—although the name had been anglicized to rhyme with "porridge." It was probably Bernard Shaw who started the more modish pronounciation with a French stress. Orage was later known even to close friends by his surname alone, and it became a sure passport to failure if someone presumed to call him "Alfred." Even the "Richard" was an addition at his confirmation, based on his schoolboy nickname of "Dicky" and replacing the original "Alfred James." In this juggling with names and in his later love of anonymity—most of his contributions to the *New Age* were signed with different sets of initials—may lie a clue to understanding the man. As his reaction to Ouspensky was to show, one of Orage's great fears in practicing the Gurdjieff Method was that he might discover that everything he had assumed to be himself—the artist, the editor—was not his real self at all. Not because he was ashamed of his early privations but because he had loathed them, the charismatic intellectual Orage—"whose very name was the Storm," as Chesterton wrote—submerged the memory of Dicky Orage, the poor scholar of Fenstanton.

Howard Coote, the son of the local squire, marked the boy out as a pupil of promise in the class he taught at a Non-Conformist Sunday School. Coote allowed him the run of his library, introduced him to the works of Ruskin, Carlyle, Matthew Arnold, and Morris—who left their ponderous traces all over Orage's less accomplished prose—and subsidized his education after the age of fourteen. Under Coote's supervision, Orage acquired French and Italian, both of which he read with fluency, although despite the long periods he spent in France, his spoken French never lost its execrable accent. The young man's zeal for self-improvement led him to study drawing and to trudge the ten miles into Cambridge to art college. In the village school at Fenstanton, he so outshone his fellow pupils that a special prize was set aside for him to prevent his competitors from becoming demoralized. Eventually he was appointed pupil-teacher, and the Coote family paid for his training as a schoolmaster proper at Culham College near Oxford. In 1893 Orage left Fenstanton for a teaching job in Leeds which the Cootes had found for him.

About this time he met his future wife, Jean Walker, a student at the Royal College of Art. They were not to be married until 1896, and their friendship was sustained chiefly by correspondence. According to his biographer, Philip Mairet, Orage's decision to marry cost him the support of his patron, who objected to the marriage as putting a stop to a promising career. But there were additional reasons for the quarrel. Coote himself had married and had a son, whom he proclaimed a future Prime Minister of England. All Fenstanton knew that Orage's hopes were blighted; and later Orage himself used wrily to end the story with the reflection, "Ce sont les premiers pas qui Coote."

Orage had thus to abandon his hopes of a Cambridge education. He remained to the end of his days a don *manqué,* and during the decline of the *New English Weekly,* he was debating with himself the possibility of getting a job at Oxford or Cambridge. In the event, the intellectual world he entered was of a peculiar kind, and Orage became a leading exponent of its tradition of thought.

The most superficial part of this world was its Socialism. Orage became involved with openair political meetings in Leeds and worked for a time with the Independent Labour Party. He met Tom Mann and other Socialists; Mairet dates Orage's real break from the life at Fenstanton from his arrival at his mother's funeral wearing a tie of a revolutionary red. Orage's politics seem to have put him in disfavor with the educational authorities; but in the main he was interested in what his friend Holbrook Jackson called "Socialism, not Socialists," and his Socialist phase represented the first stirrings of rebellion, the emergence of the thinking man. It also coincided with his marriage to Jean Walker and his escape from the tutelage of Coote. In any case, as Orage himself wrote in 1926, "Socialism was not then either the popular or unpopular vogue it has since become; but it was much more of a cult, with affiliations in directions now quite disowned—with theosophy, arts and crafts, vegetarianism, the 'simple life,' and almost, as one might say, the musical glasses."

On all these tympani Orage learned to play with scintillating effect. It was the age of Fabianism, of anti-vivisection, of Rational Dress; of William Morris and craftsmen's Utopias; of Nietzsche and the Superman; above all, of the occultists. In England the Theosophical Society combined H. P. Blavatsky's occultism with the emphasis placed on social reform by her successor, Annie Besant. It was an atmosphere in which Ouspensky would have been perfectly at home. The influence of this milieu remained surprisingly strong up to the 1930s and produced a sort of intellectual— D. H. Lawrence and Charles Williams are two other examples of the type— who remained isolated from the mainstream of thought in London or the universities. Orage was not the only thinker to have received his further education at Theosophical hands; what was remarkable was the speed with which he came to dominate his field of activity and the critical mind which refused to become the slave of Tibetan Mahatmas.

Orage had no particular religious upbringing. His mother was not religious, and his attendance at the Non-Conformist Sunday School does not appear to have produced any extraordinary piety. "I remember," he wrote in 1907, "years ago boo-ing through the keyhole of a Methodist meeting in which a Revivalist was singing, 'Where is my wandering boy tonight?' And I remember the Revivalist bounding to the door and shouting: 'Get away, you little fiend!'" But he clearly had a natural bent for mystical and esoteric works which his marriage to Jean Walker greatly strengthened—as his wife herself was a keen Theosophist. About 1896 Orage became a member of the Theosophical Society and soon created consternation by what the neophytes considered his "destructive" tendencies and an unorthodox enthusiasm for Plato and the *Mahabharata*.

Before long Orage felt descending on his shoulders the folds of the guru's mantle. His first personal forum outside Theosophical lecture platforms was a small "Plato Group" in Leeds which met weekly for several years. From the point of view of some of his listeners, Orage might just as well have talked about gardening, for in Holbrook Jackson's words: "The attraction was ultimately Orage, not Plato, or Nietzsche, or Blavatsky, or whatever it might be at a particular moment. He used philosophy as the jumping-off place for the display of his own powers and personality." Orage's personal magnetism began to attract devotees, and his long-boned, handsome physique did nothing to put them off. Holbrook Jackson remembers him as he was in 1901:

> In appearance Orage was tall and at that time slim and dark-haired. He dressed conventionally, except for a soft felt hat, then unusual, and probably an indication of social and aesthetic revolt. He had an *aura*, and impressed so much by his presence that you forgot details, even the vague birthmark which broke into his complexion like an irregular sunburn, and seemed to become deeper when he was bored or out of humour. . . . You expected a man who looked like that to talk well. . . . Even his small talk was fascinating.

Jackson, who loathed the "yoga-stricken mugwumps of Leeds," was not the only person to comment on Orage's "aura"—and his eyes. The Nietzschean Anthony Ludovici, who first met Orage in London in the late 1900s, noticed both:

> I was struck then, as I never ceased to be struck every time I met Orage, by the intense intellectuality that radiated from every part of his being, particularly, of course, his eyes. A curious disparity between the latter, whether in their pigmentation or form, only served to enhance the uncanny expression of resolute and penetrating wizardry which always suffused his face when he was speaking, and many a defeated debater must have left the bewildering man's presence with an uncomfortable feeling of having been routed as much by what he had seen as by what he had heard.

Orage's mental fireworks often had miraculous results. Jackson noted their invigorating effect on diffident young men. "And women in his presence were liable to develop what Marchbanks in *Candida* calls 'Prossy's complaint.'" But not until Holbrook Jackson himself appeared on the scene did Orage find the larger platform from which to approach his willing devotees.

In 1901 the two men met in a Leeds bookshop. Jackson had lived for a year in the town, where he was involved in lace manufacture. He was about the same age as Orage and like him found the lack of mental stimulus depressing. An immediate friendship sprang up, and a week after their meeting, a torrent of conversation was unleashed, which culminated in Orage's expounding the *Bhagavad Gita* to Jackson, and Jackson preaching on texts from Nietzsche. Orage lent Jackson the *Gita,* and Jackson riposted with *Thus Spake Zarathustra.* "Next morning," remembers Jackson, "he walked from his cottage at Chapel Allerton to mine at Headingley with a new light in his eye. He had spent the night with 'Zarathustra,' and the time for action had come—and the Leeds Art Club was born." Nietzsche had supplied the keystone for Orage's first synthesis, and Orage "went over the top." "We all developed supermania. He wanted a Nietzsche circle in which Plato and Blavatsky, Fabianism and Hinduism, Shaw and Wells and Edward Carpenter should be blended, with Nietzsche as the catalytic. An exciting brew."

The Leeds Art Club was the cauldron in which the mixture simmered. The precise ingredients were a matter of dispute among the more Theosophically inclined Orage, the Fabian Jackson and a third collaborator, A. J. Penty, an architect whose researches into the medieval guild system were to have significant political results. Later the Arts Club was stated to have "no written object," and at its foundation in 1903 the terms were already beautifully loose. Its members were to "affirm the mutual dependence of Art and Ideas. The separation of beauty from use, or use from beauty, proves in the long run disastrous to both; and only their union in a single clear purpose can restore to us the value of either. To this end it is necessary that real and enduring standards should be created anew . . ." To begin their revolution in taste, the Club held exhibitions of arts and crafts, provided a gathering place for kindred spirits and arranged open meetings in the Leeds Museum to which eminent figures—including Yeats, Chesterton and Shaw—were persuaded to come. The more intimate proceedings were dominated by Jackson and Orage, who shared, for example, a series of Friday evening lectures in April and May 1905, at which the topics were distributed as follows:

"Imaginary Portrait: The Superman as Saint"
  Holbrook Jackson
"Sentimentalism, Romanticism and Realism"
  Alfred Orage

"Art and Conduct"
Holbrook Jackson
"The Principles of the Arts Club"
Alfred Orage

The Leeds Arts Club possessed a library largely assembled by Orage, and as its premises also housed the local Fabian Society and Theosophical Society, the collection reflected the whole scope of his interests. Members of one society were quite likely to belong to another or all three. Mary Gawsthorpe, a suffragette who was a member of the Arts Club and later contributed to the *New Age*, recalls in her autobiography, *Up Hill to Holloway*, how one afternoon in the clubrooms, as she cast about among the shelves, she stumbled unwittingly from social reform to Annie Besant on karma. Regardless of how famous they later became, Mary Gawsthorpe found the members of the Club "as unique, as distinguished a group then, then not later in their lives, as I have met anywhere since. Not easy mixers, not peppy, not pollyanas, not smart, not merely brainy, they had an unmistakable quality of being mature mentally, even then, over thirty years ago. It was stimulating, refreshing, and nourishing to be a member of the Leeds Art Club circa 1904." The music and drama critic Gerald Cumberland was another member of Orage's audiences. He was less certain of the quality of his companions, which was apt to fluctuate, particularly on the occasions when Orage lectured "rather dangerously" on Nietzsche:

His gospel, always preached with his tongue in his cheek, that every man and woman should do precisely what he or she desires, acted like heady wine on the gasping and enthusiastic young ladies who used to sit in rows worshipping him. They wanted to do all kinds of terrible things, and as Orage, backed by "that great German," Nietzsche, had sanctioned their most secret desires, they were resolved to begin at once their career of licence. They used to "stay behind" when the lectures were over, and question Orage with their eyes, and it used to be most amusing and a little pathetic to listen to the gay and half-hearted insults with which Orage at once thwarted and bewildered his silly devotees.

He had in those days a wonderful gift of talking a most divine nonsense—a spurious wisdom that ran closely along the border-line of rank absurdity. The "cosmic consciousness" of Walt Whitman was a great theme of his, and Orage, in his subtle devilishly clever way, would lead his listeners on to the very threshold of occult knowledge and leave them there wide-eyed and wonder-struck.

This idolatry could not but have its effect on someone of Orage's temperament. If he was a seducer, it was not only with ideas. Nietzsche and the rebellion against Victorianism had something to do with it, as did the Arts Club which became a center for what Philip Mairet calls "not a little flouting of conventions and libertarian experiment." But Orage himself was at least as much the cause as the atmosphere he had helped engender. "He wasted his substance in talking and falling in love," wrote Holbrook Jackson. "He allowed himself to fall in love too often in those early days both in Leeds and London, and until he learnt how to canalise his passions his work suffered." Later Orage was to list "Falling in love," as his recreation in *Who's Who*, but apparently even in Leeds he had recognized a "scattering of force" which resulted from his frequent affairs. Jackson recalls a suggestive incident on the beach at Whitby, when unexpectedly he came upon Orage making a bonfire of poems and love letters.

How seriously to take his Don Juanism is uncertain. Mary Gawsthorpe records a visit to the Orage's tiny house in the Potternewtons at Leeds. She was at that time engaged, and Orage knew her fiancé as well as herself.

This did not prevent him from suddenly drawing me to him as I prepared to go. Without any warning and before I knew it, he had pulled me to him and had said, "Kiss me." I have heard the theory that "there is no seduction" discussed with warmth, but I shall stoutly declare however, that if there is such a thing as the spirit of the thing that must have been a perfect example, for I was led, and in spite of all laughs to the contrary, to do exactly what Orage asked, or commanded, that is, I kissed him.

This innocent or unconscious response, the reader making the choice, was accompanied by something so arresting I could not fail to take note of it. Swift as lightning, the taker of the kiss gave a little laugh, an elated, triumphant laugh.

It may be thought that this tells us more about the prim and prudish atmosphere of Leeds than about the motives which swayed Orage. But the question remains: underneath the urge to assert himself, was Orage really looking for a more ideal love—or a correct understanding of love? It is significant that his best-known exposition of Gurdjieff's ideas is an essay on the topic.

The marriage of Orage and Jean Walker was childless, and Jean—who had been used to living in more expansive surroundings than their cramped cottage—found the strain of poverty hard to bear. As Orage became more and more widely known as a Theosophical lecturer and the moving spirit of the Leeds Arts Club, the pressure of his adoring acolytes had a bad effect. Holbrook Jackson has recorded Orage's tendency to sulk if he were contradicted, and Mary Gawsthorpe confirms the impression that his wife's critical acumen was too developed for the budding prophet. Any blame for the separation which eventually took place was by no means one-sided; but Jean Orage's increasing intimacy with Jackson was the immediate cause of husband and wife going their different ways. Apparently, despite a series of minor crises, the marriage did not break down until Orage finally settled in London. Leeds was proving too small a stage for the self-confidence Orage's success had given him. His teaching had become irksome, his private life complicated. The Leeds Arts Club had been astonishingly successful and had spread from Leeds to Hull and Bradford, but its membership never exceeded 100, and this could not give Orage the audience he needed. At the end of 1905 he left Leeds for London, where he was joined by Jackson and Penty. For luggage he took only his three-volume translation of Nietzsche.

The world he had left behind was the greatest influence on his thought until he met Ouspensky and Gurdjieff. Jean Orage remained within that world, retaining Theosophical interests and working as an embroideress for William Morris's firm of decorators. Orage himself never lost his deep concern with the occult, and in London as in Leeds, the groups of idealistic Progressives clustered round the Theosophical Society and the fringes of Fabianism, giving him his first public. But in Nietzsche he had found both a personal justification and a bridge between the restricted world of esotericism and matters of general intellectual concern. During the bleak depression of his first months in London, when he was failing to support himself by freelance writing and living on the charity of friends, Orage wrote two small books, *Friedrich Nietzsche, the Dionysian Spirit of the Age* (1906) and *Nietzsche in Outline and Aphorism,* published the next year. In the first book, the author hailed Nietzsche as "the greatest European event since Goethe"; and his analysis of the salient points of "the philosopher with the hammer" proves how greatly this influence prepared him—as it did Ouspensky—for certain aspects of Gurdjieff's ideas. Orage hailed the coming of the Superman. But what of the rabble, the *canaille,* with their lack of taste and their gilded idols? "The multitude with their gods are indispensable to the creation of the powerful man. As a sort of battlefield and place of exercise, the populace serve the needs of the aristocrat."

Orage and Jackson began to agitate in the Fabian Arts Group, a body formed in 1907 by Fabians disenchanted with the ideas of Sidney and Beatrice Webb. Together with Penty they made overtures to the Junior Art Workers Guild, in which the architect was lecturing on the revival of the guild system. These societies provided Orage's earliest opportunities to shine in the public eye, but at the same time his Theosophical activities made him a source of controversy in the esoteric world.

By July 1905, Orage was a member of the committee of the British Section of the Theosophical Society, and on his arrival in London he resumed the Theosophical lectures which had been so successful in the north. Soon his unorthodox brand of Theosophy began to attract criticism. It was not only its Nietzschean iconoclasm which shocked the Theosophists, but its irreverent treatment of the tin gods, Blavatsky and Besant. Orage made his debut in London Theosophical circles at a time when these were considerably agitated. In 1906 a celebrated row broke out over the immoralities of Mrs. Besant's friend, C. W. Leadbeater; the following year, those who attacked Mrs. Besant for her support of Leadbeater found more ammunition in questionable goings-on at the deathbed of the President of the Society, Colonel Olcott. The Himalayan Masters who were supposed to be the powers behind the scenes were said to have appeared and appointed Mrs. Besant as his successor; there were, however, rival claimants, and skirmishing resulted in permanent divisions within the Theosophical Society, as well as the secession of several independent groups. Naturally, Orage ranged himself with the critics of the establishment.

The first of a series of articles he published in the *Theosophical Review* between the end of 1905 and the end of 1907 was an attack on the Society which was giving him column space for not living up to its principles. The last word had not been said on Theosophical matters, he reminded the more cultist of his readers. "Once one took the literature of the Society as the revelation of exact knowledge. Now one sees the literature as the forerunner of a still more splendid revelation of worlds unimagined before." As for *The Secret Doctrine*, "what in the name of Oeaohoo the Younger, does it all mean?" Was one Theosophist like any other, and was there really a "Theosophical" point of view? "Doubtless," he taunted, "with many others in the Society, I am not religious, I am not psychic, I am not scientific. I am not even ethical." He proposed a sort of Theosophical agnosticism which would prevent people from wasting their time "winding those giddy useless mazes" of *The Secret Doctrine*.

On reviewing my ten years of Theosophical reading concerning Man, I do not regret it. Certainly I have lost the hope of finding certain answers, but I have also lost the wish to find them . . . I like to live in a world of miracles and to be a miracle myself. I like to think that every pat little complacent scientific definition of man, every tin-tabernacle description of him, is superficial and ridiculous. I even like to think that the Theosophical views, the defined views that is, are ridiculous too. Man is not definite, for he is still defining himself.

This was inviting attack, and Orage was furiously assailed. Why, it was asked, did he bother to call himself a Theosophist? The future Bishop J. I. Wedgwood mocked "the Nietzschean vagaries" of "my good friend, Mr. Orage." A certain Dr. Wells told him in print that he was "not old enough." In answer to these counters, Orage further defined his position. "I am in this quandary," he explained. "I find myself believing certain things in the face of my contemporaries, in the face of a good deal of Theosophical literature and (most strange of all) in the face of my own mind. In other words, I have in some respects returned to an attitude of faith. Now temperamentally and by training I am incapable of appreciating faith at its face value. . . . I hate to believe without evidence, and still more to feel myself compelled to believe without evidence." But Orage's faith enjoined a skepticism which was too much for many Theosophists and in an article, "Occult Arts and Occult Faculty," published in January 1907, he defined more clearly his attitude toward the miraculous.

Ten years before, he wrote, such a title would have made his mouth water. "I see myself in those remote days impatiently cutting the pages, and turning the leaves to find the article itself. I see myself greedily, credulously and uncritically gulping down the rigmarole and abracadabras, the slovenly sentences and the unlovely terminologies." All this had been in the hope of miracles, of "the easy, certain and simple road to the whole cosmic conundrum." Such hopes had faded, "miracles did not happen. And as one by one the mares rose from their mysterious nests, flapped their mysterious wings and disappeared into the ridiculous void, the impression began to grow upon us that there were no secrets hatching at all . . ." In this search through mares' nests for the egg of the phoenix, Orage discarded "the whole list of magical superstitions, mystery-mongering devices from astrology to zoomancy. Note I do not deny the reality of these arts." But absorbing as such "occult arts" were, they "caught and devoured" people. "A caught and devoured person is called a crank." In contrast to the "occult arts," he defined three "genuine occult faculties": intuition, insight and imagination. These were all "our present faculties raised to another dimension." Thus, "intuition is winged thought. In an act of intuition the rational mind flies." Insight was "winged judgment" and imagination "winged sympathy." Orage wrote that he would respect the occultist who excelled in such qualities. He was "turning away from the older magic, the magic of the occult arts, with something like loathing. If to be wise I must know these things, then blessed be ignorance . . . what has been learned may be forgotten . . . faculties must be acquired, therefore they are an imperishable possession."

In the autumn of 1907 he was still writing for the *Theosophical Review*, but by that date he had more pressing concerns. On May 2, 1907, he and Holbrook Jackson made their debut as editors of a magazine of their own.

From the moment that Orage and Jackson took over, the *New Age* was a peculiar paper. Its historian Wallace Martin refers to "its unprecedented form." The distinguished contributors and the various causes for which Orage made propaganda are fairly well known, but the original purpose of the paper has been buried by Orage's later enthusiasms. In the first number of the *New Age,* the editors printed as their creed a hymn to the Life Force:

Believing that the darling object and purpose of the universal will of life is the creation of a race of supremely and progressively intelligent beings, the NEW AGE will devote itself to the serious endeavour to co-operate with the purposes of life and to enlist in that noble service the help of serious students of the new contemplative and imaginative order.

It was the feeling which Ouspensky experienced half a dozen years later. A new race of men was on the earth—and there was no limit to their potentialities. In some ways the *New Age* was the Leeds Arts Club writ large, and its stated objects bear a distinct relation to the ideas of raising human faculties to another dimension which Orage was elaborating in the Theosophical press. Soon after Orage had moved into his half of the editorial chair, the Theosophical Publishing Society issued his *Consciousness, Animal, Human and Superhuman* which states positively the Nietzschean occultism at which he had been hinting in his Theosophical articles. The book consists of lectures which Orage originally delivered to Theosophists in Manchester and Leeds, and the man who wrote it had little to learn from the basic argument of *Tertium Organum.* In many ways his analogies are more acceptable than those of Ouspensky.

Orage begins by assuming "a perfectly continuous and essentially similar underlying consciousness common to all living things visible and invisible." This "universal awareness . . . only by the particularised activities of beings becomes defined and limited into specifically human, animal, vegetable modes." Animal consciousness is a "one plane consciousness," receptive like a sheet of sensitive paper; but there is no knower of the impressions received. "In fact," states Orage, "there may be memory without a memoriser." Human consciousness can be represented by the sensitive paper folded once, so that the second plane surface formed stands for an observer of the impressions received by simple, "one plane consciousness." We decline into animal consciousness, warns Orage, in striking anticipation of Gurdjieff's terminology, "when we are not observing ourselves." The upper limit of human consciousness is illustrated by folding the paper into a sphere, symbolizing the vigilance of the ego. It is important to Orage to stress that the human mode of consciousness had been formed out of the original animal consciousness "like the embryo within the shell," because his real purpose is to predict the emergence of a Superman whose consciousness "should compare with man as man compares with the animal."

Using his analogy of the folded paper, Orage asks his readers to imagine a third fold to represent Superman consciousness. If the ego creates a human mode of consciousness by observing pure animal sensitivity to impressions, a still higher mode might be attained by contacting the higher self which can observe the ego. This is the directing overmind responsible for creative thought, and the birth of this new observer takes place in the womb of human consciousness just as human consciousness develops from the animal: an emergence represented in mystical doctrines as a rebirth or an awakening from sleep. Just as the "interiorizing" of man has resulted in the growth of mental faculties, Orage prophesies that the emergence of Superman consciousness will be accompanied by the growth of new "ecstatic faculties." He stops short of laying down the law on how this growth is to be achieved: to seek to grow in this way is dangerous and the choice of means must be an individual responsibility. The tone of the book is that of a man nursing a general hope for the promised land, but disillusioned with his own attempts to reach it. "Perhaps the sure way is to raise, to deepen, and to extend our human faculties," Orage concludes. He set about contributing to this aim in the columns of the *New Age*.

He and Jackson bought the *New Age*—then an old established weekly in severe financial difficulties—with the aid of a subsidy of 500 pounds from George Bernard Shaw and a similar sum from a Theosophical friend of Orage called Lewis Wallace. Wallace had made money sheepfarming in New Zealand and, according to the translator Paul Selver, "had white silky hair, a drooping moustache to match, a rosy face and a general air of self-depreciation no matter whom he was talking to." He wrote frequent articles of an occult cast for the *New Age* under the pseudonym of "M. B. Oxon"— an allusion to the pen name, "M. A. Oxon," of the famous Victorian spirit medium, the Reverend W. Stainton Moses. For several years he contributed 100 pounds a month to shore up the rickety finances of the magazine.

The pool of talent from which the new editors drew was that centered on the Fabian Arts Group and its allied lobbies. G. K. and Cecil Chesterton, Hilaire Belloc, Bernard Shaw, and H. G. Wells were among the earliest recruits; and their tussles in print established one thing important to the character of the paper—it was not tied to any sectional interest. Soon it became clear that the only fixed star in the *New Age* galaxy was Orage himself. In January 1906, he became sole editor when Holbrook Jackson bowed out of an undertaking which his colleague insisted on keeping independent—and, of course, Oragean—at the expense of financial stability. The "desperado of genius" had arrived.

Orage now entered on the days of his greatness which lasted until the middle of the First World War. His long apprenticeship in the provinces— he was thirty-three when he arrived in London—had developed in him the qualities which he now deployed so skillfully. As editor, he was naturally a focus of intellectual activity, but the groups which formed around him at this time greatly extended the editorial function. In the words of Professor Janko Lavrin: "One could not find so high a level of conversation anywhere in London." On Monday afternoons the circle would gather in the basement of the Chancery Lane ABC café, where the proofs of the next issue were read and the talk ranged far and wide. Once a week Orage would leave his tiny office and become the center of discussions at the Kardomah café in Fleet Street. Those who met in print in the *New Age* met in person in the editor's company. In the early days, the group would include Clifford Sharp, S. G. Hobson, the Chestertons, sometimes Wells and Arnold Bennett; later perhaps, J. C. Squire, Katherine Mansfield, F. S. Flint, T. E. Hulme, and the Imagist poets were included. Orage's love of debate encouraged him to stir up disagreement both in verbal discussion and in print. The only cloud on the horizon was his occasional prickliness when he felt his dignity threatened. It was the same Achilles' heel that Jackson had noticed in Leeds. Under Orage's successful exterior was a latent insecurity which craved the applause of others; and when the trappings of success were denied him, this self-doubt came to dominate him entirely.

The causes for which the *New Age* is chiefly remembered bear witness to his success. There were, of course, the literary or aesthetic discussions—on "the new drama" or the realistic novel—and individual publications, like Arnold Bennett's "Books and Persons" column or the stories of Katherine Mansfield, which were achievements in gathering copy rather than intellectual midwifery. But the National Guilds movement, which owed its origin to the ideas of A. J. Penty and S. G. Hobson, and the later doctrine of Social Credit, the brainchild of Major C. H. Douglas, received a great part of their impulsion from Orage's magpie brain. He was never an original thinker, and even the Swiftean prose style on which he so prided himself sometimes makes heavy reading. Orage was preeminently a man of the moment, whose chief facility was to *be there*, a snapper-up of unconsidered inspirations. Under his management, the *New Age* and its circle became the most articulate section of Progressive idealism in Britain.

The always Platonic idealism of Orage must be stressed, because it can easily be lost sight of under theories of the Guild State or a National Dividend. Ezra Pound compared him favorably with other literary figures—Yeats, Wyndham Lewis, and T. S. Eliot. They, said Pound, had "no bottom." "Orage had." A. E., who met him only in the last years of his life, recognized the voice of a fellow idealist even in Orage's prewar political "Notes of the Week." Orage began with a self-dedication to "the universal will of life," and although he may seem in retrospect to have been absorbed in the artistic and political questions of the day, the causes he adopted all took as their basis the idea of changing the nature of man in society, rather than accepting man as fallen and changing society to fit his unworthy needs.

In the Theosophical articles of 1907, he had proclaimed his disillusionment with the traditional occult arts and took refuge in Nietzsche. But by 1917 the Nietzscheanism of his New Age articles had faltered, and occultism began to creep back into the paper in the company of psychoanalysis. Orage's earlier change of attitude had reflected less a change of direction than a new personal influence, and his return from the realms of general ideals to those more specifically esoteric coincided with the removal of that influence from his life.

This influence was Beatrice Hastings, one of the principal contributors to the New Age from 1908 till 1914. Born Emily Alice Haigh in 1879, the girl who preferred to be called "Beatrice" had led an eventful early life. Philip Mairet writes of the time when she met Orage, that she was "dark, brown-eyed and vivacious, with a manner revealing intensity both mental and emotional." A South African, she had been married unsuccessfully to a professional boxer, and first met Orage at a Theosophical lecture he gave in London in 1906. She had been one of the young ladies who "stayed behind," and her appearance in Orage's life coincides with the irretrievable breakdown of his first marriage.

Beatrice Hastings possessed considerable literary talent in addition to her physical attractions. Her contributions to the New Age are prodigious in volume, although erratic in quality. Her specialty was malevolent criticism, and she exercised her abilities to such effect that several London publishers stopped sending the paper books for review. She became not only Orage's constant companion, but his literary conscience; and her flamboyant presence was a necessary part of the setting at the New Age offices or the café gatherings. After Orage's death, she published a splenetic pamphlet whose bitterness and extravagance have been made the excuse for ignoring it altogether. She claimed, for example, to have been responsible for most of the actual editing of the New Age until she left Orage, and this has naturally aroused the ire of latter-day Orageans. But even the devoted Philip Mairet admits that she had a large hand in Orage's literary decisions, and it is obvious that the quality of the editing did improve markedly as soon as she arrived. The days of Beatrice Hastings were the days of Orage's greatest success. There is some element of coincidence in this, and while several of her later allegations are preposterous, her portrait of Orage is so true to indications from other sources, as to repay the most careful study.

It says much for the temper of the times that the presence of Beatrice Hastings at a Theosophical gathering did not mean that this formidable young woman approved of the occult. Later she was to accuse Orage of "paranoiac mystagoguery," while at the same time herself writing a defense of Mme. Blavatsky. But it seems that Orage's deep occult interests had early on given her quite a jolt. About a year after their meeting, she writes, "when Aphrodite had amused herself at our expense, I found in his rooms a collection of works on sorcery. Up to this time, Orage's intimate friend was not Mr. Holbrook Jackson, who thought he was, but Mr. Aleister Crowley. . . . Well, I consigned all the books and 'Equinoxes' and sorcery designs to the dustbin. But the affair gave me such a shock that, for years, I would not hear of theosophy, spiritualism or anything to do with the occult. During my period on the *New Age*, few references, even, will be found to such things unless on a tone of superb, and I add superbly ignorant contempt."

Orage did know Aleister Crowley; and he told C. S. Nott that he had met him while Acting Secretary of the Society for Psychical Research, a post he had filled on first coming to London. Psychical research was an old interest of Orage, who had published on the subject in his Leeds days and edited a rather critical examination of Frederic Myer's *Human Personality and Its Survival of Bodily Death* in 1904. Edwin Muir, who as "Edward Moore" contributed to the *New Age*, claims that Orage "was a member of a magic circle which included Yeats." By this he means the famous Hermetic Order of the Golden Dawn which had split up into various quarreling factions in the year 1900, with Yeats and Crowley on opposite sides of the fence. The Golden Dawn had a temple at Bradford, and although there is no record of Orage's name in the membership lists of that organization, the leading Theosophical lecturer in the north could hardly have avoided coming into contact with some of its members. Yeats had been one of the literary lions to appear before the Leeds Arts Club; and his companion had been another member of the Golden Dawn, the actress Florence Farr, who added a lute accompaniment to the poet's recitation.

Until the advent of Beatrice Hastings, Florence Farr was the chief woman contributor to the *New Age*. In June 1907, she had reviewed Orage's own *Consciousness* with the remark that "Mr. Orage's mind is equipped by nature and subtle Eastern practices to give a better idea of Superman Consciousness than Shaw or Nietzsche." This confirms Beatrice Hastings's statement that in Leeds Orage had taken to Hatha yoga and breathing exercises. In the autumn of 1907, about the time that Orage was avowing his disillusionment with the "occult arts," the *New Age* published an unsigned review of *The Star in the West,* a panegyric of Aleister Crowley written by the future Major-General J. F. C. Fuller. The reviewer was concerned chiefly with Crowley, not his disciple, and made frequent references to chapter and verse which revealed him to be in possession of a set of Crowley's *Equinox.* Despite a half-hearted attempt to make Crowley appear a silly season frolic, the reviewer conceded—in markedly Oragean cadences—that he dealt "admirably" with the problems of superconsciousness. And some six months later, at the end of February 1908, David Eder contributed an obscure but apparently favorable review of Crowley's *Konx Om Pax.*

This is the last that the readers of the *New Age* heard of Crowley, and it may be presumed to coincide with the purge of Orage's magical texts carried out by Beatrice Hastings. It is not going too far to see Orage's condemnation of the occult arts as the beginning of her influence over him, and in the silence thereafter observed by the *New Age* on occult topics, her hand firmly on the reins. Crowley's "Do what thou wilt shall be the whole of the laws" came very close to Orage's own Nietzschean morality; but judging by the tones in which Orage referred to the Great Beast when talking to C. S. Nott, he had never been in any danger of falling under the spell of the man.

The arrival of Beatrice Hastings and the downfall of magic coincided with Holbrook Jackson's departure. The *New Age* gradually changed its character from a Nietzschean-Fabian magazine to a literary and aesthetic review. Its triumphs were now of a different sort. In the period up till the outbreak of the war, the *New Age* dealt most notably with aesthetic problems, and distinguished itself by discovering talented young writers. Orage began to emerge as a literary critic; and the successes of this era include the discovery of Katherine Mansfield and the elaboration of a "conservative philosophy of culture" by Orage, T. E. Hulme, and the Spanish educationalist Ramiro de Maeztu.

Orage is not diminished by insisting on the influence exercised over him by Beatrice Hastings. It was usually a personal encounter which excited him to a new phase of activity. Her beauty, verve, and fundamental amorality gave Mrs. Hastings advantages which she did not hesitate to exploit, and it is quite possible that Orage, who usually succeeded in dominating his surroundings, was intrigued by encountering an equally strong personality. Even at their first meeting, Beatrice Hastings claimed to have "rallied him, on his perverse loquacity." Under her tutelage Orage was very much the man of letters, his Nietzscheanism in abeyance, his occultism damped down.

Her departure from his life removed the inhibitions on his fundamental preoccupations. It also coincided with a series of crises in the life of the *New Age*. As a result of this combination of factors, Orage was ready for another crossing of the Rubicon when Ouspensky arrived in London. This time he was to drag a whole flotilla of souls after him.

2

Suspensk

When Orage and Jackson took over the *New Age,* they could count on a virtual monopoly of Progressive writers. The success of the magazine bred imitations: in 1911, Hilaire Belloc founded his paper, *The Eye-Witness,* and next year the Chesterton brothers left the *New Age* to join him. In 1913 Fabian pressure launched the *New Statesman,* with two *New Age* men at the helm: J.C. Squire as literary editor and Clifford Sharp as political editor. These defections deprived Orage of some of his best writers and established substantial competition to the *New Age.* The circulation dropped to less than 5,000. Nothing daunted, Orage increased the size of the paper and continued to encourage new writers. But at the end of 1913, the regular subsidy paid by Lewis Wallace ceased, and during the war printing costs rose to a level which the *New Age* could ill afford. This alteration in his material fortunes ran parallel with changes in Orage's private life.

If we are to believe Beatrice Hastings, Orage was suffering just before the war from a form of nervous prostration, which he attempted to conceal by passing it off as "overwork." He had "periodic fits of a curious mental illness."

Philip Mairet suggests that a sense of dissatisfaction was germinating in Orage; that his worldly success came increasingly into conflict with his deeper inclinations. "Tales for Men Only," of which Orage wrote and

213

published at least six in the short period 1911–12, arise directly out of his inner conflict: his sense that he had allowed a stern dedication to the purposes of Art and the Life Force to be diverted into the channels of literary fame.

The plots of the "Tales for Men Only" concern the efforts of the narrator—Orage's favorite pseudonym R. H. Congreve (later abbreviated to R. H. C.)—to break up various love affairs which threaten to absorb his friends. By the time of the sixth tale, published in November 1912, the tone is vitriolic, and the writer seems to be trying to free himself altogether from the need for female companionship.

Long after the liability to complete subjection to female illusion is over, men sometimes continue to experience perturbations of their equilibrium in the presence of women. In few instances are these perturbations violent enough to overthrow the mind entirely, but for the moment they undoubtedly do cause the judgement to reel and stagger and the resulting conversation and actions to become distorted. These residual phenomena, however, are to be distinguished from the similar phenomena of adolescence by the fact that they no longer inspire hope but disgust or, at least, annoyance.

Beatrice Hastings was not the type to take even an implied attack lying down. A satirical sketch which she published in late 1913 under the pseudonym "Robert à Field," is apparently a reply to the "Tales for Men Only." Although she refers to the piece under the title of "The Non-Committal Man," it is obviously the one printed as "Courtley Poole"—a character presented as "a fanatical bigot" with "a self-opinionated name." He is hypochondriac, neurotic, and stubborn. And there is one pertinent criticism of a failing which Orage himself may have felt keenly. This might be expressed as a "lack of follow-through." In a lawsuit, he refuses to appeal; when he takes lottery tickets, it is only a single one. "Everything which Courtley does turns out to be moonshine. Moonshine is the reward of all bigots."

Finally, "In May, 1914, domestic affairs having become intolerable," writes Beatrice Hastings, "I left for a few months' tour in order to make a break." At the outbreak of war she was living in Paris and remained as "war correspondent" for the *New Age*. But the break was not clean; bickering continued in a series of acrimonious letters.

The collapse of the relationship in 1916 was a blow to Orage's pride. Despite the vehemence of "Tales for Men Only," it seems that it was Beatrice Hastings who left *him*. To a man of overpowering attractiveness to most women—and a Nietzschean by public confession—this was a bitter sop. In this period of crisis he began to frequent the Café Royal where, as G.K. Chesterton wrote, "he presided in a sort of club." Augustus John, Walter Sickert, Jacob Epstein, and Orage's close friend, the Australian caricaturist Will Dyson, were members of this circle. It was more worldly Bohemianism than Orage had previously known, and the companionship of the Café Royal may have solaced a life which had grown lonely. His emotions seem to have been further confused by the attentions of a girl who refused to surrender to the famous charm, but preferred, in the words of Philip Mairet, "a Platonic attachment." The failure of the *New Age* to attract more new writers must also have contributed to lowering his self-confidence, and the political schemes in which he became involved brought him equally little success.

After Orage became converted to the Social Credit theories of Major C.H. Douglas, which failed to gain acceptance from the Labour Party or the National Guilds League, the *New Age* pounded out the message of Social Credit to a largely deaf nation, and the disillusionment of its editor grew. Much earlier, he wrote in 1926, he had begun to doubt whether any movement of ideas was possible among the proletariat; now he became convinced that if Douglas, "the Einstein of economics," could be rejected, "reform in any drastic sense is impossible."

Orage emerged from the war years facing frustration, insecurity, and a sense of failure. "He became unable to miss a shot at golf," writes Philip Mairet, "without glancing round anxiously in fear that some stranger had noticed the mistake." In 1919 physical troubles were added to others when he had to undergo an operation for appendicitis. His mind began to return to the more metaphysical preoccupations which the presence of Beatrice Hastings had for a time suppressed. This reviving interest in psychology and the occult made Ouspensky's teaching instantly appealing, because it seemed to answer the questions which he and his friends had been so anxiously asking: in effect, the same questions he had shelved as insoluble some fifteen years before.

The *New Age* published Ouspensky's "Letters from Russia," and Orage himself turned violently against Bolshevism, as a succession of Slav mystics, bearing their exotic gospels out of a Europe torn by war and revolution, began to appear in the *New Age* circle. Janko Lavrin discovered Nicolai Velimirović, Bishop of Zica in Serbia, who contributed a series of apocalyptic meditations to the *New Age* under his own name and the pseudonym R.A. Vran-Gavran. As early as 1915, Paul Selver had introduced Orage to Dmitrije Mitrinović, at that time an attaché at the Serbian Embassy. Mitrinović subscribed to a composite occultism based on the vision of a united Christian Europe; he occupied himself in London by trying to persuade people in positions of some influence to join him in an "open conspiracy" for the salvation of "Pan-humanity." On August 19, 1920,

Orage began a series of articles on "World Affairs" in collaboration with Mitrinović, under the pen name "M. M. Cosmoi." For a time his disciplined hand held Mitrinović's near incomprehensible rhapsodies in check; but in December, Orage unleashed the prophet who rampaged through the columns of the *New Age*, mystifying its readers and wreaking havoc with the already tiny circulation. Mitrinović's articles considered the various nations of humanity as different organs of one great World-body; thus Germany might represent the scientific intelligence, Russia the intuition of mankind, and Britain—which Mitrinović always called "Albion"—the function of common sense. Few contrived to make sense of his ecstatic parentheses, and fewer still can have come away feeling greatly enlightened about world affairs.

Another innovation in the *New Age* was an extended discussion of psychoanalysis, and this inquiry represented the true continuation of Orage's search for meaning. Psychoanalysis was still an unfamiliar subject in England, although the days of its complete disregard were over. There had been a time when mention of Freud's name was enough to incur censure. In 1911, when Dr. David Eder had read a paper on Freud's methods to a section of the British Medical Association, his chairman and the entire audience walked out in disgust. By contrast, Eder's own circle saw psychoanalysis as the harbinger of a golden age.

The group which responded enthusiastically to Freud was the same section of the intelligentsia which a dozen years earlier had combined social reform with Theosophy and the occult. Orage was not the only thinker to tire of the glamor and fraudulence of the "occult arts" and yearn for a secular occultism which could explain man, his soul, and the universe in terms which did not revolt the rational mind. He had no difficulty in forming a group with the aim of constructing a "psycho-synthesis": a solid edifice to oppose the psychic rubble generated by the analysts' quarrying. But on closer acquaintance it began to appear that psychoanalysis as it stood was not going to provide the liberating impulse for which the Progressives were looking. One of the group, Rowland Kenney, has recorded the disappointment of its members when they concluded that psychoanalysis contained no "possibilities for the building up of a new way of life":

> Perhaps because we had not grasped its deeper significance, it seemed to us that, while it might heal many psychic wounds, it would never help one to re-create one's own inner being. (It should be remembered that I am writing of the autumn of 1921.) What we wanted, we decided, was a psychosynthesist—probably what we wanted was a change, a new interest or excitement—and we tried to formulate a kind

of programme or scheme for the building up of the psyche on new lines.

The psychosynthesis group included Havelock Ellis, David Eder, James Young, and Maurice Nicoll. Mitrinović sometimes attended, and other members of the *New Age* circle like Kenney and Dr. J. A. M. Alcock were also involved. Ellis, Eder, and Orage had all been Fabians; of the younger generation, both Maurice Nicoll and James Young had studied with Jung at Zurich. Alcock, in Kenney's words, was "a young medical man . . . who had never been able to take *materia medica* seriously. He believed that in an enormous number of cases the value of a bottle of medicine depended on the faith the patient had in it." Rowland Kenney himself had been the first editor of *The Daily Herald* and was a long-standing member of the group around Orage. An air crash had left him broken in spirit as well as in body, and he hoped to find in psychoanalysis some solution to his personal problems.

The sort of psychoanalysis which the *New Age* favored was never very far from the occult. Maurice Nicoll had connections with Theosophy as well as strong links with Jung. Young hoped that occultism, understood as "self-development through deepening, or expanding the limits of self-consciousness," might merge with the new psychology. David Eder's Freudianism had anchored in a spirit which could also—as his review in the *New Age* of 1908 shows—play host to Aleister Crowley. Alcock had been born in India, and in Kenney's words, "was delighted to find that psychoanalysis linked up with yoga and other Eastern philosophies."

Orage himself was reviving old contacts. Shortly after he had abandoned Theosophy to concentrate on the *New Age*, the Theosophical Society had fragmented. In 1909, G. R. S. Mead, who had published Orage's final articles in the *Theosophical Review*, resigned to found his own Quest Society. This issued a magazine, *The Quest*, devoted to occultism, Theosophy, and scholarly work on the history of religions; Ezra Pound, John Masefield, and Professor Wilson Knight were among the contributors. It was to Mead that Orage naturally turned when he again became concerned with questions of the spirit. "What the circulation of *The Quest* is, I have no idea," he wrote in the *New Age*, "but it should be ten times greater." The psychosynthesis group and the Quest Society exchanged views: Alcock contributed to *The Quest*, while Mead himself became interested in psychoanalysis and wrote articles based on books lent him by David Eder. Two articles on yoga and psychoanalysis published under the name of "F.I. Winter" may possibly have been by Orage himself. "*The Quest*," announced Orage, "is the literary Platonic Academy of our day."

During this period of undirected speculation Lewis Wallace returned to the *New Age*. As "M.B. Oxon," he published two articles in February 1920, at the height of discussion about psychosynthesis. These were eccentrically entitled "Psycho-Egyptology," and their train of thought was soon to be incorporated in Wallace's extraordinary book, *Cosmic Anatomy*. His ideas would have been quite familiar to Gurdjieff, for example, he saw man as "a common chord" in touch with an upper and a lower world: "The fact that he is man depends on the power he has to link these two octaves." When Ouspensky arrived in London, he found the intellectual world which centered on Orage in a state of ferment and the focus of attention unsteadily shifting between psychoanalysis and mystical philosophy. Circumstances could have provided no material more aptly molded to his hand.

The impasse in which the Orage circle found itself was a particularly intense form of a condition which was affecting most thinking men and women. The Great War, that crowning futility, had just ended, and intellectuals everywhere were feeling their way in a vacuum. In his essay "The Republic of the Spirit," published in 1920 in *The Evolution of an Intellectual,* John Middleton Murry gave expression to a whole army of opinion which saw the war as an object lesson in the follies of materialism. This section of the community felt, but was not able to articulate, the four years of horror, felt it as a *sin,* experienced the shame of being less than human. "We are somehow maimed," wrote Murry, "yet how we do not know." He appealed for a new "aristocracy of the spirit" disregarding worldly rewards. These it must "replace by titles more arduous." The declaration of principle seemed absolute: "In order that it may have the strength to refuse to compromise without, it must refuse to compromise within."

Among the Orageans, the late summer of 1921 was a bleak season. On September 22, Orage warned that the *New Age* could only just cover its costs and was in danger of having to suspend publication. On October 13, the last of Mitrinović's articles appeared. The psychosynthesis group was already in difficulties. In early August, Maurice Nicoll had written in his diary a "Prayer to Hermes": "Teach me—instruct me—shew me the Path so that I may know certainly—help my great ignorance, illumine my darkness? I have asked a question."

As if in answer to that question, Ouspensky made his entrance. In June, Claude Bragdon had made contact with him in Constantinople. By July, Theosophical circles had some advance notice of his coming through an article on the fourth dimension by Mead in *The Quest,* perhaps stimulated by Lady Rothermere who at this time was scattering about copies of *Tertium Organum.* Ouspensky arrived in August 1921, and stayed at a Bloomsbury hotel. Almost immediately he began holding meetings to expound the ideas of Gurdjieff. Orage was the chief mover in securing him an audience, and Ouspensky's other Theosophical contacts proved useful. He spoke to Mead's Quest Society and to another breakaway group of Theosophists led by D.N. Dunlop—an early friend of Yeats and A.E.

The psychosynthesis group pricked up its ears. J.A.M. Alcock wrote to Rowland Kenny to tell him that the psychosynthesist had arrived. Orage went one better and sent a telegram summoning Kenney to his flat to meet Ouspensky. It became obvious that whatever Ouspensky was about, he was extremely sure of himself. He spoke not as a man inviting discussion, but as a Man Who Knows. Kenney's first meeting with Ouspensky left him "puzzled" but intrigued:

His looks did not impress me. Nevertheless, when he smiled his eyes lit up with a warm twinkle which encouraged confidence and confidences. His nose made one think of a bird's strong beak; indeed, when sitting in reflection or repose he hunched himself together and looked like a dejected bird huddling up in a rainstorm. He was obviously a man of a dominant if not domineering type of character, with determination—or obstinacy—written over his every feature.

I launched out with my views on certain recent developments in psycho-analysis and a need for a revaluation of certain psychological principles. Orage followed on until he was brought to a dead stop by a snort from Ouspensky. "Why waste time, Orage? Tell Kenney what we are meeting for."

The meeting was to establish a group to be taught, not a forum for discussion; and to the collection of dedicated talkers gathered round Orage, this dictatorial attitude was hard to swallow. Paul Selver found Ouspensky "quite monumentally boorish. He was one of those exasperating Russians who doggedly refuse to credit any other Slav nation with artistic ability. He sneered when I expressed the view that there were several Czech or Serbian poets of outstanding greatness. I had read them and he had not, but he contemptuously dismissed my remark with a sweeping gesture, as though consigning those unspeakable rhymesters to a garbage-heap." Ouspensky once more found himself in a society of intellectuals. In his last five years, he had learned much about "wiseacreing" and was evidently in no mood to tolerate it.

From the beginning of November 1921, Ouspensky began to hold meetings of his own, at first in a studio owned by Lady Rothermere in Circus Road, St. John's Wood. The initial audience numbered about twenty and consisted chiefly of readers or contributors to the *New Age*. After a time Lady Rothermere tired of her new interest, but not before she had established Ouspensky in a small flat in Gwendwr Road in Baron's Court. The meeting place oscillated between the rooms of the Quest Society, and the house shared by Maurice Nicoll and James Young at 146 Harley Street; then eventually, it became settled at 38 Warwick Gardens in South Kensington. And with Lady Rothermere's departure, the salon atmosphere created by her patronage vanished.

Gradually, Ouspensky's reputation spread. The October number of *The Quest* carried a long review by Mead of Claude Bragdon's edition of *Tertium Organum*, still the only available translation. *Tertium Organum* seemed to him "over-ambitious, too flamboyantly titled, and introduced with a superfluity of puff by the American editor. Nevertheless, Ouspensky is a serious thinker. . . ." For Mead the book fell short of the necessary sublimities. "He has thought himself deeply into things," he wrote, "but only apparently at last to make shipwreck on the bare rocks of an 'immobile universe.' He leads up gallantly to a conclusion, and then falls back, short of the beatific vision. . . ." Ouspensky replied in a letter dated October 25, defending himself against charges of pretentiousness. Neither was he, explained Ouspensky, the eminent professor of mathematics to whom his translators had ascribed the book.

His small audience grew slowly: the socialites and the merely inquisitive departed, and those who had heard of Ouspensky through the grapevine replaced them. From the psychosynthesis group came Alcock, Nicoll, Eder, and Young. Other friends of Orage, like Rowland Kenney and Carl Bechhofer Roberts, also attended Ouspensky's lectures. Orage whipped up more support from those to whom he had been a minor guru. There was interest from the Theosophists: Maud Hoffmann, who was a friend of Mabel Collins, the author of the Theosophical "classic," *Light on the Path*, and who shared the house at 146 Harley Street with Maurice Nicoll and James Young, seems to have told Nicoll about Ouspensky even before Orage. Ouspensky's audiences were composed generally of the better-off among the intellectuals: as Bechhofer Roberts wrote, "One saw doctors, psychologists, psycho-analysts, editors, writers, civil servants, theosophists of both sexes, clergymen and a sprinkling of the men and women who are always attracted by the lure of the mysterious."

Orage himself clearly expected that his relationship with Ouspensky would be along the lines of an editorial collaboration with a *New Age* contributor. Indeed, his relationship with Mitrinović had been conducted on just these terms; and the forceful personality of Ouspensky, bearing a message which demanded acceptance of a master-pupil relationship, was a profound shock. Mitrinović himself came to some of Ouspensky's meetings and fought hard to retain Orage's allegiance. But the total commitment demanded by Ouspensky overwhelmed his less impressive arguments; for although Orage may not have known it, such a commitment was what he sought.

The teaching which produced such cataclysmic effects was the teaching Ouspensky had absorbed from Gurdjieff. Man is asleep, mechanical; he has no "I" of his own. He must try to awake, observe himself, and realize his own mechanicalness and the illusory nature of the personality with which he identifies and which manipulates his life. He can do nothing, but must join a group dedicated to waking up. Perhaps then he will discover his "real I" and acquire a soul which he most certainly does not possess.

Those who responded to Ouspensky did so according to their different natures and their differing problems. Nicoll saw the new system as the continuation of his quest, Young as the next step in a scientific inquiry, and to Orage, it may have appeared as a hammer to smash through the unsatisfactory life he had created and penetrate to some truth. To Rowland Kenney, whose air crash had left him "an insomniac, a writer unable to write, a quivering jelly of fears, worries, doubts and apprehensions," Ouspensky's broken English opened doors into new rooms of thought. "My first interest was the purely practical one of the neurotic who wants healing and reassurance that not only is life going to be worth living, but that he is again going to be fit for active life. I am afraid I did not find the drastic methods of Ouspensky immediately effective. The devastating emotional upset was not a sedative for jangled nerves." The brusque treatment of irrelevant questions and the shocks administered by Ouspensky to personal vanities did, in the long run, work for Kenney who began to find his needed support in "the esoteric side" of Ouspensky's teaching. He reached the conclusion that no liberation in the social sense was possible until there had been a liberation from "the tyranny of internal things."

Ouspensky's teaching methods at this time already resembled those he would continue to use until the beginning of the Second World War. He held meetings several times a week and conducted at least two groups: a small body of hard-core enthusiasts and a larger one, probably to act as a magnet and a screening device. He also saw pupils privately. At his meetings, he expounded Gurdjieff's ideas and then invited questions and answers. This constituted the really important part of the meeting—or so Ouspensky would say in the 1930s—because the right sort of question, which was based on personal experience and sprang from a real desire for knowledge, meant that the teacher would answer from his own experience. The questioner would receive hints of where his problem fitted into the vast scheme of human psychology and the universe which was being unfolded gradually and with an irritating arbitrariness before him.

Ouspensky's methods were those of Gurdjieff in more than the system of question and answer. He would create confusion and uncertainty by changing the dates of meetings, or by telling pupils like Rosamund Sharp that he wanted to see less of them, only without warning to subject them to a battery of personal interviews. In Ouspensky's mouth, the system assumed the aspect of a scientific, rational approach to the universe and lost much of the eccentricity and exoticism which characterized Gurdjieff's own teaching.

James Young recorded the various exercises devised by pupils to assist the process of self-observation. "Some people took to doing counting exercises in the Underground, instead of staring at their fellow passengers or reading their daily papers; others tried to overcome the 'mechanism' of their dislikes in the matter of food by eating what they would not otherwise have eaten, or the 'mechanism' of their likes by abjuring favourite dishes." He thought that "on the whole, sincerity gained at the expense of material politeness," and that conversation became "more alive and real," but noticed that there was a distinct tendency to observe the mechanicalness of others rather than one's own automatism.

A fascinating glimpse of how a member of Ouspensky's audience might progress from polite interest to a complete commitment to the System is given by a series of letters which Rosamund Sharp wrote to an unnamed correspondent from October 21 to December 7, 1921. In many ways, Mrs. Sharp provides an excellent example of the sort of person attracted to Ouspensky's lectures. She was the daughter of E. Nesbit's husband, Hubert Bland, a former leading light of the Fabian Nursery, and—after an affair with H.G. Wells—had married Clifford Sharp who, by all accounts, was an unsatisfactory husband. Orage telephoned her and told her that he had found "a man I could believe in."

Expecting a psychoanalyst, she was surprised by Ouspensky, whose teaching seemed religious, philosophical, and analytical all in one. At first she felt that Orage "had let me in for a lot of stuff that I couldn't understand and that was quite probably useless to me." To her great horror, Ouspensky, evidently imitating the practice of Gurdjieff, asked to see her alone. She talked to him in a café for two hours and quelled some of her disquiet. Ouspensky was "a wonderful person. Incidentally he has the sweetest smile in the world, but that is his only attraction from an ordinary point of view, counting out his brains, of course." Suddenly she discovered an access of energy, and despite lingering doubts about her ability to understand the details of Ouspensky's exposition, life began to seem more worth living. She wrote: "If there is one grain of truth in it I'm not going to reject it whatever nonsense may surround it."

The feeling of well-being continued, but her worries were by no means stilled. Ouspensky's method of question and answer meant that the pupil must painfully piece together the complete system of thought. Rosamund Sharp worried about her own capacity to winkle out the information she needed and envied intellectuals like Orage their ability to formulate questions. She called the System "Suspensk." Her teacher became more human: the stern exterior of the lecturer with his very short sight and innumerable pairs of spectacles was softened by a visit to the flat in Gwendwr Road and the discovery of his notorious devotion to cats. Cats apart, there were also moments when she achieved real contact with the teacher, like that at the very first meeting when she had blurted out, "How can we get a will?" and "Ouspensky sort of switched round in his chair and looked straight at me and began talking about the possibility that man had to awake and for a few minutes everything became really thrilling, sort of vibrating with life."

Her anxiety mounted about the eventual outcome. She felt herself at one end of a long, dark tunnel without the certainty of light at the other. It became apparent that the discipline was changing her, and she worried about losing her friends. At the very outset, she had suspected this possibility; now she felt them slipping away. Then the real test began: Ouspensky—perhaps playing the part that Gurdjieff had played in Uch Darye—seemed depressed, talked of returning to Constantinople because things were not going well, gave her to understand that she was the only member of the group who responded more than intellectually to the true significance of his work. Rosamund Sharp hoped that if he did decide to go he would go quickly, while it was still possible for her to return to her old interests. She wondered whether she could face this. Her correspondent began feeling "change" in her, accused her of unfriendly behavior. He, too, was slipping away. She knew this and faced up to it. Her friendship with Orage was also a thing of the past, for she had stopped identifying with him. "Killed by changes in me and in him. We both know this without speaking a word. . . ."

In all his teaching, Ouspensky made no secret of the facts that the System he taught derived from Gurdjieff, that Gurdjieff was somewhere on the continent of Europe trying to establish a permanent base, and that the London lectures, the questions and answers, and the basic exercises which included "self-remembering," were only the preliminaries to proper work in a "school." In the winter of 1921–22, Gurdjieff was still in Hellerau, convinced of the possibility of starting work in Germany; but when the Hellerau project failed, he returned to Berlin. It seems to have been agreed that, because Ouspensky was having some success in London, England was the next best place to try to establish a permanent Institute. In Berlin, Gurdjieff made his pupils learn English, and in London Ouspensky prescribed Russian lessons for some of his pupils. It was Gurdjieff's own idea that he visit England, and he arrived in London in February 1922, with Mme. de Hartmann as his secretary. "I at once invited him, as a matter of course, to my lectures," says Ouspensky, "and introduced him to all who were coming to them."

Gurdjieff's first introduction to Ouspensky's pupils took place on February 13. According to Orage's notes of the occasion, Gurdjieff talked chiefly about "impressions" and "energy." As children we acquire new impressions, he said, but as we grow older, our sensitivity to new impressions weakens, and they can only be obtained by force. Similarly, energy is mechanically acquired and mechanically used; but there are methods for obtaining new energy. At this Orage commented, "pickaxe and pounder, eh?" A number of interesting observations were made by Gurdjieff that do not seem to appear elsewhere. You may study men by their postures and judge nationality by methods of dancing. Each nationality has a different number of movements and therefore of thoughts. In the same way, all our moods are the result of our experiences, and the trained eye can read them. If a man's original associations can be traced, we can create in him any emotion. These topics had obvious reference to Gurdjieff's plans for an Institute on a large scale.

Some of Gurdjieff's audience took fright. "A few timid people were scared away," wrote James Young, "perhaps by his completely shaven head." It may have been at this first meeting that only one member of the overawed group dared to ask the Master a question— "What would it be like to be conscious in essence?" He received the reply: "Everything more vivid." There were no more questions, and Gurdjieff left. The second meeting at which he confronted Ouspensky's group was on March 15. Gurdjieff talked about personality and essence. He said that in Europe the term "hypnotism" referred only to personality. One center might be hypnotized by the others. Again there was talk of a permanent Institute. Individual programs in such an organization, Gurdjieff said, could only be arranged after long study by others and by oneself.

The London Institute was destined never to materialize, although a large building in Hampstead had been found to house it. The reason was Gurdjieff's failure to obtain a visa, although Bechhofer Roberts says that he would have been allowed to enter Britain if he had left behind all the Russians who followed him from Tiflis and Constantinople. A deputation was organized by Orage, Maurice Nicoll, and some of the other doctors— including a bemused surgeon called Kenneth Walker who had been whisked from Harley Street by Nicoll and made to testify before the Home Secretary in favor of a man whose name itself was still new to him. Lady Rothermere attempted to exert pressure covertly, and another follower of

Ouspensky even mobilized a High Court judge to buttress Gurdjieff's case. The Londoners still seem to have been hopeful in late June, but by this time the Home Office was even causing trouble over a brief visit which Gurdjieff proposed to make from Berlin. On the main issue it remained adamant. The traveling circus could not enter Britain.

Part of the reason was probably Bolshevophobia. The specter of Red Revolution frightened many governments at that time, and there was a tendency to see in every Russian a bearded, bomb-secreting anarchist intent on disrupting society. No country in Europe was anxious to admit more than it could absorb of the huge numbers of White Russians pouring out of the Slavic depths. Even though Ouspensky's own position was secure, it might be that his visit to Theosophical headquarters in Adyar had somehow tainted him with the brush of sedition. Bechhofer Roberts, who had visited the Theosophists at the same time—when he was only nineteen—had been forced to demand an inquiry when he returned home in order to free himself from unpleasant surveillance. Neither can Orage's reputation have been exactly free from blemish. There had been a plot to kidnap a Member of Parliament, and the government had thought it worth while to suborn Orage's friend and colleague, J. M. Kennedy, to act as an informer on the *New Age* group.

Outweighing all considerations of logic was the fact that Gurdjieff was known to have spied for the Tsarist government in Tibet. It was in Britain on one or another of the trips he made early in 1922, that Gurdjieff was interviewed by security men, but no records are available to clarify the situation. Neither is there any evidence for Louis Pauwels's claim that the former French President Poincaré intervened personally to procure for Gurdjieff the permit which allowed him to settle in France; although, in view of Ushe Narzunoff's status as an ally of France, there would have been nothing illogical in his doing so. Somehow the permit was obtained. Gurdjieff moved his Berlin group to Paris, and again began to look for a suitable home. Very soon one was found in the Prieuré des Basses Loges, a château some forty miles from Paris, near Fontainebleau. The Institute for the Harmonious Development of Man had at last found a roof. The money to pay first for renting, and then for the purchase of the château, came from Ouspensky's friends and pupils in London. Lady Rothermere once more provided funds, but the leading contributor was a rich Yorkshire industrialist named Ralph Philipson. Mrs. Philipson even handed over a valuable string of pearls to Gurdjieff, who gave them back.

Ouspensky's own attitude toward Gurdjieff was ambivalent: he "still expected a very great deal more from his work" but saw a recurrence of "all the former obstacles which had begun to appear in Essentuki." For the moment he devoted his energies to supporting Gurdjieff's plans. Some of his London pupils, particularly the ones who had been most forward in trying to establish Gurdjieff in England, decided to "give up everything" and go to Fontainebleau. "In my opinion," wrote Ouspensky," some had been in far too great a hurry to give up their ordinary occupations in England in order to follow G." Others, who wanted their Master to make the decision for them, he told to wait until he himself had been to the Prieuré.

In the first week in July, Ouspensky went to Paris where he stayed at the Hotel Solferino in the Rue de Lille. He sent back encouraging messages, but warned his pupils that Gurdjieff's establishment was not yet fully organized. Then in mid-August, he received disquieting news from Orage, whom he had left in charge of the groups in London. Ill-disposed or panic-stricken people had been sowing rumors among the new recruits who were terrified by tales of madness, sexual scandals, and the dangers said to be attendant on self-observation. Ouspensky wrote to his senior pupils, asking them to suppress the gossip and warning Orage to keep strictly to his instructions. However, the exodus had already begun, although few of the visitors to Fontainebleau can have departed without qualms.

Almost the first to go was James Young, who left Harley Street in some confusion of mind. Was he going simply to improve his technique as a psychotherapist? Afterward he declared that he had seen in Ouspensky's exposition of the System a possible way of overcoming the problem of "failure of the will" in which he was interested. On the other hand, as an honest man, he had to admit that he could not "lay claim to such an impersonal motive." Maurice Nicoll abandoned his practice, borrowed money from his expectations under his father's will, and left for France with his wife, his sister-in-law, his young daughter, and a nanny. Several patients of Young and Nicoll followed their analysts across the Channel. Rosamund Sharp left for Fontainebleau, as did Rowland Kenney, who arrived in a mood of great surprise that he should be in such a place at all. There were numerous people whose circumstances permitted only week-end visits or short trips. One of these was J.G. Bennett, the young intelligence officer from Constantinople, who had joined Ouspensky's circle on his return to England.

The growth of interest in Gurdjieff's ideas was like the spreading out of ripples in a pool: Ouspensky's arrival in London had produced an eddy which enclosed Orage and his friends; and their conversion—for conversion it most certainly was—set off fresh waves through the intellectual world. After Orage had been won over, Gurdjieff and Ouspensky would have been names to conjure within the close-knit intellectual society of the day; but there is no doubt that it was Katherine Mansfield's death at Fontainebleau which introduced them to a wider public.

•   •   •

Katherine Mansfield was the daughter of a prosperous New Zealand banker. She came to Europe for education and stayed to experience life. Her tempestuous and theatrical prospecting for experience led to a succession of lovers, a miscarriage, an abortion, and an operation which permanently damaged her health. Somehow she contrived an area of equilibrium in the midst of all this turbulence, out of which emerged a series of meticulously observed short stories. In 1912 she met John Middleton Murry, then a hopeful young writer and editor of his own magazine, *Rhythm*. They struck up an intense and unstable relationship. They lived together, lived separately but near at hand, then each took flight from the other in order to work. Katherine Mansfield's hysterical temperament, her insistence on subordinating the responsibilities of personal relationships to a relentless pursuit of experience—an aspect caricatured by D. H. Lawrence in the character of Gudrun in *Women in Love*—complicated their lives unbearably. In 1916 they lived for a while with the Lawrences in Cornwall in an abortive experiment in communal life. After the war Katherine Mansfield's health began to break down in earnest with the onset of tuberculosis; and in the autumn of 1921, she and Murry—at last married—were living in Switzerland because of the supposedly beneficial effect of the mountain air. From their friend, S. S. Koteliansky, K. M. heard about a Russian doctor in Paris who had a new treatment for tuberculosis, and she became convinced that a cure was possible. To the great distress of Murry, who thought that her only chance lay in remaining in Switzerland, she left for London in July 1922, ostensibly in order to see a heart specialist before going on to Paris to begin treatment for her diseased lungs. In fact she had a perfectly sound heart and the real reason—as Murry afterward believed—was to renew her contact with Orage.

The relationship of the Murrys with the Lawrences is well known, but that with Orage and Beatrice Hastings was almost equally important. It was Orage who had published Katherine Mansfield's first stories in the *New Age* in 1910. Later Beatrice Hastings was to claim the responsibility. Whatever the truth, Katherine Mansfield fell for a time under the influence of the powerful Mrs. Hastings, and it was to her that she is supposed to have turned in 1911 for help in arranging her abortion. After she met Murry, her connection with Orage lapsed; for Orage had also been Murry's first publisher, and Murry's magazine, *Rhythm*, was in some ways a rival to the *New Age* in which it was bitterly attacked. However, when Beatrice Hastings left Orage and went to Paris, the two women again resumed their relationship.

When the breakup with Orage removed Beatrice Hastings from the scene in 1916, the relationship of the Murrys and Orage altered once again. Next year Orage published some stories of Katherine Mansfield's, and Middleton

Murry met him for what was only the second time in his life. Relations between the two men remained affable but distant. Murry was conscious of a relationship with Orage which resembled that of opposed magnetic poles. "He, far more than many other men whom I knew far better," Murry wrote in 1934, "was an influence in my life: a queer kind of negative influence, no doubt, for I was always resisting Orage, but a very real one."

In the autumn of 1921, Orage—probably remembering Murry's bouts of mysticism—suggested that the newly published book of Lewis Wallace, *Cosmic Anatomy*, be sent to him in Switzerland. "To such speculations," wrote Murry eight years later, "I have since learned to attach a meaning, as a sometimes useful method (if used warily) of making the borderlands of psychology accessible to thought; but at that time they meant nothing—less than nothing; they were positively repellent. I put the book aside. K.M. picked it up."

Cosmic Anatomy is a curious book. It is an open question how much Lewis Wallace was in fact the author and how much the book was cobbled together by Orage and the psychosynthesists to serve as an introduction to Ouspensky's lectures. It describes an occult system derived from Oriental religions, Rosicrucianism, and similar sources which is supposed to be linked to contemporary science—psychoanalysis, of course, and relativity. There are striking parallels with Gurdjieff's own teachings. At all events the book answered the metaphysical hunger of the times in general, and of Katherine Mansfield in particular.

From her Russian wonder doctor in Paris, K. M. fled to London, with the hapless Murry following. The goal was Orage, both as mediator of *Cosmic Anatomy* and as the magnetic personality who had dominated the *New Age* gatherings. She saw him on August 30, 1922, by which time he had almost certainly resolved to go to Fontainebleau. "She said it had been wonderful," recalled her friend, Ida Baker, "he had been so affectionate, embracing her and calling her 'darling,' as though in a return to earlier, happier days." K. M. recorded the interview in her journal. It typifies the attitude of many people who came to Gurdjieff—a general attitude, irrespective of personal problems, but here expressed with the customary Mansfield powers of observation.

On that occasion I began by telling him how dissatisfied I was with the idea that Life must be a lesser thing than we were capable of "imagining" it to be. I had the feeling that the same thing happened to nearly everybody whom I knew and whom I did not know. No sooner was their youth, with the little force and impetus characteristic of youth, done, than they stopped growing. At the very moment that one felt that now was the time to gather oneself together, to use one's whole strength, to take control, to be an adult, in fact, they seemed content to swop the darling wish of their hearts for innumerable little wishes. Or the image that suggested itself to me was that of a river flowing away in countless little trickles over a dark swamp.

They deceived themselves, of course. They called this trickling away—greater tolerance—wider interests—a sense of proportion—so that work did not rule out the possibility of "life." Or they called it an escape from all this mind-probing and self-consciousness—a simpler and therefore a better way of life. But sooner or later, in literature at any rate, there sounded an undertone of deep regret. There was an uneasiness, a sense of frustration. One heard, one thought one heard, the cry that began to echo in one's own being: "I have missed it. I have given up. This is not what I want. If this is all, then Life is not worth living."

But I *know* it is not all. How does one know that? Let me take the case of K. M. She has led, ever since she can remember, a very typically false life. Yet, through it all, there have been moments, instants, gleams, when she has felt the possibility of something quite other.

At this point, Katherine Mansfield was living in the house of her friend, the artist Dorothy Brett, while Murry rented a room next door from Boris Anrep. K. M. became completely involved with the group around Orage. This now included another old friend, the novelist J. D. Beresford, who was also attending Ouspensky's meetings. The spiritual quest on which they were embarking was contagious, but Murry remained unaffected. "I felt that the only thing that remained to me—my own integrity—was at stake. It was not that I felt superior to Orage, or J. D. Beresford, or James Young, or Maurice Nicoll, who were among Ouspensky's disciples: still less did I feel superior to Katherine. But I was certain that it would be treachery to myself to follow them. I could scarcely bear to discuss the doctrines of Ouspensky with Katherine." In despair, he began to turn more and more to the teachings of a mystic named Millar Dunning, whom he had met at Garsington, and who also counted J. W. N. Sullivan—still not yet emancipated from Aleister Crowley—among his devotees. Eventually, feeling life "a kind of torture," Murry took flight to Selsfield, the country house of his friend Vivian Locke-Ellis.

Katherine Mansfield had not quite given up hope of making him understand. She saw Orage again on September fifth and tenth; on the fourteenth she went to a lecture by Ouspensky at Warwick Gardens and met Orage on the sixteenth. Four days later, she attended a luncheon at J. D. Beresford's, about which she wrote to Murry.

K. M. absorbed Gurdjieff's ideas from Orage rather than from Ouspensky. She attended a few of Ouspensky's lectures and then came to tell him that she was off to continue her treatment with the Paris specialist. To Ouspensky, she did not seem to have long to live, but he gave her Gurdjieff's address, and on October 3 she left for Paris. The next day she protested in a letter to Murry: "I don't feel influenced by Ouspensky or Dunning. I merely feel I've heard ideas like my ideas, but bigger ones, far more definite ones. And that there really is Hope—real Hope, not half-Hope . . ."

Orage himself arrived in Paris on October 14. He was still trying to sell his share of the *New Age*, but had received a subsidy from Lewis Wallace to speed him on his quest for truth. In his brilliant variations on literature, the arts, Theosophy, and social reform, he had simply been postponing the inevitable reckoning which his nature had long since decreed. Fifteen years earlier, he had written in his speculations on the higher forms of consciousness: "Perhaps the great ways of Religion, Art and Love are also the safe and certain ways. Perhaps it is the racial experience that has named these as the chosen means, the humanly effective means. Special means doubtless exist; but special means involve special difficulties." Now special means confronted him which had none of the rigmarole attached to them of the occultism which he had earlier abandoned; and he could no longer put off the attempt.

The impact of Ouspensky's teaching on him had simply deepened after the first shock. On May 30, 1922, he had written to Claude Bragdon: "Ever since Mr. Ouspensky came to London under Lady Rothermere's auspices last August, I have been attending his lectures, and more and more and still more I find myself absorbing his teaching . . . Mr. Ouspensky is the first teacher I have met who has impressed me with ever-increasing certainty that he knows and can do." All his resistance had crumbled. C. S. Nott reports that later Orage compared his own situation in 1921–22 with that of a character called Hamolinadir in *Beelzebub's Tales*. This character represents the man who has "learned everything" and found no solutions in the knowledge of the schoolmen. "Hamolinadir," said Orage, "is a cartoon of the disillusioned modern thinker, whose reason is insufficient for objective conclusions."

Yet one cannot but feel that the intellectual baggage of Orage—like that of Ouspensky and of many of Gurdjieff's followers—had been insufficient to weigh him down. The gadfly mind seldom penetrates deeply enough into the disciplines from which it draws sustenance to deliver any sort of verdict upon them. Philip Mairet quotes a remark of Ramiro de Maeztu: "Orage knows the shapes of everything and the weight of nothing." He suggests that Orage felt the absence of a solid core of truth to be a flaw which affected both society and himself. After the flight of his mistress and in the absence of a cause to dominate, Orage sought a master and a dominating interest. The sovereign alkahest which would reconcile all social and personal contradictions must be God.

"Since in my experience," he wrote after his time at Fontainebleau, "every attempt to establish an ideal and conscious relation between man and man, without taking God into account, has failed, the only remaining hope of the serious social reformer is to 'find religion,' that is to say, find God." This has been criticized as rationalizing after the event; but it is perfectly in line with what he had accepted of Gurdjieff's ideas. How can you reform society, the argument runs, when man himself is unregenerate? Man is asleep, and you can help at best to wake up only a few. Altruists are self-indulgent people—and, of course, asleep. All you can do is try to find your "real I." "Why must you go?" asked his devoted secretary, Alice Marks; and Orage returned simply: "I am going to find God."

Orage's departure from London was viewed by a far wider circle than that of the *New Age* office as a tragedy from which the causes he had championed would not recover. Criticism began. Dmitrije Mitrinović disconsolately, but humorously, watched the man he had hoped to make his own Saint Paul submit to the dictates of another gospel. He complained to Wilma Muir that too many clever men in London were throwing up their jobs and migrating to Fontainebleau because Gurdjieff had promised that he could raise into full bloom the merest bud of a soul. Yet, after melancholy shakings of the head, Mitrinović would then gurgle with laughter and cry: "London is Looney-bin, no?"

The contrast between the view from "within" and the view from "without" is absolute. From one point of view, Orage's conversion was incomprehensible, or a matter for censure. From another, it was simply necessary. Once more he made a clean break with his past. The last time he had burned his boats, he salvaged from the ashes three volumes of Nietzsche. This time his luggage was less bulky. It consisted, as he later said, of *Alice in Wonderland* and a toothbrush.

3

The Institute for the Harmonious Development of Man

The château known as the Prieuré des Basses Loges stands at the bottom of a small hill in the village of Avon on the outskirts of Fontainebleau. The building—said to have been designed for Mme. de Maintenon—is three stories high and low in proportion to its length. The windows of the two lower stories are flanked by shutters, while those of the upper story project from a gray slate roof. Inside, the ground floor contains the once ornate Empire drawing room, salon, and library; the second floor, a set of luxurious bedrooms known by the pupils as "the Ritz," where Gurdjieff and Mme. Ostrowsky had their quarters and where visitors and new arrivals were generally lodged; and the third floor—or "Monks' Corridor"—holds attic bedrooms where most of the pupils slept.

In the courtyard at the château entrance is a fountain—out of whose circular basin Gurdjieff once heaved a car single-handedly—and on the other side of the house, beyond a terrace, is a garden supposed to have been designed by Lenôtre. In Gurdjieff's day the garden included an impressive lime avenue and another fountain used as a swimming pool. When Gurdjieff bought the property, the grounds extended beyond the 45 acres around the house to some 200 acres, bounded by a stone wall outside of which rose the trees of the Forest of Fontainebleau. Inside the demesne were various auxiliary buildings: a complex of kitchens and servants' quarters attached to the château in an ugly wing; an enormous orangery built almost entirely of glass; and a small house in the gardens known as "Le Paradou." Under Gurdjieff's régime the Paradou housed the children of the colony, who were supervised in a rota by one mother a week.

The Prieuré was owned by the widow of the advocate Maître Laborie, who had been given the château in payment for his defense of Dreyfus. After various negotiations carried out by Mme. de Hartmann, Gurdjieff first leased, then bought the Prieuré for 700,000 francs. But his hopes of immediate occupancy were frustrated, and it was not until October 1922, that he was able to move the caravanserel into his new headquarters.

The first English pupils found Gurdjieff temporarily established in Paris where he hired a house in Auteuil and used the Dalcroze Institute in the Rue de Vaugirard for teaching his movements. In August, James Young arrived to find the pupils occupied in making costumes for public performances which Gurdjieff planned to give. Metalworking, embroidery and shoemaking were some of the tasks imposed; and many of the new arrivals were strangers to any form of manual labor. As Young wrote, they suddenly had to pick up the techniques of several different handicrafts, "which meant overcoming one's awkwardness and diffidence, and some-times, be it confessed, one's indifference or even dislike. This work was carried on with feverish activity, and occupied, together with the exercises, thirteen or fourteen hours every day. The keynote was 'Overcome difficulties—Make effort—Work.' . . . You may imagine that this kind of communal work, together with misunderstandings that arose from language difficulties, called upon one's exercise of the virtues of self-remembering, non-identifying and non-considering to the utmost."

The Prieuré was fully furnished, except for the former servants' quarters, but had not been lived in since 1914. The advance party from Paris had the task of hacking the grounds into shape and renovating the inside of the building. "We weeded and trimmed up the almost indistinguishable paths," Young remembered, "washed all the glass of a large 'orangerie' or vinery, which afterwards became a workshop and smithy—and, in general, worked like demons." When the château and the grounds had been made more or less habitable, Gurdjieff and the main body of pupils arrived.

A peculiar prospectus was issued in French, entitled, *L'Institut du Développement Harmonique de l'Homme de G. Gurdjieff,* in which Ouspensky claimed to have had a hand. It began with an account of the expeditions of the Seekers for Truth in the Orient and of Gurdjieff's adventures while trying to establish himself in Russia. "The number of people interested in the basic ideas of the Institute," it claimed, "is clearly growing: there are not far off 5,000 members, scattered about throughout the world." Bechhofer Roberts, who visited Fontainebleau as an interested spectator, remarked that the numbers could safely be reduced to 500; and in fact, the inhabitants of the Institute numbered between sixty and seventy. At least half of these were Eastern Europeans; according to Young, "Russians, Armenians, Poles, Georgians, and even a Syrian." They kept themselves aloof, eating in their own dining room and separated for the most part from the English pupils by an impassable language barrier. Of the thirty-odd English residents, many are known by name. There were the doctors: Nicoll, Alcock, Young, and another psychoanalyst named Dr. Mary Bell; half a dozen Theosophically inclined ladies; Orage, Katherine Mansfield, and other literary converts like Rowland Kenney and Rosamund Sharp. There were a couple of civil servants, among them R. J. G. Mayor, and a diplomat or two. A larger floating population of weekend visitors included the faithful like J. G. Bennett, the intrigued like Clifford Sharp, and the merely inquisitive like Bechhofer Roberts. It should be emphasized that Gurdjieff's Institute—the achievement for which he is generally remembered—was a limited concern with a finite number of pupils, and that strict supervision was exercised over admission. For example, the skeptical psychical researcher, Dr. E. J. Dingwall, was refused access to Fontainebleau.

According to the prospectus, Gurdjieff accepted pupils of three categories: those who wished to undergo his educational program, those who merely wanted theoretical instruction, and those who were his patients in his capacity as physician-hypnotist. Gurdjieff later published a revised translation of parts of his prospectus—but with the idiom and the presentation somewhat altered. In the winter of 1922–23, he expressed himself in the style of the new psychology, in the tones of a prophet who would have been at home in Edwin Muir's Hellerau:

Because of the conditions of modern life, contemporary man has deviated from his original type; that is to say, from the type which should have been produced by the influence of his environment: the circumstances of the place, the surroundings and the culture in which he is born and grows up.
. . . instead of raising man completely to a new degree of development, civilization has encouraged the evolution of certain faculties at the expense of others, some of which have been utterly destroyed; . . .
Man has become an uprooted creature unable to adapt himself to life and alien to all the circumstances of his present existence.
This is what the psychological system of M. Gurdjieff asserts by means of *psycho-analysis,* showing by experiment that the world-picture of a modern man and its own effect on life are not the personal and voluntary expression of his entire being, but that on the contrary

are only the accidental and automatic manifestations of several parts of him.

The prospectus continued with a summary of Gurdjieff's doctrine of the three centers, but presented in a completely different way from the "occult" version familiar to readers of Ouspensky. Emphasis was placed on the fact that self-observation showed the centers to be uncoordinated, in perpetual conflict, and with different degrees of development. Man must bring his centers into a state of harmonious cooperation. Such a struggle could not be carried out alone, as its dangers demanded specialist instruction. *"It is indispensable,"* the prospectus concluded, *"to develop new faculties which are not given to man in life and which cannot be developed in him by general methods."*

Gurdjieff announced an elaborate program which he divided into theoretical, practical, and medical sections. The theoretical side was represented by an extensive series of lectures.

Science of *the harmonious development of man;* Psychology of man's inner development. Study of methods of knowledge and of the perfecting of the *I* according to the theories of European science and Oriental schools. Experiments and practical work. Application of the psychological method to different sciences; cosmological philosophy; universal mechanics. Science of relativity. Science of number. Science of Symbols. Astrophysics, mathematics, chemistry ancient and modern (alchemy); ancient medicine, modern Oriental medicine. Comparative study of religions. Mythology. Idolatry. Ancient esoteric schools and modern Oriental schools. Psychology of art. Ancient and modern philosophy.

The practical section comprised "harmonic rhythm," "special exercises for the development of memory, will, concentration of thought, perception, etc."; "Music, song, modelling, Oriental dances (sacred), drawing, painting, sculpture"; "Trades and applied arts—agriculture, horticulture, market-gardening; languages." It was added that "the teaching and the practice of all these subjects is carried out according to *special* methods."

Under the 'medical section' were listed an extraordinary number of "therapies," including "hydrotherapy," "phototherapy," "electrotherapy," "magnetotherapy," "psychotherapy," "dietotherapy," and something called "duliotherapy." Gurdjieff also proclaimed that the Institute contained "physico-metric," "chemico-analytic" and "psycho-experimental" cabinets. What these were was anybody's guess, but presumably they were part of the well-equipped medical department of the Institute which the prospectus announced side by side with a Journal of the Institute, "printed in appropriate characters." As Bechhofer Roberts observed in 1924, the "cabinets" had no visible existence, and the "Medical Section" was confined to "a few pieces of electrical apparatus of ordinary type."

Some of the claims in the prospectus could be justified as being allegorical. One of Gurdjieff's followers has explained "duliotherapy" as being "slave-therapy;" that is, the total submission to the will of the Master. No doubt the various "cabinets" could be similarly explained—and even the Journal "printed in appropriate characters." But it is difficult to explain away the oddest part of Gurdjieff's prospectus: the "Individual Histometric Record" designed for "patients" who were engaged on practical work on themselves, and were following a program laid down for them individually. This strange document consists of a series of blank forms on which various medical and psychological particulars were supposed to be entered. On the bottom of each page is the rubric: "For the terminology of schematic and conventional expressions see the special instructors' manual."

As far as is known, the elaborate "Record" was never used. This does not necessarily mean that it was mere window dressing—although, of course, it is quite probable that Gurdjieff was simply trying to blind the intellectuals of the West with their own science. Few detailed medical examinations ever seem to have taken place; but the divisions which the form distinguishes bear a definite resemblance to stages through which a pupil might pass under Gurdjieff's supervision. A preliminary assessment, then a two-month period of observation, during which the pupil would be switched rapidly from task to task in order to determine his problems and capacities; a revised assessment based on how the pupil behaved during the period of probation; and a definite recommendation from Gurdjieff of a particular line of work. It is interesting that the course was conceived in terms of nine months—the period of gestation, which also corresponds to the points on Gurdjieff's enneagram. It may be that the Record was never used because it was intended for pupils following an individual program— and that Gurdjieff never proceeded beyond the collective methods which he found necessary for large numbers of people. As he told Maurice Nicoll, he saw the Institute as "a hatching place for eggs. It supplies the heat. Chicken inside must try to break shell, then help and individual teaching possible. Until then only collective method."

The collective method included intense application to manual tasks. Building and carpentry—at both of which Gurdjieff excelled—were perpetually in progress. Gardening proceeded from morning to night; and if no work was needed, it was manufactured. When Professor Denis Saurat, head of the Institut Français in London, came to visit Orage, he found that his friend had been made to dig an extensive ditch in the garden—but almost at once was directed to fill it in. The pupils did the housework, made costumes for the dances, and took their turn at the onerous duty of "kitchen-boy" for which the incumbent had to rise at 5 A.M. and be responsible for feeding the entire community. A Russian bath was constructed, with steamroom, hot-room and cold-room; and during most of the first winter at the Prieuré, the pupils were occupied in erecting the building in the Institute gardens which was afterward known as the Study House. This construction was based on an old aircraft hangar which Gurdjieff had bought from the French army and which, in the fashion of the day, James Young calls an "aerodrome":

> The walls were lined within and without between the uprights with rough laths. The space between the laths was stuffed with dead leaves. The laths were then covered over inside and out with . . . a mixture of mud and straw, or hay chopped very small. Stoves were then put in the building and the walls dried and hardened before painting them. The roof was made of tarred felt nailed on to the joists; glass extended all the way round the upper half of the walls. This glazing was improvized from cucumber frames—a really good piece of work. After these had been fixed in position the glass was painted with various designs. The lighting effect was very pleasing. The floor, which was the naked earth pounded thoroughly and rolled, and dried by means of the stoves, was covered with matting, on which were placed handsome carpets; the walls below the windows were hung with rugs in the Oriental fashion. . . .
>
> Sometimes . . . Gurdjieff would have us out to work at the building until two or three in the morning with the aid of big electric lamps hanging from the rafters. . . . Everything was arranged, or rather disarranged, so that nobody should be allowed to fall into a routine. . . . For a week at a time we would not have more than three or four hours sleep at night, and sometimes even only one. My hands were often so stiff in the morning from digging or pick-axeing or barrowing or sawing or felling trees that the fingers exhibited the phenomenon which is known surgically as "snap-finger"; when one had coaxed them to a certain point they suddenly straightened out with a kind of snap. Every night in the study-house people would fall asleep during the mental exercises.

On one occasion a pupil who had been working on the Study House roof fell asleep between two beams, and only prompt action by Gurdjieff prevented a tragedy. It was small wonder that the day at the Institute began at eight or nine o'clock in the morning. "This may sound a fairly late hour for so monastic an institution," Bechhofer Roberts admitted, "but you must remember that they probably went to sleep only about four or five o'clock. It is one of Gurdjieff's doctrines that out of the seven or eight hours sleep of the normal man half are wasted in the process of 'falling asleep,' whereas the only period that matters is passed in 'deep sleep.' This last can be gained equally by spending less time abed and being more prepared to fall quickly into it from fatigue." Pupils sometimes slept four to a room, on mattresses on the floor, with no comforts—and to many of the English pupils this was unheard-of privation. Until noon there was work: in the house, with the farm animals—cows, goats, sheep, pigs and poultry—which were acquired, or in the grounds. At noon there was a meal consisting usually of bread and soup, a spare diet which greatly shocked most of the English arrivals, and which, a *Daily News* reporter complained, "an English working man would scorn."

After the meal and a short rest, the pupils returned to work for the afternoon. In the early evening, they had some time to themselves before gathering at nine or ten o'clock, occasionally for a session of questions and answers held by Gurdjieff, but mostly for instruction in his movements. At first these classes were held in the salon of the château, but after the completion of the Study House that building became the center of the most eye-catching aspect of Gurdjieff's teaching.

The Study House could hold some 300 people. Gurdjieff decorated it in a style probably based on a dervish *tekke*. Immediately in front of the stage stood a fountain which was illuminated during performances. Facing the stage at the far end of the Study House was a curtained booth in which Gurdjieff could sit partially concealed. On the balcony above hung a collection of musical instruments. Around the walls ran a continuous low divan covered with Oriental carpets on which the pupils sat to watch the others perform—men on one side and women on the other. The audience was separated from the central area of the Study House by a gangway and a low wooden railing. Above them, the ceiling was covered in swathes of material decorated by de Salzmann with a pattern in which the enneagram occupied a central position. Around the eaves of the building Gurdjieff placed a series of texts written in a peculiar script: "Here one can only direct and create conditions but not help," one ran; again: "We can only strive to be able to be Christians"; or, "Remember that work here is not for work's sake but a means."

It was the Study House which visitors remembered, whether those who came from Fontainebleau to attend demonstrations of the movements, or the interested spectators from England who were trying to learn more

about Gurdjieff's work. In February 1923, a *Daily News* reporter interviewed Gurdjieff in the Study House and found him uncharacteristically
explicit about the purpose of the exotic surroundings.

> The Study-House is not yet complete, gorgeous as is the interior.
> Gurdjieff told me that he is having built a special organ, unique in
> Europe, with the octaves in quarter tones.
>
> Much also remains to be done in other parts of the House. Soon the
> fountain will diffuse a different perfume for every hour, and other
> fountains are yet to be installed.
>
> By this elaborate combination of appeals to the senses, Gurdjieff
> believes he is providing so many aids to meditation.
>
> "The senses should be gently distracted," he said, "and then the
> mind itself untrammeled by the senses is free to work. Only by such
> means can it be brought into the way of harmonious development
> together with the body and with the emotions."

By this time it was clear that Gurdjieff's "dances" could be divided into
three groups. There were the dances, rituals, and fragments of traditional
lore which he claimed to have collected during his Eastern travels; then
there were some broadly dramatic interpretations like the one called the
"Initiation of the Priestess"; the third category of "movements" or exercises
was based on the principle of keeping the various "centres" working at full
stretch. James Young compared the effect of such exhausting undertakings
to the children's game in which you try to pat the top of the head at the
same time as rubbing the stomach with a circular motion. "The will finds it
difficult," he remarked, "to combine two such unaccustomed movements
and to keep them clear-cut and regular at the same time. The exercises
were mostly devised on these lines, and some of them required the
combination of four different movements, each of which had its own distinct
rhythm. To attempt these exercises involved great strain, and to continue
for any length of time was very fatiguing."

It was not the body alone which was exercised in this way. Some of the
movements were governed by complex counting exercises which the pupils
had to perform in order to keep in time with the others. The exercise
described by Ouspensky which entailed the repetition of a series of "Oms"
is one example; although Gurdjieff could be much more adroit in devising
aids to mental agility. As purely mental exercises, he would make pupils
learn Morse Code, or memorize lists of Tibetan words, or expect them to
know the script in which his texts were written on the Study House roof.
They were also compelled to learn an arithmetic where all the laws were
distorted. "A series of statements was made," James Young remembered,

"such as $2 \times 1 = 6$, $2 \times 2 = 12$, $2 \times 3 = 22$, $2 \times 4 = 40$, $2 \times 5 = 74$. Find the process by which these results are arrived at. In this case, to the first product 4 is added, to the next 8, to the next 16, and so on." Operations of this sort determined the movements of individual dancers who were thus forced to exercise both mental and physical "centres" simultaneously.

"No great value was attached to these things in themselves," Young wrote of the mental exercises. "The value lay in the amount of effort expended on them." But did the dances in fact transcend this limited goal of "making effort"? To some it seemed not merely that they had a validity in themselves—as an "artistic" achievement—but that in some way they aligned the pupil with the harmonies of the universe. A writer who has taken part in Gurdjieff's movements has explained this in terms of what seems a very strange coincidence. As well as the mental exercises and the physical movements, Gurdjieff would give a subject for meditation: an exercise for the "emotional centre." Once, this particular pupil was being instructed in a movement for which the meditation had not yet been given. Quite unbidden, there overcame her a feeling of extraordinary regret that her relationship with her mother had not been one of greater understanding. Then the instructor gave the subject for meditation: "the grief we have caused our parents" . . .

Yet Gurdjieff often gave only the bare bones of a movement and left his senior pupils to work out his intentions.* The same was true of the music, which was interpreted by Thomas de Hartmann from Gurdjieff's skeletal indications of melody, rhythm, and harmony. But the music, too—played either by de Hartmann or by Gurdjieff himself on his hand-operated portable organ—has been experienced as the music of the spheres: people have claimed that Gurdjieff's "Temple Music"—resembling plainsong—can provoke precise reactions in its hearers. In 1927 Carl Zigrosser visited Fontainbleau and later described the effect which the music had on him. "Usually," he wrote, "music prompts me to day-dreams and lovely fancies . . . this music did not carry me out of myself at all; it centered its effect upon my very essence, it appealed directly to my emotions. It sang as if it had a message for me alone in the world—yet others have since told me that they had precisely the same feeling. It aroused in me at will the feelings of joy, pity, sorrow, fear, struggle, and above all an exquisite yet terrible yearning . . ." However it must be said that at least to one music critic sympathetic to the Work, the Gurdjieff-de Hartmann music has very little to recommend it; and far from lifting the mind to a higher plane, anchors it

*This fact has recently been made the basis of a defense in a lawsuit between Gurdjieff's family and those who carry on his work. If Gurdjieff gave only indications of a completed movement, it was argued, can he be said to have any proprietary rights over the finished article?

firmly in the late nineteenth-century tradition influenced by Scriabin. It is certainly instructive to compare the pieces based on Oriental themes with those of de Hartmann's contemporaries—such as Dvořák—who devoted a less "esoteric" touch to compositions based on folk motifs.

To many of those who have taken part in Gurdjieff's movements, they and the music together provide the key to his teaching. Even those who were merely spectators have been transfixed. In November 1922, Katherine Mansfield described a dance of some seven minutes duration: "it contains the whole life of woman," she wrote to her husband,"—but everything! Nothing is left out. It taught me, it gave me more of woman's life than any book or poem. There was even room for Flaubert's *Coeur Simple* in it, and for the Princess Marya . . . Mysterious."

The Prieuré was a house of meanings, isolated from the surrounding world by a wall and a philosophy of detachment. To the village of Avon the inmates seemed to be a collection of millionaire neurasthenics and, apart from the tradesmen, they dismissed the Institute as a *maison des fous*. On Saturday evenings, Gurdjieff held public performances of his movements and could often count on an audience drawn by curiosity. But he attracted no real interest from the local community or the town of Fontainebleau. Sometimes the Mayor or the Prefect of Police would be lavishly entertained at one of Gurdjieff's Oriental banquets—the Master was always concerned to keep on good terms with the authorities—but in general, the house and its inhabitants were cut off from the outside world. When a new arrival approached the little gatehouse of the Prieuré and tugged at the bell-pull labeled "*Sonnez fort*," he was deliberately leaving one attitude to life for another. "I cannot develop you," said Gurdjieff. "I can only create the conditions for you to develop yourself." Upon the pupil's ability to adopt a new attitude to his experiences depended his vision of the Prieuré.

To put into words what a pupil felt went on at the Prieuré is difficult. The proximity of the Master gave an extra charge to the atmosphere, an added intensity of perception, and when coupled with the teaching of self-observation, might indeed be said to raise the consciousness of the pupils in the sense of making them more aware of their functioning as human machines. There was *meaning* in everything, particularly in one's own reaction—if the dancing of a mechanical toy could be called its own—to unusual situations, hard work, and extraordinarily complicated exercises. From the moment of entrance into the community, conditions were arranged so as to grate against a pupil's "mechanism." Maurice Nicoll was forbidden to read; another pupil who could not bear the sight of blood was given the task of slaughtering animals for food. And the most humdrum situation—which in ordinary life would have been ignored or accepted—could provide material out of which to build new meanings. Dislikes to be overcome, pettiness borne in silence, one's own worst impulses encountered face to face; every event of the day provided material for "work on oneself."

This was what Gurdjieff meant by his catchword, "intentional suffering"—voluntarily opening the psyche to those aspects which it would rather have forgotten or glossed over. "One suffers terribly," Katherine Mansfield wrote to Murry, " . . . it takes very severe measures to put one right. But the point is there is hope. One can and does believe that one will escape from living in circles and will live a CONSCIOUS life. One can, through work, escape from falsity and be true to one's own self—not to what anyone else on earth thinks it is."

Self-observation has been defined by one of Gurdjieff's followers as doing everything "as if God were watching." The activity was undoubtedly easier in the presence of God's deputy, the ever-present, awful Mr. Gurdjieff. A sober British businessman attended a demonstration in the Study House and found himself inspected by the Master. "During the performance I was confronted by Gurdjieff himself; and for one whole minute I felt myself examined and alone. All this sounds fanciful as I record it, but at the time it was a unique experience." At the same time as forcing his pupils to self-examination, Gurdjieff's mercurial changes of character baffled those who had first come in contact with the more straightforward Ouspensky. "I have seen him perform marvels," wrote Rowland Kenney, "I have known him to act like a petulant, spoilt child."

Gurdjieff was everywhere and all-powerful. He delegated the classes in movements to younger pupils, and his personal staff—the de Salzmanns, de Hartmanns and Dr. Stoerneval—acted as his deputies. Yet he did so much himself that accounts of the Institute often leave as their chief impression that of its director's manic activity. When in late December 1922, there was a fire in the Prieuré which burned out two of the rooms, Katherine Mansfield described to Murry how Gurdjieff had appeared in the midst of the chaos with a hammer, knocking down the burning wall. In February 1923, Denis Saurat watched him trying valiantly to save a burst boiler by bombarding it with lumps of clay which might plug the crack in its side. Besides these feats of inspired improvisation, Gurdjieff supervised the building projects, interviewed pupils personally, and at any moment might appear in the house or gardens encouraging the workers to "super-efforts" with cries of "Skorry!" "Queeker!" He spared no one and might rouse the whole household in the early hours of the morning to perform some newly devised task.

Gurdjieff's remarkable abilities, his ubiquitousness, and his methods of confusion gave rise to feelings of dependence which were more than a little superstitious. *Everything* was intentional, *all* difficulties were manufactured. Some pupils like James Young remained immune from the infection, and Maurice Nicoll wondered "whether the difficulties Gurdjieff knows he creates are equal in value for work with those he does not know he creates." Yet to many otherwise intelligent men and women the Master was little short of divine, and no doubt the presence of a large Theosophical element among his followers encouraged the less strong willed to couple Gurdjieff's name with those of Himalayan Mahatmas. An account of the Prieuré which Maud Hoffman published in the *New York Times* in February 1924 is so studded with enthusiastic expressions—"luxurious," "heavenly," "beautiful," and the rest—that an inquirer might feel justified in believing the worst.

Such reactions have been responsible for much of the hostile criticism which Gurdjieff encountered. When a man's powers have been exalted to the skies, when his too *schwärmerisch* supporters insist on viewing him through rose-colored glasses, critics who decide that he does not live up to the image created by the faithful are likely to be virulent. Partly this was the fault of Gurdjieff's sillier followers; but partly, also, it was a danger of his method. In 1924, Bechhofer Roberts satirized the reactions of some of the over hopeful:

> I used to hear what a wonderful worker Gurdjieff was. Rapt disciples told me with bated breath of the abnormal speed and skill with which he built paths, for example, or sawed wood, laid bricks and designed ovens and even a kippering-kiln. But recenly I have noticed an element of doubt in these accounts. The paths wear badly, the walls crack, the ovens do not function and the kiln no longer kippers. Is it possible that Gurdjieff is not the super-artisan he is supposed to be?
>
> Perhaps; but there is also another explanation for these mischances, which has often been put forward by the editor [Orage].
>
> "It is a test," he declares, explaining that Gurdjieff could, of course, do it all much better if he wished, but he is anxious to test the faith and devotion of his pupils.

In such an atmosphere it was difficult to make any balanced assessment of Gurdjieff. His rages might very well be a "test"—and more than one person has reported that Gurdjieff might abruptly switch off a flow of abuse and turn to wink at a bystander—but equally they could be real. A complete outsider might fail to grasp that anything apart from the obvious was happening at all. Or if he sensed something . . . *below the surface* . . . he felt shut out, deprived, the butt of a private joke. The businessman who had been "examined" by Gurdjieff in the Study House "felt like an outsider; like a visitor to a sanatorium." The feeling of exclusion might grow until

Gurdjieff's influence over his pupils appeared sinister and potentially harmful: the hypnotized sheep of a Black Magician. Eventually some of the pupils themselves would begin to wonder . . . and this was an effect which did not displease Gurdjieff. "Do you know," asked Denis Saurat, "that some of your disciples are close to despair?" "Yes," Gurdjieff replied, "there's something sinister in this house, and that is necessary."

The contradictory nature of the Institute could be caught in a visit of a single weekend. One pupil who arrived from Ouspensky's London group had her first glimpse of Gurdjieff in the Study House directing the movements. The pupils had to hold their arms outstretched parallel with the ground; hold them steady for several minutes, hold them, HOLD THEM — and the brutal taskmaster did not let the poor creatures relax their taut muscles until the nerves of the visitor from London were screaming their own protest, and her anger at the director of this torture chamber burst into a smouldering rage. The next morning the visitor was gathering wood in the garden when she suddenly felt the presence of someone behind her. It was Gurdjieff, who smiled—not just charmingly, but kindly, with his eyes—as he wished her good morning. She had the sensation of being confronted by two different creatures—or were they merely two aspects of the same man, whose ability to don masks at will or to mobilize functions of the human being to order, began to edge her mind toward a new comprehension of what the individual might do to become his own master?

What was going on? It took several highly intelligent men many months to discover, and in some cases to resolve their perplexity. During the construction of the Study House, Maurice Nicoll asked Gurdjieff why he did not build more solidly. Gurdjieff replied: "This is only temporary. In a very short time everything will be different. Everyone will be elsewhere. Nothing can be built permanently at this moment." Then why the whole elaborate structure of an Institute, why the publicity which Gurdjieff seemed increasingly to seek? The answers to these questions can only be suggested in terms of individual pupils who stayed at Fontainebleau. The nature of Gurdjieff's Institute cannot really be conveyed in generalities, because it dealt in specifics.

"For some of us the building is a temple; for others a theatre," the *Daily News* reporter was told by a Russian who showed him the Study House. "Some of us meditate; others dream, and many worship, but we all learn." The Institute, like its Master, is sometimes scarcely visible: now a palace, now a pigsty; sometimes an elegant château infested by a crew of intellectual riffraff, sometimes a spiritual Neuschwanstein or Fonthill, crowned with pinnacles and battlements which disappear into the mist. Materializing out of the beyond, Gurdjieff and his magic castle were somehow waiting—for particular individuals faced with particular problems. You could ring the bell of the Prieuré and enter with no particular commitment; but if you stayed you became—for a time at least— "entangled."

CASE: *Katherine Mansfield.*   PROBLEMS: *A surfeit of "life," dissatisfaction with human relationships, consciousness of an inevitably approaching death.*

On Friday, 13, October 1922, Katherine Mansfield reached Paris with her devoted companion, Ida Baker. She was still undecided whether or not to go to Fontainebleau and still concealing from Middleton Murry the real purpose of her flight to France. She took rooms in a hotel in the Place de la Sorbonne and wrote as cheerfully as she could to Murry at Selsfield, encouraging him to enjoy the pleasures of human companionship and living with wealthy friends. Yet on the very day of her arrival, she had confided to her journal that she and Murry were "no longer together"—but was she now "in the right way"? Her answer is based on a self-analysis according to Ouspensky's teaching of the "many I's." "No, not yet. . . . I feel a bit of a sham . . . And so I am. One of the K.M.'s is so sorry. But of course she is. She has to die. *Don't* feed her." Her physical distress had produced an inability to work; and gradually the cultivation of the "I" which wanted to go to Gurdjieff produced a conscious decision. This was still bound up with her hopes of a physical cure, and she wrote to Murry:

> I am going to Fontainebleau next week to see Gurdjieff. I will tell you about it. Why am I going? From all I hear he is the only man who understands there is no division between body and spirit, who believes how they are related. You remember how I have always said doctors only treat *half*. And you have replied: "It's up to you to do the rest." It is. That's true. But first I must learn how. I believe Gurdjieff can teach me.

Next day was her birthday and she replied to Murry's invitation to join him at Selsfield. "I do think Selsfield sounds perfect, but it's no good my coming there while I am a creeping worm. When I can fly I will come . . ." Flying meant being "conscious of a purpose," refusing to live life mechanically "just as the pendulum swings." Her old striving for experience now appeared only the manifestation of unconscious, mechanical existence.

That day F. S. Pinder arrived to see her with James Young, who had come up from Fontainebleau to meet Orage off the boat-train. He gave her a medical examination—probably at the insistence of Gurdjieff, who had

had a private letter from K. M.'s own doctor advising him to turn her down as a pupil. "He spent a couple of hours with me, talking about Gurdjieff and the Institute. If I were to write it all to you," she informed Murry, "it sounds fabulous and other-worldly. I shall wait until I've *seen* it. I still hope to go on Monday and I'll take a toothbrush and *peigne* and come back on Wednesday morning, only."

This was equivocation; for she was at last clear in her own mind. On the same day she made a lengthy entry in her journal, to try and organize her thoughts. "Ever since I came to Paris I have been as ill as ever. In fact, yesterday I thought I was dying. It is not imagination. My heart is so exhausted and so tied up that I can only walk to the taxi and back. I get up at *midi* and go to bed at 5:30. I try to 'work' by fits and starts, but the time has gone by." She faced the fact that she lived the "life of a corpse," and that she was still "an absolutely hopeless invalid." "What is my life?" she asked herself, and answered: "It is the existence of a parasite." Then out of her misery burst a cry from the inner depths. "I am so terrified of what I am going to do."

"Why hesitate?" she demanded. Was it not because she feared to lose Murry? But what was their relationship anyway? Murry knew her only as a dream—a dream of the day when she would be better. "Therefore," she encouraged herself, "if the Grand Lama of Thibet promised to help you— how can you hesitate? Risk! Risk anything! Care no more for the opinions of others, for those voices. Do the hardest thing on earth for you. Act for yourself. Face the truth." At first she decided that she would send her conclusions to Murry and tore the pages from her journal, adding phrases to reassure him. "And when I say 'I fear'—don't let it disturb you, dearest heart. We all fear when we are in waiting-rooms. Yet we must pass beyond them . . ."

On the seventeenth, K. M. took what she called "my first Leap in the Dark." She and Ida Baker traveled to Fontainebleau where they were met by James Young and installed in a temporary room. From afar Katherine Mansfield observed the Master. "He looks exactly like a desert chief. I kept thinking of Doughty's *Arabia*." Next day she was moved to 'the Ritz' and it was decided that she could stay for a fortnight under observation. Gurdjieff himself was fully occupied with the preliminary organization of the Institute and had only time for a few words spoken through an interpreter. "Mr. Gurdjieff is not in the least what I expected," she told Murry. "He's what one wants to find him, really. But I do feel *absolutely confident* he can put me on the right track in every way, bodily and t'other governor." She was very well looked after. "I have a lovely sumptuous room—a kind of glorified Garsington—for the fortnight. As for the food, it's like a Gogol feast." The day following—Thursday, October 19—Ida Baker made her escape in a state which she described as "emotional centres entirely out of control." She had been K. M.s last link with her old life, and on the day of her departure, K. M. wrote to S. S. Koteliansky of her own "private revolution." She had moved from the world of ordinary life into Gurdjieff's realm. Probably she had long ago abandoned any real hope of a physical cure. But if Prospero could not raise Miranda from the dead, he might be able to *wake her up*.

The world as I know it is no joy to me and I am useless in it. People are almost non-existent. This world to me is a dream and the people in it are sleepers. I have known just instances of waking but that is all. I want to find a world in which these instances are united. Shall I succeed? I do not know.

In contrast to the ordinary world, immersed in its dreams, life within the walls of the Prieuré was more intense than she had ever known it. "One has, all the time," she wrote to Murry on October 20, "the feeling of having been in a wreck and by the mercy of Providence got ashore . . . somewhere. Simply everything is different. Not only language, but food, ways, people, music, methods, hours—*all*. It's a real new life." At first she was officially on her fortnight's probation, and because her physical condition prohibited any great exertion, Gurdjieff instructed her to observe the other pupils at work. She surveyed the trench digging in the garden, watched Gurdjieff and de Salzmann perform expertly in the carpenter's shop, and sat amid the turmoil of the kitchen while the cooks clattered utensils and sang, Gurdjieff and a dog intervened to complicate the action, and "at least 20 pots" bubbled on the stove.

Gradually she was drawn into a more active role. She studied rug making, looked after the indoor flowers, learned Russian, and watched the movements classes in the salon where she also took part in Gurdjieff's counting exercises. "In fact, at 34 I am beginning my education," she informed Murry in late November; and then, ruefully, when faced with the prospect of making costumes for Gurdjieff's projected demonstrations: "All the things I have avoided in life seem to find me out here." She recorded external events for Murry's benefit, but despaired of conveying their interior content. "I cannot express myself in writing just now," she admitted on October 27. "The old mechanism isn't mine any longer, and I can't control the new." Literary ambitions occasionally resurfaced—but always in the distant future, when she should be fit to write.

Her relationship with her husband—conducted entirely through their letters—veered wildly around every point of the emotional compass as K. M. tried to come to terms with the questions posed by life at

Fontainebleau, and Middleton Murry in England attempted to define his own attitude to the life she was attempting to lead. On October 27, she suggested that Murry invite Ouspensky to dinner; then came an exhortation: "Suppose you throw up every single job in England, realize your capital, and come over here to work for Gurdjieff. Burn every single boat for once!" Next day she wrote severely about the lack of a real relationship between them; there existed only "the possibility" of a relationship. But by November 2, this was retracted in a fit of remorse, as she insisted that she was dramatizing the existence at Fontainebleau. Five days later the sense of living outside the world had returned. "In three weeks here I feel I have spent years in India, Arabia, Afghanistan, Persia . . . And how one wanted to voyage like this . . ." Part of the extraordinary atmosphere was produced by the intensity of personal contact between the inmates of the colony. She was irritated by "some of the English, 'arty' and theosophical people," but enthused over the "truly wonderful" "advanced men and women" and wrote telling Murry of her encounters with the de Salzmanns, the de Hartmanns and "Olgivanna"—Olga Ivanovna Lazovich Milanov Hinzenburg, who had joined Gurdjieff in Tiflis as a society lady with a houseful of servants and now found herself cleaning out her Master's pigs. "Friendship. The real thing that you and I have dreamed of. Here it exists . . ." By mid-November, Murry was becoming concerned that his wife was "hypnotised." She replied trying to explain her situation.

> Dear Bogey, I'm not "hypnotized." But it does seem to me there are certain people here who are far beyond any I have met—of a quite different order. Some—most—of the English here don't even catch a glimpse of it. But I am sure. I remember I used to think—if there was one thing I could not bear in a community, it would be the women. But now the women are nearer and far dearer than the men. Of course, I don't speak of Mr. Gurdjieff. I couldn't say he was *near* or *dear* to me! He is the embodiment of the life here, but at a remote distance.

Toward the end of November, Murry became irritated by the luxury of Selsfield. He decided to try and find a cottage to share with J.W.N. Sullivan, whose wife had left him after the couple had become entangled with Aleister Crowley the previous year. He and Sullivan drifted closer to Millar Dunning and began to look for a cottage near the artist's colony in the village of Ditchling where, besides Dunning, Eric Gill and his Guild of Craftsmen had settled.

Dunning was a mystic in a Whitmanesque mould. His one published volume, *The Earth Spirit* (1920), contains a series of meditations on natural landscapes interspersed with prophecies of a coming New Age. For Murry,

Dunning's importance was that he practiced Raja-yoga and provided some practical discipline which could be seen as a counterpart to the austerities which K. M. was undergoing at the Prieuré. On December 9, Katherine Mansfield wrote to her husband about a conversation she had had with Alexander de Salzmann on poverty of spirit—"To be poor in ideas, in imagination, in impulses, in wishes—to be simple, in fact." "I hope you will meet this man one day," she wrote; and Murry replied from Ditchling:

> . . . if you have your Salzmanns, whom I should dearly love to know, I have my Dunnings, whom I would dearly love you to know. And every letter of yours that I get makes me feel more than ever that we are marching along parallel paths—parallel paths which converge, and that the day is not so terribly far distant when we shall be ready for one another.

Despite K. M.'s earlier attempts at proselytizing, Murry's new occult interests rang a little strangely in her ears. At the end of November she wrote that she was glad that he was going to live near Dunning. But had he not been joking when he told her that the Prieuré might be "his Way"? "One can only come here *via* Ouspensky," she warned, "*and it is a serious step.*" Before Christmas she had accepted "your Dunnings" and Murry's aspirations. But her first reaction had been based on a surer knowledge of her husband, whose devotion to yoga proved a temporary phase. Under Dunning's tuition he experienced a vision of the *crux ansata*, but was left unmoved on being told that it was a symbol of immortality. In a fit of revulsion he abandoned all mystical practices.

He had wanted to spend Christmas with his wife at Fontainebleau, but she hastened to put him off. The hotels in the town would be closed, and the Institute itself was still in chaos, so he could not stay as a guest. She herself had been moved from "the Ritz" into a tiny room in the Monks' Corridor which she shared with Olgivanna. Her letters tread a wary path between trying to give Murry a true picture of the discomforts of her life— that first winter the cold was intense and fuel was scarce—and continuing to communicate the benefits which she felt she derived from her stay. She explained that her change of room was part of Gurdjieff's discipline: "It is a favourite habit of his to set the whole house walking. Easy to see why when one saw the emotions it aroused." But her exile from "the Ritz" lasted only for a month. On December 17, she wrote that the room had taught her "to rough it in a way you and I have never done," and continued in amazement: "But how did Mr. Gurdjieff know how much I needed that experience?" What was more, just as she felt that she had learned her lesson and was plunging into real despair, Gurdjieff himself had appeared with words of comfort and ordered her back to "the Ritz." "Sometimes I wonder if we 'make up' Mr. Gurdjieff's wonderful understanding. But one is always getting a fresh example of it. And he always acts at precisely the moment one needs it. That is what is so strange . . ."

Gurdjieff had directed a balcony to be built for his invalid pupil above the animals—three cows and a mule—in the cowshed of the Institute. On this balcony, Katherine Mansfield now spent the day lying on a divan, receiving visits from her friends and watching the cows being milked. What was the reason for this strange régime? Animal magnetism? The smell of manure? Because Indian medicine recommends the breath of cows—those bacillus-carrying animals—as a specific for tuberculosis? All these possibilities have been suggested; but not the simplest one. It had been clear to Ouspensky (and would have been even clearer to Gurdjieff, with his greater medical knowledge), that Katherine Mansfield had not long to live. Gurdjieff had agreed to admit her to his community; but although she was in need of spiritual help as well as physical, her invalid condition disqualified her from full participation. Her everyday contact with other people provided an opportunity to "work on the emotions"; but in Gurdjieff's opinion, she probably needed, as much as the latter, to regain contact with the soil and her body. She had herself felt the need to learn to look after animals, though a view from the stable balcony was as much as could be managed.

Her gallery was decorated by de Salzmann with caricatures of members of the Institute, camouflaged as birds and beasts. The canopy above was painted with suns, moons, and stars edged in red and blue. After K. M.'s death, critics singled out the apparently grotesque circumstances of her last days. Her friends at the Institute reacted by stressing how happy she had been. Some of their reports are overreactions to criticism of the "Gurdjieff killed Katherine Mansfield" variety; but it seems certain from the accounts of Olgivanna and the young Lithuanian, Adele Kafian, that the dying woman was indeed determined to find "sermons in stones and good in everything." At the same time there is an undertone of sorrow, masked a little by the festivities of Christmas which was celebrated with Gurdjieff's customary exuberance.

On December 23, Murry was told of Gurdjieff's decision that, "although there are so few of them," the English should celebrate Christmas on the twenty-fifth and not wait until the Russian Christmas in the New Year. At the Master's expense they were to invite the Russians to a feast. "And he has given us a sheep, a pig, two turkeys, a goose, two barrels of wine, whiskey, gin, cognac, etc., desserts of all kinds, an immense tree and carte blanche with which to decorate it." K. M. felt compelled to watch the slaughter of the animals for food. "I attended the obsequies of the pig this morning. I thought I had better go through with it for once and see for myself. One felt horribly sad . . . And yesterday I watched Madame Ouspensky pluck, singe and draw our birds. In fact these have been gory days, balanced by the fairy-like tree. There is so much life here that one feels no more than one little cell in a beefsteak, say. It is a good feeling."

Katherine Mansfield took part in the Christmas celebrations and watched the distribution of presents to the children of the community—always a high point in Gurdjieff's year. On her return to her room, she discovered that Adele Kafian had arranged a private Christmas tree which she had dug up in the forest. On it were burning three candles, which she had lit to symbolize herself, her friend, and Middleton Murry. The two friends sat "in silence"—in Adele's words—"looking at our Christmas tree. One candle burnt badly, it flickered and began to go out.—'That's me,' she whispered. No, No! I jumped up and put the others out first. This was her last Christmas tree. I did not know then the superstition about three candles."

At least half-consciously anticipating her death, K. M. wrote again to Middleton Murry on Boxing Day. She felt her letter to be "flat and dull," but it gives the impression of a report from some far outpost of the world—a strange place where she drank *koumiss* on her gallery while discussing astrology or watching Gurdjieff milk a goat in Arab fashion by securing its hind legs across his knees with an unbreakable grip. Somehow her experiences had produced in her an attitude of faith.

> . . . If I were allowed one single cry to God, that cry would be: *I want to be* REAL. Until I am that I don't see why I shouldn't be at the mercy of the old Eve in her various manifestations for ever.
>
> But this place has taught me so far how unreal I am. It has taken from me one thing after another (the things never were mine) until at this present moment all I know really, really is that I am not annihilated and that I hope—more than hope—believe.

It was the final letter to Murry in which she described the life of the community at Fontainebleau. Her last letter of all concerns Murry's traveling arrangements. Gurdjieff had agreed that he should come to stay for a week in January; a week which was to include the opening of the Study House on the thirteenth—the Russian New Year. K. M. waited in growing excitement for the visit to take place; and shortly before Murry arrived, she made a breakthrough which was to present her husband with a more complete person than he had previously known.

Orage recorded the nature of this breakthrough in his article, "Talks with Katherine Mansfield," which he wrote the following year. He remembered how often during their first months at the Institute he and K. M. had discussed the strange phenomenon of their vanished interest in literature.

"'What has come over us?' she would ask whimsically. 'Are we dead? Or was our love of literature an affectation, which has now dropped off like a mask?'" Occasionally he had been shown a fragment of some work in progress—which was always torn up before completion. Then very near the end, Katherine Mansfield sent for her old editor and confided to him a revelatory insight: she had discovered that a new approach to literature was possible. In his account, Orage is careful not to use Gurdjieff's terminology; but it obviously underlies the whole essay, and it was almost certainly in the language of the System that Katherine Mansfield expressed her aspirations. Her former attitude to writing had been the mechanical reaction of certain "I's." Now she proposed something new.

> I'm aware . . . of a recent change of attitude in myself: and at once not only my old stories have come to look different to me, but life itself looks different. I could not write my old stories again, or any more like them: and not because I do not see the same detail as before, but because somehow or other the pattern is different. The old details now make another pattern; and this perception of a new pattern is what I call a creative attitude towards life.

She had reached a certain stage in the *process*—and suddenly new meanings had fallen into place like the tumblers in a lock. *There were other ways of dividing up the world.* The details of how she proposed to apply her new discovery are not encouraging; she wanted, for example, to use the subtlety with which she had previously poked fun at human failings to depict a hero and heroine overtopping each other's bids in a contest of love. But the nature of her insight is much more important than its consequences. She had integrated the newfound faith of which she had written to Middleton Murry with the intellectual demands of her profession; and at last head and heart were acting in concert.

It is difficult to see how the French critic who accused Gurdjieff of making Katherine Mansfield "die badly" can have been familiar with the evidence. She had arrived at Fontainebleau in a state of terror and depression. A week before her death Gurdjieff's alchemy had turned this into a sense of purpose and near tranquillity. In view of what she so clearly sensed about her physical condition, complete tranquillity was impossible; and it was her body—about which Gurdjieff could do nothing—which failed her.

Middleton Murry arrived at the Institute on the afternoon of January 9, "Before I had time to kiss her," he wrote later, "the thought passed through my head: something has happened. By that 'something' I meant something decisive in the spiritual struggle in which she had been engaged. She had changed profoundly in the three months since I had seen her; she seemed unearthly, and I had never seen anyone more lovely than she appeared to me that day." K. M. told him that although she had gained from her experience, she did not know whether she would stay much longer at Fontainebleau. "But she had not, she said, really made up her mind about M. Gurdjieff." The couple made plans to live together in a country cottage, and during the afternoon and evening Katherine Mansfield led Murry round to inspect the work in progress, to meet her friends, and to take a hand in painting the Study House. After supper some of the pupils assembled in the salon for the nightly session of exercises. According to Olgivanna, K. M. was withdrawn and nervous, hoping rather desperately that the dancers would perform Gurdjieff's "The Initiation of the Priestess"—from which she always seemed to derive energy and exaltation. Halfway through this movement Gurdjieff stopped the dancers and ordered them back to the Study House. K. M. left the salon to go to bed. As she climbed the stairs, followed by Murry, a coughing fit began; in her room it became clear that she had had a hemorrhage. Blood gushed from her mouth, and the doctors gathered around; but by 10:30 that night, she was dead.

Murry's feelings about Gurdjieff remained for a long time very mixed, but at the end of his own life, he permitted himself a definite statement. He refused to judge the Institute. "But I am persuaded of this," he wrote: "that Katherine made of it an instrument for that process of self-annihilation which is necessary to the spiritual rebirth, whereby we enter the Kingdom of Love. I am certain that she achieved her purpose, and that the Institute lent itself to it. More I dare not, and less I must not say." Murry did appoint himself the hagiographer of his dead wife, and this must be taken into account when considering his verdict. But K. M.'s adventure at Fontainebleau seems to have left her a being who, if she had lived, would have been a ship refitted for new voyages rather than a leaking tub sailing under ragged canvas. As Olgivanna wrote, she had destroyed the world in which she had lived and in which she no longer believed. She had built another one—where there was still a place both for literature and for her love for Murry. *If she had lived* . . . and surely that is the criterion? She left the world of the Institute in a plain coffin, but even if she had known the inevitable form of her journey out, would not the journey in have been the only thing to do? Those who believe in the "other side" would scarcely deny her trumpets.

The romantic circumstances of Katherine Mansfield's death increased the curiosity of the British press about Gurdjieff and his Institute. Lady Rothermere visited Fontainebleau in the New Year of 1923, and her presence added to the newsworthiness of the Prieuré. On February 19, the *Daily Mirror* devoted its entire front page to photographs of the Study House, Lady Rothermere, and various aristocratic Russian inmates. The more intellectual *Daily News* ran a long series of articles by a special correspondent, E. C. Bowyer. The first was headlined: NEW CULT—FOREST TEMPLE OF HARD WORK AND ROUGH FOOD—FAMOUS DISCIPLES, and made great play with the names of Orage and Katherine Mansfield. Bowyer described Middleton Murry as "a constant attendant at Ouspensky's London lectures" and claimed that J. D. Beresford, Algernon Blackwood, and J. W. N. Sullivan were all "deeply interested." In fact, of all those named, only Algernon Blackwood could be described as a devotee, and although he visited the Prieuré several times, he remained true to his reticent nature. Even his unpublished papers tell nothing more of his interest.

The *News* articles ran continuously from February 15, describing quite fairly the life at Fontainebleau. On the nineteenth, Ouspensky, described as "a middle-aged, much travelled and learned Russian" and "the chief missionary for Gurdjieff's academy," was interviewed in London. He struck an eminently sober note. "I don't like to see the word 'cult' applied to the movement," he said. "We are not trying to found a church or sect, but simply to promote a method of education and study." Ouspensky was at pains to emphasize that the manual labor described at Fountainebleau had "nothing to do with a Tolstoyan love of work for work's sake." It was "merely one—often a brief—stage in the education of the student."

The *Daily News* published a half-page of photographs of pupils at the Institute engaged in dancing, sewing, cooking and building the Study House. Discussion invaded the correspondence columns. An anonymous article took issue with Gurdjieff's proclaimed intention of divesting the pupil of his personality and liberating his essence. The writer compared Gurdjieff's "essence" to the subconscious of psychoanalysis, and noted that not the "essence" but the "personality" was the repository of all civilized values. "Would it be unfair to ask Mr. Gurdjieff bluntly whether de-socialisation of the individual is the aim of his system of training?" Why, this critic asked, had the "essence" been "thrust below the surface" in the evolutionary process? "Every scientific inquirer into the nature of the subconscious has been impressed above all else by the strength of its primitive desires. If wisdom, insight and even genius also reside there, it is in association with these powerful forces." The writer argued that this accounted for the failure of previous attempts to mobilize the unconscious, and he ended his article on a note of warning. He did not suggest that Gurdjieff was unaware of the dangers confronting him. He and his colleagues appeared to be "able and honest men. But the history of not dissimilar experiments in the past suggests the need for vigilance and the advisability of suspending judgment for the present."

On February 22, letters from J. D. Beresford and J. W. N. Sullivan appeared dissociating themselves from Gurdjieff and Ouspensky. Sullivan pronounced himself unsympathetic to Gurdjieff's aims and possessing "not the faintest intention of forming any connection with his Institute." Beresford followed up his own letter with an account of why he had withdrawn from Ouspensky's lectures the previous autumn.

Beresford accompanied Katherine Mansfield to Ouspensky's lectures and took part in discussions with her and Orage about the Fourth Way.

He describes how he explained the principles of the Fourth Way to Millar Dunning, the yogi from Ditchling. Dunning listened with interest, then "without gesture or emphasis" informed the novelist that the Fourth Way might "produce the result desired; but that it was evil. He then went on to say that the successful followers of this road were those spoken of in Christ's parable as coming to the wedding of the King's Son without a wedding garment—the mystical garment of love."* Beresford admits that this statement might not impress many readers as one of great significance; but for him, it came "with a sense of revelation," and he began to feel that the teaching was "repugnant" to him. The central point of Beresford's article in the *Daily News* was a warning that the soul without the wedding garment would "suffer in the hereafter." He made a distinction between occultism—as represented by Gurdjieff and Ouspensky—and mysticism— whose representative for him was Dunning. Later he contrasted "personal and impersonal methods" and admitted that "in my own mind they have much the same connotation as Black and White Magic."

Meanwhile the Fontainebleau Institute exercised an undiminished fascination. At the beginning of March, the *New Statesman* carried an article signed "C." and entitled, "The 'Forest Philosophers.'" This was by the editor, Clifford Sharp, and was designed, so he wrote, to counteract the misleading impressions given of the Fontainebleau colony in the press. Like the *Daily News* reporter, he denied that the Institute bore any relationship to the various "experimental colonies" with which his readers were familiar. The only comparison that could be made was with the community established by Pythagoras at Samos in 500 B.C.

Sharp had been completely carried away by Gurdjieff and Ouspensky. His wife and many of his friends were at Fontainebleau, and the comparison with Pythagoras most probably originated with Orage. He himself had

* Beresford does not name his friend, the "poet and mystic." For some time, I thought that this was A. E. Waite, whom J. G. Bennett remembers stalking out of Ouspensky's meetings with the sententious phrase, "Mr. Ouspensky, there is no love in your system"; but Mr. Tristam Beresford believes it was Dunning.

visited the Institute and may have contemplated taking the plunge; for he was convinced that "Mr. Gurdjieff and his colleagues possess knowledge which is far in advance of anything that is known to European science." Gurdjieff's psychological analysis was "infinitely more subtle, more comprehensive and more scientific than the work of, for instance, William James." Gurdjieff's musical expertise indicated "a knowledge of the precise emotional effects of rhythm and tone that was never dreamed of, even by a Mozart." Sharp even swallowed whole Gurdjieff's claims about the Institute's medical section and declared that at Fontainebleau, there was "what is perhaps the most complete installation of medico-electrical apparatus in the world."

The tone of this article caused Sharp's readers some concern, and the week following its appearance, Edwyn Bevan wrote firmly to bring the erring editor to heel. Bevan (1870–1943) was a former head of the British School of Archeology in Athens, who at the time was lecturing at King's College, London. During the early 1930s, he twice delivered the Gifford Lectures and the spiritual problems which had so exercised Sharp's hero, William James—another Gifford Lecturer—were by no means foreign to him. If Gurdjieff's teaching proved its worth, he argued, it would "stand or fall on its own merits, like any other scientific theory." But, "the introduction of this 'esoteric tradition' business" aroused his suspicions. "It has been associated in the past with so much humbug." There was no evidence that Gurdjieff possessed any knowledge with which orthodox scientists or scholars were unfamiliar. "No doubt a supposed origin in a secret Oriental tradition tends to secure a much wider popularity in certain circles for any teaching," Bevan wrote; and he pounced on the very difficulty which Gurdjieff later admitted had spoiled his work: "popularity with just the wrong kind of people—the people whose adherence is *not* a recommendation."

In a second article, published on March 17, Sharp made no reply, but instead summarized Ouspensky's teaching and invited those who were interested to go to Fontainebleau and find out more for themselves. It was a valiant attempt to beat the drum for the Institute for the Harmonious Development of Man; and Sharp clearly recognized that Gurdjieff's teaching might have a mass appeal—to those literally or metaphorically shellshocked, whom Middleton Murry had described as "maimed" by the experience of war. Ouspensky had emerged from the European holocaust with a teaching which had apparently sustained him in the eye of the hurricane, and Sharp placed particular emphasis on his explanation of war as the necessary consequence of man's unconscious state.

CASE: *Dr. James Young.*   PROBLEMS: *intellectual curiosity, dissatis-*

faction with psychoanalysis, a vague suspicion that Gurdjieff the Master does after all possess Powers.

Once the Institute was fairly launched, James Young was able to look about him and analyze what he found. He was distressed by his fellow pupils who "fell short of the standard of culture which Ouspensky had led me to expect. However, I tried to reassure myself with the thought that we were all 'machines', and that one machine is as good as another so far as 'mechanical' life is concerned. I don't think I quite succeeded, and certainly I had grave doubts when I listened to the never-ending chatter of some of the women, which struck me as the essence of 'mechanism.'" For some time he let his scientific conscience sleep undisturbed; but after six months, he found it impossible to go on pretending to himself that he was observing Gurdjieff as a psychological phenomenon.

Gurdjieff decided to buy a car. There was a certain subdued excitement about this for many, probably because unconsciously it stood for the inclusion of something human and commonplace in a world which was rapidly becoming inhuman and outside reality. It was understood that Gurdjieff had never before driven a car, which was probably true. It was believed by many, including presumably intelligent English women, that Gurdjieff would not have to learn to drive in the ordinary way. He would be able to drive, so to speak, by inspiration. . . . When there was a ghastly noise suggestive of tearing of gear-wheel cogs, the faithful insisted that it was a test of faith for sceptics such as myself. . . . I soon discovered that it was impossible to cope with such sophistry and "will-to-believe." . . . I could not but be impressed by the power which accrues to a man once he has been invested with the magical attributes of the "all-powerful father" or has had the "magician" archetype projected into him, as Jung would say. People in the grip of such a transference are oblivious to criticism. . . .

Another example: the parents of an imbecile child got it into their heads that Gurdjieff might be able to help this child in some mysterious way, and brought it all the way from England. It had an attack of diarrhoea soon after arrival, probably due to change of diet. In this case I was really astonished to find that people who might have known better said that Gurdjieff had begun to "work" on him. They meant that by some mysterious means best known to himself he had produced the diarrhoea.

Young's skepticism provoked accusations of spiritual pride from his fellow pupils, and the doctor confided his disillusionment to a friend, "a man of letters," who occasionally came to stay at Fontainebleau. This was almost certainly Bechhofer Roberts. Their correspondence confirmed Young's suspicions of the Institute. Bechhofer was clearly influenced by the warnings of Dunning and Beresford but felt that 'the place is *real*." He thought that Gurdjieff was probably able to teach methods of self-development, but only to those who would cooperate with his personal plans. After awhile he became seriously alarmed. "In my own mind lies no longer any faintest doubt about Gurdjieff and his Institute. Signs of hoofs and horns are all over the place, and my deep and instant distrust, which increased with every day I spent there finds confirmation whenever I return . . ."

A specific incident was needed to catalyze Young's decision to leave Fontainebleau. A woman member of the Institute was taken ill and, according to Young's observation, vomited blood. Young diagnosed an intestinal ulcer. Gurdjieff denied that the woman had vomited blood at all and produced, in Bechhofer's words, "quite a different diagnosis"—his reticence might conceal every sort of obscenity or irrelevancy. Shortly afterward an operation in London proved that Young was right. When the doctor taxed Gurdjieff with the affair, he was upbraided for lack of trust; and Orage, with whom Young shared a room, maintained that it had merely been another test. Young could take no more and left at once.

This seems to be an open and shut case. Even if Gurdjieff had intended his remarks to Young as a "test," he must have realized that in the climate which he had deliberately created such a gambit might substantially decrease the sick woman's chances of a cure. But soon after Young's departure, Maurice Nicoll noted in his diary: "Jimmy has left. G. gave lecture on importance of remembering that we came here with a definite object . . ." This lecture was delivered on August 21, 1923, and it answers almost all Young's objections to the life at Fontainebleau.

Gurdjieff began by attacking one section of his pupils—those who had forgotten why they came. They were supposed to be at the Institute to "work on themselves" and they were supposed to have come because they realized that ordinary life could not provide the special conditions necessary for such work. But once at the Institute they forgot all their resolutions and refused to see that Gurdjieff was actually creating the necessary conditions around them. Gurdjieff proposed that pupils unable to make use of this opportunity leave at once and stop wasting his time. Those who stayed must use everything which happened as a means to work on themselves—and this meant not caring for the opinions of fellow pupils or for those of Gurdjieff himself. He emphasized that many states were produced artificially in people by the unusual conditions he created for them, and that attempts to "help" people over their emotional crises might nullify all the work which had gone into creating them. It didn't matter, he explained—answering James Young's as yet unvoiced objections to the "mechanically-twittering" ladies—who was mad, who was clever, who was a decent sort, and who a bounder. If they were tempted to think that their fellow pupils were a collection of fools, Gurdjieff told his audience, this was because the Institute existed to create the sort of conditions which would expose the worst sides of people, principally so that a pupil would see his defects for himself. When someone came to Fontainebleau, he left a world which accepted a man's valuation of himself. No wonder, when he first found himself in an atmosphere which encouraged a deeper examination of human behavior, that he imagined that he was locked up with a band of rogues and idiots.

Gurdjieff ended by saying that the Institute, instead of being a corrective to everyday life, had turned into something worse than everyday life. His pupils were occupied with scandalmongering, judging others, "considering," and forming cliques. In fact—although he did not say this—his Institute had become like institutes the world over.

Thus, the case of Dr. Young is not entirely open-and-shut. It still demanded a large amount of trust from a medical practitioner to assume that Gurdjieff's medical knowledge was as great as his own. But it could well have been that the lesson Gurdjieff was trying to teach was that Young should assert himself more—rely on his professional competence when he knew himself to be right. There remains an element of doubt; but the evidence is weighted on Gurdjieff's side. It was not necessarily Young's diagnosis with which he took issue, but with the doctor's own psychology. The fact is that, whatever Gurdjieff said, the sick woman was operated upon, and his pronouncement did not prevent her from having medical treatment. It may have delayed treatment; in which case Gurdjieff is certainly to be blamed—but, as he told his pupils, they were supposed to take no account of his expressed opinions except as a stimulus to their psychological work. The trouble was, as he himself recognized, that he was naturally a figure who inspired uncritical obedience and attracted to himself people in search of a pair of shoulders broad enough to carry their burdens.

Young admits that he was not completely free from the hypnotic trance in which many of Gurdjieff's pupils lived. His search for a Master did not end with his leaving Gurdjieff, and for a time, he was closely connected with Dmitrije Mitrinović. He became Middleton Murry's closest friend, and for the rest of his life practiced as an eclectic psychiatrist in London. He did not regard his time at Fontainebleau as wasted. "I am convinced," he wrote, "that much that was valuable was met with on the way"; and it was Young whom Dorothy Brett selected to enlighten D. H. Lawrence on the Institute for the Harmonious Development of Man.* It is a moot point whether Young was a "failure" from Gurdjieff's point of view or whether Gurdjieff was a failure from Young's.

CASE: *A.R. Orage*.   PROBLEMS: *as stated in previous files*.

When Orage arrived at the Prieuré with *Alice in Wonderland* in his pocket, he found that, far from disappearing down magical rabbit holes, he was expected to dig them. Gurdjieff forbade him to smoke which, he said, "almost killed" him. "I was told to dig," he told C. S. Nott, "and as I had had no real exercise for years I suffered so much physically that I would go back to my room, a sort of cell, and literally cry with fatigue. No one, not even Gurdjieff, came near me. I asked myself, 'Is this what I have given up my whole life for? At least I had something then. Now what have I?'" The *Daily News* correspondent contrasted the corduroys and calloused hands of this new Orage with the elegant Bohemian of the Café Royal. Denis Saurat, who came to see his friend on February 17, 1923, was amazed by the physical change he found. "I used to know him when he was almost fat," he wrote, "when his tall, bony frame supported a body of some 85 kilos weight. But to meet me came a thin, almost emaciated Orage with a troubled face. Seemingly a taller Orage, whose movements were quicker and stronger; in better health, but unhappy."

In early 1923, puzzlement seems still to have been Orage's prevailing emotion. He was resolute enough to give the *Daily News* correspondent an account of what he believed to be Gurdjieff's objectives, but hinted that he had become a member of the Institute more out of hope than from any definite expectation. "There are men in London who are already as 'clever' as it is possible to be for men under ordinary conditions," he told Bowyer, "and who are asking themselves whether this is the ultima thule—whether they have reached the final limits of their evolution. We believe that there is something more, and so we are here." Bechhofer Roberts approved of Orage's "half-tolerant, half-sceptical tone" when confronted with certain irregularities at the Institute, but later became impatient with the editor's insistence on explaining away every one of Gurdjieff's inconsistent actions. He decided that Orage and most of the English intellectuals at Fontainebleau were waiting "like mystical Micawbers—for something superconscious to turn up."

Denis Saurat's story of his visit to the Institute reinforces the impression

---

*An unsuccessful attempt, like all those of Lawrence's friends, to interest him in Gurdjieff. Brett's tea party was interrupted by the arrival of Carrington and her brother Noel, who talked at such length about India that the party broke up.

that Orage and his friends were confused. On the night of the Frenchman's arrival, Gurdjieff sent him a bottle of vodka to share with Orage and the other English. No one wanted the vodka, but because the pupils were scared of Gurdjieff, they refused to let Saurat tip half the bottle out of the window, and instead, forced the spirit down their reluctant throats. "All these people were disconcerted," Saurat recalled, "prey to a mixture of shame, fear and inarticulate hope." Saurat had an interview with Gurdjieff, after which he repeated to his friends the Master's admission that the Seekers for Truth had made some of their discoveries in books. This irritated the English pupils. One of the doctors wondered what they were all doing at Fontainebleau if the tradition was to be found in books. Another Englishman suspected that perhaps there was no secret tradition after all. They were all very struck by Gurdjieff's admission that "there was something sinister" about the Prieuré. "They wondered a little whether they were dupes," reported Saurat, "but they still preferred to be victims. However, they were afraid of being exploited by Gurdjieff for his occult ends."

Depressed, confused, and suspicious Orage may have been, but he still believed sufficiently in Gurdjieff's ideas to resent a joke at their expense. Saurat confided in a reporter that he was a professor at the University of Bordeaux and could assure him that all the inmates of the Institute were mad. The journalist repeated this to Orage, who took ten years to forgive Saurat his act of betrayal. And Orage's commitment was in no doubt to Middleton Murry when he had to refuse the editor's offer of the *New Age*. Murry saw the older man as reduced to essentials. "It seemed to me," he wrote, "that a very fine simplicity had descended upon his complex nature . . ."

The period of uncertainty and despair must have lasted at least for Orage's first four or five months at the Prieuré. Then he made a breakthrough. "When I was in the very depths of despair," he told Nott, "feeling that I could go on no longer, I vowed to make extra effort, and just then something changed in me. Soon, I began to enjoy the hard labour, and a week later Gurdjieff came to me and said, 'Now Orage, I think you dig enough. Let us go to café and drink coffee.' From that moment things began to change."

Presumably this means that Orage entered a new phase of his instruction. In whatever manner, "things began to change" for him, and the alteration concerned his relationship with the Master. From quite early in their association, Gurdjieff developed an affection for Orage, whom he later said he had "loved as a brother." Orage no doubt "worked," in Gurdjieff's sense, very hard; his background in Theosophy gave him certain common interests with Gurdjieff; he had also, as Murry said, "burned his boats," and was prepared to dedicate himself to spreading Gurdjieff's ideas. But underneath the professional relationship between the two men grew up a certain camaraderie, apparently based on Gurdjieff's side upon a genuine feeling of friendship. One result was that Orage—whose mind could gallop where Gurdjieff's could merely canter—soon held something of a privileged position at the court of Fontainebleau. During the later 1920s he was even known to exploit this at Gurdjieff's expense. "You know, Orage," Gurdjieff would say portentously, "oranges grow on trees." "Do they really?" Orage would drawl. "I thought they came from boxes." From under their simian brow ridge, Gurdjieff's eyes would look momentarily puzzled; had the favorite son really been so stupid?

By what stages Orage progressed from a relationship of awed obedience to one of banter, we cannot know; but the first steps in his future intimacy with his teacher must have been taken during the spring and summer of 1923. Orage was certainly among the most able of Gurdjieff's pupils in a conventional sense, and his skill as a propagandist was to prove invaluable. When Gurdjieff selected him to accompany Dr. Stoerneval—his oldest follower—to the United States, he was, in fact, the obvious choice as ambassador. He set sail for New York in the autumn of 1923 to edit souls.

America had begun to appear to Gurdjieff as a necessary step for two related reasons. The first was financial. Although most of the cost of buying and refurbishing the Prieuré had been met by Ouspensky's pupils, Gurdjieff was still faced with a considerable financial burden. According to the *Daily News*, the general rate for a pupil at the Institute was seventeen pounds ten shillings per month, although visitors who stayed in relative luxury in "the Ritz" or came simply to be cured by Gurdjieff of various ailments, might be charged as much as forty or fifty pounds. But the majority of Gurdjieff's pupils, though comfortably off, were not rich, and well over half the total complement of the Prieuré were Russians who relied entirely on the Master's charity. Into the bargain, since the Prieuré had become his home, Gurdjieff had sent for his family from Georgia, and they arrived in the summer of 1923 to increase the number of his dependents. To supplement his income, Gurdjieff had resumed his profession of "physician-hypnotist" and spent considerable time in Paris—where he established an "office" in the Café de la Paix—plying his trade for the benefit of drug addicts and alcoholics. At the same time he undertook various business activities, including a profitable deal in oil shares and the establishment and sale of two restaurants in Montmartre.

Together with the organization of the Institute and the demands of the pupils who arrived there, it is not surprising that all this activity wore him down. In "The Material Question," Gurdjieff writes that his health began to concern him, and he realized that he would have to take a rest. He had been planning a trip to the United States in the more distant future; but he now decided that if he made the expedition sooner, it could serve the dual purpose of fund raising and holiday. "I was beginning to hope," he writes, "that my pupils would now be capable of organizing various lectures and demonstrations in America by themselves."

As a dress rehearsal for his transatlantic venture, Gurdjieff decided to risk his remaining capital on a series of demonstrations in Paris over the Christmas season of 1923. These were organized through Alexander de Salzmann's acquaintance with Jacques Hébertot, the director of the Théâtre des Champs-Elysées, where the performances took place irregularly between December thirteenth and twenty-fifth. Expansive as always, Gurdjieff had the small fountains in the foyer run with red and white wine. "The Art of the Antique Orient Revived," proclaimed the *Echo des Champs Elysées*, and promised further revelations from "the mysterious heart of Asia" in seasons to come. For the moment, the publicity announced, the Institute for the Harmonious Development of Man was confining itself to three programs: a demonstration of movement, a program of music performed on Gurdjieff's collection of Oriental instruments, and an exhibition of "religious phenomena, consisting of tricks, half-tricks and real phenomena observed in religious ceremonies of the ancient East." The "tricks" of which the advertisement spoke were conjuring tricks of the sort performed by stage illusionists, and Gurdjieff had already used them to enliven his Saturday night demonstrations in the Study House. Apparently the members of the Institute were proficient conjurers—as anyone must be who is interested in "psychical phenomena." It is unclear what Gurdjieff meant by "half-tricks"; and the "real phenomena"—sustained exercises in the direction of consciousness—were not obvious to the general public.

The demonstrations of movement created great interest. Gurdjieff's program included the "Stop" exercise, "The Initiation of the Priestess," and gymnastic exercises said to derive from a "school called 'The Seers'" which had "existed from antiquity in large artificial caverns in Kafiristan, on the heights of Kijera." There were "movements" from monastic orders in Chinese Turkestan, Kafiristan, Tibet, Caucasia, and Kashgar; "work-dances," prayers and fragments of ritual. The program concluded with an item called *Pythia* described as "part of a ceremony like that M. Gurdjieff witnessed in the Sanctuary of Houdankr in the Lotko country in the Chitral."

The interest which Gurdjieff aroused was of a rather ambivalent sort. Yet despite an equivocal press, the very fact of the performances—together with the mystery attached to Gurdjieff himself, and the impact of the "Stop" exercise wherever it was demonstrated—made the Fontainebleau Institute once more a talking-point. From the almost furtive character he had impersonated in Moscow, Gurdjieff had apparently turned himself into a publicity-seeking—though no less mysterious—impresario.

Ouspensky observed the transformation with mixed feelings, as once more all the doubts which had assailed him in Essentuki and Constantinople reasserted themselves. In January 1924, he watched Gurdjieff leave with his troupe for the United States; and in his mind was the memory of their parting in Essentuki. On his return to London, he told his pupils that the association with Gurdjieff had ended. To those who asked whether they should go to Fontainebleau or stay in London, he replied that the break was total: "Either go to him or stay with me. If you go you not see me again. If you stay and I am wrong you will pay for it and I too." Ouspensky did not specify the reasons for his renewed mistrust of Gurdjieff, and his public statement in *In Search of the Miraculous* is the bare record of his announcement "that my work in future would proceed quite independently *in the way it had been begun in London in 1921.*"

Meanwhile Beelzebub, twirling his mustaches and with his karakul cap perched jauntily on the side of his head, sailed indomitably off to America.

4

A Crack in the Times

The New York in which Gurdjieff arrived with Orage as his herald was a city which, intellectually speaking, was living on capital borrowed from Europe. A favorable exchange rate had persuaded many writers and artists to leave an exclusively business-oriented society. The 1920s were the great years of the American in Europe: the time of gatherings of intellectual expatriates in Paris and the fluttering of social butterflies along the Riviera. The Bohemians and the cosmopolitans could not always be told apart; for the artists needed the patronage of the wealthy, and the rich socialites enjoyed the cachet of being considered patrons of the arts. Europe was a cloud on the horizon of Washington Square.

It was the age of the great Atlantic liners, symbolizing the proximity of Europe to the United States: Jean Toomer, who became a leading exponent of Gurdjieff's ideas, wrote an abortive novel called *Transatlantic* set on such a ship. It was the age of prohibition, when, "if you point your fourth finger," wrote Gurdjieff, "and covering one half of your mouth with your right palm, utter the name of any liquid you fancy, then, immediately and without more words, that liquid is served at table—only in a bottle purporting to be lemonade or the famous French Vichy." It was the age of jazz, and of Gurdjieff's phobia, the foxtrot. A time of characteristics sharply defined in retrospect but in fact as evanescent as champagne.

For those intellectuals who were unable to emigrate or who resisted the pressures to do so, there were less obvious temptations in the sort of "inner emigration" which became familiar in Germany during the 1930s. Malcolm Cowley writes in *Exile's Return*, "The bohemian tendency triumphed in the Village, and talk about revolution gave way to talk about psychoanalysis. . . . After the War the Village was full of former people. There were former anarchists who had made fortunes manufacturing munitions, former Wobblies about to open speakeasies. . . ." The general turning away from politics was occasioned partly by left-wing disgust at the war and the Versailles peace, partly by right-wing horror of moral chaos and Bolshevism. Psychoanalysis was only one of the panaceas which captured the attention of the intellectuals and, as Cowley realized, "the implication of all these methods is the same—that the environment itself need not be altered. This explains why most radicals who became converted to psychoanalysis or glands or Gurdjieff gradually abandoned their political radicalism."

An entire milieu was introverting, as the nation itself veered into isolationism. In the late 1920s, an extraordinary underground influence was exercised by Orage's teaching of Gurdjieff's ideas. Although psychoanalysis was a more enduring movement, in Orage's New York heyday the revelations of Professor Freud were no match for his captivating charm.

The ground for Orage's mission had been prepared by Claude Bragdon's publication of *Tertium Organim*. On its publication in 1920, *Tertium Organum* sold so well that Bragdon had to turn over the list of his Manas Press to Alfred Knopf for fear that his other activities would be swamped by his spare time publishing. Meanwhile through Ouspensky's "Letters from Russia" in the *New Age*, he made contact with Orage, who replied that he himself had lost touch with Ouspensky after his flight from Ekaterinodar. Eventually an American devotee of *Tertium Organum* called at the London headquarters of the Theosophical Society, where a friend of Ouspensky told him that Ouspensky was in Constantinople. Bragdon was able to open communications and to send Ouspensky a check for royalties.

It rapidly became known among the devotees of Ouspensky's book that the author was associated with Gurdjieff. The vagueness of most people about this association is illustrated by Bragdon's reaction when he heard from Orage—with whom he had corresponded since his first inquiry about Ouspensky—that Gurdjieff was arriving in the United States. Orage wrote from Fontainebleau, on November 26, 1923:

I expect to be sailing for New York on Dec. 15 to spend a few weeks in preparing the way for Mr. Gurdjieff's visit in January (you know of course all about Mr. Gurdjieff and Mr. Ouspensky). Naturally I look forward to meeting you, and, in fact, I should come with even more timidity if I did not expect to find you there.

Bragdon wrote later, in his autobiography, *The Secret Springs,* "Although I knew nothing of Gurdjieff and his Institute, I did know of Ouspensky's connection with it in some capacity or other, and that by my publication of *Tertium Organum* I stood more or less committed to its general philosophy. Nevertheless something deep within me demurred, and so I did not take any action, even to the extent of meeting Orage at the dock as he had suggested." However, as soon as Orage landed, he came to see Bragdon and spent "several hours" trying unsuccessfully to persuade him to support Gurdjieff's demonstrations in New York. Despite this reverse, Orage and Stoerneval managed to excite some interest among intellectuals and the press.

The program of Gurdjieff's displays was an expanded version of that given in France. The first demonstration was held on January 23, 1924 in a ballroom known as Leslie Hall at 260 West 83rd Street, and was followed by other performances at the Lenox Theatre (end of January), the Neighborhood Playhouse in Greenwich Village, and a grand demonstration at Carnegie Hall on February 9. There may also have been other performances in the Astor Hotel and a "Webster Hall." Orage then left to prepare the way for demonstrations in Boston and Philadelphia, and Gurdjieff followed with his pupils. They performed in Chicago and returned to New York for a final demonstration at Carnegie Hall on March 3.

The demonstrations were the sensation of the hour. Reports varied from the partisan article by Maud Hoffmann which appeared in the *New York Times* of February 10, to the most extravagant sensationalism. *The Bookman* occupied the middle ground:

We were very much puzzled and a little impressed by sacred temple dances, ritual movements, dervish dances, etc. While the dancers exhibited great muscular control, the music oppressed us and the movements themselves seemed jerky and utterly lacking in grace. However, many other persons seemed moved, and the audience represented widely diverse interests. In the large and darkened hall one caught glimpses of Theodore Dreiser, Fannie Hurst, John O'Hara Cosgrave, Gloria Swanson, Rebecca West, Elinor Wylie, Mrs. Thomas Lamont, young Alan Rinehart, etc., etc. How important such a movement can be we are not capable of judging. Somehow, we suspect that the greatest artistic work is never done by the man who becomes a complete disciple of any cult.

This more or less open-minded comment was in marked contrast to the stories invented by the sensational press. The *American Weekly* carried a story under the headline: "DR." GURDJIEFF AND HIS MAGICAL SECRET OF LIFE—HOW TO BE A SUPER-MAN OR SUPER-WOMAN BY FEEDING PIGS, DANCING WEIRD DANCES ALL NIGHT AND OTHER FANTASTIC ANTICS. The journalist's climax was an account of how in the evenings at Fontainebleau "scores of patients of the asylum—institute—eddy out like gentle ghosts at twilight." To the strains of music—"exotic, sensuous, mystical, provocative"—played by hidden musicians, Gurdjieff apparently gave commands from within his curtained booth in the Study House, "'Dance!' he cries from behind the curtain. 'Dance as your souls dictate! Dance—dance—dance to freedom!'"

The journalist William Seabrook attended the demonstrations out of a fascination with matters mystical and occult. He was mildly interested in the conjuring parts of the program, although he found them little different from the feats performed by Houdini, who claimed no supernatural powers. But he was deeply impressed by Gurdjieff himself, whom he met the night after his arrival and engaged in an all-night conversation. "Whether his power lay simply in the fields of hypnotism and autosuggestion, or went beyond it into authentic telepathy and clairvoyance," Seabrook mused, "or even further into the Tibetan and Yoga fields of alleged occult miracle-working, I never became convinced—for the reason that I've never yet become convinced that power in these latter categories can exist at all. But whatever category Gurdjieff's power may have lain in—in those days he had power." Seabrook was disconcerted by the discipline of Gurdjieff's pupils. "They were like a group of perfectly trained zombies, or like circus animals jumping through hoops ringed with fire, or like the soldiers of Christophe who marched without breaking step off the parapet of the citadel on that sheer mountainside in Haiti."

The most spectacular demonstration of Gurdjieff's authority was a breathtaking variation on the "Stop" exercise:

> The troupe was deployed extreme back stage, facing the audience. At his command they came racing full tilt towards the footlights. We expected to see a wonderful exhibition of arrested motion. But instead Gurdjieff calmly turned his back, and was lighting a cigarette. In the next split second an aerial human avalanche was flying through the air, across the orchestra, down among empty chairs, on the floor, bodies pell-mell, piled on top of each other, arms and legs sticking out in weird postures—frozen there, fallen, in complete immobility and silence.
>
> Only after it had happened did Gurdjieff turn and look at them as

they lay there, still immobile. When they presently arose, by his permission, and it was evident that no arms, legs, or necks had been broken—no one seemed to have suffered even so much as a scratch or bruise—there were storms of applause, mingled with a little protest. It had been almost too much.

The vision of the Master as a Man of Power, which had proved so attractive in Russia, left in the United States an impression of mild distaste. The British writer, Llewellyn Powys, visited the Neighborhood Playhouse and observed Gurdjieff: "His general appearance made one think of a riding-master, though there was something about his presence that affected one's nerves in a strange way. Especially did one feel this when his pupils came on to the stage, to perform like a hutchful of hypnotized rabbits under the gaze of a master conjuror."

Claude Bragdon approved wholeheartedly of Powys' imagery, and agreed that there was "something disturbing" about Gurdjieff. "He impressed me as a man of power," he wrote, "but at the same time I was a little repelled; I did not want to be drawn into that particular net." The actor, Walter Hampden, was even more outspoken. He had attended a late night session of questions and answers conducted by Gurdjieff, and remarked afterward to Bragdon: "Claude, no one need tell me that this man is a Master. The mark of a Master is mastery, and Gurdjieff cannot even make himself understood—no Master would come here so unprepared as that."

The demonstrations did serve a purpose, although not that of raising funds. The last performance at Carnegie Hall was the only occasion on which seats were sold, and this was not a financial success. But the irritating questions posed by Gurdjieff himself had been enlarged by the unfamiliar quality of his music and the movements. And in New York—as earlier in Russia and London—the Work split into two parts. There was the puzzling figure of the Master himself, the source of knowledge and the creator of confusion; the glyph incarnate, a living parable. And there was the reasonable voice of Orage to explain the inexplicable. To one recalcitrant pupil who objected that Gurdjieff would not answer her questions, he once burst out: "Can't you just watch him?"

To supplement Gurdjieff's teaching there always emerged explicators, who repeated what they themselves had understood—perhaps what they had gleaned from Gurdjieff's hints and chance droppings of advice or remembered from talks he had given when it had suited him to teach explicitly. Orage was there in one sense to tell his pupil to watch Gurdjieff, to seek for something behind the literal understanding which he imagined to be the limit of comprehension. He was responsible for interpretation and administration, as well as beating the drum. As in England, it was he who made the contacts which gained Gurdjieff a following. The responsibilities which he had assumed of necessity were to hang like an albatross around his neck for the next seven years.

The view from outside—of the mission of Orage and Gurdjieff, of the sensation caused by the dances, of the subsidence of a nine days' wonder—is again quite different from the internal landscape which the two men really inhabited. They stepped through a crack in the times.

During the decade which separated the end of the First World War from the stock market crash of October 1929, American intellectuals tried uneasily to find a compromise with the disturbingly successful philistines riding the business boom. In an article written in March 1932, from the far side of the Depression, Edmund Wilson analyzed the "superficial" nature of such intellectual attitudinizing:

> We can see now that they all represented attempts on the part of the more thoughtful Americans to reconcile themselves to a world dominated by salesmen and brokers—and that they all involved compromises with the salesman and the broker. Mencken and Nathan laughed at the broker, but they got along with him very well, provided he enjoyed George Moore and had pretensions to a taste in liquor; . . . the poets and philosophers hid from him—and the physicists grew more and more mystical in the laboratories subsidized mainly by the profits from industrial investments; the humanists, in volume after volume, endeavoured by sheer hollow thunder to induce people to find in the stock exchange the harmony and dignity of the Parthenon.

Wilson later reprinted this article as part of a longer piece on "The Literary Consequences of the Crash" in which he associated the success of Gurdjieff and Orage with the schizophrenic climate he described. But the "more thoughtful" Americans whom he pilloried as unhappily straddling the gulf between Fantasy and Mammon must sometimes have been conscious of the precariousness of their stance. It was unsatisfying, it was compromised from the points of view both of culture and of cash, and it provided no real solution to what Gorham Munson was to call "the dilemma of the liberated." In the book which Munson published under that title in 1930, he summarized the problem confronting a generation which had lost faith in its early enthusiasms and was discontented with superficial rebellion. "The intelligent modern man feels liberated from petty social conventions, narrow theological views, discredited authorities, the grosser popular superstitions, but liberated for what? Only, it seems, to face a darkened problem of choices, with many strong reasons for distrusting every alternative offered."

The appeal of a theory which seemed to advocate harmony and integration—which pointed the way toward some ultimate synthesis—was strong. The New World was still in the process of establishing a solid identity vis-á-vis the Old; and despite the birth pangs of a new literature, it had scarcely begun to compete in the cultural field. It appeared to some intellectuals—and Orage fostered this belief—that the next step might prove to be the Gurdjieff Method; that in some way, there was a specifically American mission to adopt the strange discipline which Gurdjieff advocated and bring it to an unimaginable fruition. Conditions for Orage's success in New York were similar to those which had favored Ouspensky in London. Within a general climate of opinion, there were particular groups whose own search for values had approached the point at which they might rise to the bait thrown out by the Master and the steady fishing of his disciple. The three most affected were the literary group which in 1923 was more or less under the influence of Waldo Frank; the circle of writers and publicists centered on Herbert Croly and the *New Republic;* and the staff of the avant-garde *The Little Review*, edited by Margaret Anderson and Jane Heap. These groups were in close contact—Waldo Frank published in both *The Little Review* and the *New Republic*—and Orage's success cut a broad swathe through the intelligentsia of New York.

The Frank circle of 1923 included Hart Crane, Gorham Munson, Jean Toomer, and Kenneth Burke. All were in some way affected by Gurdjieff and Orage, although Crane very quickly, and Frank later, rejected the influence of Fontainebleau and its Master. Waldo Frank (b. 1889) was the literary lion at the time of Gurdjieff's arrival. He had graduated from Yale in 1911 and worked in New York as a journalist before taking to the life of a freelance writer. In 1916 he was one of the founders of the review, *The Seven Arts*, and soon his novels began to earn him a reputation as a prophet. In France, he was looked upon as the voice of the new American literature and became the American correspondent of the *Nouvelle Revue Française*. At the end of 1916, he married Margaret Naumburg, who two years earlier had founded the progressive Walden School in New York, where the teaching was based on the principles of psychoanalysis and the New Education. But even at the time of his greatest success as an interpreter of America to itself and to Europe, Frank was turning toward mysticism.

At Yale he had investigated the mystics, Oriental religion, and the new psychology. His marriage increased his interest in the internal world, and at the very time (1919–20) when his book *Our America* was enjoying a huge success, Frank was traveling the country absorbed in the study of medieval Cabalists. *Our America* established his reputation; and it was the book of a seer of eternal values. "Ours is the first generation of Americans consciously engaged in spiritual pioneering," he proclaimed. His contemporaries were in search of a "mystic Word." "We go forth to seek America. And in the seeking we create her." Under this influence of Whitman he declared: "The one true hierarchy of values in the world is the hierarchy of consciousness"; and implied that his generation was reacting towards a "four-dimensional" consciousness—an idea he must have derived from the books of Claude Bragdon.

In February 1920, he had a series of visionary experiences in Richmond, Virginia, which induced a burst of creative activity resulting in his novels *Rahab* and *City Block*—both published in 1922. Some time after his illuminations, Frank read *Tertium Organum*, and lost no time in passing on his enthusiasm to his friends. The group adapted catchwords from Ouspensky in phrases like "the new slope of consciousness," "the superior logic of metaphor," and "noumenal knowledge"; *Tertium Organum* seemed to provide the basis for the leap into that American superconsciousness which Frank so hopefully expected.

It is not clear whether Frank discovered Ouspensky for himself, or whether he was directed to *Tertium Organum* by one of the book's leading propagandists, the poet Hart Crane. Crane became eloquent over the virtues of *Tertium Organum*, and—perhaps stimulated by Ouspensky's arguments—he too underwent mystical experiences. In June 1922, he was writing to his friend, Gorham Munson, about his experience of "the higher consciousness" under anaesthetics the previous winter. Munson told the poet's biographer, John Unterecker: "You cannot overemphasize the importance of that book. Crane hounded me to read it. And he kept after me to read it until I finally did."

Munson himself was born in 1896 and graduated in 1917 from Wesleyan University. In 1921 he married the dancer Elizabeth Delza. Like his associates, he made his name in the world of the little magazines. In the spring of 1922 he founded *Secession* which he published from various towns in Austria, Germany, and Italy before returning to the United States, where the last number of his magazine appeared in April 1924. At the time of Gurdjieff's arrival in New York, Munson was Waldo Frank's closest follower, and in 1923 had published *Waldo Frank, a Study*, a laudatory essay which he afterward described as "premature." He was to become one of Orage's right-hand men.

The American who most fully committed himself to Gurdjieff was another disciple of Frank, Jean Toomer. Toomer is now remembered only for his one published novel, *Cane*, an account of life in the southern United States. Critics of *Cane* bemoan the fact that its always elusive author seemed almost to disappear soon after his impressive debut in the world of letters. The lack of creative writing during the last third of Toomer's life can be explained by perpetual illness; but his earlier disappearance was into the Work. Until the mid-1930s, he remained the most important figure after Orage in the teaching of Gurdjieff's ideas in America.

Jean Toomer (1894–1967) was born Nathan Eugene Toomer. Through his mother he derived his ancestry from P. B. Pinchback (1837–1921), who was briefly Governor of Louisiana in the 1870s. Toomer is thought of as a Negro novelist although, in fact, his ancestry also included Welsh, Dutch, French, German, Jewish, and Indian blood. This mixture of so many races of the earth produced in Toomer a human being of great attractiveness. Like his mentor Orage, he seems to have found his path strewn with willing conquests, although his graceful physical type was at the opposite pole to the angular Englishman. Like Orage too—like almost all men of impressive personality—he provoked opposition.

In the unpublished book "From Exile into Being," which Toomer began in 1938, he analyzes the reasons why he entered the Work. The metaphor which governs his account is one which Gurdjieff took from Buddhist imagery. Life consists, he said, of two rivers in one or another of which a man belongs. One of these rivers flows into the common pool of unevolved life force which is distributed throughout newly created beings. The other river flows into the ocean, otherwise the energy source from which the water is transformed to higher grades of being. "A man who has in his common presence his own 'I' enters one of the streams of the river of life; and the man who has not, enters the other." Toomer sees his progress toward Gurdjieff in terms of the drop of water to which Gurdjieff compared the would-be individual trying to move from one stream to the other. The second chapter of "From Exile into Being" is entitled "Unease in the First River." Although it was written after a long period spent under the Gurdjieff discipline, the tone of moral earnestness seems to have been characteristic of Toomer at all stages of his life.

At the age of nineteen, Toomer wrote, he experienced a great "moral awakening." What *ought* he to do? What were the moral imperatives which should govern his life? He decided to try to learn scientific agriculture, but neither this nor attempts to study law proved successful. He left the universities of New York and Wisconsin because they failed to provide what he was looking for, and only several colleges later did he succeed in recovering a sense of purpose. His unanchored situation was made even more insecure when he was rejected for military service in the First World War on grounds of physical fitness. "So I looked," he wrote, "so I tried. I tried this. I tried that. Not this. Not that. I got jobs. I quit jobs. I rejected and was rejected." He decided that the world was engaged in a conspiracy to pretend that people "were making the best of an inevitably bad lot" in order to hide "the certain knowing that they were misfits and *should* be misfits in this world-as-it-is, in this life-as-it-is." As he put it in his privately published book, *Essentials* (1931), "The open conspiracy: 'Let's do outside things; inside things are too difficult.'"

At the end of the war, Toomer "overnight" lost his faith in God under the influence of scientific and evolutionary thought. But "a month or so after I lost God I found my mind." He discovered Whitman and Goethe and began to make contact with American writers, including Lewis Mumford and Waldo Frank. At last he had an objective, and he began a period of intense work in order to learn to write, although writing alone could not satisfy his hunger for fundamentals. He began to feel that "higher attainment" was the goal of existence, and for such attainment a technique was necessary—as literary technique had to be learned, so he must find a teacher of higher consciousness. Toomer found himself "reading the mystics, the philosophers and religious writers of America and Europe," as well as those modern authors "whose books were creating a new literature, and indeed a new culture in this land." The greatest influence on this curriculum was undoubtedly Waldo Frank; and Toomer's catalogue makes it clear how the Frank group could see the new literature which they were striving to create as inseparable from an extension of personal consciousness. *Tertium Organum* had answered what it was possible to see as a specifically American need.

And then there was *Cane*. Waldo Frank was Toomer's literary sponsor, and in the last half of 1922 spent some time with his protégé in the South, where Toomer in his turn helped Frank with the dialogue and speech rhythms of his novel *Holiday*. The following year *Cane* appeared and had an instant critical success. Toomer was not really a natural novelist, and his unpublished works are chiefly remarkable for their psychological insight. When he spreads himself, he has a tendency to become turgid and imprecise. Yet his feeling for words is still evident in the book of aphorisms, *Essentials*, which was provoked by his Gurdjieff experience, and compression and discipline worked in his favor. *Cane* showed these virtues, and its impressionistic account of Negro life is vivid, rich as molasses, and filled with a sense of natural beauty. Although Toomer may have lost his early faith, he retained—or had possibly regained—an appreciation of the highly emotional Christianity of the American South. It was on its own merits and not as a result of Waldo Frank's foreword that *Cane* earned its success. As a result, its author found himself engulfed in the excitement of the new literary movement. He had arrived.

"To arrive" meant a great deal in those days of the early '20s. If you were doing anything worthwhile in any of the arts and in the modern idiom, to arrive meant that you were welcomed into the most remarkable upsurge yet to occur in our national culture. . . . You were part of a living world of great promise. And in this world, if you so felt it, there was not only art but something of religion. A number of us, including Gorham Munson and Hart Crane, came to sense that we were as men with missions pioneering up "the new slope of consciousness."

Like Crane and Frank, Toomer entered the life beyond life. He went through an extraordinary experience in which he felt at one with *his* people, with *all* people, with all the world. "I was *in*," he wrote. "All I had formerly thought and felt *about* a larger being and a higher consciousness became for me a living reality of higher experience." The experience was so intense that it became "unbearable," and Toomer was thankful when it departed, leaving "an unforgettable taste, a burning memory of how it had been when my soul visited me."

Toomer began to see life as a religious process. He rediscovered God, and wondered how he could ever have had the temerity to put pen to paper. "In my present condition I simply wasn't up to writing. Writing, real writing, it now seemed to me, presupposed the possession of the very things I knew I lacked, namely self-purity, self-unification, self-development. I wasn't fit to write." His success had turned to ashes as he tasted it. One day his self-analysis reached the point at which he asked the question, "*Who* am I?" At once this "perfectly natural . . . but very startling question" became the center of gravity in his discussions with his friends. The conclusion which he reached was that "one must become a man before he can become an artist." After a succession of failed attempts to persuade his friends to join him in an effort to achieve self-mastery, he decided that the only solution was to seek a master himself. He saw "a trip to Europe and to India as the next logical inevitable step." But at this point Orage arrived in New York and—miracle of miracles!—the mountain came to Mohammed sailing in a first class cabin on the French Line.

The Frank circle was the most obviously "prepared" segment of the intellectual world to respond to the message of Orage. However, there were other groups of literary men who were also "looking for something" and could not in all honesty ignore Gurdjieff's ideas. One responsive lobby was formed by the disappointed liberals of Herbert Croly's *New Republic*. Croly (1868–1930) is best known for his two books, *Promise of American Life* (1909) and *Progressive Democracy* (1914), which earned him respect as a theorizer on the new America but small commercial success. In 1914 he founded the *New Republic* with the aid of wealthy backers. During the war years, his magazine was popularly regarded as the mouthpiece of President Woodrow Wilson, and Croly played a leading part in securing United States intervention in the First World War. He lost much of his popularity by opposing the signing of the Versailles agreement. This break with the policy of the Wilson administration cost the *New Republic* half its circulation and much of its prestige, so that in 1919, Croly found himself in a position similar to that of Orage in London.

Disillusioned with politics, he turned his attention to the prospects of reconciling religion and science. Edmund Wilson—who was the literary editor of the *New Republic* and set his face firmly against the influence of Orage and Gurdjieff—refers scathingly to the "inhibited personality and unsatisfied religious instincts" which laid Croly open to conversion; long before the advent of Orage, Croly's *New Republic* articles had begun to discuss topics of a more or less religious nature, and he had even assembled the materials for a religious book. Orage's approach to similar problems—as a fellow publicist and literary man—was naturally attractive. Other associates of Croly were ready for Gurdjieff's ideas. Among these were T.S. Matthews, son of the Episcopal bishop of Princeton, who was then working on the *New Republic* and later became editor of *Time*, and Amos Pinchot, a lawyer and publicist, whose brother Gifford Pinchot had been a member of Woodrow Wilson's cabinet. Edmund Wilson's criticism of the vogue for Orage occasionally assumes an embattled tone.

There were other groups who came to Gurdjieff chiefly by default. Perhaps their personal idols had crumbled, or they apprehended in a dim way that their gods were substitutes. Perhaps they had been soured by success and had lost their sense of purpose. One such circle was formed by the staff of *The Little Review*. Essentially this consisted of the editors, Margaret Anderson and Jane Heap, and whatever friends they were able to influence. If in capturing the attention of the Frank circle, Gurdjieff secured a hearing for his ideas in America, the friends of *The Little Review* made his name a byword among the studios and studies of cosmopolitan Bohemia.

Margaret Anderson founded *The Little Review* in Chicago when she was twenty-five. Born in Indianapolis in 1889, she went to college in Ohio, and escaped from her country club background to work on a magazine in Chicago. There followed a brief career in journalism and a period on the staff of *The Dial* before *The Little Review* burst out Athena-like in 1914. From the start the magazine bore the unmistakable imprint of its originator's enthusiasm for Art; it was as if the whole fabric of dullness, prudishness, and rectitude which American artists felt encumbering them had been banished by the force of her lone enthusiasm. The first volume of Margaret Anderson's autobiography, *My Thirty Years War*, begins with her self-appraisal: "My greatest enemy is reality. I have fought it successfully for thirty years." Throughout the life of *The Little Review*, its founder crusaded valiantly in all directions.

The Little Review was, if anything, more astonishing than Orage's *New Age*. Unhampered by any consistent editorial policy, it simply concentrated on publishing what its editors found worth publishing—and on one occasion, when Margaret Anderson and Jane Heap decided that literature was temporarily moribund, there appeared a sixty-four-page blank number prefaced by an announcement that there was nothing fit to print. There were other little magazines—and as 1920 approached, many more, like Waldo Frank's *Seven Arts* and Munson's *Secession*, were founded in imitation of *The Little Review*—but few approached the success of their model, and none gathered so distinguished a list of contributors. The first poems of T. S. Eliot, the serial publication of James Joyce's *Ulysses*, and the poetry of Ezra Pound (who for some time was the magazine's European editor), appeared alongside the work of Wyndham Lewis, William Carlos Williams, and later of Frank, Kenneth Burke and Jean Toomer. *The Little Review* was indispensable in bringing the culture of Europe to America and in assisting the new literature which America was incubating. It may seem a jaundiced and European view to say that *The Little Review* and modern American letters were released together on an unsuspecting public, and it is of course exaggerated; but the remark is in the spirit of the magazine, and in certain moods, its editors would probably have agreed.

Margaret Anderson was a young woman of striking good looks. Ezra Pound's good angel, John Quinn, who helped *The Little Review* financially in New York, thought Jane Heap "a typical Washington-Squareite," but wrote that Margaret Anderson was "a damned attractive young woman, one of the handsomest I have ever seen, very high-spirited, very courageous and very fine." The attentions to which she was no doubt subjected simply increased her sense of independence. "I am no man's wife," she thundered in *My Thirty Years War*, "no man's delightful mistress, and I will never, never, never, be a mother." Her energies were entirely devoted to the life of art, which she later defined in Jane Heap's *Little Review* motto:

TO EXPRESS THE EMOTIONS OF LIFE IS TO LIVE
TO EXPRESS THE LIFE OF EMOTIONS IS TO MAKE ART.

The temperament of its founder made *The Little Review* both invaluable and infuriating. Its *joie-de-vivre* did not exclude a serious purpose, although in the early numbers that purpose was somewhat in doubt. For a time Emma Goldmann and anarchism provided a center of gravity, but although *The Little Review* always remained sympathetic to the anarchists, its real direction was dictated by the forceful personality of Jane Heap.

More successfully than any of Gurdjieff's famous followers, Jane Heap contrived to disappear. Once she committed herself to the Work, she made a remarkable break with her past life—and became invisible. Academics in search of information never persuaded her to divulge her personal history, and it is impossible even to discover the exact year of her birth. The date, November 1, was not known until after her death in June 1964, and her age she kept a closely guarded secret. She was probably born around the middle 1880s in Kansas. Both her parents had emigrated from Europe to the United States; her father from Cheshire and her mother from Norway. Her grandmother was a Lapp, and that branch of the family had lived three days' journey beyond the Arctic Circle.

"There were many fascinating stories of her earliest life in the Middle West," writes one pupil,"—the hard conditions—the fierce weather—and many unusual experiences of great range and intensity." One particular set of experiences was provoked by her father's job. He was the warden of a lunatic asylum. In March 1917, Jane Heap published an article in *The Little Review* describing the loneliness and isolation of her upbringing.

"There were no books to read in this place except the great volumes in the Patients' Library," she wrote; "and I had read them all. There was no one to ask about anything. There was no way to make a connection with 'life.' Out there in the world they were working and thinking; here we were still. Very early I had given up every one except the Insane." In this stifling and hallucinatory environment, one thing alone supported her: Art. "Who had made the pictures, the books and the music in the world? . . . And how could you tell the makers from just people? Did they have a light around their heads?" Then one day a real live Artist visited the United States— "'Sarah Bernhardt.' Even when *they* said it the name had a light around it!" The little girl decided to walk all the way to St. Louis where the "wicked French actress" was appearing; but thought better of it, and resolved: "Some day I would go to Paris. Other people had got that far. I would go on living for that."

And then she came again! I was there, the first night, sitting in the balcony with some other art students. We had sold our futures to sit so close . . .

It was only the beginning. Jane Heap succeeded in reaching Europe and she succeeded in making art. The details of her education remain obscure, but she and Margaret Anderson met in Chicago in 1916. "Jane and I began talking," Margaret Anderson wrote. "We talked for days, months, years . . . We formed a consolidation that was to make us much loved and even more loathed." Eventually Jane was persuaded—much against her will—to write for *The Little Review*. The relationship of the two editors was conducted through a volcanic eruption of conversation. "There is no one in the modern world whose conversation I haven't sampled, I believe," wrote Margaret

Anderson in 1930, "except Picasso's. So I can't say that it isn't better than Jane Heap's. But I doubt it in spite of his reputation."

The topic of conversation, of course, was "Art"; or rather, the psychology of artists. Jane Heap's "uncanny knowledge of the human composition" steadily pushed their dissection of the artist-type toward a study of universals. As Margaret Anderson later put it: "We had never thought of art simply as painting, poetry, music, sculpture. We thought art was an expression, through the arts, of a need for something else." To both of them, art had represented an escape from childhood; now it began to seem a beginning.

Jane Heap was far from what would be called a "happy" person. In California during the summer of 1916, she delighted in keeping Margaret Anderson on edge by constant threats of suicide. The next year, when the pair moved *The Little Review* from Chicago to New York, "jh" was plunged into such despair that she spent most of the eighteen hours after their arrival face-down on her bed. But in Margaret Anderson's opinion, it was the state of desperation which gave Jane Heap her drive.

This unhappiness was not just a fashionable *Angst* about the human condition, but had its personal aspects. In the blunt phrase of T. S. Matthews, "she was the first full-blown Lesbian case I ever saw." Part of her legend lay in her unusual appearance—in Margaret Anderson's words: "handsome features, strongly cut, rather like those of Oscar Wilde in his only beautiful photograph." For evening dress she would appear in tuxedo, black bow tie, and long black skirt. It was making an eccentric virtue out of necessity; but even in the early 1920s, the strain must have been excessive, and was probably responsible for the frustrations and bursts of spleen for which she was noted. Something of this emerges from the pen-portrait of "jh" by C. S. Nott, who met her in New York in 1924. She "had the most stimulating and penetrating mind of any American woman I have ever met, and like all people with strong positive vibrations her negative ones were equally strong. She could be quite ruthless and regardless of near friend or old foe when she wanted something. She had a strong masculine side; as she said to me, 'I'm not really a woman.' . . . ." Margaret Anderson explains the deflationary tactics of her friend: "She never had the sardonic pleasure in it that was often attributed to her. She regarded the pricking of the bubbles of self-illusion—helping people to distinguish between wish-fulfilment and reality—as essential to the race."

In New York *The Little Review*, with its oddly assorted directorate, went from strength to strength. But the value placed by posterity on the magazine is in inverse proportion to its financial success. Sometimes there was very little money. Trouble with the Society for the Suppression of Vice over the publication of James Joyce's *Ulysses*, a poor diet and—despite the importance of *The Little Review* in avant-garde circles—a predictable lack of response from a hostile environment at last took their toll. Matters came to a head in the winter of 1922. Jane Heap complained that artists in the United States had still to make any recognizable impact; for Margaret Anderson, it was the last straw. "For a number of years life had had the aspect of a polar expedition," she wrote, "—all life serving only to maintain life. It was time to change such an existence. It was time to bring *The Little Review* to an end."

Jane Heap refused to accept this decision; and so Margaret turned the direction of the review over to her co-editor. "I didn't know what to do about life," she admitted, "—so I did a nervous breakdown that lasted many months." To one who had always given thanks for her "unaccountable inner happiness," the experience must have been both painful and puzzling. In her autobiographical *The Fiery Fountains*, she records her transition from a state of supposed euphoria to a confrontation with her "enemy," reality. "The impression persisted: 'I am so happy, I have always been so desperately happy.' (As unhappy as that?) Orage said." In 1922 she was confused and directionless, her questionings were inchoate, and only by degrees did a positive aspiration take form.

An encounter with W. B. Yeats—an early and constant contributor to *The Little Review*—ignited a new enthusiasm for Europe, and a meeting with Georgette Leblanc, who for twenty years had been the mistress and the inspiration of Maurice Maeterlinck, resulted in a new friendship that stimulated Margaret Anderson's religious instincts.

Greenwich Village was discovering French Symbolism for itself at about this time, and *The Little Review* had begun to draw on esoteric sources. Margaret Anderson and Georgette Leblanc began to pursue their interrogation of the cosmos in terms more directly religious. They were inspired by the Bible but not to any positive activity; they recoiled in alarm from the terminology of Eastern religion. But both editors of *The Little Review* had read Claude Bragdon's edition of *Tertium Organum* and considered that "we had found a contemporary author with a great mind." They heard a rumor that Ouspensky was writing a book to be called *The Unknown Doctrine* about his association with Gurdjieff. Then Gurdjieff's personal emissary arrived.

When Orage landed in New York his task appeared unenviable. As he had failed to persuade Claude Bragdon—his only apparently solid "esoteric" contact in the city—to lend his support, he was forced to fall back on his literary reputation. He somehow discovered the Sunwise Turn Bookshop at 2 East 31st Street, which is described by Carl Zigrosser as having been "much more than a bookshop; it was a clearing house for ideas, a meeting place for free spirits." Its proprietors were a retired English teacher, Madge Jenison, and a retired art teacher, Mary Mowbray-Clarke. They published Coomaraswamy's *The Dance of Siva,** and advertised in *The Little Review*. "The shop was animated more by crusaders than commerce," writes Zigrosser. "The sagging financial structure was shored up by taking in a succession of moneyed people as partners." From this center of the Progressive world, Orage made propaganda.

It is ironical that at the very outset of his mission in the United States, Orage met the person with whom he was to find the ordinary and important fulfilments of life, and who would eventually prove to be the most important influence in detaching him from his Master. Jessie Dwight had bought a share in the Sunwise Turn, and happened to hear Orage's initial lecture on Katherine Mansfield. Next day Orage met her in the shop and asked whether she had enjoyed the talk. According to Philip Mairet, the reply was, "No, not at all." From this promising beginning a friendship developed which culminated in Jessie Dwight's becoming, first Orage's secretary, and afterward his wife.

A prospectus for the Institute was circulated—a translation of the French original. Margaret Naumburg found a copy at the Sunwise Turn, and passed it to Jean Toomer who was intrigued and wanted to examine the doctrine of Ouspensky's teacher. His projected journey to the East was now unnecessary; equally, it had just begun. "I began reading it," he writes of Gurdjieff's prospectus. "The first words made me feel that I was close to what I sought. I read with eagerness. I read with glow. I gave cries of joy as I came upon statement after statement that said what I wanted to hear said. Here it was. This was it. At last I had come upon something that 'spoke to my condition.'"

Margaret Anderson gives an account of "Orage's first lecture" in New York, which seems to refer to an occasion which preceded the arrival of Gurdjieff and his pupils:

Orage walked out upon the stage. He was tall and easy, but quick and sure—the most persuasive man I have ever known. He sat down and began to tell, simply, why he had come. Claude Bragdon interrupted by standing up to say that he had a letter from Ouspensky which he would like to read. It was a conventional letter, everyone was bored, Bragdon was unaware of boredom as he began commenting on the letter. Orage stopped him expertly and went on with his talk. But the ease and flow of the evening had been broken. "Talk louder," someone called out. "And be more interesting," Mrs. Lydig said loudly. This

---

*Coomaraswamy became a friend of Orage, although according to Mrs. Jessie Orage, he thought Gurdjieff "a bit of a charlatan."

made me angry. "Don't do that," I whispered to her—"What's the matter?" she said, still loudly, "don't you agree?"—"Of course not," I said, "just wait, he'll be so interesting he'll be incomprehensible." But he wasn't. He had no intention of being merely "interesting."

It was the ideas they heard from Orage which impressed Margaret Anderson and her friends, not the dances which fascinated the town. Jean Toomer's reaction to the prospectus had also been primarily intellectual; but this did not exclude a highly emotional reaction to the movements. A slightly damaging fact was that Waldo Frank's literary patronage had resulted in an intimate association between Frank's wife, Margaret Naumburg, and Frank's protégé, Jean Toomer. The pair attended one of the demonstrations together which, according to Toomer, was held in Webster Hall. He was impressed by the figure of Thomas de Hartmann at the piano—"a monk in a tuxedo," he thought. More impressive still was the figure of Gurdjieff, walking up and down the aisles, inspecting the audience. Toomer had tried German and Swedish gymnastics as well as the system of F. Mathias Alexander; and he and Margaret Naumburg decided that Gurdjieff was "co-ordinated" in Alexander's sense.

I saw this man in motion, a unit in motion. He was completely of one piece. From the crown of his head down the back of the head, down the neck, down the back and down the legs, there was a remarkable line. Shall I call it a gathered line? It suggested co-ordination, integration, knitness, power . . . I was fascinated by the way the man walked. As his feet touched the floor there seemed to be no weight on them at all—a glide, a stride, a weightless walk.

The unusual nature of Gurdjieff's deliberate gait impressed many who met him, "Like the hind legs of a cat," says Mrs. Jessie Orage. "He looked," recalls a man who knew him during the 1930s, "as if he were walking at the head of a parade." Was this the new kind of man of which *Tertium Organum* had spoken? "I was already convinced," writes Toomer, "that some men, men never heard of by the general world of men, had attained various of these higher states, had come into possession of a superior knowledge and wisdom, a superior power, an almost incredible mastery. They were variously called Masters, Adepts, Mahatmas. I believed that men of this category had existed in ancient times and that there must be some existing at this time. G., I felt, could be a Master. Certainly not a saint . . . Not a holy man, not a yogi, but—a Master?"

In the dancing itself, Toomer found an unexpected release of emotion:

To my mind they were amazing events that satisfied and exceeded anything that I could have asked for. I was in the audience but I saw and felt what went on as if I were already one of the participants. The performances began at theatre time and continued on and on as though the pupils were capable of endless endurance. By 12 o'clock most of the onlookers had left. The demonstrations continued. I stayed to the very last, for I was endlessly fascinated, and would have been happy if the performance had gone on through the night, every night.

As when Ouspensky came to London, the test of commitment seemed to be the giving up of everything and a pilgrimage to Fontainebleau. Toomer was still unconvinced that he could not succeed independently in the sort of "work" advertised by Gurdjieff. He projected his feelings outward, in the form of a mild distaste for Orage and a sneaking mistrust of Gurdjieff, the Man of Power. He had a number of talks with Orage, who after enlarging on the miserable condition of mechanical man, slipped his qualification into the conversation: "Yes, *but there is a way out.*" "That was just what I wanted to hear," wrote Toomer, "in just so many words, from him. I myself was intuitively certain that there was a way out, but I wanted it said by someone who impressed me as having found it." Such reassurance could not conquer the fear he felt of Gurdjieff. "He seemed to have everything that could be asked of a developed human being, a teacher and a master. Knowledge, integration, many-sidedness, power—in fact he had a bit too much power for my comfort. . . . I held back, G.'s power disturbed me. I was not sure of it, and I wanted to be sure before I placed myself wholly in his hands. This at any rate was how I explained it to myself." He reacted in the fashion which Jane Heap later called "the bolting of beginners," and fled New York while the demonstrations were still in progress.

Gurdjieff moved his troupe to the small Neighborhood Playhouse in Greenwich Village, which had been lent to him by a wealthy family who were friends of Mary Mowbray-Clarke of the Sunwise Turn. Here, he began to concentrate on screening likely candidates for the Institute. The Neighborhood Playhouse was well known to New York intellectuals—Gorham Munson's wife, Elizabeth Delza, had danced there—and admission was by invitation only. Gurdjieff stood in the foyer of the theater scanning his audience. Again, the susceptible were impressed by his mere presence. "He had a presence impossible to describe," writes Margaret Anderson, "because I had never encountered another with which to compare it."

The Neighborhood Playhouse demonstrations separated the likely candidates from the less hopeful prospects. Once again Orage acted as the interpreter, and from the small audiences of 100–150 there began to emerge those who became his chief supporters. The Munsons were overwhelmed; on the night of her first visit, Elizabeth Delza could scarcely sleep for the "revivifying" effect of the dances in which she discovered "a unique theatrical experience." Hart Crane arrived, and some witnesses thought he was drunk, although it may have been excessive devotion to Gurdjieff which exaggerated his condition. His companion of the evening, Susan Jenkins Brown, remembers merely that "Hart and I were irreverent but well-behaved. . . ."

Irreverent or not, Crane was, at the time, extremely impressed: "Things were done by amateurs," he informed his mother, "which would stump the Russian ballet, I'm sure."

It is easy to give the false impression that "all New York"—to quote Margaret Anderson—was reeling under the impact of Gurdjieff. "All New York" was interested in the initial sensation, but the lasting impact of the 1924 visit was limited to the small groups of intellectuals who have been mentioned. Conditions were, in fact, not very bright for Gurdjieff and his pupils in February 1924. "As time passed," Thomas de Hartmann wrote, "there were fewer and fewer people in our audience; and we had no further prospects. Our food ration diminished day by day." Gurdjieff ordered everyone to find work. In the nick of time, de Hartmann renewed an old acquaintance which enabled him to make a booking for Chicago. Orage was dispatched with C. S. Nott, a young assistant from the Sunwise Turn, to prepare the ground in Chicago and in Boston and Philadelphia on the way. The pupils followed, and Jessie Dwight offered Gurdjieff a large contribution to the Institute in exchange for permission to accompany him.

Despite the tours, and even a letter printed by the *New York Times* from novelist Zona Gale appealing to the public to support the final demonstration at Carnegie Hall, the expedition had been, in Claude Bragdon's phrase, "disappointing, even disastrous," and as Bragdon noted, when the party returned to Fontainebleau, Orage was left "to devise ways to pay their debts and to continue the campaign." At least he was left with a base on which to build. Groups began to form for the study of Gurdjieff's ideas. One began to meet in the Jane Heap house on East 9th Street. Membership cards were issued to those who subscribed to the Institute for the Harmonious Development of Man. They read as follows:

> G. Gurdjieff's Institute for the Harmonious Development of Man
> Certificate of Membership No. . . .*
> Valid for one year from June 1st, 1924–1925
> The bearer of this, a member of the GURDJIEFF Institute has the following privileges:

> Free residence, with all the rights of permanent members, at the chief centre of the Institute at Fontainebleau, as well as at the

---

*Jessie Dwight was No. 606, Jean Toomer, No. 619.

Institute's boarding houses in other places; free attendance at all classes, lectures and conferences whenever held under the auspices of the Institute, except those lectures, etc. specially held for permanent members; free subscription to the Institute's journal and all the literature issued by the Institute.

The right of enquiry and reply concerning the ideas of the Institute.

Any member may, if he or she wish, use any of the sanatoria or hotels of the Institute for him or herself, and family, at one half the regular rates.

> Annual subscription $120.
> (Signed) Founder G. *Gurdjieff*
> Person issuing A. R. *Orage*

This document is authorised for American citizens only over the personal signature of one of the following persons:

Mrs. Rublee, 242, E. 49th Street, New York. Professor Comstock, Harvard University, Boston. Edgar Hamilton, 245, N. Kenilworth Avenue, Oak Park, Chicago Mr. A. R. Orage, c/o Mr. F. R. Whiteside, 1510 Waverly St., Philadelphia.

The reference to "sanatoria" and "boarding houses" was no doubt intended to reinforce the illusion which Gurdjieff loved to perpetuate, that he had opened branches of his Institute in "the chief European cities." Was this fraudulence, a test, or for some unfathomable purpose? There is a suspicious likeness to Aleister Crowley's famous advertisement for his magical order of the Astrum Argentinum, which also refers to sanatoria and other imaginary facilities. . . . And is this likeness intentional?

The crack in the times swallowed people up, as recruits mustered the courage to travel to Fontainebleau. Margaret Anderson and Georgette Leblanc left for France and took a farmhouse at Passy from which they could commute to the Prieuré. For the moment Jane Heap bided her time. She was still attached to the world of Art; that very year she opened The Little Review Gallery. C. S. Nott decided to go to Fontainebleau. On the other hand, when Gurdjieff directed Jessie Dwight to follow suit, she returned to Orage and scoffingly told him of the magisterial command. She, go to France? Orage looked at her sadly and said: "But you must." So she made the crossing in the company of Olgivanna.

Jean Toomer postponed the evil day as long as he could, and a letter he wrote to Gorham Munson betrays his attempts at temporizing. At the same time as he asked for information about Gurdjieff and the Institute, he tried to cover himself by telling his friend that "I just may have a chance to learn something of the Rosicrucians, first hand." Eventually he overcame his revulsions and returned to New York. On July 9, he wrote to Orage that he regretted having missed "the most intensive work of the Institute, together with your evening at the Munsons." The impulses which had been warring within him had settled their differences. "I have now ended a phase of many years' duration," he told Orage, "and am open with no backward reservation whatsoever, to the next discipline." At this stage he intended to book himself on the first possible ship to Europe. He had taken six months to make up his mind, and was eager to be off.

Most of his friends were unavailable. Margaret Naumburg was in Reno from where she wrote him agitated leters, inquiring whether Orage knew of the relationship between her and Waldo Frank, and informing Toomer that she had just finished reading *Isis Unveiled*. The various obstacles in the path of her own projected visit to Fontainebleau were gradually being cleared away. Toomer did seek out Hart Crane. "My feeling for Hart was as warm as ever," he later noted, "and I had a sense that this might be the parting of our ways. Crane was moving further away from Gurdjieff and was soon to start an attempt to dissuade his friends from having anything to do with the Institute or with Orage. Gorham Munson and his wife were out of town for several weeks, and a tortured correspondence flew between him and Toomer. How did the discovery of a Master affect relations with the doyen of their literary circle, Waldo Frank? Frank, after all, had assumed the airs of a prophet and they were in a sense deserting a standard to which Hart Crane was remaining loyal. Was all their writing, Munson wondered, based on self-deception? Toomer was little help; for now that he had made his commitment, he rested in its security. On July 17, Toomer wrote to Munson: "I did not ask you to choose between Waldo and Gurdjieff. I simply stated an opposition as I saw it . . . to me Waldo stands for what *not* to do, whereas Gurdjieff stands for what *to do*." This was an opinion to which Munson soon became converted, and in a few years' time he would be broadcasting his convictions from the housetops.

Orage replied "promptly" to Toomer's request for an interview, and the novelist was quickly enrolled as a member of the Institute. He passed the time before his boat sailed by attending Orage's groups as a preparation for the Prieuré. His originally cool attitude to Orage grew steadily warmer, until just before his departure, he was inspired by the older man's exhortations about the value of his forthcoming experience. "I can still see him seated there in that hot New York room," Toomer wrote, "he in shirt sleeves and wearing suspenders. His eyes were keen and sparkling and his face aglow, all of him alive with zest for the ideas and the work."

Unfortunately for those intent on penetrating Fontainebleau itself, an event—quite unknown in New York—had occurred before Toomer set sail which profoundly affected Gurdjieff, all his pupils, and would-be pupils. It altered the entire tenor of his work. The reverberations settled the course of Orage's life for the next half-dozen years and were as influential for Ouspensky and his followers in England. In the afternoon of July 5, 1924, Gurdjieff's car left the road from Paris to Fontainebleau at the junction with the N 168 road from Versailles to Choisy-le-Roi, and crashed into a tree. *The Master was dangerously ill.*

5

A Chapter of Accidents

Gurdjieff's accident had a significance for his followers far beyond the material and philosophical difficulties which were its natural result. A simple car crash—and the lives of a number of people seemed to hang in the balance, poised dizzily between reality and unbelief. Within the framework of Gurdjieff's System the accident assumed a new meaning, an embarrassment of meanings, a confusion in which many possible interpretations took root and sprouted consequences like tropical vines.

It was Gurdjieff's custom to spend two days in the week away from Fontainebleau and to drive back to the Prieuré in the afternoon. During the hectic period after the purchase of the Prieuré, he often made this journey. In "The Material Question," he tells how the organization of his new establishment and the demands of his practice as a hypnotist so tired him that he fell asleep at the wheel one afternoon and awoke in his stalled vehicle at ten o'clock the next morning. Perhaps what Gurdjieff called his "'charge-and-crash' with my automobile at full speed into a tree standing silently, like an observer and reckoner of the passage of centuries at a disorderly tempo" was the result of another such incident. On the other hand, he was an appalling driver, and this was only the first of at least four crashes. "He drove like a wild man," wrote Kathryn Hulme of her meeting with Gurdjieff in 1932, "cutting in and out of traffic without hand signals or even space to accommodate his car in the lanes he suddenly switched to

Portrait of Ushé Narzunoff, supposedly taken in 1898, and published by the French scholar Joseph Deniker.

Unpublished photo of Narzunoff's two sons with their lama "educator," from the collection of Joseph Deniker.

Narzunoff and his wife in Verknie-Udinsk, November 1908.

Above: Agwan Dordjieff, a Tsanit Khanpo who was at the right hand of the Dalai Lama. *Right:* Prince Ukhtomsky, head of the Department of Foreign Creeds during the period of the Great Game and a powerful supporter of Buddhism.

Graphic photograph of members of the Dordjieff mission, which included four Russians and three Chinese. Narzunoff is second from left.

The young Ouspensky in about 1912, impassioned by his own "search for the miraculous." *Below:* Backcloth for the ballet *The Struggle of the Magicians* first performed in Tiflis in 1917.

Gurdjieff as he appeared sometime during the 1920s.

The château in the village of Avon on the outskirts of Fontainebleau, afterwards known as Le Prieuré to the followers of Gurdjieff.

Followers of Gurdjieff erecting the framework of what was to become known as the Study House.

Gurdjieff, no doubt giving directions, inside the Study House during its construction.

An unidentified pupil standing with a pole on a platform in the Study House. *Below:* Another pupil on top of a ladder, illustrating well the story told about a pupil falling asleep from exhaustion and being rescued by Gurdjieff.

Another view from inside the Study House with fences in place for dancing. Gurdjieff is in center. *Below:* Gurdjieff as he appeared in his passport photo in the 1930s.

Jean Toomer, author of *Cane,* and
the most senior advocate of Gurdjieff's ideas in the United States.
Below: Orage, holding his first child,
during the happy period that preceded his final break with Gurdjieff
in May 1931.

Lynne Place in Virginia Water, the center for Ouspensky's teachings from 1935 until his death in October 1947. *Left:* Ouspensky, as he looked during his prime.

Gurdjieff's pantry in his apartment on the Rue des Colonels Renard in Paris which served as study, storeroom and confessional combined.

Ouspensky, holding one of the cats that so frequently accompanied him. *Below:* Rodney Collin, the most ardent of Ouspensky's followers and the disciple of the Work in Mexico City.

Gurdjieff and Mme. de Saltzmann, now the only surviving member of the original Tiflis group. *Right:* A more mellowed Gurdjieff as he appeared during his last years in Paris.

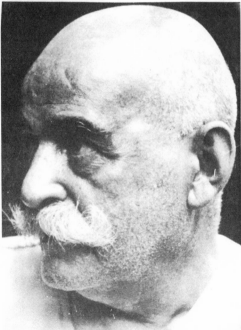

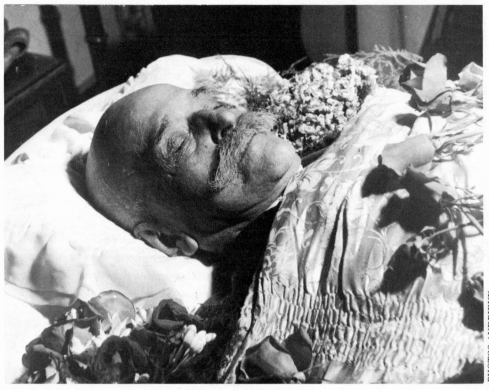

. . . the chances he took overtaking buses and trucks were terrifying." On the day of his accident, Gurdjieff had had lunch in an Armenian restaurant before leaving Paris for Fontainebleau; and, if large quantities of spirits had accompanied the meal, perhaps the consequences were predictable. Mme. de Hartmann blames the accident on the steering wheel which was found to be broken after the crash. She is the chief witness to the events of that day.

And very odd they were.

Mme. de Hartmann was still acting as Gurdjieff's secretary and steward. On the morning of July 5, 1924 she called for Gurdjieff at his new Paris apartment on the Boulevard Péreire. They had planned an expedition from Paris to inspect some equipment which she had ordered for the Prieuré, but Gurdjieff abruptly postponed the tour of inspection. This astonished her because of his customary considerateness to those with whom he had dealings outside his work. She was then told to persuade her parents to emigrate from Russia to avoid a famine which Gurdjieff predicted. More interesting still, she was given Gurdjieff's power of attorney. She was to tell the mechanic in the garage where Gurdjieff kept his Citroën to check the car thoroughly, especially the steering wheel. Then her plans for the day were further disrupted. Instead of traveling with Gurdjieff to the Prieuré by car, she was told to make an inventory of his apartment and to return by train. Gurdjieff departed, leaving her disgruntled at the prospect of a stifling railway journey in midsummer.

During the afternoon she fell asleep at her task and was awakened by what sounded like Gurdjieff's voice calling her name, "Olga Arcadievna!" By her watch it was 4:30, half an hour before she had to catch her train to Fontainebleau. On her arrival she learned that Gurdjieff had been taken to the hospital, and at the hospital she found her husband and Dr. Stoerneval. It appeared that Gurdjieff had "severe head injuries and lacerations of the hands." No bones had been broken and the skull was sound. Gurdjieff's case was turned over to two Russian doctors, and the next morning he was brought home—apparently still concussed and unconscious—in which state he remained for five days.

While helping to nurse Gurdjieff, Mme. de Hartmann had to hold his wrist. Although he was unconscious, she felt "his fist clench with great force." There are other rumors that even while unconscious Gurdjieff told his attendants where to massage him. Jessie Dwight was present when Gurdjieff arrived back from the hospital and saw him look at her. A passage from C. S. Nott's book, *Teachings of Gurdjieff*, describes the immediate impact of the news:

> Gurdjieff was brought out on a stretcher, his head covered with bandages; he was unconscious, but he murmured, "Many people, many people." He was carried upstairs to his room.

A hush descended on us; everyone went about his work quietly and seriously. A few were weeping, though there was a complete absence of conventional expressions of sorrow. Gurdjieff's condition was very serious; the doctors were not very hopeful for his recovery; the wonder was that he had not been killed instantly.

Later in the day I went up to the garage in Fontainebleau to get something from his car, a small Citroën, which had been towed there. The radiator was crushed, the engine was off its seating, the steering column was broken, screen and doors and windows smashed, the front axle and wings crumpled. Gurdjieff had been found lying on the grass verge on the road that runs from Paris to Fontainebleau, his head on a cushion of the car. How he had got out of the car, whether he had got himself out or was carried, was not clear.

The life of the Institute was dislocated. "There was silence in the Prieuré," writes Nott, "we spoke with lowered voices; the bell in the belfry no longer rang; there were no dances or music in the Study House and everyone wished with his whole being for Gurdjieff's recovery . . . it was as if the mainspring of a great machine had broken and the machine was running on its momentum. The force that moved our lives was gone." The real extent of the crisis for the Institute's inhabitants is shown in the account of Margaret Anderson's young nephew, Fritz Peters. Fritz and his brother Tom had been adopted by Jane Heap after the breakup of their parents' marrriage and, with the conversion of the editors of *The Little Review*, found themselves living at the Prieuré—a somewhat extraordinary boarding school. The brothers had arrived just before the crash and had time to see something of the ordinary operations of the Institute. "The very existence of the Institute depended entirely on G.'s presence," wrote Fritz Peters. "It was he who assigned work to every individual—and up to that moment he had supervised personally every detail of the running of the school. Now the imminent possibility of his death brought everything to a standstill. It was only thanks to the initiative of a few of the older students, most of whom had come to him from Russia, that we continued to eat regularly." The boy had been told to mow the lawns every day, and continued to perform what he regarded as a sacred obligation despite the threats and ostracism from the pupils in authority. Having given their wills into Gurdjieff's keeping, it seems that the disciples had little common sense left . . . or was there some deeper reason? As Peters writes: "What surprises me now is that I was not categorically forbidden to continue, or even forcibly restrained. The only explanation that I can find is that his power over his pupils was such that no single individual was willing to take the responsibility of totally denying what he had told me."

Mme. de Hartmann took over the administration of the Prieuré, while her husband and Mme. Ostrowsky helped Dr. Stoerneval to nurse Gurdjieff for the month or so before he was up and about. Jean Toomer, who arrived in the aftermath of the tragedy, found that "gloom hung over the place. Little or no work was going on and that half-heartedly." The responsibility of deputizing for the Master, and even of caring for him, almost overwhelmed the older disciples. According to Thomas de Hartmann, "We felt we had to protect him, though we might be wrong. We did not know his real condition. How could we? But to let him do everything like a healthy person—as for instance, to drive a car again quite soon—we felt obliged to stop him. We had to do it and to try to do it in such a way that no one could notice it and that he himself would not realise our intention if he really were still not quite recovered."

Gurdjieff at length appeared in the gardens. "His head was bandaged and his eyes concealed behind dark glasses. His sight was so impaired that he did not recognise us," writes Nott. "Against the doctor's instructions and warnings he had made a tremendous effort to get up. At first he would take a few steps, then stop. After fifteen minutes he was taken back to bed. But each day he stayed a little longer and walked a little further." It seemed that Gurdjieff's proverbial contempt for his body's demands was once more being demonstrated as he urged it on its unwilling passage. Jean Toomer felt a terrible disappointment when he compared the man of power he had admired in New York with this pathetic figure "who bore almost no resemblance to the Gurdjieff I had seen moving around. . . . Once begun, Gurdjieff's daily walks with his two companions continued rain or shine. My impression was that he took each walk as he took each step, deliberately and with unswerving determination. He did not speak to anyone—or show any recognition of their existence, if he saw them at all."

The second phase of Gurdjieff's recovery, as his pupils saw it, began when he was able to superintend work from his chair. He directed that large numbers of trees be felled and burned before him; and it was thought that he drew a form of strength from the blaze. "This continued," in Nott's words, "until it looked as if we should have to cut down half the forest to keep the fires going." At length Gurdjieff called a halt, and more general work began. The Prieuré regained something of its former animation. Toomer found that "things began to hum."

It was perfectly amazing what his presence did. Extra life, extra zest, extra power, extra will sprang up in us. Everybody worked hard all day long and sometimes into the night. The project was to clear a space in the woods along the road for a new kitchen garden. I sawed the trunks of felled trees into three-foot lengths. At the other end of the two-man saw was an Englishwoman with more stamina than five men. She was the pacemaker, and I had to keep up.

By the autumn, Toomer felt in magnificent physical condition. He wanted no other life. Nott reports that everyone was hoping that the Institute would resume its normal functioning. But there was another shock in store, what Toomer called "a bolt":

> Gurdjieff one fine day called every person on the place to gather round him. Then he simply announced that he would close the Institute— "liquidate" it was his word. Would we please never again refer to it as the Institute. That was finished. It was to be known from now as *Le Prieuré* only, his home where he would invite those sympathetic to him personally. "All my life I have lived for others," he said. "Now I will live for myself a while."

The pupils were given two days to move out. Nott and his friends were flabbergasted: "We did no more work that day, but talked among ourselves, trying to discover if anyone understood what it was all about. 'Is this,' we asked, 'the end of all the hopes that have been raised in us? Has everything really come to an end? Is his work really finished?' Everyone was mystified—old pupils as well as young."

According to Nott, most of the Russians and some Americans left the Prieuré for good. "They took him literally." Everyone, except for Gurdjieff's family and his closest associates, did leave for a short time; but gradually the more obstinate came drifting back. Nott's account treats the dispersal as an obvious "test"—rather as Thomas de Hartmann had treated Gurdjieff's announcements in the Caucasus that he was going to abandon work. But despite the Chekhovian sadness of the Russian pupils, it may be wondered whether Gurdjieff's directive was not—at least as far as it concerned them—intended to be taken at its face value. He was undoubtedly still supporting many of the general mass of Russians at the Prieuré; some had no great interest in his work, but for a Russian emigrant in the early 1920s it was next to impossible to find lucrative employment. Life inside the château walls was almost certainly more tolerable than life outside it, even if the provider of life's necessities exercised an incomprehensible discipline within his domain. Jessie Dwight's memory of the dismissal is that Gurdjieff's sense was clear: he would have no more parasites. And indeed, those summarily evicted had quickly to find jobs in Paris. Olgivanna became an attendant in a women's lavatory.

The "test" aspect was certainly present. As the more obstinate pupils drifted back, it emerged that Gurdjieff would allow the Americans to stay.

Jessie Dwight had been directed not to take part in the general exodus, and both Nott and Toomer remained with some half-dozen younger recruits from the United States. It was announced that Gurdjieff was to go away to take a cure, and that the remaining faithful would be granted interviews before he left. Toomer's apprehensiveness overcame him: "I was to confront a man whose knowledge and power I reverenced, who was not himself. I had no means of measuring to what degree he was not himself." In his terror, his questions vanished—a common occurrence with pupils who confronted Gurdjieff, and one which happened on this occasion to Nott also. It was decided that Toomer might stay, but after reflection the novelist concluded that, as the situation stood, he would gain more from an association with Orage in New York. He "was hungry for ideas, real ideas." Nott had decided to leave in order to establish himself in business. Gurdjieff apparently succeeded in persuading even the most tenacious that their proper place was not in the Prieuré.

The obvious reluctance of Gurdjieff to continue teaching as before prevented further neophytes from crossing the Atlantic. Margaret Naumburg had spent most of the summer trying to leave; and now, by the autumn, found that events had forestalled her. Until the last minute, she was hoping to sail, despite her knowledge of the accident and the possibility that Orage—who had gone to France to see Gurdjieff—would forbid any further visitors to Fontainebleau. On October 3, 1924, she wrote to Jean Toomer who was still at the Prieuré that she was on tenterhooks lest Orage's return prevent her own departure. She was apprehensive about the effect the news of Gurdjieff's condition might have on the converts in New York, but expected that Orage would say as little as possible.

Orage's position was decided for him by necessity, which meant money. For the work to continue, an incapacitated Gurdjieff must be kept in funds and sometime in the autumn after the great dispersal, Orage set sail for France to discover how matters stood. He was probably at the Prieuré by the end of September or the beginning of October. On what basis affairs proceeded between him and Gurdjieff, we can only guess, but the upshot was that he returned to New York in November with Jessie Dwight to carry on groups started by Orage after the demonstrations of the winter and early spring.

Between midsummer and autumn of 1924, the fact of Gurdjieff's accident completely altered the complexion of his work. The interpretation of the accident altered it still further.

Was it an accident? Gurdjieff's reputation as a dangerous driver, his heavy meal, and the possibility of overwork could all point to pure mischance. He may have had the car checked carefully because he had simply felt that there might be something wrong with the steering. Innumerable causes of a completely accidental nature could have sent him off the road into the tree.

If it was an accident, this was a real shock. Jean Toomer's reaction was shared by most of the disciples. "I did not believe it," he wrote. "I did not believe that a man of G.'s order was subject to the accidents that befall ordinary men." This was not mere hero worship, but followed from Gurdjieff's proclaimed doctrine. "Man lives in life *under the law of accident*," he had told Ouspensky in Russia. Ordinary sleeping man could begin to free himself from all the mechanical influences which determined his actions only through other influences which had their source "outside life" in the "inner circle" of humanity. This meant, to all intents and purposes, Gurdjieff's Work. By "work on himself," man could escape from the mechanical law of accident and place himself under the law of fate which governed his real essence. Surely the Master himself had escaped from mechanical laws?

Ouspensky remembered what Gurdjieff had taught, and his own teaching transmitted the doctrine of accident and fate. His later position is recorded in the book, *The Fourth Way*.

Questioner: When do we cease to be under the law of accident?
Ouspensky: When we develop will. To be completely free from the law of accident is very far, but there are different stages between complete freedom and our present position. . . . The theory of accidents is very simple. They happen only when the place is empty; if the place is occupied, they cannot happen. Occupied by what? By conscious actions.

Some days after the car crash of July 5, Ouspensky came to France. His stepdaughter and Mme. Ouspensky were still at the Institute, but as Ouspensky himself had now broken publicly with Gurdjieff, he had to content himself with telephoning them. He visited the crossroads where the Citroën had crashed, in the company of Boris Mouravieff, who remembered him as:

. . . despondent and crushed. After a prolonged silence, he said to me: "I'm frightened. . . . This is dreadful . . . Georgeivanitch's Institute was established to escape from the influence of the law of accident under which men spend their lives. Well, see how he himself has fallen under the influence of this very law . . . I still wonder whether it's really a pure accident?—Gurdjieff used always to make light of honesty together with all the rest of human personality. Has he not gone too far?—I tell you, I'm terribly afraid!"

Mouravieff lunched with Ouspensky in Fontainebleau, and during the meal his friend kept returning to the question of integrity. "Obviously," wrote Mouravieff, "the problem formed for him a sort of axis. And in consequence of for me unfathomable reasons, he would link the question of integrity and the accident which befell Gurdjieff." Later Mouravieff remembered a conversation which he connected with this concern of Ouspensky's. They had dined well in the Place Saint-Michel and had adjourned, as was Ouspensky's custom when in Paris during the 1920s, to the bars of Montmartre. Since his breach with Gurdjieff, Mouravieff had been trying in vain to persuade Ouspensky to discuss his former Master. Without warning, he asked him directly why he avoided such a discussion.

> Suddenly, his expression changed. I had the impression that before me there was *another man*, and no more the one with whom I had spent the whole of a pleasant evening in the most interesting discussions. He turned abruptly back to me and said in a strange tone of voice: "Imagine that a member of the family has committed a crime. In the family, one doesn't talk of it!"

Mouravieff is certain that the question was intimately related in Ouspensky's mind to the accident; and it seems as if Ouspensky thought it possible that the disaster was in some way a punishment for Gurdjieff having offended against heaven. Had they been wrong all this time, had they failed to recognize something fundamentally evil in this teaching? Gurdjieff had said that his Fourth Way was "against Nature, against God." Was this "accident" a proof of his infallibility—or was it divine punishment for his distortion of the truth?

Whatever interpretation is put on Ouspensky's strange conduct, even a strictly materialist view of the accident itself could lead his followers into the empyrean. Another explanation went the rounds: Nott attributes it to a "fanciful lady, a theosophist," who "spoke mysteriously of the 'dark brethren' who were trying to destroy Gurdjieff's work." He does not reveal the full details of the plot; but it has been enlarged by word of mouth until the dark brethren are said to have suborned the trees themselves to bend down and sweep Gurdjieff off the road. It is an uncomfortable fact that in his *Third Series*, Gurdjieff gave some countenance to the babblings of the lunatic fringe; but the question of why he did so is—as always with Gurdjieff—problematic. Apparently, it suited him once more to play the "maestro of the supernatural." He may have wanted to batten on to one particular fantasist. Or it may have been a test to single out sheep from goats. Or, of course, he may have meant it, and we may all be finding excuses for him to save our own self-images.

Accept a completely normal interpretation of the accident—mechanical failure, bad driving, bad luck, or drowsiness. There is no puppet master pulling the strings, no cosmic significance attached to the crash. Gurdjieff has collided with a tree, severely lacerated his hands and is concussed for five days. Afterward he is seen not to be the same man: virtue has gone out of him, and he completely changes the pattern of his life. There is a perfectly simple explanation for this, and it has been eagerly adopted by certain followers of Ouspensky who wish to justify their teacher's break with his master: Gurdjieff sustained severe injuries to his head, and was never the same man again. His mind deteriorated and he ended in delusion.

Even so, there are some inexplicable features of Olga de Hartmann's story of July 5. Gurdjieff seemed to make provision for work to go on in his absence, he required a careful check of his vehicle and he sent Mme. de Hartmann home by herself. Did he foresee the accident? The voice, too; what about the voice which called "Olga Arcadievna"? The Great Magician has crashed, and anything is possible.

None of the accounts of the incident has ever been fully explicit, but through them all runs a suspicion that everything was not what it seemed. The evidence points to the fact that Gurdjieff knew he was going to crash. He made his legal disposition and sent home the secretary who in the normal course of events would have traveled with him. Thomas de Hartmann remembers that when he returned from the United States, Gurdjieff regarded his pupils "with a very serious expression." The composer connects this with the accident which followed: "We did not know then what awaited us." This is typical of the masterly equivocation with which some of the memoirs of Gurdjieff are written.

Gurdjieff must have arranged his accident himself.

The crash itself is easily explained, but not certain aspects of it. Gurdjieff's car had after all been checked thoroughly—particularly the steering gear which Mme. de Hartmann suggests caused the accident. If Gurdjieff had been proposing to crash his own car, he would have had to be quite sure that it was in perfect working order. A slight misjudgment, and he would have been killed. Nott's account of the state of the Citroën admittedly shows that if Gurdjieff staged an accident, he did it thoroughly; although what else would one expect from a man who used the Russian Civil War as a backdrop to his productions? He was found lying by the side of the road with his head on a cushion and supposedly no memory of how he had gotten there. The Sly Man would not have been above a little comfort while he waited. His injuries are rather mysterious. Lacerated arms and hands could be inflicted on himself by a particularly strong-willed man; and there should be no doubt that if Gurdjieff was no magician, he was at least extraordinary enough to disregard physical pain for the sake of his work. Head injuries appear to have been limited to severe concussion. Note well—there was no objection to Gurdjieff's leaving the hospital; and there were no bones broken. Then, as soon as possible, he was removed from external medical care and placed, first under the supervision of two Russian doctors from Paris, next under the charge of Mme. de Hartmann, Dr. Stoernaval, and Mme. Ostrowsky. Apart from the possibility of collusion with his staff and the doctors, Gurdjieff's own medical knowledge probably extended to counterfeiting the symptoms of concussion for a nonmedical audience, and may even have helped him to judge the impact of his car against the tree.

Now reconsider the events of his arrival back at the Prieuré. He looked directly at Jessie Dwight, who also remembers Dr. Stoerneval slamming the door of the car which brought him home—in a manner not calculated to help a patient suffering from concussion. Jean Toomer's comments on Gurdjieff's recovery are couched in suggestive language. The italics are mine. "What I saw, *as my impressions registered it,* was not a strong man, not a great man, not a man. *I saw* a little shrunken old person. . . ." Some people may have wondered whether the accident was genuine, but we are not told directly. At least to the sharp-eyed Fritz Peters, there was an element of doubt. He thought he had seen Gurdjieff watching his stubborn lawn mowing from a window. Some months after the great man emerged, Peters was detailed to walk behind him carrying a chair on which he could rest. Gurdjieff told his attendant that he was "almost blind" and that he did not want to worry the others. In his *Boyhood with Gurdjieff,* Fritz Peters wonders whether or not this was the case, although at the time, he writes, "I was sufficiently convinced of his blindness, because he frequently wandered from the path."

The accident was a large-scale test for all Gurdjieff's pupils and camp followers. If the de Hartmanns are sincere in recording their consternation, it seems to have worked even on those close to Gurdjieff. An experiment, then, to see how the menagerie would function without its keeper; to see who would obey instructions given them before the accident and who would forget in the crisis induced by the tragedy. It does not seem that many people passed the test, and this must have interested the Sly Man profoundly. How would his personal staff behave: An Armenian pupil called Mme. Galumnian, in fact, started classes in movements, and Thomas de Hartmann played Gurdjieff's music. The rest seem to have waited upon the Master. How would the younger pupils behave? It is clear that without

Gurdjieff's physical presence few intimations of new meaning could be extracted from physical tasks.

On a broader canvas, the accident furnished a magnificent source of worry and friction to the more credulous. Who had in fact learned anything? Gurdjieff would be able to see the position of many of his disciples more clearly than before; and by such a large shock, he would be able to test the temperature of his work as a whole. Who needed it, who were freeloaders, who were devoted to him personally and who to his ideas?

A thought that is perhaps unworthy—but maybe merely realistic— crosses the mind. It might have been very convenient for Gurdjieff, just at this juncture, to change his spots. He had overworked himself to bring his pupils up to the standard required for a fund-raising and publicity tour. This had not been a huge success from the material point of view. It was time for a number of his subordinates to take some responsibility for the Work, and he would "live for himself" for a period. He now had a pleasant house and a possible source of income which could be tapped at any time by his appearance as the Great Magician.

Or simply, he may have wanted a change in the repertory. Perhaps he had seen that the methods which he had intended to use would not prove effective in the delicate business of enlightening the West. His brief acquaintance with Europe and the United States may have caused him to revise his plans—what were his plans?—and decide that his methods would turn his disciples into a troupe of performing animals. The silly sheep did as they were told. Another production was called for, with a much smaller cast. It may be, after all, that the burst of publicity which Gurdjieff had invited was designed to attract a large number of people for a short time, so that he could filter them quickly through a fine mesh. Who would commit themselves wholeheartedly to the task which he proposed?

All these possibilities are implied by the idea that Gurdjieff faked his accident, and by its predictable results. On the widest scale the changes were decisive. For Gurdjieff himself it meant a completely altered pattern of activity, for Ouspensky an intense inner crisis, for every pupil or prospective pupil agonized heart-searching as all the conflicting possibilities were passed in review. For Orage it meant that he was on his own in a foreign country.

Gurdjieff's own comment on the incident, in *Beelzebub's Tales*, refers to his deliberations three months after the crash. "I then reflected," he writes, "that the attempt to preserve the existence of this institution would, in the absence of real people round me and owing to the impossibility of procuring without me the great material means required for it, inevitably lead to a catastrophe the result of which, among other things for me in my old age as well as for numerous others wholly dependent on me, would be, so to say, a 'vegetation.'"

So variety is the spice—the red pepper—also of the spiritual life? Or did he not mean what he said? There is a final possibility more confusing than any yet mentioned. Gurdjieff may have arranged his "accident" badly. The evidence indicates that he had staged the scene—but perhaps he had miscalculated and hurt himself in sober fact.

6

Per Americam ad Beelzebub

For the second time in his life Orage found himself a "pupil-teacher." The phrase was his own; and his early experience as a schoolmaster should not be forgotten. For all the brilliance of his career in the great days of the *New Age*, it is the late 1920s which appear as Orage's apotheosis—the time when his real inclinations operated at their greatest power and to maximum effect. For nearly five years, he had the American field to himself and built up a personal following as devoted as any he had inspired in Leeds or London.

For much of the 1920s, Gurdjieff existed for American followers of his ideas chiefly as a subject of rumor and speculation. Some people had met him on the 1924 trip, and a few paid visits to Fontainebleau; but it was only the Master's shadow which stretched across the Atlantic to reinforce with its obscurely menacing authority Orage's own. Orage's teaching was quite individual, and one of his pupils dubbed it, "the Oragean Version."

In November 1924, Orage began his career as an independent teacher of Gurdjieff's ideas. That month *Century* magazine published his "Talks with Katherine Mansfield," and on December 3 the *New Republic* printed his essay "On Love." Before Orage's visit to Fontainebleau, Herbert Croly had published two scenes of "Unedited Opinions" in which the Englishman had confined himself to literary matters, and on December 31, Orage contributed another column under this heading. This time the motive was frankly propagandist. His topic was "Religion in America." As Orage saw it, the Americans had confused humanitarianism with the central object of religion, which was "the divinisation of man." By this he meant "the development in man of relatively divine qualities and, particularly, of a relatively transcendent and divine state of consciousness."

The assumptions, implicit and explicit, of all religions are, first, that our present normal state of consciousness is not enough, however developed, to satisfy the demands of the perfect life; and second, that there are special means or, if you will, exercises and modes of living, comprehended as religion, designed to enable man to attain a higher state of consciousness in this life.

America did not seem prepared, Orage remarked, to "*risk*" very much on religion; all the disciplines which achieved popularity—such as psychoanalysis and Christian Science—promised immediate benefits. He admitted that no European country had adopted religion in his sense of the term, "but the tradition lingers like the warm ashes of an old fire. An individual can still catch a flame from it . . . Europe is rapidly losing what America has never had. The only question is whether America can snatch the torch before it is cold." There may have been more to this appeal than Orage's immediate mission. Gurdjieff himself later placed great stress on America as a field for spreading his ideas, and it may be that even at this stage—perhaps particularly because of the unsettled political condition of Europe—the United States had assumed this importance in his eyes.

An undated circular among the Toomer papers sets down the principles on which Orage based his organization. "It is proposed to form a number of small groups for the study of the Gurdjieff system," it begins. The groups were to consist of both men and women and number between six and ten people. Meetings were to be held weekly, and Orage would "attend as many meetings as possible." There was one strong prohibition: "Nobody should attend more than one group."

The greatest success of the spring demonstrations had been to interest the duennas of the salons, and Orage built on these earlier conquests. He numbered among his devotees Mrs. Meredith Hare, Muriel Draper, and the ubiquitous Mabel Dodge Luhan, who for a dozen years had been superintending a literary salon intended to rival that of Gertrude Stein in Paris. Groups met in Jane Heap's house on the Lower East Side, in the homes of Meredith Hare and Mabel Luhan, and also in Margaret Naumburg's Walden School. Sometimes Orage supervised weekends at Mabel Luhan's house at Croton-on-Hudson. In the event, his groups were considerably larger than the cells of six to ten people which the circular had envisaged, and his audiences numbered between thirty and fifty. Gorham Munson has described one assembly at Muriel Draper's which included himself and his wife, Mabel Luhan and her husband Tony, the artist Boardman Roginson, the art critic Carl Zigrosser, the poets R. Elsworth Lawson and Schuyler Jackson; Rita Romilly, Edwin Wolfe, and Helen Westley from the theatrical world; and such oddly assorted characters as Edna Kenton, Jean Toomer and the Pinchot brothers; Herbert Croly and T. S. Matthews; Jane Heap and *The Little Review* "office boy," Caesar Zwaska. At the same time, writes Munson, another group which included Waldo Frank and John O'Hara Cosgrave was meeting at the house of Meredith Hare.

The roll call includes both the eminent and the eccentric. Jeffrey Mark, another member of the groups, who at the time was head of the music section at the New York Public Library, decided that he and his associates had a better claim to the title of "the hundred neediest cases" than the usual beneficiaries of Christmas charity. An editorial in the *New Republic* for January 14, 1925 took up the remark shortly after Orage had begun his ministry. "At some future time when the world has grown wiser, the hundred neediest cases for whom aid and sympathy are asked at the Christmas season, will not be composed of those suffering merely material and physical ills. It will be realized that spiritual misery is the truly heart-rending form of need, and its victims have the greatest claim upon human sympathy."

The meetings presented a bizarre appearance. Some of the participants remember Jane Heap arriving in tuxedo smoking a cigar, Muriel Draper wearing a turban of silk stockings and—the totem and prize exhibit of the groups—Mabel Dodge Luhan's exotic Indian husband, Tony. Claude Bragdon recalled him "wrapped in his imperturbable dignity and bright red blanket. I could not but contrast the made-up, strained faces of most of the women present with his bronzed, calm, inscrutable mask. The air was thick with cigarette smoke, the raucous noises from the street competed with the voice of Orage as he lighted one cigarette after another—and from another—while he told about (sic) the necessity of self-observation to the rest of us—including Tony. It was primitive man and civilised man in dramatic juxtaposition."

For three years Waldo Frank attended one of Orage's groups. In a sketch entitled "Mystery in a Sack Suit," published under the pseudonym "Searchlight," Frank directed the attention of *New Yorker* readers to:

> . . . little knots of people scattered about town in comfortable places— very intent, largely silent . . . . editors, wives of Wall Street, professors, novelists, single girls, restless businessmen, artistic youths.

Here were true intellectuals who despised Greenwich Village. Here were socially elect who looked down upon Park Avenue as a gilded slum. . . . listening with passionate concern to a man they call Orage (pronounce it precisely like the French for *storm*). . . .

"With a most humane smile," writes Frank, "Orage blights the claims of humaneness. With valedictory sentiment, wipes sentiment off the slate. With logic swift as a machine, he discredits logic. With courteous manner, drops spiritual bombs into the laps of ladies who adore him." In the words of Elizabeth Munson, Orage had "a terrible eye for the otiose": a trait which Frank noticed also. "Orage looks like a boy and his shoulders are sharp. They have a way of shrugging—shrugging off fads and facts and systems at a pace poor slow old England could not hope to keep up with."

Although the lecturer's charm was having its customary effect, there were a few dissenting voices. Frank had to defend Orage against critics who despised the worldly brilliance of his following, and reminded them that the Buddha had been supported by "snobbish Brahmins and the rich youth of Benares." The more disillusioned Orageans—those who wryly considered themselves "the hundred neediest cases" or in T. S. Matthews' phrase, "a pretty job lot"—might wonder a little about the degree of consciousness exhibited by their spell-binding instructor. The chain smoking which nicotined his fingers, his manner of lighting one cigarette from another with "slightly trembling hands"—was Orage entirely conscious of these deeply ingrained habits?

Among Orage's critics was Edmund Wilson, who resisted the pressures put on him by the *New Republic* circle to join a group. Orage appeared "a funereal and to me distasteful person." Another critic was Orage's old companion of the Café Royal, Jacob Epstein, who arrived in New York in 1927 and was most unfavorably impressed by the adulation given to his friend by "cranks of all sorts."

The audiences which came under Orage's goad in fact represented considerably more than the predictable collection of Theosophists, camp followers, and adoring spinsters. Besides the more or less literary and artistic celebrities, there were a number of men of a scientific bent, including John Riordan, a young engineer who was a friend of William Carlos Williams, and Charles Daly King. Daly King (1895–1962) became an important commentator on Gurdjieff and Orage; and in fact was one of the few people to develop the ideas derived from Gurdjieff in a novel direction.

He is described by Dr. William Welch, who became his pupil in the mid-1930s, as "at heart a romantic, a lovable, pugnacious, well-to-do semi-dropout from the world of conventional ideas." "Daly"—as he was known—had first been attracted by the demonstration of Gurdjieff's movements, and was encouraged by Jessie Dwight to attend Orage's groups. He presents the interesting spectacle of a psychologist—a maverick, it is true, but still a psychologist—who chose his profession as a result of the Work. He appointed himself the custodian of Orage's teaching, and in 1951 issued a summary under the title of *The Oragean Version*. One hundred copies were printed, most of which were given to former Orageans or presented to public libraries. Apart from some jottings made by C. S. Nott, it is through Daly King that Orage's technique has been preserved.

The lucid and contemporary form in which Orage presented Gurdjieff's ideas gave an unnerving complexion to his meetings; for whoever heard of a guru more concerned with Eddington and Whitehead than with mystic verbiage and asceticism? There was little of the wild-eyed desert father or the sitter on bo trees in Orage; yet he spoke familiarly of the wisdoms of antiquity and brought into the conversation Christianity or the *Mahabharata*. In his *New Yorker* article, Waldo Frank hit on the uncanny effect which this created: Orage was "mystery *in a sack suit*," a contradiction in terms. There was something slightly terrifying about him. "He believes in literally nothing. *Nothing that is*, I mean. This is what makes him so detached. . . ."

The teacher was playing a role and impressions of him varied. One pupil remarked on his "steely toughness," another on the "quiet brilliance" which taught "pacifically" without undue pressure. Another noted his "ease of manner" and the simplicity of presentation which concealed the depths of what he taught. Yet to another he seemed a man with "great patience and understanding" but "terribly involved."

The meetings were usually scheduled for eight o'clock, although Orage rarely made his appearance until an hour later. They lasted for two or three hours and took the form of an extended discussion—sometimes prolonged for a select band into the early hours of the morning. Orage never "lectured," although he "talked" at length, and his old skill—developed in the *New Age* gatherings—at subtly organizing debate came back into play. His technique is outlined in a note of Toomer's intended as an *aide-memoire* for his own teaching:

In special terms the effort should be to impregnate a conception. Since the terms that are familiar to those present are unknown, since the special type of ideas that appeal to each are likewise unknown, it is necessary to broadcast, to speak with many terms and ideas in the hope that conception will take place in all. I should hold clearly in my mind the attitude of the "I" that is to be conceived, this being separate from and capable of development separate from the organism—the aim being to conceive it, develop it, in order that it may control the organism.

Gorham Munson remembers that Orage's cunningly hidden hand gave the discussions "much more shape than is common . . . he usually kept things related to a basis for discourse and manipulated them towards a definite conclusion." Because of this fluid approach, we can form no idea of the sequence of Orage's exposition; and *The Oragean Version* is no help, because Daly King was unable to do more than synthesize the essentials.

How Orage began a session would probably depend on the mood of the group. Perhaps it would be a striking phrase like that remembered by T. S. Matthews: "There is not a soul in this room." One of his favorite introductions is recorded by Daly King, and it is straightforward Aristotle. This is the division of reality into categories of the Actual and the Potential. At one particular moment, for example, we are occupied in reading a book. But we might be holding, instead of the book, a glass of beer, a fishing rod, or a rifle. In certain circumstances these are all possible objects for us to hold, and we are even quite likely to take part in the activities which they suggest. Thus in Orage's distinction, if the Actual state of reality consists in our holding a book and engaging in the activity of reading, all these other objects and activities form part of the Potential state. Excluded from the Potential are examples of the manifestly impossible—for example, the idea that we are holding a railway engine or the remarkable interstellar communicator invented in the year 3000 on Procyon 4. Reality, in Orage's definition, includes both that which is happening and that which may happen; while unreality includes all impossibilities—whether actual impossibilities or potential. Accepted science treats man only as he actually exists, and takes no account of his potential existence. In the syllogism, science, therefore, only considers one part of human reality and ignores the other. Orage admitted that this might be quite right and proper, but insisted that Gurdjieff's singularity was to consider man also *as he may become*. Not as "man in quotation marks," in other words, but as Potential Man.

The Oragean Version begins with a brief introduction to Gurdjieff's Laws of Three and Seven, and with a vague reference to the source of this knowledge in "Esoteric Schools." This sets the tone of Orage's treatment of the forms of the ideas themselves: Gurdjieff plus Ouspensky. Orage had absorbed Gurdjieff's ideas at the source, but had also experienced them filtered through Ouspensky, and some of Ouspensky's own preoccupations, such as eternal recurrence, found a place in his exposition. He was sparing with his material, but his treatment of the structure of the human machine and the plan of the universe follows his teachers in almost every detail.

His presentation, however, was founded on a metaphor of his own. The image is that of explorers setting out to investigate an unknown continent. They have never been there: in the last resort all they have to prove the existence of the *terra incognita* is a map, and they cannot test its accuracy until they undertake the voyage and can match the features of the landscape against the printed contour lines. But a map they must have, even to execute a landing, and the expedition would be impossible without it. Orage provided his followers with two "maps." The first was Gurdjieff's account of the human machine: the three centers, with their different parts; the mechanicality of man; the various sorts of "food" which the organism must ingest. The second—a larger projection altogether—consisted of Gurdjieff's cosmology with additional material in the form of Ouspensky's speculations on time and recurrence. But the distinguishing mark of the Oragean version was the vessel in which his disciples were to sail. Explorers must have a ship to transport them; and the ship of which Orage was captain was called "the Method."

He customarily led up to the Method by stressing the mechanicality of man. He was greatly helped by the popularity of behaviorist psychology as purveyed by Dr. John B. Watson; and newcomers would be cast into the depths of despair by Orage's picture of man as a machine. Then came the punch line: the Method provided a way out of man's desperate situation. The Method was the center of gravity of Orage's teaching, and as a catchword, it came to be synonymous with his name or that of Gurdjieff. In Daly King's record, it is divided into two parts which the psychologist assumed were not complete.

The first part consisted of the activity which Ouspensky has made familiar—self-observation. But according to the Oragean version, Ouspensky left out most of the details of this process. Simple "self-observation" is only the first of three processes which must be experienced. Orage began by stressing the Pythagorean precept of "Know thyself" and holding his pupils to it most literally. He advised them to get on terms with the self with whom they would have to live most of their life. They were to start with basics—what did they look like, for example? They were told to list their physical characteristics, and if possible to have a friend film their movements. A questionnaire was suggested—what does this creature X (yourself) like, dislike, look forward to, fear? What would he like to be, to know or to do? What have been his happiest and unhappiest moments, what are the characteristics of his personality, and how does he assess them? Why does he fear to die? There were further tasks: such as a survey of one's life conducted as impartially as possible, and another which involved a nightly review of the events of the day imagined as the unrolling of a cinema film. These exercises were designed to give the pupil an idea of himself in his mechanical state and were mere preliminaries to Self-Observation.

The technique was usually known among the Orageans as "Self-Observation without identification"; but the phrase, "without identification" was only one of a number of strictures by which Orage defined this very troublesome activity. Self-Observation implies the separation of the sense of "I" from the physical body. The observing "I" must not "identify"—in Gurdjieff's phrase—with the thing observed. Neither must there be any inclination for the observer to criticize what it sees, to alter what it dislikes, or to analyze what it finds. Self-Observation must take place in all conditions at all times; for this is the Method of the man in the world, the Fourth Way. Orage enumerated the various aspects of human activity to which Self-Observation might be applied. The recommended categories were posture, gesture, movement, facial expression, and tone of voice. The exercise was also to be conducted with all possible senses. An example given in *The Oragean Version* is the observation of one's crossed legs. They are easily observed visually; but another source of information is provided by muscular tension. Orage's catalog of senses spilled over from the accepted five to include temperature, pain, the sense of balance, and the pulse. The core of the matter was that the observing "I" should not identify with the data which it contemplated. The technique applied only to the physical body and, at least to begin with, the pupils were not deemed advanced enough to be able to observe an emotion or a thought. An undated note by Jean Toomer on the sort of activity attempted is glossed, "All in all, the most vivid bit of observation to date."

> I had been trying to pay attention to what Orage was saying and at the same time to do another thing. This effort rendered some part of the organism quite sensitive. Then Grace Potter asked Orage if he would mind repeating what he had just said. I remembered what he said. Orage implied refusal to do this by stating that she, Grace, was at perfect liberty to ask anyone present . . . to do this. The prospect of being called on neither alarmed me nor caused the pattern and essential conduct of his discourse to fade from my mind. Grace turned around and named Jean Toomer. This act shocked the organism, made it tremble, quiver, grow extremely nervous. But still my mind retained the necessary data. But I experienced considerable difficulty in speaking. And at the same time, quite outside the organism I observed it, the whole scene, with unusual clarity (I doubt that the observation itself came from conscious effort). I observed the effort made. The first

words spoken. I observed the quiver in the voice. [A footnote: the posture of the body. The movement of an arm, holding a cigarette, to knock the ashes in an ash tray. The lampshade. The table. Surrounding faces.] I observed the organism's nervousness as the formulation proceeded. I was aware of instinctive interference with the mental processes. I observed the cerebral center try to subdue and control the instinctive. I observed the cerebral being worsted in this battle. Finally some word was needed. The mind could not find it. Pause. Blank. I and everything was drawn to find this word. After a while it came from nowhere. Not the right word; but an appropriate one. And soon the task had been completed. Then I made the effort to listen to Orage. I caught his comment. But what he said immediately after that was not recorded. The organism was still all a-tremble. The cerebral still seeking to control it. I could hear or see nothing of externality because of this conflict. Nevertheless I did observe it, and this time consciously. Finally the trembling subsided, the stupor passed away. Again the organism functioned in the group.

Self-Observation was only the first part of the first stage of Orage's Method. It was supposed to be carried on while the further steps were practiced. The second of these was known as Participation, and was subject to the same qualifications as Self-Observation; that is, it had also to be practiced without identification, without analysis, and in accordance with all the other precepts which defined the first activity. Participation meant not merely observing a given notion, movement or position, but consciously taking part in it, consciously inhabiting the action which was being observed. A third step marked the end of the first stage of the Method. This was called Experiment. Experiment concerned change—or at least attempted change—of the mechanized functioning of the human being. This was change not for the purpose of reform, but for Experimental purposes only: to gain more knowledge and thus a greater consciousness. Suggested subjects for Experiment were drinking habits, smoking, and the number of hours of sleep taken at night; even the order in which the shoes were put on in the morning could be altered—and then, when the reverse order became customary, the original unconscious habit could be reinstated as a conscious activity. Another form of Experiment, directed to building up an effective Will, was the taking and keeping of vows.

Experiment in its fullest sense meant the playing of roles. Within the structure of the Oragean Method this activity can be seen in its logical and necessary place, not merely as an example of Gurdjieff's erratic virtuosity. In order to discover his own nature and that of other people, the experimenter adopted roles quite alien to his normal inclinations. Extend such activity into dramatic terms, and it is possible to see Gurdjieff's car crash, his sometimes inexplicable conduct, and other strange events in different terms.

The second part of Orage's Method is much quicker to describe than the first, and consists of the two activities which Gurdjieff called "Voluntary Suffering" and "Conscious Labour." The first stage of Voluntary Suffering was the suppression of the symptoms of negative emotion—an activity stressed by Ouspensky. An example is to remain externally calm in the face of preposterous insults. The object of this exercise of severe self-restraint is to produce friction, which is said to promote otherwise unobtainable changes in the personality. The category of Conscious Labor seems at once more definite and more specious. The first step is said to consist of "Pondering," of weighing intellectually the sort of problems normally thought of as "imponderable" and arriving at a solution which is entirely one's own. Orage dictated a list of subjects for Pondering, which included the questions—"man," "sex," "consciousness," "the world," "the universe," "nature," "God"; Gurdjieff's ideas—"the octave," "essence and personality"; and topics which seem simply to have interested him personally— "the Bible and other Sacred Books," "Incarnation and Reincarnation," "Spiritualism." The object was to arrive at an interpretation of these questions which satisfied the essential man; to resist the opinions implanted by associations, by upbringing, by education—and perhaps by the system of unlearning provided by Gurdjieff himself.

Other branches of Gurdjieffian knowledge entered the curriculum of Orage's pupils. Classes in Gurdjieff's movements were conducted by Jessmin Howarth, who had been at Fontainebleau, and in 1927 Orage introduced a series of "psychological exercises" based on Gurdjieffian principles and designed to flex the unused muscles of the mind. A simple example is the sort of counting in unaccustomed ways which Gurdjieff imposed on the performers of his movements. Such a series might vary from the comparative simplicity of 1-2-3-4- 4-3-2-1- 2-3-4-5- 5-4-3-2- 3-4-5-6- 6-5-4-3 to the increasingly complex 1-100, 2-99, 3-98, 4-97. In April 1927 Orage wrote to Jean Toomer announcing that he was beginning classes in his exercises that June—"two nights a week of three hours each"—and inviting him to attend. After these classes, fortified by halva, black coffee, and chili con carne, the Orageans became absorbed in discussion. The morning after such a conversation, one participant discovered she had left her car near Orage's flat and somehow found her way home without it. Such absorption was not purely intellectual; it extended to the person of Orage himself. His magnetism at times produced unwelcome results. "He seemed to know the answer to every question," Nott writes; "his replies were so right that many of us got into the habit of talking everything over with him—mundane problems as well as psychological ones. In the beginning this helped very much, but some of the weaker ones came to rely on him entirely, and consulted him in everything." Philip Mairet describes how a woman pupil "insisted on his prescribing a diet for her indigestion, and he, either in desperation or drollery suggested stout and oysters which, as it turned out, actually did her good." Orage was often exasperated with his pupils' demands, and in April 1927, he was complaining to Jean Toomer that "a professional 'psycho-analyst' would make a fortune in my situation; but it brings me nothing whatever except experience."

Placed on a pedestal though he might be, Orage taught with Gurdjieff's unavoidable gaze peering over his shoulder, and the strange Caucasian accents of his Master began to mingle rather oddly with the voice of reason.

Between November 1924 and the spring of 1929, Orage was responsible to himself alone for the conduct of his groups in New York. In self-imposed isolation, Gurdjieff maintained a reduced establishment at Fontainebleau, answering—as he later explained—only those letters with enclosures which bore figures ending in a satisfactory number of zeros. He was immersed in literary activity. This new venture had begun soon after the car crash, and his American followers were first to feel the effects of their Master's industry. Gurdjieff was writing what proved to be *Beelzebub's Tales to his Grandson*. Sometimes he dictated in Russian to Mme. de Hartmann, sometimes he scribbled in notebooks in Armenian. His efforts were roughly translated by Russian- and Armenian-speaking pupils, and sent across the Atlantic to Orage. Orage improved the English of the translations and made use of Gurdjieff's bottomless allegory in his groups.

Beelzebub's Tales is a leviathan of a book. The printed edition is over 1,200 pages long. P. L. Travers has described it as "a great, lumbering, flying cathedral" and the prose as "labyrinthine." The subject matter comprises the explanations given by Beelzebub—a wise and ancient being who is at last returning to "the place of his arising" after expiating the sins of his youth—to his favorite grandson Hassein. The pair are traveling through the universe in a space ship with Beelzebub's faithful servant Ahoon, and Beelzebub whiles away the lengthy flight by answering his grandson's questions about the nature of the cosmos. Hassein has developed a particular interest in the state of affairs on the planet Earth where, according to Beelzebub, conditions of life are quite peculiar, with the natural order turned topsy-turvy because of a mistake on the part of certain cosmic authorities. The language used by Beelzebub is labored, the periods are few and far between, and to reach Gurdjieff's meaning, the reader has to hack through a jungle of verbiage apparently arranged so as to lose him in a thicket of subordinate clauses. The whole is spiced with Gurdjieff's cumbrous sense of humor and flavored with terms coined from every language under the sun. If the reader were patient enough, he would discover the doctrine which Gurdjieff had stated simply in Russia camouflaged under a mass of new terms. The book can have no casual readers because it is frankly impenetrable; and although Orage's followers might have found both the form and the substance of Gurdjieff's teaching in *Beelzebub's Tales*, the dim religious light of Gurdjieff's "flying cathedral" must have come as a shock after the bright illumination in the orderly building of Orage's mind.

Orage himself was baffled by Gurdjieff's first attempt to give literary form to his vision. Nott—who is often far from accurate—says that the first installment of *Beelzebub's Tales* arrived from France in March 1925, and that Orage sent it back as completely unintelligible. Then a revised version arrived which Orage read to his pupils, remarking that this was an entirely different matter. "We could not make much of it," admits Nott. "Soon, however, something began to work in us; and as more chapters came over, the impact on our feelings became stronger." Orage suggested interpretations of the puzzling text and emphasized the overriding importance of subsidizing Gurdjieff while he completed his great work. A memorandum of Jean Toomer's, dated December 28, 1925, records Orage as stating that such support was perhaps the most important task for any of Gurdjieff's followers. Of the chapter in *Beelzebub's Tales* called "The Holy Planet Purgatory," Toomer noted: "Orage says that he has read thousands of books and nothing in philosophy, nor Plato nor Plotinus, compares in lucidity, concentration, subtlety, etc., with this chapter. It leaves all philosophy behind."

At first, Orage or Jessie Dwight read *Beelzebub's Tales* to the groups, but in later years, Orage confounded the book's confusion by making his pupils—quite literally—fit it together piece by piece. A set time would be appointed when he would leave his office door unlocked. The pupils were made to come and "steal" cyclostyled copies of the translation which were scattered around the room in disorder. In fact, they would have paid a fee of ten dollars before performing this act of "theft." In consequence, copies of what became known simply as THE BOOK were highly prized, and a complete copy was a rarity to be treasured. It was a tragedy when Schuyler Jackson left his laboriously collected typescript on a train from New York to Trenton and never recovered it. Reference to THE BOOK became common in some intellectual circles as dark hints about the Method. Edmund Wilson was supremely irritated:

> I did not read *Beelzebub's Tales*, but I did read *Das Kapital*. Not that I want to compare the two works, but there *was* a certain similarity in

the way in which people then approached them; and I was surprised to find that an apparently social evening that would turn out to be a conspiracy to involve one in some Communist organization resembled a dinner I had once attended at which I was chilled to discover that the springes of Orage had been laid for me—and these both recalled to me an earlier occasion on which a literary conversation in the rooms of the proselytizing rector of the Episcopal Church at Princeton, had been prodded by amusing remarks in the direction of the Christian faith. People did want faiths and churches badly. . . .

As *Beelzebub's Tales* crossed the Atlantic in one direction to create fresh problems for the eager student, Orage's pupils made the crossing in the other. Orage himself was reluctant to send pupils to Fontainebleau, and even when he relented sufficiently to give them a letter of recommendation, he usually began by trying to discourage the man or woman who was eager to "give up everything" to live at the Prieuré. For one thing, Gurdjieff had officially closed the Institute and discouraged visitors. For another, a request for an introduction to Gurdjieff might show what Orage called "the fallacy of Going-to-Tibet." To one pupil—who eventually lived at the Prieuré for some four or five years—he asked tellingly: "Why do you want to go? I'm teaching you here."

On the other hand there were those, like Margaret Naumburg, who had been fascinated by the spectacle of Gurdjieff himself, and whom only ill luck had prevented from traveling to France. The wish to sit at the Master's feet was one which Orage himself certainly understood; for this was exactly what he had done when he left Ouspensky for Gurdjieff. During his first four years in the United States he regularly closed his own groups in the summer and left for the Prieuré, where he renewed his own contact with Gurdjieff and worked on the translation of his writings. Not just Orage's authority, but his very life was rooted in the soil of Fontainebleau. His letters to Toomer show that he dreaded the prospect of returning to America from his French retreat. At the Prieuré—as Gurdjieff was later to say of his flat in Paris—was "quintessence," a rarified atmosphere; a far country of the spirit as well as of geography. The exotic associations of the only non-English-speaking country Orage ever visited could only have heightened his sense that the Prieuré was "special place."

The summer of 1925 was the first after Gurdjieff's car crash and visitors were few. When the Irish poet, Monk Gibbon, arrived, the château and its grounds presented a desolate appearance. He found only two disciples, "a very serious-looking young man, with sandy hair, from the English Midlands, and a young girl with flaming red hair from America. They were both in their early twenties, slightly lost lambs, typical of hopeful, questing youth in search of the philosopher's stone." Gibbon was told that Gurdjieff was in bed and writing. He was shown the Institute's prospectus and lectured on the happiness of Katherine Mansfield. Then he was taken by the Englishman—probably a pupil called Bernard Metz—to see the Study House.

> The interior suggested a Turkish bath that had fallen on evil days. Someone had whitewashed the walls and strewn a few worn carpets about the floor. Someone else had begun a series of garish, oriental wall-decorations which had not got very far. Despite the brightness of the colours an air of intolerable melancholy streamed from those uneven white surfaces, those brilliant garish blues and sombre reds.

This depressing picture of neglect and inactivity is confirmed by Margaret Naumburg's letters to Jean Toomer, in which she reported on the comatose condition of the Prieuré, and the equivocal status of the summer visitors.

Margaret Naumburg arrived on June 14, 1925 to find that her coming had been announced by Orage. She was met by Mme. de Hartmann who told her that she would probably be able to stay, but that this depended on Gurdjieff. In the upshot, Gurdjieff's reaction was: if Orage approved, so did he. Margaret Naumburg heard his voice dictating late at night when she was in bed, but her first sight of the Master was almost as worrying as Toomer's had been. She was told he was recovering, but he looked dreadful and moved with difficulty. However, he clearly retained all his old relish for discomfiting his pupils, and made Margaret Naumburg's first meal a misery by filling her full of whisky.

Just before her arrival, the practice of movements had started in the Study House directed by Mme. de Salzmann; and there were readings from Gurdjieff's writing in progress, including the tale of his Universal Travelling Workshop. Gurdjieff's nephews and nieces, Mme. de Salzmann's daughter and Mme. Ouspensky's grandson were being instructed in movements. The children disliked this and became bored and fractious. Gurdjieff's method of dealing with insubordination was original. He did not punish the children, but put Bernard Metz on the stage of the Study House and made him hold a difficult position for a considerable time. The children were told that this would be their own fate if they misbehaved again.

To Margaret Naumburg, impatient for "practical work," everything seemed lackadaisical. She felt that her own instruction in the movements from the Englishwoman Elizabeth Gordon was rudimentary. Work was further impeded by the death of Gurdjieff's mother, which necessitated a complicated ritual carried out in the Study House during a storm.

Margaret Naumburg eventually had a conversation with Gurdjieff, who was lying in bed. He seemed to confuse the relationship between her and Toomer—perhaps on purpose. He had been announcing for the past five months that his book would be finished in a few days' time. "What would he do when it was completed?" she asked him. Gurdjieff answered that he did not know. Perhaps he would go away and rest, perhaps he would go to Egypt—perhaps, just *perhaps*, he might take some people at the Prieuré, only not—like the year before—those not seriously interested.

Orage and Jane Heap arrived in mid-July, but Margaret Naumburg still felt deprived of what she had come for. She informed Toomer that both Jane and Orage were complaining that everything was rundown. Apart from these old friends, she moaned, there was no conversation to be had. The older pupils were arrogant. They seemed to consider everyone else mentally defective, and their criticism of Orage smacked of jealousy.

As the summer wore on, her disappointment increased. There had evidently been some doubt as to whether Orage would return to New York to carry on his teaching for a second year. On August 18, she informed Toomer that this had now been resolved, and Orage would after all continue. But she suspected he would try to divert the New Yorkers from work in a practical sense, and talked of going off to Ouspensky next spring. Her time had been wasted, and she wrote resignedly that Toomer had been right to stay in the United States.

Orage and Jessie Dwight returned to New York via England, sailing on October 3. The teaching continued, but next summer there were no new residents at the Prieuré. The château remained wrapped in an enchanted slumber, and when Daly King tried to gain admission he found no one who seemed to be in authority.

Two events of some importance took place that year. The first was the visit of Aleister Crowley. Crowley knew the town of Fontainebleau well—in 1924 he had spent a tormented period there in an attempt to cure himself of heroin addiction. The Great Beast was a familiar figure in Paris expatriate circles, and Nott met him in the capital while himself staying at the Prieuré. Crowley's interest was aroused either by a general occult curiosity or by Gurdjieff's reputation as a specialist in curing drug addiction; and he soon afterward turned up at Fontainebleau, where he was the object of some amazement. To one of the inmates, the Wickedest Man in the World seemed overfed and inoffensive—with the exception of his almost colorless eyes, the antipodes to Gurdjieff's heavy gaze. The published accounts of Crowley at the Prieuré speak only of a brief visit and a vaguely sinister impression. Nott records that Crowley spoke to one of the children present about his son whom he was teaching to be a devil. "Gurdjieff got up and spoke to the boy, who thereupon took no further notice of Crowley." But the magician's visit was extensive, and his confrontation with Gurdjieff of a more epic nature.

Crowley arrived for a whole weekend and spent the time like any other visitor to the Prieuré; being shown the grounds and the activities in progress, listening to Gurdjieff's music and his oracular conversation. Apart from some circumspection, Gurdjieff treated him like any other guest until the evening of his departure. After dinner on Sunday night, Gurdjieff led the way out of the dining room with Crowley, followed by the body of pupils who had also been at the meal. Crowley made his way toward the door and turned to take his leave of Gurdjieff, who by this time was some way up the stairs to the second floor. "Mister, you go?" Gurdjieff inquired. Crowley assented. "You have been guest?"—a fact which the visitor could hardly deny. "Now you go, you are no longer guest?" Crowley—no doubt wondering whether his host had lost his grip on reality and was wandering in a semantic wilderness—humored his mood by indicating that he was on his way back to Paris. But Gurdjieff, having made the point that he was not violating the canons of hospitality, changed on the instant into the embodiment of righteous anger. "You filthy," he stormed, "you dirty inside! Never again you set foot in my house!" From his vantage point on the stairs, he worked himself up into a rage which quite transfixed his watching pupils. Crowley was stigmatized as the sewer of creation was taken apart and trodden into the mire. Finally, he was banished in the style of *East Lynne* by a Gurdjieff in fine histrionic form. Whitefaced and shaking, the Great Beast crept back to Paris with his tail between his legs.

The second significant event of the summer of 1926 was the death of Mme. Ostrowsky. Fritz Peters calls her "the most impressive permanent resident at the Prieuré." Katherine Mansfield had written that "she walks about like a queen exactly"; and Peters confirms this observation:

I remember being particularly fascinated by the way she moved; she walked without any perceptible movement of her head and without the slightest jerkiness in her movements; she was never hurried, but at the same time she moved at incredible speed; every movement she made in whatever she was doing was absolutely essential to that particular activity.

During the early summer of 1926, this silent but imposing woman became increasingly ill. She took to her bed and was put on a special diet that included large quantities of blood pressed from meat. It became known that she had terminal cancer, and Gurdjieff told his pupils that she was living "through him." Her doctors had put her under sentence of death, he said, and he had been able to extend the time limit through his own efforts.

"She live many lives, is very old soul; she now have possibility ascend to other world," he told Fritz Peters. "But sickness come and make more difficult, make impossible for her to do this thing alone. If can keep alive few months more will not have to come back and live this life again."

An episode in *Beelzebub's Tales* must refer to Mme. Ostrowsky's death. In the chapter called, "The Bokharan Dervish Hadji-Asvatz-Troov," the dervish tells Beelzebub of a European friend who succeeded in discovering a cure for cancer, but almost immediately became the victim of tragedy. Cancer was diagnosed in his wife, but he himself had a road accident which prevented him from putting his cure into effect. When he recovered from his accident, he saw with horror that his wife was so far advanced in the disease that all he could do was to try European medicine. The European doctors recommended X-ray treatment, but this only resulted in fresh outbreaks in other parts of his wife's body. Casting caution to the winds, the husband decided not to spare himself and channeled his energies to effecting some slowing down of the cancer. He managed by this means to keep his wife alive for almost two years.

This tale so closely corresponds to the circumstances of Mme. Ostrowsky's death as to leave no doubt that Gurdjieff is referring to himself. Olga de Hartmann claims that once during Mme. Ostrowsky's last days, Gurdjieff caused a marked improvement in the invalid's condition by making her drink a glass of water which he had held for a few minutes in his hands. Are we to understand that he really believed he had a cure for cancer, that his knowledge of vibrations or Tibetan medicine was in fact superior to Western science? What is clear from his manner of telling the story is that Gurdjieff felt great affection for his "wife" and that her death was a personal tragedy for him. Fritz Peters had described how, after her death on June 26, 1926, Gurdjieff retired to his room and saw no one for two days. He emerged to greet the archbishop who came to preach the funeral service. "There were no manifestations of sorrow, no tears, just an unusual heaviness about him, as if it required a great effort for him to move."

Gurdjieff further confused his pupils by devoting the day of the funeral to embarrassing the archbishop and preventing expressions of grief over Mme. Ostrowsky's death. He described what he said was a traditional funeral custom from more enlightened times. After a death, Gurdjieff claimed, the friends of the dead person would spend three days remembering the evil deeds committed by their acquaintance during his life. They would then begin to concentrate on the fact of their own mortality. A newly arrived recruit to the Prieuré was completely bewildered by the funeral feast, during which Gurdjieff kept up a running stream of curses on God.

Very soon afterward he began living with another woman, who soon became pregnant.

It was the following summer that the real influx of visitors from the United States began. American memories of the Prieuré are usually of the years 1927 and 1928. The real reason why Orage persuaded Gurdjieff to allow visitors during these years was financial. The master was concentrating on literary work which excluded other money-making activity; and at the same time, the cavalier attitude he showed to substantial sums he did receive from his supporters made it seem that subsidizing his activities was like trying to fill a bottomless pit. Until his marriage in 1927, Orage lived in what seemed to many of his New York pupils very straitened circumstances in a tiny apartment in Chelsea. Money from admission charges to his meetings went largely to the Prieuré. But by the spring of 1927, Orage— perhaps slightly annoyed that friends like Daly King had been refused admittance, and certainly determined that Gurdjieff could do something toward his own keep—was writing to Jean Toomer:

As for American visitors to the Prieuré this summer, I have written finally to G. for an official permit to authorise such proposals. Lots of people want to go from here; but so far I have said neither yes nor no . . . I'm not disposed to countenance formally any such visitations without *some* assurance from G. that at least they will be admitted or at least considered.

He told Gurdjieff that an American would pay an average of 100 dollars per week, and this was the decisive factor. For the next four years, a small but steady trickle of pupils crossed the Atlantic with letters of introduction from Orage—or sometimes from Toomer, who was prone to announce his protégés in the style of a minor prophet. "TO GEORGE IVANOVITCH GURDJIEFF—GREETING!" began one hortatory letter with which the Chicago poet, Mark Turbyfill—a contributor to *The Little Review*—arrived at Fontainebleau. Despite such impressive credentials, a candidate for admission could never be certain, when he walked up to the doorway with "Sonnez Fort" written beside it, that he would penetrate the enchanted castle itself.

A new arrival at the Prieuré would be greeted by one of the senior pupils and probably—unless there was a particularly full house in summer—given a room in "the Ritz." He was now in a place where everything was uncertain, where the possible meanings jarred in hideous confusion, where he never knew precisely what might happen at any moment. When

Gurdjieff deigned to take notice of a newcomer, he might meet him in any one of his unpredictable roles. One of the 1927 arrivals was unable to approach the Master during the first twenty-four hours of his stay because, whenever he came anywhere near, Gurdjieff turned and shouted at him. Then at the first of the lavish dinners which the pupil attended, he suddenly felt that Gurdjieff's eye was on him, and on looking up received a beatific smile of welcome. Or, Gurdjieff might be in a more quizzical vein. When Carl Zigrosser first encountered him in June 1927, he had just been given a conducted tour by Thomas de Hartmann.

> When we came near, he opened the conversation by saying, "I smell American." I had been prepared for this sort of greeting by the reports of previous visitors, so I was not as startled as I might have been. He went on to explain in his curious English: "You no take bath here last night; I smell American smell." After some conversation he asked if I could drink. When I replied that I hoped I could, he invited me to sit beside him at dinner—a place which I learned later was reserved for those who drank. He laughed and added that he liked three kinds of people; those who could drink, those who could tell stories—and the third he would tell me about some other time. A few minutes later, he left us and went to his room.

Almost as disconcerting as the Master himself were encounters with other pupils. What did they know that the neophyte did not? How should the newcomer behave toward them? A new arrival often felt in the position of a specimen under examination. Nott records that his every action after he arrived was reported to Gurdjieff. Alternatively, like Toomer in 1925, the neophyte could approach his new acquaintances from a superior height: he was "one of the chosen; most of the others could not possibly be."

In the late 1920s the permanent population of the Prieuré was about thirty people. Until 1929 the de Hartmanns and Mme. de Hartmann's parents, the Schumakers, lived in the château. The Stoernevals with their son Nikolai, and Mme. de Salzmann with her two children lived in the Paradou. Alexander de Salzmann worked in Paris during the week and commuted to the Prieuré on weekends. Another visitor from Paris was Adele Kaffian, who had been such a friend of Katherine Mansfield. A more infrequent bird of passage was Mme. Galumnian or Chaverdian, an Armenian who took a leading part in the translation of *Beelzebub's Tales*. Although her husband lived in Soviet Russia, she was able to visit Gurdjieff for long periods until the early 1930s. Then there was Gurdjieff's family— his sister and her husband, his brother Dmitri with his wife and four children; also another nephew, Valya, who had made his way alone from Georgia to Fontainebleau.

A few other Russians remained from the great dispersal. The duties of concierge and mechanic were performed by the Merkouroffs, and the Prieuré horse had as its attendant, one Andrei Andreivitch—upon whom Gurdjieff once performed an extraordinary cure for sciatica after anaesthetizing him with Armagnac. Then there was the former barrister Rachmilievitch, in whose flat the Moscow groups had at one time met. He was an eccentric who Gurdjieff claimed to keep at the Prieuré for the express purpose of annoying everyone else. Rachmilievitch must have been the only pupil who ever tried to extract the truth from Gurdjieff by force. On one occasion he chased Gurdjieff up a tree, and on another, when a party were bathing in the River Loing, he grasped the Master's head and threatened to hold him under the water until he was enlightened.

A few English remained with Gurdjieff from the period when his following had been recruited by Ouspensky. Three single ladies—Misses Gordon, Merston and Alexander—attended to household duties or supervised the gardens. Bernard Metz, who made the original English translations of *Beelzebub's Tales* which Orage reworked, was the only Englishman among the permanent residents. From America several young men arrived to stay for different periods, including Caesar Zwaska, the "office boy" of *The Little Review*. Jane Heap's adopted sons, Tom and Fritz Peters, added to the population, and other visitors arrived for weekends or for longer periods. Some of these came because of an interest in the teaching, but others came to be cured by Gurdjieff of various complaints. During the later 1920s, the life of the Prieuré revived.

The atmosphere was less frenzied than during the period of the Institute for the Harmonious Development of Man. Pupils were less likely to be dragged from their beds in the middle of the night to practice movements, and indeed instruction in the movements often completely lapsed. The course of the week ran to a more leisurely pattern, with Saturday night an evening of festivity. All afternoon, Dmitri Gurdjieff stoked the boilers which heated the water for the Russian baths, and in the evening men and women separately visited the bathhouse. One weekend Zigrosser joined the party:

> The women took their bath at five o'clock. When they had finished, and everybody had eaten a light supper, all adjourned to the study-house for coffee, some time between eight and nine o'clock. There everyone sat about while a chapter from Mr. Gurdjieff's book was read aloud or—as happened the first time I was there—Mr. de Hartmann

played the organ. Then, when Mr. Gurdjieff gave the signal, men and boys went to the bath-house. The bath was the regular Russian steam bath, accompanied with much joking and story-telling; but sometimes Mr. Gurdjieff's most valuable remarks came out in the course of this apparently casual conversation. He used to call upon each newcomer to tell two or three stories as a payment for his bath.

On more than one occasion these storytelling bouts provided an opportunity for Gurdjieff to insert a couple of barbs through the chinks in a pupil's armor. A monk from Mount Athos was a guest in the bathhouse, and Gurdjieff persuaded him to take part in a battle of "anecdotes." These grew more and more ribald until Gurdjieff turned on the visitor and denounced him for obscenity. The monk was struck dumb; and Gurdjieff's comment to Orage was, "I wished to show him he was no monk."

At about midnight the feast would be held in the dining room of the Prieuré. Gurdjieff sat in the middle on one side of a long oval table with his pupils ranged around him. Exotic dishes appeared, beginning with large quantities of Russian hors d'oeuvres accompanied by raw herbs—tarragon, fennel, mint, or parsley—which were eaten by hand. Often a sheep's head would be placed in front of Gurdjieff—who would extract the eye and offer it to a newcomer. Those familiar with his stratagems watched as eagerly as the Master to see how the hapless guest would react. Would he refuse brusquely? Would he try to be polite? When pressed by Gurdjieff, would he cave in abruptly or become angry? More important than the sheep's head were the spirits which circulated with the meal. Gurdjieff disliked wine and frequently played the trick of decanting *vin ordinaire* into superior bottles to deceive important guests. He preferred Armagnac or, if that was unobtainable, Vieux Marc. In these fiery spirits were drunk the famous "toasts to the idiots."

The duty of proposing the toasts was usually delegated to Mme. de Hartmann's father. Each member of the company was assigned a category of "idiot." Gurdjieff used the expression in a dual sense to denote both the various brands of stupidity to which his followers were individually prone and the Greek meaning of idiot signifying a "private person." Zigrosser records a sequence of seven "idiot toasts" which was used consistently when he visited the Prieuré: "all idiots," "ordinary idiots," "the candidate for idiocy," "the superidiot," "the archidiot," "the hopeless idiot," "the compassionate idiot." In addition, there were "squirming idiots" and idiots both "round" and "square," each category supposedly conveying something to the people to whom they were applied. For example, at one period in the late 1920s, Dr. Stoerneval was an "arch-idiot," and Orage was the "superidiot." A "squirming idiot" was supposed to be someone confronted with a particularly unpleasant personality trait; while the round and the square idiots might be identified by reference to Gurdjieff's teaching on the symbols used to denote the developing man.

"Always when presiding at a table," Jean Toomer wrote, "G. has a certain charm and lordliness. He devours his food and thinks well of you if you do likewise." From Toomer's notes it seems that he took part in more expansive dinners than many other followers of Gurdjieff, for he records some interesting information about the upper reaches of the idiot range— even about the twenty-first idiot whom Gorham Munson understood to be "His Endlessness" or God himself. But Gurdjieff, recalled Toomer, called himself "the unique idiot. The unique idiot is twenty-one on the scale. You seldom reach a toast to it. Should you, G. guarantees that while everyone is under the table, he will dance on the tabletop. Also, by the way, it is generally understood by those who dine and drink with him that God is his heir and that when he dies God will then become the unique idiot."

Only once did a pupil dare to interrupt the sequence of toasts and propose one himself. Predictably, this was Rachmilievitch, and his toast was to the Master who so infuriated him. The dinner party was larger than usual and had failed to respond to Gurdjieff's prodding. In the middle of the toasts, Rachmilievitch raised his glass and addressed Gurdjieff: "God give you the strength and the manhood," he said, "to endure your lofty solitude." Gurdjieff looked at him—in the words of a pupil to whom Rachmilievitch wrote describing the incident—"kindly, without smiling." After a momentary silence, the toasts to the idiots resumed.

The society of the Prieuré has often been called patriarchal, and the patriarch ruled with a rod of iron. At first Gurdjieff even banned women from his Saturday feasts until two, less in awe of him than the rest, decided to organize a women's feast among themselves. They sat down to eat in one of the bedrooms—having sent the redoubtable Jane Heap to persuade Mme. Ouspensky (who for a long time was a permanent resident) to join them. As the feast began, the door opened and Gurdjieff's portentous figure appeared in the doorway. Looking surprised to see Mme. Ouspensky, he promptly identified the culprits and denounced their illicit celebration. "Never such thing again in my house," he proclaimed. Next Saturday the women joined the company in the dining room.

Certain pupils, like Orage and de Salzmann, enjoyed the privileges accorded to court jesters, and Gurdjieff's response to a real challenge from another quarter was usually delighted surprise. At dinner one night Mme. Stoerneval disgusted him by remembering at great length the excellence of chocolate as it was made in St. Petersburg under the old regime. He embarked on a tirade against the follies of a St. Petersburg education and the trivialities which it encouraged. Mme. Stoerneval left the room; shortly afterward Schumaker, who announced that he could not approve of

Gurdjieff's discourtesy, followed her. Schumaker must have told his wife, who had not been at the meal, for she soon appeared in front of Gurdjieff, highly enraged. "I will wager you," she said, "that if someone had brought you your Perrier water even five minutes earlier, this would not have happened." Gurdjieff looked up, "absolutely delighted," and at the first opportunity took her into Fontainebleau where he loaded her with delicacies at the finest patisserie in town.

Gurdjieff was now a writer, as well as being a "teacher of dancing" and of other things not in the curriculum of a normal educational establishment. It was to be expected that his writing methods would be as unconventional as the rest of his activities. During the period after his accident he had written chiefly at night, but as people once more began to dog his footsteps, they were swept up into his irregular routine. He might work at home at the Prieuré—in his room if it were winter, or outside on the terrace in the summer. Or, he might take it into his head to go into Fontainebleau, where he sat in the Café Henri IV—scribbling illegibly in notebooks. He claimed that the spectacle of the world as a passing show encouraged concentration and detachment.

In addition, he led another life quite independent of the Prieuré. During the 1920s, he had an apartment in the seventeenth arrondissement of Paris where he spent two nights a week. Carl Zigrosser once ate a picnic supper there with the Master and Alexander de Salzmann: "I shall never forget the picture of Mr. Gurdjieff reclining on the bed, as only an Easterner can, a glimpse of his hairy chest showing through his open shirt, his frame shaking with laughter at some story told by Mr. Salzmann." When in Paris, Gurdjieff did his writing in the Café de la Paix, sustained by Armagnac and coffee taken with lemon. He liked to spend the evening at a Montmartre restaurant called L'Ecrevisse where he invited groups of friends to eat crayfish, of which he was particularly fond.

The exoticism and inspired chaos which surrounded Gurdjieff were raised to new heights when, after Mme. Ostrowsky's death, he began taking pupils on motor trips through the French countryside. After his "accident," many people might have had doubts about the Master's driving ability, and if they remained sanguine, a single expedition would have disabused them of that confidence. As Ouspensky said, Gurdjieff drove a car as if he were riding a horse, and Jane Heap's fright when she discovered that he had locked the doors from the outside was not at all assumed. Gurdjieff did come to grief, but although on one occasion he collided with a poplar at fifty miles an hour, the most severe injury among his pupils was a broken shoulder blade. From the Citroëns of his early motoring days, Gurdjieff graduated to a big, heavy Fiat in which the back seat could be curtained off so that the staff of secretaries and translators might labor undisturbed by the passing landscape.

For THE BOOK went with them. Perhaps with Mme. de Hartmann acting as Gurdjieff's amanuensis, Jessie Dwight typing on a small portable typewriter, those temporarily responsible for the translations disputing the correct word for some abstruse expression, and assorted other pupils confusing the issue, the Fiat would lurch forth on to the high road. ("How very convenient," de Salzmann once remarked as he surveyed a neatly laid out cemetery several thousand feet below the car window in a vertical drop.) As was usual when Gurdjieff was writing, he invited reactions from his audience and was particularly insistent that the translators find the right equivalent for a Russian or Armenian phrase. On one occasion the expression at issue was the English "so to speak." The young American who had charge of the English translation stuck to his guns in the face of Gurdjieff's vehement declaration that he meant "so to say." "I read famous English writer, Algernon Blackwood," he proclaimed. "He say, 'so to say.'" "It is 'so to speak,' Mr. Gurdjieff," insisted the young man in frosty tones. Tempers mounted. Then Gurdjieff broke the tension. "Idiot," he said quietly. "For you I tell."

"Short of any mechanical breakdown," Fritz Peters writes, "we seemed to have an unusual number of unnecessary experiences on the road." Gurdjieff would appoint a map reader—and decline to consult him. He would refuse to stop for gas until he ran out—whereupon one of the passengers would have to trudge back to the nearest village. He never carried a spare tire, and so, if a puncture occurred, the tire had to be repaired, not replaced. During all these complications, Gurdjieff sat by the side of the road working on *Beelzebub's Tales*.

Food—in huge quantities and unfamiliar shapes and sizes—accompanied the expeditions. Gurdjieff loved picnicking and was skillful at discovering Russian and Oriental delicacies in Paris. He carried strips of bear's meat which he pressed upon his companions—although he seldom ate much himself. On the other hand, if a pupil particularly liked a delicacy, he or she would be lucky to be offered it.

When the party arrived at a hotel, life became even more complicated. It would undoubtedly be too late for the hotel management, and a respectable-looking ambassador had first to soothe those in authority and reserve the rooms. Then the party disgorged itself from the Fiat, festooned with fragments of cold meat and *Beelzebub's Tales*. On one occasion, at a very smart hotel, the hall porter opened the trunk of the car to take out, as he thought, the luggage. He was met by the debris of a Gurdjieffian picnic, and a half-melon rolled out on to the ground at his feet. Then Gurdjieff himself emerged, unbuttoned, shabby, clutching a battered briefcase containing heaven knew what. . . .

In the dining room of the hotel, things would not be much better. Gurdjieff—as on one occasion in Vichy—might be even more unbuttoned than he had been when he entered the hotel. Dinner progressed as it did at the Prieuré: with particular tidbits reserved for favored pupils, with Gurdjieff haranguing his companions, with the toasts to the idiots drunk in Armagnac. By the end of the meal the entire dining room was silent with all ears tuned to catch everything that was said. Then the *coup de grace*. Gurdjieff belched loudly and looked around. This was the cue for others to do the same. Seated at his right hand Orage followed suit—and so on around the table until a fusillade of belches had emptied the dining room.

How did he get away with it? One reason is that he was a very heavy tipper. Sometimes colossal sums would be added to the bills of very modest restaurants—sums exceeding the total of the bill itself. On one occasion Gurdjieff bestowed an unthinkably large tip on the head waiter of a restaurant which produced an execrable lunch. Afterward he explained that he had his reasons. If the lesson struck home, the waiter would encourage the cook to serve other parties as they had served his entourage. People would soon stop visiting the restaurant and Gurdjieff would be magnificently revenged by ruining the man who had ruined his meal.

It was not entirely a matter of money, although when he had money, he was very free with it. There was undoubtedly a certain magnetism, compounded of charm and sheer bravado, which allowed Gurdjieff to sail unscathed through most social irritations. Tipping of elevator men and porters, for example, was often accomplished with a handful of pistachio nuts—mingled with fluff and old pieces of tobacco—which Gurdjieff produced from his pockets. The cheek of the man—for his self-assurance was sometimes less than absolute—was more than that of a mere flouter of convention. Gurdjieff entered the conventions and somehow bent them in his direction, leaving behind him some very puzzled guardians of things as they should be done. There is an absurd magnificence in a man who decides that alcohol is necessary to keep his car radiator from freezing in the Swiss mountains—but it must be alcohol in its sweetest, stickiest, most expensive form: green Chartreuse.

Gurdjieff's motor tours were usually to Vichy, the South Coast towns, or Switzerland—for he loved the mountains—and to Normandy and Brittany. Once it was arranged that a party would leave for Algiers. They reached Marseilles with no more than the usual complications, but in Marseilles Gurdjieff decided that they would not go on board ship. After he returned to the Prieuré, he wrote a piece of music about the journey. It was called, "Departure for Algiers."

7

The Prior of Avon

Are we dealing with a mere joker, an inspired zany with a marvelously developed knack of persuading other people to pay for his amusements? There was a part of Gurdjieff which relished the pleasures of the game and the deception, but he cannot be explained away so easily. At the risk of anticipating the final verdict, we must make some partial assessment of what Gurdjieff was trying to do.

He said that one stage of his operations was intended to produce in his victims the sensation of their own nothingness: he wanted a pupil "not to be nonentity," so first he made him "feel nonentity." Frequently people came to him because they sensed that something was out of joint, whether they located the trouble within themselves, or projected it outward on the nature of the world and indulged in a fit of prostration at the universal misery. Out of the ashes of the old personality with which they were identified, a new individual might grow. The insults, the occasionally childish behavior, and the elaborate jokes were not only part of Gurdjieff's expansive individuality, but helped to create around him the atmosphere of double meanings, extraordinary significance, withdrawal from the ebb and flow of ordinary living. Within Gurdjieff's orbit all things were possible, because reality was marginally shifted out of phase so that the connections of cause and effect were altered and the pupil could eliminate conditioned reflexes and—in an effort to find his way through the maze of paradox— become himself.

It was possible to ignore this side of his work altogether, or to be totally repelled by it. Georgette Leblanc had a disastrous first weekend at the Prieuré. Afterward she was driven to the station at Avon by a visitor who had been summoned by Gurdjieff to act as chauffeur. "Impossible walk," he had informed her. "She too angry." All the way to the station the irate Mme. Leblanc wondered volubly how anyone could stay at the Prieuré under that unpleasant charlatan Gurdjieff: but later she came back and became one of his most devoted followers. Her friend Margaret Anderson prints an account by the American novelist and publisher's editor, Solita Solano—who met Gurdjieff for the first time in 1927—of a similar experience, pitched in a lower key.

> I hoped for a demigod, a superman of saintly countenance, not this "strange" ecru man about whom I could see nothing extraordinary except the size and power of his eyes. The impact everyone expected him to make upon me did not arrive. In the evening I listened to a reading from his vaunted book. It bored me. Thereupon I rejected him intellectually, although with good humour. Later in the study house (how annoyed I was that women were not allowed to smoke there) I heard the famous music, played, I believe, by M. de Hartmann. This, almost from the first measures, I also rejected. A week or so later in Paris I accompanied Margaret and Jane, who had not quite given me up, to a restaurant where *écrevisses* were the specialty which Mr. Gurdjieff was coming to eat with about twenty of his followers. He seated me next to him and for two hours muttered in broken English. I rejected his language, the suit he was wearing and his table manners; I decided that I rather disliked him.

Seven years later Solita Solano also went back to Gurdjieff "in a crisis of misery." There undoubtedly had to be a need—although the nature of this need might be quite undefined—before a pupil would commit him or herself to his rugged ministry. The testimony of his pupils shows that they believed themselves to have discovered much that was of value in their contact with him. To history it may seem that nothing very much was going on; but if the pupil opened himself to the new meanings, and tried to balance on the knife-edge between yes and no, he might discover within the fabric of historical "events" another texture, other potentialities: new uses for the input of human experience. Perhaps buying a bottle of green Chartreuse to use as an antifreeze seems a schoolboyish prank; but it was a fragment of a larger characterization, part of the regalia of the invisible man.

You cannot come OUT if you have never been IN. The experience of two

Americans as different from each other as chalk from cheese, who lived for periods at the Prieuré, shows how life with Gurdjieff could be conducted on completely different levels.

One spent the time from spring to autumn of 1931 at Fontainebleau. He had joined Orage's groups in New York chiefly because he was in hot pursuit of a girl who went on to become a pillar of the Work. He had a healthy respect for Gurdjieff as a practical psychologist and certainly as a man who was able to "get his number." He suffered from no great existential anxiety, and took no deep interest in the philosophical problems raised by Gurdjieff's ideas. But once at the Prieuré, his money ran out, and he was marooned—a rather irreverent acolyte—within the château grounds. Quite cheerfully he would weed paths and perform his share of the work—after all, it was summer, wine was cheap, there were companions of his own age, and the Master was often away. He became known chiefly for composing a Prieuré song with a chorus which ran: "Trootitoot-toot; rootitoot-toot, we are the boys of the Institute!" Then one day while washing up, he confided to the woman pupil who was helping him that he personally was "not going anywhere." The woman promptly informed Gurdjieff, who sent for him next morning. When the summons came, the composer of Institute songs was amusing himself by trying to catch the goldfish in the fountain. Gurdjieff seated him, gave him a cup of coffee and remarked: "I think you leave now. I think you try somewhere else." The young man left the Prieuré within the hour. In Paris he found a job playing professional hockey, and with his first pay check went to see Gurdjieff at the Café de la Paix. Their relations remained amicable for some time, and the renegade received practical advice which he valued from a man whose pretensions to cosmic knowledge concerned him not at all.

A complete contrast is provided by the story of how another young American left the Prieuré. He had become interested in Orage's groups while still at the university, and being of a literary and philosophical turn of mind belonged to the generation influenced by *The Little Review* and its attempt to penetrate the thick skin of American philistinism. He became deeply committed to the practice of Gurdjieff's ideas and lived at the Prieuré almost continuously from the autumn of 1927 to that of 1931, taking over the English translation of *Beelzebub's Tales* from Bernard Metz. When he decided that it was time for him to leave, he approached Gurdjieff and told him that he wanted to go and live by himself in Paris. "This all right," replied Gurdjieff, "only I give you exercises." The pupil wanted no exercises and refused them. Gurdjieff flew into a passion. He was wasting everything he had done, he cried. The results of four years' work would be dissipated. When the pupil showed no signs of giving in to this line of attack, Gurdjieff changed his strategy. From a drawer in the table at which he was sitting, he took out an automatic. "Take with you," he commanded, "you will want to shoot yourself." The pupil threw the revolver back to the other side of the table and stalked out.

He had no communication with Gurdjieff for several years, and his interests turned to nonesoteric subjects. But from Rachmilievitch, he received a letter describing an occasion when he and Gurdjieff had been discussing "good pupils" and "bad pupils." Rachmilievitch had put his name forward as that of a "good pupil." Gurdjieff had not answered, but "benevolently smiled."

From one point of view this story contains everything. But in the last resort, the possibility of any verdict on the *process* depends on our assessment of Gurdjieff's motives. We may concede that pupils did derive benefits from his instruction, possibly that they found what they were looking for. We may even admit that it is possible to catch a hint of the nature of their experience. But in the last resort, the personality and motives of Gurdjieff must be brought into question, for it was on his manipulative skills that the process depended. It could and did go drastically wrong.

The many conflicting Gurdjieffs who appeared to different disciples theoretically ensured that the teacher himself remain invisible. But instead, these mysteries, doubts, and contradictions produced a composite "Gurdjieff"—a slightly bearlike animation of the archetypal Fool, the Jester, the Trickster, a man with whom no one was ever entirely safe. Thus a man who had made his business the destruction of illusions was to some extent defined by his public image; and in considering Gurdjieff, of all people, it is important to distinguish between image and reality.

Gurdjieff acquired a reputation, and often rumor rather than experience etched its outlines. In 1952 *Time* commented that he "seems to have been a remarkable blend of P. T. Barnum, Rasputin, Freud, Groucho Marx and everybody's grandfather." As a snap judgment this is not inaccurate, and it sketches the sort of image which now confronted those who approached the Master. The production was no longer the play of the professional hypnotist—unless a particular candidate opted for that play—but its central character was no less enigmatic than the magician of St. Petersburg. The Fontainebleau papers called him "the Magus of Valvins"; and when Zigrosser published his account of how Gurdjieff had met him with a deflating "I smell American," the *New York Times* described this as "Fe-Fo-Fumism." The comment was jocular, of course, but it indicated the unconscious image of Gurdjieff as the ogre at the top of the beanstalk.

The image was one of great power, even among those who were kept informed of the Master's activities. By 1929, D. H. Lawrence was

endorsing Mabel Luhan's verdict that Gurdjieff was "an imaginary incarnation of Lucifer." Rumor was quite specific about Lucifer's misdemeanors.
The poet H.D. (Hilda Dolittle) was said to have extemporized:

> In the house of your Sphinx
> The whores
> Scrub the floors
> And buy their own drinks.

Although Gurdjieff's reputation was always equivocal, the effect of his
personal presence never diminished. One former Oragean remembers
how, before Gurdjieff's visit to New York in 1929, rumors had been
circulating about the "mysterious and wicked" figure of the Master of
Fontainebleau. The groups had heard of his "wickedness with women" and
his ceaseless demands for money. But when Gurdjieff faced Orage's New
York groups for the first time, all the rumors "were erased like chalk off a
blackboard." The reaction which this particular pupil experienced was
exactly that of Ouspensky fourteen years before. She put it in different
words: "He's hiding."

Gurdjieff was hiding behind the various roles which he assumed, but he
was also concealed behind the leading role of the Master. His own
personality quite naturally affected his functioning as a teacher; and puzzled
disciples have often followed Ouspensky in separating Gurdjieff the human
being with all his many defects from the system of ideas which he taught.
Zigrosser warned in 1929:

> If one places too much emphasis on Gurdjieff the man, responding,
> pleasantly or otherwise, to his rich, incalculable personality, but
> making no attempt to divine his ideas, one misses practically every-
> thing of value in the contact . . . he is also expounding certain ideas, a
> certain standard of values, certain attitudes to life, and a certain
> technique for meeting it, which I, among others, have found extremely
> interesting and, as far as I have been able to try them out, sound.

The "rich, incalculable personality" was on occasion purely mischievous.
Fritz Peters, whose *Boyhood with Gurdjieff* conveys the impression of
Gurdjieff the man, calls his private character "complex." "At times," he
writes, "it seemed to me that . . . playing with people was literally nothing
more than a diversion for him, something to take his mind off the
continuous pressures under which he worked." If he had no other claims to
fame, Gurdjieff would still be justly celebrated as one of the great masters
of the practical joke.

The exaggerated respect shown to Gurdjieff did not conceal a certain shiftiness which occasionally characterized the man. His most alert pupils were by no means uncritical. Beryl Pogson speaks of the "curious impression" given by Maurice Nicoll's diary of his time at the Institute. The doctor noticed Gurdjieff's "weightless eyes, his blushes, his hesitation, his strange power." T. S. Matthews noticed that "everyone, including Orage, was afraid of him, didn't understand him, and never knew what he would do next." Matthews identifies an important feature of Gurdjieff's character with his description of the "sly, peasant-shrewd sayings" of *Beelzebub's Tales:* for there was in Gurdjieff a considerable element of peasant cunning, which compensated for a mind which was not of the first order. "Thinking," says one former resident at the Prieuré, "was not G.'s thing." The wily Levantine, the haggler over prices, the man constrained by circumstances to become an acute practical psychologist—there was much of his origins in Gurdjieff. Toward the end of his tenure at the Prieuré, one of the inmates remembers him returning from America very short of money. The baker in Avon had become pressing about the settlement of his small account. Miss Merston tried fruitlessly to postpone the reckoning; but just then, Gurdjieff walked by, discovered the situation, and quickly charmed the irate baker into submission—although he admitted to the tradesman's face that he had no money. The witness was astounded: "It was pure artistry."

If the virtues of the Sly Man were larger-than-life adaptations of those he had acquired in his native Caucasus, his vices were equally the vices of his native land. The pashalike manners which T. S. Matthews observed, his reputation as a connoisseur of wine, women and song, his insistence on traveling accompanied by a train of followers, show that Gurdjieff brought the manners of a successful Middle Eastern businessman to Europe. The man behind the mask could sometimes be seen peering through the eyeslits. But granted his natural cunning, his coarseness, his sensuality— why should these *per se* disqualify him from the task he was attempting? The charges against him must be considered one by one.

He was a gormandizer, a fleshly man, not a spiritual teacher. Gurdjieff certainly always enjoyed his food and drink, although he was never the bibulous glutton of popular imagination. Ever since the early days in Russia, observers noted that he sometimes ate very little at the feasts over which he presided, and he undoubtedly used the euphoric effects of alcohol to loosen up the company for his inspection. Several pupils have noted a peculiar effect of the alcohol consumed at Gurdjieff's table: no one became drunk until the Master had left the room. On one occasion, Gurdjieff even threw a glass down the table at a woman pupil who had helped herself to a drink out of turn. But it is true, on the face of things, that Gurdjieff does not measure up to conventional standards of how spiritual leaders ought to behave.

Another charge against him is that of cupidity. Was he out for money? He may have needed large sums for his work, but it is undeniable that he did somehow acquire a château—which he called "my house." At different times he maintained various flats in Paris, and except for short periods, he did live off his pupils. But is this so very reprehensible? His profession was that of "teacher"—whatever we may think about what he taught—and it was logical that his pupils should support him. As a writer in *The Times Literary Supplement* once remarked, it is impossible to imagine him piling up loot in some Swiss bank. For long periods he supported hordes of indigent Russians; and followers unable to pay for themselves were often maintained at the common expense. After Gurdjieff's death his family were by no means left in easy circumstances, a fact which is at once explained by Gurdjieff's seignorial attitude to any funds he happened to have in his possession. After constant pressure and reminders of the dire straits in which the Master was placed, a supporter might contribute a large sum only to find it dissipated on what appeared to be some quite trivial undertaking. Once Gurdjieff bought the whole population of the Prieuré bicycles—and made them learn to ride. Another time he gave all his followers opera glasses. He installed intercoms throughout the Prieuré; and on more than one occasion spent the whole of a generous subsidy on a gargantuan meal for his followers.

Nevertheless, the impression remains that he was, as J. G. Bennett once admitted, "by Western standards, a shark." This is possibly because of his undoubted cunning in wheedling money out of people—not because of suspicion that he operated as a shearer of sheep through base motives. Sometimes he may have been teaching the penny-pinching or the gullible lessons in the use of money; sometimes, no doubt, the sheer pleasure of the game impelled him to see how far he could push his luck. Material survival was never greatly in question; for Gurdjieff could have earned his living in any one of a half-a-dozen ways.

Then there is Gurdjieff's conduct with women. This is less likely to shock people today than it did in the 1920s and 1930s when the avant-garde sometimes hid beneath its daring cleavage the heart of a Victorian prude. And perhaps Gurdjieff was not as black as he is painted. At least twice he asked women to marry him (although one was the wife of the Swiss consul in New York). But there is no doubt at all that Gurdjieff had sexual relations with many of his pupils. The important questions are: under what conditions did these relationships take place and what was the effect of Gurdjieff's promiscuity on the women who became his sexual partners?

If Gurdjieff merely used the power of his position to persuade girls to sleep with him, is this a serious offence? This of course depends on who the girl was and on the degree of her willingness. Some women asked for nothing better than to throw themselves at the Master's feet; but failure to comply with Gurdjieff's plans often led to exclusion from the Work altogether. Gurdjieff was certainly a sensual man, and enjoyed the pleasures of the bed as much as those of the table. Fritz Peters was familiar with the aspect of his room at Fontainebleau:

> There were rumors at the time, and I am in no position to deny them, that a great deal more went on in his rooms other than drinking coffee and Armagnac. The normal state of his rooms after one night indicated that almost any human activity could have taken place there the night before.

As any reader of *Beelzebub's Tales* will become aware, Gurdjieff disapproved of contraceptives, and the natural result of his sexual athleticism was a fair-sized family of natural children. Weighing certainty with gossip, it is clear that there are now living about half-a-dozen of his children by various women in his circle. Again Fritz Peters is fairly specific in a reference to the children at the Prieuré. "With the exception of my brother and myself," he writes, "all the other children were either relatives—nieces, nephews, etc., of Mr. Gurdjieff—or his natural children." T. S. Matthews confirms that the size of Gurdjieff's extended family was quite obvious to members of the New York groups. "His women followers obviously adored him, and some of those who had found favor in his sight had visible mementos: swarthy and liquid-eyed children."

Gurdjieff did heap presents on his "calves"—as he called his children (their mothers were "cows")—when he remembered. But his attitude was at bottom careless and negligent. Of course, there may have been an esoteric reason to justify the magisterial antics. One woman follower of Gurdjieff has been reported as saying that "Gurdjieff used to take us girls into intimacy with him. It was his way of helping us." Other suggestions have been made that Gurdjieff's sexual activities were a result of his "secret" sexual teachings—perhaps a form of Tantrism which he had picked up in the East—but this seems intrinsically unlikely. Without knowing any more details, it is difficult to avoid the suspicion that, after all, physical gratification did play a large part in his motives. There may even creep back suggestions of that otherwise inaccurate comparison with Rasputin.

Criticism of Gurdjieff as a cynical materialist takes no account of what he said he was trying to do, and far more serious questions are raised when we come to consider his methods of "awakening" his pupils. In administering his "shocks," he could often be brutally harsh—and sometimes he over-stepped the limits. Even if we admit the validity of his objectives, it must also be admitted that in a number of cases Gurdjieff's methods ended in tragedy. Either he made a false assessment of a particular pupil, or he was guilty of criminal negligence toward him. He was playing with fire and the game in which he invited his pupils to take part was a dangerous one. In Gurdjieff's view it was better to die than to remain asleep.

But a great deal of nonsense has been put forth about his ruthlessness. Ranging from the accusations that he killed Katherine Mansfield to the latest notion of him as "a strange Messiah who let others die in his place," these visions represent the idea of Gurdjieff as Lucifer pushed to the ultimate. Although a number of people may have killed themselves as a result of contact with him, there is no way of telling how many desperate folk were saved from self-destruction by the mere fact of having a Master-figure to lean upon. If casualties and salvage jobs were placed on the scales, it is probable that the balance would tilt significantly in Gurdjieff's favor. This in no way excuses unprincipled conduct toward a pupil at any time.

There are two definite cases of suicide from the 1920s which clearly illustrate the problems with which the moral censor must deal. I have cut—both here and in later references—any information which would enable a casual inquirer to identify the persons concerned. It would be quite possible for a seriously interested researcher to discover—in time—to whom the names "Mr. X" and "Mrs. Y" refer.

Mr. X was a British diplomat, described by a man who knew him as "the Harold Nicolson of the F.O. of these days." He was born in the late 1880s, took a Double First at his university and led the field in the Foreign Office exams of his year. His chief work took place during the series of peace conferences which followed the First World War, and his achievements were recognized by the award of a decoration. It is clear that he was a brilliant man and might confidently have expected to add a knighthood to the letters which he placed after his name. It may have been through Rowland Kenney—who went from journalism to the Foreign Office—that he came into contact with Ouspensky and Orage. At all events, the diplomat was possibly the most distinguished recruit to the Prieuré, which he seems to have visited during 1924.

This means that he would have been there at the time of Gurdjieff's "accident" and the resulting confusion. In describing life at the Institute, J. G. Bennett writes: "Some people went mad. There were even suicides. Many gave up in despair." When pressed on the question of suicides,* he mentioned, without naming him, the figure of Mr. X, and hinted that the

---

*In an interview with the author.

effects of Gurdjieff's closing his Institute were even more shattering than can be gathered from Nott or the de Hartmanns. It may well have been the depression caused by Gurdjieff's announcement that he was shutting up shop which drove the less well-balanced of his pupils over the brink. This makes sense in terms of what little more we know about Mr. X, and it emphasizes the point that, with a large number of pupils, Gurdjieff could not keep track of each individual's personal situation. Enough is now known about the dangerous effects of breaking off a psychoanalysis while the patient is still in a dependent state to make it clear that even an exceptionally intelligent man like Mr. X would not be immune from the feeling that the sun had gone out. His obituary stated that all his friends and colleagues had been surprised by his urgent request for transfer to the Middle East. They would have been even more surprised if they had known that Ouspensky had given him the task of contacting the Mevlevi dervishes and finding out all he could.

On his way to his new posting in the summer of 1925, the diplomat and his wife stayed for a few days at the Prieuré, which was at this time in a state of suspended animation. They were befriended by Margaret Naumburg who saw Mr. X as a "typical" member of the English upper class; he possessed, she thought, one side of complete conventionality and another which was uncertain and questing. From her letters to Jean Toomer, it is plain that the diplomat was distraught, although there is little to show what was really responsible. Margaret Naumburg succeeded in shocking him severely with the bland statement that his profession must give him an unrivaled opportunity of practicing Gurdjieff's theory of role playing. But despite her feeling that Mr. X was trapped, even she was unprepared for the news reported by a London daily newspaper that he had shot himself two days after his arrival in the East.

We do not know what motives were behind this, although acquaintances hint at prior unbalance. It may even be that his conversation with Margaret Naumburg was the straw which broke the back of his tottering self-esteem. Gurdjieff's teaching cannot be shown to have played any specific part in this suicide; and Gurdjieff might merely have been one ingredient in a personal crisis whose main constituents were quite different. But it is at least highly probably that Gurdjieff's standards and orientation induced a state of desperation in which a brilliant man took his own life. The episode does provide a warning that not even the most highly trained intellect was proof against the gloom which attacked less endowed disciples.

A second tragedy took place in the summer of 1927. This was the death of Mrs. Y, a former dancer at the Paris Opéra, who had become intrigued with Gurdjieff's ideas through an interest in the movements. She stayed at the Prieuré until the demonstration in the Théâtre des Champs-Elysées at

Christmas 1923, and was then persuaded by her husband to abandon the American expedition and to return to London. It was probably in late 1923 that Mrs. Y was involved in an incident with Gurdjieff which has been described as "near rape." Her husband came to Ouspensky's lectures in Warwick Gardens, had nearly entered the Prieuré himself, and is discreet: "There were strange rumours about G.," he writes, ". . . I had a profound mistrust of the whole venture." Behind this reticence is concealed the gravest scandal to trouble the Work until the mid-1930s. The reverberations were echoing round the walls of the Institute when the first Americans arrived in the spring of 1924. Even if we excuse Gurdjieff's conduct by the sort of double-thinking which rationalizes him out of so many scrapes, the results in this case were appalling. Mrs. Y seems to have been rendered permanently unstable by her experience, and may have made an attempt to return to Fontainebleau. Certainly, during 1927 she was again in France. Her husband met her abroad and was shocked to discover how "ill" she was. Mrs. Y returned to England, where in the late summer of 1927, she fell from an upper-story window in a south coast boardinghouse and was killed. The coroner recorded a verdict of suicide "whilst of unsound mind." Mr. Y refers guardedly to his wife's condition: "Most of those who left the Prieuré, or were banished from it by Gurdjieff himself, had the greatest difficulty in readjusting themselves to ordinary life. It was as if they had seen the vision of the new world, only to be rejected and thrown back into the chaos from which they had tried to escape. This too often resulted in tragedy in their own lives."

Mrs. Y's death occurred some eighteen months after she had given birth to a child. We do not know whether her final rejection by Gurdjieff took place before or after the birth. Under other circumstances it might be argued that if Gurdjieff had banished her from the Prieuré, this was because he considered it her role to look after her husband and family—indeed cases could be cited in which he did exactly this. But there is also the "near-rape" to be taken into account, and its effect on a young woman who, as Mr. Y wrote, thought she had "seen the vision of the new world, only to be rejected." Gurdjieff certainly showed a hardness of heart which was quite out of the ordinary. Later he referred to Mrs. Y as someone who "made trouble" for him.

It is always possible that by his own remorseless ethic Gurdjieff had committed no sin. *Wake up—or be damned: it is better to die than be damned*. The trouble is that it was not only to his pupils that Gurdjieff might appear capable of no wrong. It was an inevitable risk of the function he had taken upon himself that he might come to believe his every action justified by the ends it was designed to attain. If the pupil accepts that the Master is necessary to shock him out of his mechanical state, it is possible to see how he can also accept the need for implicit obedience; for without such docility, how is the Master to engineer the artificial crises which are such an important part of his discipline? But for the Master there are dangers in receiving such complete devotion. He may come to believe that it is his right and due. Then his conviction that such methods are necessary to help people "wake up" may grow progressively stronger—together with the accumulating pressures which encourage him to half accept a reflected and exaggerated estimate of his own powers.

Did the ogrish side of the enigmatic Mr. Gurdjieff sometimes take over— as if Mr. Hyde had been the deliberate creation of Dr. Jekyll, or Frankenstein's monster a projection of part of Frankenstein? Had Gurdjieff invented his role and then begun to identify with it in earnest? It is a question which some of his disciples must occasionally have asked themselves. What conclusions they reached largely depend upon their answers to that incessantly recurring enigma: "What is the Work?"

8

Art, Science, Religion and Gymnastics

The conversion of Orage, the death of Katherine Mansfield, and the success of Gurdjieff's ideas in the United States all meant that Fontainebleau and its Master were topics for discussion in café society. Outside the circle of the converted, there was not likely to be much comprehension, and Gurdjieff's tactics were designed to discourage casual inquirers. Nott has told the story of how two visiting psychologists were kept at arm's length by Gurdjieff's impersonation of a genial but bumbling idiot, and it is scarcely surprising that the most curious stories circulated in the artistic world.

Before Monk Gibbon paid his visit to the Prieuré, he had discussed Orage's conversion with A. E. and W. B. Yeats. Yeats too, had played the part of Doubting Thomas and tried to communicate to Gibbon something of his own disillusionment with his magical adventures. "I have had a lot of experience of that kind of thing in my time," he told the young man, "and my advice to you is—leave it alone. I know how such sects become priest-ridden and fall into the hands of charlatans." But even well-intentioned warnings sometimes stirred the curiosity, and through the society of the salons and the cafés, Gurdjieff's ideas found their way to potential converts. One pupil first heard the phrase "self-observation without identification" at a weekend party given by Dorothy Coates, the mistress of John Quinn. Another—who spent several years living at the Prieuré—became intrigued by a story he heard from a friend who was a devotee of Gertrude Stein. One evening the great lady was said to have sat fixedly in her chair without turning her head to left or right. "Perhaps," said the friend, "this was something Gurdjieff had told her to do."

This was not entirely improbable. When Jane Heap moved to France in the late 1920s, she became close friends with Gertrude Stein, and Leo Stein—although he remained critical—was familiar with the content of Gurdjieff's ideas. Gertrude Stein and Gurdjieff once met. According to Alice B. Toklas, "She had nothing against him." That the rumor of some connection between the two may well have been true shows how the mediation of Orage had made the ideas of his Master common currency among the influential avant-garde.

Orage's teaching was a lucid presentation of a practical discipline; but it also had about it a self-justificatory flavor. He was advocating a philosophy to which he had been drawn for reasons which were by no means purely intellectual; and of this he was probably aware. This does not mean that his reasons were in some way invalid: his own nature, and that of the audiences whom he had to interest, demanded a justification of the way of life he recommended in terms of contemporary rationalism. The result was the creation of a body of literature, part propaganda, part apologetics, which formed a definite "Oragean" school of thought. The theme was always the same. Why should writers, scientists, or publicists abandon their absorbing occupations and fix their gaze on the stars? The answers were always similar: we need a return to first principles.

Approaches varied; and in the end, some of the intellectuals who had surrendered to Orage's persuasiveness concluded that they had been mistaken, that for all his logic, Orage was wrong. They returned to their former occupations, although not entirely unmarked. Their situation was similar to that of Middleton Murry and the *Adelphi* group in England who, after teetering perilously on the edge of the abyss, had fled in alarm. The influence of Gurdjieff, Ouspensky, and Orage as forces to reject is often as significant as their positive role.

Jean Toomer was—at least apparently—a model for all thinking men and women of the Oragean persuasion. He had become seriously involved with the ideas at the height of his literary success with *Cane*. He had accepted one of the standard arguments—that the writer should become a man before he write—and his dedication seemed to be absolute. But even Toomer wavered at times from the narrow way on which he had set his feet; and the story of his association with Gurdjieff is a paradigm of the relationship of the spirit and the world.

In November 1924, Toomer returned to the United States with a hunger for "real ideas" which he felt Orage could satisfy. His impatience evidently got the better of him for, on December 8, Orage was admonishing him that "for a long time our *chief* concern is to listen, to learn to listen, as G. used to say." By January 9, 1925, Toomer was writing repentently to Orage that he would "like to learn from you, to work with you, more than formerly. . . . Substances in me are turning to Gurdjieff, and, more immediately, to you." His ambitions changed direction. He wanted to become an esoteric teacher. Specifically, he wanted to be like Gurdjieff.

The first reward of his new commitment was permission to conduct a group in Harlem. This was not a success, and toward the end of 1925, Toomer left New York for Chicago. When Orage returned from spending the summer and autumn of 1925 at the Prieuré, he wrote to his prize subordinate: "I am very much interested how affairs are proceeding with you in Chicago. Very little indeed of what you are doing has come to my knowledge; and a little of even that is only gossip about a girl! What I should like to hear is how many groups you have, their numbers and quality. . . ."

Toomer's main achievement was not in building up a circle of proselytes, but rather in playing a fish long-since hooked by Orage. The pair had designs on Mabel Dodge Luhan and her house in Taos, New Mexico, where she and her husband lived in an isolation sometimes shared by the D. H. Lawrences—and an increasing number of intellectuals. Taos was fast becoming an artist's colony, filled with refugees from the big cities who were concerned to return to the primitive virtues. The Harlem poet, Langston Hughes, wrote a sultry evocation of the place called "A House in Taos," and at once it was assumed that this house was Mabel Luhan's.

Mabel Luhan had been caught by the mission of Orage and Gurdjieff in early 1924. When she had first heard of Gurdjieff's Institute, she wrote to D. H. Lawrence, who at that time was in his most splenetic mood against all things Gurdjieffian. He had replied in January 1924, that he had "heard enough about that place at Fontainebleau . . . to know that it is a rotten, false, self-conscious place of people playing a sickly stunt. One doesn't wonder about it at all," he emphasized. "One knows." Nevertheless, sometime toward the end of January 1924, the Lawrences visited the Institute on their way to Baden-Baden. The expedition did nothing to allay Lawrence's mistrust of Gurdjieff, and Mabel Luhan devoted reams of paper to an attempt at persuading him to try again. These letters read as an appeal for information; but in fact they were probably an artfully conceived campaign to draw Lawrence into the net. For by the spring of 1926, the writer had long since gone beyond providing house-room for Orage's nestings in New York.

Her enthusiasm for Gurdjieff's ideas had a personal aspect: Jean Toomer, who she had probably met at Orage's meetings. A letter of January 8, 1926, which she wrote to Toomer from a hotel in Santa Fe, shows to what lengths her infatuation had gone. It had become entangled with her interest in the ideas which Toomer represented, and she suddenly decided that it was vital to start a branch of Gurdjieff's Institute in Taos with Toomer as the chosen instructor.

The practical outpouring of her devotion becomes clear in the correspondence between Toomer and Orage. Mabel Luhan had offered her ranch to Gurdjieff to house a full-scale Institute on the lines of Fontainebleau. She had probably also given—or been one of the leading spirits in raising—the sum of 15,000 dollars, which had been handed over to Toomer as Gurdjieff's representative. Toomer was in communication with Mme. de Hartmann, who was still Gurdjieff's secretary and administrator. He sent 1,000 dollars to her and asked what he should do with the remaining 14,000 dollars. His own suggestion was to start a branch of the Institute in Taos. He wrote to Gurdjieff that he had inspected the property, which was suitable for encouraging hard work, although too isolated from ordinary life for a school of the Fourth Way. Of Mabel Luhan he wrote: "I can hope for her, just in so far as she will persist in her present idea of following your method—but I could not persuade myself to certainty in regard to her constancy."

On February 1, Gurdjieff broke his self-imposed silence with a long letter of thanks to Mabel Luhan. He wrote in the lengthy Armenian sentences of Beelzebub, and the letter was translated by Mme. Galumnian. He explained his rule about not answering letters and said that nevertheless, when Mme. de Hartmann handed him the money, he felt he must write personally. He explained that he was at last struggling free from the problems created by the liquidation of the Fontainebleau Institute—and maintained the fiction that he was also liquidating its various branches throughout the world. He had no time to devote to the money-making activities which could support an Institute, he explained; neither could his writing be interrupted. He was therefore compelled to refuse the offer of the Taos house.

Toomer had lost his chance to establish the well-endowed Institute of his dreams. The 14,000 dollars went into a fund for the publication of *Beelzebub's Tales*, and the Taos plan was abandoned. This no whit diminished the enthusiasm of Mabel Luhan. On April 3, she replied to a letter from Lawrence which ended with the reflection that "we are all changing pretty drastically"; and again, her tone is eager to engage Lawrence.

Her letter makes suggestive reading and explains Gurdjieff's enormous appeal to those jaded by life's more obvious stimuli. The attempt to convert

Lawrence was made very much in terms of the Oragean version. "So that's his Method," Mabel Luhan wrote. "Self-observation. First with *non-identification*, then *participation*, then *experiment*." She tried to persuade her friend to sound out Gurdjieff for her; and as she suspected that the Master was at that moment on the French Riviera on one of his chaotic expeditions, might not Lawrence be able to cross the Italian frontier and interview him? Keeping up the pretense that she was asking a favor, she cajoled Lawrence by protesting her trust in him. She might visit Fontainebleau "for a week or two in May," she wrote; "but I'd rather wait to hear from you first."

Lawrence had no intention of succumbing. He was tolerant of her interest, and even prepared to investigate it. But he was fundamentally opposed to the ideology of expanded consciousness, believing that the way to cosmic awareness lay through the unconscious. His annotations of *Tertium Organum* show a total opposition to Ouspensky, and "As for Gourdjieff and Orage and the awakening of various centres and the ultimate *I* and all that," he wrote, "—to tell you the truth, plainly, I don't know . . . There is no way mapped out, and never will be." Mrs. Luhan could retrieve her own game; Fontainebleau might do her good. The last word from the Lawrence side of the correspondence came from Frieda Lawrence, who wrote discouragingly in July: "I don't like the Gurdjieffs and the Orages and the other little thunderstorms."

Meanwhile, Toomer continued his spiritual odyssey. Increasingly, he felt himself detached from life, his values rooted in the values of the Work. A memorandum, dated April 10 and 11, 1926, indicates the state which he was seeking: "the planet Karatas" to which he refers is mentioned in *Beelzebub's Tales* as Beelzebub's home planet from which he was exiled for presumption, and to which he has painfully won the right to return.

I have an intimation that this Earth, instead of being my home planet—as Toomer assumes and feels that it is and as it is for the planetary body—will become strange, foreign and remote, while at the same time I will increasingly feel Karatas or the Sun-Absolute to be my home. This, in the reality of fact, knowledge, attitude, realisation; not in mere words or fancy. . . .

Let me observe where *this* remote being, Toomer, dwells, what he does, where he goes, what things he uses, and how he lives, in general. Let me likewise observe the life of these other remote beings, bipeds, quadrupeds, insects, etc., seeing them all as *remote*, distant from my native planet, friends, associates and surroundings. If I can hold this state, wherein this Earth—all of it, New York and Toomer's room and friends in New York included—is *really* the remote place, whereas Karatas is *really* home, the chief feature will then at once wish to leave this place and will become nostalgic, will wish to reach Karatas. And in this way, it can be used to aid my return.

In his notes for conducting his own group, Toomer had reminded himself to bear in mind "the nature of the I that is to be conceived." Now, in his increasing internalization, he admonished himself: "Transfer all dependence and expectancy from the external world, and from organism, to I." He became awed with the idea which Orage transmitted as "man can become a cell in the mind of God."

Hitherto I have held the attitude that life would help the organism, that the organism must be helped by something external: this has been my dearest attitude. Now I say that I must help it, and must prepare myself in order to help God. This prospect is at once terrifying and liberating.

He is a remote being. *I* am responsible for him and I am responsible for myself throughout all time. I am obliged to make all possible effort in all circumstances to preserve, improve and develop him. I am responsible for my own realisation.

The nearest practical equivalent to "the planet Karatas" was the Prieuré, where Toomer spent the summer of 1926. He returned to Chicago in September, and a circular announced his first meeting on October 3. There were to be groups for both old and new members and a special group to listen to readings of *Beelzebub's Tales*. "Events at Fontainebleau this summer which have a bearing on the work in America will be mentioned." The nature of these mysterious events is not stated; and probably the sentence was used by Toomer simply to excite interest in his return from France. A month or so later Orage wrote urgently from the Prieuré—or "Château Gurdjieff," as he liked to call it—in the terms of *Beelzebub's Tales* to ask "how you are getting on during your first descent to the planet 'Earth'?" Toomer replied that he confronted "a strange composite of positive and negative feelings towards the work, with very few clear conceptions of what it is about or how it is conducted in groups." He found that many people were friendly to him personally, but balked at the mention of his mission in Chicago. The "planet 'Earth'" was not a hospitable place for a pupil-teacher of Gurdjieff's ideas.

Next summer he returned to Fontainebleau, partly at the request of Orage, who had decided not to cross the Atlantic that year and wrote that he would feel "easier in his mind" if Toomer were at the Prieuré to superintend the summer visitors. In 1927 there were a great many

Americans at Fontainebleau, and Toomer was the senior American pupil present.

It seems that, in his elliptical fashion, Gurdjieff indicated that great things were in store for him; but there is little further information about his relationship with Gurdjieff until the summer of 1929 when he was again at the Prieuré. He was suffering from a prolonged bout of depression which had begun when his novel *Transatlantic* had been rejected the previous year; and in a note dated September 20, 1929, he analyzed his feelings. He had returned to Fontainebleau "after some months of having been comparatively asleep in the objective world." The French Line turned down a scheme, which he had hoped to arrange, for him to write factually about life aboard one of their ships. This jolted him "from my comparative state of not feeling reality and made me again conscious of life as it is, of the real difficulties involved in managing this organism named Toomer." He was depressed about sex problems and money. He got drunk repeatedly and wrote of vomiting and nausea in a paroxysm of self-disgust. While waiting for the publishers Harcourt Brace to pass verdict upon the rewritten version of *Transatlantic*, he made an entry in his notebook which shows how "the planet Karatas" was now becoming the alien world. His feet were once more touching the surface of that much despised planet Earth.

> In the midst of my great work I am becoming literary.
>
> This idea was formulated one chill rainy twilight as, with two grogs aux [sic] rum under my belt, I walked through the avenue of plane trees from the gare at Avon to Le Prieuré.
>
> It was caused (1) by a recognition of the increasing value I am giving to all that has to do with writing, (2) by a realisation that many of my inner experiencings are automatically relating themselves to literary forms, (3) that I again see, sense, feel, understand the world from the point of view of a literary artist, (4) that my literary work again has a living atmosphere.
>
> I accept it. I accept it because I understand it is an aspect of my necessary contacting with the ordinary and practical worlds.
>
> This begins the period of my great writing.
>
> Years hence I will again emerge into the world of pure being.
>
> This is an eclipse of Jean the saint, an emergence of Jean the man in the world and artist.
>
> Salzmann: "Once you were an eagle. Now you are a sheep."

The mood of jubilation was shattered by the renewed rejection of *Transatlantic*, and his problems came crowding in on him. He felt that he had cut himself off from human experience. All his plans were being delayed, in particular his wish to project an image of himself as an American novelist, not the Negro author of *Cane*. Worse still, he saw things *repeating . . . and repeating* in the pattern of his life, in a minuscule reminder of eternal recurrence. Once more he would be returning to Chicago from Fontainebleau, having failed to have a novel accepted. Resignedly, he sailed for the United States in October to resume his groups. "Imperfect though it is," he wrote, "I leave my form in Chicago. In Chicago I am and possess all that having a form implies. The minute I leave Chicago, my form tends to dissolve."

Just as he had reconciled himself to the world in the hopes of success with his novel, he accepted his role as a spiritual director when that success was denied him. Although he was far from downing his pen, *Transatlantic* was Toomer's attempt at the sole literary form in which he had achieved success. Afterward he burrowed deeper into the core of Gurdjieff's ideas, and his later writings almost all relate to the discipline which he continued to teach. He made his most original contribution to the Work in 1932— some three years after he had temporarily folded his wings and decided to join the common herd.

With unintentional irony—for he was necessarily ignorant of the battle with literary ambition which Toomer was fighting—Gorham Munson published an essay on "The Significance of Jean Toomer" in his book *Destinations* (1928). He held up his friend as an example to all American writers. An artist fully conscious of the responsibility which his gifts entailed, Munson wrote, was forced, like Toomer, to seek the solution to the universal questions. He was morally bound to seek for unity in himself, so that the voice his readers heard would be genuinely his own. Harking back to the days when they sat together at the feet of Waldo Frank and looked on *Tertium Organum* as their Bible, Munson wrote of the potential of this new sort of artist, and the reader of *Destinations* is left in no doubt that in its author's eyes the correct destination was Toomer's indefinable goal.

In another essay in the book, "American Literature and the Unattainable," Munson pointed the way in more general terms. He appealed to the disillusioned but not disheartened man; "the man who has lost his illusions concerning wealth and sex and art and social reform, but who has turned searcher with a vengeance, who is desperate and practical, skeptical of himself, energetic to the point of gratuitous effort and unified by his object, which is self-knowledge and self-development towards a clear but utterly remote standard." This might stand as a definition of Oragean Man, and Munson proposed it in direct opposition to the ideal of the whole man embodied in the romantic vision of the artist. As a leading supporter of the romantic heresy, he selected Waldo Frank. This onslaught on his former mentor was the first of several; for the coming of Orage had fairly split the "Art as Vision" circle, and Munson conceived it his duty to show Frank the error of his ways.

Munson was less prominent than Toomer in the Work hierarchy, but was very active on Gurdjieff's behalf and became the unofficial treasurer of the Gurdjieff fund in New York. Kenneth Burke was certainly interested in the ideas and may have conducted a group at some time before he turned Marxist in the 1930s. Hart Crane was the only one of the original circle to hold out staunchly for a more personal vision. "Your comments on Gorham's shrine and gland-totemism," he wrote to Allen Tate early in 1927, "convince me that Orage talked as vaguely and arbitrarily in your presence as he did in mine on a similar occasion." A longer letter to Ivor Winters, written on May 29 of the same year, complains that his friends' missionary zeal has broken the ties between them. For even Waldo Frank had become swept up by the Oragean tide.

A month or so after Crane decided that he could no longer understand his friends, Frank arrived at the Prieuré to stay for a weekend with his second wife, Alma; both Toomer and the Munsons were at Fontainebleau, and Frank's discomfiture was widely observed. According to Munson, he was little the wiser for his experience in Orage's groups and seemed unaffected by Gurdjieff's scorn for intellectual posturing; he appeared to believe that the Master would welcome him as a fellow-sage. Instead of meeting Gurdjieff as an equal, he had found himself led on a lengthy tour of the Prieuré grounds by Russian pupils. Eventually, Frank was introduced to Gurdjieff, who thoroughly confused him by talking in his usual garbled English about the still less comprehensible *Beelzebub's Tales*.

The Saturday routine wore on, with the bath in the late evening and the feast held at midnight in the "English" dining room. The Franks were seated on each side of Gurdjieff, who presided patriarchally over a gathering sixty strong. During the meal there was a lull in the conversation, and into this Gurdjieff interjected a passage which in Munson's account is slightly confused. However, the incident was recorded by another pupil, and Gurdjieff seems to have been implying that Frank treated Alma as a substitute for Margaret Naumburg, not as an individual in her own right. "You not marry Blondine," he said to Frank, "why you tell me so? Better you stay with Jewish wife. For Jewish man only Jewish woman corresponding. In bed he take woman like handkerchief. Truth I tell, woman squirm, she know, truth I tell."

This is strong medicine—unless Gurdjieff is to be considered infallible—and it may be thought questionable. It is all very well for Munson to write that "Gurdjieff's diagnosis was confirmed by their separation two years later," and for another pupil to claim that he never knew Gurdjieff to be the cause of a broken marriage. Granted that Gurdjieff had achieved his customary psychological precision in his assessment of the Frank's relationship, by what standards was he acting? Was it in the best interests of either Waldo or Alma Frank to have their troubles aired in public? By the standards of his Work, the standards of impartial self-assessment and self-development, Gurdjieff may have been perfectly correct. But we have no guarantee that the drastic treatment at Fontainebleau did not contribute of itself to the breakdown of Frank's marriage.

The moral question aside, this thrust undoubtedly told. The rest of the evening seems to have been devoted to testing the Franks. A reading of *Beelzebub's Tales* dragged on until nearly four in the morning. Eventually Waldo Frank cracked and asked permission to go to bed. Gurdjieff instantly gave it and invited both Franks to one of his crayfish dinners. A very short time after the couple had gone to bed, Gurdjieff stopped the reading and dispersed the company.

According to Gorham Munson, Frank's final brush with Gurdjieff took place in L'Ecrevisse. A companion of Gurdjieff was witness to this scene. Gurdjieff was nervous, she records, and his writing was apparently going badly. He was so distracted that he began to sharpen a pencil, although his breast pocket was full of pencils which were already sharp. Waldo Frank was expected, and eventually arrived. "Shaking with rage, he raised his fist and, shaking it at Gurdjieff, yelled, 'Go back to your hell, you devil, and leave us alone.'" "Unfortunately," remarks Munson, who heard a version of the story from Alma Frank, "Frank's voice tended to be light and high and the performance was shrill." Gurdjieff looked up innocently. "What angry man say? I not understand." Waldo Frank made a dramatic exit, and Gurdjieff turned to his companion with whom he had planned a shopping expedition, "Miss, you pay, eh?"

Munson's epilogue to this story consists of a remark made by Gurdjieff on an expedition to Mont-Saint-Michel a few days later. Talking of Waldo Frank and Margaret Naumburg, he made the comment: "Her I like. But he is squared idiot."

The squared idiot had had enough of Gurdjieff—and took refuge in his former interests. The novel which he planned to complete during the summer of 1927 was never finished, and his notebooks merely contain what one critic describes as jottings on mysticism. It may be that the shock of his weekend at the Prieuré was responsible for Frank's re-emergence as the prophet of the New America. Investigation of the possibilities of becoming a more perfect individual had halted, and he reverted to the possibilities of the nation as the more perfect communion of the individual with his kind. During 1928 he produced *The Rediscovery of America*, which the *New Republic* printed chapter by chapter with Frank's ink scarcely dry on the manuscript. His new vision was based on an analysis of the American situation from a neo-Oragean viewpoint, although the influence of his wide mystical reading was also marked. Frank saw in true Oragean fashion "a uniform people, an unconscious people, a people enslaved to the monotone of industrial 'advance' which is the domination of *things*." To this he opposed his ideal nation composed of "a conscious people, a varied and integral people, the symphonic nation in whom all selves adumbrate to wholeness."

The whole trouble, he thought, lay in the fickleness of the self. He took his stand on Gurdjieff's teaching of man's "many I's." "The usual 'self' is a flashing and fusing of words, a flux of memories and behaviours split from the unity of life." No nation could be composed from such impermanent individuals. In order to create a group, the individual first needed to reform himself. His argument was that which Munson had used a year earlier in *Destinations*. "What is needed," wrote Frank, "is a method for achieving specific controls within us, as sure as the method of the modern chemist." He debated Buddhism, Pythagoras, and the Cabala as disciplines for achieving self-knowledge and unity with the whole. "The archaic methods are barred," he concluded, "for their values and ends are not ours." But America could learn from the East the "applied science" of which it stood in need. Frank then outlined a vague and inflated method for achieving what he called "the image of wholeness." He warned his readers that there were various dangers to the semi-mystical practices which he recommended. As an example, he criticized the Method derived from Gurdjieff, whose followers formed the only "Eastern cult" with which he had had contact. "It is vitiated," he wrote, "by the doctrinal separation of the observing 'I' from the observed organism." He ended by acknowledging "my debt to Mr. Orage, whose dialectic stimulated me, often through disagreement, to come to my own conclusions."

Frank's more detailed criticism of the Gurdjieff technique is very acute: he had in fact stumbled on the central trick of the Method and decided that he did not like the direction in which it was leading him. To those who remained in every sense disciples, this exhibition of—dare one say—free will, appeared as a return into mechanicalness. They began to accuse Frank of plagiarizing Gurdjieff. Having come *in* he was now going *out* again; but down and out from the point of view of a true believer. It was clear that he must be censured.

In 1930, the year after *The Rediscovery of America* was issued in book form, Gorham Munson published *The Dilemma of the Liberated*. In many ways this was a covert reply to Frank's apostasy; but whereas Frank had used Orage's Method as a possible aid in his self-imposed task of constructing a distinctive "Americanness," Munson argued from current intellectual questions to the necessity of the Method. The Oragean attitude appeared to him as a necessary outcome of the Humanist philosophy propounded by Irving Babbitt and Paul Elmer More.

Munson opposed the Humanist position to the conventional attitudes of the Romantic. The Romantic "resigns his Ego to his organism" and "like a child led by its nurse" he travels along the road mapped out for him by nature. The logical end of this progress was Freud, whom Munson rather oddly saw as a prophet of sensuality. Munson addressed those attracted by Babbitt's doctrines of "restraint" in tones which only a knowledge of the Work can discern as a sales pitch. "The New Humanist feels that his real, deepest self is somewhat apart from his natural mechanical self. He wants to be the driver of his machine, not a mere intoxicated passenger in a runaway vehicle."

The Humanists, Munson felt, were obviously halfway to his own position. They appreciated the need for a salutary discipline; but they stopped short of taking the vital step. The liberated man would consider Humanism with sympathy, but his own aspirations were set on higher things. For the Humanists in the last resort were only "pseudo-liberated" and—of course— they lacked a Method for developing the Will which was to exert the discipline they preached. Munson thought the Humanists had restricted "the length of our tether." His appeal would be familiar nowadays, and in Europe the phrase, "expansion of consciousness," had long been current in the society frequented by Ouspensky and Orage. Munson put his "disagreeable" proposition in more homely terms. "The Great Revolt will be the revolt against the limits of Humanism as new vistas of action, thought and being become discernible beyond the end of the tether." The real lesson was to be learned from "the resolute disposition of the genuinely religious to go to any lengths, if necessary." A truly liberated human being was religious by definition.

The Dilemma of the Liberated was an appeal to the man who had freed himself from convention and inheritance, but who had come to see that self-indulgence was not the way out. In many ways it is a remarkable book which would have been prophetic if it had been less shackled to the intellectual controversies of the time. As it stands, it is the attitude alone which remains prophetic; and the attitude is derived almost entirely from Orage. *The Dilemma of the Liberated* is very much the sort of book Orage would have written if he had written sustained criticism. It was Gurdjieff and Orage applied; a sort of public version of the appeal with which every teacher of the Gurdjieff ideas begins his campaign: "What do you want? Humanism, as a civilized doctrine which joins ethics and common sense? Hmmm, very well. How will you exert that discipline? You need a technique. . . ."

• • •

By the time Munson published *The Dilemma of the Liberated*, *The Little Review* was no more. Again the Oragean magic had convinced a group of intellectuals that art was not enough. Among them, Margaret Anderson leaves no doubt that it was Orage, rather than the "baffling" Gurdjieff, who initiated her into "the art of life." When in 1925 she visited the Prieuré, Gurdjieff was still almost incommunicado, and Orage's adroit manipulation left her "slightly hysterical"; "I wanted to shake Orage and shout: tell me what it is you know that I don't! Next I wanted to weep, as a token of my admiration." Instead they discussed her reactions, and Orage dangled before her the carrot of a less "subjective" state of being. Then he cross-examined her on what she wanted from life:

> What is your object in playing the piano?
> As nearly as I can define it, playing the piano is the logical way to recapture continuously that state of ecstasy without which life is not worth living.
> That is not an object, corrected Orage. If you say you are playing the piano to make money or to give concert tours you have named objects.
> And then he added the five words that have changed my outlook upon life:
> Act, said Orage, don't be acted upon.
>
> *   *   *   *
>
> I saw Orage again. This time he said seven words:
> Remember you're a pianist and not a piano.

Orage's influence was also the deciding factor for Jane Heap. In 1926, after visiting the Prieuré several times, she allowed space in *The Little Review* for a rather heavy-handed article by Orage called *"A Theatre for Us,"* in which Orage described Gurdjieff's theory of the three centers of man.

Orage added that he did not undertake to write a Gurdjieffian play, but he would go to see it. It is small wonder that his English friends considered that his judgment had faltered; for if they took this covert piece of propaganda at its face value, they must have formed a poor opinion of Orage's artistic standards. Literature and art had been completely subordinated to the world view of Gurdjieff; and the appearance of this article in *The Little Review*—the magazine of all the little magazines which most exalted the role of the artist—shows clearly how the artist was coming to distrust his own most cherished illusions. The article speaks "as an intelligent to the intelligent," it addressed an "in-group," and with hindsight it appears as the forerunner of *The Little Review*'s capitulation to the pressure of the times and Orage's remorseless logic.

During the years 1928–30, Margaret Anderson and Georgette Leblanc lived in a lighthouse at Tancarville in Normandy and wrote their memoirs. Georgette Leblanc admitted that her *Maeterlinck and I* was an act of exorcism, but Margaret Anderson's *My Thirty Years War* was equally an attempt to annihilate the past by comprehending it. "Each day," wrote the creator of Mélisande, "I feel that I leave myself a little more, the better to go towards my encounter with myself." The founder of *The Little Review* put it more simply: "I am trying to become a new human being." Then at last Jane Heap agreed with Margaret Anderson that *The Little Review* must end. All their strivings and aspirations had become transmuted. Their attention had passed through the glass of art and fixed itself on the view beyond the window.

Margaret Anderson returned to her magazine to write a last editorial in the spring of 1929. She had begun *The Little Review*, she wrote, because she "wanted an intelligent life." Only the very best artists could give her this life; and so she created a magazine for them. But now she had come to the conclusion that "even the artist doesn't know what he is talking about. And I can no longer go on publishing a magazine in which no one really knows what he is talking about. It doesn't interest me." She could imagine only one sort of magazine which would be interesting to publish, one which would be "about people."

> Only, don't let me hear any more about "it's the artist who transforms life." I know it. But I'm not particularly interested at the moment in transformation. I want a little illumination.
>
> Of course I won't start that other kind of review. I wouldn't really have the patience: everyone becomes too angry when expert opinion is brought to bear upon his pretences, his satisfaction in living the human clichés. It would take years to get down to a little decent discussion of the world psyche.
>
> In the meantime I shall search psychological conversation.

Jane Heap's farewell was less tumultuous and more concerned with the artist's predicament. Headed, "Lost: a Renaissance," it recalled that *The Little Review* had been the standard-bearer of "the revolution in the arts, begun before the war." Hope of this renaissance had faded, she wrote, just as the hope of a better world after Armageddon had vanished soon after the signing of the Versailles peace. Her editorial explains better than any analysis why American intellectuals fell headlong into the arms of Orage; and it indicates that the reasons were not so different from those which drove Europeans into embracing totalitarian politics or the Catholic

Church. There was one obvious difference: the Gurdjieff discipline promised a way of escape for individualists.

> We have given space in the Little Review to 23 new systems of art (all now dead) representing 19 countries. In all this we have not brought forward anything approaching a masterpiece except the "Ulysses" of Mr. Joyce. . . .
>
> Self-expression is not enough; experiment is not enough; the recording of special moments or cases is not enough. All of the arts have broken faith or lost connection with their origin and function. They have ceased to be concerned with the legitimate and permanent material of art.
>
> I have not come to this opinion hastily nor through any habitual pessimism, but only after years of observation, revaluing, and learning. I hold no disappointment, despair, or fears for the future. I hold no negative emotions. The actual situation of art today is not a very important or adult concern (Art is not the highest aim of man); it is interesting only as a pronounced symptom of an ailing and aimless society.
>
> This is the situation as I see it. My "luminous certitude" that it could be changed made of me a victim of the Little Review. . . . In spite of logic, deprivations, financial catastrophies and Mr. Sumner, we have gone on running the Little Review: or I thought I had until I found that it was running me. I was a victim as much as any saint, savant, or business-man. But my idea of victimization had been enlarged. It is this that now needs my attention . . .

The final number of *The Little Review* in which these editorials appeared is an extraordinary document. The bulk of the issue was taken up by the replies made by past contributors to a questionnaire sent them by the editors. This was an adaptation of the standard questionnaire which Orage gave to his pupils as a preliminary exercise in self-knowledge; and the editors printed a letter from Orage which correctly prophesied the sort of answers they received:

> I doubt whether you will get any sincere answers to these questions. After all, the stuff of the answers is the stuff of which "literature" is the disguise—and as your questioners are mainly literary, they will naturally preserve their private capital. I wouldn't answer the questions in public myself for anything. Why? The public doesn't deserve my answers. And couldn't make me any equivalent return. In a small

group, sworn to secrecy and eternal friendship, these mental con-
fessions would be salutary and in fact necessary—but where, even, is
such a group?

The contributors divided themselves into several factions: those like
Picasso and Shaw who were too busy and eminent to reply; rumbustious
correspondents like Ben Hecht and Richard Aldington who took the
questions at their face value, and others who filled in the answers in an
excess of humor (some of the jokes were quite good: Question—Why would
you not change places with anyone?—Allen Tanner: "Ah, because I am
myself and *intensely* under my influence"); a group which included André
Gide and Aldous Huxley who caught some idea of the underlying intention;
and the *Little Review* set who were pupils of Orage and Gurdjieff and wrote
in the private language of their ideas.

Of these some, like Munson, answered in the Oragean mode. Why
should he make strangers privy to his dearly bought self-knowledge?
Others, like Solita Solano and Georgette Leblanc, answered straightfor-
wardly that they wanted to be "more conscious" human beings, and the rest
of their answers followed according to the canon. There was an astoundingly
sophisticated—and Gurdjieffian—reply from Fritz Peters, aged fifteen.
Mark Turbyfill contributed a dolorous lament for his will-less "puppet-
hood." Gertrude Stein was more than usually enigmatic ("Jane, Jane come
away let the garden come and stay came late to stay in the morning came
late to stay the first day in the evening"). Margaret Anderson regarded the
answers as confirmation that even artists did not know what they were
doing. Jane Heap announced that she had found her own answers to some
of the questions and that these provided the best reason for abandoning art.

But none of the really eminent contributors followed suit. The real
creators—those who were still convinced that they could in fact create—
remained unmoved by the arguments about the necessity of going "beyond
art." The critics were drawn to Orage by intellectual honesty; the minor
writers perhaps because they lacked the final obsessive conviction which
drove the greater artists. It was those who had been defeated by the 1920s
who joined the Oragean caucus.

The release experienced by the intellectual who discards his rigorous
standards is often of an intensely emotional nature; and the devotion which
Orage inspired was more than a little religious. To Herbert Croly,
Gurdjieff's approach seemed to provide the contemporary philosopher's
stone, the union of religion and science. During 1925 and 1926, his *New
Republic* editorials made frequent concealed reference to Orage's technique, and Croly moved into the open with his article "Religion as

Method," of June 30, 1926. "The only trustworthy knowledge of God," he declared, "is derived from a kind of contemplation which includes and combines the results of mystical experience and scientific method." He distinguished two possible ways of "being aware." The first—in which the "individual organism" was supposed to deepen its contacts with the "total environment"—is related to the "method" of Waldo Frank. The second was simply the Method as taught by Orage.

Croly himself seems not to have pursued his discipline to the end. Perhaps the vacillation between Frank's mysticism and the Method which can be seen in his writings of 1926 shows that he never committed himself wholeheartedly to Orage and Gurdjieff. In 1928 he had a stroke which Robert Morse Lovett, in his own book, *All Our Years*, connects with his practice of the Gurdjieff Method. The same year the *New Republic* published Waldo Frank's *The Rediscovery of America;* and when the work was issued in book form in 1929, it bore a fulsome dedication to Croly, whose association with the renegade Frank indicates that he had at last decided against Orage. "Croly was a fastidious man," writes Edmund Wilson, "and in the long run he found Orage grating." The founder of the *New Republic* died in 1930, by which time Orage's authority in intellectual circles was in any case on the wane.

However, Croly's hope for a scientific religion was shared by committed Orageans. Jane Heap was fond of emphasizing the technical aspect of the discipline; in Orage's words, it was "a technique of techniques." Margaret Anderson makes frequent references to "the Gurdjieff science." The best apology for the scientific attitude of Gurdjieff's approach was made by the recorder of *The Oragean Version,* Charles Daly King.

In 1927, at the height of Orage's success, Daly King published a short book called *Beyond Behaviorism* under the pseudonym of Robert Courtney. It begins with an acknowledgment to Orage and a dedication "to my old friend and frequent companion, M. N. Eddin"—the Mullah Nasr Eddin whose unconventional drolleries pepper the pages of *Beelzebub's Tales.* The Orage groups considered the book to be their justification in terms of contemporary psychology. Psychoanalysis was not worthy of their steel; it was merely another product of the Western life of illusions, but Behaviorism and its leading popular prophet, Dr. John B. Watson, were other matters. If men were no better than Pavlov's dogs and if psychology must confine its attentions to recording observable behavior, the position of Western man might seem more hopeless than ever. This was where the Oragean stepped in. Of course, man is mechanical, ran the argument; of course, he is conditioned by physique, inheritance, and education: *but there is a way out . . .*

Like Croly, Daly King saw the Method as a possible junction of religion and science. He began with the parable of the emergence of the butterfly from the chrysalis. In the course of his argument, this comparison was applied to the new men who were to emerge from the old automatic men, and to the new science which was to spring from the ashes of the old. Daly wanted "bigger and better men" as the only possible solution to the problems of industrial society.

> Presently, so it is said, within a few generations, we shall face a bankruptcy of brains that will cause our food and water supplies to become uncertain, epidemics to sweep our crowded cities, and our whole, vast, complicated fabric of life to decompose in such a welter of blood and misery as the world has never seen.

He accepted many of the Behaviorists' arguments, but these merely increased the sense of hopelessness. "Is our civilization doomed?" This question was dismissed as too vast for individual consideration. The individual must therefore concentrate on himself. Religions—which had held out the hope of a soul only if a man worked to obtain it—had degenerated into mere altruism. "As if, forsooth, by a figurative enlargement of the visceral system a man could become a god!" Daly shaded the desperate situation of humanity in the darkest possible tones. If religions and psychologies provided no solution, where could the inquirer find hope? At this point he introduced the idea of self-observation. "Here," he announced, "we have the very secret itself!" "That 'I' am indeed a thing distinct from my body (or any or all of its functioning parts) is evident from the fact that it is *possible* for 'I' to observe its behaving body with completely impersonal non-identification." The practice of this method would result in the metamorphosis of the human butterfly. "This method is the technique of techniques. If we can make progress with this, all other processes, from play-writing to carpentering, will become *ipso facto* much easier for us to master."

The summer after he had published *Beyond Behaviorism*, Daly—now with a degree in psychology—went to California as assistant to Dr. William M. Marston, under whom he had studied at Columbia. Here he worked with Marston in developing the system of "Integrative Psychology." Marston's position was that, although the Behaviorists were correct in attempting to measure only what was measurable, this did not mean that the phenomena of consciousness should be excluded from the province of psychology. He argued that Behaviorism was a valid branch of physiology and not part of psychology at all. His own theory was that consciousness was what he called "psychonic energy" which resulted from the functioning of synapses in the brain.

Daly collaborated with his former teacher in various papers and a book on the theory of Integrative Psychology. From his point of view, the most important aspect of Marston's work was that it rescued the phenomena of consciousness from the Behaviorists, who had tried to exclude the topic from all academic consideration. He set to work to incorporate this helpful new approach within the structure of the Method. The result was another book, *The Psychology of Consciousness*, published in 1932.

This is "a much more detailed, technical and expanded version" of *Beyond Behaviorism*. Gone are the literary conceits of the purely Oragean work; gone are the mournful reflections on approaching doom. In their place is a closely argued justification for the method of self-observation. The first part of the book contains a critique of Behaviorism and other schools of psychology. It ends with an outline of Marston's ideas. Having restored consciousness to the center of attention, Daly parades across the field the question of the "I." He then pounces on the defects which he finds in all the current theories of the nature of the "I"—the soul-theory, the mind-theory and the body-theory" with all their variations. Then once more, taking care to distinguish it from "the fallacy of introspection," he produces like a rabbit from a hat, the Method of Gurdjieff and Orage.

Daly King's description of the technique of self-observation is taken directly from the material which he had derived from Orage and later published in *The Oragean Version*. The importance of *The Psychology of Consciousness* is that it provides a rational justification for the process—and a superficially impressive one. Daly liked to claim that self-observation was "the only extant proposal for psychology which is at the same time both scientific *and* psychological." Somewhat naturally, there is no evidence that he derived any support from the psychologists at whom he directed his arguments; they were likely to be wedded either to the physiological or the philosophical schools. What he was proposing—and it must have seemed all the more extraordinary to readers who knew nothing of Gurdjieff or Orage—was an activity neither philosophical nor physiological, but which he claimed as truly scientific. The defects of his book are obvious enough: there is a suggestion of cultishness, and topics which only an Oragean would consider relevant intrude into the discussion. But *The Psychology of Consciousness* is an astonishing proof that it is possible to argue strongly for the "scientific" status of the discipline brought to Europe and America by a man popularly considered as a crank and a charlatan.

By the end of the 1920s there had grown up a distinctive "Oragean" standpoint. No one could claim that this had much influence outside a small circle; but it was an honest—at times a painfully honest—attempt to come to terms with reality. If detached critics like Edmund Wilson could see the attitudes of the early 1920s as outworn by the end of the decade, the situation for those who had been most deeply involved in that hopeful rebellion was both more personal and more desperate. The Augustan critic could call for new solutions; but to romantics who had experienced the poverty of their own former attitudes, there were few courses open in a sceptical world. Munson saw the year 1929 as a turning point for the twenties generation. He pointed to the final number of *The Little Review*, to the appearance of books like Walter Lippmann's *A Preface to Morals* and Joseph Wood Krutch's *The Modern Temper*, which recognized the prevailing atmosphere of blighted hopes and called for new standards. Krutch's book was influential in its day, and despite Munson's subpoena on its arguments, these were in one place directed at the weakest spot in the Oragean armor.

It is difficult to believe that Krutch did not have the Orageans in mind when he analyzed the pressures making for a new religiosity. He detected a general belief in a discontinuity between the human and the natural world. If this belief ever came to be accepted, he wrote, the door into the unseen world would be open once more and religion might well flourish quite as luxuriantly as it did in former times. But Krutch saw a basic implausibility in this attitude. It was really a "philosophy of the 'as if.'" "We may reasonably doubt," he wrote, "whether men can actually live by any faith so tenuous." He saw two results of the flight into materialism: to win for the old creeds a small number of troublesomely vacillating recruits; and considerably to increase the number of people interested in metaphysics considered rather as a game than as a means of arriving at truths relevant to the life in which we live.

It is noticeable that most of the Orageans came to their discipline—or at least argued in support of it—from despair. *There was no hope*. Therefore they would try a more hopeful path. This approach seems very much a "philosophy of the 'as if,'" and however Orage had begun his spiritual journey from the office in Chancery Lane, such an attitude of willed acceptance did come to dominate his relationship to the Work. In his posthumously published *The Active Mind*, he makes a plea for adopting the Gurdjieffian point of view in an essay called "Life as Gymnastics."

Can we alter our attitudes at will? asks Orage. If we establish control over our emotions, we can feel about any event as we please. Any "method aiming towards betterment" must start by correcting the attitude to life. "What is our imagination of life? What do we take it to be? Is it a coiled rope or a snake? It may prove in the end impossible to know for certain what life is; but in that case, we are free to imagine it to be something *useful* to us." Orage suggested that "in the present epoch the image of life as a gymnasium is a greatly needed tonic." The gymnasium, he reminded his readers, had been the symbol of life itself for the Pythagoreans, "whose God ran this planet as a gymnasium for the exercise of men."

It is difficult to see in what other direction we moderns can look for a new image and therefore attitude towards life. We have no longer the possibility of religion in the traditional sense. Ordinary goodness—in the sense of doing what others call good—has no intelligent appeal. And after the still recent Great War, the belief in progress is superstition. But the clean, strong, idea of life as a field of exercise for the development of all our muscles—physical, emotional and intellectual—has still the unspoiled quality of manly or womanly idealism. And life lived in that attitude would certainly be interesting as well as profitable.

Was the whole fabric of Oragean intellectualism built on so fragile a foundation? If the teacher were playing a role not out of an overriding sense of personal conviction but for the sake of encouraging a "right attitude" toward life—then perhaps this attitude was all that was taught? Or was Orage's almost cynical point of view an act of superrealism? There is no indication when he wrote "Life as Gymnastics" but it is probable that he grew toward these opinions as his association with Gurdjieff progressed. So far we have seen Orage as the pupil-teacher, the figurehead, the Master in his own right. We have ignored the progress of the actor behind the role. He can no longer be neglected, for in 1929 Gurdjieff once more appeared in New York, and Orage's very ability to perform his task was called into question. Two years later Orage left America to the mercy of Gurdjieff and the Depression. The circumstances of this parting can be interpreted in many different ways; sometimes, it seems, in several different ways at once.

Time, taught Orage, following Ouspensky, is "the potentiality of experience." In *The Active Mind*, he wrote: "Time as succession is simply the actualisation of one possibility out of each successive moment. Could we actualise two possibilities, or three or four at once, we should be living in two or three or four different streams of time." Go back to his introduction—the division of reality into the Actual and Potential. In terms of time, extending our potentiality must have something to do with simultaneity . . . there are so many possibilities. . . .

9

The Dominion of Heropass

"The Heropass"—or to give the process its full fearsome title, "our ALL-COMMON MASTER THE MERCILESS HEROPASS"—was Gurdjieff's term for the flow of time. Unlike many of the words he used in *Beelzebub's Tales,* the meaning is easily guessed. For Gurdjieff himself, for his leading followers, and for their pupils also, the years 1929–34 were a period of great changes. Perhaps these resulted from the natural effects of the passage of time. Perhaps they arose from an artificial disturbance in it.

Orage's letters to Jean Toomer provide a good index of his changing attitudes. On January 5, 1926, he wrote to Toomer enclosing "the remaining" chapters of THE BOOK. There was one section still unwritten, and the conclusion of the chapter on Art had to await Orage's return to Fontainebleau. Gurdjieff did not propose to publish the first series of his writings until the second and third were complete in Russian and English translation.

> You will see that the Greek Kalends will come first! However it is nothing to us personally; and in fact, it is something of a privilege to be able to prepare an understanding of the book before (if ever) it is published. . . . I haven't plumbed the depths of G.'s thought and

probably never shall; but at last certain meanings and interpretations of the colossal parable I now begin to understand.

Orage wrote that he was starting a group for all previous members of his and Toomer's groups, and had already begun one for newcomers. There was a third group to occupy his attention; but even with some income coming from these sources he was hard pressed. "I already see," he wrote, "that it will leave me far too short a time to worse than waste. In short, I must have something to do that will be profitable." When he left Fontainebleau around Christmas time, he had given Gurdjieff 500 dollars of his own money. "The Prieuré was in debt, Gurdjieff had not a penny and nothing had arrived. . . .

Financing the importunate Gurdjieff was almost the chief subject of the correspondence between Orage and Toomer. Sometimes we may suspect Orage of passing on to his junior colleague the pressures which were put on him; but although a measure of acting may intrude into the situation, there is no doubt of the incessant demands made by the Prieuré.

By late spring 1926, the question arose of Toomer's becoming responsible for the publication of *Beelzebub's Tales*. In May, Orage wrote putting at his disposal 3,000 dollars, if this should arise. This seems to have been in return for Toomer's releasing approximately that sum from the publication fund established with Mabel Luhan's donation. This sum found its way to Gurdjieff and his administrators, but it did not support the Prieuré for long. On November 12, 1926, after Toomer had left the Prieuré for Chicago, Orage wrote from Fontainebleau telling him how much Gurdjieff had appreciated his "parting present" of money. This seems to have consisted of another 2,000 dollars from the printing fund, of which some had already been given to Gurdjieff and some was promised; and Orage wondered anxiously: "God knows how you are going to make up to the printing fund the $2,000 you have given to G. but I presume that you like, as I do, something to work against." He then tightened the screws further. "Anyhow, it went very quick, and just as a dog soon learns where he last got meat and expecting returns for more without enquiring *how* it got there, G. and Mme. H. sit as it were looking you-wards in their hunger."

On teaching matters Orage was still hopeful about the publication of *Beelzebub's Tales*. He wrote that Gurdjieff proposed to go to Dijon "to consult about format, etc." He advised Toomer "to begin at the beginning and only to 'rustle' the book at first, Get along with the elements, just as you did in your New York group—and in the meanwhile, create an interest in the book by seldom speaking of it. Then a little later, as a special favour, you might consent to reading the chapters to groups specially collected and, as it were, privileged." Orage wrote that Jessie Dwight, Jane Heap, and

Elizabeth Gordon had left for New York to take temporary charge of his own groups. He himself had evidently had to stay to work on *Beelzebub's Tales*. There creeps into his letters a hint of frustration and the suspicion that Gurdjieff is "holding out" on him.

> I still am not sure of my return to New York at Christmas—but I hope to go, and to find much new material ready to my hand. All the same, my feet get very cold occasionally when I think of beginning groups all over again—because I doubt whether the "ancient" groups would profit us or themselves by more attention.

During late November and early December Orage wrote several times bemoaning Gurdjieff's slow progress on THE BOOK and trying to squeeze money out of the unfortunate Toomer. Gurdjieff "quite expects the remainder of your nest-egg at any moment." He "looks for the post, so to speak, in expectation of 'America send cheque, finish $2,000!!!' as Beelzebub would say." On December 6, Orage announced his own return to New York where he hoped to be useful in attracting income; "and certainly I do not consider any money too high to pay—if only we can get it!"

From his letters to Chicago in the early part of 1927, it is clear that Orage was becoming increasingly impatient of Gurdjieff's incessant demands. His appeals during the previous months may have been an attempt to persuade Toomer to overcommit himself so that he should have "something to work against"; but in New York he was once again himself in the firing line. On January 17, he wrote that "things are *not* going with a mighty flourish here either. The wind has dropped a good deal since last June. . . . However, the work is to go on *as if* circumstances were completely favourable . . ." The depression was only momentary and on February 11, he reported that, "with a good deal of effort," the situation has improved. "Like a fool" he had sent more of his own money to Gurdjieff—and during the spring of 1927 the financial situation continued to dominate his correspondence.

> Gurdjieff is really quite extraordinary about money—but not, unfortunately, unique; we've known many people at college and in life equally extraordinary. However, I'm giving him still the benefit of the doubt, and I'm only sorry I cannot give him a million if only to see if he could be impecunious within a month or so of receiving it.

Largely through Munson's efforts, Gurdjieff was now receiving 1,000 dollars a month from New York. Orage wrote that Toomer should save his contributions and take them with him when he went to Fontainebleau in the summer. His warning was not in time to prevent Toomer succumbing to the plaintive demands of the Prieuré; and on April 8, Orage was writing again: "I still think you should have resisted the appeal. After all, $1000 a month is not starvation. . . ." Only eight days later, Toomer was informed that "there has been another wail last week from G. via Miss M[erston]. He has had to give up his Paris flat!" Despite his friendly warnings, Orage had not curtailed his personal contributions to Gurdjieff's upkeep. At the end of May he wrote that he had personally sent 2,500 dollars since January, and that he was having trouble making ends meet. He had been forced to turn a deaf ear to a cable appealing for more. The Prieuré would have to take summer visitors to make up its cornucopian budget, and it was now that Orage held out to Gurdjieff the prospect of American disciples paying 100 dollars each.

Apart from the financial considerations, Orage's letters of early 1927 betray a certain uneasiness at his position in New York; an uneasiness which stemmed from the same sources as had made him doubt whether his groups would really benefit from his return in the winter of 1926. In February he was writing to Toomer—perhaps in an attempt to rally his spirits—"I tremble to anticipate each succeeding week. If I don't make the ideas interesting, the group would fall flat, but if I make them too interesting, the group would fall flatter, perhaps would never rise. G.'s noose-dance is no joke!" In early April his mood was of resigned determination; the sigh and the setting of the jaw can almost be heard:

It is not plain sailing to interpret G.; and I'm usually in despair before the lecture and in a state of self-disgust after it. All the expressed admiration in the world doesn't affect my feelings. At the same time I'm glad to be up against anything so impossible and intriguing.

On May 12, soon before the summer recess, his mood was even blacker. "I'm profoundly dissatisfied with my attempts to get anywhere near the bottom of the damned BOOK."

The summer of 1927 was significant for Orage's relationship with Gurdjieff. Instead of traveling to the Prieuré with the main influx of summer visitors, he and Jessie Dwight went on holiday in Canada with the Daly Kings. That August Orage sailed for France alone, and stayed at Fontainebleau for ten days, then returned to New York. Soon after his arrival—on September 24—he and Jessie Dwight were married.

Some Orageans noticed that their leader became less accessible after his marriage. This was only natural, but it shows how Orage's priorities had begun to alter. His essay "On Love" was written while Jessie Dwight was at the Prieuré in 1924, and it marks an important point in the development of his ideas. The essay is based upon Gurdjieff's teaching about the three kinds of love: instinctive, emotional, and conscious. Instinctive love is a matter of chemistry or biology. Emotional love is an aberration. Conscious love—rarely if ever attained—is the only true form of loving. A conscious lover works on himself in order to help the loved one: "If I am not sure what is proper to her perfection, let her at least have free way to follow her own bent. Meanwhile, to study—what she is, and may become; what she needs, what her soul craves and cannot find a name, still less a thing for. To anticipate today her needs of tomorrow. And without a thought all the while of what her needs may mean to me." The attitude is the same as Katherine Mansfield's when she planned to describe a "contest of loving." "On Love" takes up the idea, develops it, and applies it to the author's own situation.

Orage's embarkation on a phase of happy family life was the natural outcome of this attitude; and it marked the end of his total dependence on Gurdjieff. But he was by no means free of his Master yet; and Gurdjieff knew it. The Orages sailed again for Fontainebleau on New Year's Eve 1927. When they arrived in France, Gurdjieff kissed Jessie Orage, declaring that she was half his now, whether she liked it or not.

Mrs. Orage's relationship with Gurdjieff was ambivalent. She had first gone to the Prieuré only at her husband's express urging, and although she took a leading part in the typing and translation of *Beelzebub's Tales*, she also stubbornly went her own way. She overrode Gurdjieff's rather schoolmasterly "rules" and avoided the tasks which more conscientious converts fulfilled. So, for example, when all the other pupils removed their shoes for the movements in the Study House, she left hers outside the building so as not to be seen recovering them when she slipped away. Gurdjieff seems to have respected her attitude, and his eye was lasciviously fixed on her. After one occasion on which she evaded his invitation to his flat in Paris, Gurdjieff discovered her reading letters from Orage, and promptly issued an edict that all mail was to pass through his hands. She was always more detached from the Work than her husband. Her independence grated on some of Gurdjieff's followers. When Gurdjieff introduced his idiot toasts, Mrs. Orage was put in the "squirming idiot" category; and Alexander de Salzmann once burst out in exasperation, "If you'd only admit that you're a squirming idiot, what a marvellous initiate you'd be!"

From one angle it seems as though Gurdjieff resented her claims on Orage and exerted himself to be unpleasant. Once, when the couple were returning from France to the United States, they went to say goodbye to the Master at the Café de la Paix. "Did you ever hear of a man called Y?" asked Gurdjieff (it had been Mrs. Y who threw herself out of the boarding house window). "His wife make trouble for me. She commit suicide." The reference was to a real suicide, known as such, and the impact on Gurdjieff's listeners was horrific. But was the remark dictated by jealousy and self-interest—or was this another "shock" administered for the Orages' benefit?

If Jessie Dwight had resented Gurdjieff's influence over Orage, as Jessie Orage she resented it still more. In the days before they were married Gurdjieff went out of his way to underline his ascendancy over his "super-idiot"; and afterward he placed great strains on the relationship. Once in the early days Gurdjieff and the Orages were touring in Gurdjieff's car on a chaotic journey with typewriters and picnic baskets. Gurdjieff discovered a four-day-old jar of caviar among his provisions and gave it to Orage to finish. To Jessie Dwight's annoyance, Orage meekly ate some of the decrepit contents, and Gurdjieff underlined his victory with an airy: "I'll give the rest to Lady Rothermere." An incident from the winter of 1927–28 illustrates Gurdjieff's continual goading. The scene was the dining room of the Prieuré, with Orage seated on Gurdjieff's left. The "introduction of the noble French armagnac" into the systems of the diners had been rather more concentrated than usual. A pupil who was present remembers a commotion around Gurdjieff which resolved itself into the Master dangling a small object which he had snatched—probably a watch or a locket belonging to Jessie Orage. Orage, says the pupil, had a "tiger-like" look on his face and sat watching Gurdjieff play with the object he had captured with "polite patience." Suddenly, he pounced to recover the locket; but Gurdjieff—although he was supposed to be very drunk—was even quicker, and whisked his prize away from Orage's lunge.

This acting—or was it acting?—increasingly determined the relationship between the Orages and their Master.

Gurdjieff grew increasingly impossible, and the final straw was a terrifying experience when the couple were leaving Paris for New York in February 1928. Gurdjieff transfixed Jessie Orage with his gaze. He seemed to immobilize her, and she could not breathe; for a moment she was convinced that he was going to make her lose consciousness altogether. Then he spoke: "If you keep my super-idiot from coming back to me, you burn in boiling oil." Orage had gone to sleep. But he was finally persuaded by his wife's insistence that this time Gurdjieff had gone too far. It was the last visit he ever paid to Fontainebleau, and the Orages saw nothing of Gurdjieff for almost a year.

From the spring of 1928, they were back in the United States, and in the early summer, Orage wrote two letters to Toomer which refer clearly to the financial extremities in which Gurdjieff found himself and his own new detachment from the demands of Fontainebleau. "I have a feeling that something will happen to the Prieuré this summer," he wrote on May 5.

"Supplies are *really* short . . . the situation is slated for drastic change; and I should have liked one of us—and not me—to be there to witness it." Just over a month later another resigned letter arrived in Chicago. "I suppose you can't contribute *immediately* and substantially towards the sum of $10,000 which G. has called for? No? Well, anyhow, I send the S.O.S."

In the middle of June 1928, the Orages left for California via Taos, and in the autumn Orage tried to start groups in San Francisco. But after two months of effort his audience was only thirty or forty for a weekly group, and by the end of October, he decided that it would take six months to arouse any general interest. He had heard of Jean Toomer's renewed literary ambitions and wrote that he was "reviving my own interest strangely enough." He proposed a competition to see whether he or Toomer could make more money by writing before June the following year. This is extremely significant, for next year (1929) Toomer was to write the memorandum which might—if *Transatlantic* had been successful—have signaled his emergence from the Work. In the event, Toomer returned to Chicago reflecting that there he had left "his form." Orage now had a form—a marriage—apart from and even antagonistic to the Gurdjieff ideas, and to this he held. He was clearly beginning to feel that he had been *in* long enough; and that it was time to come *out*. Perhaps Gurdjieff had some inkling of this. Certainly he knew that the 10,000 dollars for which he had asked had not arrived. The only solution was a personal trip to New York.

Gurdjieff arrived in New York on January 23, 1929. Three days later, Orage informed Toomer: "As you can guess, G.'s main purpose in being here is money; and he wants $10,000 within three weeks." He himself was suggesting privately to several people that they borrow 10,000 dollars to provide "this colossal amount." The Master was in top form. "G. is more himself than ever—that is to say, he is more impossible than ever. But certainly New York needed a shaking up; and I too must have needed it. . . ." Five days later, Orage wrote again to suggest that Toomer use the idea of financing the publication of *Beelzebub's Tales* as an excuse for levying contributions. The New York groups were nearly mutinous. "We are all making a special—and for most—final effort." By the middle of the month Toomer had decided to come to New York, and Orage told him that he would be "twice welcome bearing gifts." He was to raise 1,000 dollars in Chicago "so to say, as security for *your* return to Chicago with G.'s fresh material, etc." Apparently Orage was still prepared to absorb the shock of Gurdjieff's demands into the attitude of the Work. On April 22, after Gurdjieff's departure for France, he wrote to Toomer that a monthly sum had been guaranteed him from the New York groups. "I find myself no end pepped up by G.'s visit; and I'm sure you find yourself the same. He got his 'roses,' I may say . . ."

So had the letter writer; but in a different sense. On April 5, 1929, Gurdjieff had sailed for France. After the ship moved out, Orage danced for joy on the quay. "Thank God I'm free again!" he said. A fortnight later his first child, Richard, was born, and this all but set the seal on his liberation from the Master.

Orage's personal interests were expanding again. In 1929 he began to conduct a writing class and revived his own literary efforts. He collected short passages of criticism from the *New Age* and published them with a few more recent essays under the title, *The Art of Reading*. One of the *New Age* articles he reprinted was an assault on the inadequacies of rationalism; and the final essay in the book advocated a return to the cultural standards of ancient India. Such ideas recalled the position he had occupied in pre-Gurdjieff days; the days of T. E. Hulme and his return to the irrational during the Great War. They were not likely to strike any chord in his readers. Orage was staunchly out-of-date; and when *The Art of Reading* was published in the summer of 1930, the reviews showed it. There was general approval of Orage's critical powers, but many reviewers began to ask what all the fuss had been about. C. H. Grattan in *The Nation* expressed the prevailing disillusionment: "A. R. Orage has a vast reputation for profundity, and indeed is more than a literary critic in the eyes of his intimates: he is a sage. But I fail to see what it is that so interests our Columbuses of the spirit, for I can find nothing in the man except an Englishman who happens to be a fairly interesting critic." The feeling that the Orage bubble had burst was expressed even more powerfully when Farrar and Rinehart issued his *Psychological Exercises* in the autumn. Again it was *The Nation* which was most deflating:

> This book ends a mystery in none too impressive a fashion. It reveals just what Mr. Orage's initiates meant when they spoke of his "psychological exercises." For a long time those who have stood apart from the Orage furor have imagined that these were something pretty impressive, but now anyone can consult this book and find that they are no more remarkable than cross-word puzzles, anagrams, and other parlor games that involve a certain literacy. One can imagine idle people having fun with Mr. Orage's exercises, but they won't one fears, become much wiser in consequence.

By the time these unflattering notices were published, Orage had returned to England. Before he left, he had to submit to one last invasion by Gurdjieff, who landed in New York on February 15, 1930. His arrival had been announced in two ambiguously worded cables. One—which had probably been edited by a member of Gurdjieff's entourage—read:

BREMEN BRINGS THOUSAND KILOS DISILLUSION; HUNDRED KILOS MOMEN-
TARY HAPPINESS, AND TEN POUNDS RETRIBUTION. SIGNED: AMBASSADOR
FROM HELL. The other—addressed personally to Orage—indicated that
Gurdjieff himself had been let loose among the liner's telegraph equip-
ment. IF LOVE NOT DISSIPATED it ran, ARRANGE BATH AND PARTY. SIGNED:
GRANDSON AND UNIQUE PHENOMENAL GRANDMOTHER.

The chaos threatened by such communications quite naturally materialized. Orage wrote to Nott that Gurdjieff was once more in search of
funds, "though I doubt whether this time he will get much. His coming has,
of course, bust up my group meetings and left me desperately placed for
income, but I must be 'clever,' I suppose and find a substitute." At the end
of May, he closed his meetings and left for England with his wife and son,
intending to spend the next six months writing for American magazines. He
told Nott that he would not hold "any groups whatsoever," and it is difficult
to avoid the impression that one reason for the trip was to avoid the
pressures imposed by Gurdjieff's presence in New York. The family settled
near Rye in Sussex, and although the writing went badly, Orage spent the
summer and autumn unmolested by Beelzebub and his importunities. But
by the beginning of December 1930, Orage's indecisions had again
propelled him across the Atlantic.

Gurdjieff's own account of his break with Orage is contained in the first
chapter of his privately published *Third Series*. Although there are several
typescript versions of this chapter in circulation, the outline of events is not
in doubt.

Gurdjieff begins by recalling the circumstances of his "accident," and the
closing of the Institute at Fontainebleau. This, he writes, dispersed his
pupils throughout Europe, and many of them became teachers of his ideas
in order to support themselves. Because they were insufficiently prepared,
this merely increased the misunderstandings which already existed about
him. Eventually, he concluded that all the various groups which had grown
up while he was writing his book had become more or less insane.

Gurdjieff claims that when he arrived in America on November 13, 1930,
he saw from the faces of his reception committee that they too had
developed this form of madness. The Americans had become concerned
exclusively with a small part of his teaching on self-observation, which was
itself a very preliminary exercise. Accordingly, Gurdjieff writes, tongue
almost projecting from cheek, he reversed an earlier decision to exempt
Orage's pupils—to whose contributions he already owed so much—from
the sheep-shearing which was the purpose of his expedition.

Gurdjieff then recalls how he summoned five of the leading members of
the New York groups to a confidential meeting. He told them that as he had
now finished the first book of his proposed writings, he was able to devote

his attention to reorganizing his work on the original plan which had been interrupted by the car crash. Because of the support they had given him, he was going to begin with the Americans. Gurdjieff informed the group of five that, regrettably, he would be forced to reject many of their fellow Orageans. He proposed to treat those who were rejected so that they should be completely disillusioned both with his ideas and with Orage himself. His five leading henchmen were warned not to tell anyone of this projected piece of theater.

On November 21, when Gurdjieff delivered a lecture in the apartment where he was staying to all Orage's pupils who could attend, he told them that he had intended to divide the pupils at Fontainebleau into three categories. When Orage came to New York, he had become a candidate for the middle group—but that was all. The results of Gurdjieff's "accident" had left Orage high and dry in America and Gurdjieff without a source of income in France. Orage had behaved much better and with less cause than some of his other pupils, said Gurdjieff; he had immediately begun to send him money. For his part, he was compelled to turn a blind eye to various misinterpretations of his teaching until his health was fully restored and he could divert his attention from his writing.

After this acknowledgment, Gurdjieff's next words seem at first sight completely inexplicable. In an early version of this chapter he is especially virulent against Orage. Orage had made various collections, a portion of which he had sent on to Gurdjieff—Gurdjieff implies that he had kept large quantities of money for himself—and in order to justify the levying of contributions had started unauthorized classes for Gurdjieff's movements, directing his own groups, using only the various preliminary instructions which he had absorbed in his short time as a pupil. This was all the material with which Orage had to work, and his pupils had therefore been driven mad: it was as if they were trying to become generals by constantly practicing the introductory drill for raw recruits. Gurdjieff added some gratuitous insults about Mrs. Orage, a cause apparently of Orage's vast expenses which obliged him to continue manipulating the small amounts of material already in his possession. . . .

To his New York audience, most of whom must have been baffled, annoyed, or shocked by his denunciations of their beloved leader, Gurdjieff then announced the plan of which he had told five selected pupils: reorganizing his work in a new form. No one could join the new group, he said, who failed to sign a form of obligation which he dictated. This forbade members of his projected new group to associate with any of the Orageans except those who were named in a list which Gurdjieff proposed to distribute. They were also prohibited from having anything to do with Orage himself.

While Gurdjieff discoursed to the select band who had at once signed the obligation, his original audience had been decimated by the fervent Orageans who were suspicious of Gurdjieff and wanted to remain faithful to Orage alone. There was a third group which came in for Gurdjieff's most ponderous irony: they sent a telegram, asking for the advice of Orage, who was on his way from England. These ditherers tried to postpone their decision whether or not to sign until Orage himself landed. He arrived at the beginning of December and promptly asked for an interview.

Gurdjieff replied that, being a man of his word, he could not possibly meet Mr. Orage unless he also signed the obligation imposed on all the other members of the New York groups.

To the astonishment of Gurdjieff's entourage, Orage at once signed the obligation, although it appeared quite absurd to ask him to promise to dissociate himself from his pupils—even to break with himself. But, according to Gurdjieff, Orage found nothing contradictory in the request. He explained that for a long time he had felt the contradiction between his inner uncertainties and the part of the omniscient Teacher he had to play. He had wanted to put an end to the charade much earlier, but circumstances had prevented him from making a final decision. Now he would take the opportunity of signing the obligation to make a clean break with the people whom he had lately taught—as a teacher; and to have nothing to do with A. R. Orage—the Orage who had formerly existed. He asked to be allowed to join the new group as an ordinary member.

Gurdjieff describes his reactions on hearing of Orage's surrealistic decision. He was concocting one of his exotic dishes when the news was brought to him, and when it had sunk home, he was so affected that he broke down completely. He rushed into his bedroom in a flood of tears, and had to be rescued by Dr. Stoerneval with whisky. Despite the ever-present possibility that this story is one of Gurdjieff's mystifying parables, there is evidence that for once he is speaking of real events.

After Orage's signature, those pupils who had been holding back rushed to sign the obligation, and Gurdjieff established a scale of fines according to the resources of each defaulter. His next lecture was given to a full house, which included Orage and most of his disconsolate supporters, who had now been well and truly shorn.

To Daly King, who had been among the diehard Orageans, the whole farrago seemed a pointless bluff, and he consigned Gurdjieff's exercises to the kindergarten. He and the other recalcitrants were permitted to attend all Gurdjieff's meetings as usual, and he therefore concluded that Gurdjieff's repudiation of Orage had no real significance. But later he changed his mind; and from the drama Gurdjieff staged in the winter of 1931 arose countless confusions which nearly submerged the Work in the United States.

Gurdjieff's activities continued in their elliptical fashion. His apartment on West 59th Street was filled to bursting with pupils, acquaintances, and the smell of cooking. Readings of the first and second series of his writings were held in Studio 61 of Carnegie Hall, with Mme. de Salzmann in charge of the first book and Gurdjieff's German secretary, Louisa Goepfert, in charge of the second. The *Third Series*—which may have consisted only of his lectures—was read in Gurdjieff's apartments by Dr. Stoerneval. The fees for attending public readings were two, three, and four dollars respectively, and private readings were also held—at which presumably Gurdjieff presided—for higher fees. This wholesale takeover of his pupils left Orage in a by now familiar but still precarious position. "I've led the life of Jack-in-the-Box since my return here," he wrote to Nott on March 1. To make ends meet he "had to conduct four literary classes a week," as there was no income from his old groups, and Gurdjieff had chased three-quarters of his followers away with his perpetual demands for money.

G. talks as if he expects me to carry on as before; but in spite of my constant association with him, I'm not feeling even warm about group work. He has a miracle to perform in ten days. He has the intention, it really appears, of publishing part of *Beelzebub's Tales* here in New York. That will be something tangible if it comes off. But he is making such impossible conditions that no publisher will accept them; and, in fact, G. cannot really expect it. All the same, I do think we are near publishing something!

It is doubtful whether Gurdjieff was serious about publishing *Beelzebub's Tales*. Orage had always wanted the book published, and it might be that Gurdjieff was simply humoring his subordinate. Nott tells a story about Alfred Knopf which seems to show that Gurdjieff was not exactly pressing hard for publication. As the publisher of *Tertium Organum*, Knopf approached Gurdjieff to see whether he could add *Beelzebub's Tales* to his list. He was told by Gurdjieff: "First clean your house, then perhaps you can have my book." This story may well be apocryphal, and Nott's statement that Gurdjieff left America without selecting a publisher because "the time for publication was not come" piously wishful thinking. On March 20, Orage wrote to Toomer that Gurdjieff had left him with a selection of chapters "to get published *or* to publish." He wrote that Knopf had the typescript and that "after him I will send it to others." Eight days later, Toomer was told that Knopf had turned it down and that *Beelzebub's* epic voyage had continued to Doubleday. "I share your opinion that no publisher will accept it." Orage concluded that they would have to issue it themselves.

Despite his apparent cooperation with Gurdjieff's plans, Orage himself had been irritated. "The situation is anything but bright," he wrote to Jean Toomer on March 28, "and I confess to a little fatigue with Gurdjieff and his ways. Perhaps that is because I've just had to find over two hundred dollars with which to discharge the debts he failed to remember!" By April 10, he had still not been able to hold a group meeting. He wrote to Nott of "the paralysis left by G." This was only cured by the prospect of his own permanent departure; and at the end of May he held his final meeting in Muriel Draper's apartment. Carl Zigrosser remembers this last exhibition of the maestro's virtuosity: "He rang all the hortatory changes, he played on all the emotions. He was witty, subtle, ironic, sarcastic, noble. He was prodigal with memorable phrases and precise formulations. He beseeched and scolded like an elder brother. It was a brilliant performance." On July 1, a farewell party took place at Muriel Draper's. Orage's former pupils mingled with his literary friends, among whom Zigrosser mentions E. E. Cummings and Lincoln Kirstein. Two days later the Orages left New York to live permanently in England.

Thanks to Gurdjieff's machinations, Orage left virtually nothing behind him—little, that is, of an organized sort, nothing except those intangible "influences." On his arrival in England, he had a conversation with Nott which that kindly Boswell has recorded.

He said that he felt that his work with groups in America had come to an end, and another phase was beginning; that to every pupil the time comes when he must leave his teacher and go into life, and work out, digest, what he has acquired. Then he can return to his teacher, if necessary, on another level. It was not that he had left Gurdjieff or the Teaching, but because of both he had reached a certain stage, and it was necessary for him to stand on his own feet.

Nott's opinion provides the "orthodox" verdict from the viewpoint of a pupil of both Orage and Gurdjieff. Orage's group had "got stuck" and needed to be shocked. Orage himself was not fired, repudiated or driven away by Gurdjieff, but brought to renounce his former self and to emerge a better and more self-reliant man.

There is one item of evidence which this possibility ignores. Why did Gurdjieff collapse in a paroxysm of weeping when he heard of Orage's subtle decision to have nothing to do with himself? Was it because, despite unbearable provocation, Orage had understood so correctly what was required of him?

Or was it because Orage had not understood at all?

Gurdjieff was clearly trying to destroy all traces of Orage's work in New

York, and—perhaps equally important to him—to send the Orages away for good. It may be that Gurdjieff was finding it next to impossible to relieve Orage of his dependence on him. This would explain his threats and insults to Mrs. Orage: they were attempts to provoke Orage into standing up for himself and his wife; ultimately perhaps into leaving. It also explains Gurdjieff's collapse in New York. For by signing the obligation imposed on all his former pupils, Orage—slippery as a philosophic eel—had wriggled out of a position in which he seemed certain to be forced to break with Gurdjieff. He had detected a symbolic significance in Gurdjieff's demands which had never been intended—Gurdjieff's account of his request to Orage can be read to mean that he acted as a joke. Perhaps Gurdjieff broke down and cried because of his real affection for his super-idiot and his apparent inability to get that idiot to see two things: that he must take responsibility for himself, and that his quicksilver mind was not the answer to all problems.

Orage said goodbye to Gurdjieff for the last time on May 24, 1931. Later in England he received a number of communications from the Master asking him over to France, such as a letter of August 1932 requesting him to come for a day, or at least to send Jessie. Orage replied: "There was a time when I would have crossed oceans at your bidding. Now I would not even cross the Channel."

There are a succession of postscripts to this story. An almost identical situation had arisen in Gurdjieff's relationship with the de Hartmanns—and at virtually the same time. Both husband and wife had accompanied Gurdjieff to New York on the trip early in 1929, and during this time Gurdjieff had spoken at length to Thomas de Hartmann about the need to establish his career independently of the Prieuré. On their return from New York, he began to make life very unpleasant for the de Hartmanns. Eventually, "after a very strained and difficult conversation," they felt forced to go. Thomas de Hartmann was so affected that he hovered on the brink of a nervous breakdown, and was never able to mention Gurdjieff's name again. But Olga de Hartmann continued to visit the Prieuré and accompanied Gurdjieff to Berlin in the autumn of 1929. All the time Gurdjieff put her under pressure.

One evening after their return from Berlin, she was with Gurdjieff at the Prieuré. He asked her to do something which she felt unable to do and told her that if she refused some terrible event would befall her husband. She traveled back to Paris in great agony of mind to discover her husband calmly asleep. Then came the final parting. When Gurdjieff was on the point of leaving for New York in October 1929, he began to tell Mme. de Hartmann how invaluable she and her husband were to him; they were to make arrangements and sail to join him in a week. This was clearly impossible, and in response to Mme. de Hartmann's anguished protests, Gurdjieff declared that if they did not come, she would never see him again. Poised in the carriage doorway, he made a dramatic exit as the boat-train steamed out of the station. Olga de Hartmann returned home and lay in bed for four days before she could face the reality of the world outside.

The de Hartmanns do not specify what pressures Gurdjieff exerted on them, and it does not matter. Without minimizing the distress which his technique caused, it should be noticed that—if we admit the possibility that Gurdjieff was trying to engineer a break—his methods were very similar with the Orages. To the de Hartmanns also, he sent messages asking them to return. And although they remained faithful to Gurdjieff's ideas, they too, resisted any attempts to entice them back.

There is a story which shows that Orage took his separation from Gurdjieff in the same positive sense—despite his angry telegram. A pupil was sent by Gurdjieff from Paris to London with a typescript for Orage to correct or translate. She was directed to travel by train and boat, as Gurdjieff had—or pretended to have—a great mistrust of aircraft. Despite the forceful courtesy with which Gurdjieff escorted her to the door of her railway carriage, she was determined to save time by catching a plane to London. Dutifully climbing into the train, she climbed straight out again on the other side and made off in triumph to the airport. On her arrival in London, she delivered her parcel to Orage and told him of her exploit. To her surprise, instead of laughing or registering astonishment, he became ferociously angry, and left his visitor in no doubt that she should on no account have disobeyed Gurdjieff. On her return to Paris, she confessed her stratagem. Gurdjieff appeared a little irked by her cunning. "So you think you smarter than Gurdjieff!" he repeated in the tones of a Chicago gangster. Then, becoming serious: "By this I know that Orage still friend."

But his verdict was not completely favorable, as Jessie Orage found when she visited Gurdjieff's Paris flat after the Second World War. The usual feast was in progress, and a short conversation took place during which Gurdjieff said to her: "Jessie, you have my plate, my dinner."

"No, I've had it," she answered.

Gurdjieff then began to talk about a man whom he did not name. This man knew everything but lacked "the simple understanding. . . . He tried for such," said Gurdjieff, "and was too intelligent to grasp it."

She began to cry. Gurdjieff never took his eyes off her.

On returning to England, Orage's first thought was to buy back the *New Age;* but Arthur Brenton, who had edited the paper since shortly after Orage went to Fontainebleau, refused to sell. Orage's old colleagues in the Social Credit movement were at first wary of him. His articles on "An

Editor's Progress"—which had been published in the *New Age* during 1926—seemed to argue that he had renounced political problems for good, and he was resented as an opportunist and a turncoat. A certain amount of lobbying took place on his behalf. According to the poet Hugh McDiarmid, the return of the prodigal was enveloped in mystery. "When news got about that he was back," he writes, "a mutual friend offered to motor me down to the out-of-the-way Sussex farmhouse where he was living. Great secrecy was enjoined on me and the visit was given all the trappings of melodrama. But I was not disappointed. Orage was well worth meeting under any circumstances."

What the doubters perhaps did not know was that Orage had returned to the cause of Social Credit in New York, and as a result, a New Economics group had been formed with Gorham Munson as the editor of its paper, *New Democracy*. From his sympathizers in the United States, Orage raised a subsidy of 1000 pounds for a new magazine to be run from the Social Credit viewpoint. From offices in the building in Chancery Lane where he had edited the *New Age,* Orage brought out the first number of his *New English Weekly* on April 21, 1932. His "Readers and Writers" column revived his old pen name of "R. H. C," and the very first article began in a way which seemed to show that the old Orage was back in fighting form. "As I was saying ten years ago," R. H. C. remarked, "when my literary studies were suddenly lifted to another plane, Mr. Ezra Pound is one of our very few men of letters."

To some people it seemed that this was indeed the same Orage. Paul Selver's heart had sunk when reading the "bewildering" series of auto-biographical articles on "An Editor's Progress." They appeared to him to show an intellectual and stylistic softening; and there is some truth in this criticism, for Orage's fastidious prose was markedly less taut in the scattered articles which he wrote during his long sabbatical. But when Selver actually met Orage again, all his doubts vanished. "Yes, this was the Orage to whom I had always paid homage. No decline whatever. Not changed in the slightest." Others thought differently. Nott saw him as "a humbler, bigger, more understanding and a more youthful man."

This was not only the impression of those who were informed as to his activities since 1923. Eric Gill wrote after Orage's death: "I do not know what gift or what grace he received at Fontainebleau. It is certain that his deep appetite for religion was there, in some manner, satisfied." To Philip Mairet, who had passed the years since Orage left England close to Dmitrije Mitrinović, the new Orage "had a new and deeper kind of wisdom. If in conversation he showed less brilliance for the love of it, his fewer words had more weight. Of the more than occasional arrogance of former days there was scarcely a trace: his judgments were as quick and accurate, if delivered from a higher and more detached point of view. I believe that he now thought always in Gurdjieff categories, except when he put himself in the frame of mind for writing his aggressive editorials."

Despite some minor successes, the *New English Weekly* was never the paper the *New Age* had been. Orage's lucidity of mind earned the renewed applause of such natural sympathizers as T. S. Eliot; and he continued to discover young writers—including the eighteen-year-old Dylan Thomas. But he failed to mobilize support of the quality he had formerly commanded. "His return was the signal for a welcome," wrote his old ally, Maurice Reckitt, "the extent of which may have surprised him, but the practical results of which did not amount to much. The prophet was not wholly without honour, but he was still almost without disciples." Philip Mairet reports that the *New English Weekly* started life with a larger circulation than the *New Age* had boasted when Orage sold it; but the earlier target would not have been difficult to match and, after his ten years of exile, Orage had lost touch with literary fashion. As before, he had now to depend on private subsidies to support his journalism, and the *New English Weekly* consistently lost money. For contributions, he had often to rely on his American friends and former pupils—sometimes the products of his writing school.

Lack of material success or any real recognition of his new venture depressed Orage. Nott saw a great deal of him at this time and recalls that he felt trapped by his political "Notes of the Week." Orage slightly scandalized his friend—an ardent Social Creditor—by admitting that his interest in monetary reform was only a "pseudo-interest." Philip Mairet had become sub-editor on the *New English Weekly*, and he noticed the stresses under with Orage's work as a publicist now placed him. "If the tension between this public work and his other-worldly aspirations had much to do with his previous flight from London, the gulf between them was now wider still. He was indeed better able to bear the strain; only once did he allow me to see something of what it cost him; but there can be little doubt that it shortened his life."

One result was that Orage began to contemplate the chances of an academic post. Another was that his interests turned again toward the transcendental.

During its first year, the *New English Weekly* had avoided anything which suggested the occult. Orage had received a warning that his unorthodox interests were unpalatable to the circles in England which he wished to influence; for soon after his return, he had greatly alarmed a Social Credit audience with a dogmatic statement about different human types. Apart from a lighthearted recommendation of the anthologist of inexplicable happenings, Charles Fort—Gorham Munson was also a Fort enthusiast and compared him to Gurdjieff—Orage contented himself during 1932 with a single printed statement on his esoteric standpoint. Although this may have been designed to placate his critics, it shows without any ambiguity the effects of his time with Gurdjieff. His credo took the form of a note on the Jubilee of the Society for Psychical Research:

> After years of search and research my conclusion upon the three greatest and most important questions—survival after death, immortality, the meaning and aim of existence—is that I do not know. The worst of it is that I do not know either whether anybody has ever possessed such knowledge or even whether such knowledge is possible.

Although Candide-like he advised his readers to "cultivate their gardens," in the last half of 1933 he gave increasing evidence of a return to the interests which predated Gurdjieff. For a brief period he was associated with Dmitrije Mitrinović in the latter's ambitious "New Britain" movement. In the *New English Weekly*, James Young made a reappearance— although with a savage attack on spiritualism. But by 1934, even "M. B. Oxon" was back in Orage's columns, indomitably discussing the time theories of J. W. Dunne. From August 1933, Orage also began to contribute regular articles to *The Aryan Path*, the Theosophical magazine whose presiding spirit was J. D. Beresford, another old friend from the days of Ouspensky's first arrival in London. These articles continued until the month before his death, and were cast in a familiar mold.

To Philip Mairet the beginning of 1934 signaled the appearance of Orage in detached and philosophic mood. He spent much time listening to the long monologues of A. E., in whom he discovered a kindred spirit. He discussed immortality and Jung, and no longer always changed the subject when Gurdjieff and his ideas were mentioned. In the second edition of his *Memoir*, Mairet cuts a passage which is remarkably interesting for the light it sheds on Orage's philosophy immediately before his death. "I will not attempt to recall, for fear of misrepresentation," he originally wrote, "some things he said of Jesus Christ, except that some of his supporters would have been shocked at their relative orthodoxy, theologically speaking—but not moralistically so, for he had no use for a humanist Jesus." Such a simple attitude—the apprehension of new meaning in old truths—seems quite often to be adopted by those who pass through the Gurdjieff mill.

Through Rosamund Sharp, Orage made contact with Ouspensky, but declined the latter's invitation to visit him and dubbed the typescript of *A New Model of the Universe*, a "new muddle." He did not hold completely aloof; for although he refused a former pupil of his own in New York an introduction to Ouspensky himself, he did pass her on to Ouspensky's secretary, Mme. Kadloubovsky. Both Mairet and Nott were under the impression that during the last year of his life Orage hoped to alter completely the nature of the *New English Weekly*. He spoke optimistically of the conclusion of the struggle for Social Credit and hinted that he was planning to introduce social and literary criticism based on Gurdjieff's ideas.

What were Orage's feelings toward the man who had dominated so much of his life? "He left Gurdjieff," says Mrs. Orage, "but he stayed with the System." One American pupil of both Orage and Gurdjieff remembers a conversation between the two men—probably in the winter of 1929–30—during which Orage appears to have told Gurdjieff that although he had helped the Work, he had not been given the help which he himself needed. If Nott is to be believed, Orage's position in 1934 was still the same. He confessed that he had never been able to decide whether Gurdjieff was a saint, a charlatan, or a mixture of both. This attitude seems to be reflected in a short sketch printed in the *New English Weekly* not long before his death. This is called "A Dealer in Immortality," and is by one "Edward Farrell." It is set in the United States and concerns a Gurdjieff-type figure who claims to confer immortality by leading his clients along a philosophical path toward a recognition of the mystic unity of things. The story ends with the arrival of a telegram accusing the dealer in immortality of fraud and the hurried departure of that individual for France. As a literary effort, it is poor stuff; and it is left unclear whether "Edward Farrell" thinks that his metaphysical huckster is a misunderstood genius or a crook.

Nothing definite can be inferred from such ambiguous hints; but it would probably not be far from the truth to say that Orage's attitude to Gurdjieff approached the "reverent agnosticism" which he then found so admirable in Julian Huxley. Nott maintains that, for all his doubts, Orage was convinced that "something had changed" in them as a result of their work with Gurdjieff. Together they speculated about recurrence. Next time . . . perhaps they would be able to develop more quickly, perhaps their places in the cosmic scheme would be taken by others and they themselves liberated from the demands of the machine. . . . Orage might not know the answers he had sought—and might admit to not knowing—but he had no regrets. A week before his death he exclaimed to Nott: "You know, I thank God every day of my life that I met Gurdjieff."

By this time it appears that Orage knew that he was under sentence of death. His health had deteriorated in the early part of 1934, and he suspended publication of the *New English Weekly* during August. On returning to work, he caught a cold and began to suffer from an acute pain below the heart. His exhaustion was apparent to Ezra Pound from the tone of his letters and from their uncharacteristic carelessness.

He had written to me during the last year when his hand was weary from physical labour of writing. A dozen others must have known the same thing, and known that he had a specific sense of his mission. That both he and I were fatigued should be apparent from an egregious typing error in the last issue, that I should have written it, from fatigue, and, as I had no proofs in Rapallo, that he should have passed it, warned me that I needed rest, but he, apparently, did not take similar warning.

On October 10, Pound received a letter containing one of the mistakes of which he writes. It ended, "perhaps I write not for men, but for God! Yours ever, A. R. Orage." "With the full signature, as valediction," Pound remembered, "where he signed normally with initials."

Whether or not Orage's heart trouble was an old illness, even the skeptical Paul Selver found his death disturbing: "To describe it as merely tragic is not enough. If such an event had occurred in a novel, reviewers would have dismissed it as being too obviously contrived."

Orage had been asked to broadcast on Social Credit. This coup was regarded both as a personal success and as a feather in the cap of Douglasites generally. He prepared his speech with great care, and delivered it on the night of November 5. During the talk he was sharply attacked by the pain in his heart, but the broadcast was accounted a success. That night he died in his sleep. The play called "A. R. Orage" had ended with the precision of his own most mannered sentences.

To Nott there had appeared signs and portents. About a fortnight before Orage's death he had watched his friend talking to a group in the Chancery Lane ABC café. "A pale yellow light issued from Orage, a nimbus, not only round his head, but around his whole form . . . When Orage came back to my table, his face had a sort of radiance of youth." And on the night when Orage died, Nott dreamed of his face, "smiling in a mass of glowing coals."

The shock of Orage's death produced an eloquence of grief. Orage was sixty-one, and the period of his greatest editorial brilliance was twenty years behind him. His mourners were not lamenting the editor of genius or the publicist of Social Credit—however much they pretended that this was what they were doing. The "Memorial Number" of the *New English Weekly* and the number following were packed with tributes to a remarkable human being, one who for all his failings had the capacity to inspire and then to justify affection. T. S. Eliot praised him as "a man who was seeking the essential things," Llewelyn Powys wrote that he combined "the head of a man of science with the heart of a saint," and A. E. testified to his many-sidedness: "Almost everywhere I explored his mind I found the long corridors lit." Many obituarists praised his integrity, and Will Dyson spoke for his friends when he called Orage "the secret standard by which we judged ourselves." His devotees mourned the loss of their guide and mentor. David Eder caught the essentials:

> Was he a mystic? Only in 'the sense that we are all mystics. At the bottom we know so little and the philosophies are all so futile; A. R. O. never deluded himself with knowledge when sense existed, never pretended that things were what they were not. The ugliness of the world was all his and he would not move a hair's breadth towards glossing it over with a false word, or a pretended belief.

The *New English Weekly* survived Orage and for a brief time an Orage Society met to commemorate him. His most tangible memorial is the impressive headstone for his grave in Hampstead Churchyard on which Eric Gill carved the enneagram and, underneath, a verse from Orage's cherished *Mahabharata*.

> The wise grieve neither for the living nor for the dead.
> Never at any time was I not, nor thou,
> Nor those princes of men, nor shall they ever cease hereafter.
> The unreal has no being
> The real never ceases to be.

10

What Struggle? What Magicians?

The insubstantial quality of Orage's last years may suggest a withdrawal from the world into disillusion. If so, this was not accompanied by bitterness, but reflected a positive nature resting after the tumult of its Gurdjieff adventure. To allow Orage to sink into some pit of piety is to detract from the essential excitement of his time with Gurdjieff: he had been *exercised,* made supple, stretched—until, according to some, the light shone through.

The explicit character of Orage makes clearer, however, the problems which surround the more reticent Ouspensky. The accepted explanations of why Ouspensky and Gurdjieff parted company show a clear division between the disciples of the two men, and—particularly among Ouspensky's more superstitious followers—the situation is sometimes represented as a mysterious esoteric duel; a struggle of the magicians. But the complexities which surround Orage's break with Gurdjieff should warn the inquirer against accepting too facile an interpretation.

The case from Gurdjieff's side has been made by Nott, who relies partly on information from his friend, F. S. Pinder. It appears that after Gurdjieff's London visits in February 1922, he made another trip later that winter, taking Pinder with him as interpreter. At a meeting of Ouspensky's pupils, Gurdjieff dismayed the audience by turning on their revered teacher and tearing him to shreds. He was too intellectual, declared

Gurdjieff; if he really wanted to understand, he must go back to the beginning again, and "work on himself." A little later, when Ouspensky was visiting Fontainebleau, Gurdjieff used Pinder to interpret a lecture in the Study House. When Ouspensky objected to some of Pinder's translations, Gurdjieff turned on him with, "Pinder is interpreting for me, not you!" The Pinder-Nott version of the break is that Ouspensky was mistaken in thinking that he understood "Gurdjieff's inner teaching." They argue that he saw himself as a religious philosopher in the tradition of Vladimir Soloviev and was determined at all costs to found his own school and have disciples sitting at his own feet. Nott maintains that it was Gurdjieff's trip to London in late 1922 which really caused the break, and reports a remark made by Gurdjieff to Pinder on their way back to France. "Now," he said, "they will have to choose a teacher."

There are several different interpretations of the "Gurdjieffian" school of thought. Ouspensky is sometimes seen as being both lazy and a thief. In Nott's words, he "had a perfunctory fling" at the movements, then abandoned them as unproductive. He was a writer when he met Gurdjieff, and he remained a writer—"stealing" Gurdjieff's material and manufacturing a "System" which was never intended to be systematized or even made public at all. In fact, he was what Gurdjieff called a "hasnamuss"; a man lacking conscience or any sort or scruples.

More frequently Ouspensky is seen as someone who failed the tests which Gurdjieff set him. According to this interpretation, he could not withstand Gurdjieff's onslaughts on his self-importance and over-intellectualism. The attitude treating Ouspensky as a "failure" sometimes mellows into understanding and sympathy. Gurdjieff's "shocks," it is emphasized, were often really intolerable; and Ouspensky was essentially a nice man whose conscience might have been offended by any one of Gurdjieff's outrageous actions. It should be clear by now that part of the Gurdjieff discipline consists in confronting the pupil with what for him are the worst things in the world: things which for him at that moment represent limitations of his nature to which he cannot admit—of which he is possibly even unable to conceive. It may be that there is no limit to how far this can be carried, and there have certainly been catastrophic failures. There may have been simple conflict between Ouspensky's preconceptions—which he may never have recognized as such—and the deliberate actions of his unpredictable teacher. Perhaps, it is suggested, there was some action— immoral, unforgivable, criminal—which Ouspensky recognized might have its place in the context of the Work, but which he could not himself accept.

However, the suspicion that Gurdjieff had tried to drive away Orage and the de Hartmanns can lead to a very different interpretation of the evidence of Nott and Pinder. Ouspensky's withdrawal might have been exactly the result for which Gurdjieff was striving. Ouspensky broke with him at Essentuki, rejoined him at Constantinople, and once more returned to work with him in London and Paris. Would he never learn to stand on his own two feet? It is conceivable that Gurdjieff reasoned in this fashion and forced his pupil into making the final separation for himself. There is also the consideration that Ouspensky's followers might have been thoroughly confused by an apparent contradiction between their teacher's methods and the more outlandish tactics of Gurdjieff. There are indications that Ouspensky partly agreed with this estimate of Gurdjieff's purpose. He writes that Gurdjieff asked him to come and live in Fontainebleau several times during the period between the acquisition of the Prieuré and his departure for America. "There was a good deal of temptation in this." The term "temptation" is always used by Gurdjieff and Ouspensky to signify a process of deliberate deception carried on in "esoteric schools" to test the pupils; and both Orage and the de Hartmanns were exposed to the identical "temptation." Ouspensky clearly made the same deduction as had Orage and the de Hartmanns: the break must be absolute. Thus he returned from France after Gurdjieff's departure for the United States and told those who wanted to work with him that "my work in future would proceed quite independently *in the way in which it had been begun in London in 1921.*"

In the rather doctrinaire atmosphere of his London groups, the ominous "G." was legislated out of existence, although Ouspensky never denied that what he taught derived from him. On a number of occasions he amplified what he said in *In Search of the Miraculous* about his break with the Master. It is necessary to examine in more detail the idea that Ouspensky was able to break away on his own as a result of what he learned from Gurdjieff, rather than as a reaction against it.

In Search of the Miraculous concentrates on his separation of the man Gurdjieff from the ideas of Gurdjieff. From what we know of Orage's life after his parting with the Great Magician, it seems that he too may have performed such a painful division. While the Man Who Knows still seemed to know a lot, he himself appeared less admirable than before. "I saw clearly at that time," Ouspensky had written of his break at Essentuki, "that I had been mistaken about many things I had ascribed to G." In the language of psychoanalysis, we should say that the effects of the transference were wearing off.

Ouspensky's idea of the perfect master had been strongly influenced by Nietzsche. "Men who seek for a real, living superman in the present," he wrote in *A New Model of the Universe*, "somehow thereby reveal a higher principle in their souls." Ouspensky's discovery that the seeds of a new humanity were latent in the individual came as the result of his search for a superior breed of human being already in existence: "Man finds superman within himself when he begins to look for him outside himself, and he can find superman outside himself when he has begun to look for him within himself." Almost certainly the "things I had ascribed to G." had to do with Ouspensky's vision of Gurdjieff as a representative of superhumanity. Discussion with the visible superman threw him back on the superman within—his own higher forces, that superior self which he had felt assert itself during the sad and dangerous winter of 1919.

When he broke with Gurdjieff in Essentuki, Ouspensky reverted to his earlier esoteric interests and continued his search for the miraculous. On the appearance of his *A New Model of the Universe* in 1931, he remarked to Kenneth Walker that he hoped to make contact with an "esoteric school" as a result of its publication. This prompts the question: to what did he think he had belonged during his time with Gurdjieff? Orage considered the Prieuré an "esoteric school," although Gurdjieff had always proclaimed that his groups were only an outer, or at best, a central ring on some occult target. Perhaps Ouspensky's image of an "esoteric school" was destroyed at the same time as his image of the Master. Or, perhaps he decided that Gurdjieff's "school" was, as Gurdjieff claimed it to be, a preparatory school for higher things.

By February 1923, when the London *Daily News* interviewed him, Ouspensky had become careful not to present himself as in any sense Gurdjieff's subordinate. "Gurdjieff and I have reached our present stage of knowledge by long and hard work in many lands," he was quoted as saying; and his interviewer reported that "in Gurdjieff he found a kindred spirit who had gone farther on the same road." This raises a second crucial question: now that we are more familiar with Gurdjieff's tactics in presenting his ideas favorably to those he considered likely to respond, had Ouspensky ever been justified at all in thinking that he and Gurdjieff were in fact traveling the same road? Perhaps their objectives had only coincided for a time; or perhaps Ouspensky's aims—the attainment of "cosmic consciousness," the achievement of freedom in a universe of many dimensions—had never been the same as those of Gurdjieff? The Master had emphasized *"the teaching by itself cannot pursue any definite aim. It can only show the way for men to attain whatever aims they might have."* Ouspensky had passed through a *process*, reached a point at which, after protracted anguish, he made a decision and emerged on the other side of the tunnel. He may have thought that Gurdjieff's more experienced followers would leave after the expedition through the mountains from Essentuki because they, too, would recognize the nature of the process they had undergone.

This possibility is supported by the fact that Ouspensky made a division between his own ideas—like those on eternal recurrence—and Gurdjieff's

System. He and his pupils were engaged in dual activity. On the one hand, Ouspensky taught Gurdjieff's System; and on the other, he enlisted his pupils' help in his own search for the miraculous. The ideas of the System were sound, but the source from which he had received them had become tainted. Accordingly, they must all search for the Source from which Gurdjieff himself had received the ideas. In a private conversation in the winter of 1924, Ouspensky replied to J. G. Bennett's enthusiastic affirmation that the System could lead to "Consciousness and Immortality" in terms of the most stoical pessimism:

> We were in his little sitting room in Gwendwr Road, West Kensington. He stood with his back to the gas fire, peering at me as usual through his powerful pince-nez. He sighed deeply, and said: "You say that you are sure that this work can lead to consciousness and immortality. I am not sure. I am sure of nothing. But I do know that we have nothing, and therefore we have nothing to lose. For me it is not a question of hope, but of being sure that there is no other way. I have tried too much and seen too much to believe in anything. But I will not give up the struggle. In principle, I believe that it is possible to attain what we seek—but I am not sure that we have yet found the way. But it is useless to wait. We know that we have something that has come from a Higher Source. It may be that something more will come from the same Source."

Ouspensky had really made two separations: he had separated the man Gurdjieff from Gurdjieff's ideas, and he had separated his own theories and aspirations from Gurdjieff's System. In public he never criticized his old teacher; but in private, he found fault with Gurdjieff's conduct, on Gurdjieff's own terms. In October 1935 and October 1937, he detailed his objections. In the beginning, he said, Gurdjieff had laid down three principles for the Work which he contradicted by his later behavior. The first was that no one must do anything without understanding why they were doing it. The second was that no one should take anything on trust, but must verify any statement of Gurdjieff's from their own experience. The third principle was that the leader of the Work must never produce infatuation in his disciples. Ouspensky stated bluntly that in Essentuki Gurdjieff had begun to ignore these principles by demanding and accepting faith and blind obedience. He had therefore broken the contract which bound his pupils to him by betraying his position of authority.

Ouspensky told his followers that, as well as his moral scruples about Gurdjieff's conduct, there was a further problem which had made him decide on the break in January 1924. Gurdjieff had begun accepting people who were totally unprepared to benefit from the Work. Ouspensky said that the help he had given Gurdjieff in 1922 was a final test, a gamble to see whether anything would come of the Institute at Fontainebleau—a format about which he had all along had the gravest doubts. He had collected money and sent people to Gurdjieff, but in the resigned anticipation of failure.

All this is relatively mild, and may only have been the story which Ouspensky related for general consumption. His public loyalty to Gurdjieff was extraordinary, and he permitted himself full liberty of expression only within his closest circle. Orage's explanation of the split is therefore of great interest. He always maintained that it was Gurdjieff's near rape of Mrs. Y in 1923–24 that finally decided Ouspensky. The date tallies, and the scandal was of such proportion that the explanation is very plausible. If Orage were right, this would explain Ouspensky's obsession with Gurdjieff's "integrity" in his conversation with Boris Mouravieff after Gurdjieff's crash; and why— out of loyalty to his teacher, as a "member of the same family"—he refused to tell Mouravieff why he had decided to work alone.

So who is the Black Magician—Ouspensky, the thief; or Gurdjieff, the monster of depravity? The situation is more complicated than is clear from any partisan point of view. For although Ouspensky implies that the break in January 1924 was complete, he quite definitely did continue to see Gurdjieff from time to time. He often traveled to Paris, where *A New Model of the Universe* and *In Search of the Miraculous* were being translated under the supervision of Baroness Rausch de Traubenberg, and these absences effectively concealed such contact from his own pupils. For his part, Gurdjieff became increasingly careful to hide Ouspensky's arrival from the inmates of the Prieuré. Margaret Anderson was surprised to find Ouspensky at Fontainebleau in the spring of 1924—after the supposed break had taken place. He was there again for Mme. Ostrowsky's funeral in 1926. At various other times during the 1920s, Ouspensky was seen at Fontainebleau, although Gurdjieff did not allow him to mix with his pupils and saw him only in the salon behind closed doors. The possibility of collusion—even of some master plan—cannot be ruled out.

In about 1930 Ouspensky told several of his older followers that for the previous seven years he had been lying quiet in the hopes that something might come of Gurdjieff's work, much in the spirit that he had cooperated in the establishment of the Institute for the Harmonious Development of Man. Certainly, during the 1920s his activities had about them a quality of wait-and-see, and he kept them on a very modest scale. His pupils numbered between forty and fifty, and his meetings continued to be held at 38 Warwick Gardens in South Kensington.

Kenneth Walker, a Harley Street surgeon who joined the group in 1923, condenses his memories of the unvarying nature of Ouspensky's meetings. The entry past Mme. Eugenie Kadloubovsky, the wife of a former Russian diplomat, who acted as Ouspensky's private secretary and administrator; the austere schoolroom atmosphere; the slightly uncomfortable and tense mood of Ouspensky's audience as they waited for their lecturer—who was inevitably late, as Gurdjieff and Orage were always late for their meetings— are all of a pattern. The silent and almost imperceptible appearance of Ouspensky—as Rom Landau described him, "white-haired, clean-shaven, above middle-age, bespectacled, stout"—and the introductory, "Well" are later confirmed. It was always difficult to discover when the next lecture was scheduled, but the routine of the meeting itself scarcely varied. Some ten years after Walker's introduction to Ouspensky's lectures, Rom Landau found virtually the same arrangements. Ouspensky's notes seemed to him to serve as "a focus for his eyes" rather than as an aid for the memory; and if he ever, in fact, needed to refer to them he disconcerted his audience by removing his spectacles altogether and bringing the manuscript right up against his nose. His heavily accented English and his staccato delivery made it difficult to follow what he was saying, but somehow this did not detract from the total effect of his manner.

If the meeting were devoted to one of the introductory lectures which Ouspensky wrote, he would speak for three-quarters of an hour. More commonly, the talk would last from five to ten minutes and be followed by another silence, apparently endless, until a pupil summoned up enough courage to ask a question. When he was once asked if he intended to publish his lectures, Ouspensky replied, "What is the use? What is important is not the lectures, but the questions and answers," and this warning note is inserted by Mme. Kadloubovsky at the beginning of her selection from Ouspensky's talks entitled *The Fourth Way*. Landau makes it clear that the success of the meeting depended on the nature of the question:

Mere literary or philosophical questions were not welcome, and the effect of such a question was invariably devastating. Ouspensky was never rude, nor even ironical—but he was cruelly matter-of-fact, and would not tolerate questions that did not betray an honest desire to know more.

Someone would ask, after Ouspensky had discussed the various states of consciousness: "Is Buddha the seventh state of consciousness?"

Ouspensky, without even looking up to see who had asked the unfortunate question, would only answer: "I don't know." He then remained silent, and you felt that in his thoughts he probably continued, "and I don't care."

This method of question and answer reproduced in a formal fashion the means by which Ouspensky and his companions had been forced to extract information from Gurdjieff in Russia. For although pupils might attend "lectures," they were never spoon-fed, and Ouspensky emphasized that originally it had been no part of Gurdjieff's plan to teach a "system." As Rosamund Sharp found, a pupil had to probe and prod to complete each facet of the Ouspenskian universe.

Undoubtedly this contributed to the excitement and the sense of purpose experienced by Ouspensky's followers. Their teacher was doing his best to reproduce for them his own experience. But because of the conditions under which he worked, the ideas were easier to assemble than they had been when he learned them from Gurdjieff. As he told his pupils: when he first met the System, he had been urged to "remember himself" for two years before it was finally revealed that man does *not* remember himself. What his follower, Rodney Collin-Smith, later dubbed "this strange unfolding of possibilities which went by the name of O's lectures" proceeded quickly enough to provide a sense of achievement, the feeling that something had been accomplished in the knowledge of the human machine. Rom Landau came as a journalist, but stayed out of fascination. He noticed practical results "even within a single year's work."

Ouspensky's conception of "the System" was inseparable from his concept of "school." His obsession with the latter idea can be traced back to his own erratic education; and it was always associated for him with the idea of a definite structure. The System as taught in such a school demanded a discipline on the part of the pupils. "If there are no rules," said Ouspensky, "there is no school." There were rules for a number of reasons. The first was to create friction so that the pupils would have to make efforts to overcome their negative emotions. Because the pupil must put himself in the hands of the teacher, "one can only enter a school when one has lost, or is prepared to lose, a certain amount of self-will." And certain rules—such as that about not talking to strangers about their esoteric studies—were designed to prevent the Work from suffering. If they talked, their own valuation of their activities would suffer, and they ran the risk not only of distorting the ideas by transmitting them ineptly, but of broadcasting material which should be kept for schoolwork.

Such considerations produced the rule-dominated structure of Ouspensky's following. While some rules stemmed from the ideas of the Work itself, others seemed to have more to do with Ouspensky's rather formal correctness—perhaps a reaction against the flamboyance of Gurdjieff. People were not allowed to address each other by their Christian names, and the custom of "Misters," "Madams," and "Misses" continues today. Other rules were probably the result of Ouspensky's Russian upbringing, with its restrictions on free intellectual discussion, and his consequent fear of police of whatever nationality. Pupils attending meetings at Warwick Gardens had to leave their cars several blocks away, so as not to draw attention to the building. If they met each other in public—in the street or at a theater, for example—they were forbidden to recognize each other for fear of provoking a conversation with third parties about Ouspensky's work. For similar reasons they were not to mix friends "in the Work" with friends outside it.

The rules certainly served to provoke friction; and they produced the "secret society atmosphere" which grated on outsiders like Nott. They could result in ludicrous situations. A regular attender at Warwick Gardens who wished to lunch with a fellow Ouspenskian might feel compelled to do so in a suitably clandestine rendezvous; and one furtive publisher took to telephoning his acquaintances "in the Work" from public phone booths in order to circumvent possible eavesdropping from his office switchboard. The rules were open also to some potentially harmful applications. There was one, which had originated in St. Petersburg, that if a member of a group decided to leave, he should be ostracized by the remaining members. Gurdjieff had explained that the purpose of this regulation was to prevent errant pupils from being scared of returning. But in the later stages of Ouspensky's own work and under his successors, this rule was applied so that the offenders found themselves cut dead by numbers of people whom they regarded as their friends.

Nothing could have been further from Ouspensky's own intentions. His essential kindliness overrode all other considerations. A pupil once came to him to announce her engagement to another of his followers. His face wreathed in smiles, Ouspensky said: "In that case, of course, there are no rules."

Indeed the hallmark of his teaching when contrasted with Gurdjieff's was its gentleness. As one of his American followers expressed it: "Ouspensky omelette—not too tough." He refused to batter his pupils, and this decision dates back as far as the preliminaries to his "miracle" in Finland, when he arrived at "the esoteric principle of the impossibility of violence." This did not mean that Ouspensky would not occasionally fry the omelette a little longer if the need arose. As one of his old pupils puts it: "He was unfailingly courteous, but when it was absolutely necessary, he could also shout 'Moscow-fashion'—a sound which 'split the air' and shocked into awareness the day-dreaming pupil for whom it was intended."

To all appearances—apart from the role of the teacher—Ouspensky seldom indulged in the more theatrical techniques used by Gurdjieff. But it is very difficult to know where to draw the line in terms of theatricality. The sensation that the teacher was playing a role was never so marked among Ouspensky's pupils as it was among those of Gurdjieff; but Ouspensky possessed a verbal dexterity which could amount to the same thing. When combined with his skillful assessment of a pupil's psychological state, this could produce effects similar to those which Gurdjieff achieved with more toil, sweat and pyrotechnics. Ouspensky's methods could be extremely subtle. For example, once during the 1940s he was telling his pupils in New York about the doctrine of the "many I's": "He scolded us severely," one pupil writes, "saying that we must never say 'I' before we knew what we were saying":

> "Look what happened to the devil," he said. And I protested: "But Mr. Ouspensky, God said to Moses on Mount Tabor, 'I am that I am!'"
>
> I was sitting in the first row. He paused, and looked at me for a while, and then said tenderly and very softly:
>
> "Yes. But you, you see, you are not God. In you there is no 'I.' You must work. Work hard to have 'I.'"
>
> "If only I had enough energy to work!" I said sincerely.
>
> "You have it," he assured me. "You waste it in arguments." He gave me a long look, and then indulged in the shadow of a smile.

Behind the stern figure of Warwick Gardens, there was still the charming and affable Ouspensky of earlier days. He was now "taking serious things seriously"—and this may account for the slight oppressiveness of his System when contrasted with the jovial performance of Gurdjieff—but he still enjoyed good food and wine, still took pleasure in art and poetry, still displayed the sense of humor which he had shown Bechhofer Roberts in Rostov. In London he patronized a Chinese restaurant in Oxford Street, and his taste in tea became so celebrated that Twinings of the Strand regularly invited him to their major tastings.

Some of his pupils found it hard to realize that he was a man like any other. Bennett remembers an expedition to buy prints of St. Petersburg for Ouspensky's flat, when he found himself unable to accept that this was not in some way a teaching expedition and that the Master needed relaxation like any other human being. By virtue of the teaching role, and the need to play a part to sustain it, the inevitable transference took place. One evening in Paris, Ouspensky and Mme. Ouspensky were sitting in a café with some of their pupils. Ouspensky was withdrawn, rugged, and Russian. "Very hard to make a friend of Mr. Ouspensky," said his wife; and what was perhaps merely a dig at a husband's moroseness thereafter came to be repeated as an element of the teacher's mystique.

Ouspensky saw his pupils privately in his flat in Gwendwr Road. The building is now demolished, but Kenneth Walker remembers it as "a rather somber Victorian house in an equally dismal road." His description of Ouspensky's rooms gives the impression of a vaguely rundown atmosphere. "There was a divan-bed, a bookcase, two chairs near to the gas-fire, and a large mahogany table on which rested a type-writer, writing materials, a camera, a galvanometer and some scientific apparatus of an unfamiliar nature. On the mantlepiece lay a half-finished tin of sardines, the remains of a loaf, a plate, knife and fork and a few morsels of cheese. . . ." Until the late 1920s, this unremarkable haunt of bachelor Bohemianism was Ouspensky's only home.

Then sometime between 1929 and 1931, he came to a decision. His routine altered, and it was never the same again. In the autumn of 1930, he told J. G. Bennett and other leading followers that since the results he had expected from Gurdjieff's work had not materialized, he would therefore no longer apply the brake to his own activities. His last visit to Fontainebleau was in 1931. On this occasion Gurdjieff did not even allow him as far as the village of Avon, and their conference took place in the Café Henri IV at Fontainebleau. This meeting marked more decisively than the apparent break in 1924 Ouspensky's complete separation of his work from Gurdjieff's. From this time on, his disappointment with Gurdjieff was more openly—and sometimes bitterly—expressed. He spoke of Gurdjieff's "failure" as a catastrophe greater than the Russian Revolution. On several occasions he was even more emphatic. To one pupil who asked him privately what must have become a wearisome question, Ouspensky said quite simply: "Well, he went mad, you see."

Another complication is created by the role of Mme. Ouspensky. It has already been mentioned that the Ouspenskys' marriage was an unusual arrangement and that when Ouspensky first arrived in London, his wife did not accompany him. Until about 1924–25, she lived at the Prieuré. Gurdjieff is then reported to have sent her away, saying that her husband needed her. Mme. Ouspensky left Fontainebleau, but instead of going to England—a country she loathed and whose language she never made any great effort to learn—she took a flat for several years at Asnières near Paris. She did establish a working relationship with her husband: some of the London pupils came to Paris to help with the translations of his books and formed a Work group under the direction of "Madame."

When, about 1927, Mme. Ouspensky at last nerved herself to cross the

English Channel, the relationship of husband and wife remained as distant as before. Mme. Ouspensky used to say that Gurdjieff was her teacher, and for his part, Ouspensky had at least one mistress. In the various country houses in which the couple lived during the 1930s, they had separate quarters.

These houses were Mme. Ouspensky's contributions to the Work in England, and gradually she drew in to her hands the reins of a communal activity of the sort that Gurdjieff had created at Fontainebleau. At first she came to England only for part of the summer, and the country houses which she supervised were taken in the names of one or other of Ouspensky's pupils. There was a house in the southeast of England, another called Pound Scots at High Wycombe, next the Oast House at Trosley in Kent, and in 1930 an increased number of pupils gathered in Wendover. At this succession of establishments, Mme. Ouspensky set herself to reproduce Gurdjieff's assaults on his pupils' prejudices and self-images—in fact to provide the necessary friction for people to apply the principles which Ouspensky outlined.

She still kept communications open with Gurdjieff in France, and Nott and Mme. de Salzmann were among those who acted as couriers. Ouspensky was as interested as his wife in tales of Gurdjieff's activities; and his pupils remember how he sometimes turned a blind eye to emissaries who were "smuggled" into Mme. Ouspensky's presence. But was this only a blind eye? It remains possible that the breach between the two Masters— even the apparently definite breach of 1931—was deliberately arranged: a play, rather as Gurdjieff's passage of arms with the Orageans that same year was a play. And perhaps the play was not even for the benefit of Gurdjieff's or Ouspensky's immediate followers, but for later generations. The idea of the struggle of the magicians creates an almost mythical polarity. To say that the pious comedy—the *ludibrium*—was designed to provide the focus of a new religion may not be too wide of the mark.

Let us remember the lack of evidence we possess for the historical reality of events before 1919. How far does the play extend? Ouspensky's role may have been conceived as in some way mitigating the difficulties which Gurdjieff's methods inevitably created. Such a role might have the appearance of treachery, and might even appear treacherous to Gurdjieff himself. It may have been that Ouspensky saw himself in the role of Judas to Gurdjieff's Christ.

Gurdjieff taught in Russia—and repeated in *Beelzebub's Tales*—that the accepted view of Judas Iscariot was completely wrong. In reality, he said, Judas had been the closest and most faithful disciple. The fact that Christ had to die was known to all the disciples beforehand: it was a necessary part of the mystery play which they had determined to act out. Without the selfless performance of the traitor's role by Judas—who knew he would go down in history as a villain—the Christian drama would not have reached its necessary conclusion.

Gurdjieff's favorite term of abuse for followers who began to teach his ideas was "Judas-Iscariots"; and we know that his vilification of Orage as a plagiarizer and as an ambitious man was not the condemnation which it sounds. Ouspensky was obviously another of the "Judas-Iscariots" at whom Gurdjieff aimed his shafts. If they were in collusion to perfect their drama, it is possible that Ouspensky's apparent defection was part of the design, that he was the closest and most trusted disciple despite all appearances— or even that it was on his initiative that the drama was played in the manner in which it was.

Ouspensky might well have thought that Gurdjieff needed a loyal opposition; and he might even have brought Gurdjieff himself around to this point of view. Shortly before his death Ouspensky told one of his pupils that "she would understand"—what, he did not say—if she read *Old Diary Leaves*. This is Colonel H. S. Olcott's six-volume history of the Theosophical Society. Knowing Ouspensky's methods—he once told a pupil to read the New Testament in every translation she could find, solely to draw her attention to a passage halfway through St. Matthew's gospel—we might expect the solution to be fairly near the beginning of Olcott's saga. In the foreward to the first volume of *Old Diary Leaves* (1895), the Colonel explains his reasons for speaking out.

> The controlling impulse to prepare these pages was a desire to combat a growing tendency within the Society to deify Madame Blavatsky, and to give her commonest literary productions a quasi-inspirational character. Her transparent faults were being blindly ignored, and the pinchbeck screen of pretended authority drawn between her actions and legitimate criticism. Those who had least of her actual confidence, and hence knew least of her private character, were the greatest offenders in this direction. It was but too evident that unless I spoke out what I alone knew, the true history of our movement could never be written, nor the actual merit of my wonderful colleague become known.

One must still explain the abuse on both sides: Gurdjieff's castigation of Ouspensky as a "weak man," and Ouspensky's seeming anger against Gurdjieff's "paranoia." It may well have been a case similar to that of Gurdjieff and Orage—but with a different and perhaps a larger end in view. Like Gurdjieff's characters "Yelov" and "Pogossian," Ouspensky and Gurdjieff may have flung mud at each other with the tacit understanding that they were acting for each other's benefit. The opposition between the two figures has been made overacute by some of their followers, although such partisanship may in fact be designed to conceal the true nature of the game in progress.

Of course, just as in the case of Gurdjieff's accident, it is always possible that a plan was made and then miscarried; that both Gurdjieff and Ouspensky began to identify with their roles vis-à-vis each other; that Gurdjieff became in truth the strict chastizer of the erring disciple and Ouspensky grew more and more into the part of the disillusioned renegade. And although Ouspensky recorded Gurdjieff's teaching about Judas in *In Search of the Miraculous*, he himself maintained an opposite view in *A New Model of the Universe*. Does this counteract the previous argument; is it a deliberate contradiction inserted by the author—or is it his indirect confession, left behind for those who run to read?

Judas is simply a small man who found himself in the wrong place, an ordinary man, full of distrust, of fears and suspicions, a man who ought not to have been among the apostles, who understood nothing of what Jesus said to his disciples, but a man who for some reason or other was accepted as one of them and was even given a responsible position and a certain authority. Judas was considered one of the favourite disciples of Jesus; he was in charge of the apostles' domestic arrangements, was their treasurer. Judas' tragedy is that he feared to be exposed; he felt himself in the wrong place and dreaded the idea that Jesus might one day reveal this to others. And at last he could bear it no longer. He did not understand some words of Jesus; perhaps he felt a threat in these words, perhaps a hint of something which only he and Jesus knew. Perturbed and frightened, Judas fled from the supper of Jesus and his disciples and decided to expose Jesus. . . . He needed to accuse Jesus and his disciples of crimes in order to feel himself in the right. Judas' psychology is a most human psychology, the psychology of slandering what one does not understand.

There may be no deceptions at all. Alternatively, everything may be deception.

11

Real Psychology

When in 1930–31, Ouspensky told his senior pupils of his decision to wait no longer for results from Gurdjieff's work, he added a strange corollary. Perhaps, he said, the expansion which he planned would attract the attention of the "Inner Circle," the invisible esoteric hierarchy which he appeared to believe was the source of Gurdjieff's teaching. How seriously he took this hope is hard to say. Was the "inner circle" of humanity merely another carrot dangled before the noses of his expectant donkeys?

The formation of some sort of organization to support the Work was an old project of Ouspensky. He told his pupils that this was his contribution to what Gurdjieff called "the third line of work," that is, "work for the benefit of the school." "From the moment I met the system," he said, "I felt that it was more important than anything I ever knew and, at the same time that it was known only to a small group of people. There were no organizations behind it, no help, no nothing . . . I decided to work on this line." But many of his associates thought that the pressure for expansion came largely from his wife. One former pupil writes: "She might have been said to have bullied all of us into pressing this idea on O., who gradually gave way." As the Ouspenskys' own organization expanded, all efforts to make contact with the "Inner Circle" were abandoned. Mme. Ouspensky succeeded in converting most of her husband's pupils to a belief that they themselves would eventually constitute an "inner circle," and that a large organization was necessary to screen possible recruits. Ouspensky himself was never completely won over, and insisted that the idea was his pupils' responsibility. However, in the autumn of 1930, he began the program of expansion with a series of public lectures under the title "The Search for Objective Consciousness." His audiences grew steadily.

One result of the increasing number of pupils was that more people wanted to work with Mme. Ouspensky in her country establishments. In 1931 a house called The Dell was taken at Sevenoaks; and although several pupils were driven away by the ferocity of "Madam's" treatment, next year a still larger house was found to be necessary. Sophia Grigorievna Ouspensky was to all outward appearances a termagant. "She was, in every act, a great lady," Bennett writes. Nott calls her "always the Grand Duchess." She would never accept the title of "teacher" but always referred to herself as "nurse." Nevertheless, her methods were modeled on Gurdjieff's; and she pulled no punches. Incongruously, her public mockery of her followers had at first to be carried out through an interpreter.

This was Gurdjieff—but Gurdjieff without the subtlety or the warmth which redeemed all but his most outrageous violations of conventional human relationships. It is true that Mme. Ouspensky took on her shoulders all the odium generated by the unpleasant aspects of the Work: Ouspensky even stopped seeing all but his closest followers privately in Gwendwr Road and sent those who came to him with personal problems to his wife. So the contrast between the shrewish exterior of Sophia Grigorievna and the consideration shown by Pyötr Demianovitch is a little unfair. But there is no doubt that if Mme. Ouspensky assumed the martyr's role, its vindictive side "did not," in the words of one who suffered under her, "conflict with her private inclinations." Neither was she above using people in Gurdjieff's most unscrupulous manner. When toward the end of the 1930s she took to her bed, it became apparent that she had been training members of her entourage with just this eventuality in mind.

Relieved of his tutorial activities, Ouspensky was able to devote more time to his literary work. In 1927 Ouspensky decided to revise *In Search of the Miraculous* and eliminate from it all confusion between his ideas and those of Gurdjieff. This was a task in which he could never entirely succeed, but any developments of his own ideas—on the fourth dimension, eternal recurrence or the Superman—found their way into the book which was eventually published as *A New Model of the Universe;* a better subtitle than the one given it would have been, "applications of the third canon of thought."

Only one of Ouspensky's changes in terminology is significant. This is the introduction of the phrase, "the psychological method." When *A New Model of the Universe* was published in 1931, the expression gave reviewers great trouble, and as the book was subtitled, "principles of the psychological method in its application to science, religion, and art," this was serious. In the early editions of *Tertium Organum* Ouspensky had not used the phrase at all. Instead, he talked of the limitations of scientific reasoning and the necessity of going *beyond* in terms of "objective" and "subjective" knowledge. Scientific investigation proceeds by the objective method. Where this fails, the only solution is to transcend the limitations of the human psyche by expanding "the limits of receptivity." He had originally discussed this process as "the possibility of the expansion of subjective knowledge." But by the 1923 edition of *Tertium Organum* this had become "the possibility of the expansion of the application of the psychological method."

Thus the daunting "psychological method" grew out of the earlier "subjective knowledge." It was really an extension of Ouspensky's memorandum to himself to "think in other categories," just as *A New Model of the Universe* was an outgrowth from *Tertium Organum* and the illumination which accompanied it. "The psychological method," Ouspensky explained, "is nothing other than the revaluation of all values from the point of view of their *own* psychological meaning and independently of the outer or accompanying facts on the basis on which they are generally judged." To take a literary analogy, this is an argument for revaluation of experience according to the sort of standards for which C. S. Lewis argues in *An Experiment in Criticism:* that is, standards of literary appreciation referring only to the book under discussion. Kenneth Burke once gave an example of the psychological method from the realms of mystical experience. "If one under gas dreamed a metaphysical 'revelation,' we could not dispose of the 'revelation' by saying that the man was under gas; it would remain a revelation regardless of the 'facts.'" The use of the psychological method effectively puts its user beyond criticism.

In the second edition of *A New Model of the Universe,* Ouspensky attempted to clarify his argument. A logical mind is all very well and most useful for certain operations. But as soon as this logical mind has the courage to recognize its limitations, it becomes a "psychological mind." This is what he had meant by saying that the psychological method "aims at keeping the mind itself constantly in its field of view, and at regarding all conclusions and discoveries *relatively to the state or kind of mind.*" Then he makes one of his familiar paralogical leaps:

> The psychological method is first of all a method of distinguishing between different levels of thinking, and of realising the fact that perceptions change according to the powers and properties of the perceiving apparatus. The psychological mind can see the limitations of

the 'logical mind' and . . . it can understand the reality of the existence of a higher mind and of esoteric knowledge and see it in its manifestations. This is impossible for a merely logical mind.

Up to a point his reasoning is clear. Always to keep in mind our state of mind at the time of making an observation; always to bear in mind the limits of logic; always to remember the possibility of the third canon of thought. We can see how he arrived at this position through the logic of *Tertium Organum* and his ideas of the fourth psychological dimension. It is also quite in harmony with Gurdjieff's teaching on self-observation. But why must the psychological mind realize the reality of the existence of esoteric knowledge? Ouspensky is once more indulging in dogmatic imperatives where he should have only expressed possibilities.

The clue lies in the original term, "subjective knowledge." The subjectivity with which the *New Model* deals is Ouspensky's; and the arguments for the existence of esoteric knowledge which its author finds compelling need convince no one but himself. "The idea of the existence of a hidden knowledge," he writes, ". . . must grow and strengthen in people's minds from the realisation of the insolubility of many questions and problems which confront them." This expresses his own driving force in a single sentence. He never accepted the idea that, objectively, there might be *no* solutions and, where logic failed him, he took refuge in a private world. As long as the *New Model* is read conventionally, as an expression of objective and universally valid truth, it must seem absurd. But if the reader applies Ouspensky's "psychological method" to the text, the book becomes merely an invitation to enter its author's subjective world. *A New Model of the Universe* is Ouspensky's application of the third canon of thought to his personal obsessions. As an indication of possibilities open to the untrammeled mind, it proved an intoxicating experience for many of its readers.

As the author once remarked, it is "a very long book." Most of the subject matter had been touched on in *Tertium Organum,* and what is new is the manner of presentation. The book possesses little consecutive argument, but it is rather the introduction to a state of mind. Some of its original fascination is lost today in a world familiar with the mind-stretching concepts of science fiction; and it is significant that ideas derived from the *New Model* have formed a quarry for several science fiction writers. Ouspensky evidently hoped that some of his readers would follow him into his personal universe, and because this was by definition a universe where ordinary logic did not apply, he had to provide some hypothetical framework to provide an illusion of security for those who took the bait. So—very much on the principle by which Orage had dubbed Gurdjieff's cosmology "the Greater Map"—Ouspensky projected such a framework in the title chapter, "A New Model of the Universe."

He began by discussing the ideas of Newtonian physics and showed how the universe of scientific laws had been upset by the Einsteinian universe of relativity. He then proposed "a new model" which could disrupt existing physics just as the old physics had earlier been overturned. This "model" had in fact been completed by 1912, and Ouspensky had since been encouraged by Gurdjieff in the belief that the "period of dimensions" which he postulated expressed the same idea as Gurdjieff's Ray of Creation. In his earlier writings, Ouspensky had discussed five dimensions: the zero dimension, the conventional three, and the "fourth" of Time. In his "new model" he postulated two more. If we imagine Ouspensky's fourth dimension, the Long Body of Time, stretched like a clothesline before us, the short fifth dimension runs perpendicular to it—like a series of monstrously elongated clothespins, with each clothespin representing one particular moment—say 10 A.M. on April 10, 1980. This is the dimension of the Eternal Now, and if each clothespin were crossed by other lines of Time, it would still and forever represent 10 A.M. on April 10, 1980. But at each moment in Time—at each moment when the clothesline is broken by the clothespin—a man's actions may affect what happens next, and thus the structure of the clothesline, the shape of the Long Body, and also each subsequent moment of time, each Eternal Now, each clothespin following. But at each moment, there are also a number of possible courses of action open to us. Some are not selected and therefore are not actualized in the line of time along the clothesline. Ouspensky then postulated a sixth dimension, one at right angles to the clothesline and clothespin, which actualized all possibilities—whether selected or not selected—at once.

This ingenious piece of speculation was linked to the idea of eternal recurrence. If a man recurs and recurs, the only means of altering the remorseless cycle is to make different choices: that is, to select different possible courses of action at any moment in time. Thus by changing the *future*, by altering the shape of the Long Body as it will reveal itself *after his choice*, a man will also be altering his past—the configuration of the body of Time as it existed the last time he traveled this way. Accordingly, the next time around more new choices may be possible, and further change.

And further on (it is implied)—with unlimited change at each moment in time, when we are free of the tyranny of both past and future, when we arrive in the psychological dimension of absolute freedom and contain within ourselves all possible worlds—this is indeed the wisdom of the gods.

A New Model of the Universe had a mixed critical reception. It was agreed that Ouspensky's essay on yoga was very fine, but the rest of the book met with general incomprehension, and the "New Model" chapter was severely criticized. *The Times Literary Supplement* remarked that the book was "very good when the author is telling us about himself; it is mostly very bad when he is telling us about anything else. . . ." *The Nation* came even nearer the mark: "the only knowledge that a non-esoteric reader will derive . . . is about the psychological workings of the esoteric mind." Ouspensky had one panegyricist, John O'Hara Cosgrave in the *Saturday Review of Literature,* who wanted to force the *New Model* on "every college professor and author of books and writer for newspapers and magazines." In the *New Republic* Kenneth Burke recalled the impact of *Tertium Organum* on his circle, but described the *New Model* as "beyond 'argument.'" For his revised version of the universe he preferred Blake or Milton.

In England there was a second edition in 1934, and despite the obvious intellectual pitfalls, the book served very well what might easily be supposed to be Ouspensky's purpose. He had designed it for a popular audience and had hoped for a popular success; indeed he was dissatisfied with the high price of the handsome Routledge volume* and wanted a cheap edition. Who would bite on the lures he had strewn about so plentifully? He had talked in terms of religion, biology, mathematics, occultism, and philosophy; he had discussed sex and politics; he had indulged the most romantic fancies of journeys to the East. Behind it all, however, was an implication that there were particular secrets to be learned.

In a note prefacing the *New Model,* Ouspensky promised the publication of another book telling of his discoveries "during the time from 1915 to 1919." Three times he referred to the existence of a "special doctrine accessible only to a few" in places where his readers might make some connection with ideas of self-development. This was the opposite of the technique which he had used with his band of forty to fifty pupils in 1924. They had been given the task of distinguishing between Gurdjieff's ideas— referred to as "Special Doctrine"—and the "New Doctrine" for which Ouspensky was responsible.

Ouspensky once answered the question whether he had "altered the teaching much" that he had not altered it at all. He went on: "But I prefer . . . to start with the psychological side." He defined psychology as "study of oneself." This leads first to the recognition of the multiplicity of "I's"; and second to learning methods of self-observation—for which a man needs to know Gurdjieff's working diagram of the human machine. "Real psychol-

---

*A *New Model of the Universe* was published by Routledge and Kegan Paul largely through the influence of Herbert Read, a director of the firm.

ogy," Ouspensky said, begins when a man is told to "remember himself" and realizes that although he cannot do this in his present state, he might succeed with effort. This was the nub and axis of the System as he taught it, and even when he had led his pupils on some cosmological sally, he never tired of reminding them that "Only with the help of the psychological study shall we really increase our knowledge; without it we shall only be learning words."

After the publication of the *New Model* in 1931, and still more after the second edition of 1934, recruits came in droves to Warwick Gardens. Ouspensky instructed his pupils to approach friends who might respond to the System, and he began to hold meetings on more than one evening a week. In 1934 he wrote a series of introductory lectures, which were later published under the title of *The Psychology of Man's Possible Evolution*. These served both as an introduction to the ideas of Gurdjieff and—because they were frequently repeated—as a means of reminding pupils of the principles they were studying. To repeat these lectures and also to save time in answering questions about the basic outline of the System, Ouspensky made use of his most senior pupils. These included one man who had been with him since 1924, a journalist who was one of his older followers and a member of the Royal College of Physicians named Dr. Francis Roles.

At the same time Ouspensky delegated his authority to two other followers. The first was a very qualified delegation and simply involved the recognition of an already existing situation. J. G. Bennett—to whom Ouspensky was indebted for having arranged his visas from Constantinople—enjoyed an ambiguous relationship with his teacher, and from 1925 to 1930 had no direct contact with him at all. By the summer of 1930, Bennett had established a small discussion group which met regularly, and of whose activities he sent reports to Ouspensky.

The second delegation of authority was made by Ouspensky in a quasi-official manner. On September 9, 1931, he was talking to his closest pupil and friend, Maurice Nicoll. Then he said: "Nicoll, you had better go away. . . ." In the silence after his words, Nicoll was left contemplating his boots. Ouspensky completed his sentence. "Go away," he said, "and teach the System."

At first Nicoll's teaching was on a very small scale and had to be combined with the demands of his profession as a psychiatrist. His earliest pupils often found themselves sitting among the patients in the doctor's waiting room. The nucleus was formed by a few old followers of Ouspensky. These brought their friends, and outsiders might be introduced to the regular meetings. As the number of pupils grew, Nicoll divided his groups. There were meetings in his consulting rooms, in the flats of group members, in a physical culture studio run by a devoted follower named Fulford Bush, and in a dancing school in the Finchley Road.

Nicoll's experiences as a psychiatrist fitted him much better than Orage or either of the Ouspenskys to crack the whip if necessary, and it does not seem that his teaching ever incurred the casualties inflicted by Gurdjieff and Mme. Ouspensky. The impression remains that the doctor was remarkably skillful in tempering the wind to the shorn lambs under his charge.

We imagine the 1930s as a period dominated by industrial depression, unemployment, and mass political movements. But the slump affected intellectuals in different ways. Some turned toward the realities of this world, others withdrew from it precipitately. Ouspensky's teaching seemed to provide a way of detachment from the world which did not require subscription to apparently outmoded creeds. His decision to expand coincided with the beginning of the recession, and his success certainly owed something to the troubled state of Europe. It was in this psychological climate that Rom Landau wrote a bestseller, *God Is My Adventure,* and came himself to hear Ouspensky. In his *New Statesman* review of *The Fourth Way,* Rayner Heppenstall places Ouspensky's readers among that section of the avant-garde who had never been quite certain whether or not their place was in the arrière-ban:

> For quite a lot of people the years before Hitler's war were still dominated, not by the new Oxford communist poets, but by Central European mystagogues with more or less eye cocked on the mystic East. . . . In many a Garden Suburb sitting-room, beside the nature cure pamphlets and the outlines of Adlerian psychology, lay a copy of *Tertium Organum* or *A New Model of the Universe*. People were bent on awakening their higher centres, emerging from the prison of mechanicalness, being at one with the One, achieving synthesis and breathing correctly.

After the publication of the *New Model,* Ouspensky's lectures began to attract the attention of the *literati*. His shadowy presence in London was known to many intellectuals, and despite the secrecy of meetings at Warwick Gardens, the departure of Orage and Katherine Mansfield for the Prieuré had inevitably placed Ouspensky on the literary map. Although *Tertium Organum* never achieved the success in England which it enjoyed in the United States, it had a wide circulation in Progressive circles; and one of its most fervent devotees was Mrs. Bernard Shaw. But during the 1930s the literary men who attended Ouspensky's meetings came less frequently from the Progressive camp than from the fringes of Bloomsbury.

In those high and far-off days, contact between "intellectuals" and "society" was very close, and there was still a small circle within which fashions traveled fast. Nicoll, with his literary connections and parties at the Café Royal, moved in several strata of society and was the natural choice when Edwin Muir needed psychiatric help. Kenneth Walker (d. 1966) was an eminent surgeon, fellow of innumerable Royal Societies, and three times Hunterian Professor—the last two occasions in 1922 and 1924. He was introduced to Warwick Gardens by Nicoll, whose friend he had been at Cambridge and whose neighbor he was in Harley Street. Walker himself was no stranger to Bloomsbury and was a friend of Goldsworthy Lowes Dickinson. Mrs. Beatrice Mayor was a friend of the Huxleys. Her husband, R. J. G. Mayor (1869–1947), was a prominent civil servant in the Department of Education and was also a follower of Ouspensky. He was a member of the famous Cambridge "Apostles," and a peripheral figure in the circle of Lytton Strachey, who disapproved violently of his attempts to discover Truth. Aldous Huxley, Gerald Heard, and Christopher Isherwood also attended Ouspensky's lectures; both Huxley and Heard went several times to talk with Mme. Ouspensky in the country, although they never took part in the regular Work activities.

Some traces of Ouspensky's influence may be found in Heard's *The Third Morality* (1937), but Huxley was the most obviously affected of the group— although the impression remains that he reacted unfavorably to the Work, perhaps because he believed that Gurdjieff had been the cause of Katherine Mansfield's death. One obvious example of Huxley's borrowing is his use of the term "negative emotions," which occurs in *The Doors of Perception* (1954), to describe the unpleasant states of mind which are accentuated by hallucinogenic drugs. While he was writing his *Ends and Means* (1937), Huxley consulted the bookseller John M. Watkins of Cecil Court about the sources of "the perennial philospophy," and followers of Ouspensky maintain that his attendance at Ouspensky's lectures was also in the nature of a research expedition. Certainly the argument, if not the details, of *Ends and Means* with its declaration that "The ideal man is the non-attached man," is strikingly similar to what Huxley might have heard at Warwick Gardens.

The character of Mr. Propter in Huxley's *After Many a Summer* (1939) is sometimes taken as a portrait of Ouspensky. Propter is a man capable of withdrawing from personality. His method entails helping a man to "unlearn a lot of things he now regarded as self-evident and right." In Mr. Propter's conversation can be found hints of Gurdjieff's "objective moral- ity." "All personality is a prison. Potential good is anything that helps you to get out of prison." And in his lecturing of the "middle-aged English scholar," Jeremy Pordage, the reader finds a transposition into literary terms of the Ray of Creation, with its successively increasing number of mechanical laws. "Most of us live on the mechanical level," says Mr. Propter, "where events happen in accordance with large numbers. The things we call accidental or irrelevant belong to the very essence of the world in which we elect to live."

The promiscuousness of intellectuals toward Ouspensky did not result in a literary movement like that which Orage had inspired in the United States. The reason was Ouspensky's inflexible ban on writing about the System without his permission. When his followers asked—as they did at regular intervals—for news of when he intended to publish *In Search of the Miraculous,* Ouspensky would temporize and say that it was in their interests to keep the ideas for their own work rather than to let the world into their secrets. This prohibition was extended to prevent his pupils from writing altogether. One example is that of the novelist Bernadette Murphy, who was directed to abandon her writing and become secretary to Kenneth Walker. A few stray references did escape Ouspensky's net; only in the case of Aldous Huxley was the leakage considered serious, and the faithful erupted in loud cries against plagiarism of the Work.

The writing which Ouspensky did permit is so allusive as to give nothing away. Frequently it would be impossible to tell that an author had been in touch with his teaching. Robert Mayor's posthumously published *Reason and Common Sense* (1952) is the sort of philosophical treatise one would expect from a former Fellow of King's. Beatrice Mayor's *The Story without an End* (1940) is a mawkish allegory of spiritual progress dealing with the attempts of Betsy, denizen of Lowland, to climb the Great Slope. R. R. Merton, the translator of the *New Model,* published a volume called *Sons of the King* (1940) which contains Ouspenskian ideas filtered through a rather woolly mind. Almost nowhere is there to be found the life-giving impulse which animated the Orageans, and the contrast between Orage's fertilizing influence and Ouspensky's impersonation of a hen brooding on a clutch of eggs is telling.

The single exception to this melancholy rule was a book published in 1936 by Kenneth Walker, whose only previous literary work had been a children's story. Called *The Intruder** and subtitled, "an unfinished self-portrait," this is an interesting attempt to base an autobiography on the doctrine of man's "many I's." Walker introduces himself as his own experimental rabbit, and declares that "the study of psychology should begin, not with the examination of the broken clockwork that is brought to the psychotherapist's consulting room, but with a careful observation of the wheels and springs of action working within one." He confines himself to

*Later rewritten as *I Talk of Dreams*.

observing four different "I's," "so immersed in their dreams that they represent sleep rather than awareness"; but over and above his multiple ego, Walker makes out another entity whom he christens "the Intruder." The Intruder corresponds to what Ouspensky called "Big I," and Walker sees him as the agent of that fuller consciousness which alerts him to the cavortings of the marionettes who normally manipulate his life.

Just as the presence of Ouspensky in London acted as a compelling magnet for some intellectual circles, *A New Model of the Universe* provided a similar lodestone for a wider audience. In 1931, the year the *New Model* appeared, Charles Williams—whose secretary, a Miss Ripman, belonged to the Work groups and so had prior knowledge of Ouspensky's ideas—published his novel *Many Dimensions*, which contains much speculation on time and dimensions, and even a character who is trapped in a "perpetual recurrence." Britain in the 1930s had developed an appetite for the mysteries of time. J. W. Dunne published his *Experiment with Time* in 1927; and the same year Wyndham Lewis argued in *Time and Western Man* that time was the obsessive preoccupation of the age (and even the inspiration of Charlie Chaplin). John Buchan—adept as always at picking incipient fantasies from the void—published *The Gap in the Curtain* in July 1932. It is difficult to believe that he had not read the *New Model* and heard something of Ouspensky. *The Gap in the Curtain* tells of a house party at which the lion of the weekend is Professor August Moe. Moe selects five members of the house party for an experiment, all of whom are tired, nervous, or ill. They must not be men "too deeply sunk in matter." After a period of fasting and drug taking, Moe's subjects sit holding pieces of blank paper cut to the size of the *Times*. The object is to visualize the text of the newspaper one year from the date when the experiment takes place; and the story is concerned with what the characters do with the information they receive.

The interesting feature of *The Gap in the Curtain* is not the pseudotheory of reading the future, which is an amalgam of Dunne and Ouspensky. It is the character of Professor August Moe. Moe is the first appearance in the popular literature of the 1930s of a character who became archetypal for the decade. A brooding, powerful, Central European—or perhaps Scandinavian—genius with the ability to cast an intellectual spell over his listeners, Professor Moe is a sensationalized version of Ouspensky's public image. He shares with Ouspensky the technique of presenting his case in different ways to different people; and he shares his fascination with time. Professor Moe anticipates another fictional genius: in this case one whose ideas were admittedly borrowed from Ouspensky, and whose appearance gives substance to the idea that a vague image of Ouspensky himself formed part of the mental furniture of the late 1930s.

Visitors to the Royalty Theatre in London for the first night of J. B.

Priestley's *I Have Been Here Before* on September 22, 1937, would have seen Lewis Casson in the role of Dr. Görtler, and read the unfamiliar name of Ouspensky in the program. In the published version of the play, Priestley makes his acknowledgment as follows:

> For some of Dr. Görtler's theories of Time and Recurrence, I gratefully acknowledge my debt to P. D. Ouspensky's astonishing book, *A New Model of the Universe*. It must be understood however, that I accept full responsibility for the free use I have made of these borrowed ideas, and that it does not follow because I make use of them that I necessarily believe in them.
>
> J. B. Priestley

The play is set in a lonely Yorkshire inn and the basic plot is a contemplated adultery. The situation is complicated by the appearance of the mysterious Dr. Görtler, hinting darkly at the theories of eternal recurrence. Some of the characters decide that they have "been here before." It emerges that Görtler has intervened to halt a succession of misfortunes which will occur if the wife goes off with her lover. The affair will end disastrously, the lover's career will be ruined, the forsaken husband will shoot himself, and various subsidiary characters who depend on the protagonists will be caught up in the general tragedy. In the last act it appears that Görtler failed, because the lovers elope as they had done "before." But the wife returns repentant to find that Görtler has persuaded her husband not to commit suicide. The result is that the husband is reconciled to the loss of his wife; thus saving his own life and her happiness, as well as the career of his wife's lover, and the well-being of those who would also have been affected. It is a neatly moral application of Ouspensky's theories.

The play was commercially successful, and it certainly helped the sales of the *New Model*. A common reaction must have been that of David Hughes in his book on J. B. Priestley: "One cannot help being interested," he writes; "however much, for the sake of intellectual dignity, you pretend to wriggle in your seat, the attention is held throughout the piece, and you go away from the theatre muttering comments that sound vaguely like threats, determined to have a look at Ouspensky and see what possible truth it contains, even if you stick at the first thirty pages." In Warwick Gardens there were outraged cries about plagiarism which Ouspensky met with equanimity. He was used, he said, to people stealing his ideas. Although Priestley had freely acknowledged his source, he never succeeded in meeting Ouspensky, who regarded him as a potential menace to security. But the impact of the *New Model* had a lasting influence in turning

Priestley's mind toward the books of Gurdjieff, Ouspensky, and Nicoll, with results which became apparent in his later fiction.

Behind the mystery-making which produced such excellent entertainments, Ouspensky's reputation grew. Regarded by outsiders as a mysterious underground eminence, he was increasingly revered by his disciples, and the strange sort of success he enjoyed by proxy in the personae of Professor Moe and Dr. Görtler, may unconsciously have colored the pupils' images of the Master.

The notoriety which the *New Model* and Ouspensky's lectures brought the Work resulted in a further increase in the number of people who wanted to spend weekends under the eagle eye of Mme. Ouspensky at Gadsden. In the autumn of 1935, a larger house was taken at Virginia Water in Surrey. This was Lyne Place, a sizable Regency building with a farm. Perhaps harking back to the Tolstoyan fashions of his youth, Ouspensky decided that Lyne should be as self-supporting as possible. His pupils worked: making hay, growing fruit and vegetables, and keeping bees, with the dual objects of producing food and generating the friction which their discipline demanded. Later on, classes were held in Gurdjieff's movements. Some twenty people lived in Lyne Place itself, others bought houses in Virginia Water, and by 1938 about a hundred people were arriving to work on Sundays. This expansion brought with it effects which some of the older pupils noted with chagrin, among them, Kenneth Walker:

> One of the most obvious losses was that because we were now so many, we saw much less of the two Ouspenskys. This meant that we received less personal guidance from them, and were left more to our own devices. We were no longer a big family, but were now acquiring the attributes of an Institute. Yes, the older amongst us were forced to accept the fact that we had lost something by becoming bigger.

Lyne Place was organized with the mixture of elegance and austerity which was the Ouspensky trademark. Visitors complained of an atmosphere of tension. One was even convinced that the regime was vegetarian—which was not true, although the impression can be explained in terms of its puritan associations. Little conversation at meals, no laughter, the deadly seriousness of the pupils immersed in their struggles to "self-remember"; this was undoubtedly one aspect of the life at Lyne Place. In contrast, if there was a celebration of some kind, no expense was spared: Ouspensky enjoyed large, formal dinner parties, and his country house provided an excellent setting.

C. S. Nott visited Lyne Place in the late 1930s, and found the Ouspenskys comfortably established. He had the impression that despite all the outward trappings of success, Ouspensky—who was drinking heavily—was living in the past. This is an accusation also made by J. G. Bennett in connection with a drinking session in 1933: "He then had the habit of sitting up half the night drinking claret and, nearly always, of talking about his own early days in Russia. He seemed to have been obsessed with the need to put himself back into the life he was living before he met Gurdjieff in 1915."

This may have been so; but Ouspensky's manner of teaching and the material he used made him live not so much in the past as in a sort of continuing present. By the very fact that he was teaching a system which resulted from his time with Gurdjieff, he had created a kind of canonical period and ceaselessly reconcentrated his mind on its events. This impression was intensified for his pupils through readings from the typescript of *In Search of the Miraculous*. By inviting people to enter his private psychological world in the *New Model*, Ouspensky created around him an atmosphere which reinforced the Russian associations of the *New Model's* subject matter—which came chiefly from the years between 1908 and 1912. As he gradually gave more prominence to his personal ideas, his pupils heard of the role of the devil in preventing human evolution, discussed Ouspensky's theory of an "esoteric school" which had inspired Ibsen, Rossetti, and Alexis Tolstoy, and practiced exercises of "repetition" and "stopping thoughts" with which their teacher had experimented long before. For them Ouspensky's own search was a historical glyph; yet that search had not ended, and perhaps Ouspensky had begun to look back toward the direction in which he had first set out.

The impression that he was disappointed in the results of his personal quest is given by another story told by Bennett, whose wife had an interview with Ouspensky soon after she recovered from an overdose of drugs. The tale of her ecstatic experiences when close to death brought Ouspensky to the verge of tears. He told her that since his youth he had been hoping for such an experience but that he had remained unenlightened. A sense of having been cheated by fate may have lain at the back of his increasing dogmatism. It had always been a feature of his character to entrench himself in strange positions, and as the 1930s wore on, his stubbornness grew.

One frequent source of conflict was provided by Ouspensky's views on evolution. In the *New Model* he describes the universe as a "Great Laboratory." He believed devoutly in the inheritance of acquired characteristics and argued that certain forms of life had been created solely to develop a particular characteristic which was needed for the creation of the culminating life form—man. Man was the prize exhibit in the laboratory, for he was nature's attempt to manufacture a self-evolving creature.

Ouspensky followed a bizarre but common occult theory that animals are degenerated men—perhaps failed experiments.

He had some equally unorthodox ideas about personal evolution. Three categories of men were distinguished according to sexual behavior: men of supra-sex, infra-sex and normal sex. Humans afflicted by infra-sex were symptoms of race-degeneration; and among these Ouspensky included both the sex-obsessed and the sexually "abnormal" of any description. Beings of supra-sex were those who had mastered the art of transmuting the sex-energy into a means of personal evolution, and Ouspensky printed a list of the "thirty-two signs of Buddha-hood"—actually deriving from a Chinese astrological manual—as an indication of what these supermen might look like.

From his earliest days in London, Ouspensky's refusal to admit orthodox concepts of evolution had brought him into conflict with his more scientifically trained followers. His views on the sexually "abnormal" were unshakable; "and may," one former pupil writes, "have been genuinely naïve." In answer to a question about homosexuality, he once replied that he knew very little about it, because it did not exist in Russia; and in *A New Model of the Universe* he inveighs against psychoanalysis for providing a justification for homosexuals. Such traits belong to the caricature reactionary, and it is evident that Ouspensky intensely and increasingly disliked his own time. It would be wrong to see this as a blind revulsion from a world which had turned against him. What was happening was that the psychological method had got out of hand.

Ouspensky even used the latter to justify his hatred of Bolshevism. In *A New Model of the Universe* there is a chapter called "Eternal Recurrence and the Laws of Manu," in which Ouspensky couples his theory of recurrence to the caste divisions laid down by Hindu tradition. These laws, he said, represented "an ideal social organisation in accordance with esoteric systems" because the division into four castes of Brahmins (priests and scholars), Kshatriyas (warriors), Vaisyas (merchants), and Sudras (servants), was a natural division. Whether people liked it or not, they belonged to one or another of these classes. A man might move up a caste the next time around the circle of recurrence. Here Ouspensky could not have differed more from Gurdjieff, who denounced the "maleficent castes" of society. Ouspensky admitted that modern society offered no examples of "correct" division into castes. But "the most brilliant periods of history" occurred by accident when the social order approached the caste system yet still allowed some flexibility. One of these periods had been "the beginning of the 20th century in Russia." Ouspensky appeared to regard the Russian intelligentsia as potential Brahmins, characterized by the wish for "disinterested activity" and "personal freedom." This is really an adaptation of his early presentiment that he belonged to "a new race of men." In the 1931 edition of the *New Model,* Ouspensky incorporated a long note denouncing the "pseudo-intelligentsia," a class he described as "the worst, *outcaste* element of Vaisyas and Sudras." He characterized these—still using the Russian example and obviously with the Bolsheviks in mind—as intellectuals "who do not become the intelligentsia"; that is, intellectuals who disagreed with his concept of the role of an "intelligent."

By the time the second edition of the *New Model* appeared three years later, Ouspensky had obviously come under fire about this rather strange sociological theory. He altered the text of his chapter on the Laws of Manu, but inserted a new preface—whose purpose was chiefly to explain his ideas of the "psychological method"—a further condemnation of Bolshevism. It appeared that, according to the psychological method, Bolshevism was evil incarnate. But the merely "logical"—as opposed to "psychological"—mind would never see this.

> The man of logical mind who demands proofs for everything . . . looks for the cause of the world economic and political crisis everywhere except where it actually lies.
>
> And even if he were told that the causes . . . lie in the existence of the Soviet government in Russia, and in the recognition and *support* of this government by other governments, he would never understand it. He is accustomed to think in a certain way and he is unable to think differently. For him the bolsheviks are a "political party" like any other party, and the Soviet Government is a "government" like any other government. He is unable to see that this is a new phenomenon different from anything he knew before.
>
> Where are the proofs of this? he would ask.
>
> And he will never see that this needs no proofs. . . . "proofs" are by no means always necessary in order to accept or to deny a given proposition. There are "psychological proofs" which mean much more than facts because facts can lie and psychological proofs cannot lie. But one must be able to feel them.

Why must one be able to feel them? The answer is because Ouspensky felt them. Because he regarded Bolshevism as the dominance of the criminal element in humanity and its leaders as renegade Brahmins, the psychological method—supported by esotericism—dictated that everyone else must feel this too. Ouspensky made a rule for his followers about not becoming involved in "criminal politics"—which included not only fascism and Communism but the English Labour Party. This bore heavily on some of his followers—for example, Bennett, who had been offered a parliamentary seat by Ramsay MacDonald.

Dogmatism did not matter when Ouspensky was teaching the System, because he faithfully insisted that his followers must verify everything for themselves. But it came to mean an increasingly dictatorial attitude toward more general matters. For example, Kenneth Walker, besides being a surgeon, was one of the pioneers of popular sexology, and in 1940 published one of the first paperback books on sex. Then on one occasion at Lyne it was discovered that he had given a young Ouspenskian advice on some sexual problem. Ouspensky's rage was colossal—although it appeared to have little impact on a blandly smiling Walker.

The influx of new disciples had repercussions for Ouspensky's London lectures. By the autumn of 1937, he found himself overwhelmed with meetings, and told his senior pupils that they must share the burden. Apart from delegating some of the routine work, he wanted to devote more time to writing. He was becoming anxious that he had not published anything for a long time and needed to keep his name before the public. He also had to find a larger house for the meetings, if possible with a hall where Gurdjieff's movements could be taught. By the spring of 1938 the problem had been solved.

The building which Ouspensky and his followers acquired is known as Colet House and stands in Colet Gardens opposite the old site of St. Paul's School. It had belonged to the ballet school of Nicholas Legat whose wife, Nadine Legat, was a pupil of Ouspensky and had evolved a gymnastic form of dancing incorporating Gurdjieffian principles of self-observation. The large hall was ideal for the movements, and there was ample room to hold much larger meetings. Ouspensky moved a private press, belonging to one of his pupils, into the basement where it functioned as a means of "work" with a particularly pointed moral. For when the proofs were pulled—in the words of a pupil who was concerned in the project—"every literal [misprint] was an unmistakable example of sleep."

Ouspensky insisted that this enlargement of his activities should have some outward cover to satisfy the police that nothing subversive was in progress. The result was the formation of a society called the "Historico-Psychological Society," whose numbers were fixed at 300. The committee consisted of the two Ouspenskys, some half dozen supporters from Lyne, and a strong medical lobby from the Harley Street district, including Kenneth Walker and Dr. Francis Roles. Other members were the journalist who had taken meetings for Ouspensky and Robert Mayor who acted as librarian and treasurer. The Society's objects again hint at a vision of "real psychology":

1) The study of problems of evolution of man and particularly the idea of *psycho-transformism*.
2) The study of psychological schools in different historical periods and

in different countries, and the study of their influence on the moral
and intellectual development of humanity.

3) Practical investigation of methods of self-study and self-development according to principles and methods of psychological schools.

4) Research work in the history of religions, of philosophy, of science
and of art with the object of establishing their common origin where
it can be found and different psychological levels in each of them.

Under this rather unwieldy umbrella, Ouspensky's organization took
shape. By 1938 he seemed to have attained much of what he had set out to
achieve for his "third line of work." If Gurdjieff's Institute had failed,
Ouspensky now had a substantial London base and an organizational
framework; while at Lyne his wife put his pupils through the hoops about
which he told them theoretically. Despite the hints that he was a
disappointed man, Ouspensky had many more material advantages than he
could have hoped for twenty years earlier. He had an estate where he lived
the life of a country gentleman and indulged his hobbies. He kept horses
and his increasingly portly figure was a familiar sight in the saddle. He
made a collection of antique firearms and held sessions of target practice.
His sense of irony prevented him from taking his organization too seriously.

Neither did he encourage uncritical adoration of himself. Once at a
meeting he had a question about "invisibility"—had he ever been "invisible"? he was asked. Ouspensky replied cuttingly that he could tell them
anything he liked and they would still have to believe him. It was the same
with people who tried to invest him with miraculous powers. Nevertheless
some did so, and the circumstances surrounding his death were to give
them cause to reassert their opinions. "Ouspensky had powers," one young
disciple wrote. "He kept his powers hidden, however, and they were
manifested only very rarely, and then most subtly and never for show. His
integrity in these and other matters was absolute, and he was incorrupti-
ble."

If there is something of Dr. Görtler and Professor Moe in this picture of
Ouspensky, it is an image which was common to a number of his pupils. In
contrast, while magical powers never seem to have been attributed to
Mme. Ouspensky, she was not averse to a certain amount of adoration. This
may have gathered about her by association; for although Ouspensky
sometimes discussed religious topics with his pupils, and went everywhere
accompanied by a "much-thumbed New Testament," he drew a definite
boundary between religion and the System. This was not true of his wife.
During the weekends at Lyne, she would organize readings from the
sayings of Buddha, or the Sufi poet Rumi, or the Russian compilation of the
Fathers known as the *Philokalia*, which she had translated into English by

Mme. Kadloubovsky—all of which she accompanied by a commentary pointing out the resemblances to the System.

People best remember the Ouspenskys as they were in 1938 and 1939. These were the great days, when their work was outwardly successful, and apparently harmonious. But the distinct separation between Ouspensky's personal following and "Madam's people" encouraged some internal dissension and faction fighting. One recurrent problem was that of Mme. Ouspensky's grandson, who lived with the community at Lyne. He made incessant demands on the patience of the Ouspenskys' pupils, and many thought Mme. Ouspensky blind to his faults. However, to some of "Madam's people," Lonya's behavior seemed to be yet another deliberate provocation in the sense of the Work. Ouspensky himself admitted that his step-grandchild was a thorough nuisance, but in this—as in other matters—allowed himself to be swayed by his wife.

Ouspensky's difficulties were compounded by his wife's taking to her bed. He discussed her illness with a psychiatrist pupil and both concluded that the cause was a form of neurasthenia. Yet even though she spent an increasing amount of time in her room, Mme. Ouspensky's influence grew increasingly powerful, and Ouspensky came under attack for his apparent subservience. Maurice Nicoll once visited Gadsden and once Lyne for special celebrations; and on both occasions—after a large quantity of drink was consumed—Nicoll became highly critical. At Gadsden, the evening ended with Nicoll, Ouspensky, and a senior pupil of Ouspensky's drinking together. Nicoll stated "violently" that Ouspensky had "gone soft" and was too much under his wife's influence. He tried unsuccessfully to persuade the third man present to break with Ouspensky and start a group of his own.

It is known that Nicoll kept in touch with Gurdjieff despite the appearance of complete separation. Was this a further act in the play? Was Nicoll playing Judas in his turn? Or was his role that of the slave who rode in the chariot of the Roman Emperor whispering: "You too are mortal"? Certainly, there was a suggestion of the imperial about the Ouspenskys in the late 1930s. They enjoyed the status which had belonged to Gurdjieff in the early days at Fontainebleau. The contrast between their circumstances and those of their old Master was considerable. It might almost be seen—by those eyes peering at the historical glyph—as a morality.

12

The Bone Beneath the Mountain

Gurdjieff's *coup de théâtre* of 1931 nearly wrecked his work altogether. His material fortunes had been closely bound up with those of Orage; and most of his remaining pupils had been Orage's also. Although his apparent ill-treatment of his leading henchman did not of itself result in many defections, it introduced an element of doubt into the Master's relations with his American followers which had not been present when the persuasive Englishman had been available as mediator.

To those in close touch with Gurdjieff, there was really little doubt that there was "business as usual." He carried his personal atmosphere around with him, and on his visits to New York the hotels in which he stayed were crowded with the apparatus of Oriental cooking. He rose early—about 6 or 7 A.M.—and spent the morning writing in the Childs restaurants which he used as "offices." Then he went shopping for the ingredients of an exotic lunch. The meal, with its accompaniment of vodka and applejack, might last till about 2:30, after which Gurdjieff would rest for an hour. In the evening he would return to Childs and perhaps again play host to his pupils at dinner, prolonging the session into the small hours by recitations on his hand organ.

Some former Orageans remember farewell ceremonies for Orage instigated by Gurdjieff both in New York and at the Prieuré. There was a general impression that no division of interests separated the teacher and his pupil.

Yet Orage had gone; and he had certainly expressed some doubts about his old Master to several of his American pupils. Because Gurdjieff now had to take responsibility for raising money himself, this meant trips to the United States at least once a year between 1930 and 1934. Personal contact with Gurdjieff in his role of sheep-shearer naturally increased whatever doubts a pupil might have had about entrusting himself to an "esoteric teacher." Seen from the New World, Gurdjieff's fortunes appeared to be undergoing a rapid decline.

In England historical circumstances seemed to play into the hands of the Ouspenskys. In America, although Gurdjieff quite obviously expected the Depression to bring many more recruits to the Work, economic hardship and uncertainty had precisely the opposite effect. This may have been partly because Orage's success in New York was associated with the sort of intellectual attitudes which came to be considered particularly "Twentiesish"—the complex of humanism, hedonism, and unorthodox psychology which Edmund Wilson denounced. In England, Ouspensky escaped identification with outmoded attitudes because he had begun on a very small scale. But the early successes of Orage in New York effectively discredited Gurdjieff's ideas for Americans of the 1930s.

There was no one to replace Orage, although several small groups came into existence under directors like Schuyler Jackson. A number of Gurdjieff's leading followers in the New York area formed a "Committee for the New York Group," which took on the thankless task of trying to organize financial support for their prodigal Master. But after Orage's final departure, the most senior "pupil-teacher" of Gurdjieff's ideas in the United States was Jean Toomer in Chicago. It was during 1931 and 1932 that Toomer emerged with a personal initiative which attracted widespread notice, as it was linked to a romantic and tragic development in his personal life.

The expedition which he made to Fontainebleau in 1929 was to prove his last. Next year Gurdjieff visited the group in Chicago, and Toomer himself visited New York and Montreal. In 1931 he did not meet Gurdjieff, and the Toomer papers provide little information about his activities; but he once more appeared in print for the first time at any length since the publication of *Cane*.

Toomer's *Essentials* was issued privately in Chicago. Its author described it as "some 300 crystallizations in words of observations and understandings which have arisen in me during a five-year period." The book is a collection of aphorisms and would probably be inaccessible to anyone unfamiliar with Gurdjieff's ideas. "We have many reformers, few transformers," Toomer wrote; and "We want to be free from the things we want." There is something about the Work which encourages its devotees to make epigrams about it. Jane Heap was another coiner of phrases; and the idea may be to provide mnemonics or texts to be mulled over. Those contained in *Essentials* are often well-turned or witty and provide enduring food for thought. "While an increasing number of materialists are committing suicide because they believe they have no soul," Toomer proclaimed, "an increasing number of spiritualists are going crazy because they believe they have one." There is much more in the same vein, and no single aphorism could be chosen as displaying the theme of the book. But one short passage, less epigrammatic than many, does seem to provide an indication of how Toomer had come to understand the Work. He wrote that he saw the emergence of a new type of man, a "psychological type." "This is a psychological adventurer: one who, having had the stock experiences of mankind, sets out at right angles to all previous experience to discover new states of being."

There are no detailed records of how Toomer conducted his groups in Chicago. Fritz Peters met his pupils in the autumn of 1931 when they numbered about twenty-five and was not impressed by their quality. "They seemed to me to have been attracted to his teaching for a variety of not very good reasons—because of loneliness, or perhaps because they considered themselves misfits or outcasts. Most of them had dabbled in the arts, theosophy, the occult or something of the sort, and had come to Gurdjieff as if in search of another 'cure' for their life problems . . ." Toomer's meetings consisted of readings from *Beelzebub's Tales* followed by discussions in which the participants tried to relate the book to their personal situations. Gurdjieff's "impartially objective criticism of the life of man" became a justification for anything avant-garde. "Any radical social behavior became almost automatically justified," Peters writes, ". . . the prevailing attitude of this particular group of followers was that of substituting new values for old by rote." What is clear is that Toomer's group had struck out on their own line; and this was not very acceptable to a fundamentalist.

For two months in the summer of 1931, Toomer lived with several members of his group in a three-room cottage at Portage, Wisconsin. He began with four of his closest associates, and on weekends the numbers were increased to thirty by the addition of other pupils from Chicago and some interested locals. To the newspapers he described the object of his summer at Portage—still hazily referred to by literary historians as "a cottage experiment"—as being "to keep a number of 'intellectual' men and 'intellectual' women in close proximity and observe the psychological effects."

Among his group were a bank cashier, a salesman, a reporter, a clubwoman, a justice of the peace, and a businessman. There was also a native of Portage named Margery Latimer. She had first become interested in Orage's groups in New York and had joined Jean Toomer's in Chicago when she returned to Portage from leading the literary life. Margery Latimer was a promising young writer, the author of *We Are Incredible* (1928) and the even more highly regarded *Nellie Bloom and Other Stories* (1929), which contains several traces of Gurdjieff's influence. She was probably responsible for the site chosen by Toomer for his experiment; and also for igniting a fresh spark of interest in Portage's most celebrated lady of letters and her own literary godmother: Zona Gale.

Zona Gale invited the townsfolk of Portage to her home to hear Toomer lecture and succeeded in arousing a degree of interest. A few sober citizens were persuaded to attend talks which Toomer delivered in the woods nearby, but a small number of interested locals did not prevent rumors circulating about the doings in the cottage by the river. About a year after the experiment, a reporter from the *San Francisco State Journal* interviewed the acting Chief of Police in Portage. Did he remember Jean Toomer?

"Yes," said the chief, puffing at his pipe. "I remember him well. Tall fellow, pretty dark. Yesh, we had an idea he was part Negro all right. Lots of people here did."

"What kind of place did he run, chief?"

The chief thought for a moment and replied: "I don't know much about it, but from reports we got there was some damn funny things going on out there. He was some kind of philosopher. I never did figure it out."

Over in the corner a man, hidden behind a newspaper, suddenly said: "Why I heard they were climbing trees out there just like squirrels."

"Yes sir," the chief said solemnly, "just like squirrels."

Apart from climbing trees and shocking the bourgeoisie, what was Toomer doing?

He called the account he wrote of the episodes "Portage Potential," and subtitled it "An adventure in human development." He constantly emphasizes that the experiment was his personal creation: "I was building a world. I was creating a form. It was to be my own." His methods bore some relationship to those of Gurdjieff but are recognizably original. He introduced *games*—deck tennis and swimming in the nearby river—which provided excellent material for observing the natures of group members. He named the members responsible for various activities—cooking or housework—"Chiefs" (and how did they respond to the suggestion of authority?). He delivered lectures on the particular sort of tail which each of his pupils possessed. Short and curly? Twisted? Diabolically straight? His contribution was intended to be more than simply personal; Toomer being who he was, with a particular interest in creating Americans out of a bouillabaisse of peoples, saw it as a particularly American form. "The Portage cottage was a nursery school, and we its members. It was a school for Americans—a place where those who had been conditioned by America could work the bad of America out, the good of America in, and become human beings of the given types as developed in America." He had at last begun to give expression to the ideas of a nation of regenerated men which he had absorbed from Waldo Frank.

It is a great loss that "Portage Potential" has never been published; it is unique in portraying the uncertainties and extemporizations on the part of the teacher as well as the reaction of the pupils to the shocks he administers. From the teacher's side, it is clear that some of the most powerful effects he produces are unintentional. Toomer admits that one talk he delivered—chiefly on "negative emotions"—had a completely unforeseen impact upon Margery Latimer. In the typescript she is referred to as "Marion Kilburn."

> The effect of this talk was experienced most by Marion Kilburn; and in her there was produced a series of experiences considerably beyond anything that I had planned or could possibly have controlled. The results in her, indeed, came about only because my, for me concise formulations, but for her more than random shots, happened to crystallize materials for certain experiences, materials gathered by her unusual person over a number of years.

Judging by the list of testimonials from his pupils which Toomer attached to the text of "Portage Potential" he succeeded in inducing experiences of great intensity in a considerable number of people. He concluded that his experiment had shown four things: "That through self-knowledge man can become man"; "the possibility of change"; that "people can be consciously energized"; and that it was possible to create a "conscious form" in which all these things could take place. For public consumption he put it more simply: "As a result of the experiment," he told a reporter, "I am satisfied that it is entirely possible to eradicate the false veneer of civilization, with its unnatural inhibitions, its selfishness, petty meanness and unnatural behavior, under proper conditions. Adults can be reeducated to become as natural as little children, before civilization stamps out their true subconscious instincts."

This sort of language was not calculated to soothe the critics who suspected that, without the veneer of civilization, moral anarchy would break loose. By the time this interview appeared, Toomer had come under heavy fire.

As the summer of 1931 passed, the curiosity of the local press increased. It was hinted that the inmates of the cottage formed a "free love" colony, and increasingly vicious attacks were made on Toomer's Negro ancestry. Whether or not Fritz Peters is right in attributing deliberate flouting of convention to the members of the Chicago group, Toomer's associates were certainly used to more Bohemian standards of behavior than the citizens of Portage; and Toomer's own attractiveness to women had before 1931 led to awkward situations. The result of the Portage experiment as far as the outside world was concerned was to make Toomer notorious as an arcanely corrupt "philosopher"—although few readers of the many newspaper reports can have approached an accurate conception of what the experiment had been about.

In October 1931, Toomer and Margery Latimer were married in Portage. Baulked of their free love scandal, the press began to make life in the town increasingly unpleasant for the Toomers and their protectress, Zona Gale. Everywhere the couple went they had to face hostile inquisitions from reporters. Even six months later, on their arrival in the artists' colony at Carmel, California, they were subjected to a barrage of questions on the Portage experiment. How had chaperonage been observed? Did they believe in nudism? And pounding away beneath the more salacious speculations was the drumbeat of a manufactured public opinion demanding the ostracism of the Toomers for marrying across the color line. It is considered that this persecution helped to cause Margery Latimer's early death, which took place in 1932 after she had given birth to a daughter. Her husband called the child "Margery" and dedicated "Portage Potential" to "Margery of Portage."

"Portage Potential" was finished in the autumn of 1931. But no publisher would accept it, and on February 9, 1932, Toomer wrote to Gorham Munson asking his opinion of the manuscript and enclosing the verdict of one publisher's reader: "I believe very deeply that since *Cane* (which had genius in it) you have traversed the wrong road."

In the correspondence which followed, Munson's objections amounted to a request that Toomer suppress his work for political reasons. He disliked the testimonials which Toomer had appended to the book and advised his friend to cut all reference to emotional entanglements between members of the Portage group. He wrote forcefully about the unwisdom of mentioning Gurdjieff's name in connection with the experiment. Toomer had loyally avoided connecting his unpopular activities with Gurdjieff in any interviews he gave to the press, but evidently felt that he could scarcely write a book about his summer colony with no mention of the source of his ideas. As it turned out, *Portage Potential* remained unpublished, although its author formally registered the copyright. He may have been influenced by Munson's urgent appeals against trying again for publication after a lapse of time.

From Munson's description of Gurdjieff's reputation in New York, his advice was justified. Munson also hinted that renegades from the Work were causing trouble for Gurdjieff's loyal supporters.

The sort of rumors spread by disillusioned Gurdjieffians can easily be imagined. Fritz Peters has recorded several incidents which blackened Gurdjieff's reputation. Two of these were the result of his unorthodox medical treatments. In one case Gurdjieff prescribed a limited amount of alcohol for a woman supposed to be a semi-alcoholic on the grounds that without it she would die. Her doctor had forbidden her to drink as part of his treatment for another illness and was naturally furious when he discovered that his patient had forsaken him for an illicit medical practitioner. He restored the regime of abstinence, and the woman duly died. A second *cause célèbre* concerned another woman who was dying in the hospital. Gurdjieff diagnosed her trouble simply as a death wish and prescribed enemas of olive oil which she was to administer herself with a syringe smuggled into the ward. Supposedly this was to remove a particularly vile form of constipation from which the patient suffered; in fact—as Gurdjieff might well have intended—the syringe was discovered by the hospital authorities. When the woman eventually left the hospital, she bitterly attacked Gurdjieff for causing trouble. Gurdjieff on his side claimed that he had now given her cause to live—by provoking her to a positive hatred.

Of course it is easy to claim responsibility after the event; and it may be wondered whether Gurdjieff's olive oil enemas did not fall into the same category as Orage's stout and oysters. But although he may occasionally have been driven to prescribe unlikely remedies by the clamor of his disciples, as the decade wore on—and particularly after 1933—Gurdjieff came increasingly to rely on his unorthodox medical treatments as a source of income. He has always had his advocates as a physician, and during the later 1930s, he was virtually supported by contributions from one young American who had arrived at the Prieuré to be cured of a drug addiction. The role of the physician-hypnotist which had served him so well in Turkestan, Constantinople, and Paris, was transferred to New York. Peters remembers Gurdjieff's complaints that, because of lack of interest on the part of his disciples, he was forced to earn money for himself. At this time he was living in a fifth-rate hotel, and the ambivalent tone of his activities depressed the young man who had known him as the Master of the Château du Prieuré. "I was glad," he writes, "when he emerged from this rather woebegone characterization of a kind of quack doctor living in shoddy circumstances."

This progressive deterioration in Gurdjieff's circumstances was just beginning when Gorham Munson advised against the publication of *Portage Potential* in 1932. A more serious cause for concern was provided by rumors of his sexual misdemeanors. Along with the usual stories of women being invited to his hotel room at unlikely hours of the night, there was a dinner party to which Gurdjieff asked a number of reporters and writers. Before the party he persuaded Fritz Peters to "teach" him all the most Anglo-Saxon terms he knew for sexual activity—although afterward it appeared that he not only knew the four-letter vocabulary well, but had played this scene with other people. During the dinner party Gurdjieff subtly switched roles from that of perfect host to that of satyr, making use of the coarsest expressions he had been "taught." The result was the beginning of an orgy. Gurdjieff eventually stopped proceedings by ridiculing his guests and directing them to see from their conduct what they really were. He told them that, as this was an important lesson, he deserved to be paid; and according to Peters collected several thousand dollars.

Such proceedings were open to grave misunderstandings. But one specific case brought home to America the possibile consequences of Gurdjieff's capacity to inspire devotion. This concerned a young woman who met him in Chicago and followed him to New York. She was considered a "semi-invalid," and was evidently crippled by shyness and feelings of inadequacy. According to Peters, Gurdjieff told his associates that he could both help the girl with her problems and cure her infatuation. However, the girl's family arrived from Chicago, accused Gurdjieff of seducing their daughter and had her committed to a mental hospital. In the hospital the girl committed suicide. Gurdjieff's followers split into two camps; and at the instigation of his opponents, the Master was imprisoned for several days on Ellis Island. His supporters finally secured his release, but Gurdjieff had to return to France, and later found it difficult to reenter the United States.

The steady decline of Gurdjieff's reputation extended over several years. After the excitements of 1930–31, the New York group had been prepared for anything when Gurdjieff arrived for the winter of 1931–32, and it was in tones of amazement and relief that Gorham Munson described the visit to Toomer in Chicago. Gurdjieff was affable, approachable and open. This extraordinary improvement was maintained right up until his departure on the *Bremen* on January 16, 1932. If Gurdjieff had been intent on papering over the cracks caused by the fracas of the previous winter, he seems partly to have succeeded, although Munson, for one, had no illusions about the purpose of his Master's visit. As he wrote to Toomer, Gurdjieff announced his departure immediately after securing what he had come for. As in the days of Orage, sheep-shearing took priority over enlightenment.

Next winter Gurdjieff was again in the United States and visited New York and Chicago. The trip of 1932–33 marks the point at which relations between him and his American followers began to deteriorate in earnest, and several were driven away filled—in Toomer's words—"with disgust and anger and the conviction that he was using his power merely in order to obtain money, money and more money without cease." Money was urgently needed. In the spring of 1933 a shocking telegram arrived in New York announcing that Gurdjieff was "absolutely destitute" and that the Prieuré was about to be sold. Nothing could be done, for Gurdjieff had exhausted not only the patience of his followers but the fund of goodwill on which they in turn could draw. Toomer was approached by the New York "Committee" about the large gift made by Mabel Luhan, for which he had acted as trustee in 1926, and replied that "the sum no longer exists." He did not state how the money had been spent, but most of it must have dribbled from the publication fund into the coffers of the Prieuré.

The Gurdjieff who arrived to winter in New York in 1933–34 was a man with all the accoutrements of failure. The noisome reputation he had gathered, the seedy appearance of his doctoring and hypnotizing, the feeling that the Prieuré and the good days were now in the past, all contributed to a slightly unhealthy atmosphere which impressed itself on some of those who met him. It seemed undeniable that his health was poor—he already looked terrible in the winter of 1932–33—and he had grown very fat. He had totally confused his pupils by publishing a strange book called *Herald of Coming Good*. As far as the public was concerned, the image of Gurdjieff the ogre was in the ascendant. Rom Landau flew the Atlantic to see him and was almost frightened out of his wits. Before his interview he had lunch with an American writer who had followed the progress of the Work for several years and who confirmed Landau's worst suspicions with an extraordinary piece of gossip. Landau's informant had last seen Gurdjieff at a reception in the spring of 1933. He had been sitting at a table with a woman friend, a novelist.* Gurdjieff caught her eye and began to breathe in and out in a peculiar fashion. The novelist turned pale. After a few minutes, she recovered and admitted to him that whatever Gurdjieff had been doing had "struck her right through her sexual center." In plainer language, she had been given an orgasm by remote control.

Landau's visit to the Great Northern Hotel on West 57th Street where Gurdjieff was living proved sufficiently alarming. He was admitted to the

---

* Landau does not name either of the characters, but the man was probably Bragdon and the woman Zona Gale.

Master's shabby rooms by a young man with eyes which "glowed feverishly" and who gave the journalist the impression of "having just seen a ghost." The interview with Gurdjieff went badly. Landau was discomposed by having unwanted cigarettes pressed on him, and Gurdjieff clearly did not intend to answer his questions. Even worse, the journalist appeared to be falling under some "hypnotic influence" or "electric emanation" which deprived him of the power to move from his chair and gave him a feeling of "acute nervousness" in the pit of his stomach. Gurdjieff looked "the perfect Levantine, evasive in his answers, hyperbolical and anxious as to what effect he was producing." Released from his psychic disablement, Landau was sent home with a copy of *Herald of Coming Good*. After the encounter, he returned to his hotel where he "felt a strong desire to wash my hands. I washed them in very hot water for about five minutes, and then felt better. . . ."

Gurdjieff could not be washed away by soap and water. He might be temporarily cast down; his appearance might have deteriorated; but even at his seediest, a taste of the old mastery was still in evidence. Claude Bragdon caught a glimpse of him in early 1934 through the plate glass window of the Hecksher Building Childs Restaurant which Gurdjieff was then using as his New York "office." "He had grown fat," Bragdon wrote, "he looked untidy; time had turned his long, black ringmaster's moustache to grey; but he was unmistakably a personage, and the old, arrogant, undaunted look shone forth from his eyes."

Toomer's reaction to this mercurial Falstaff was confused. Perhaps what had appeared right and proper in the castle of the Great Magician seemed mean and petty in the United States. At all events, when he met Gurdjieff in New York in the spring of 1933, he was disconcerted. "He was in a bad way. His health was poor. He looked it, however, looked as if he had been through a mill. . . ." Gurdjieff's behavior was as appalling as his physical condition. It was unprincipled, unpleasant, and absurd. Toomer felt "a great relief when I left New York and thus left him. To me he seemed a changed man, changed for the worse. I felt his work was dead. Whether dead or not there was no place or function for me in it. It was a travesty and hollow mockery of the work I had entered in 1924 with all my heart. I would have nothing to do with what was going on at present. I would have something to do with future work—if there was a future work—on the critical basis as if I were meeting him and his work for the first time, taking nothing for granted."

During the summer of 1933, the scandalous rumors about Gurdjieff began to spread. Toomer recorded the speculations of some disillusioned disciples that Gurdjieff himself was out of control and smashing everything. "He seemed to be tearing down everything he had created," he wrote disconsolately. "His life seemed a blight, he was alienating people and throwing them off right and left. . . ." Yet he refused to condemn. He still possessed a legacy which he treasured in the form of the ideas and *Beelzebub's Tales*. He could not pass judgment on the man who had given him these; but he could stand aside. The lieutenant resolved not to bring any new recruits to his tricky general.

This resulted in an ironical state of affairs. Those whom Toomer himself had introduced to the ideas began to lecture their former teacher. "I found myself in the role of a student to my own former pupils who had now risen above me," he commented wryly, "because they saw and believed whereas I was blind and skeptical. The situation was not without its humor."

There was an obvious parallel to the dilemma which Gurdjieff had presented Orage two years earlier; and Toomer's resolution of the problem recalls the fate of his old friend and former teacher. Orage's establishment as the father of a family had helped to loosen the ties which bound him to Gurdjieff; and in early 1934, Toomer had moved to New York where he met Marjorie Content—one of the earliest partners in the Sunwise Turn—and the pair decided to marry. Toomer wrote to Gurdjieff requesting an interview. He explained that his "center of gravity" had first been in Gurdjieff's work, then in his first marriage. After this, he wrote, he had gravitated back into the Work; but now he proposed to marry again. He approached Gurdjieff in a valedictory mood, although he was still prepared to discover the old fascination.

At their first meeting Gurdjieff told him that he was leaving for France the next day. Toomer knew that he was short of money and gave him 200 dollars. Gurdjieff immediately began to work on him for more. They met again in Gurdjieff's apartment. Toomer found the rooms piled high with the normal rubble of Gurdjieffian living; it was clear that their occupant had not the slightest intention of leaving America for many weeks to come. Gurdjieff put pressure on his visitor for a sum of over 300 dollars, giving his "essence-word" that he would be paid back in four months' time, and that he would have "a place in his future creations." These tactics immediately reawakened all Toomer's distaste of the previous spring, and the reasons which had driven him away again became compelling.

What could be in the man's mind? Who and what was he? What were his purposes? What aims did he have for me, if any? What aims for the people of the world? Was I a mere tool? Was I not even that, so nothing from his point of view that he need not even consider the way he used or misused me? Was he the supreme egotist? Was he, as some claimed, insane? Did he, as some also claimed, know psychic laws but was essentially stupid in his practical dealing with people? If he knew anything at all about me, how could he fail to know that I was ready and willing to do all I possibly could as regards any real need of his that I could grasp and understand, whereas just these tricky manipulative tactics were sure to throw me off.

Or, on the other hand, was he, under the guise of this, to me, distasteful proposal, trying to do something for my good?

The sickening feeling of uncertainty allowed for no firm decisions. Perched on his fence, Toomer wavered now this way, now that.

This is what is so awful about the situation with G. The situations themselves are always taxing—and you can arrive at no sure reconciliation or fixed understanding because for every fact there is a counter-fact, for every reason a counter reason, for every bit of "bad" behavior another bit of "good" behavior, for every son-of-a-bitching thing a counter saintly thing.

All of a sudden his resistance collapsed. He felt that he himself was insignificant—so why not give the money? The Gurdjieff he now saw was in improved health, full of vitality, altogether a return to his former self.

Insane? He was in full possession of every one of his extraordinary faculties. Debauched and slovenly? Nothing of the sort. Afraid of the dark and being alone? It was ridiculous. Whatever he had gone through, the thing that showed plainly was a decided improvement in every respect.

Toomer admitted his bafflement over Gurdjieff's antics. He decided that some of the deceptions were so transparent that those who fell for them deserved no sympathy. "Why does he work in this way?" he asked. "Might as well ask the sphinx." But the sphinx had become a little more communicative, and as the result of answers Gurdjieff gave to his pupils' questions, it began to be rumored that he would begin a new phase of work on his "birthday," January 13. He had ended a phase of writing and recuperation which had begun with his accident in 1924. After the accident, said Gurdjieff, he had been compelled to "produce energy artificially." He announced expansively that he had consumed enough drink to fell ten men, and also forty pounds of opium. In order to restore his body, he said, he had been doing things which would make him suffer when he remembered them. Toomer's comment was that this explanation said nothing about "the benefits or distastes experienced by those others who were parties to his Gurdjieffian nights."

To Toomer, Gurdjieff became quite confidential, and the American plucked up courage to ask whether Gurdjieff remembered a time when he had promised to make him "ruler of Africa." Gurdjieff smiled: "Something went wrong," he said. Toomer's psyche was *African*. At this Toomer was puzzled, remembering that at different times Gurdjieff had told him that he was both English and American. He quizzed the Master again.

"You not as I counted," he said.
"How do you mean?"
"In the very beginning I counted you." I suppose he meant, "got my number." He went on, "You not as I counted."
"How do you mean?"
"You manifest differently at different times, different from what I expected. You not as I counted and I get angry."
"Angry? Why?"
"You not as I counted."

Gurdjieff remained in New York until the late spring of 1934, and Toomer was approached for more money on at least one other occasion. But despite his renewed affection for the Master, he was not back in the fold. Like Orage before him, he had a sense that he was up against a brick wall. In 1935 he was married and detached from his roots in Chicago. He wrote: "I have reached the limit of my possibilities for the present. I can do no more for myself in the way of having new experiences. In the immediate future I, myself, personally, do not exist." In 1936 he and his wife moved to Doylestown, Pennsylvania, and for a time, all contact with Gurdjieff and his pupils ceased. It should be said, however, that late in life Toomer returned to the fold, and that his last years were spent working with a Gurdjieff group.

By 1934 the Work in America was in a fragmented state. During the 1920s, it had seemed that the Master and his subordinates were determined to extend their activities at least among the few deemed capable of appreciating what they were up to. Now it began to seem that—since the break with Orage—everything that had been achieved had been sacrificed. In New York there was a divided group of perhaps fewer than thirty followers. Toomer no longer superintended affairs in Chicago, although a Chicago group continued to exist and Gurdjieff visited the town, trailing chaos in his wake, both in 1932–33 and in 1933–34. In various other American cities, there were small groups who remained interested in Gurdjieff's ideas. But the most impressive result of his influence had appeared in the work of another man, Frank Lloyd Wright.

The marriage of the distinguished architect to Olgivanna Hinzenberg in August 1928, resulted in a close relationship between the Lloyd Wrights and Gurdjieff. The couple had attended Toomer's Chicago groups, and Frank Lloyd Wright announced the foundation of his Taliesin Fellowship in 1932—the year in which Toomer left Chicago. The Fellowship was announced as teaching "essential architecture," and Gurdjieff was one of its first guests. Olgivanna Lloyd Wright's book, *The Struggle Within*, was not published until 1955, but the philosophy which it embodies, and which inspired the community from the start, derives quite obviously from Gurdjieff. "Our survival," she begins, "lies in the destruction of the false self." And from this precept flows the familiar ideas of suffering, conscious effort, and self-knowledge which she had imbibed from her master.

During the 1930s, Wright often accompanied his wife to Gurdjieff's table in New York or Paris, and Gurdjieff visited Taliesin several times. The relationship of the two men was one of mutual respect tinged with suspicion; Wright did not willingly play second fiddle to anyone. Yet he cooperated loyally during the Master's last visits to the United States. During the Second World War, Taliesin provided a congenial refuge for the de Hartmanns, the Notts, and other followers of Gurdjieff who fled Europe in the face of Hitler. Taliesin is still run according to Gurdjieffian principles. It was largely because she disagreed with these that Stalin's daughter Svetlana left the community after her flight to the United States.

The situation foreshadowed what was to emerge after the deaths of Gurdjieff and Ouspensky. The influence of the Work has often been most pervasive in the areas where it is least obvious—not in the groups or societies formed to perpetuate the ideas, but through more underground connections.

Gurdjieff had driven away the de Hartmanns, Orage, and most of his other close pupils. In America he behaved so badly that he reduced some of his former supporters to supporting a prosecution. And Ouspensky's pupils agreed that it was at about this time that their teacher ceased to keep a weather eye on Gurdjieff.

No one knew what Gurdjieff intended. Toomer was far from alone in his perplexity over the Master's future plans. Rom Landau tried to find out something in 1934 and was unsuccessful. He was told by a pupil of Gurdjieff's that many of his followers had been waiting for years for answers to such questions.

No one was even sure what had happened already. Gurdjieff was as isolated as a tight-rope walker who has ceased to believe in the tight-rope which supports him.

The view from Europe provides no simple answers. The main problems are posed by the sale of the Prieuré and the publication of *Herald of Coming Good*.

The sale of the Prieuré was a curious affair. It does not seem that mortgages were the primary cause, although Gurdjieff's long-term financial obligations were probably irredeemable. The immediate reason for the sale was a bill from the local coal merchant: Gurdjieff owed 200 or 300 francs. He had managed to avoid paying much greater bills and could no doubt have sidestepped this one. But it seemed that he had ceased to care: the bill remained unpaid, and the debt was bought by a Paris banker, who foreclosed. The Prieuré—with all its contents, including the furniture which had come with the original purchase from Mme. Laborie—was sold.

Gurdjieff appeared to have lost interest in his château. His apathy was so complete that his followers had to rescue trunks filled with musical manuscripts from under the noses of the auctioneers. Had he really been planning "work on a big scale" for the next year as Alexandre de Salzmann had told Nott? Had the Prieuré served its purpose and become a millstone round his neck? Or was the episode the result of that decline in Gurdjieff's energies which was so noticeable to his American supporters?

Nott was as depressed as Gurdjieff's American followers with the Master's physical condition. He found him irritable, silent, and morose. But as always, there are contradictions. It seems from Nott's account that Gurdjieff was quite aware he was ruining his health by eating too much fat, and he even had unflattering photographs taken which he stuck on packets of sweets and gave away. This supports the idea that, for reasons of his own, Gurdjieff had decided to place himself in as bad a light as possible, and at the same time, to make a clean break with the past phases of his activity.

But if we accept that he had deliberately allowed the Prieuré to slip from his grasp, we must explain away the fact that in 1934, the year after the sale, Gurdjieff was angling for a permanent base in America. He remembered Mabel Dodge Luhan's offer of 1926 and delegated Toomer to see whether her house in Taos was still available. On August 18, 1934, Toomer had to report that the chatelaine of Taos now showed no noticeable enthusiasm for the project. During the mid-1930s, Gurdjieff made at least one other attempt to tap the bank balance of a rich woman in order to reestablish himself in a large house. Did he regard the loss of the Prieuré in a serious light, or was this simply a stratagem to raise money? This question is crucial to the interpretation of that eccentric work, *Herald of Coming Good*.

This first published writing of Gurdjieff is dated from the Café de la Paix on January 13, 1933. It is subtitled, "First Appeal to Contemporary Humanity," and was priced at "from 8 to 108 French francs." The "good" which Gurdjieff announced to the world was the coming publication of the books on which he had been engaged over the past seven years, principally the (now completed) "First Series" known as *Beelzebub's Tales*, of which *Herald of Coming Good* included a synopsis. Appended to it were seven forms of registration on which the purchaser was supposed to write his name and address, how he had acquired the book, the particulars of whoever had recommended it to him, and the price he had elected to pay. The object of all this rigamarole was to give Gurdjieff some idea of the size of the audience he could expect for *Beelzebub's Tales* and to make sure he would reach the people who had already responded to his ideas. Unfortunately, there is no doubt that *Herald of Coming Good* was one of the factors which substantially reduced his prospective readership.

The style and the presentation were intimidating. The prose was, if anything, more rambling and less consequential than that of *Beelzebub's Tales*. Gurdjieff now had no Orage to structure his sentences for him, and an uninitiated reader like Rom Landau might well be forgiven for thinking that at best he had stumbled on the folly of a peculiar monomaniac. The little book was put together in haste, and its author had second, third, and fourth thoughts. A substantial section merely reproduces the English translation of the prospectus for the Institute for the Harmonious Development of Man. As well as the body of the text, there are two prefatory notes, a printed "circular letter," added after the book had gone to press, and a "supplementary announcement" tacked to the end.

The opening section of *Herald of Coming Good* contains the first information about himself which Gurdjieff made public. If the reader avoided becoming trapped in the oxbow lakes sometimes formed by Gurdjieff's sentences, he would have discovered a sketchy narrative of the author's search for knowledge in the East and his career as a professional hypnotist. This last piece of information caused great consternation when it became known among his followers; and it has often been insinuated that copies of *Herald of Coming Good* are rare as a result of a campaign to suppress this damaging evidence. Even more shocking to Gurdjieff's pupils was the admission that he regarded them as experimental animals. He stated bluntly that he had founded his Institute "for purely personal ends" and roundly abused the people who had supported him after his "accident." Coming in the midst of Gurdjieff's apparently most unscrupulous behavior, *Herald of Coming Good* seemed to confirm the worst suspicions of his disillusioned followers, and its appearance in the spring of 1933 coincided with the biggest exodus of his American pupils.

But if Gurdjieff were really the unprincipled cynic he seemed to be, why did he suddenly confess everything? It could be that he had tired of the game, that he proposed to let the illusion of his master dissolve altogether. It could also be that this was a deliberate shock gauged to "test" his followers. Or, may it have been simple misjudgment?

It is clear that at the time of his writing of *Herald of Coming Good*, Gurdjieff anticipated continued contact with his disciples. Apart from announcing the publication of *Beelzebub's Tales*, he provided an explanation of his idiosyncratic behavior—the story that for the past twenty-one years he had been living an artificial life in order to prevent his guinea pigs from idolizing him. "Believe me," he writes, "during the whole period of my relations with you, my inner world never harboured either egotistical or altruistic impulses." He also announced plans for the continuation of his work; but as for any perceptible effect on his followers, these might as well have remained unvoiced. Aside from the details of the plans, there were one or two indications that Gurdjieff himself did not share the exaggerated view of his abilities held by some of his pupils. He admitted to possessing "weaknesses" and referred to "undesirable manifestations of my nature." He also explained some of the principles of teaching and role playing upon which he claimed to have based his recent conduct.

Gurdjieff talks of a principle which he expresses in a single hyphenated sentence: "To-be-patient-towards-every-being-and-not-to-attempt-by-the-possibilities-in-our-power-to-alter-the-consequences-of-the-evil-deeds-of-our-neighbours." During the previous four months, he writes, he has tried to put this principle into practice himself and encouraged others to do the same. He chose three pupils for this experiment. One he influenced "by means of almost uninterrupted, kindly-intentioned persuasions and conscientious exhortations," the second "by threats of the terrible future awaiting him," and the third "by means of various hypnotic suggestions." During the same period, while maintaining his "inner benevolence" to the best of his ability, Gurdjieff writes that he set himself the task of quarreling "ruthlessly" with all actions inspired by people's vanity, but always "under a mask of serious irritation." Whether the three subjects he describes ever existed is questionable, for *Herald of Coming Good* is no freer from preposterous and unverifiable statements than any other of Gurdjieff's writings. But the three different techniques of manipulation are those Gurdjieff consistently employed: for one man the carrot, for another the stick, for a third hidden persuasion. Any of Gurdjieff's pupils might have found in *Herald of Coming Good* the keys to a dozen puzzling experiences.

If they had chosen to look, that is. For most of them did not. It is frightening to think that one has wasted a great deal of time entirely under the influence of a skillful puppet master and much more consoling to believe that one has been the dupe of the devil, or is immersed in a cosmic mystery of unfathomable proportions. The most significant fact about *Herald of Coming Good* is that it was ignored or rejected. Two attitudes were common: either Gurdjieff was seen as a phony of the most obnoxious sort or he was taken at face value, his every claim accepted. Whether he was thought to be a hero or a villain, the result for his followers was the same: oversimplification, stupefaction, and—as he would have said—"sleep."

Gurdjieff had given away his secret; and perhaps the reaction made him decide that his disclosures had been premature. In New York in 1934, only a year after publication, he was at work on an "Introduction" designed to replace the *Herald* and was recalling all unsold copies. Originally, he spent a lot of money on the production and hoped to market the book commercially, but later he simply gave it away. Nott and Elizabeth Gordon sent copies to all Ouspensky's pupils, and Ouspensky had it read to a gathering of his closest circle. The general opinion was that the tract was "almost paranoiac," and Ouspensky suggested that perhaps Gurdjieff had syphilis. All copies of *Herald of Coming Good* in England were rounded up and destroyed.

There is a widely believed story that Gurdjieff intended *Herald of Coming Good* to shock Ouspensky. This does not seem to go far enough. The booklet would have served as a "shock," not only to Ouspensky, but to other close followers whose dependence on him Gurdjieff had not been able to cure. By revealing his secrets Gurdjieff might have expected to encourage a proper comprehension of his ideas in those who were able to understand him—and to disembarrass himself of followers whose credulity passed all bounds.

Of course, it might have been a quite straightforward appeal. The "Supplementary Announcement" gives some support to this theory. It is dated March 7, 1933, from the Grand Café, Fontainebleau. Gurdjieff writes that this postscript is "evoked" by "the events of an economic, political and social character taking place in the past few weeks." At first sight this seems to mean that the economic and political crisis—which, for example, brought Hitler to power in Germany—had resulted in Gurdjieff's addressing an appeal to former members of the Institute. He announces that from June first, he proposes to reestablish the activities of the Institute as they had existed before his "accident" and to resume the life he had led before deciding to concentrate on writing. But it may be wondered whether Gurdjieff's notion of "economic and political crises" extended further than the coal bill and the mortgages on the Prieuré, and whether this last section of his odd pamphlet is not a simple appeal for money to save the château.

And of course *Herald of Coming Good* might have been simply a *jeu d'esprit*. Gurdjieff announced a new and improved Study House which he claimed was to be erected that April. It was to be equipped with the most splendid devices. There were to be three laboratories dealing with branches of science previously unknown on earth; "namely the 'magnetic-Astral,' the 'Thoughthanbledzoin,' and the 'Mentaloethero-winged.'" Two inventions of Gurdjieff were to be set up in the new building: the "Luminous Keyboard" and the "Retro-rebounding-Echoraising Organ." It is impossible to believe that Gurdjieff himself took these impressively titled inventions seriously, or that he expected others to do so. But, was there a purpose in these absurdities? If Gurdjieff had *Beelzebub's Tales* read aloud to his pupils and the meaning was too readily understood, he would alter the offending passage in the book, lengthen his already endless sentences, and conceal entirely the already obscure symbolism. "Must dig dog deeper," he would say; and his pupils would have to scrabble for the bone. Gurdjieff's literary work and his personal teaching were very similar. He would help a pupil toward a valuable insight, and then try to confuse the issue by talking nonsense for hours on end. In *Herald of Coming Good* he revealed some of his trade secrets—and then buried the bone under some obviously fraudulent claims about his invention of the "Luminous Keyboard."

Whether or not *Herald of Coming Good* had any significance for Gurdjieff's plans for the immediate future, it could not prevent the loss of the Prieuré. Gurdjieff retired to Paris, where he lived for a time in the Grand Hotel. The sale of the Prieuré and his trip to America in 1933–34 mark the end of a period of turmoil which had begun in 1929.

About the year 1930, Gurdjieff wrote a piece of music called "As if the difficult years had passed." Whether in his own estimation the difficult years were already over or were still to come, the 1930s were trying enough. The decade took permanently some of his closest companions.

Memento mori . . . people had begun to die. Alexandre de Salzmann died in 1933, Orage in 1934; and during the later 1930s, Gurdjieff's brother Dmitri and Leonid Stoerneval also died. Gurdjieff's personal circumstances were less favorable than at any time since his arrival in the West, and he seemed to have exhausted the energy which usually enabled him to rise above misfortune.

After the sale of the Prieuré he was more than ever dependent on his remaining American pupils. From midsummer 1933 until midsummer 1935, he spent most of his time in the United States. For six months he stayed with Fred Leighton—a wealthy adherent whose allegiance dated back to the Oragean groups of the mid-1920s—and made several efforts to reestablish himself in the style to which he had become accustomed during his occupancy of the Prieuré. It was during this period that Toomer approached Mabel Luhan on his behalf and, according to J. G. Bennett, a number of other attempts were made to find support for his plans. One project foundered when the plane carrying a senator on his way to meet Gurdjieff exploded in midair. Another was prevented by the refusal of the Soviet authorities to allow Gurdjieff to teach his System in the USSR. He sailed for Europe some time in the summer of 1935, apparently in a despondent state of mind; after a visit to Germany, he returned to Paris.

Bennett believed that between May and July 1935, Gurdjieff succeeded in returning to Central Asia. He produces no evidence to support this assertion, beyond his own recollection that toward the end of his life, Gurdjieff spoke of a trip he had made to Persia—which Bennett somehow associated with this stage in his career. But we know for certain only that he returned to Europe after his plans had apparently been frustrated at every turn.

In the late summer of 1935, Gurdjieff reappeared in Paris. For a time he lived in a flat in the Rue Marchand, then in one in the Rue Labis. In 1936 he moved to his best-known address at 6, Rue des Colonels Renard, in what was then the Russian quarter just north of the Etoile. He was more elusive than before, and traveled widely: to Vichy, where there lived a number of Russians who had formerly been at the Prieuré; to the hotels on the Riviera where he seemed to feel at home; to Normandy to visit the Stoernevals; also to Germany and the Low Countries. He kept in touch with the small number of followers left in New York and a few old pupils in England like C. S. Nott, who occasionally visited him in Paris. Elizabeth Gordon from the Prieuré remained with him; and a number of Americans, inspired by the teaching of Jane Heap, took the Master by storm. The Gurdjieff whom they knew was a man more obviously benevolent than his younger self. It was as if, having buried his bone hundreds of meters deep to confuse history, he allowed his followers closer to the larder than they had been for a decade.

The final number of *The Little Review* had symbolized a complete break with its editors' previous lives. It was a confession of faith in the Work; and, once committed Jane Heap in particular devoted the whole of her powerful energies to the cause. She became the intermediary between Gurdjieff and the expatriate community of Paris, and from as early as 1927, she supervised an "artist's group." In many ways she took over the function of Orage as the missionary to the intellectuals; and she came to occupy a place in the affections of her pupils not far removed from the niche reserved for her initiator. Margaret Anderson ranks her with Orage as the best "introducer" to the System, and it was largely Jane Heap's doing that Gurdjieff's "reputation loomed in Left Bank conversations" (to quote his follower Kathryn Hulme) "in a persistent hush-hush way, like a cloud enveloping a Jehovah."

From 1932 Jane Heap's group began to meet in a more regular fashion in her apartment in Montparnasse. It included Solita Solano and also Georgette Leblanc and Margaret Anderson, when they visited Paris. In *The Unknowable Gurdjieff* Margaret Anderson prints a series of aphorisms made by Jane Heap in her exposition of the Work, and these remain the only published records of her teaching. Kathryn Hulme—at that time writing her first two novels and acting as companion to a wealthy milliner who wanted to see Europe—was introduced to the group by Solita Solano with the claim that in the Montparnasse flat "the only important thing in Paris" was going on. The size of Jane Heap's group and the names of others who comprised it remains a mystery. Janet Flanner—author of the "Genet" columns for the *New Yorker* and translator of Georgette Leblanc's *Maeterlinck and I*—and Djuna Barnes—the author of *Nightwood*—were friends of *The Little Review* circle, and may possibly have been among her group. For just as the Prieuré had been part of "Paris in the Twenties" first Jane Heap, and then Gurdjieff himself, were part of "Paris in the Thirties": a Paris where the wine tasted a little sourer than in the previous decade; the Paris of *Nightwood*, which T. S. Eliot published in 1936, with an introduction hinting that the perversions of the novel's characters stood only for the wider situation.

Jane Heap—whose "personal magnetism was almost visible"—provided a sheet anchor for a number of displaced persons. In late October 1936, she left Paris for London on Gurdjieff's orders to begin teaching there. Her Paris group was left, as Kathryn Hulme writes, "high and dry"; she had always discouraged them from meeting Gurdjieff personally, on the grounds that his role playing would put them off the Work. But three or four of her stranded pupils, including Solano and Hulme herself, refused to be daunted, and bearded the Master in the Café de la Paix. Gradually, with the addition of Elizabeth Gordon, and later Margaret Anderson and Georgette Leblanc, this circle became a regular group under formal instruction from Gurdjieff. It was a group which Gurdjieff kept strictly to itself, a group composed of women of a certain type—literary, sophisticated, and single—whether divorced, deserted, unmarried, or frankly Lesbian. Casual visitors who asked to be allowed to join the Work were met with a blank refusal.

Kathryn Hulme in *Undiscovered Country* and Margaret Anderson in *The Fiery Fountains* have both described the Gurdjieff of 1936–38. The Master who emerges is essentially a kind and charitable man. He could be terrible: raging at his pupils for some fault real or imaginary; exacting; giving them strenuous exercises for the development of their "inner worlds"; or contradictory in familiar fashion. But an atmosphere of mellowness surrounds him—as if the difficult years had indeed passed. He was no longer the grasping entrepreneur, but the charitable man, consoling the lonely women for what was lacking in their lives; no longer the ogre, but the man known as "Monsieur Bonbon" from his habit of giving away sweets to shop assistants, lift boys, and casual passersby. His hospitality was as extravagant as ever, his charity overstepped the bounds of his pupils and friends, and gradually the walls of his flat began to fill with oil paintings of all sorts—

most of them excruciatingly bad—which he bought in order to keep the artists alive. Until the end of his life, the traffic of pupils and patients in and out of his apartment was swollen by those to whom he referred as "mes parasites."

If he was more genial, he was also more straightforward than before. It may be that the records of this period are written by people who were in particularly close contact with him, but the Gurdjieff of their accounts is less confusing and more paternal: he gave direct instructions for performing exercises—for example, with rosaries such as the ones "Ushe Narzunoff" is holding in his photograph; he was concerned less with the intricacies of cosmology—he had abandoned his writing for good—and more with practical instruction. There were still the familiar, enormous, and taxing lunches with the traditional idiot toasts. The same extraordinary ability to assess psychological states was brought into play as Gurdjieff christened his pupils with animal names, names which he said expressed their "inner natures." Once more the hair-raising motor expeditions set off for Vichy or the South Coast—where in Monte Carlo Gurdjieff gave all his "children" money and sent them off to play at the Casino. In the Rue des Colonels Renard, his eccentric scheme of decoration, his Oriental cooking, and his perpetually shuttered windows plucked his pupils from the heart of Paris into another world.

At about the same time that Jane Heap's group of Americans began to meet regularly in her apartment in Montparnasse, the Work at long last began to penetrate the Parisian intelligentsia. This was the responsibility of Alexandre and Jeanne de Salzmann.

The group which Alexandre de Salzmann gathered round him in 1932 was the second which he and his wife brought to Gurdjieff. About 1928 the de Salzmanns visited Alphons Paquet in Frankfurt, and together with Louisa Goepfert, they began group readings from *Beelzebub's Tales* in the Paquet household. Paquet himself visited Gurdjieff only once, shortly before the closure of the Prieuré; but in the autumn of 1932, his wife and one of his daughters came to Paris to study with the Master.

In his turn, Gurdjieff visited Germany on several occasions. Paquet's daughter, Frau Henriette Klingmüller, remembers his first appearance in Frankfurt, when all her sisters were tipped by Gurdjieff—but she herself left out. "You not necessarily money," remarked the Master, "you my godchild"; and proceeded to concern himself especially with his goddaughter whose dowry he apparently withheld.

Apart from the Frankfurt group, de Salzmann's services were rendered chiefly at the Prieuré. As the life of the Institute ran down, de Salzmann left Fontainebleau and went to live in Paris, where he at first made his living by interior decorating, then went to work for an antique dealer. The group which collected round him in the two years before his death in 1933 arrived largely by accident.

The literary-philosophical group known as the Grand Jeu originated in the friendship of four Rheims schoolboys, René Daumal, Roger-Gilbert Lecomte, Roger Vailland, and Robert Meyrat. All except Daumal—the youngest by a year—were born in 1907. They became bored and world-weary at a precociously early age. They called themselves the "Phrères simplistes," cultivated a morbid sense of humor, and experimented with alcohol and the occult.

By 1927 the group were living in Paris and had made contact with kindred spirits. The enlarged circle decided to publish a review. This was called *Le Grand Jeu*—but significantly, it had originally been entitled *La Voie*. "We believe in all miracles," proclaimed the manifesto. "Attitude: one must enter into a state of complete receptivity, be pure in order to do this, having created a void within oneself. *From this stems our ideal wish to place everything in question at every moment. . . .* We do not accept because we no longer understand anything." The signatories of the manifesto sought the "eternal moments" which nourished the spirit. "It is in such moments that we absorb everything, that we swallow God so as to become transparent enough to disappear."

By the end of 1930, the Grand Jeu was in a state of decay. Vailland and Lecomte were continually in and out of the hospital; the Surrealists had finally withdrawn the hand of friendship; and there was a conflict between a left-wing political element and the esotericists within the group. Daumal himself was living in poverty, drifting from place to place, beginning to lose his teeth, and taking to his bed. He later admitted that he was "close to madness and death." At this critical point, he was introduced to Alexander de Salzmann.

The intermediary was the Czech artist Josef Sima, who was one of the signatories to the *Grand Jeu* manifesto. One evening, after a meeting of the Grand Jeu at Sima's, the group encountered de Salzmann in his usual café on the Boulevard St. Germain. The artist always sat alone, smoking from a long cigarette holder, drinking a mixture of calvados and beer—of which he would consume perhaps a dozen glasses each evening. His hands would be occupied with a pencil—continuously designing what looked like Oriental calligraphy. Daumal was bowled over, and de Salzmann came to seem—in the words of the poet's biographer, Michel Random—"the man who could save everything." De Salzmann's puckish sense of humor evidently influenced his relationship with the younger man—and Daumal wrote enthusiastically that the artist was "a former dervish, former Benedictine, former professor of jiu-jitsu, healer, stage-designer, not a tooth left in his head, an incredible man." "We no longer understand anything," the *Grand Jeu* manifesto had declared. In contrast, for Daumal, de Salzmann was the Man Who Knows. Other members of the Grand Jeu were less sure of the Russian's omniscience, and Daumal reproached a friend for his lack of perception; "You still have only the reflection of a shadow of a vague feeling of the *Personage* he is. I look forward (wrongly) to witnessing the moment at which you realise this. But it is certain that you will find him on your way— as if by chance—the very day on which you need him. . . ."

The advent of de Salzmann hastened the breakup of the Grand Jeu. This finally came about at the beginning of 1932, when the political and mystical wings of the group clashed over the question of militarism. By this time, René Daumal was living with Vera Milanova, the young Russian whom he subsequently married; together the couple spent entire nights discussing the Work with de Salzmann. In 1932 Vera traveled to the United States and Daumal took a job as a press agent to the Indian dancer Uday Shankar in order to tour America with his troupe. In New York he composed *La Grande Beuverie* ("The Great Drunk") as his farewell to the complicated literary and occult world of the Grand Jeu. It comprises a denunciation of the ordinary apparatus of communication; a description of the "artificial paradises" created by those who see through such illusions; and a recommendation of a superior world of reality. This is the world of the awakened man of the Work, and it is not to be gained without a struggle. The agent of this struggle is the Master Totochabo—perhaps de Salzmann, perhaps what Daumal had heard of Gurdjieff from de Salzmann—who appears with the familiar message: *"There is a way out."*

In 1933 Alexander de Salzmann died of tuberculosis. The Prieuré had not yet been sold, but he was living in a hotel in Fontainebleau. He was quite alone, and Gurdjieff refused to visit him. One of the inmates of the Prieuré used to call on him in the evenings with presents—halva and other delicacies—smuggled out from Gurdjieff's table. De Salzmann lay in a darkened room, his skin a bluish-gray. He was clearly dying, but still Gurdjieff would not come to see him. Eventually, the sick man summoned up the strength to rise from his bed and sought out Gurdjieff in the Café Henri IV. The pupil who had brought him halva was sitting at the next table, and it seemed to her that Gurdjieff was "not very kind" to the man who had made such an effort to see him. A few days after the interview, de Salzmann died. It is said—but also vehemently denied—that his last words were: "I'll know on the other side whether he's a Master or a demon."

Gurdjieff's apparent cruelty may have conveyed something to de Salzmann which is closed to outsiders, but to an outsider it cannot seem that he acted in a particularly admirable fashion. What passed between the two men is unknown; but the incident must remain one of the blackest marks against the Gurdjieff of "the difficult years." Neither is it known what effect the death of the Man Who Knows had on René and Vera Daumal; for by 1933, their loyalty had passed beyond devotion to a man and become devotion to a teaching.

On their return to France from the United States, they settled down in Paris, where Daumal worked on the *Encyclopédie Française* and achieved some fame in 1936 with the publication of his volume of poetry, *Le Contre-Ciel*. In 1935 they visited Geneva to work with Mme. de Salzmann, accompanied by the Orientalist Philippe Lavastine—at that time a publisher and the first French recruit to the Work from outside Daumal's immediate circle. But from 1934 until the outbreak of the war, the headquarters of the new group which formed around Mme. de Salzmann was in Sèvres.

The house at Sèvres, writes Jean Biès, "reproduced in miniature the Prieuré of Avon." The building stood in the middle of a derelict park and contained a large room for the movements and semi-permanent quarters for Mme. de Salzmann, Daumal, and Lavastine. Every evening the Daumals would travel out from Paris to take part in movements classes—which lasted far into the night, like Gurdjieff's at the Prieuré. There were readings from the chapters of *Beelzebub's Tales* which had been translated into French; there was housework; and on weekends the house filled with visitors. According to Biès, the group began to disintegrate about 1937, although it did not finally break up until two years later.

When the Sèvres group had been established for some time, Gurdjieff reappeared in Paris, and Mme. de Salzmann began to bring her pupils to him. Gurdjieff sat—a Caucasian minotaur—at the center of a labyrinth of initiations. Pupils approached him through "exoteric," "mesoteric," and "esoteric" groups. The favored, like Daumal and Lavastine, were sometimes invited to meals at the flat in the Rue des Colonels Renard. By the outbreak of war the pattern of future activities had become established: a pupil would be introduced to the Work by Mme. de Salzmann, and only after some months—or even years—might be selected to meet the Master himself. It was an external form for an idea which animated each pupil, however he or she expressed it: that gradually they were penetrating to the center of the secrets of the universe.

Later, Daumal constructed an allegory of this spiritual progress in his most famous work, *Mount Analogue*, which he did not live to complete. *Mount Analogue* is described as "a novel of symbolically non-Euclidean adventures in mountain climbing," and in its allegorical and elliptical style, there are frequent traces of Daumal the 'pataphysician. The book is dedicated to Alexander de Salzmann, who may be portrayed under the name of Pierre Sogol (Sogol = Logos), a "Professor of Mountaineering." In the story, Sogol assembles a band of would-be mountaineers to climb Mount Analogue, which stands on an island hidden from observation by the curvature of space. "Everything takes place as if Mount Analogue did not exist." In order to reach the island "one must assume the possibility and even the *necessity* of reaching it."

The 'pataphysics with which Sogol "reasons" himself and his team on to the island are expertly deployed; and the characters of the various mountaineers are described in the same tradition. The rewards of climbing Mount Analogue are represented in "peradams," precious and almost invisible pieces of crystal. Clearly they are spiritual rewards, and for that reason indefinable—except in allegorical terms. But what if Daumal had all along been deluding himself? What if there were no peradams—no bone beneath the mountain at all?

If Sogol does represent de Salzmann, and not some more abstract figure—say a composite of Gurdjieff and de Salzmann, or simply an archetype of the Work teacher—the beginning of *Mount Analogue* provides some interesting indications of how the painter might have become estranged from Gurdjieff. Sogol tells his prospective pupil that he had yearned for "something more" in life and that at one stage he thought that he had found this in religion. He "entered a monastery; a very strange one . . . it belonged to a distinctly heretical order." Every day one of the brothers was selected—unknown to the others—to play the role of the Tempter. "One thing proves to me," Sogol says, "the diabolical nature of this custom: not one of the brothers ever refused to accept the role of Tempter. . . . The Tempter was himself the victim of a monstrous temptation." Sogol is persuaded by a Tempter to design machines for waking people up; but when he himself becomes Tempter, he realizes the childishness of his inventions and the ignominy of his role in the monastery. He goes to the Superior and tells him that he can no longer play the devil: "He spoke to me with mild severity, perhaps sincere, perhaps professional. 'My son,' he concluded, 'I see that there is in you an incurable *need to understand*, which must prevent you from remaining any longer in this house. We shall pray God to call you to him by other paths.'"

Might this not, in the language of *Mount Analogue*, be Daumal's record of how de Salzmann parted from Gurdjieff? If so it does not seem that the artist's difference of opinion with his Master was over much more than methods. But if the quarrel was a more serious affair, it is ironic that it was through de Salzmann, and afterward through his wife, that Gurdjieff was left with any pupils at all.

Gurdjieff—at least in the opinion of one person who knew him well during the late 1920s and early 1930s—was growing old and tired; and he certainly had little inclination to proselytize for himself. After the United

States entered the Second World War, the group which included Kathryn Hulme and Margaret Anderson scattered to the four winds. Elizabeth Gordon remained in Paris until she was interned by the invading Germans. Jane Heap, in England, was as cut off from Paris as if she had been in New York. According to Nott, Gurdjieff had made plans to visit Lyne Place, in an attempt to cure Mme. Ouspensky of her illness. But the outbreak of hostilities prevented all contact with his followers abroad. On the other hand, the disastrous course of the fighting in France helped to turn the minds of French intellectuals to things of the spirit. It was through the group which formed around Daumal and Lavastine that pupils were led to Mme. de Salzmann, and then to the old magician of the quartier du Ternes. Wartime conditions once more acted—in Ouspensky's words—as "a gigantic *memento mori*"—a reminder that time was always running out.

13

The Strange Death of Pyötr Ouspensky

The time of the Munich crisis must have presented a familiar sensation to Ouspensky. It was almost as if events were repeating, and repeating, and the cycle of recurrence could not be broken. When several intellectuals—including Aldous Huxley, W. H. Auden, and Christopher Isherwood—made emigration fashionable around 1938, Ouspensky resisted the persuasion of his supporters to follow suit. You could be too clever, he said, in anticipating political events. He had in any case his own theory of what might happen. If England and France declared war on Soviet Russia, who by the Pact of Steel had revealed herself as Germany's ally, everything would be over within a year. Neither did he like the idea of behaving like a rat leaving a sinking ship. He quite obviously enjoyed his way of life in England, and his stoicism in the face of physical dangers was in marked contrast to that of his wife. When the first air raid sirens blew over Virginia Water, she made precipitately for the cellars and needed no inducement to leave for America.

But for all his reluctance, Ouspensky again found himself overtaken by "events." The sensitiveness to official disapproval which he shared with Gurdjieff had to withstand constant exposure. Although he probably did not know it, from 1937 he was under Home Office surveillance, and after the German attack on Russia his position as an anti-Bolshevik Russian made him potentially suspect of treasonable activities. In fact, he narrowly avoided being interned and had to live permanently at Lyne when the flat at Gwendwr Road was totally destroyed by a bomb.

So it was that, just as the effects of Ouspensky's decision to expand began to make themselves felt in increased interest in his teaching, events conspired to prevent any real exploitation of these gains. Insecurity created a situation very like the early days of Ouspensky's own contact with Gurdjieff, and gradually even the questions at his meetings became devoted to the problems of war. Could war be stopped? he was asked. Ouspensky repeated what he had been told by Gurdjieff in 1915. Man can *do* nothing. Everything *happens*. To people who were convinced that the war was a simple case of right and wrong, he answered that there was no question of this, but that they had seen only a fraction of the truth. Hitler was the necessary outcome of the failure of the West to stop Bolshevism in Russia. Both Fascism and Communism were "criminal" parties. He recalled how, when he had returned to St. Petersburg on the outbreak of the First World War, everyone had been concerned with what they would do when the fighting ended. But an end to hostilities had not meant that the war was over.

Gradually, his bitter anger against the Bolsheviks developed into a pessimism which saw Europe being engulfed by "criminal elements," even if the Allies should win. His ideas seemed, if anything, to have hardened since 1919, and doubtless the memory of past hardships rose to the surface of his mind. Bolshevism had always existed everywhere in different forms, he proclaimed, sweeping Herriot, Daladier, Blum, H. G. Wells, Bernard Shaw, and the Labour Party into one cosmic incinerator. He defined Bolshevism as essentially a will to use violent methods to compel other people to accept one's ideas. Ouspensky's abhorrence of violence and his fear of a society dominated by "criminals" and Sudras combined with the disruptive effects of the war to force him inexorably toward America.

On January 4, 1941, Mme. Ouspensky left for the United States. J. G. Bennett's wife was one of the farewell party at the station, and returned depressed by the total dependence exhibited by "Madam's people" on their teacher. Then on January twenty-fifth, Ouspensky announced his own departure. He told his assembled pupils that he could do nothing more in England; the outbreak of war had finally put an end to the possibilities of continuing. He compared conditions to those he had experienced in the Caucasus. Quite possibly they were witnessing the end of one particular historical period and the beginning of another.

Although they must have expected it, the announcement hit his followers like a physical blow. The record of the farewell meeting shows how hard they found it to accept the idea of taking any individual initiative. Ouspensky told them that they must try to maintain both Lyne Place and

Colet Gardens; if they could keep up some level of activity under wartime conditions, this would in itself be a useful exercise. He would keep in contact by letter and might send them some material to read. If they wanted to engage in any personal work, he advised them to try "stopping thoughts." It was little help to the lost sheep he was leaving behind.

Mme. Ouspensky had equipped Lyne Place so that when the war broke out as many families as possible could be evacuated from central London; and under the direction of a couple who had joined Ouspensky in 1924, a small community assembled to wait out the war. At much the same time, Maurice Nicoll's followers were evacuated to Gloucestershire from their farm in Essex. In London, J. G. Bennett and Kenneth Walker continued to hold small groups to discuss the System. But to all intents and purposes— and with the exception of the Nicoll household in Gloucestershire—the departure of the Ouspenskys left a vacuum in England.

Some of Ouspensky's followers began maneuvering for jobs which would allow them to follow their teacher to America. Ouspensky's directorate was split between the emigrants and those who stayed at home. Besides Walker, Bennett, and the couple who had taken charge of Lyne, the home guard included Dr. Francis Roles. The disciples who succeeded in finding jobs in America included Lord Pentland, the journalist who sometimes deputized for Ouspensky, and a comparatively new recruit to the circle at Lyne Place named Rodney Collin-Smith, better known under his pen name of Rodney Collin.

Rodney Collin was born in Brighton in 1909, the eldest son of a retired wine importer. During childhood he became an omnivorous reader. At the age of eighteen, he spent several months walking in Andalusia and gathered the material for a book of travel sketches published in 1931 under the title of *Palms and Patios*. During the three years he spent at the London School of Economics, he began to write for newspapers, and when he graduated, he became a freelance writer. He founded *The Rucksack,* the journal of the Youth Hostels Association of which he was secretary, and worked for the *Toc H Journal*. On a pilgrimage organized by Toc H in 1930 to attend the Passion Play at Oberammergau, he met his future wife, Janet Buckley, who was eight years older than he.

Although they did not marry until 1934, this meeting seems to have marked an alteration in Rodney Collin-Smith's interests. All his loves seem to have been idealistic; his involvement with Toc H and the Youth Hostels movement gave place to a devotion to the Peace Pledge Union and its *Peace News;* and in 1932 he contributed an article to *The Aryan Path* appealing in a very Ouspenskian fashion for a sane world government by a spiritual aristocracy. This probably means that he had come in touch with the Theosophical wing of the Peace Pledge Union—of which J. D. Beresford was a member—and it is certain that it was a member of the P.P.U. who introduced the Collin-Smiths to Ouspensky's lectures in the autumn of 1936. The previous year they had attended several lectures given by Maurice Nicoll, which had not roused in them any particular enthusiasm. But from the time of their meeting with Ouspensky, both husband and wife devoted themselves entirely to the Work.

They bought a house at Virginia Water in order to be close to Lyne Place. Janet Collin-Smith worked in the house, and her husband returned to work in the gardens at Lyne during the evenings. He spent his spare time in the British Museum studying the history of psychological systems on the lines worked out in the program of the Historico-Psychological Society. At Lyne he developed a taste for "super-effort" in Gurdjieff's sense; and this was to color his later application of the ideas which he learned from Ouspensky. "Rodney had a leaning towards effort, struggle and self-discipline," writes his sister-in-law, the novelist Joyce Collin-Smith. "He was by nature a school man and he took to the Fourth Way teaching with enthusiasm. . . ."

When the war came, his wife traveled with Mme. Ouspensky to the United States. At first the group took a series of temporary houses in New York, and for a time based themselves at Rumson on the New Jersey coast. Then, with the help of Schuyler Jackson and other former Orageans who had already scoured New Jersey to find a refuge for Gurdjieff, a substitute for Lyne was found. Eventually Franklin Farms at Mendham—a former residence of the Governor of New Jersey—was bought, largely out of money provided by Janet Collin-Smith. Her husband secured a job on the British Purchasing Commission, which sent him to Bermuda and Mexico before finally producing, about 1942–45, the hoped-for transfer to New York. Collin joined his wife and the daughter who had been born in 1937 at Mendham and began again the routine of commuting to his office and returning to work in the gardens of the community.

He was still very much a junior member of Ouspensky's circle, although chance had given him an opportunity to approach his teacher more closely than he would otherwise have done. By a coincidence, both he and Ouspensky traveled from Liverpool to New York on the *Georgic*. Because the ship had to zigzag to avoid U-boats, the voyage was longer than usual, and the young man came to know Ouspensky moderately well during the passage. However, for some time after his arrival at Franklin Farms, Collin was shy of presuming too much on this acquaintance. Frequently, his office work combined with the physical labor of gardening wore him out so that he felt incapable of attending Ouspensky's evening lectures in New York. "He normally lay awake," writes his sister-in-law, "until the lights of the returning car swung into the long drive. Ouspensky would then go into the big kitchen and sit drinking wine and talking philosophy until the early hours." Then, one night Collin realized that his lassitude was not simply the result of physical exhaustion:

> I jumped out of bed and flung on my dressing gown . . . and with the cord trailing behind me, I ran downstairs in a way quite contrary to the controlled discipline of the household. Before my courage failed me, I flung open the kitchen door. I expected to see a number of people more important than myself, sitting at the long table. Instead, "O" was alone, drinking wine. Before I could stop myself I shouted at him loudly: "Why am I afraid of you?" He looked at me calmly and answered: "Why did you say 'I'?"

There are two interpretations of the subsequent rapproachment between the two men. One, which emanates more or less from Ouspensky's directorate, maintains that Rodney Collin took advantage of the circumstances which thrust him into Ouspensky's company from the time they sailed together on the *Georgic* and that the apparently close relationship which grew up between them was unwished for by Ouspensky. The other holds that as a result of the incident in the Kitchen at Franklin Farms— which, as Joyce Collin-Smith writes, Rodney Collin "looked back on . . . as a time of revelation"—Ouspensky began to take particular note of his young follower. "Thereafter he gradually drew Rodney nearer himself, as his chauffeur, personal attendant and intimate pupil. Ultimately almost as his son." The truth may lie somewhere in between the two versions, and— predictably—on the truth may depend yet further conflicting possibilities. What is indisputable is that Rodney Collin saw a great deal of Ouspensky. His own view of the developing relationship is given in a biographical note, probably based on information provided by his wife:

> . . . he spent more and more time with Mr. Ouspensky, driving him to and from New York for his meetings and usually spending the evening with him in a restaurant or in his study at Franklin Farms. He became deeply attached to Mr. Ouspensky in a way that included without being limited by, personal affection and respect. While formerly he had concentrated on Mr. Ouspensky's teaching, it was now the teacher and what he was demonstrating which occupied Rodney's attention.

As the wording of this note implies, the Ouspensky who arrived in America was a little more accessible, a little less the magisterial source of wisdom of whom everyone in England stood in awe. Partly this was because he was in the United States (Russians are crows, Gurdjieff remarked about his supporters, English sheep, and Americans burros), and the role which he had to play was different. Partly there may have been a sense of relief at escaping from his large organization.

In America Ouspensky had his own reputation apart from any association with Gurdjieff. *Tertium Organum* still lingered in the minds, and in the libraries, of a whole generation of intellectuals. In an article which appeared in the *South Atlantic Quarterly* in October 1941, nicely timed to coincide with the beginning of Ouspensky's lectures in New York, Sarah Newmayer described how *Tertium Organum* had provided a rational justification for her belief in immortality. She recommended the book "to all those who . . . must bring even the hope of immortality to the bar of reason"; a powerful argument in time of war. Also, the *New Model* had been received more sympathetically in the United States. But on the one hand, Ouspensky was meeting less reverent questioners—like the one soon after his arrival who asked what evidence there was that a cat really did have an astral body (to which Ouspensky answered unconcernedly that it all had to do with the connection of centers)—and on the other, there was some trouble with former supporters of Orage.

C. S. Nott had also emigrated from England and set about collecting Orageans for Ouspensky's lectures. Both the Ouspenskys banned any mention of *Beelzebub's Tales*—THE BOOK with which both Gurdjieff and Orage were identified in New York. And there were times when Orage's teaching clashed directly with what Ouspensky now taught. For example, in mid-July 1941, Ouspensky was faced with a question which centered round Orage's dictum that "individuality is consciousness of will." He replied that this was a mere form of words unrelated to what Gurdjieff had said. The remark was Orage's alone; and Orage had forgotten a lot and had had to make things up.

Ouspensky arrived in New York in March 1941, and his lectures seem to have begun that summer. They took place in a studio in an apartment house on 78th Street between Lexington and Third Avenues where the incessant noise from the Third Avenue El provided a jarring accompaniment to Ouspensky's heavily accented voice. His audiences numbered between thirty and fifty; but he found great difficulty in collecting a permanent group of followers. In the first year perhaps only half a dozen lasted the course.

Gradually the Ouspenskys' activities once more expanded. In late 1942, Franklin Farms was acquired, and Ouspensky began to select people from his audience to spend weekends at Mendham. The pattern of life at Lyne was reproduced, with farmwork and housework for the pupils. Gurdjieff's movements were taught by two former colleagues of Orage. Even the magnificence of the dinners at Lyne was translated to the New World, and a party for Mme. Ouspensky's name-day would see all the guests in formal evening dress. As in England, there was a definite split between "Mr.

Ouspensky's people" and "Madam's people"; and once more, Ouspensky seems only with reluctance to have accepted his wife's insistence on a large organization. At Mendham, he kept to himself and did not even appear for the meals at which his wife would apply the lash of her tongue to selected victims. One of her pupils, who also met Gurdjieff, has remarked on the similarity between Mme. Ouspensky and her Master:

> I can still feel the sensation that crept along my spine when I heard Madam approaching, her cane announcing her as she came closer and closer to the terrace of the dining room. Although small in stature, she looked and towered above us all through the sheer strength and poise that radiated from her presence. When she reached the long narrow tables at which we sat, everyone remained motionless, eyes glued to one spot, simultaneously wishing to draw her attention and yet to become invisible to her.

To some of those who were closer to the milder and more sinuous approach of her husband, Mme. Ouspensky appeared as a terrible and vengeful mother. In America the contrast between her ferocity and Ouspensky's "elegance and eloquence" as a human being became increasingly marked. One pupil, who used to dine on prawns with Ouspensky in one of the Longchamps restaurants, remembers him chiefly not as a teacher, but as a gracious host, a kind and feeling person, of "infinite charm." "There was a refinement and a lovely decency about him." In contrast, Sophia Grigorievna appeared to be a dark manipulator of occult forces, and Ouspensky's own "innocent" disposition seemed "bewildered and terrified" by his wife. His dining companion of the war years recalls "a man still in search" of something he had not found: "He died in sadness."

As he grew older, Ouspensky withdrew more and more from human contact. He would sit for hours with a few of his pupils, drinking wine in total silence. Some pupils considered this a teaching gambit; but it could as well be seen as the watch spring running down. And Ouspensky's calm was broken by outbursts of a frustration which had been mounting since before he left England. He had been very gloomy during his last months at Lyne, questioning whether he would ever make contact with the elusive "Inner Circle." On one occasion when his step-daughter was very depressed, she asked him for advice. Ouspensky shouted at her, "Pray, Lenotchka, pray!" If he had begun to believe that his own objective—the attainment of the higher consciousness which he had so restlessly pursued in Russia—was unattainable, prayer may have come to seem the only way out.

Nott used to visit him during the war in his New York apartment. He found that Ouspensky's drinking had become even heavier: ". . . he was drinking strong concoctions that I could not take. 'You must have a stomach of iron,' I said one day when he offered me one of them. 'It's too strong for me.' He said, 'It's the only thing that relieves the boredom and depression that comes over me at times.'"

A new printing of *A New Model of the Universe* appeared with a publisher's notice stating that Ouspensky was working with Gurdjieff in a community near London. Ouspensky was furious and wanted to withdraw the book or give a press conference to correct the false impression. His outbursts of temper became more frequent, and a challenge to his position in England by J. G. Bennett did not improve matters. In 1941 Bennett and some of his pupils spent a holiday in the Welsh mountains where Bennett had undergone a series of visionary experiences. These seemed to him to reveal the secrets of universal order, and he began to explain the visions to his group, making use of the terminology of the System. Reports of this reached Ouspensky in America, and a letter of May 1942 reminded Bennett of the rule that no one was to write anything without permission. Ouspensky forbade public use of the System and disparaged Bennett's speculations in multidimensional mathematics. "He then went on to say," Bennett writes, "that nothing new can be found by intellectual processes alone, and that there is only one hope: that we should find the way to work with the higher emotional centre. To this he added the sad comment: 'And we do not know how this is to be done.'"

Reverberations of this quarrel reached New York. People who attended Ouspensky's meetings heard loud condemnations of Bennett's plagiarism and perfidy. Ouspensky's suspicions were fanned by distance, and as Bennett continued to follow his own line, the reports from those in England who were content merely to wait for their Master's return made matters worse. The climax of the quarrel came in the middle of 1945, when Bennett was unable to contain his frustration at the lack of initiative shown by the guardians of Lyne Place, and positively invited repudiation by giving a series of public lectures on the System to a large audience. At Ouspensky's command he was summoned to Lyne, where the senior members of the directorate took him to task. He then received a letter from Ouspensky's solicitor demanding that he return all the material—in the form of lectures and manuscripts—which he had received from Ouspensky. The Lyne contingent were forbidden to have any contact with him on any subject whatsoever.

This seems the act of a failing and jealous man, even though it is quite clear that Bennett had transgressed. But was he the plagiarist and "thief" whom Ouspensky vilified in New York? In Bennett's protest against the stagnant attitude adopted by the orthodox lies the germ of conflict between those who were to struggle during the next ten years to "keep the System pure" and those like Bennett who saw the material they had been given as incomplete and demanded the right to supplement it. This shows more clearly than anything that Ouspensky's presentation encouraged at least two views as to the nature of the System. Orage saw a Method at the root of the teaching. Ouspensky saw a System; but systems can either be ends in themselves or foundations for new and improved systems: true pictures of the world or means to attaining a true picture. It is always possible that Ouspensky was taking steps to ensure that Bennett struck out on his own. In *Witness*, Bennett describes several occasions when he was told by Mme. Ouspensky that he must try to be more himself; that in his work with his group he was not to imitate his teacher's methods. It is not outside the bounds of possibility that this was the sort of dismissal received by Maurice Nicoll.

There is also the possibility that Ouspensky was what he appeared to be: an old and disillusioned man, suffering from insecurity and illness. But what are we to make of this semblance of age and disappointment? Near the end of the war the couple who had superintended the community at Lyne made their way to Mendham against innumerable difficulties. They found Ouspensky disabled "as if by a stroke" and "a sort of prisoner" at Franklin Farms. He told the husband that he had little time left to live. He was to return to England, derequisition Colet Gardens from the Navy who had occupied the building, and restore it as quickly as possible in preparation for Ouspensky's arrival. There were considerable obstacles in the way of this project; but, to the accompaniment of incessant complaints from Ouspensky that the task was taking too long, it was eventually carried out.

Ouspensky gave his last lectures in New York in the summer of 1946, and announced to his followers—who by this time numbered about sixty—that he was returning to England. Those who went to Mendham would be taught by Mme. Ouspensky, but the others would have to "find their own bearings." The effect on his pupils was cataclysmic; several ambled aimlessly from philosophy to philosophy until finally coming to rest with the remaining New York followers of Gurdjieff. From evidence of the pupil who was directed to restore Colet Gardens, it is clear that Ouspensky's return was long premeditated and part of a deliberately conceived plan. But there are other rumors that he decided to base himself in Britain because his wife had invited Gurdjieff to Mendham; and if she had done so, Ouspensky's reaction would have been consistent with his decision in 1922 that if Gurdjieff settled in London, he would go to Paris or the United States.

Ouspensky landed in England in January 1947. His state of health profoundly shocked his closer disciples. They had heard that he was ill, then that he was better again. Kenneth Walker saw him as "aged" many years, "both in mind and in body, and there were other changes in him as well. . . . It was . . . obvious to us that Ouspensky would be unlikely to be able to carry out whatever he intended to do . . . he appeared to me to be a man who had lost all of his former enthusiasm and drive." The nature of Ouspensky's illness was not known at the time, as he refused to submit to treatment; but it was in fact a form of kidney failure exacerbated by his drinking habits. He was driven directly to Lyne Place from the ship at Southampton and emerged into the public gaze only for six momentous meetings at Colet Gardens.

The question which faced his pupils was: what would become of the teaching which they had used as a life belt for so long? They had relied completely on their teacher and obeyed his prohibitions on taking in new recruits. With the exception of Bennett, they had waited patiently for their Master's return. Since 1941 very little had happened. Kenneth Walker, feeling some of the same pressures that affected Bennett, had published three books which referred peripherally to the System. His *Diagnosis of Man* (1942) had been written during the Blitz and appealed for world reform by means of internal rather than external change. The same year *The Circle of Life* discussed "the circle of recurrence"; and both books made great use of the *New Model*. By 1944, in *Meaning and Purpose*, Walker was already beginning to repeat himself, and all three books merely posed gigantic questions that revealed an underlying desperation on their author's part. Ouspensky's British followers were in a bad way, and the return of the Master was to have provided artificial respiration.

Dr. Francis Roles had collected three hundred people—the number at which the membership of the Historico-Psychological Society had been fixed—and the shock which Ouspensky's appearance gave this wider audience was as great as that to the inner circle of his pupils. Perhaps because of infirmities which prevented him from hearing correctly, perhaps because of some purpose of his own, Ouspensky used a Miss Quinn, who had accompanied him from America, as a "transmitting station" between himself and his pupils. If she could not understand a particular question, it was deemed unanswerable; and very few questions met with approval. Ouspensky appeared to be administering to his audience *en bloc* the treatment which overimaginative or pretentious inquirers had received before the war. Questions were bounced back like balls hitting a blank wall. Added to this was the difficulty of hearing Ouspensky, who spoke in fragments and even more ungrammatically than usual. What precisely did he mean by his conduct at these final meetings?

The writer J. M. Cohen had first heard of the System during the war years and was one of the newcomers who were prepared to meet the exalted figure of prewar legend. In a broadcast talk entitled, "In the Work," he has described his impressions of the first three of Ouspensky's last series of meetings:

> The room contained upwards of three hundred people, all of them middle class. The atmosphere was tense in a way that I came to recognise as characteristic; the ticking of names on attendance sheets was performed with ritual gravity. When we had been sitting silently for perhaps ten minutes, Ouspensky mounted the two steps to the stage. He was short, iron-grey with a very stern and straight glance, and he walked with a stick. Every movement was clearly a painful effort. He was a very sick man. . . . Ouspensky asked for questions. They came in the jargon of the System, . . . but each one was stonewalled. "Be simpler," rapped the commanding voice with the strong Russian accent. "Start from what you know." "What do you want? Be simpler and we can begin." But nothing did begin . . . one question stands out from those three evenings. It was asked by Kenneth Walker, the surgeon, who was one of Ouspensky's oldest pupils. "Do you mean, Mr. Ouspensky, that you have abandoned the System?" The answer was a thunderbolt: "There is no System."

What did the Master—or the sick man—require of his pupils?

The first three meetings took place on February 24, March 5, and March 12. At the first, Ouspensky refused to tell his questioners what he wanted from them. He had given them no plan of activities when he left for America. What was this "teaching" to which they referred? He had given no teaching. He refused absolutely to answer any questions posed in the terms which he had used before the war. He asked his audience what they wanted: if they told him, if they gave him material to work on, he might be able to do something. At the second meeting, the audience tried hard to discover the terms in which they must put their questions in order to receive an answer. Again, Ouspensky scoffed at questions about "mechanicalness" and "self-remembering." What did these terms mean? Who had told them that they were mechanical, he inquired, and why did they believe this? They must not believe anything. Questions posed in more general or more indefinite ways were treated with similar sarcasm. Those about the meaning of Christianity were dismissed as great imponderables. No one would ever know what Christ really taught, just as no one would ever know what life was all about. He, Ouspensky, could not go on repeating the same things over and over again. He possessed nothing of any importance to give them; indeed, he said, he owned nothing at all.

In one of his published letters, Rodney Collin recalled how his Master answered a pupil who asked, "How can one find harmony?" Ouspensky replied: "This is your question? This is my question now, and I have no answer." Another questioner: "What is meant by harmony?" Ouspensky: "It is a musical term, nothing more."

From the first two meetings, two themes emerged which threw the pupils back upon their own resources. They must have an aim, a straightforward everyday aim. And only *by oneself* could any effort be made to achieve anything. This seemed to overthrow the whole elaborate idea of "school" and "rules" which had existed before the war; and by the third meeting, the implications of this train of thought were becoming clearer. Some years ago, said Ouspensky, they had had a "system" which they discussed; but at the outbreak of the war they had come to the conclusion that this would not help. He had never known even what the first step along the road to self-mastery should be. Now he no longer believed in the possibility of change. And to a worried lady who asked why he would not help them, Ouspensky returned bleakly that he could help no one, because he had no help to give. Finally, he closed the meeting because he said that there were no simple questions and that therefore he could not answer anything to the purpose. He might come again if his audience wished it.

After a long gap, two more meetings were held on May seventh and twenty-first. These were much shorter than the first three, but Ouspensky seemed better pleased with the questions which were asked. Then came the last meeting on June 18. Although obviously failing and unable to answer clearly, Ouspensky did appear to provide one guideline: a simple reinforcement of his instruction to each person to find out what he or she wanted: to try, test, and sample life to discover one's true inclinations. He closed this final meeting with the hope that he might see them again if he remained in England. Perhaps, he said, some time was left him. Afterward he had to be helped from the lecture room and—out of sight of his audience—was given an injection.

The plan of returning to The United States must have already formed in his mind, and it has been suggested that he had resolved to try the same gambit in New York which had so disconcerted his English pupils. He shut himself up at Lyne Place and announced that he would sail to America on September 4. "On that day," writes Rodney Collin, "we went to Southampton, put our luggage on board, and were ready to leave. A few hours before the boat was due to sail, he arrived at the dock and suddenly said quietly, "I am not going to America this time.' It was like the 'stop' exercise on the scale of the whole Work. A stop was made in many lives, everyone's personal plans were turned upside down, and a space made in the momentum of time where something quite new could be done."

The last month of Ouspensky's life is the most extraordinary and problematic time in his entire existence. To say that his followers were shaken and puzzled after the meetings at Colet Gardens is understating the case. The sudden countermanding of the American trip was left until the last minute; the dock gates had even been opened so that the invalid's car could drive directly up to the liner. It was yet another dislocation in the expected pattern of events; and already among those who hoped to begin again where they had left off in 1940, a number of conflicting interpretations of what Ouspensky meant at his final meetings had begun to gain ground. And possibilities multiply once more. . . .

The differences of opinion were supplemented by private conversations which members of the old directorate had with Ouspensky. Kenneth Walker felt that Ouspensky's private utterances confirmed the impression that "he was a very deeply disappointed man. Something had gone wrong, and somebody had failed but who it was that had failed was never very clear to me. In all probability we were all implicated in the failure which Ouspensky seemed to be feeling so deeply." Had the System failed to come up to Ouspensky's expectations? Had his pupils failed to make proper use of it? Or had they failed to understand anything at all?

On the other hand, to the pupil who had organized the restoration of Colet House, it appeared that sometimes Ouspensky could overcome his physical disabilities and make contact with a deeper and more powerful sort of knowledge than ever before. He felt that Ouspensky had wanted to ensure that no activities would ever be carried on in his name; that in fact he had meant what he said when he denied the usefulness—and even the very existence—of the System. This point of view was supported by Ouspensky's emphatic declarations that In Search of the Miraculous was not to be published. Others agreed that Ouspensky had wished to call a halt to activity of the kind which had become familiar, but argued that this was because he wanted to give his followers a fresh start and encourage new approaches. During the last month of the Master's life, the uncertainty generated by his last meetings produced a uniquely charged atmosphere among his followers.

To Rodney Collin the dying man was transformed into a repository of new meanings, significance incarnate. Even before the abortive expedition to America, the force had been accumulating around Lyne. Ouspensky "hardly spoke at all even to the people who were eating and sitting with him," Rodney Collin writes. "Yet one had the sense that everything that was done was a kind of demonstration, and gradually an atmosphere developed which can hardly be described. . . . He showed the few who were with him, without explanation, what it means for a man to pass consciously into the realm of the spirit."

The strangest feature of Ouspensky's last month was that he and his followers took long car journeys—often through the night, always without food, and with the Master's cats accompanying him—to parts of England which he had previously known. He drove to West Wickham, to Seven-oaks, to Gadsden, and to Maurice Nicoll's old seaside cottage. The expeditions were seen as of portentous significance by some members of the entourage. On one occasion the group returned to Lyne and parked in front of the house. Ouspensky did not climb out with the others but stayed in his seat surrounded by his cats. He remained in the car all night, and one of the more dramatic ladies looking after him stood motionless at the window, her arm ceremoniously raised in salute.

Two prominent followers of Gurdjieff visited Ouspensky in his last days and came away with the impression of an invalid making prodigious efforts to overcome physical disability. If meaning is read into everything, there is a risk that it may be read wrongly. And there is a version of Ouspensky's death which holds that he did not agree to the lengthy and laborious expeditions, that he was too ill to know what he was doing, and that it was largely the idea of Rodney Collin to make those curious pilgrimages.

The generally accepted view is that Ouspensky wanted to fix in his mind the places he had known with a view to "remembering" them in his next recurrence. Kenneth Walker writes that he often spoke of recurrence to his pupils in the last weeks of his life. They had the impression that there was something Ouspensky "wished fervently to change" the next time around.

Ever since the publication of *A New Model of the Universe*, Ouspensky had been plagued by questions about recurrence. He always emphasized that the theory was not essential to the System, although he had synthesized it satisfactorily with Gurdjieff's ideas. The condition of mechanical man is that of ceaseless repetition; but someone who wants to wake up may perhaps be able to change the cycle. His ideas had altered considerably since writing *Ivan Osokin*, and the pessimism inherent in the idea of recurrence was harnessed to the System. It provided both the stick and the carrot: the motive for waking up and the goal at which to aim. The prison house in which man was confined could be seen as a fortress constructed of recurring lives. Like "people of *byt*," people connected with the "events" of history could never hope to escape from the place they occupied in the gigantic construction, otherwise the whole edifice would collapse. But the "invisible" man, who had avoided becoming a cornerstone of history, would have comparatively little difficulty in escaping. No one would notice a pebble dislodging itself from the mortar between the massive blocks.

Ouspensky taught that the possibility of escape from recurrence came when a man met an esoteric school. He rewrote the early draft of *Ivan Osokin* inserting the character of a magician to whom Osokin goes after his love affair appears to be ending unhappily. The magician represents the Work. He has certain characteristics of Gurdjieff and some of Ouspensky's own: he is something of a *bonviveur;* his room is hung with Oriental carpets, and he favors cats. It is this magician who sends Osokin back in time and allows him to watch himself make the same mistakes all over again. Ouspensky recommended an analogous practice to his pupils, advising them to relive the events of their lives in order to avoid the repetitions—or "recurrences"—which provide each person with his personal blind alleys. His character Osokin decides after all not to shoot himself, and the magician gives him the opportunity to escape from his cycle of languid failures. The solution for Osokin is to devote fifteen years of his life to study with the magician. And he is warned that, for those who have guessed "the great secret," "time is counted." They either evolve or degenerate very quickly in their cycles of recurrence—and finally they cease to be born.

What was it that Ouspensky wanted to change in his next recurrence? Did he want to take up "school work" at an earlier period next time around? Walker half implies that his break with Gurdjieff lay on his conscience, but other witnesses declare that Ouspensky wished to free himself from the specter of Gurdjieff in any future life. At the beginning of *Ivan Osokin*, the disconsolate hero tells a friend of his feeling of being "cut off from life." "You have your life now," Osokin says "and a future ahead of you. I tried to climb over all the fences and the result is that I have nothing now and nothing for the future! If only I could begin again from the beginning!" This is the statement of a man disillusioned both with "life" and his attempts to reach beyond it. Did he simply want to relapse into conventional existence?

This is doubtful, because the whole idea of recurrence had by 1947 become indissolubly linked to Gurdjieff's teaching on self-remembering. In System terms, Ouspensky declared that what recurred was a person's essence. But although *essence* could only recur, *memory* could become immortal. Mere moments of self-remembering were relatively useless. "The whole thing is to create a continuity." A continuous memory might help in remembering, in waking up next time. It was here that the vividness of his own childhood memories assumed a particular importance.

During his last years in New York, Ouspensky was preoccupied with the theme of developing memory in recurrence. In the fragmentary records of his talks from late 1944 to late 1945, the topic predominates. He said that he was preparing a book on memory and declared that even theoretical knowledge of recurrence could alter the facts. On another occasion he revealed that he had once advocated teaching the System to imaginative people who could acquire some understanding of the concept. He even told one group that for them, recurrence was the most important idea of all.

At what stage do we step off the endless belt? When do we become free? For the members of the directorate and for the helpers who lived at

Lyne, the tensions mounted. The sick Master ended his expeditions and retired to his room. It is hardly possible to call what took place "events"; for whatever was going on became confusing, even distressing, to those who were present. Memories of the period are clouded; more than one person has claimed that Ouspensky died in their arms; and as to what it all meant, no one not present would be able to pass judgment. Several interpretations of the circumstances surrounding Ouspensky's death sprang up—but because these are based on participation in an unimaginable atmosphere, it is quite impossible to say what really happened. One passage in literature seems to correspond to the hints and brief writings about the period. It is the section of *Memories, Dreams, Reflections,* in which C. G. Jung records the circumstances in which he began his *Seven Sermons to the Dead:* "The whole house was filled as if there was a crowd present, crammed full of spirits. They were packed deep right up to the door, and the air was so thick it was scarcely possible to breathe. . . ." The forces which had taken Lyne Place in their grip—whether they were subjective or in any sense "objective"—came from the world of the miraculous which the dying man had sought so long.

Communication went beyond the verbal threshold. Some people felt that knowledge came seeping through the limits of the three-dimensional world by some divine osmosis, that they were in touch with "the inner circle of humanity." The dying man seemed able to communicate his ideas telepathically, to such an extent that one of his attendants, scared of becoming the victim of her own imagination, asked that he use words alone. Ouspensky accepted this reasoning and complied.

The house was overshadowed. One witness remembers Ouspensky sitting in the Green Drawing Room, when a powerful presence seemed to press upon his companions. Ouspensky spoke: "You notice?" he said. Was he the vehicle for forces greater than man? "What was going on," says one pupil, "was God's business." In the words of another: "He was an *angel:* don't you understand that?" In the terms of the System, Ouspensky had equated the "angels" of the Christian hierarchy with the degree of being represented as "planets" on Gurdjieff's Ray of Creation. There was a sense that in some way those at Lyne were participating in an ascension.

Also that it had been planned before. In the days of 55a Gwendwr Road, a pupil had gone to the flat to find the door opened by Ouspensky himself. "I only know," said the pupil, "that I have to be with you when you die." "Quite right," said Ouspensky, and so it proved. In his later New York lectures he had often returned to the theme of "miracle," defined in the terms of the System as "the laws of a higher cosmos operating in a lower." There was a sense that in the miracle of his death, Ouspensky was somehow creating a mystical body of which his followers were part. "'I will always be with you,' he too could say," Rodney Collin remembered, "but lightly and smoking a cigarette so that none noticed."

One of those present at Lyne declares that he "saw him succeed during the last month of his life in his life-long aim of experiencing 'cosmic consciousness.' During and after this experience two more eye-witnesses agree with me that he was a completely changed man—no longer the man who wrote the books or conducted the groups in London and New York." But to Rodney Collin, the miracle appeared to be enacted also for the benefit of Ouspensky's pupils. It was partly the culmination of the teaching which Ouspensky provided merely through existing, partly the last act in a gigantic mystery play.

The idea of the mystery play derives from Ouspensky himself, but is indirectly influenced by Gurdjieff's teaching of the uses of the stage in antiquity. When in *A New Model of the Universe* Ouspensky discusses the parts men play in the cycles of recurrence, he refers to the particular sort of roles acted by men who are members of "esoteric schools." These men are more conscious than the *corps-de-ballet* of mechanically repeating people, and their roles are consciously directed. The perfect instance of a drama connected with an esoteric school is "the drama of Christ." Ouspensky connected the Gospel drama with the Greek mystery plays, which for him represented the outer courts of an esoteric school which trained candidates by "a consecutive and gradual introduction to a new cycle of thought and feeling." The purpose of the theatrical representation of the mystery schools and the historical drama of Christ was the same; the difference was "that the latter was played in real life."

Under the circumstances it was not unnatural to compare the death of a revered teacher in apparently miraculous circumstances to the Crucifixion scene of the Gospel drama. Rodney Collin saw Ouspensky's death as providing an equivalent experience in the drama of the Work, and he applied his Master's dicta about Christ to Ouspensky himself. He wrote an account of Ouspensky's last days called *Last Remembrances of a Magician,* which still exists but is inaccessible. After Ouspensky died this was circulated in typescript until objections—quite possibly to the part allotted to its author—forced Rodney Collin to withdraw it. He then issued another version with the offending passages blocked out in the style of a wartime censor. This account has never been published.

Rodney Collin's version of events is complicated by the fact that he saw himself as having an important part to play in the drama of Ouspensky's death. This part demanded that he supplement the failing resources of his Master with his own. Just as the Work teacher created situations which would tax his pupils' predispositions to the utmost, Collin saw it as his duty to force Ouspensky to act counter to his "automatic" instincts—the feelings and sensations of a very sick man. By resisting the "normal," mechanical imperatives of a diseased body, Ouspensky might remain conscious in his last hours, and at the last "die consciously." The struggle for full consciousness was an additional reason for the long motor drives and the minor exertions which filled Ouspensky's last days. Collin believed that his teacher had explicitly delegated this task to him; but those who object that Ouspensky was bamboozled into taking his motor expeditions would also object that Rodney Collin's behavior just before Ouspensky's death bore little relationship to the facts of what occurred. *Last Remembrances of a Magician* is a title, one of Ouspensky's former followers writes, "which at any rate until he was too ill to know what he was doing or saying, Ouspensky would have loathed and repudiated." What we know of Collin's conduct gives a certain weight to this idea.

He returned to England with Ouspensky in January 1947, temporarily leaving his wife with Mme. Ouspensky at Mendham. There is some evidence that his attentions were unwelcome—that the intimate position which he felt himself to occupy was not a matter of choice on Ouspensky's part. One particular incident demonstrates this. Sitting in the drawing room at Lyne, Ouspensky became extremely angry with Rodney Collin and started shouting at him, ending by hitting him across the face. Collin interpreted this in his own fashion, and "completely slap-happy," turned around and delivered a stinging blow to the head of Dr. Francis Roles, which broke the doctor's eardrum.

The episode was construed by Collin as a form of initiation, and shortly afterward, he acted on this assumption. He caught a plane across the Atlantic and went posthaste to Mendham. Later he wrote that Ouspensky "possessed" him "with his own mind" during the flight. On his arrival at Franklin Farms, he considerably scared Mme. Ouspensky by assuming the manners and voice of her husband and implying that the mantle of the dying Master had fallen on him. Nothing more is known about this interview, except that, after it had taken place, Collin returned to England and the house of miracles at Lyne.

Lyne Place was overshadowed. . . . In November 1951, Collin wrote: "Among the many extraordinary impressions at the time of Ouspensky's death there was—particularly at one period—the immensely strong feeling of some great power or being, some Christ-like being, as far above Ouspensky as Ouspensky was above us, presiding over all that was being done." And in March of that year, he summed up in a single letter the theology which he developed from Ouspensky's last days:

> All the literally miraculous things that happened at Ouspensky's death, and everything that has developed since—both for me personally and

in relation to his work as a whole—convince me that he did not die as ordinary men die, but that he reached a level where a man becomes immortal, or at any rate where he is not confined to time as we know it, but can act and make connections through time. . . .

Further, if he did so become independent of time, or if he had acquired fourth body (if you like to be technical) then he is accessible now to anyone who desires his help with sufficient urgency and belief.

The lectures, the whole system as he explained it, were indeed the explanation of how to do the impossible, of how miracles are achieved. How then should we be surprised that Ouspensky himself actually put this knowledge to the use for which it was intended, and evidently expected those who followed him to take it the same way? Looking back I am appalled to remember how we took it all as a method of making slight adjustments to our personal psychology. . . .

But what actually happened? Without a blow-by-blow account of events, there is little to be said. Few people know the answer, and some of those who do have put forward the most disturbing ideas. Rodney Collin, of course, described Ouspensky's conduct as an example of "work"—of "super-effort," as Gurdjieff would have said—a demonstration of how to turn the most adverse circumstances to good account. "One of the most extraordinary things was to see how he turned every unfavourable trick of fate—separation from his friends, distortion of his ideas, physical weakness and pain, into advantages, and by willingly abandoning normal powers and faculties was enabled to achieve supernormal ones of infinitely greater value."

Even if we do not dispute the miraculous which engulfed Lyne Place, it is easy to see how Rodney Collin might have read into Ouspensky's slightest actions the sense of an event which he already half-expected. For example, if Ouspensky had been trying to keep him at arm's length, the following sentence from a letter of July 15, 1949 is easily explained: "In Ouspensky's last months one saw how he accepted being old, sick, ugly, helpless, in pain, misunderstood, and indeed did everything to prevent others comforting him, to suffer consciously, to make it more difficult for him to be understood. . . ." Was it not simply that the disciple's advances had been rebuffed in irritation? Collin admits that faith alone kept at bay disillusion and bewilderment. "While if for a moment that faith was lost, what was being done actually became for the doubter no more than the vagaries of an old man who had lost his mind."

Whatever possibility is accepted, it is clear that Ouspensky was making stupendous efforts to force his weakening body into extended activity. In

The Theory of Eternal Life Rodney Collin describes how, after his journeys through England, his Master continued to exert himself gratuitously.

> When almost unable to set one foot before the other he would make his dying body walk step by step for an hour at a time through the rough lanes; force it to rise in the small hours, dress, descend and climb long flights of stairs; turn night into day; and require of his companions in order to remain with him, such feats of endurance as they in full possession of health and strength were scarcely able to accomplish.

And again in a letter of August 23, 1952:

> A little before his death Ouspensky after having spent a whole night forcing his dying body to walk, and waking us in order to make many experiments, said to me: "Now do you understand that everything has to be done by effort or do you still think that things come right by themselves?"

A fortnight before his death, Ouspensky assembled his inner circle and told them that they must "not be afraid to take second step." They must reconstruct everything for themselves"—from the very beginning."

His companions were convinced that their Master was undergoing the transmutation before their eyes. The unseen presences attended them; for the wall between here and *there* had been breached. Telepathic effects reached far beyond Lyne itself, as dimensions and cosmoses merged to produce their miracles. The epigraph to *Tertium Organum* had looked forward to a day when "there shall be time no longer." The words of one Apocalypse contained the shadow of another.

On the last day of his life, Ouspensky got up and dressed. Brushing aside all restraint, he came downstairs and summoned the household for a final briefing. To Rodney Collin it seemed that "he was able to communicate many ideas in such a way that each perceived in them the solution of his own problem."

Ouspensky returned to his room. At dawn the next day, October 2, 1947, he died. In the opinion of his companions this was a "conscious death."

When his body had been removed for burial at Lyne Church, Rodney Collin went to the bedroom where his Master had died and locked himself in. He refused to come out, despite persuasions which became increasingly angry and hostile. The household was already prostrated before the blankness of the future and had no time for an absurd young man compounding their grief. A ladder was placed against the window ledge, and an attempt was made to reach the man inside. The ladder was pushed away from the wall. Six days later the bell of Ouspensky's room rang downstairs in the kitchen. Janet Collin-Smith, who had by now arrived from America, was sent to her husband. She found him sitting cross-legged on Ouspensky's bed, in the words of his sister-in-law, "emaciated, dirty, unshaven. He bore all the signs of having been through a tremendous traumatic experience. He had had neither food nor drink during his time of solitude. He asked for lime juice. He adopted a gentle, child-like attitude to those who came to look after him, unlike his usual forthright manner."

Patently something had happened to him; but what he thought this was became clear only later. From this six-day fast a whole new development was to result. For a time, however, there was only confusion and dismay. Ouspensky had departed. What were his followers to do? To some, the sun had suddenly ceased to shine; but to others, it seemed that the sacred time, the time of the miracles, might not be over. The miraculous had extended its influence beyond Lyne, both before and after Ouspensky's death. "That morning dead," Rodney Collin wrote of his teacher, "he walked with a traveller crossing London Bridge; and to another at the wheel of a car showed the secrets of this universe."

Neither was he the only member of the group at Lyne who felt the continuing presence of Ouspensky. The strangeness of the attendant phenomena continued to haunt one participant long after 1947. She discovered certain parallels in sacred literature and decided that Dr. W. Y. Evans-Wentz, the editor of *The Tibetan Book of the Dead*, spoke with the voice of authority. Eventually, she ran Evans-Wentz to earth; he lived on a mountain sacred to the Indians on the Mexican border. During their conversation Evans-Wentz tried to give his mountain away; but this concerned Ouspensky's old pupil less than his reaction to her account of Ouspensky's death. "I always thought Ouspensky was an Arhant," he remarked: "now I know that he is."

Just before Ouspensky died, the printing of *Strange Life of Ivan Osokin* on the private press used by his followers was completed. Although a copy was taken posthaste to Lyne by the printer, Ouspensky died before he could see it. At his funeral the printer discovered the novel in the glove compartment of the car.

"Do you remember the end, the very end?" asked Osokin.

"Yes, I remember," and slowly she recites the end of the tale: *And the King's daughter of Duntrine got her to that part of the beach where strange things had been done in the ancient ages; and there she sat her down. The sea foam ran to her feet, and the dead leaves swarmed about her back, and the veil blew about her face in the blowing of the wind. And when she lifted up her eyes, there was the daughter of a*

*King come walking on the beach. Her hair was like the spun gold, and
her eyes like pools in a river, and she had no thought for the morrow
and no power upon the hour, after the manner of simple men."*

Ouspensky had told his pupils to "begin all over again," to "reconstruct
everything from the beginning." When they had recovered from shock,
there would be various interpretations of what this meant. Had they been
freed from the repetition of fixed forms or not? And for a few, who had been
affected by the sense of the miraculous, the same question posed itself for
the Master. How to account for this sense of his continuing presence?
Perhaps his last heroic days had freed him from recurrence. Perhaps he had
gone *further on*, to some inconceivable new beginning.

*"One life ends and another begins. One time ends and another begins.
Death is really a return to the beginning."*

14

The Last Suppers

During the period of indecision after Ouspensky's death groups gathered round two figures, Dr. Francis Roles and Rodney Collin. The directorate could see only one course open: to ask Mme. Ouspensky for help. Mme. Ouspensky's own wishes were clear, but shocking: they were to contact Gurdjieff in Paris. There was renewed dissension. Then Mme. Ouspensky wrote to say that plainly, no one had understood anything; it was nonsense that Ouspensky had abandoned everything by which he had lived since meeting Gurdjieff. They were to sell Lyne Place and end their own activities.

Gurdjieff himself took a hand in the game. A communication arrived at Lyne reading: "You are sheep without a shepherd. Come to me."

This new development caused almost as much consternation as the successive blows of Ouspensky's last meetings and death. His pupils had been forbidden to think of Gurdjieff for so long that those who did think of him at all imagined that he was probably dead. Others decided that Ouspensky really had meant that Gurdjieff was mad. To others he was something approaching the devil incarnate; at the very least a Black Magician. When an artist sketched Ouspensky's death mask, one of the Russian's devoted followers suppressed the picture for fear Gurdjieff might acquire it and so obtain a magical hold over Ouspensky's soul. At all events, Ouspensky had parted from Gurdjieff for reasons which no doubt seemed good to him; and who were his pupils to question the decisions of a man from whom they had learned so much? The section which was united in devotion to Ouspensky divided into two main bodies of opinion: those who supported Roles's view that he had a mandate to carry on Ouspensky's work, and those who believed that Ouspensky had tried to put an end to everything. But about half of Ouspensky's former disciples, under Kenneth Walker, decided to obey the instructions from Mendham.

In the spring of 1948, Mme. Ouspensky herself decided to reestablish contact with Gurdjieff and dispatched presents of 300 dollars and a roll of silk. These were regarded as grossly inadequate; but in answer to a query whether Mme. Ouspensky should be written to and trounced for her niggardliness, Gurdjieff replied: "No. You out of mouse make elephant." The lines were open between Paris and Franklin Farms.

Ouspensky's death also affected J. G. Bennett, who had expanded his teaching activities. In 1941 he had acquired a large house called Coombe Springs, standing in extensive grounds in the London suburb of Kingston-on-Thames. This became the center of his group which styled itself "The Institute for the Comparative Study of History, Philosophy and the Sciences." By the mid-1940s, two to three hundred pupils were visiting Coombe Springs for the sort of activities which had prevailed at the Prieuré or Lyne Place.

Bennett had resolved to take the bold step of publishing a book mentioning the System. At the inauguration of his Institute in 1946, he had delivered a series of lectures entitled *The Crisis in Human Affairs*, based partly on a private theory of history and partly on the System. *The Crisis in Human Affairs* appeared in July 1948—at the precise moment when Bennett learned that Gurdjieff, far from being dead or relapsed into senility as was the common assumption, was very much alive and kicking. On a business trip to the United States he visited Mme. Ouspensky at Mendham and received the same advice as had been given to the emissaries from Ouspensky's English groups. Trembling inwardly at the thought of confronting the terrifying phenomenon he had last known at Fontainebleau, he returned to England and left with his wife for Paris.

Bennett and the Ouspenskians were Johnny-come-latelies as far as Gurdjieff's personal following was concerned. As soon as wartime conditions permitted, Gurdjieff's pupils had begun to converge from every point of the compass on the Rue des Colonels Renard. Two of the earliest comers had strange tales to tell.

Fritz Peters was serving in the American forces in Luxembourg. He had fallen into a trough of depression induced by a series of apparently miraculous escapes from death and a mounting disgust at the horrors of warfare. Eventually he secured leave and headed for Paris "very close to what I would have to call a form of madness." Gurdjieff welcomed him with literally open arms, took in his condition at a glance, and directed him to lie down and rest. Peters was refused aspirin for his headache and was given scalding coffee instead.

> I remember being slumped over the table, sipping at my coffee, when I began to feel a strange uprising of my energy within myself—I stared at him, automatically straightened up, and it was as if a violent, electric blue light emanated from him and entered into me. As this happened, I could feel the tiredness drain out of me, but at the same moment his body slumped and his face turned grey as if it was being drained of life. I looked at him, amazed, and when he saw me sitting erect, smiling and full of energy, he said quickly: "You all right now—watch food on stove—I must go." There was something very urgent in his voice and I leaped to my feet to help him but he waved me away and limped slowly out of the room.

A quarter of an hour later Gurdjieff returned to the room. "He looked like a young man again," Peters writes, "alert, smiling, sly and full of good spirits." The reunion was celebrated uproariously and accompanied by copious quantities of armagnac. Gurdjieff sent Peters away "convinced . . . that he knew how to transmit energy from himself to others . . . at great cost to himself."

In the summer of 1946, Kathryn Hulme visited Gurdjieff. She took with her a young Belgian nurse—an ex-nun—with whom she had been doing relief work in Germany. During their conversation, Gurdjieff appeared to fall asleep, and the Belgian girl whispered that perhaps they had better go. Gurdjieff awoke, smiled at her and—in spite of his total ignorance of her past—named the precise Order of which she had been a member: "Petite soeur de . . ." As Kathryn Hulme writes, he could have just been commending his visitor's compassion; but this was not an explanation which she would readily accept.

Entire groups of pupils arrived at the Rue des Colonels Renard. An ambassador from Jane Heap's London group arrived in 1946, and in the autumn of that year, Gurdjieff was surprised by roars of laughter which greeted his onslaught on a hapless newcomer who had endured identical treatment at the hands of Jane Heap in London.

Building up gradually to a crescendo toward the end of 1948, Gurdjieff's former pupils—with *their* pupils, and their friends, relations, and children—poured into Paris to sit at the Master's feet. They found him a little older, a little more tired, but recognizably the same man. Indeed, to Fritz Peters it seemed that, except for the lack of a house and grounds in which to work, the teaching was proceeding exactly as he had known it in the Château du Prieuré. But complications were created by the arrival of so many former disciples. There was considerable agitation among Gurdjieff's French pupils, who were reminded that the play in which they had taken part was only the latest in a line of long-running successes. The new arrivals created a crowd scene where before there had been tasteful *soupers intimes*.

Gurdjieff's wartime teaching had not been exactly clandestine, but neither had it been widely advertised. Rumors branching from the circle of Daumal and Lavastine invaded the intellectual community. "His name passed from mouth to mouth," explains Pierre Schaeffer, who met Gurdjieff in 1943; and although no single approach to Gurdjieff was ever exactly like another, Schaeffer's situation at the time may indicate the more general reasons which brought others to Gurdjieff. Within the space of a few years, he had had to withstand "a war lost, a general mistake in orientation, a naive belief in the possibility of changing the world." Gurdjieff saved him from despair. "You didn't go to Gurdjieff because you wanted to meet him," Schaeffer told the writer Elizabeth Antébi, "it happened to you to meet him through a third person."

With a relatively small number of pupils gathered in this fashion, Gurdjieff had returned during 1943 and 1944 to holding sessions of questions and answers—as he had in Russia and as Ouspensky had done in his memory for so many years at Warwick Gardens. "He would propose a field of observation," says Henri Tracol, who came to him during the war. Discussion of the results formed the basis of meetings, and the Master might occasionally recommend exercises for particular individuals. He seems to have abandoned the occult cosmology recorded in *In Search of the Miraculous*, but he was never averse to flashes of Magery—to playing the Man Who Knows, allowing his hieratic manner full rein. There was one pupil, for example, who had scarcely begun a question—"M. Gurdjieff," whom the Master interrupted, grandly and mysteriously: "It is a long time now, since I was Gurdjieff . . ."

With the increasing demands on his time and on the floor space of his tiny flat, Gurdjieff reverted to more general methods—as he had done when he first arrived in Western Europe. He was now teaching in a more sedentary fashion than before, presiding as a domestic patriarch over a rapidly increasing family. To make up for the lack of a Study House there was the Salle Pleyel, where nightly sessions of the movements were held, which Gurdjieff rarely missed. He retained all his old skill as a "teacher of dancing" and his poise and presence in the classes never failed to make an impression. "He came in," one remembers, "like a great red light . . ." With minor variations his routine was the same as it had been for twenty years, though by the late 1940s it had attained the sacrosanctity of ritual.

There was the flat itself—of which every detail impressed itself on visitors. It stood on the first floor in the Rue des Colonels Renard, on the right as one entered the building. The block itself was massive and functional, a warren of small flats like Gurdjieff's own, the street a high-walled gulley admitting little light—even supposing that Gurdjieff did not close the shutters, in order (as he once wickedly explained) "to prevent the vibrations from escaping." The flat itself was unprepossessing. A hallway, which bent to the left, turned into a passage leading to Gurdjieff's room and a spare bedroom. On the right of the hallway was the sitting room, decorated in the most extraordinary fashion. Its walls, like the walls of the hallway, were covered with the paintings of his "parasites"—not a square inch of wall space was untenanted.

On each side of the sitting-room fireplace hung twin representations of the enneagram, made of mother-of-pearl, sewn to fabric-covered black disks. Under one of these, the Master himself would sit, observing his disciples as they crouched on low, uncomfortable stools during interminable readings from *Beelzebub's Tales*. Behind them, in the corners abutting the street, were two strange and glittering artifacts. One was a sort of stylized Christmas tree, made out of some gold-colored metal or gilded wood, which gleamed in the light reflected from countless prisms of glass. The other was a cabinet containing a large collection of dolls dressed in different national costumes and an assortment of keepsakes: pipes, musical instruments, Orientalia. When the room was properly lit, the skill of Gurdjieff as a stage designer became as obvious as it had been in the Study House at Fontainebleau. The cheap materials scintillated and sparkled like Aladdin's cave.

Encased in their private fantasies—more like the Forty Thieves in their jars than Aladdin's genii—the pupils sat under the Master's eye. That is, if they were not next door, in the dining room, where the pictures still clustered thickly on the wall, and there was scarcely room to breathe if Gurdjieff had a full house. This was where the toasts to the idiots were drunk, as they had been ever since Fontainebleau. The toasts were proposed by a director—not now the long-dead Schumaker, but an incongruous Paris banker or an English technologist. It was at Gurdjieff's table that some pupils felt most keenly the intensity of the experience—and an extraordinary parallel was born in the mind of more than one. Here Gurdjieff would make ritual offerings of dainties to his guests, abuse or comfort his visitors, compel the drunkards to abstain from alcohol and the teetotalers to down glass after glass of armagnac or peppered vodka.

The food for Gurdjieff's feasts would proceed across the hall to the dining room by means of a human chain, which originated in the diminutive kitchen. Here Gurdjieff cooked his highly spiced dishes on a coal stove, and his pupils washed up in the most primitive of sinks. Next door to the kitchen, and directly to the left of the entrance to the flat, was what for many pupils was the most significant room in the house: Gurdjieff's pantry.

This room was a study, storeroom and confessional combined. Its shelves were crammed with bottles and jars, and from them dangled rings of sausages and sheaves of dried herbs. Nudging the delicacies were reminders of Gurdjieff's occupation: rosaries or chaplets hanging from nails. On the little table beneath might lie a pile of papers, relics of Gurdjieff's literary work, and a vacuum flask of hot coffee. Kathryn Hulme first knew the pantry during the 1930s; on her return in 1946, she found it "a Lucullian treasure room, its tiers of shelves stacked with boxed, bagged and tinned goods, while overhead hung from the ceiling were garlands of spice bouquets, strung red peppers and imported sausages of every size and colour." In this aromatic confusion Gurdjieff would give advice to individual pupils, prescribe exercises or listen to their problems.

If the French had to reconcile themselves to sharing Gurdjieff with others, the English and Americans, who had been receiving his teaching irregularly or at second or third hand, were forced to adapt themselves to his unpredictable behavior. Those who had been familiars of Gurdjieff before the war noticed few changes—but several faces were missing from his board. Georgette Leblanc, for example, had died in 1941, watched over by Margaret Anderson. In *The Fiery Fountains* her friend has recorded how the dying woman made prodigious efforts to "die consciously"—to watch the core of her being through death. Just before the end she was told that Gurdjieff had called her "friend" and seemed overjoyed by the news. "Alors," she inquired, "nous allons mourir sans mourir?"

Memento mori—and there was Gurdjieff himself, widely believed to be in his eighties. "What shall we do when you die, Mr. Gurdjieff?" asked one of his pupils. "I Gurdjieff," the Master replied furiously, "I *not* will die." But the question remained. Pierre Schaeffer attended the meetings with the perpetual conviction that the Master would die before he, Schaeffer, would have time to ask him his own question. The fact of death and Gurdjieff's attitude toward it hung suspended over the whole company.

A complicated relay of cause and effect was set off by the death of René Daumal in 1944. Daumal had finally been conquered by tuberculosis and malnutrition—Max-Pol Fouchet, who visited the Daumals in 1942, found them drinking hot water to fill their stomachs. Daumal died in the faith, in the middle of composing *Mount Analogue* while believing himself to be only a beginner on the slopes of his mountain. But he died pitied by his former friends, who saw him as betrayed into folly by the Work. He may have believed that the Work disciplines would save his life; and certainly the contemplation of his death caused others to reconsider their attitude toward the remorseless ethic which they believed had compounded his ruin.

A few days before he died, Daumal was photographed by another group member, Luc Dietrich. Dietrich was so affected by the death of his friend that he underwent a crisis, as a result of which he abandoned everything and rushed off to Normandy to study the behavior of madmen in a mental hospital. During the Allied bombardment of the village in which he was working, he developed an abscess on the brain. He died in August 1944, after three weeks of agony. Gurdjieff came to visit him in the hospital and brought him two oranges. He placed one in each hand of the invalid with the benediction: "All your life has been a preparation for this moment." One of Dietrich's friends was struck by the last tortured glance which the dying man cast at his teacher who stood at his bedside, calmly engaged in his favorite pastime of handing out sweets.

This friend was Lanza del Vasto, and the sinister impression which Gurdjieff made on him had considerable consequences for the Master's reputation. Lanza and Dietrich had been close friends in the days when Dietrich was a poverty-stricken young writer seeking a mentor. Lanza held a degree in philosophy and tended toward mystical speculation; he was soon to become known for founding the mystical order "L'Arche" and publishing a celebrated narrative of his journey to India, *Pèlerinage aux sources* (1943). While Lanza was in India, Dietrich met Philippe Lavastine, who introduced him to Mme. de Salzmann, and eventually to Gurdjieff. On Lanza's return he found Dietrich converted to the Work; and for a time, he, Dietrich, and Lavastine formed a group under Gurdjieff's instruction. Then he became uneasy and tried unsuccessfully to drag Dietrich away.

Lanza del Vasto's suspicions of Gurdjieff were significant because of his mystical proclivities. There was already some disquiet about the Work in the French occult world. This may have originated in a feud between Alexander de Salzmann and the leading French esotericist, René Guénon (1886–1951). Guénon is said to have admired de Salzmann and sought a meeting; but all attempts at a rapprochement were spoiled by de Salzmann's wicked sense of humor. Guénon was fond of parading his lack of concern for his selfish ego—"Il n'y a pas de René Guénon," he would say, implying that he was at one with the infinite and personally unworthy of the reverence which his disciples bestowed on him. "Il n'y a pas de René Guénon? Helas," said Alexander de Salzmann, the follower of Gurdjieff in search of his "Big I." It is uncertain whether this tale had anything to do with Guénon's injunction to his disciples to "flee Gurdjieff like the plague," but relations between the Work and the French esotericists were already strained by the 1940s. When Lanza became eminent in French mystical circles after the publication of *Pèlerinage aux sources*, the addition of his voice to those of Gurdjieff's other opponents meant that the whispering campaign against the Work increased in volume.

There was another disturbing death—closely connected with the death of Luc Dietrich. Gurdjieff had singled out Dietrich as a compulsive Don Juan and condemned him to have one woman a day "and not prostitutes, that's too easy." In the early spring of 1942, Lanza, Dietrich, and the Daumals were together on the plateau of Assy in Savoy, in an atmosphere reminiscent of Thomas Mann's *The Magic Mountain*. Assy was an area where consumptives came to be cured and this was the reason for Daumal's presence there. A young convalescent named Irène-Carole Reweliotty arrived at the spa: a woman of twenty-one who had suffered from heart trouble since puberty. She had literary ambitions and fell quickly under the spell of Dietrich, the published writer and the accomplished charmer. Dietrich introduced her to the Gurdjieff groups, an event which Irène, at the time, regarded as the turning point in her life. She recorded her struggles in a diary, published in 1946 as the *Journal d'une jeune fille*. They are struggles familiar enough from the writings of Margaret Anderson and the papers of Jean Toomer. She was a machine, she could not write—for what should she write about? She hated herself and next, by a swift reversal, hated the Gurdjieff groups. Then Daumal died and after him Dietrich, her protector and "elder brother" in the Work. Shortly before his death he had written to his protégée advising her to distance herself from the Work; but despite her doubts, Irène-Carole continued to attend the groups. Eventually in 1945 she received an invitation to dinner at the Rue des Colonels Renard.

During the course of the meal Gurdjieff spoke to her in Russian, a language which none of the others present could understand. He directed her to pretend to leave with the others and then to return to the flat. Accordingly she left, but instead of returning, she telephoned Gurdjieff from a café and told him that she could not come as her mother was expecting her. Gurdjieff insulted her "in terms," Louis Pauwels writes, "which seemed to conceal nothing of his intentions." The next day, Irène, in a state of shock, went to the disciple who had introduced her to Gurdjieff and announced her departure from the Work. She was turned away in a manner which Pauwels does not specify and thrown back on her own resources, which threatened to abandon her altogether. The bottom had fallen out of her world. In the hopes of reconstituting her universe she returned to Assy where she died unexpectedly of a heart attack. Her last letter to her mother contained the sentence, "I'll end by thinking that G. has cast a spell on me."

The wildest rumors circulated after her death. It was said that her brother had had a vision of Gurdjieff—whom he had never seen, but whom he nevertheless recognized—when he entered the room where his sister had died. There were rumors that inquiries into the case had been suppressed. The image of the Black Magician rose like some diabolical phoenix out of the ashes.

Once more—as in the examples of questionable conduct during the 1920s—there is an element of uncertainty. Even if we discount the recurrent vision of Gurdjieff as Bluebeard or Rasputin, there are still disturbing factors about this case. It does seem that someone had bungled—whether Gurdjieff or the pupil-teacher does not matter. It may be that Gurdjieff did want to sleep with Irène-Carole, but that is not in itself a crime. Neither can it be said that he directly caused her death. But there can be little doubt that the Work in general and the contretemps with Gurdjieff in particular caused a nervous breakdown; and that this reactivated a dormant physical or psycho-physical ailment. The dark side of the Work was again in evidence. And, of course, suspicion of Gurdjieff was strengthened in occult and mystical circles.

It was not as if his reputation was spotless, even on a strictly material plane. Wartime conditions had provided Gurdjieff with a superb opportunity to stir the pot of violent emotions; and at the same time, no doubt, to indulge his roguish temperament. His lavish hospitality struck a jarring note at a time of material privation: for even if the Master expended a great deal of time and money on his pupils, just how, in that occupied city, had he acquired the vodka and the delicacies which gave his feasts their memorable flavor? He did of course levy dues on his followers—but on at least one occasion he lived fully up to the precepts which he embodied in the story of "Abram Yelov" and "Peter Karpenko." Looking at the company around his board, he lashed out: "You eat good soup, cost eighty dollars. And you nothing give. You parasites." The instructor of the group reminded the Master of a 2,000 franc contribution which had been handed to him on the group's behalf. Far from being ashamed, Gurdjieff launched into the most withering verbal assault, and acted his role with such conviction that one of the instructors seceded altogether from the Work, taking along a body of pupils.

But was he acting? There were objections on the grounds of patriotism as well. Gurdjieff admitted to working the black market and collaborating with the Germans. He could feel no particular loyalties to either side in the conflict and had enough experience of war and revolution to give him an enviable sangfroid in dealing with the problems of material survival. When his American pupils returned after the war, they expected to find him ill and starving; instead, they found the pantry fully stocked and Gurdjieff well supplied with cigarettes. He had indeed taken one gamble—that of mobilizing as much credit as he could. He told shopkeepers that he had inherited an oil well in the United States, and that after the war he would pay them everything he owed. The returning Americans bailed him out— and Gurdjieff was able to stalk proudly into his creditors' shops or offices and announce the arrival of his legacy.

But he was sailing close to the wind. Soon after the war the police searched his flat and discovered under his mattress quantities of foreign currency—gifts from pupils which he had hoarded illegally. The mystery was that Gurdjieff had been warned of the authorities' intention to search the flat, and not only had he done nothing about the warning, but he announced to all and sundry that nothing compromising would ever be found. J. G. Bennett, who tells the story, repeats Gurdjieff's statement that his motive had been to experience prison from the inside—although his experiences in both India and Georgia might well have given this tale the lie—and adds that Gurdjieff's "dossiers with the Sûreté Publique and the Prefecture of Paris were bulging with reports of unlawful activities of all kinds." This was the Sly Man's ambiguity on a quite basic level.

There was also the ambiguity of the man-monster. Gurdjieff, after all, was the Great Magician, the Man Who Knows and the fountainhead of the teaching. Numbers of Bennett's pupils were shocked and distressed by Gurdjieff's bad language and his terrorizing tactics. One lady who had made the trip from England was so overcome by her first impressions that she stayed away from her next appointment in the Rue des Colonels Renard. Eventually she summoned up her courage and returned, apologizing to Gurdjieff for not staying the course. "Your loss," said Gurdjieff, severely, bidding her farewell, "your loss."

Memento mori—would you save your life or lose it? Propelled once more by the friction of affirmation and denial, the timorous and the foolhardy sat and sweated—both literally and metaphorically—through the ordeals in Gurdjieff's flat. But Gurdjieff could wear another face. The French called the lunches and dinners agapes, or love feasts. Pierre Schaeffer's essay "A Modern Thaumaturge," provides the best evocation of their atmosphere. "I feel obliged to state," Schaeffer writes about Gurdjieff's hospitality, "that anything (gherkin or pimento) can, with the necessary concentration and human tension, become the way to communion . . ."

This great feast—can I say it without shocking?—reminded me of another. It was impossible not to think of the Last Supper. Bludgeoned into life, we were taking part in tragic agapes. We dipped our hands in the dish with a Master. The figure of Judas or of the favourite disciple was enough to give one a fit. Our indomitable friend, the Banker, whose face was aglow with the vodka that he detested ("you drink another toast, Director, you not drink anything!") was Peter. There were swooning Mary Magdalens, incorrigible Marthas and Nicodemuses painfully full of goodwill. Was Gurdjieff himself aware of these resemblances? The very act of eating, if surrounded by rites, however incongruous, could not fail to make us think of Holy Communion.

The quality of the occasion, the intense meaning which suffused the suffocating, aromatic flat, Gurdjieff's conduct at the table—these are indications of the many levels on which life at the Rue des Colonels Renard was conducted. As at Fontainebleau, the Master's presence brought extra significance to every remark, every minor incident. Gurdjieff's last suppers were Last Suppers in the Biblical sense. What else could they be? After Gurdjieff's death, Schaeffer became a Catholic. He later confessed that he could never go to Mass without thinking of Gurdjieff. "Had he not invited me to the last hours in the Upper Room?" He laments: "Last Suppers, alas, are always among the last moments of the Masters, they will be their memorials."

As the remark implies, Gurdjieff was moving on to an ecclesiastical plane.

There were so many people: former Ouspenskians, former Orageans, those who had known Gurdjieff personally or through his disciples, pupils of J. G. Bennett whose connection with the Work was more peripheral. Whether or not Gurdjieff wished it to happen, they formed what one commentator has called a "spiritual empire." The lone adventurer of the Himalayas, "the tiger of Turkestan," was a long way away. Now there was an old man, a Man of Power, who inspired both terror and affection and controlled the allegiance of a sizable number of people.

It seemed that the emperor was taking steps to consolidate his dominions and that he intended to leave behind him some organization to perpetuate his teaching. After the war Gurdjieff made at least two plans to establish himself in large houses in the country: once in a vast nineteenth-century château and once in a disused hotel on the Seine. His pupils remain doubtful how seriously he intended these projects to be taken; perhaps, like the chores at the Prieuré, they were merely an excuse for "work." Gurdjieff also decided to publish *Beelzebub's Tales*. When F. S. Pinder asked the Master why he intended to issue a work which—for all the repeated revisions—was still riddled with mistakes, Gurdjieff replied that it was a "rough diamond." "Now necessary to publish."

He was slowing up perceptibly. When Dorothy Caruso, the widow of the great tenor, first met him in the summer of 1948, she saw "an old man, gray with weariness and illness." Why did he not give up? "I thought, 'The kind of force he is using is wearing him out. Why must he go on doing it? Why do they let him? We should go home, we should not ask this tired man for anything.'"

Another accident took place. Gurdjieff's car was rammed by a drunken driver. Bennett saw him return home afterward and thought he had seen a corpse walking. Gurdjieff had fractured ribs, had cut and bruised himself severely, and had sustained dangerous internal injuries. Despite his doctor's orders and in danger of death from countless different causes, he held a dinner that night as usual, telling his pupils that he must force his body to walk. For several days he was very ill, but continued to lever his battered frame into the dining room and play host. Gradually his bruises faded, and he was cured. The words of one follower—"cured himself"—do not seem too wide of the mark for this occasion. "His recovery was so complete," Dorothy Caruso writes, "that he looked younger after the accident than before . . ." The mishap did seem to reinforce whatever resolutions he had made about the future, for three or four days afterward, he summoned Bennett and directed him to bring as many pupils as he could to see him in Paris.

A fresh influx began. Bennett brought some sixty of his pupils during the summer of 1948, and weekend visits to Paris became the rule for him and his wife. Bennett's role in events was becoming crucial, for a variety of reasons. He was available, devoted to Gurdjieff, and possessed of extraordinary energies. In England he had an established center at Coombe Springs—a body of pupils as extensive as any Ouspensky had ever commanded—and the organizational abilities which went with so large an undertaking. If C. S. Nott is to be believed, Gurdjieff told him that Bennett was "useful for money" but that the majority of his pupils would be useless for the purposes he had in mind. Gurdjieff might have had many different reasons for making this statement, but to take the cynical view, he might also have seen Bennett as a link with those who had been taught in the very different manner of Ouspensky. Such a conjunction was certainly in his mind, and he had even instituted readings from the typescript of *In Search of the Miraculous* as a change from *Beelzebub's Tales*.

In the summer of 1949 Bennett was at a meal in the Rue des Colonels Renard, when Gurdjieff began to talk to him "in rather a low voice" about the role of Judas at the Last Supper. He reminded Bennett of his teaching about Judas and asked him if he agreed. Bennett replied that he thought Gurdjieff was right. "I am pleased that you understand," said Gurdjieff; and in answer to another pupil who asked him to repeat what he had said, he returned: "I speak only for him." Bennett calls Gurdjieff's words "enigmatic," but it is clear that they had great significance for him; and elsewhere he commends the role of "Judases" in general. They are the "near-heretics" who make the work of their masters live. This is worth bearing in mind when considering the history of the Work after Gurdjieff's death.

On October 30, 1948, Gurdjieff sailed for America once more. His pupils had to bring very high-level pressure to bear on the French authorities before they would grant him a reentry permit, and there may also have been difficulties about landing in New York. Once there, Gurdjieff ensconced himself in the Wellington Hotel and resumed his American routine. The meals in the hotel, the sessions in various Childs Restaurants, and the visits to the baths in the company of the men unrolled as before. Gurdjieff scandalized devoted Ouspenskians by his apparently ungrateful attitude toward their teacher who he said had "perished like a dog." Others again were prepared to be terrified by a man whom they knew simply by the reputation he had acquired during the early 1930s. Most were pleasantly surprised by the mellow Gurdjieff they encountered.

During his visit, Gurdjieff addressed an appeal "to all my present and former adepts" on the subject of *Beelzebub's Tales*. He announced its forthcoming publication and asked all of those who felt that they had derived benefit from the study of his ideas to pay 100 pounds for a copy of the first printing. The appeal was written by Bennett, who claims that he was not aware of what he was writing and that the manner and vocabulary were completely alien to him. He concludes that he "had been made the victim of one of those tricks of thought transference, or suggestion, that Gurdjieff loved to play."

There were just over nine months of Gurdjieff's life to run. In the New Year he returned to France and resumed the familiar pattern of his existence. Hordes of pupils crowded into his flat, or took part in chaotic motor expeditions so like those of the 1920s that only Gurdjieff's age and corpulence betrayed the difference. All this time he continued his practice as a "physician-hypnotist" and the constant procession of his patients was a familiar sight to those who visited him in his capacity of Master.

Throughout the summer of 1949, Gurdjieff drove himself against what was clearly a mounting burden of pain. He grew thin and pale. To the question of a pupil about whether he would not go to California for a rest— "the kind of question Gurdjieff never answered," says Dorothy Caruso—he replied: "Perhaps California, perhaps further."

Those around him refused to accept the nature of his illness. He had weathered so many storms that he seemed to be indestructible. Surely he would cure himself again? *Beelzebub's Tales* was on the point of publication, and negotiations for the château were on the brink of success. There were so many people who wanted to see him and so many who hoped for great things from his work. An atmosphere of high expectation developed.

In London Bennett gave weekly lectures from the third to the twenty-fourth of October 1949, ambitiously entitled "Gurdjieff—The Making of a New World." He appealed to "a world on the brink of disaster, unable to believe and not daring to hope" and offered Gurdjieff as the guide through the perplexities of life in the shadow of nuclear destruction. In connection with Bennett's lectures, Mme. de Salzmann flew to London to give instructions in the movements. The response was gratifyingly large.

Gurdjieff had been booked to leave for the United States on October twentieth, four days before Bennett delivered his last lecture. But, as in the case of Ouspensky on a very similar occasion, the sea voyage never took place.

From what Gurdjieff said to followers like Fritz Peters, it seems that he must have known for some time that death was approaching. William Welch records an odd incident, about two weeks before Gurdjieff's death, when the Master drove to the Russian church in the Rue Daru with four or five companions, and for an hour sat silently outside it. "They remembered it only later and wondered about it when they found themselves in that same cathedral standing around his bier."

Gurdjieff treated his doctors abominably, ignoring or refusing their advice. Eventually the newly qualified Dr. William Welch was sent for from America to take over from the corps of distinguished physicians who had been repulsed by the Master. Gurdjieff now seemed to have little will to live, and the doctor removed him without difficulty to the American Hospital at Neuilly. There he prepared to tap Gurdjieff's dropsy. "Only if you not tired, Doctor," the Master told him.

Gurdjieff died at 11 A.M. on October 29, 1949.

"Do you want to die like a dog?" he had thundered at his quivering pupils; and Pierre Schaeffer asserts that Gurdjieff's own death was far from the bestial fate he predicted for the mass of mankind. "He didn't die like a dog," Schaeffer writes. "In death he made a difficult, indefinable movement with his extraordinarily contorted muscles. There was a force behind the mask, apparently so calm, a gaze behind those lids that would never open again. This gaze imprinted itself on our pupils. Every eye caught a gleam and we assimilated this food too." Dr. Welch was at the death bed, but he excuses himself from giving a medical opinion on the facts. "Although I was present," he writes, "and the events that occurred were unique in my experience, I do not know their significance and have no way of expressing them in a proper context. . . . For myself what I must acknowledge is that the death of Gurdjieff was the death of a man 'not in quotation marks.' And I have seen many men die."

It is said that as he lay dying he murmured to the crowd by his bedside:

"I'm leaving you all in a fine mess!" When I asked Henri Tracol if this story were authentic, he smiled and spread his hands.

"He did *not* say that," he answered and paused, before continuing: "—but it was true!"

It was the final coup. The old blister, the sainted *gaffar*, the Great Magician had—*in his death*, done it again!

15

The Quest for Harmony

Gurdjieff's obsequies were celebrated by a crowd of devotees, who were left wondering what the next step was to be. According to Dr. William Welch, on the Thursday before his death Gurdjieff had summoned Mme. de Salzmann to his bedside and issued instructions for the continuation of his work. On the evening of the Master's burial in Avon—where he lies between two great menhirs of undressed stone—she spoke to about fifty pupils and announced her program. She told them that a teacher of Gurdjieff's stature could never be replaced. Their one chance was to work together: to create the conditions which Gurdjieff had been able to manufacture by himself, but which could not now be engineered by a single person. J. G. Bennett had already been approached by French rebels against her authority, and he knew full well the differences of opinion which divided both the English and the American followers of Gurdjieff and Ouspensky. "Having seen the friction between those who had been closest to Gurdjieff," Bennett writes, "I could not but marvel at her optimism; yet I was bound to agree that in unity lay our only hope."

The Masters might be gone; but there were Mistresses to take their place. The forces attempting to weld Gurdjieff's fragmented legacy together were dominated by four remarkable women. Two—Mme. de Salzmann and Mme. de Hartmann—have been active, up to the present time (Mme. de Hartmann died in September 1979), while Mme. Ouspensky died in 1963 and Jane Heap the following year. The organization which they jointly created owes general allegiance to Mme. de Salzmann in Paris and has increasingly developed the characteristics of a church. It is known simply as "the Work" and has been able to bring multifarious points of view under a common umbrella. For example, attempts to bridge the gap between Maurice Nicoll and the orthodox Gurdjieffians had been made even before the doctor's death from cancer in 1953. This was important, because after the deaths of his own two teachers, Nicoll had increasingly come into the open. With a following of about six hundred people, a headquarters at Great Amwell House in Hertfordshire, and some influence on the journalistic world, his support was significant. Volumes I–III of what eventually became Nicoll's five-volume *Psychological Commentaries on the Teaching of G. I. Gurdjieff and P. D. Ouspensky* was first privately printed in 1949. These were followed by his *The New Man* (1950), a volume of Gospel interpretations inspired by the psychoanalytical interpretation of dreams, and *Living Time* (1952), an extension of Ouspensky's time speculations with the aid of classical philosophy. The *Commentaries* received an enthusiastic endorsement from Mme. de Salzmann, and for his part Nicoll was careful to deny that his own works had any authoritative nature. They were mere "personal contributions." In view of their teacher's attitude it is not surprising that by 1960 Nicoll's successors had joined the Paris-oriented London Gurdjieff Society.

On the other hand there were the bodies of opinion which would have nothing to do with Gurdjieff's successors and were mostly headed by Ouspensky's former pupils. There were the Society for the Study of Normal Man—founded in 1951 by the adherents of Dr. Francis Roles—the London-based School of Economic Science; and by 1955 the supporters of J. G. Bennett, who had seceded from the Paris-controlled groups. Some disciples in the Ouspenskian line of succession have wanted to preserve the teaching as they received it from their Master—in their phrase, to "keep the System pure"—while others believe that Ouspensky's exposition of Gurdjieff's ideas had all along had "something missing." Still others have been inspired to add their own contribution to the Work ideas. It would be possible to write another entire book about the bewildering variety of quests on which the independent groups have embarked; and here it can only be said that these have embraced Greek Orthodoxy, Hinduism and the Whirling Dervishes, as well as resulting in a four-volume survey of the whole human knowledge by Bennett and the introduction to the West of the Indonesian religion Subud and the Transcendental Meditation of the Maharishi Mahesh Yogi.

It would also be possible to trace the widespread literary influence of the Work, ranging from the outright condemnation and bitterness of Paul Serant's *Le Meurtre Rituel* (1951) through the covert influence of the idea of "awakened men" in the Zimiamvian fantasies of E. R. Eddison, to the permeation by Work theory of the later poems and plays of T. S. Eliot. But a halt must be made somewhere: although even a book which takes the deaths of Gurdjieff and Ouspensky as its historical conclusion would be incomplete without at least one postscript indicating some of the directions in which it was possible to travel after the great men were gone. One of the most intriguing journeys—incorporating within itself so many possibilities—was the personal odyssey of Rodney Collin. If any one of the disciples' spiritual journeys suggested ways of fashioning harmony out of discords, it was this extraordinary pilgrimage.

For Rodney Collin the time of Ouspensky's death remained the focal point in the history of the Work, the core of all meanings and the source of future inspiration. Long afterward he still found himself "looking back at all those years of Ouspensky's work between the wars as *preparation*— preparation for something that was actually conceived in the end. . . ." In November 1949, he had expressed the sense that all times and all possibilities were somehow contained in Ouspensky's passage from this world to another. Death, he wrote, was "the greatest mystery, in which everything becomes possible, *nothing is impossible*."

The miracles surrounding Ouspensky's death had proved the quality of the event; and Collin had experienced his own personal miracle. When he had locked himself into the room where Ouspensky had died something had happened to him—or, more precisely, something *came* to him.

I always disliked and still do dislike the idea of "communications." For although such things are certainly possible from higher man they are inevitably understood wrongly, and immediately they are spoken about give rise to superstition in some and incredulity in others. And in due course the superstitious and the incredulous inevitably quarrel.

But I have to tell you a story. Not long after Ouspensky's death I went to his bedroom and sat down there in a rather curious, superstitious mood. After a minute or two a voice in me—it could have been a memory of Ouspensky's voice—said with the chuckle which I also remember very well: "You want a communication from the dead. Well, you won't get one!"

During his six days of isolation Rodney Collin clearly thought that he had received, if not a "communication," at least some insight or information into the state of the universe. He moved into a flat in central London and completed a book he called *The Theory of Eternal Life*.

This was based on the visions which had come to him during the six days at Lyne. It possesses the extremely brittle coherence of many visionary works—like, for example *Tertium Organum*, with which it can be compared. Some tremendous upheaval, some gigantic implosion of *new meanings* has transformed the author's universe, and suddenly everything he ever knew realigns itself to support his new vision of the world. Like *Tertium Organum*, *The Theory of Eternal Life* can be frequently faulted where it tries to be most "scientific"—a mistake in the first chapter ruins the supposed mathematical basis of the argument—but its author's intense conviction of the importance of his miracle provides—as it provides for *Tertium Organum*—a justification for the book.

The Theory of Eternal Life in a sense *was* Rodney Collin's miracle, or a central part of it. The first edition was printed privately and issued anonymously in 1950. Collin could not be induced to put his name to it, as he maintained that he had no right to claim authorship. The unanticipated result was that *The Theory of Eternal Life* sold heavily on the basis of a rumor that it was by Ouspensky. Many people who knew Collin have asserted that he rose above his natural capacities to write this book, and the conclusion of *The Theory of Eternal Life* shows that he agreed. Referring to Ouspensky, he writes: "Of his achievement then let this present book stand witness, written this year following his death, of knowledge undeserved by me. Let him who can understand understand. For so it is."

He begins *The Theory of Eternal Life* by dividing human life into nine periods, which he imagines to be related on a logarithmic scale. The enneagram is clearly in the back of his mind. Each period of human life is used to develop a higher function: thus the period of gestation produces the physical body, the first seven years of life elaborate the personality, and maturity is the time when the soul should be developed. Then comes the first covert reference to Ouspensky's death: "We have every reason to believe that the impact of ever higher energies at successive stages of life does not end at . . . the prime of life." The "prime of life" is the penultimate point on his scale; and the last point is death. At death—when according to Ouspensky the death agony merges with the ecstasy of conception for the next recurrence—the energy released is *"too intense* to be contained within a body of cellular structure," which naturally dissolves.

With these principles established, the author turns to religious and mythical writings. Traditional wisdom teaches that a period of time elapses between death and the allotting of a new body to the soul. St. Makary of Alexandria, *The Tibetan Book of the Dead*, and the Platonic myth of Er, all demonstrate that the soul does not immediately reincarnate. To discover what happens in the intervening time, Collin projects his logarithmic scale into a diagram of what he calls "the invisible worlds," which had come to him during his vigil at Lyne. This diagram consists of four circles or rings interlinked as if a figure eight had been transfixed by the sign for infinity— or another figure eight at right angles to the first, joining it at the central point. These four circles represent the four possible worlds. The first circle is the "cellular" world in which we live; its sibling on the lateral figure of eight is a world of higher energy, the "molecular" world; above both soars the "electronic" world of extremely rarified matter; and below everything at the bottom of the vertical figure eight lies a heavy, nearly inert world of mineral existence. In religious terms these worlds correspond to Earth, Purgatory, Heaven, and Hell. In the interval between death and birth, a man lives in the invisible worlds.

The "soul" is born at the physical death of a man and serves as the vehicle of consciousness in the molecular world, or Purgatory. Before death, some men develop a soul, which has "the freedom of the Earth world"; that is, it can pass through physical objects. Similarly the "spirit" is the body or vehicle of consciousness in the electronic world. The spirit is composed of a degree of matter equivalent to light and possessing similar freedoms; for example, travel in three dimensions. By projecting the logarithmic scale which governs his division of the visible life of man into different periods, Rodney Collin even arrives at the average lifetime of these more rarified bodies. "Man's individuality," he writes, "which inhabits a physical body for 76 years, has previously inhabited a soul for one month and before that a spirit for forty minutes. And birth into that spirit was simultaneous with the death of the previous physical body."

But entry to the electronic of Heaven-world presents such a shock to the individuality that most men awake from death only in the latter stages of their sojourn in the world which follows (the world of the soul, or Purgatory). Apparently deriving his idea from Plato, Collin maintains that in Purgatory time is reversed. The originality of this conception staggers him. "It is an idea of such power, intensity and far-reaching effect that it could not be invented. It is too strong for human imagination, which of itself can only produce weak ideas, enervating thoughts." In the world of Purgatory causes become effects. "I create the kind of world in which I live . . . the murderer gives birth to the murdered man and is responsible for the latter's life." This unnerving prospect has been exploited in Philip K. Dick's science fiction novel, Counter-Clock World (1968). Memory of the counter-clock experience, Collin thinks, would explain why the saviors of humanity feel that they were responsible for all the suffering and evil in the world, when from the opposite direction of time they appear to assimilate it.

The Heaven-world stands above Earth and Purgatory—at right angles to all Time, outside Time and contemplating its flow. Beneath the worlds of Time lies Hell, the destination of degenerating souls, where Time flows slowly and interminably.

Legends of the Last Judgment in fact represent the moment when a soul, having traveled through the invisible worlds, passes into a new physical body. The stumbling block to the whole argument is the absence of memory in the ordinary man, reborn man—a fact to which legends of the River Lethe refer. The problem, as Rodney Collin saw it, is to develop memory so that it can survive the shock of the transition into the invisible worlds. First a man must "develop the film" of his own memories—a doctrine which the author derived through Ouspensky directly from Gurdjieff. "Memories—of people, places, critical and trivial incidents—which are ordinarily evoked in him only by association, must be brought back sequentially and by will." A man must concentrate on every single event in his life: "Particularly those *which he is reluctant to recall.*" It is the unpleasant memories, the memories of mistakes and weaknesses, which will lead a man to remember the reasons for his embarrassments and failures, and therefore give him the possibility of change in the next recurrence. This is linked to Ouspensky's teaching that every life has its "cross-roads": points where different courses of action can make or mar the life. The man desiring to change his next recurrence must clearly note these crossroads in his newly developed memory:

Perhaps he may go back to the actual scene of some mistake or opportunity, and striving with all his force to remember himself, endeavour to attach to some wall or tree engraved upon his memory the understanding which he wishes to transmit. He may tell himself that when he stands there *in his next life* the sight of this tree must *remind him to remember.*

It will then be borne upon him that his only chance is to become conscious *now*. He will understand practically the principle that our only way of communicating memory to another life is by the force of consciousness in this. And he will see that the purpose of acquiring consciousness in life, is *to remain conscious through death.*

In the colossal task of maintaining the thread of consciousness through death, only the most severe measures are likely to succeed. Rodney Collin suggests that *suffering* provides the necessary fixative. Christ, Socrates, Buddha, and the Tibetan yogi Milarepa all seemed to invite martyrdom. This then was the explanation for the curious activities of Ouspensky's last days: *they were a preparation for self-remembering through death*. To Collin it seemed that if Ouspensky had been preparing for the conscious acquisition of spirit, he must also be helping his followers to acquire souls. This was an application of the principle which the Master had often repeated: in order to move up the ladder of being a man must put someone in his place. Everyone concerned is therefore "moving up one"—being dragged up by the teacher's cosmic ascent. This complicated process shatters the world fixed in its normally unalterable recurrence. It can take place only at the death of the teacher and—it is never clear precisely why, except that Ouspensky had thrown out the idea in the *New Model*—this requires the performance of "a tremendous cosmic drama" in which "the chief event will be the death of the producer."

Ouspensky's name is never mentioned. During one short section the Russian appears as "a man I knew"; but it is doubtful whether *The Theory of Eternal Life* would make sense to anyone unaware that it sprang fully fledged from Ouspensky's deathbed. The statement that the drama which precedes "transfiguration into the electronic world" can only be organized telepathically, remains an additional extravagance if the reader does not know that telepathy was commonplace at Lyne in September 1947. References to the miraculous appearance of Christ after the Crucifixion seems to be gratuitous wonder-making—until we remember that Ouspensky was thought by some of his followers to have appeared or at least made his presence felt after his death.

Rodney Collin drew several conclusions from his continuing sense of the miraculous. The first was that miracles occurring after a transfiguration were a sign that the experiment had succeeded. They were also designed as a final test for a teacher's disciples—to see whether they possessed sufficient faith to follow where the teacher led. The transfiguration had opened "a crack through all levels of matter," through which "for all beings there now lies a way of escape which did not exist before." On these principles he proposed to organize the rest of his life.

While her husband was writing, Janet Collin-Smith had been standing guard over him, preventing him from being overwhelmed by visitors who sought in his newly discovered certainties an authority to replace that of Ouspensky. But he seemed to have little wish to teach, although at least one friend felt that he was "going somewhere very fast." In a letter of July 30, 1948, he wrote

> It is interesting . . . that people say: "Collin-Smith is teaching, will teach, won't teach. They don't understand that I am *learning* and this is the only way that I or anyone else can do so. I remember very clearly sitting with Ouspensky at Longchamps in New York sometime about 1942, I think, and asking why everything seemed to have come to a stop. He said: "You forget one thing; many people forget it—to learn more you have to teach."

By the time this was written, Collin was in Mexico. In the drab period following the end of the war, many of Ouspensky's former followers considered emigration. There was rationing at home, a Labour Government which some of the better-off no doubt wished fervently to avoid, and after their teacher vanished, there seemed little reason to stay. Some emigrated to South Africa, others to the United States—where Mendham still held open its doors. Rodney Collin had grown to love Mexico during his wartime stay in America, and after a period of indecision, he left with his family and a small number of followers for Guadalajara, where *The Theory of Eternal Life* was finished in November 1948, and then moved into an old hacienda in Tlalpam on the outskirts of Mexico City. They rented a flat in the center of Mexico City where meetings were held which attracted Mexicans and members of the local expatriate society. Their community at Tlalpam was joined by a few more disoriented Ouspenskians from England.

Until 1954 Rodney Collin did his best to project the vision of a sacred drama and to take the role in it which he understood had been allotted to him. Underneath the part he was playing—and this was a role half-deliberately conceived on a grand theological scale—what was there? "A very fine man," says one person who knew him. To a woman who knew both Nicoll and Ouspensky, Collin seemed "the most lovable and the warmest of them all. He had charity to the tips of his fingers." He seems always to have found it easy to attract friends; yet until he met Ouspensky, he had no fixed center of gravity. From then on a great earnestness drove him.

It may have driven him too far. There are critics who say that he eventually went mad. Another faction maintains that earlier in his life Rodney Collin had been a skillful hypnotist and accused him of using hypnotic powers on people "in the Work." Tall, charming, and considerate, the contours of his face particularly English, he seems the most unlikely figure to invest with the cloak of a Svengali; and the accusation is denied by those who knew him best. But outside the closed circle of "Work" values, divorced from the intensity of his private experience, what sense does he make? The conclusion is inevitable: only within the context of the role he envisaged for himself can he be understood.

In the letters he wrote from Mexico to his numerous correspondents, he enlarged upon the theme of the miraculous. Ouspensky had gone in search of the miraculous and had enabled others to experience the miraculous for themselves. Just as Ouspensky's death was for him the key point in time, the state of mind he had experienced with some of the others at Lyne remained the key attitude to life. In one aspect he saw his mission as being to break down resistance to the miraculous. In November 1951, he wrote: "My own aim is to live permanently in this miraculous atmosphere; or at least permanently in the knowledge and memory of it. At such times it is less and less the need of *personal work* I feel, and more and more the urgency of acting as a pure and understanding instrument in the realisation of a great plan." In July 1953, he used a metaphor which leaves no doubt of how he saw the situation: "All work for the creation of groups on earth is concerned with the building of arks to be navigated from a higher level. But my experience is that navigation may be far more exact and meaningful after the Teacher achieves and dies. For then he sees further and wider; yet his work must still be with the ark he made. . . . The difference is like navigating with a great captain, and then navigating under the first mate with radio."

Rodney Collin was content to be an instrument, and to encourage in others an apprehension of the realm of wonders he himself had contemplated. The great energy released by Ouspensky's death could still give "understanding and direction" to those who had felt its effects. By June 1951, he had come to consider that "the question of actual contact with Ouspensky—through time or however it is—seems to be the key question, and no longer for a few lucky individuals but on a larger scale." His part of the Work could form part of a mystical body connected with Ouspensky through the crack in matter which his death had opened up, and maintaining its connection through the emotional support it gave to the teacher who had gone ahead. "Those who believe in him become part of his work, and he in turn becomes responsible for them."

The essential for this was what Ouspensky called "positive attitude," which is nothing more nor less than faith. Rodney Collin's advice to more orthodox Ouspenskians was in the uncompromising terms of a fundamentalist, berating Doubting Thomas. To those who floundered about wailing that their teachers had been taken from them, he wrote in tones of incomprehension. "If we ever had a teacher we have one now. If we have not one now, did we ever have one?"

His answer to the more staid—those without "positive attitude" toward the facts of Ouspensky's death and who by implication questioned his own sanity—applied both to the last days of his departed teacher and to his own condition at the time of writing:

All that Ouspensky said and did at that time seemed to me to have exactly this purpose and effect—to sort out the people who could respond to the miraculous from those who could not. . . . It was very clear that if a man in a higher state of consciousness acts directly from the perceptions of that state, . . . he will seem mad to men in an ordinary state.

By July 24, 1953, his impatience with the custodians of inherited tradition had broken all bounds and he rebuked the reactionaries who refused to take up the challenge of the new age:

It was put into our hands to be the agents of miracles. And we tell people to control the expression of their negative emotions, not to push, and to form an orderly queue for an unknown bus, which may one day take them a twopenny stage nearer heaven. I wonder that a great voice doesn't come out of heaven thundering: "O ye of little faith!"

When will people understand that a new age has really dawned? When will they stop sealing up the terrible crack in heaven which Ouspensky has made with precautions and good behaviour? We must allow divine madness to take possession of us now, before hell freezes!

With Rodney Collin's increasing emancipation from the letter of the law as Ouspensky preached it, the routine of the community at Tlalpam departed from the pattern of Lyne Place. Activity centered around an extraordinary project which originated in the visions experienced by its designer in the week after Ouspensky's death. This was for a "three-dimensional diagram" to symbolize the laws governing universal harmony. In 1949 a field in the mountains outside Mexico City was bought, and work began on a building which became known as the Planetarium of Tetecala. Tetecala—meaning "stone house of God"—was the name of the field on which the building stood. The site was perched dramatically 9,000 feet above sea level, with a magnificent view over the valley in which Mexico City lay 2,000 feet below, and the design of the building was equally remarkable. The ground plan was based on two chambers hollowed from the lava rock on which the Planetarium was to stand. The larger area— forty-three feet in diameter—was named the Chamber of the Sun. Linked to it was the smaller Chamber of the Moon. "Between the two in a small space," Joyce Collin-Smith writes, "a great upturned shell received the sun's rays through an aperture, at the Summer Solstice. Round the chamber ran a passage-way, the walls of which were lined with mosaic designs drawn and laid by himself, depicting all levels of organic life, from the primordial to the perfect Man. Above ground, the planetarium itself was to have been flanked by the library, and a room for Mexican dancing, lectures or theatre performances."

The community at Tlalpam planned to build their own houses beside the Planetarium. A clinic and dispensary were established for the local *peons*. The strange immigrant band began to integrate themselves with the life of the country. Rodney Collin established an English bookshop in Mexico City and made plans for marketing Mexican arts and crafts. He set up a publishing firm, Ediciones Sol, to issue his own books and Spanish translations of Ouspensky and Maurice Nicoll. He felt that he, the Work, and Mexico were all on the edge of a new beginning. On February 22, 1950, he wrote: "It is very difficult to convey the strange springtime feeling of certainty, of beginning from the beginning, of a new unspoiled start, which one gets in Mexico just now. Everything is growing, expanding, developing . . ." By abandoning the System, Ouspensky had set his followers free to travel their own paths. "The idea of reconstruction seems to be endless," Collin felt. "It will be different for each person according to his knowledge and capacity."

The new beginning in Mexico was watched with some trepidation from the Old World. To some it seemed that by erecting the Planetarium, Collin was embalming the Work in a stone coffin. On the principle that there should be no permanent forms, no tangible monuments, no direct literary representations of the teaching, this was unanswerable. Yet when the Collin-Smiths traveled to Europe in 1952–53, few voices were raised against them. Rodney Collin was invited by Maurice Nicoll to lecture at Great Amwell, and he remained in contact with Francis Roles and the more orthodox Ouspenskians. He also visited Paris where, through the Librairie Véga, he bought a large private library of occult books to be housed at the Planetarium. He took part in the work of the Paris groups; and with the single exception of J. G. Bennett—with whom he appears to have quarreled—he was in contact with all the different strands of activity deriving from Gurdjieff or Ouspensky. His own task began to seem more and more a work harmonizing apparently conflicting points of view.

Harmony! What to others appeared schism and dissension, seemed to Collin a necessary division of functions, the extension of a sphere of influence rather than a proclamation of dogmatic "teaching"; the provision of many different but complementary points of view. At first, with the memory of the apocalypse of Lyne upon him, his perception of the unity underlying all things had been expressed in terms of the union of Ouspensky's followers with their transfigured Master. As the impact of the experience faded with time, his sense of harmony seemed more and more to refer to the Work as a whole, to all the influences stemming from Gurdjieff and Ouspensky. This larger idea of harmony had in fact been born soon after Ouspensky's death. In August 1948, he had answered one inquirer that progress was necessary—but at the same time, that the growth of a living organism had been in the plan of the Work from the beginning.

What he was doing was providing the theology to support the work of Mme. de Salzmann and Mme. Ouspensky in bringing the scattered groups together—although he saw more unity in diversity than other leaders of the Work. He set out deliberately to write scripture, revelation, and commentary all at once; and he found his inspiration in *A New Model of the Universe*. When Ouspensky refers in the *New Model* to "the drama of Christ"—the mystery play acted out on the stage of the world—he says that no one can now tell if any of the actors in that play stumbled over their lines or missed their cues. All mistakes were corrected in the Gospels, which presented a perfect picture so that the play should have its intended effect. As early as February 1949, Rodney Collin had committed himself to the task of ensuring that the drama of Ouspensky was presented as flawlessly as possible.

> I am sure that it is in some way an esoteric principle that records have to be "made right." It is not a question of hiding mistakes or unpleasantness or anything like that. But if someone in the play acts outside of character, so to speak, the record has to correct it. The text of the play has to be more perfect than the play itself. How this can be is practically impossible to say. The New Testament must be the perfect example: *everything* is right.

Collin embodied his convictions in a pamphlet, *The Herald of Harmony*, which Ediciones Sol published in 1954. With its title harking back to *Herald of Coming Good*, it proclaimed that its author's allegiance was no longer simply Ouspenskian. The pamphlet made huge claims for the mission of Gurdjieff and Ouspensky. Each age had had a messenger sent out by "the Hierarchy," which Collin also called "Great School." The last age was that of Christ with his message of love; but that age had lacked the element of harmony. Gurdjieff and Ouspensky were the messengers of the Hierarchy for the new era, and their complementary qualities formed a polarity on which their work was based.

The deaths of the two Masters still appeared of transcendental significance, although *The Herald of Harmony* was a little doubtful about that of Gurdjieff who, "joking up to heaven, escaped with but the slightest singeing of his wings, a drift of unearthly music echoing in his trail." Both Gurdjieff and Ouspensky now took their places as spiritual influences on the coming age. The destiny envisaged for the Work was enormous. "Its interdependent parts—now single men, now groups—later must grow to nations, beliefs, whole races and their destiny." It was to be the fertilizing agent for the whole new era.

Everything, as Rodney Collin had written in 1951, was "part of a great and foreseen plan." His own role in the plan was to proclaim harmony, and in carrying out this task, he claimed the same poetic autonomy as in the creation of the Planetarium. As he wrote in the foreword to his play *Hellas* —written in 1949 and published the next year—"So much was put into the fashionable jargon of our day—in scientific terms, with electronic matter for divinity, and nuclear fission for its attainment. But not everyone is at home with molecules, and those that are grow tired of them at times. So now we must return to legend, striving to reanimate a more attractive form." He was dramatizing the mythical possibilities inherent in the historical situation; and in his own activities in Mexico, he tried to keep alive the sense of the miraculous and the perception of harmony by activating the oldest of all harmonic myths: the relationship between man and the stars.

In 1954 his long book, *The Theory of Celestial Influence*, was published in English. He regarded *The Theory of Eternal Life* as a condensation of some ideas contained in the larger book, and *The Theory of Celestial Influence* also had its roots in his visions at Lyne. Its author even saw it as the fulfillment of a promise made to him by Ouspensky on the first occasion they had met privately in Gwyndwr Road. He had told the Master that he was a writer by nature and asked his advice about his journalistic career. Ouspensky's reply had been, "'Better not get too involved. Later we may find something for you to write.'" It was a rule that if one asked Ouspensky's advice, that advice had the force of law, and Collin had written nothing for the next ten years. "But in the end," he noted, "O. kept his promise. And the outline of the present book was written in the two months immediately before his death . . . as a direct result of what he was trying to achieve and show at that time."

Written, Collin seems to have believed, under the direction of Ouspensky, *The Theory of Celestial Influence* is an ambitious attempt to link the ideas of the System with the findings of science and to calculate the cycles which govern the workings of nature. But whereas Ouspensky had drawn Gurdjieff's Ray of Creation as a diagram of various degrees of matter, Collin was concerned not with degrees of matter expressed as "all suns" or "all worlds," but with the actual physical planets. He calculated the life of the solar system; correlated planetary cycles with the functions of the human organism; coordinated cosmic factors with the rise and fall of civilizations; and in general, attempted to produce a contemporary version of the Renaissance philosophy of the harmony of the spheres. The world is one united organism, and man is a corpuscle in the world body. Such corpuscles are called "cosmoses": "The possibility of self-evolution or self-transcendence implies a very special plan and structure which some creatures have and others do not have. Thus man, who possesses the possibility of perfecting and transcending himself, can be called a cosmos, whereas a dog, which seems to be a finished experiment with no further possibilities, cannot."

The designation can also apply to groups of men. Under normal conditions, man develops in response to influences created in the conventional processes of nature. But these are much too slow to permit real growth. The result is the appearance of "schools of regeneration" which stimulate natural processes to encourage quicker development. The appearance of such schools is governed by the 165-year cycle of Neptune. By calculating from 30 B.C. Rodney Collin arrives at various dates which can be associated with "esoteric schools." Thus the builders of the Gothic cathedrals, who so interested Ouspensky, flourished circa 1125; and after a number of 165-year periods, the Rosicrucians appeared about the year 1620. Never stated, but always implied, is the most recent date on the cycle of Neptune: 1950. It is safe to imagine with what esoteric school this is associated.

A true school, Rodney Collin writes, "endeavors to simulate and in successful cases *actually creates a cosmos.*" Members of the school act the parts which in the great body of the universe are taken, for example, by the planets. In this replica of the cosmic dance the teacher *is the Sun.*

The Theory of Celestial Influence is dedicated to Ouspensky: "Magistro Meo, qui Sol fuit est et erit . . ."—Ouspensky, "who was, is, and will be the Sun." In *The Theory of Eternal Life*, Rodney Collin argues that the world of the spirit is the world of electronic energy. In several places Collin elaborates on the role of the Sun. Most importantly he writes that although man can imagine an infinity of Absolutes, for all practical purposes, the Sun is God. The implications are extraordinary, especially in view of the astonishing dedication to Ouspensky, *who was, is, and will be the Sun.*

It was Collin's personal truth and quite "beyond argument." Whatever may be thought of his harmonious universe, it has a poetic consistency which, although less compelling than Ouspensky's, required a similar leap of the imagination to perceive and to sustain. But by 1954 something of his earlier frenzy was leaving Rodney Collin. The language of *The Herald of Harmony* is false, stilted, and sugary, however real the convictions which inspired it. And, *The Theory of Celestial Influence*, although written years earlier, shows the gaps in Rodney Collin's armor, which could be ignored in the eccentric ecstasy of *The Theory of Eternal Life.* The longer work was written at high speed and is full of factual errors, but it is the nature of the mind behind it which is called into question. The book gives the impression of a man striving, and failing, to be a polymath. "He did not possess," says one acquaintance, "the intellect for what he was trying to do." Rodney Collin had a journalist's training and a large store of general knowledge: he had, among other jobs, worked on the research staff of the *Daily Express Encyclopedia* in 1934. But general knowledge does not produce generally convincing explanations of the universe. Rodney Collin is more impressive in his theological context, as the man who could live in the miraculous and who wished to inspire others with his version of harmony.

Miracles still pursued him through the last two years of his life. For example: one evening in 1954 or 1955 a companion was seated with him in his study. In amazement she saw his features dissolve and reform into an "Oriental" face. Then it became difficult for her to focus on the face at all, and it seemed as if Rodney Collin were an old man with a fluffy white beard. "It's only because I haven't shaved for some days," he said. Then his face became that of Ouspensky before shifting rapidly through a succession of unfamiliar masks—some Oriental, some simply unknown. When Ouspensky's image appeared, his companion cried out, "You are Ouspensky!" "Very likely," was the calm reply.

And again in a restaurant, the same companion noticed the same phenomenon. "I can see a face again," she said; it seemed to be Chinese. "I think, Tibetan," said Rodney Collin. Then: "Don't be frightened, the curtain of time grows thin, that's all."

But even in the realm of the miraculous, by 1954 something had failed; the batteries were running low. People began to speculate: had he lost his connection, was he mixing the levels of experience? Even—had he begun to *pretend?* He had given up listening to his own voices and begun to rely on others. Compared to what had gone before, he had walked from the Chamber of the Sun into that of the Moon.

Among those who were attracted to the meetings in Mexico City were an Englishman and his Mexican wife. Mrs. D. was a spirit medium, and soon after her arrival in the community at Tlalpam, she began to bring through messages from Ouspensky and Gurdjieff. How are we to account for the fact that the navigator listens to her, unless his radio is not working?

Mrs. D. was an impressive personality and a powerful medium. Her renderings from Gurdjieff and Ouspensky were accompanied by the appropriate manifestations; she would walk like a man, her face would seem to contort into the outline of Gurdjieff's or Ouspensky's, and her voice grew harsh and guttural, even rendering Ouspensky's famous chuckle. She had been known to exhibit the stigmata and, according to some reports, could open the wounds "at will." She had been brought up in the intense atmosphere of Mexican Catholicism, and it was to be expected that her messages would contain the flavor of authoritarian Christianity.

A whole mythology grew up from the stories told by her voices, which supplemented Rodney Collin's interpretation of the mssion of Gurdjieff and Ouspensky. Behind the great Masters, and in some way supporting them, were a pair of early Christian saints—Cosmas and Damian, the medical saints who were the patrons of the Medici. Ouspensky, of course, was named "Pyotr Demianovitch" and it was rumored that the name of "Cosmas" was somehow associated with Gurdjieff. Behind St. Cosmas and St. Damian was a mysterious character called "Ivan Ivanovitch," who appeared at odd times in history, and inspired all Ouspensky's heroes—the "Rome School," Stevenson, Nietzsche, Gurdjieff, and Ouspensky's grandmother—and eventually by some mystical subterfuge, turned out to be St. Luke himself. . . .

In 1954 the house at Tlalpam was sold and the community dispersed into family units in Mexico City, although the Planetarium remained the focus of their activity. A Christian note, pitched in an uncertain key, began to be heard in the publications of Ediciones Sol. In *The Herald of Harmony*, Rodney Collin claimed his harmonious gospel as the "New Christianity." The same year, he published another pamphlet called *The Christian Mystery*, which included a "Litany for the Enneagram." Yet another pamphlet called *The Pyramid of Fire* was withdrawn after publication.* An encounter with Catholicism became inevitable.

In the summer of 1954 the Collin-Smiths, accompanied by Mrs. D., made an expedition to Europe. The voices traveled with them; and the little group was directed from country to country on a mysterious occult quest. "We went looking for traces of schools in the past," Rodney Collin wrote, ". . . and in a way difficult to describe, one seems also to make a living connection through time back to those experiments." The quest was not altogether successful. They visited Seville, where the voices told them to look for a particular text in a specific book in a certain library: but the book was not there. After Holy Week in Seville, they traveled through the Greek islands, Egypt, Syria, Lebanon, Persia, and Turkey before returning to Mexico through Rome, Paris, and London. "Although we didn't fully understand this when we started," Rodney Collin wrote the following year, "it is now clear that this last trip was a journey in search of the Passion."

For the voices had not entirely failed, although they were not to be relied on for the exact page references of esoteric scholarship. The party had halted at Rome, and here Rodney Collin was received into the Catholic Church. It may be suspected that the voices—although they appeared to be indicating the Pyramids or the Mount of Olives—had actually been whispering "St. Peter's" all along.

On his return to Mexico, Rodney Collin found that many of his more educated followers had drifted away. He had to defend himself against charges of superstitious reliance on the voices of Mrs. D., and compared the lady's mission to that of Joan of Arc. He also had to defend himself

---

*A fate which met several of the Ediciones Sol pamphlets. The earliest to be withdrawn was supposed to have been written by Ouspensky, *Notes on Saint John's Gospel*. This was a manuscript discovered by Rodney Collin among Ouspensky's papers, but which was in fact the work of another pupil who had submitted it to him. Collin issued it believing it to be Ouspensky's work, but withdrew it when he discovered his mistake. Why the later booklets were withdrawn is a matter for conjecture.

against accusations of turning his coat. In October 1954, he issued what reads as a general statement on his conversion:

I realized many years ago that our work is not a substitute for religion. It is a key to religion, as it is a key to art, science and all other sides of human life . . .

By temperament, inclination, study, and by the country in which I have to work, I became a Roman Catholic. I had already anticipated this several years ago. It only needed the right moment and opportunity. For this time is a crossroads.

Other people, at the same crossroads, might join different religions, though it seems to me that Roman Catholicism has the greatest reserve of esoteric truth. In any case, whatever religion they chose, it would be the esoteric part which they joined. . . . For the esoteric parts of all religions are connected. . . .

A year later he reassured a correspondent that although he was now a Catholic he still belonged to the Fourth Way, and "no one either in or out of the Church" could persuade him of a contradiction. But relations with the more orthodox followers of Gurdjieff and Ouspensky had by now become strained. Those who had earlier been prepared to extend an understanding tolerance now felt that he had lost his way.

In South America, however, his influence was widespread. Besides the Mexico City group—by now chiefly Mexican in nationality—groups had been started in Peru, Chile, Uruguay, and Argentina (to the last of which arrived Jorge Luis Borges, perambulating the corridors of his eternal Library). In Mexico itself, Collin's joint activities with Mrs. D. entered the public eye, as they busied themselves in welfare work among the poor. At the Planetarium, movements were taught and theatrical performances given—which significantly, included Anouilh's play about St. Joan, *The Lark*—and Rodney Collin involved himself in a ceaseless round of activity. He was becoming increasingly simple and childlike. Some people see him as a Schweitzer-figure; others would say that he became increasingly suggestible. He drove himself harder and harder, tiring himself by responding to every call upon his time; sleeping little, growing exhausted in the thin atmosphere after long expeditions through uninhabited country with little food or rest. One such walk lasted for several days during which he ate only a handful of raisins. His personal "super-efforts" were intensified by prayer and meditation; and he began to take part in the traditional pilgrimages to the celebrated shrines of Mexico.

He issued a "Programme of Study" directing his followers to study themselves under different varieties of law—as unity, duality, trinity, as an interplay of the numbers seven and twelve, as multiplicity. The program explained what this all meant to him, and the results of his own inquiries are to be found in *The Theory of Celestial Influence*. The only new development during 1955 was a pervasive emphasis on the term "Hierarchy." The expression had appeared in *The Herald of Harmony*, and in his letters of 1955 it became increasingly important as the bridge between the ideas of Ouspensky and the Catholic Church. It was "the Hierarchy" which had sent Gurdjieff and Ouspensky to earth:

> There exists an invisible Hierarchy of spirits who order and direct all the different aspects of life on earth and humanity. That which Ouspensky calls the Inner Circle of Humanity, that which the Church calls the Church Triumphant, that is what we call the Hierarchy.
>
> The Hierarchy consists in Our Lord Jesus Christ, the spirit and redeemer of our universe, and all his conscious helpers, great and small.

He was straining now to fit the old pattern on to the new, and even the attempts at synthesis grew more and more reluctant. He had found his own home in the Catholic Church, and his letters are almost free of the complicated terms of the System. There are strong suggestions that, having performed a long and complicated journey *in*, Rodney Collin was at last coming *out*. We might assume that he had emerged from the cavern into the light of common day—but during the autumn and winter of 1955, a fresh sense of urgency appeared to strike him. Something was at last going to happen, the new age was really going to dawn. On October 3, 1955, he wrote: "I think we have come to a cross-roads on many different scales. Some tremendous opportunity is preparing." From his Planetarium he scanned the night skies and plotted an extraordinary astrological portent: on January 21, 1956 all the planets would be arranged in the form of a cross, in "the arch-sign and promise of harmony for the age to come." That same January, he led a night pilgrimage from the Planetarium to the shrine of Our Lady of Guadelupe. The walk was thirty miles, and during Mass in the Basilica, he fainted. This may have been the first of a series of heart attacks brought on by overexertion.

In March and April 1956, he concentrated on setting his business affairs in order, observing that all debts must be paid before embarking on a new undertaking. He told his friends that something momentous was about to happen, but he still did not know what it was. There had to be *something new:* but what this was he could not see. When, at the end of April, he left with his wife, and other followers for Lima, the expedition was made in an atmosphere of baffled anticipation. Rodney Collin expected great things from his visit to Peru; but his vision had clouded and he could not see *beyond*.

His exhaustion was intensified by a week's hard work with his Lima group. He held classes of movements, saw pupils individually and superintended general meetings. On May 2, the party left for Cuzco in an unpressurized plane, and during the journey through the mountains, they had to take oxygen from tubes. Cuzco itself is at a height of 11,800 feet and, after their arrival, the Collin-Smiths had to rest to recover from the altitude. Rodney Collin remarked that he felt "rather strange," and much to his wife's surprise—for usually he had no truck with medicines—he took several doses of the coramine that had been prescribed to relieve the effects of altitude sickness.

That afternoon he went out alone into the streets of Lima, where he discovered an orphan beggar boy named Modesto. The boy had a deformed leg which caused him to walk on the toes of his right foot: nevertheless, he accompanied Rodney Collin on a climb up to the huge statue of Christ which stands on the mountain overlooking the city. Here they prayed that Modesto might be healed. When Janet Collin-Smith emerged after the siesta hour, she found a crowd gathered outside a draper's shop where her husband was buying the boy clothes. It appeared that, after the expedition up the mountain, the two had gone together to the public baths where, in a ritual of purification, Rodney Collin had washed the beggar boy and dried him with his own shirt. In the street he spoke to the onlookers and told them that the boy was their responsibility. "You must learn what is harmony," he told them, "you must learn to look after each other; you must learn to give—to give." The predictable retort came from the crowd: "That's all very well for you, you're rich." Rodney Collin replied: "Everyone can give something. Everyone can give a prayer. Even if you can't give anything else, you can always give a smile; that doesn't cost anything." Then he took the boy off to buy him shoes and feed him.

That night he woke his wife. He told her that he was afraid. It had seemed so important that Modesto be cured that he had offered his own body in exchange for the boy's. Afterward he had realized that he was intended to do other work. His wife asked whether he thought that God would change His plans at his request, and Collin replied that those who had invoked the Holy Trinity as he had done were certain to have their requests granted.

On the morning of May 3, Rodney Collin went to Mass and prepared for a trip to some Inca ruins in the hills. Before the party left, Modesto arrived and took his benefactor off to show him where he lived—high up in the cathedral bell tower beneath the bells. The morning's sightseeing went as planned, and the Collin-Smiths returned to their hotel. During the siesta, Rodney Collin went out again as he had done the previous day.

From various accounts which his wife and friends pieced together afterward, he seems to have gone straight to the cathedral to find Modesto in his belfry, ninety-eight steps above the cathedral square. He sat down on a ledge below the parapet, and began to tell Modesto how he was going to arrange for an operation to be carried out on his twisted leg. All the time he was talking, he kept his eyes fixed on the statue of Christ on the mountain opposite. Suddenly he stood up, gave a gasp, and lurched forward on to the top of the parapet, grasping with his hands the two beams which supported the arch above it. Then his head struck one of the beams, and he fell into the street below. An old woman who saw him fall said that he fell feet foremost, his arms outstretched in the form of a cross, and his head canted backward as if his gaze were still fixed upon the statue. He lay on the ground in a peculiar cruciform position, with his right leg drawn up just as the cripple boy's had been. He was smiling.

"It is not unusual," Janet Collin-Smith remarks, "for a man to die of a heart attack after climbing a long flight of steep stairs at such an altitude after weeks of physical effort in a state of exhaustion. It is the natural consequence of physical conditions. It is also natural, on a different level, for a man who has believed with all his being that the object of life is to give all he has for the love of God, in the end to give himself." In what manner Rodney Collin may have "given himself" she does not say. His death could have been an accident, act of God, or the grateful surrender of an exhausted spirit into his Savior's keeping. It could have been a death chosen in accordance with the theories of *The Theory of Eternal Life:* part of a mystery play, part of a process designed to fix his memories through the invisible worlds. Or, it could have been connected with his confession to his wife that he had offered his body in exchange for the health of the beggar boy.

In November, the previous year, a correspondent had asked him about escaping from eternal recurrence. He replied that this could only be done "by sacrificing one's unicellular 'liberty' and becoming absorbed into a higher organism with a higher aim." He had always considered that the little human cosmos should join with a greater whole, and tried to live his life in a universal context. Somehow—in obedience to the laws of harmony he had so laboriously plotted—the universe demanded his death.

The town of Cuzco requested that the foreigner be buried there, and in the presence of a fair-sized crowd, the body was interred in the graveyard of the cathedral. His wife and friends arranged for a tablet to be laid in the square where he had fallen with the inscription: "Here Rodney Collin gave his life to project harmony."

After his death Mrs. D. assumed the direction of his Mexican followers. First one, then another, successor was tried; but no one had the magnetism to hold the group together. There were quarrels and doubts. A prominent member of the Mexico City group wrote letters to Europe claiming that Rodney Collin had gone mad. The voices ordered, countermanded, and ordered again. As a body of people following the Fourth Way, the group disintegrated, and the last book issued under Rodney Collin's name is to be mistrusted. *The Mirror of Light* (1959) is supposed to consist of extracts from his notebooks; but even the editors admit that it is impossible to say which he wrote himself and which came from other sources. Eventually, Mrs. D. founded a Catholic lay order to do good works in Mexico City and became the inspiration of a circle of young Mexican priests. The Chamber of the Moon at Tetacala was turned into a Catholic chapel.

On Rodney Collin's grave in Cuzco blue flowers were planted. Straining for *correspondences, links, perceptions of true relationships*, the devotee of miracles had once sought the key to the operations of immortality. "It's got something to do with blue flowers," he said, ". . . but I can't get further than that." On the headstone was inscribed a prayer he had written two months before he died:

> I was sent to earth;
> My wings were taken;
> My body entered matter;
> My soul was caught by matter;
> The earth sucked me down;
> I came to rest.
>
> I am inert;
> Longing arises;
> I gather my strength;
> Will is born;
> I receive and meditate;
> I adore the Trinity;
> I am in the presence of God.

3

First and Last Things

Timaeus: Don't therefore be surprised, Socrates, if on many matters concerning the gods and the whole world of change we are unable in every respect and on every occasion to render a consistent and accurate account. You must be satisfied if our account is as likely as any, remembering that both you and I who are sitting in judgment upon it are merely human, and you should not look for anything more than a likely story in such matters.

—PLATO, *Timaeus*, 29
translated by H. D. P.
LEE
(Harmondsworth, 1965)

1

The Sources of the System

1. Gurdjieff and Tradition

There is a distinction between the forms and content of Gurdjieff's teaching—or to use the theological terms, "substance" and "accidents." When Gurdjieff was actually engaged in teaching, the accidents may not have affected the substance of what he taught. But for anyone approaching his ideas in historical perspective, such accidents are a stumbling block.

Although he varied the forms within which he worked, Gurdjieff did make consistent use of an elaborate cosmological scheme. This is expressed in the palate-shattering language of *Beelzebub's Tales*, but it is better known through Ouspensky's *In Search of the Miraculous*. Many people fascinated by Gurdjieff approach him through this book. The result is that the cosmology which he taught to his groups in Holy Russia has become fixed in the imagination as an integral part of "what Gurdjieff taught." Ouspensky was particularly interested in Gurdjieff's theories on the cosmic relations; and successor teachers of the ideas have made use of the enneagram, the Cosmic Octave, the Table of Hydrogens, and the rest of the esoteric paraphernalia with which the name of Gurdjieff is associated.

Gurdjieff "remains one of the great enigmas of our time," writes Professor Needleman. "What sources did he draw on for his ideas, his music, and sacred dances, his method of life?" Research into the sources of Gurdjieff's System has been going on ever since he arrived in the West, but very little has been published that is not deliberately misleading. J. G. Bennett writes that "95% of what he taught can be found elsewhere," and followers of Gurdjieff and Ouspensky must at least have traced the sources of the cosmology. Discovering the sources of the cosmology makes it much clearer what Gurdjieff was about, although we must beware of assuming that the cosmology alone is "what Gurdjieff taught." In *Glimpses of Truth* Gurdjieff cautions the narrator against imagining that he would have expressed himself in occult terms to everyone who came his way:

> The fact of the matter is that in occult literature much that has been said is superfluous and untrue. You had better forget all this. All your researches in this area were a good exercise for your mind; therein lies their great value, but only there. They have not given you knowledge. . . . Judge everything from the point of view of your common sense. Become the possessor of your own sound ideas and don't accept anything on faith; and when you, your self, by way of sound reasoning and argument, come to an unshakable persuasion, to a full understanding of something, you will have achieved a certain degree of initiation.

The details of Gurdjieff's cosmology belong primarily to the accidents of his teaching. Whether or not Gurdjieff himself took seriously his more occult ideas is another question. Any attempt to trace these ideas to their sources in occult tradition does show that Gurdjieff himself had read or studied deeply in such sources, or that he accepted the findings of people who had done so. When the cosmology recorded by Ouspensky is combined with various other hints dropped by Gurdjieff and what little we know of his life, a fairly accurate picture can be formed of the sources of Gurdjieff's System. This suggests a surprisingly coherent and plausible interpretation of Gurdjieff's intellectual development; although it is as well to remember that any particular feature of his teaching may have come from friends who were more expert in certain subjects—or languages—than he.

Although the game of origins is fascinating and informative, it at once becomes futile when it is used to argue that Gurdjieff derived his ideas from any one particular source. This is why, for example, nothing will be said about the possibility that Gurdjieff took ideas from any Sufi order, though certain Sufi methods—most notably the "Stop" exercise—were clearly important to him, and it is possible that several ideas which will be discussed in a European context—such as Cabala or numerology—were first imbibed by Gurdjieff in an Islamic (that is to say Sufic) form. The apparatus of Traditional wisdom exists in all cultures and in every language.

The idea of Tradition has been made familiar by poets and philosophers, and disreputable by occultists of every description. The essence of the concept is expressed in Gurdjieff's word, "legominism": knowledge transmitted not by written instructions but by personal contact—too limiting to say by word of mouth—from generation to generation. Very often there is a corollary to this: what might be called the theory of degeneration of knowledge. In contrast with our normal ideas of acquiring knowledge through the orderly progression of inquiry and experiment we associate with the scientific method, the Traditionalist holds that our real knowledge—and our understanding of what knowledge we still possess—is steadily diminishing. The inheritors of Traditional wisdom are illuminated by the eternal flame of ancient knowledge which they guard for a time and then pass on.

In this century there have been several attempts to make this idea respectable. Philosophers like René Guénon, students of religion like Mircea Eliade and Henri Corbin, and poets like Kathleen Raine have argued movingly for the transmission of knowledge within closed groups. On the other hand there have been countless cultists and occultists—what Gurdjieff called "initiates of new format"—whose claims to possess Traditional wisdom are of the most doubtful nature. Some would place Gurdjieff and Ouspensky in this category. What is true is that twentieth-century Traditionalists—whether phony or sincere—rely much more than they like to admit on the revival of occultism which took place during the last quarter of the nineteenth century.

This phenomenon has been mentioned in connection with Gurdjieff's search for truth. The late Victorian occult revival drew the materials of its religious syntheses from sources beloved of Traditionalists throughout all Western history. In a sense the Victorian occultists were correct; their Traditions did represent a continuing line of knowledge which had remained rejected from the mainstream of European culture because of historical accident.* They sought inspiration in a perennial underground of "rejected knowledge" which has broken through the established culture of the West only at points of crisis. The turn of the century was one of these; another was that of the Renaissance and Reformation. The earliest detectable crisis in which the Traditions broke the surface was the period of some 400 years centered on the birth of Christ. This is the real canonical period of occult tradition. Oriental mystery religions were engulfing the Roman Empire; in Egypt the cult of Thrice-Great Hermes and the "science" of alchemy arose; Gnostic prophets of every description vied with each other for a receptive audience. Through historical accident, it happened that one Oriental religion, institutionalized Christianity, won a

---

* See my *The Flight from Reason* (London, 1971), published as *The Occult Underground* (La Salle, Ill., 1974).

sweeping victory and in so doing annihilated not only its opponents but certain Traditionalist tendencies within its own ranks.

Occult or Traditional positions have their roots in the systems of thought which the Christian Church conquered. It would take too long to describe the common characteristics of these ideas. They often appear widely diverse, yet share some basic assumptions. The chief is that the soul or spirit is a spark of the divine entrapped in matter, and it is the business of the adept to exert himself by religious exercise and mystical practice to return his spirit to its divine condition (re-ligare, "to reconnect": compare the idea of yoga, signifying "yoke").

There is a great difference between recognizing the existence of a continuous body of Traditional wisdom and deciding that this means that such ideas must be true in an absolute sense. Occultists often make this assumption unquestioningly—and there is a depressing tendency to incorporate every fragment of rejected knowledge into individual versions of Traditional wisdom. Gurdjieff—witness his remark about the time he wasted on H. P. Blavatsky's The Secret Doctrine—had as much trouble as any other inquirer in sifting the grain from the chaff. Nonetheless, he began with the Traditions, the supposed repositories of that "secret knowledge" to which he turned when disillusioned with both religion and science.

There are therefore three main periods of history to be examined for parallel doctrines: the three known periods when occult ideas burst through from underground to influence the established culture of the West.

2. Mystical Mathematics

"All things began in order, so shall they end, and so shall they begin again, according to the ordainer of order and the mystical mathematics of the city of heaven." In The Garden of Cyrus (1658), Sir Thomas Browne was expressing the vision of the universe common to modern Traditionalists and to all sections of educated opinion—both orthodox and heretical—in the prescientific age. Number was not seen just as the means of performing mathematical calculations but as a reflection of the divine ordering of the universe. The number 1 was not the mere integer but the Monad itself, the primordial unity which existed before, around, and through the diversification of things.

The tradition of regarding the universe as composed of numbers is known as arithmology, and for the English-speaking reader the best exposition of the arithmological point of view is Theoretic Arithmetic published in 1816 by Thomas Taylor, the Platonist. Taylor made a digest from the more famous classical arithmologists, and gave his explanations a Platonic cast. He saw the basis of the "Pythagorean" position in the separation of the One from the Many in the world of form. "The Pythagoreans, turning from the vulgar paths and delivering their philosophy in secret to those alone who were worthy to receive it, exhibited it to others through mathematical names. Hence they called forms, numbers, as things which are first separated from impartible union; for natures which are above forms, are also above separation." From the very first the tradition of mystical mathematics was closely bound up with the philosophical sources of Traditional doctrine: the Platonists, Neo-Platonists, and rank Gnostics of the first and second centuries A.D.

The mysterious Pythagoras was the father of a long tradition of number symbolism. According to legend, he traveled in the East—perhaps to the further Orient, perhaps to the sanctuaries of Egypt—before founding his community at Crotona in Italy in the sixth century B.C. From Pythagoras one tradition of mystical mathematics passed through Plato and the famous calculations in the *Timaeus* into Judaism by way of Philo Judaeus and into Christianity through St. Augustine. Between the first and the fifth centuries A.D., the Pythagorean tradition influenced various schools of thought. One of the most occult writers on number was Nicomacus of Gerassa (*c.* A.D. 100), author of a work entitled *Theologumena Arithmetica*.

The arithmological view of number sees *meaning* and not *use* in number. There are obvious parallels with Gurdjieff's usage. For example, the doctrine that three forces must be present to form any given phenomenon is an arithmological commonplace. The "octave" of the Ray of Creation derives directly from Pythagoras. Gurdjieff's diagram of the relationships of different substances in the universe was expressed in terms of "triads" of forces—carbon, nitrogen, and oxygen blending to form a given substance: the hydrogen. Arithmologists of a Gnostic or Neo-Platonic bent used the same symbolism. From the Monad—the Absolute in Gurdjieff's terms— emanated various divine "hypostases" or forces, which in combination produced other forces and so on into diversity, with each successive emanation passing further away from the Source—or, if you prefer it, descending the Ray of Creation. Gurdjieff used arithmology to support his idea of a hierarchy of being: in one aspect this is what he meant with his Ray of Creation and the Table of Hydrogens. In the *Theologumena* of Nicomacus will be found a table of the numbers from 1 to 10 considered as various grades of being.

We are approaching Gurdjieff's presentation of Traditional wisdom from the point of view of number. But Traditional ideas are so widely diffused that Gurdjieff's use of them could be compared first of all to the philosophical position of, say, Plato, Proclus, or Plotinus—all of whom made some use of arithmological argument. Gurdjieff was never primarily an arithmologist; however, a general philosophical position is less easily identified than a particular attitude to number. One final example may make clear how Gurdjieff used his Traditional sources. This is a lecture on symbolism recorded by Ouspensky in *In Search of the Miraculous* which Gurdjieff also delivered in the days of the Institute for the Harmonious Development of Man.

Ouspensky illustrates his record with pictorial symbols of the numbers 2, 3, 4, 5, 6. These are a pair of straight lines, a triangle, a square, a pentagram (five-pointed star), and a hexagram (six-pointed star or Solomon's Seal). In other words, the numbers 2, 3, 4, 5, and 6 are being considered arithmologically and not arithmetically: the symbols represent not the arithmetical numbers, but the arithmological *ideas* of duad, triad, quaternity, pentad, and hexad. Gurdjieff's interpretation of the progression from duad to hexad was an allegory of human development. Normally man is a duality, consisting entirely of pairs of opposites. When he begins to recognize that his nature consists of mechanically conflicting impulses, he may set himself the conscious aim of overcoming them. "The creation of a permanent third principle in man is for man the *transformation of the duality into the trinity*." A strengthening and application of this conscious resolution results in the trinity becoming the quaternity. The next transformation—from quaternity to quinternity—entails the construction of the pentagram; and Gurdjieff interprets this as the proper activation of all five lower centers. Once man achieves such harmony he is in contact with higher consciousness. The symbolic result is that he proceeds from pentagram to hexagram:

> And then man becomes the *six-pointed star*, that is, by becoming locked within a circle of life independent and complete in itself, he becomes isolated from foreign influences or accidental shocks; he embodies in himself the *Seal of Solomon*.

This interpretation is, of course, Gurdjieff's alone, and it is made in accordance with his ideas about human development. But to show how he had framed his conclusions in accordance with Traditional doctrine, it is useful to compare what Nicomacus of Gerassa has to say about the hexad and the development of man in a passage from the *Theologumena*:

> In another way soul is capable of articulating and arranging body in the same general way that psychic form is capable of doing so to formless matter; and in general no number is more able to fit the soul than the hexad; no other would be called so much an articulation of the universe set up as maker of soul and discovered also capable of instilling the condition of life, whence it is called "hexad." That every soul is a harmonising element . . . is evident; for when it is present it makes

peace, and orders well and fits best together the mingled opposites in the living thing, which yield and follow it, and it instills in this way health into the combination . . .

The most important use which Gurdjieff made of number symbolism is the figure of the enneagram, which he said contained and symbolized his whole System. His enneagram consists of a circle with the circumference divided into nine points which are joined to give a triangle and an irregular six-sided figure. Gurdjieff said that the triangle represented the presence of higher forces and that the six-sided figure stood for man. He also claimed that the enneagram was exclusive to his teaching. "This symbol cannot be met with anywhere in the study of 'occultism,' either in books or in oral transmission," Ouspensky reports him as saying. "It was given such significance by those who knew, that they considered it necessary to keep the knowledge of it secret." Not only did the enneagram express what Gurdjieff taught, but he claimed it as the final arbiter of esoteric knowledge: two men could decide by drawing the enneagram which was the master and which the pupil.

Because of the emphasis which Gurdjieff placed on this diagram, his followers have sought high and low for the symbol in occult literature. Bennett claims that it cannot be found anywhere; and if disciples of Gurdjieff have in fact discovered the figure, they have kept it very quiet. But Gurdjieff himself was denying the truth of the matter when he said that the enneagram could not be found in occult literature. Representations— although not as Gurdjieff drew it—can be found, and the figure would be quite well known to anyone who had bothered to study arithmology.

The traditions of classical arithmology survived through the Middle Ages in various forms. The work of Boethius (early sixth century) was much translated, and from this source as well as the Christianized versions of arithmology, ideas of the significance of number passed into common usage. When the men of the Renaissance enthusiastically rediscovered their classical inheritance, those of a mystical bent pounced eagerly on Neo-Platonism, Hermetism, and the Cabala to justify their transcendental impulses. The arithmological tradition was resurrected beside the other aspects of "divine philosophy" beloved by thinkers of the sixteenth and seventeenth centuries.

The enneagram forms the center of the magnificent frontispiece to the *Arithmologia* published at Rome by the Jesuit, Athanasius Kircher, in 1665. Kircher (1601–80) is a figure of great significance for the origins of Gurdjieff's ideas. He was typical of the Renaissance man of learning and a prototype of the scholarly Jesuit of later days. Kircher busied himself with experiments in the natural sciences: magnets, acoustics, and medicine all

occupied his attention. He even had himself lowered down the crater of Vesuvius to investigate the effects of an eruption. His chief concern was Orientalism, and he published records of the Nestorian inscriptions in China as well as rather fanciful attempts to decode Egyptian hieroglyphics. His Egyptology was overlaid with the customary reverence for the Cabala and Thrice-Great Hermes: and the whole had a further gloss of submission to the General of his Order and the Pope. It would be fair to describe him as presenting esoteric traditions in a Christian guise.

In the *Arithmologia*, there is a figure called an "enneagram" composed of three equilateral triangles. At the apex of the triangle which corresponds to the completed triangular figure in Gurdjieff's enneagram—where Gurdjieff places the *do* of his octave and the number 9—Kircher has the Greek inscription: "hierarch." Within the symbol there is a smaller equilateral triangle.

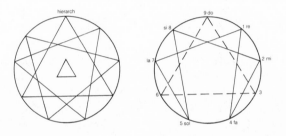

Kircher's explanation of "the mysteries of the ennead" is similar to that of Thomas Taylor. The number 3 is particularly sacred ("The Holy Tri-amazikamno"), and the 9 trebly so.

> The ennead results from the triad multiplied by itself, and has all the more arcane significance because it thrice contains the triad. While making the square of the triad it contains within itself the greater mysteries.

The number 9, the Triple Ternary, has pride of place in Kircher's occult system. In his *Iter Extaticum coeleste* (1660), he tells us that the universe is composed entirely of triads, and that the ennead governs the angelic worlds. Five years later the frontispiece to the *Arithmologia* expands this cosmology into a gorgeous emblem of the triadic operation of the universe. It should also clarify—for those who have no idea what Gurdjieff and Ouspensky saw in their Rays of Creation—what the cosmology of *In Search of the Miraculous* is pointing at. Kircher's explanation of his emblem would have been quite comprehensible to an audience educated in the compressed vocabulary of esoteric convention, but today, itself needs interpretation.

The Triune Monad, symbolised by an equilateral triangle, flows by differentiation into the intellectual world, which consists of nine choirs of angels in three degrees, represented by the same number of imaginary equilateral triangles connecting them; these instill themselves through the intellectual or angelic world into the astral world and thence into the elements in a miraculous and ineffable fashion. For all things are constructed according to the three categories of number, weight and measure, according to the creative wisdom of the Three-in-One. The Jewish, Greek and Arab Sages of Antiquity sniffed out the mystery, and were of the opinion that they could explain the construction of both the intellectual and the physical world in no better fashion than by abstract numerical arguments of this sort.

Kircher ends his description—and his book—with an attempt to derive Scriptural support for his arithmological universe. And in case it is thought that his reference to the Sages of Antiquity is intended in a scathing as opposed to a complimentary light, his valediction leaves no doubt that he felt himself to be revealing hidden doctrine. It is italicized, as is the description of the Triadic universe—but not his pious reference to Scripture. *"And I have exposed to the curious reader things which are told to few. Farewell, and guard your tongue."*

In fact Kircher's description covers only the early stages of what Gurdjieff would call the Ray of Creation, and he no doubt assumed that the rest of his emblem would be understood by an audience alert to every esoteric allusion. The Monad, which is also the Holy Trinity, is represented by the eye in the triangle at the center of the enneagram. The "nine choirs of angels" are joined in three degrees of trinities by triangles of fire.

The engraver's art is used to lead the eye from the element of *fire* through the *air*—in which there are birds flying—above the ocean on whose *waters* a ship is sailing to the *earth* which forms the foreground. We have a complete picture of the Traditional doctrine of the four elements which Gurdjieff symbolized by the terms "carbon," "oxygen," "nitrogen," and "hydrogen." The astral or sidereal world is borne up by Jehovah's wings—a common symbol in Rosicrucian literature. The emanations from the hierarchy of the angelic world flow into nine planetary spheres. In the *Iter Extaticum* Kircher names these: first "Empyrean Heaven, the Court of the Eternal King," then the region of the fixed stars—Saturn, Jupiter, Mars, the Sun, Venus, Mercury, the moon. Then there are the sublunary grades of being. As for the Ancient Sages in the foreground, the one on the right demonstrating a well-known theorum is obviously Pythagoras; and the cherub above his head carries a Pythagorean magic square. The other might be any other noble pagan—Moses, Solomon, Zoroaster, or even the Thrice-Great Hermes himself. I cannot discover whether the cat is associated with any one of them.

There are many other representations of the Neo-Platonic cosmology of the sixteenth and seventeenth centuries, but Kircher's has been neglected. We have by no means done with his fiery enneagram or the hurtling spheres of his astral world. The most obvious question is: if this is the figure known to Tradition as an "enneagram," why is Gurdjieff's different and what might this signify?

3. *The Harmonious Universe*

Pythagoras is the source of a number of other ideas associated with arithmology which have particular relevance to Gurdjieff. All theories of "objective art" based on mathematical canons of proportion can be derived from Pythagorean principles, and there is little doubt that Gurdjieff's conception of art came from the same ultimate source as his numerology. Pythagoras is supposed to have invented music to cure physical illness and what Iamblichus calls "the passions of the soul." Both in his writings and in his life, Gurdjieff gave ample proof that his own conception of "objective music" was Pythagorean. In *Meetings with Remarkable Men* he discusses the effects of music on human beings and other living objects. The companions of the Seekers for Truth were almost reduced to tears, he writes, by the monotonous music played in one particular monastery. These musical investigations—which are all concerned with the effects of music on the human psyche—reveal Gurdjieff to have known a fair amount of musical history.

No one knows where Pythagoras found his musical ideas. Scholars have guessed at both Babylon and Egypt. His theory was based on the discovery of the monochord—to which Gurdjieff refers in *Beelzebub's Tales*. The Pythagorean monochord was a single string stretched like the string on any modern stringed instrument and divided by seven frets. It was found that when the string was plucked and held at different frets to produce a musical note, the vibrations of the monochord increased or decreased in a precise mathematical ratio. From this discovery the Pythagoreans deduced far-ranging theories.

The universe was thought of as a harmony composed of such vibrations. The sort of cosmos which Athanasius Kircher depicted was essentially *harmonious* as well as arithmological; for number expressed the nature of the celestial harmony which governed and maintained all things. The tradition of musical analogy went hand in hand with that of arithmology. From Plato the arguments spread throughout the Mediterranean, collecting certain additions and alterations on the way. Proclus had the idea of simplifying the calculations of musical intervals by eliminating fractions. He therefore replaced the numbers from 1 to 7, which Plato had used to mark the divisions of the octave, with a scale whose highest number was 384. When the number 384 is divided into proportions corresponding to the ratio of vibrations which relates the notes in the octave, the resulting scale expresses their relationship in whole numbers. If this reform is compared with the Table of Hydrogens recorded by Ouspensky, Gurdjieff can be discovered performing a similarly useful simplification.

Throughout the Middle Ages the idea of the harmony of the spheres was preserved and accommodated to a Christian universe. The various grades of angels—Seraphim, Cherubim, Thrones, Dominations, Principalities, Powers, and Virtues—formed a descending octave from divinity, while the heavenly spheres of the planets could be manipulated into order, perhaps by assigning a special status to the moon and representing the earth as the silence after the echo has died away. Like the tradition of arithmology, the harmonial view of the universe came into its own in the crisis of Renaissance and Reformation. Francesco Giorgi—a canonist so eminent that Henry VIII wished to consult him about his divorce—published in 1525 the work *De Harmonia Mundi* which served as an underground influence on many of the thinkers of his time.

De Harmonia Mundi is written in three "songs," each divided into eight "notes." The very first note discusses the Pythagorean view of the connection between number, music, and the symbolic interpretation of the universe. The ancients, writes Giorgi, spoke enigmatically in parables. The universal harmony is "the concert of all strings in pure measures with no discords." But disharmonies have crept into this cosmic plan, and remain a puzzle for philosophers. In *De Harmonia* are to be found all the essentials of Pythagorean world view, distilled from the arithmologists, the Platonists and Neo-Platonists, and spiced with Cabala.

Countless examples show how the philosophy elaborated by Giorgi is the source of Gurdjieff's cosmology. This does not mean that he had read the book; for the influence of *De Harmonia Mundi* seems to have been greatest indirectly, as the source for the late Renaissance harmonial philosophy. Francesco Giorgi incorporated his Pythagorean views into a deeply orthodox Christian piety; but others whom he influenced showed less respect for the Church. Among these were the Rosicrucians with whom Gurdjieff was certainly familiar and in whom the doctrines of *De Harmonia* were widely diffused.

During the 1930s several pupils of Ouspensky in London became interested in the origins of the System which they were being taught. Research in the British Museum soon brought them to Robert Fludd, the eccentric English mystic whose great work, *Utriusque Cosmii Historia* (1617–24), contains among other things two representations of the "monochord of the world." Apart from the fact that Fludd specifically denied being a Rosicrucian, he did acknowledge his debt to Giorgi. Between 1619 and 1622, he became involved in two controversies with opponents who denounced his use of the octave as absurd mystification. One was the astronomer, Johannes Kepler, who was trying to show that the planets—the physical, astronomical planets—moved according to the principles of harmony.* Another was the French monk, Marin Mersenne, who, although a devotee of Giorgi, was concerned to purge Fludd's ideas of their magical accretions. It is typical of some latter-day Ouspenskians that they have pounced on the most occult and eccentric use of a well-known idea.

Although Athanasius Kircher does not acknowledge Giorgi as a source for his *Arithmologia*, there can be little doubt that he borrowed extensively from his predecessor. From *De Harmonia*, Kircher's universe, dominated by the Triple Ternary of the enneagram, receives a fuller explanation: we learn that the first triad produces the angels, the second the heavens, and the third the four elements. On the authority of Plato, Giorgi maintains that the octave can be used to scrutinize the human soul; for as man is constructed as an image of the greater world, the same laws apply to him as to the cosmos. *De Harmonia* argues the true Traditional position on the return of the spirit to its divine source. "Just as the Supreme Creator descends into us by the stairway of the angels . . . so we may return up them to that from which we came."

Kircher's experiments into the effects of sound on matter went further than any of his predecessors in arguing that the universe was based not only on number and harmony, but on sound itself. In his *Musurgia Universalis* (1622), he discusses the monochord, the question of intervals, and the effects of sound on matter and mind. In 1673 he published a work under the title of *Phonurgia Nova*, which defines the science of "phonurgy" as that of "miraculous faculties working by means of sounds." Apart from a predictable interest in the fall of Jericho, Kircher is chiefly concerned with musical medicine. He maintains that music can cure werewolves and madmen and gives a musical cure for a tarantula bite.

There is no doubt that Gurdjieff made thorough researches into musical literature, and although he might have picked up the principles of Pythagorean harmony from the classical texts, the version which he

---

* In the course of this, he drew diagrams based on the division of the circle resulting from the inscribed regular polygons. These diagrams have also been found suggestive by followers of Gurdjieff. As far as the enneagram goes, Kepler made no use of it, as it did not fit his theory.

expounded quite definitely derives from the revival and adaptation of that philosophy in the late Renaissance. The portable organ, like Gurdjieff's own but with an assembly of pipes, was known to both Fludd and Mersenne; while many of the miracles which Gurdjieff attributed to "Essene" music are discussed by Kircher. It is much more likely that the teacher of an "esoteric Christianity" would have taken his version of the harmonial philosophy from the more orthodox writers and practically certain that Gurdjieff's interest in the effect of sound on matter would have led him to Kircher. What of the enneagram—the blazing Triple Ternary that dominates the frontispiece to the *Arithmologia* of that learned Jesuit?

Kircher's universe is governed—as Gurdjieff would have said—by the Law of Three. From the intellectual world the astral world depends—and such is the engraver's skill that it seems to spin in the emanations from the ennead. But this cosmos is governed not by number only, but also by harmony and sound.

Francesco Giorgi had admitted that there were inexplicable discords in the universal harmony. But surely the true canon of proportion according to Pythagoras excluded any variation? Gurdjieff, the twentieth century Pythagorean, had his answer: "intentional inexactitudes." The members of his society of the "Adherents of the Legominism"—in other words, Traditionalists—had introduced into their works of art deliberate variations from the proportions which would have given perfect harmony. But the universe of the *Arithmologia* is a perfect universe and Kircher's enneagram is composed of three self-contained triangles linking heavenly choirs belonging to the same angelic orders. If a circle is drawn through the points of the enneagram, it will be seen that Gurdjieff's symbol uses the same divisions of the circle as Kircher: but that the two nethermost triangles have been opened out, and the lines which in Kircher's diagram join points 6 to 5 and 8 to 9, now join 6 to 9 and 8 to 5.

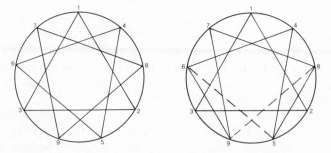

Is this an "intentional inexactitude"? According to Ouspensky, Gurdjieff called his enneagram "an incomplete and theoretical form." Perhaps he hoped that his pupils would themselves be able to complete the symbol and restore the original harmony. He interpreted the hexagonal figure in his diagram as representing man, and the triangle as standing for the external principles: the completion of the enneagram could well have been intended as signifying the union of man with the divine. Gurdjieff also called his symbol "a moving diagram," and based at least one of his dances on it. In Kircher's enneagram, "motion" is possible only within each triangle, but in Gurdjieff's, the six-sided figure allows continuous motion by reason of its isolation from the triangle in the center. Perhaps when the discords in creation—which so troubled the Renaissance Pythagoreans—were healed by a complete conformity with the divine plan, the motion of humanity would cease to be isolated from the working of the eternal principles within it.

Whatever Gurdjieff's intention in adapting the enneagram to his own synthesis, or even whether he inadvertently destroyed its original significance, it seems clear that the function of the enneagram is linked closely to another esoteric diagram: the Cabalistic Tree of Life.

4. *The Tree of Life and the Art of Ramon Lull*

In *Meetings with Remarkable Men*, Gurdjieff introduces his imaginary "Sarmoun Brotherhood" with the remark that he and his friend "Pogossian" had discovered the name in "the book called *Merkhavat*." If this refers to anything, it points to the Merkhabah texts of Jewish mysticism, which were the forerunners of medieval and Renaissance Cabalism. The Merkhabah mystics based their practices on an attempt to attain a vision of the throne of God which is described in the first chapter of Ezekiel; more accurately, they aspired to a vision of the "throne-*world*" which Professor Gerschom Scholem equates with the Gnostic pleroma with its various potencies and powers. Scholem suggests that there was considerable contact between Jewish, Hellenistic, and Christian Gnostics; and there is little doubt that the universe of the Jewish "Descenders to the Throne" would have been easily recognized by the mystics of the first few centuries A.D.—or by their successors of the Renaissance.

Although Cabalists claim to find their traditions in the Mosaic books, the text on which later Cabalists have mostly relied is called the *Sepher Yetzirah* or Book of Creation. This was elaborated by another text, the *Sepher Ha-Zohar* or Book of Splendor, written in thirteenth century Spain. These developed the ideas inherent in Merkhabah mysticism to the point at which they could be expressed in one elaborate but comprehensive symbol, known in the West as the Tree of Life. This is a diagram—as the title, "Book of Creation," makes clear—of the descent of divinity from the Godhead to Earth: what Gurdjieff called the Ray of Creation and the process from which Kircher symbolized in his engraving in the

Arithmologia. But the Tree of Life is a much more complex hieroglyph than the Ray of Creation. It also symbolizes the attributes of divinity and the forces which in combination form the universe. These elements of creation are called the *Sephiroth* (singular, *Sephirah*) and they form the symbolic "leaves" on the Tree of Life. Conventionally they are represented by nine or ten circles arranged in a particular pattern and joined by twenty-two "paths." On one level the Tree of Life forms a map by which the aspiring mystic can attain a knowledge of the whole of creation and ascend to the Godhead; on another, the symbol can be said to represent the interaction of the forces which produce phenomena. Each *Sephirah* is identified by a system of correspondences or attributions which by their associations suggest the nature of the forces which the *Sephirah* conveys.

Such a symbol corresponds to other definitions which Gurdjieff gave to his enneagram. It was "perpetual motion"—the Great Dance of the universe. It was "the fundamental hieroglyph of a universal language, which has as many meanings as there are levels of men." Twice in *In Search of the Miraculous*, Ouspensky records Gurdjieff talking of Cabala, and in his lecture about man's symbolic progress from duality to the hexad, Gurdjieff added a very suggestive comment which was deleted from the published account. After describing how his octave with its two shocks symbolized what Kircher would have called the Triple Ternary, Gurdjieff remarked that those of his audience who were familiar with the Cabala might compare the Cabalistic symbolism of ninefoldness.

A recent book called simply *Tree of Life*, written by Z'ev ben Shimon Halevi, does not conceal its author's familiarity with the terms of the System as taught by Ouspensky. In the text and in several of his diagrams, Halevi attempts to correlate Gurdjieff's use of the terms triad, octave, and interval with the traditional interpretation of the Tree of Life. It is significant that a modern interpreter of Jewish traditions has discovered similarities between his own attempts to reformulate traditional doctrine and the presentation of ancient wisdom in new guise made by Gurdjieff. In the *Arithmologia*, Kircher was quite explicit that his enneagram was equivalent to the Hebrew Tree of Life, and the diagram of the Tree places some of the "correspondences" which he lists as appropriate to each *Sephirah*.

It is impossible to explain the functioning of the Tree of Life in a few paragraphs. There is a vast literature on the subject. Above Kether, the Crown, are set three facets of Divinity. They may be compared to the divine triangle in the center of Kircher's enneagram. Kether is the point at which divine energy enters the highest of the Cabalistic worlds, and descends into the lower degrees of matter along a zigzag course which modern Cabalists call the Lightning Flash. The lowest point on the Tree is

The Tree of Life

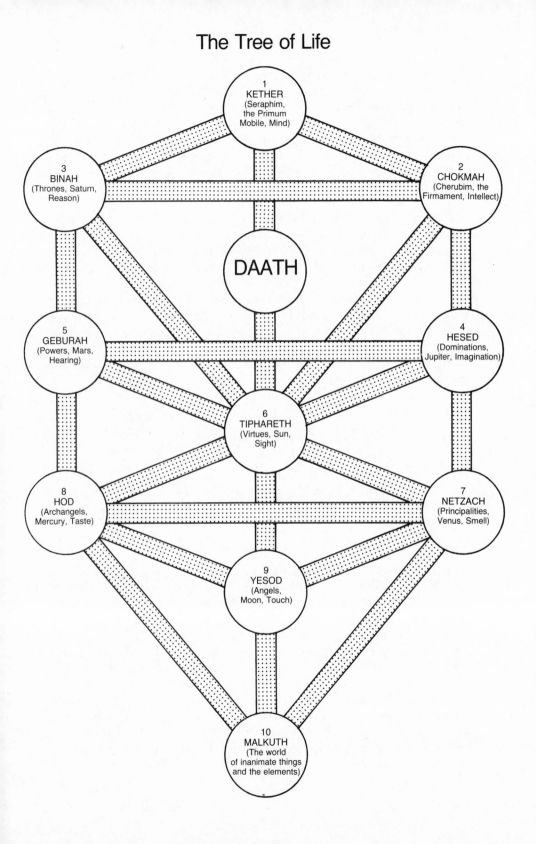

Malkuth, the Kingdom, the highest concentration of matter—to all intents and purposes the physical universe. Halevi's book uses the idea of the monochord stretching from heaven to earth, and he applies Gurdjieff's Law of the Octave with its two intervals to the descent of the divine energy into matter down the Lightning Flash. From our point of view, a reverse comparison is more significant: the application of the Tree to the enneagram.

The key to this equation is found in the frontispiece to the *Arithmologia*. Around the points of the enneagram Kircher's engraver has placed numbers. In the diagram of the Tree of Life numbers are traditionally allotted to all the *Sephiroth* except Daath, or Knowledge, a mysterious or "invisible" *Sephirah* which is often omitted. The particular numbers are fixed and certain; they form part of the system of correspondences which assigns, for example, planets, colors, metals, emotions, or personal characteristics, to the influence of a particular *Sephirah*. So if we have reason to believe that Kircher's enneagram represents the Tree of Life in another form, it is likely that the numbers surrounding the symbol are simply the shortest way of denoting the different *Sephiroth*.

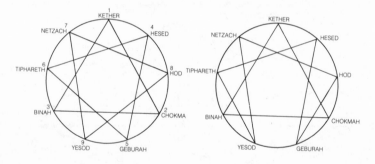

In the *Arithmologia*, Kircher explains the three triangles of his enneagram as representing the "three degrees" into which the "nine choirs of angels" are divided. In this figure, the three *Sephirah* highest on the Tree of Life—Kether, Hochmah, and Binah—form the triangle which stares directly out from the page. The other two triangles contain the triads of the Hesed-Geburah-Tiphareth and Netzach-Hod-Yesod. Malkuth, the Kingdom, is the sphere in which man views all the cosmic action; in Gurdjieff's enneagram it would be represented by the circle joining the points. Kircher's symbol signifies the descent of the divine energy into matter through the creative action of triads. The first triad of Kether-Chokmah-Binah, the second of Hesed-Geburah-Tiphareth, the third of Netzach-Hod-Yesod, make up the Triple Ternary of the divine descent contemplated from the Earth or Malkuth.

When the *Sephiroth* are transferred to the corresponding points on Gurdjieff's enneagram there is a peculiar result which can only be intentional. Whereas Kircher's diagram is a picture of "three degrees of angels," Gurdjieff's is "a moving diagram," and the direction of the movement is marked by Ouspensky with arrows. The movement within the six-sided figure representing man runs Hesed-Geburah-Hod-Netzach-Yesod-Tiphareth. On the orthodox diagram of the Tree of Life, this represents motion round the paths of the square centered on the sixth *Sephirah*, Tiphareth: this is known to Cabalists as the Yetziratic World, and is sometimes said to represent archetypal man. There is no space to explain what these designations mean, as it could only be done by reference to the rest of the Tree of Life. The important thing to notice is that the six-sided figure in Gurdjieff's enneagram refers to a particular division which makes sense on the Cabalistic Tree.

The triangle which remains isolated in Gurdjieff's "moving diagram" is that of Kether-Chokmah-Binah, the three supreme *Sephirah*. Together they form the world of Atziluth or emanations from the divinity. When Gurdjieff's octave with its intervals is distributed around the outside of his enneagram of this supreme trinity, only Kether—the Crown, the point at which the divine emanations enter the worlds of the Tree of Life—has a note allotted to it. Appropriately enough this is *do* which begins each new octave, and by beginning signals the end of the preceding one. The other points of the central triangle—said by Gurdjieff to represent the divine or eternal principles—are marked with the intervals in the octave. At these intervals, Gurdjieff taught that a shock was necessary to help the process over the point where "vibrations become retarded." But in fact, he displaced the second interval from its natural position between the notes *si* and *do* and inserted it between *sol* and *la*.

At first sight this appears to have been done simply to satisfy the demands of symmetry. In *In Search of the Miraculous* Ouspensky records Gurdjieff as justifying this adjustment by a series of abstruse arguments which may or may not make sense within the context of his cosmology. But he did state that "the apparent placing of the interval in *its wrong place* itself shows to those who are able to read the symbol what kind of 'shock' is required for the passage of si to do." An "intentional inexactitude," perhaps, but it is clear that Gurdjieff intended to signify the *degree* of force necessary. The adjustment attributes the *do* and the two intervals in Gurdjieff's enneagram to the triad of Kether-Chokmah-Binah. This trinity of *Sephiroth* from the world of emanations inserts its influence into Gurdjieff's enneagram where he placed his intervals; which makes perfect sense in his terms, as he said that the first interval, *mi-fa*, was filled by "the will of the Absolute." Not only does this refer to the Triangle of divine principles which his diagram isolates from human processes, but it should probably have been written by Ouspensky as "the *Will* of the Absolute." On the Tree of Life Chokmah—which fills the gap in Gurdjieff's enneagram corresponding to the Will of the Absolute—is known as "Wisdom," but it denotes the *active* intelligence, the dynamic or creative thrust of Will.

One could explore endlessly the possibilities which are opened up by the discovery that Gurdjieff's enneagram is an adaptation of the Tree of Life. But it may be wondered whether Gurdjieff's alterations resulted in a distortion from the original Tradition: in some cases in an oversimplification, in others a complication of an already complex symbol.

Were these divergences invented by Gurdjieff, or did they come from a Traditional source? We cannot say for certain that Gurdjieff did take his cosmology from Athanasius Kircher. Kircher believed himself to be revealing a secret knowledge in his *Arithmologia,* and it is quite possible that he simply represented a tradition which Gurdjieff could have encountered elsewhere. It must remain a matter of opinion. I believe that in the *Arithmologia* Kircher was expressing a final synthesis of Renaissance mysticism and that Gurdjieff's cosmology somehow derives from it.

One final element of Kircher's system must be discussed, because it accounts for the form in which he chose to express his Tree of Life. This is the influence of Ramon Lull and his *Ars Magna.* Both Kircher and Giorgi were devoted Lullians, and Kircher's enneagram derives from one of the symbolic figures of the Lullian Art.

Ramon Lull was born about 1232 in Majorca, which had only just recovered from three centuries of occupation by Islam. After a riotous and conventionally misspent youth, he had a series of visions and decided to devote himself to Christ. In order to achieve his ambition of converting Mohammedans, he learned Arabic and set about a synthesis of Islamic and Christian thought. The result was his immense Great Art, a symbolic system owing much to Christian Neo-Platonism, something to the Moslem saint and Sufi al-Ghazzali, and something to the Jewish Cabala. Lull was in relations with both Sufis and Cabalists; in the words of a leading Lullian scholar, "Lull in preparing to combat Islam, had steeped himself for years in its literature and mysticism. He had taken many of his arms from his adversaries."

The object of Lull's Great Art was to demonstrate the truth of Christianity by means of symbolic diagrams illustrating the combination of forces which create phenomena. The background against which he worked was the cosmology accepted by Jew, Arab, and West European Christian alike: the descent of the Godhead into matter through various grades of being. The result was a symbolic system based on two main figures. In the final form of the Art, the *Ars generalis ultima* of 1305–08, the principles which in combination govern the universe are said to number nine. They are known as the Dignities of God. The number 9 is suggestive to anyone with even a slight knowledge of Cabala, and the nature of the divine Dignities appears to be exactly the same as that of the Cabalistic *Sephiroth*. One of the two main diagrams used by Lull in demonstrating how the combinations of the Dignities operate in the universe is known as the figure T, and it is this figure which Kircher used as the basis of his enneagram. The second important Lullian diagram is called the Figure A, and it is based on the interconnection of all points on a circle whose circumference is divided by 9. It is easy to see that a particular conjunction of these points gives in one form Kircher's, and in another, Gurdjieff's enneagram.

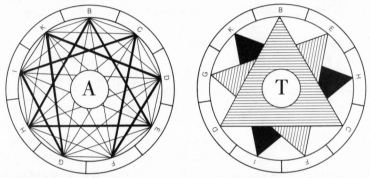

It will be remembered that in *In Search of the Miraculous* Ouspensky records several conversations with Gurdjieff on the subject of a universal language. Gurdjieff denounced all concocted universal languages, and declared that in any case a valid universal language already existed. When he introduced his Russian groups to the enneagram, he defined it as "the fundamental hieroglyph of a universal language." This description would apply very well to the Tree of Life; but it applies even more accurately to the Art of Ramon Lull. The Lullian Art was known to Gurdjieff's St. Petersburg group—it had been rediscovered by Anna Butkovsky and Anthony Charkovsky—and this fact alone may have been responsible for Gurdjieff's use of the enneagram in conversations with those pupils. However, we do know that Lull deliberately constructed his Art to provide a universal language which would unite men of all creeds under a single God. If he did in fact make use of Cabalistic traditions—and although there is no final proof, it is almost certain—he was in many ways anticipating the Christian Cabalists of the Renaissance. The synthesis of Lull precedes that of Kircher by three and a half centuries.

5. *Esoteric Christianity*

In *Meetings with Remarkable Men* Gurdjieff describes—allegorically or in historical truth, it does not matter—how he grew disappointed with the efficacy of Western science and turned to religion, only in the end to become disillusioned with established churches. Yet to his pupils in Russia, he admitted that his System could be known as "esoteric Christianity," and he told Boris Mouravieff that Christianity was "the ABC" of his teaching. In *Beelzebub's Tales* the inquiring Hassein is informed that although most of the great religions have degenerated, the teaching of Jesus Christ has secretly been preserved. It is the only occasion on which Beelzebub seems actually to recommend any religious group.

> . . . among a rather small religious group of terrestrial beings the teaching of Jesus Christ was preserved unchanged, and, passing from generation to generation, has even reached the present time in its original form.
>
> This smallish group of terrestrial beings is designated "the Brotherhood of the Essenes."

In *Meetings with Remarkable Men* Gurdjieff introduces the "Essenes" into his discussion about the miraculous effects of music. He claims that, thanks to an introduction from one of his childhood tutors, "I had been among the Essenes, most of whom are Jews, and . . . by means of very ancient Hebrew music they had made plants grow in half an hour." The miraculous accelerated growth of plants is a marvel which Kircher mentions in his own comments on the effects of sound. It is highly unlikely that Gurdjieff had really discovered any "Essenes." Quite probably, Gurdjieff merely intended an allegorical brotherhood, although it seems that he did conceive of an inner teaching within Christianity which had at least informed the System which he taught.

He could have found this idea in any of the Renaissance texts he might have studied; but another possible source is indicated in *Meetings with Remarkable Men*. Gurdjieff talks about his attempts to recover the secret knowledge of past times and his conclusion that if a school of the sort of knowledge which he sought had ever existed, it must have been among the Assyrians or "Aissors" among whom he had a number of friends. This form of Christianity had (and has) a claim to be considered the most ancient and the most pure.

After the Jewish wars of c. A.D. 70, Jewish Christianity ceased to exist. With one exception, all later Christian churches derive from the Church of Antioch in Syria, which was wholly Greek and within the Roman Empire. The exception was the Church of Edessa, the capital of a small principality called Osrhoëne situated in the Euphrates valley east of the river.

Tradition dates the beginning of the Church of Edessa to the coming of Mar Addai (the Apostle Thaddeus) in the first century. The Edessan Church was fairly certainly evangelized from Israel, and its liturgical tongue, Syriac, was similar to that of Palestine in the time of Christ. To Gurdjieff, a zealous seeker for the original and undistorted form of ancient wisdom, both the derivation of the Edessan Church and the language of its Assyrian members would have provided a powerful reason for thinking that an "Aissor school" might possess the solutions which he was seeking.

The particular strangeness of the doctrine of the Edessan Church was that it confined baptism to celibates. All the lusts of the flesh were considered evil, and only gradually were married Christians admitted to Church membership. It must be conceded that Gurdjieff gave no sign of observing these standards—although there is an echo of severe asceticism in "Ozay's" "cessation to the utmost limit of diet, breath and sex." But we are not looking for a single source of Gurdjieff's teaching, merely at the signposts on the way. One of the signposts points from the Church of Edessa—which could be seen as embodying an "esoteric" Christianity—to the "esoteric Christianity" of the late Renaissance.

Because of an error in the earliest writings on the Edessan Church, it was widely believed until the early twentieth century that the Syriac of the Peshitta—that Church's equivalent of the Authorized Version—was the very language spoken by Jesus himself. The standard English work on the canon of the Bible was still perpetuating this mistake in 1896. Current scholarship would therefore have supported an interest in the Assyrians. What is more, the early 1890s were a time of great excitement in Syriac studies. In the context of the romantic archaeology of *Meetings with Remarkable Men*, it becomes significant that in 1889, adventurous scholars penetrated the Syriac library of the Convent of Saint Catherine on Mount Sinai. Two years later, in this library there was discovered a palimpsest containing the Syriac version of the New Testament. While it would be wrong to see Gurdjieff as taking a scholarly interest in New Testament studies, he might well have taken the interest of an esoteric antiquarian.

Stimulated either by personal acquaintance with his "Aissor" friends, or by contemporary interest in Syriac, Gurdjieff might have turned to the Peshitta itself. Its first editor was the German humanist, J. A. Widmanstetter (1506–57), who originated the notion that the language of the Peshitta was that of Christ. With Widmanstetter we are back in the atmosphere of Renaissance mysticism of which Kircher was almost the last representative. Widmanstetter studied Hebrew and learned Arabic. Then in Italy he accidentally met an old man who showed him the Syriac Gospels and claimed to be the sole remaining expert on the language. The result was an edition of the Peshitta which Widmanstetter published in Vienna in 1555 in collaboration with the legate of the Patriarch of Antioch. This text was certainly known to Kircher. His fellow Orientalist, Andreas Müller (1630–94)—a correspondent of Kircher who successfully exposed the fantastic nature of the Jesuit's imagination—made a study of Syriac based on Widmanstetter's Peshitta. Not only does Gurdjieff's fascination with the Church of Edessa fit with contemporary interest at the end of the nineteenth century, but it had also been a preoccupation of the seventeenth-century Jesuits whose work almost certainly inspired his own cosmology.

In Widmanstetter's Peshitta there is an elaborate and suggestive diagram of the Tree of Life. It is all the more interesting because there seems no reason whatever for its inclusion in the text. The representation of the Tree is said to be that of "John, the apostle of Jesus Christ," who was recalled "from Asia" by his bishop. He then climbed a mountain near Ephesus and had a vision in which were contained the opening words of his Gospel: "In the beginning was the word . . ." The diagram shows the rest of his vision, in which the *Sephiroth* of the Tree of Life are associated with the wounds of Christ on the Cross. From the point of view of Gurdjieff's teaching, the interesting feature of this Tree is that around Malkuth—the Kingdom, the physical world, the bottom *Sephirah*—is curled the crescent moon. From *In Search of the Miraculous* and the whole tenor of Ouspensky's teaching, we know that for Gurdjieff the moon was the last note on the Ray of Creation, deep in matter, the realm of inorganic life. Although in some Cabalistic systems the moon may be attributed to Malkuth, it is far more often given to Yesod—the *Sephirah* above Malkuth, the realm of reflection and imagination. Here, in the pages of the Syriac Peshitta, is a Tree of Life attributing the moon to Malkuth, and linking all at once Gurdjieff's Ray of Creation, the Christianity of the Aissors, and the Cabalistic mysticism of the Renaissance.

It is most unlikely that Gurdjieff stumbled upon Widmanstetter's Tree— although there remains an outside chance that, surrounded by a bewildering conflict of beliefs, and searching for an unpolluted tradition of Christianity, he might have been attracted to a version of the Great Hieroglyph somehow associated with the Church of Edessa. What the coincidence does show is that in the crisis of the Renaissance and Reformation, men concerned to mend the once seamless robe of Christ and retrieve meaning out of chaos made use of a syncretism based on Cabalistic and Pythagorean principles which it seems legitimate to call "esoteric Christianity." Confronted with a similar crisis of consciousness, Gurdjieff may well have responded in a similar fashion—either by consciously imitating the example of that sort of esoteric Christianity represented by Kircher, or by making his own synthesis with similar motives and with similar results.

It is just possible that Gurdjieff did find some secretly preserved version of Christianity in his travels through the Middle East. The Mandaeans—a

Qui expanfis in cruce manib°,
traxifti omnia ad te SECVLA.

In principio erat
verbum.

sect of Gnostic Christians allotting a special role to John the Baptist—were not discovered by scholars until comparatively recent times. Gurdjieff himself tells us that, after he had exhausted the possibilities contained in the relatively obvious forms of Christianity with which he came in contact, he abandoned the present for "legominisms" from the past. In his quest for origins, he would certainly have pushed his inquiries as far back historically as he could go. And he could scarcely have avoided the religious and philosophical tumult of the first two centuries after the birth of Christ, when the sects known as Gnostic flourished throughout the eastern Mediterranean.

There is no agreement as to the origins of Gnosticism. Professor Hans Jonas insists that the distinctively Gnostic doctrines derived neither from the established philosophies of the Hellenistic world, nor from the established religions of the East. The Gnostic faiths seem to be rooted in a syncretism of religions—but the more occult, the more hidden, the more mystical currents of theological speculation. Professor Jonas thinks that there is a definite link between the beginnings of Gnosticism and the beginnings of Cabala; and whatever their origins, the Gnostic systems embody the doctrine of the divine ensnarement in matter. In the Neo-Platonic philosophies, this is found in an abstract and sophisticated form. In the Gnostic religions the idea occurs in a more magical and occult version.

Both Margaret Anderson and C. S. Nott have traced Gurdjieff's teaching back to the Gnostics, who in a sense provide the most obvious parallel, particularly if we are to take seriously Gurdjieff's statement that he taught "esoteric Christianity." For in the early years of the Christian religion, before Church councils and power struggles had codified theology, there was considerable doubt as to what Christianity was. Whereas virtually all theologians might accept some version of the hierarchical universe emanating from the Godhead, the conclusions to be drawn from this cosmology were a matter for dispute. The version of Christianity which triumphed was one which affirmed in a limited fashion the virtues of the world; and the Gnostic Christians, the representatives of the more magical and world-rejecting points of view, were defeated.

Of all the Gnostic systems, the most Christian and the most impressive is the powerful vision of Valentinus, whose thought Professor Jonas calls "the culmination of . . . the Syrian-Egyptian type of Gnostic speculation."

Valentinus taught in Rome for some twenty-five years before A.D. 160, and a succession of disciples elaborated his system. The Valentinians seem to have aimed at establishing an inner circle of "true Christians" within the orthodox Church, and this particular version of esoteric Christianity provides a suggestive parallel to the efforts of Gurdjieff nineteen centuries later. One of the most notable Valentinian converts was Bardaissan of Edessa, who had belonged to the "Aissor" Church and made a journey to

Armenia. His views on what Gurdjieff called "the law of fate and the law of accident" are virtually identical to Gurdjieff's own teaching.

Gurdjieff certainly knew much of what could be known in his day about the Gnostic systems. It is possible to find a great deal of what he taught in one or another of the great heresiarchs—or in the Christian writers like Origen and Clement of Alexandria, who inclined more than a little toward ideas of a Gnostic nature. How Gurdjieff became attracted to the Gnostics we cannot know for certain; for there were countless possible avenues down which his mind could have traveled. But the most likely possibility is that this quest for a primordial version of Christianity led him to the Gnostics via the "esoteric Christianity" of the nineteenth-century occult revival.

In Western Europe the phrase "esoteric Christianity" is associated with the names of Anna Kingsford and Edward Maitland. Anna Kingsford (1846–88) was a leading light of the Victorian occult world, an ardent antivivisectionist, and a friend of Mme. Blavatsky. The visions which she experienced under ether were elaborated by Maitland and herself into an occult system based on alchemy and Gnosticism. To this they gave the name of "esoteric Christianity," and the expression became a commonplace among the occult groups of London and Paris. As far as their system was Christian at all, it represented Jesus as a Gnostic magus who had sojourned in the wilderness of the Essenes and returned to preach an esoteric doctrine in Israel. In 1891 Maitland founded an "Esoteric Christian Union," but the new gospel spread chiefly through the medium of the Theosophical Society—in 1901 Annie Besant published a book of her own called *Esoteric Christianity*—and in Europe the theory became known through the hugely successful *The Great Initiates* (1889) of the French Theosophist Edouard Schuré.

When he described his System as "esoteric Christianity," Gurdjieff might merely have been bowing to the need to define himself in a way which could be accepted in Holy Russia. When the fashion for mysticism swept into St. Petersburg from Paris, the commonplaces of Western occultism became fused in an unlikely alloy with the more superstitious traditions of the Orthodox Church. The idea that there existed hidden *startzy* fascinated those who were seeking for a Master, and the semi-occult vision which this produced led to the rumor that these "invisible" holy men represented the esoteric tradition in Orthodoxy. Gurdjieff was dealing in familiar ideas, and the associations of the phrase "esoteric Christianity" would have been perfectly well known to Ouspensky.

6. *Esoteric Buddhism*

To a believer in "esoteric Christianity"—or to someone obsessed with the need to discover the original forms of religious traditions—a progression from Christianity to Buddhism was not the unlikely journey that it seems.

In 1894, the year before the Seekers for Truth are supposed to have been founded, the Russian N. A. Notovitch published in Paris his *The Unknown Life of Jesus Christ*, which had a substantial impact on Theosophical thought. Notovitch also wrote books on the political role of Russia and was much concerned with the conflict of interests between the Russian and British Empires in Central Asia. It is quite possible that he was involved in the Great Game.

In *The Unknown Life of Jesus Christ*, Notovitch claims that after the Russo-Turkish War of 1877–78, he began a period of wandering "without any definite plan" through Central Asia. In *Herald of Coming Good*, Gurdjieff uses almost the identical phrase about his own travels in the same parts of the world;* and the expression chimes all too well with the apparently purposeless meanderings of an information-gatherer to be altogether ignored. Notovitch's own route led him over the Caucasus and through Persia to Afghanistan and India. He probably made several journeys, for the trip on which he claimed to have discovered his controversial material supposedly took place in late 1887. Traveling through Ladakh, he injured his leg and made an enforced halt in the Buddhist monastery of Himis, near Leh. He discovered that this monastery had in its library copies of texts preserved at Lhasa concerning the activities of Jesus Christ in India. Notovitch claims that he persuaded the abbot of the monastery to read him the texts, while he transcribed the translation made by his interpreter.

Jesus, whom Notovitch's text calls "Issa," is supposed to have left Palestine at the age of thirteen and traveled with a group of merchants to Sind. He spent six years in Jagganath, Rejegriha, Benares, and "the other holy cities" where he studied the Vedas. He began preaching to the lower caste Vaisyas and Sudras, denouncing the caste structure and the many gods of Hinduism. This aroused the anger of the Brahmins and Kshatriyas who planned to kill him, but Issa was warned by the Sudras and fled to the Himalayas. Here he learned Pali and studied the Sutras for another six years. When he had completed his Buddhist studies he left the hills and traveled westward, denouncing sacrifices and idolatry. Notovitch's account ends with the "Tibetan" version of Jesus' trial and crucifixion. This asserts that Pilate sent his troops to remove the body of Jesus from the tomb which was becoming a symbol of resistance to Rome.

The foreword to *The Unknown Life of Jesus* claims to describe the reactions of various dignitaries of the Church to Notovitch's discovery; one and all, they tried to discourage him from publishing his material. It is quite probable that he was a hoaxer; for although the legend of Jesus' Indian

---

*In another book, *Alexander III et son entourage*, Notovitch has a chapter on "Some Remarkable Men."

journey is quite well known in Kashmir, such a publication fits suspiciously well into the anticlerical and Theosophical agitation of the 1890s. The book was immediately successful, appeared in English and American editions, and provided Theosophists with an effective argument for the theory that all religions derived from the East—perhaps ultimately from some hallowed center of occultism in the Himalayas. The Issa of whom Nikolai Notovitch informed the world appears in Annie Besant's *Esoteric Christianity*.

Whether or not *The Unknown Life of Jesus* contains an accurate transcription of material Notovitch found in Ladakh, Gurdjieff had certainly read the book or knew and believed its arguments. In Tiflis he told Carl Bechhofer Roberts as a fact that Jesus had studied in a Tibetan monastery. The romantic tone of the discovery in a remote monastery of documents vital to an understanding of the origins of Christianity would certainly have appealed to Gurdjieff; and Notovitch would undoubtedly have been discussed in Russian Theosophical circles even if no closer contact had existed between the two players of the Great Game. The idea that the real, the "esoteric," Christianity had derived from Buddhism would explain precisely what Gurdjieff was doing in Tibet as the pupil of Agwan Dordjieff. It may also explain quite a lot about the relationship between Dordjieff, the convert to Orthodoxy Shamzaran Badmaieff, and Prince Ukhtomsky, the Theosophist—who, although he announced himself as a practising Buddhist, was once described by Badmaieff in a letter to Nicholas II as a good Christian.

At this point there is an unexpected link between the esoteric Christianity of Athanasius Kircher and the exploits of "Ushe Narzunoff" in Tibet. Before Narzunoff's photograph of the Potala was published, the only picture which Europe possessed of that impressive building was a drawing in Kircher's *China Illustrata* (1670). This volume formed part of the Jesuit's work as an Orientalist and contained accounts of Tibet by missionaries belonging to his Order. Before the epidemic of Tibetan voyages at the close of the nineteenth century, Kircher's book was still much more than a curiosity for travelers to Central Asia, and it is quite possible that Gurdjieff first became interested in the Jesuit scholar by way of his *China Illustrata*. Joseph Deniker reproduced Kircher's illustration of the Potala in his edition of Narzunoff's travel diary in *Le Tour du Monde*.

Waldo Frank thought that Gurdjieff's system was "clearly derived" from Buddhism. He may have made his own investigations, but most probably based this opinion on the idea current among Orage's groups that the technique of self-observation was outlined in a Pali scripture translated by F. L. Woodward in his *Sayings of the Buddha* (1935), where it is known as "The Only Way." Orage's friend, Professor Denis Saurat, thought Gurdjieff "a great connoisseur of Buddhism":

Some highly educated Orientals with whom I have discussed Gurdjieff
go so far as to maintain that he was simply a Buddhist who for personal
reasons settled in the West and tried to teach some of the simplest of
the methods and truths known in the Far East. . . . Gurdjieff's book
shows no prejudice in favour of Buddhism, on the contrary he seems
expressly to condemn the spread of Eastern ideas towards the West.
He told me himself that he aimed at achieving a synthesis of Western
science and technique on the one hand, and Eastern spirituality on the
other, but he did not necessarily mean Buddhism, and was even of the
opinion that all religions found in Asia today are degenerate forms of an
ancient revelation.

Ouspensky once told his followers that the ideas of the System could be
recognized in Buddhism. A former pupil writes that "he did not say what
kind of Buddhism, but I supposed that he referred to the Pali texts
translated by Rhys Davids in Volume II (Dialogues of the Buddha) of
Sacred Books of the Buddhists, because I thought I had seen that book on
Mme. O.'s bedside table." The European who became the Lama Angarika
Govinda quotes Ouspensky in support of the techniques of the Pali
scriptures for orienting oneself in a universe of many dimensions, and it
would be natural to find correspondences in the Pali texts—of which "The
Only Way" is one—because for several reasons these could have appeared
to Gurdjieff as the repository of the earliest and most esoteric Buddhist
teachings.

For centuries after the death of the Buddha in 480 B.C., the scriptures
were not written down and the Pali Canon took form in the first century
A.D. It is divided into three groups, of which the most "esoteric" is the
Abhidamma-Pitaka, a collection of books on "further doctrine" or "the
super-doctrine." Professor Edward Conze explains that these were meant
for "the very core of the Buddhist élite." Anyone familiar with the
techniques outlined by Orage for the detailed practice of self-observation
would recognize a less sophisticated form of the analysis decreed by the
Abhidamma. Anything a person may think of as his own is analzyed into its
"ultimates" excluding any ego over and above these elements. The first five
ultimates are known as the Skandhas—the material attributes, feelings,
perception, impulse, and act of consciousness. Professor Conze gives an
example of an analysis of the phenomenon: "I have a toothache."

1. There is the *form* of the tooth as matter.
2. There is a painful *feeling*.
3. There is a sight-, touch-, and pain-*perception* of the tooth.

4. There is by way of *volitional reactions:* resentment at pain, fear of possible consequences, greed for physical well-being, etc.
5. There is *consciousness*—and awareness of all this.

While nothing we know of Gurdjieff's theory approaches the complexity and sophistication of the *Abhidamma,* his general approach was based on a similar attitude, and possibly he borrowed certain specific ideas from the esoteric teaching of the Pali texts: for example, the fourth book of the *Abhidamma-Pitaka* is a treatise on human types. But he may have picked up theory from many different varieties of Buddhism, including odd sects like the Tantrics, and there is one influence on his technique which is glaringly obvious: the heterodox Buddhism known as Cha'an or Zen.

When one of his pupils once asked him whether the System had anything in common with Zen, Ouspensky replied, "With Buddhism, but not with Zen Buddhism." On the other hand, when D. T. Suzuki attended a demonstration of Gurdjieff's movements in New York, he is said to have called the System, "Zen for the West." Margaret Anderson writes that Eugen Herrigel's book, *Zen in the Art of Archery,* parallels in a striking way the method of Gurdjieff's teaching. And once more, if Gurdjieff did take ideas from the Zen Masters, there might have been some stimulus for his believing that Zen represented an esoteric tradition within Buddhism. This point of view has been put forward by Alan Watts, and may represent the legacy of Theosophical opinion.

In *Meetings with Remarkable Men* Gurdjieff describes a game which he says that his father played with his friend Dean Borsh, and which he calls *kastousilia.* This procedure is so much like that of the Zen stories known as *mondo* or "question-answer" as to be no coincidence—*and there are of course no coincidences.* Gurdjieff's example is of Dean Borsh suddenly asking his father where God was at that moment. Gurdjieff's father replied that God was in the forest region of Sari Kamish. The Dean asked what God was doing there. The answer was that God was making double ladders on the tops of which "he was fastening happiness." Gurdjieff remarks that the two men used sometimes to carry on long conversations in this idiom, which would have seemed quite mad to an outsider. He adds: "Many of these conversations which then seemed to me so meaningless grew to have a deep meaning for me later when I came across questions of the same kind. . . ." He might well have found such questions and answers in a Zendo in China or Japan. An example from Suzuki shows the similarity:

Shi, of Yang-shan, was washing his robe when Tan-yüan came along and asked: "Where is your thought at this moment?" Shi at once retorted: "At this very moment what thought do you want me to have?"

The correspondence between Gurdjieff and Zen seems to have been most pronounced toward the end of his life; but D. T. Suzuki's description of an irate Master of "primitive" Zen equally well describes the inconsistent and combative character of Gurdjieff at Fontainebleau. In the Zen monastery physical labor is considered important, a particular status is ascribed to those performing kitchen service, and there is constant sutra-reading, which does not require that the listeners grasp intellectually what they hear. Most interesting of all, the parallels between the routine of the Prieuré and the practice of the Zendo is the ritual of the bath. One Bodhisattva is said to have attained enlightenment while bathing, and several Zen Masters have made symbolic use of the bath in their teaching. Even the apparent conflict of opinion among Gurdjieff's followers as to the significance of Gurdjieff's ritual baths corresponds to the conflicting answers of two Zen Masters to the question, "Why all this constant bathing?" One replies: "Even the idea of cleanliness is to be done away with." And a second contradicts the first: "Just a dip, and no why."

When Gurdjieff arrived in the West no knowledge of Zen existed in Europe or America. On the other hand, the origins of mainstream Buddhism in the "Eightfold Middle Path" taught by the Buddha would have been well known; and the idea of the Middle Way transposes accurately into that of the harmoniously developed man, the apostle of the balance. Gurdjieff was not seeking a union of all religions, as were so many Theosophists of his day. Rather does he seem to have been reconstructing—as he told Denis Saurat—the "original revelation" from which he assumed all the great religions to have been derived. Pushing farther and farther back, following occult Traditions to their sources, he would have found an "esoteric Buddhism" as he would have found an "esoteric Christianity."

And although he was not seeking a union of all religions, his search for a primordial wisdom must have led him to the publications of the Theosophical Society. From their headquarters at Adyar, from their American, British, and French branches, from their underground cells in Russia, the Theosophists acted as the central clearing house for all esoteric ideas. Although they snapped up Anna Kingsford's "Esoteric Christianity," their own teachings first came to the attention of Europeans under the name of "esoteric Buddhism." In the book which he published under this title in 1883, the journalist A. P. Sinnett summarized the cosmology which H. P. Blavatsky later embodied in *The Secret Doctrine*. The idea of esoteric Buddhism was as well known to occult circles as that of esoteric Christianity, and Ouspensky's stay in Ceylon in 1913 was dominated by the impression that he could discover some secret teaching beneath the established religion of the Theravedins. Similar ideas probably influenced

Gurdjieff's own search, and he certainly found inspiration in the conflicting theories of the nineteenth-century occultists.

7. *The Occult Revival*

Most of the materials for Gurdjieff's cosmology can be found in the teachings of the late nineteenth-century occult revival; and contemporary occultism could easily have suggested lines of research leading to ideas which other investigators ignored. Number symbolism is an example: several tomes on the subject appeared in Germany during the nineteenth century. In 1882 the Austrian spiritualist Baron Hellenbach published his *Magie der Zahlen*, which could have led the seeker at one remove to Athanasius Kircher; for Hellenbach often refers to the *Gesetz der Quadrat* of the Viennese surgeon, Franz Liharzic, which contains a reproduction of Kircher's enneagram with a reference to the *Arithmologia*. And far from being as unfamiliar to his contemporaries as Gurdjieff pretended, the enneagram was well known to the "magicians" of the Hermetic Order of the Golden Dawn, based in London. In their published rituals will be found the lecture given to initiates on "Polygons and Polygrams"—of course, from an arithmological-occult point of view. The lecture describes the magical attributes of the enneagram, which is associated with the moon and the *Sephirah* Yesod on the Tree of Life.

This does not mean that Gurdjieff read Baron Hellenbach or was initiated into the Golden Dawn. It shows simply that others were working the same quarries, and that his cosmology was part of a general revival of interest in Traditional doctrine. For example, the Golden Dawn lecture on Pythagorean figures was partly based on the researches of one of its founders, the London coroner, William Wynn Westcott. His *Numbers, Their Occult Significance and Power* was published by the Theosophical Society in 1890 and contains a reference to Kircher. Westcott also used a symbolism of squares, triangles, and geometrical figures to indicate different stages of human knowledge.

Such ideas were the common property of occultists in London, Paris, Vienna, Prague, and St. Petersburg. Everyone in these small circles knew, or knew of, each other; and every new contribution was eagerly assessed to see how it could be fitted into the huge syntheses which most of the occultists were engaged in constructing. A couple of years of occult reading—for he would not have been encumbered by much modern occult lunacy—would certainly have equipped Gurdjieff with all the material which he was likely to need.

To take a few examples from many that could be given: Gurdjieff's technique of disciplining his unharmonious pupils by assigning them to unwelcome tasks was anticipated by the strange occultist, Thomas Lake

Harris, who established his community of "The Use" on the shores of Lake Erie in the late 1850s. Harris's most famous convert was the Scottish Member of Parliament, Laurence Oliphant, whom he compelled to sew and to peddle food on the local train. Two genteel ladies were made to act as cook and chambermaid in a hotel, and a Quaker deputed to act as barman. Gurdjieff's deliberately eccentric use of European languages was quite probably modeled on the tactics of the eighteenth-century occultist, Martinès de Pasqually, who was a hero to the Symbolist mystics of the 1890s.

The most unexpected occult source for Gurdjieff's ideas is the American "Rosicrucian," Paschal Beverly Randolph, who flourished in the third quarter of the nineteenth century. Randolph was a talented and extraordinary figure. Half-Negro by birth, he made a reputation as a lecturer on the American Civil War and other patriotic subjects, but felt always that his ancestry prevented his real merits from being recognized. Eventually he relapsed into a welter of occultism and quack medicine. The essence of Randolph's teaching was sexual. Gurdjieff sometimes gave personal advice on sexuality by word of mouth, but his general teaching was clear enough. Sex was a sacred function of which there should be two results: the procreation of children and the "coating and perfection of . . . 'higher parts.'" In Russia he taught that the most refined substance produced by the body was sperm, and that it was the sperm which formed the fourth body which made man immortal. This is Randolph's doctrine in all respects.

The detail which really ties Randolph to Gurdjieff is the American's constant references to "Ansairetic Mysteries" said to be secrets of "the Syrian mountaineers." This associates him directly with Gurdjieff's emphasis on the role of the "Aissors" in *Meetings with Remarkable Men*. Unfortunately for any theory which would make Gurdjieff and Randolph heirs to the same esoteric tradition, the latter decided to reveal the source of his wisdom in *The New Mola* (1873). "Early in life," he wrote, "I discovered that the fact of my ancestry on one side, being what they were [sic] was an effectual estoppal on my preferment . . . So I called myself The Rosicrucian, and gave my thought to the world as Rosicrucian thought; and lo! the world greeted with loud applause what it thought had its origin and birth elsewhere than in the soul of P. B. Randolph! . . . Precisely so was it with things purporting to be Ansairetic. I had merely . . . got hold of a new name; and again mankind hurrahed for the wonderful Ansaireh, but incontinently turned up its nose at the supposed copyist."

At first it may seem obscurely shocking to find Gurdjieff linked to Randolph, who is an interesting and neglected figure, but very definitely an "occultist." The resurrection of Traditional wisdom by the late Victorians ' ' be tolerated—but what of the deliberate invention and peddling of esoteric doctrines by the self-confessed fake? It is difficult to see where else Gurdjieff could have derived his doctrine; and from relatively respectable and earnest seekers for truth, he evidently turned to the most dubious members of the esoteric fringe. The vision of Gurdjieff as the representative of centuries-old wisdom is once more clouded by doubt—was he, after all, just another of the false prophets who were spawned by the turn-of-the-century passion for things occult?

With the exception of sex magic, most occult ideas somehow found their way into the large body of literature published by the Theosophical Society. From the Theosophical presses poured volume after volume confounding Western Traditional knowledge with Buddhism and the religion of the Vedas. Gurdjieff used the Theosophical terms "astral body," "mental body," and "casual body," and it was almost certainly through Theosophical references that he developed his teaching of the seven centers of man. Without much question these are based on the Tantric *chakras*, the centers of force in the human body, which first became known in the West through the works of Sir John Woodroffe and which Theosophists like the notorious Bishop Leadbeater incorporated into the occult canon. There are examples of the seven centers in the works of Renaissance mystics, and near analogies like those of Francesco Giorgi who applied the octave to the human being; but the most likely route by which the seven centers arrived in Gurdjieff's teaching is through Theosophical sources.

It is also likely that the stray Hindu elements in his ideas arrived by way of Theosophy: such as the idea of food as the prime matter of the universe and the comparison of the Self with the owner of horse, carriage and driver; both of which are found in the *Upanishads*. It has been suggested that Gurdjieff's doctrine of the "three forces" implies a debt to the Samkhya philosophy; but the three *gunas* of Samkhya were well known to Theosophists, and appear in the book which probably provided a starting point for Gurdjieff's own occult synthesis. This is H. P. Blavatsky's monumental *The Secret Doctrine* (1888). In its weighty bulk are to be found references to the four bodies of man, to the "ray" of creation, to number symbolism, including a reference to Hellenbach's *Magie der Zahlen* which would eventually have led the reader to Kircher, applications of the octave to the chemical elements and the musical scale. . . . And apart from Gurdjieff's admission that he did follow up Mme. Blavatsky's references, there is one striking plagiarism. This is the renaming of the four elements "hydrogen," "nitrogen," "oxygen," and "carbon," which was first accomplished on page 593 of the second volume of Mme. Blavatsky's masterpiece.

When Ouspensky describes the lecture in which Gurdjieff first introduced this terminology, he notes that Gurdjieff confirmed that "carbon," "oxygen," "nitrogen," and "hydrogen" did correspond to the ancient elements of fire, air, earth, and water. He adds that "although G. had definitely promised to explain precisely why these names were taken and not others, he never did so. . . . Attempts to establish the origin of these names explained to me a great deal concerning the whole of G.'s system as well as its history."

We may begin to wonder why so much insistence is placed on the unprofitable nature of research into the origins of the System, and why several modern suggestions seem designed to divert inquiry on to the wrong track. Ouspensky's inquiries must have turned up a great deal of evidence—he knew all the Theosophical literature and much other occult literature as well. Other researchers must also have stumbled on clues to the origins of Gurdjieff's cosmology; and despite some odd antics, his followers are very far from all being fools or knaves. If this is kept in mind, we shall come very much nearer the nature of Gurdjieff's Method.

8. *Psychology, Religion and the Work*

"There is nothing so explosive as old ideas restated in contemporary terms," P. L. Travers has written of Gurdjieff. But was Gurdjieff expressing old ideas—in the sense of old theories—or was he in fact expressing something else, something far older; a series of wisdoms as old as the first wise man? Because the teaching was presented differently by different teachers, and because they all had to have regard to their own nature and the nature of their pupils, the introduction was made in different forms relating to the time and place. This simply means that the terms of the situation must always be contemporary; they must be those which seem to have meaning. If the pupil finds the ambiguities of *The Secret Doctrine* relevant to his personal situation, that is where the teacher starts.

The Victorian occult revival certainly colored Gurdjieff's own early search for truth. But was it a flight from reason or a return from alienation? In one aspect, it was an attempt to transpose the topics which had been traditionally the province of religion and the priest into the age of science and the scientist. The whole spectrum of subjective experience—of being-in-the-world, of mental phenomena also—had been excluded by the uncompromising materialism of early Victorian science. The religiously inclined, and the few with a real interest in questions of being-in-the-world, struggled with the task of translating the events of the psyche into a language which would have meaning for a society conditioned by the scientific miracle.

The continued advance of science has made the premature efforts of the occult revival both out of date and emotionally suspect. Science moved on from its primitive dogmatism, the theory of Relativity made its appearance, and the protests of occultists against materialism no longer tempt the

serious thinker. Yet the occult attempt to restate the perennial problems
has had two important results.

The first was the appearance of a small number of thinkers who tried to
develop the approach of Victorian occultism in a more sophisticated way.
There were a bare half-dozen, of whom Gurdjieff may have been one.
Hermann Keyserling and Rudolf Steiner are two others. Gurdjieff can be
quite easily compared to Steiner, who also passed through the influence of
nineteenth-century occultism before extracting the material which he
elaborated into his "spiritual science," Anthroposophy. There are certain
similarities in the approach of the two men; the search for a form to suit the
times, the use of movements à la Dalcroze, the theme of the Struggle of the
Magicians.

A second result of the internalizing of thought was the psychoanalytic
movement. There is evidence which suggests that Freud had a closer
contact with the occultists of Vienna than has ever been admitted,* and in
the school of analytical psychology stemming from C. G. Jung, attention
swung back to a consideration of topics treated by alchemy, Swedenborg,
and the Gnostics. Although approaching from the opposite direction, the
new psychologists were perplexed by the same sort of problems as troubled
the spiritual teachers, and they were under similar influence. While the
Steiners and the Gurdjieffs searched through tradition for forgotten
knowledge, the psychologists rediscovered the forbidden area of being-in-
the-world and proposed to subject it to the scientific method. In both cases
there was bound to result a restatement of old ideas in contemporary terms.

Because Gurdjieff's System was intended to be in a form "accessible to
contemporary man," and also because it had been worked out through the
sources to which contemporary man naturally turned, it has some correspondence with other serious attempts to redefine intangibles. Ouspensky
used to recommend the study of the "older" psychology and certain
Theosophical works. The threefold division of man into body, emotions,
and intellect was a commonplace of prescientific psychology. It is also found
in Laurence Oliphant, Vladimir Soloviev, Papus, Steiner, and countless
occult writers. In the interesting system called "Statuvolism," constructed
in the 1870s by the American hypnotist and phrenologist, William Baker
Fahnestock, can be found many resemblances to Gurdjieff's psychology.
On a more occult level, Annie Besant's A Study in Consciousness (1904)
contains some interesting ideas as well as much talk of "ultimate atoms." It
is subtitled "a study in psychology."

More conventional psychology has left fewer traces in Gurdjieff's
teaching. The discussions of laughter in In Search of the Miraculous were

*See The Occult Establishment.

probably inspired by Henri Bergson's writings on humor. Gurdjieff and Ouspensky always gave psychoanalysis a very bad press, regarding it as further involving man in the unreal world, but Kenneth Walker in his *The Conscious Mind* has compared Freud's views on psychology with those of Gurdjieff. Apart from their agreement that "wrong sex" forms one of the chief sources of human misery, there is little to justify the comparison. The parallel with Jung is much more exact. The similarity is sometimes so marked that the two are said to have met; but Arnold Keyserling once secured a denial from Jung himself. The parallel stems chiefly from Jung's own occult reading, and particularly from his reliance on the Christian Gnostics.

Of all the twentieth-century psychologies, the approach apparently closest to Gurdjieff's is Behaviorism. In its insistence on the mechanical conditioning of man—that man cannot *do*, that he is *done to*—and in its utter materialism, the System as defined by Ouspensky seems to have much in common with the theories made popular by J. B. Watson. It was not entirely wishful thinking which made Orage's followers see their Method as "the step beyond Behaviourism."

The origins of Behaviorism lay in Russia, in Pavlov's famous dogs, and the language of Behaviorism belonged at first particularly to Russian thought. If Mme. Blavatsky was in one sense the protest of the religious conscience against Darwin, Gurdjieff representes the first adjustment of the "spiritually-minded" to Pavlovian psychology.

All these similarities are in theoretical terms. It is when we move from theory to practice that the Gurdjieff Method appears most individual, and in so far as there *is* a consistent method, this is provided by the theatrical element, the philosophy of role playing which derives from Gurdjieff's own impersonation of Everyman and Superman. But the very term "role playing" is not peculiar to Gurdjieff's System, and the emphasis which his followers place on the idea seems to be a relatively late development. It was in 1923 that the whole idea of role playing as an explanation of psychological problems and as a means of curing them was broached by the Rumanian psychoanalyst, Jacob L. Moreno.

In that year Moreno published his book, *Das Stegreiftheater* (Theatre of Spontaneity), based on experiments which he had begun in Vienna two years earlier. He had started with the idea that actors on the stage experienced a great conflict between their own interpretations of a part and what Moreno called "role-conserves"—*type* roles artificially embalmed in the text of the dramatist. "I remember the struggle in Eleanora Duse between herself as a private dramatis persona, and the roles she had to impersonate; the struggle between the role-concepts created by the playwright and the concepts she had of these characters." From this starting point, Moreno developed on the one hand a theory of roles in society, and on the other, a whole series of techniques based on the dramatization of the patient's problems. Even the names of his techniques are suggestive: "role-reversal," the "mirror-technique," "double ego," "psychodramatic shock." "Psychodrama," Moreno writes, "is the science of the actor. . . . The actor must become an observer of himself."

Moreno's techniques and terminology are so similar to the vocabulary of "playing a role" that there must have been some contact between the followers of Gurdjieff and the theories of psychodrama. As to Gurdjieff himself, it is impossible to say. It does seem unlikely that he would pay much attention to a European who had developed for himself some of his own techniques; but without implying any debt to Moreno, Gurdjieff's Method can be described as a particular form of psychodrama.

And what is real in a universe where everything is theatrical? What is and what is not meant to be taken seriously? Gurdjieff's world is one of doubts, of the shadows of ideas, of uncertainty over the most normal-seeming appearance. What is the role of the cosmology in this altered version?

9. *Theater and the World*

Moreno's psychodrama is not the only contemporary development with which Gurdjieff's dramatic experiment can be compared. It seems certain that there must have been contact with the ideas of Konstantin Stanislavsky (1863–1938), whose book, *An Actor Prepares*, was originally published in Russia as *An Actor's Work on Himself*. Stanislavsky's Method involves, like Gurdjieff's, concentration of the attention and relaxation of the muscles. "Our type of creativeness," he writes, "is the conception and birth of a new being—the person in the part. It is a natural act similar to the birth of a human being." In another book Stanislavsky holds out to his actor the possiblity of expanding his awareness. "Only the actor whose development proceeds along harmonious lines can, quite independently and through his own acquired experience, raise himself step by step to a wider consciousness."

Other developments in the Russian theater may have been equally significant; in particular the work of N. N. Evreimoff (1879–1953). Carl Bechhofer Roberts met him in Petrograd in 1915 and published translations of two of his plays in the *New Age*. Evreimoff is celebrated for his invention of "monodrama," an idiom in which the internal drama of an individual's conflicting impulses is externalized on stage. Orage's *Little Review* article of 1926, "A Theatre for Us," suggesting a representation of the three centers of man, was derived entirely from a remembered performance of Evreimoff's monodrama *The Theatre of the Soul* at the Little Theatre in London on March 8, 1915. In theoretical terms, Evreimoff's chief argument was that all human life is governed by the theatrical instinct; and here he influenced Ouspensky, who recommended his book *The Theatre in Life* (1927) in *A New Model of the Universe*. Evreimoff ends *The Theatre in Life* with a confession of faith in his God, "Theatrarch" : "I believe that having played thousands of roles, more and more difficult, I approach closer and closer to him, my director, until, perfectly trained in the dramatic cycle of the cosmos, I became at last his inseparable and worthy colleague."

This idea of a theatrical universe is an old one. We can date it back at least as far as the Hindu idea that the universe consists of the "days and nights of Brahma," of plays enacted by the god for his own amusement. E. R. Eddison bases the fictional world of Zimiamvia on the same poetic conception. Neither is the idea of a purgation by role playing confined to men of the theater. Herman Hesse uses it in very much the same sense as Evreimoff in his novel *Steppenwolf* (1927). Harry Haller, the Wolf of the Steppes, the lonely visionary Outsider, prowls around the palisades of life until he discovers the magic theater. There is a notice above the door. It reads: MAGIC THEATRE: ENTRANCE NOT FOR EVERYBODY. With his attempts to gain entrance to the theater, Harry begins a surrealistic spiritual quest. Toward the end of the book he enters a booth marked "Guidance in the building up of the personality." Here he learns that "man consists of a multitude of souls, of numerous selves." But he forgets the lesson that he plays many parts and begins to take things too seriously. In the end he commits a murder—a theatrical murder—and is found guilty of "the wilful misuse of the magic theatre."

Theater in the unusual sense of the term has found a place in the communal activities of the various groups deriving from Gurdjieff. Presumably ordinary dramatic productions are thought to provide material for self-observation as valid as that given by "spontaneous" theater. Kenneth Burke has inaugurated a whole new school of criticism based on the dramatic metaphor and probably deriving from Gurdjieff. At the same time there have been attempts to show that the use of theater to shock people, to disrupt what Moreno would call their "role-conserves," derives from Traditional wisdom.

Gurdjieff's "Society of the Adherents of Legominism" used the theater as a vehicle for self-development. Orage may have been repeating something he heard from Gurdjieff when, toward the end of his life, he referred in *The Aryan Path* to "one of the lesser-known traditions of the Greek drama—that its actors lived to create it"; for it is a tradition quite unknown to historians. Two expressions from Greek theater are suggestive: the "persona" or *mask* worn by the actor; and the actor's original designation as "hypocrite," meaning "one who answers" (the chorus).

We do not know where Gurdjieff got his ideas about using dramatic situations. Every academic work on the history of the theater enshrines one or another theory about the relationship between religious ritual and the origins of the drama. A student of occult Tradition would find the image of the world as a theater a philosophical commonplace. It is to be found in Plato and Plotinus; the Renaissance attributed the idea to Pythagoras. There is an ecclesiastical tradition which originates in St. John Chrysostom; and by the late Renaissance the rapid growth of theaters was being defended against the self-righteous by the argument that the stage was a force for moral education—as Gurdjieff would have said, a "reflector-of-reality." Dr. Frances Yates has shown how the idea of the world as theater was transposed into the idea of the theater of the world, and contends that the theaters of the late Renaissance were an integral part of the occult-philosophical world view.

But the real justification for linking Gurdjieff's use of theater to occult Tradition concerns the glyph—the "mystery-play" in Ouspensky's sense—for the beholder at a distance in time the perception that *everything falls into place* in the emblem of events; that the Passion of Christ happened in the only—emblematic—way which it could have happened; that the drama of Ouspensky's death was in some way blazoning out the heraldry of the universe. It is a quality of perception which is genuinely experienced by substantial numbers of people. This idea, which leads us to the Rosicrucian fracas of the seventeenth century, is almost more incredible than a belief in indiscriminate miracles. The stage management of history is something which it is difficult to accept—even if the play being produced has in the relative sense a very small cast indeed.

The Brotherhood of the Rosy Cross announced itself to the world in a series of manifestoes printed in Cassel in the years following 1614. A barrage of literature and counter-literature sprang up from people denouncing, acclaiming, and seeking out the mysterious Rosicrucians, who proclaimed "a general reformation of the whole world." But the Brotherhood remained elusive, and it has often been wondered if it ever existed. Dr. Frances Yates in *The Rosicrucian Enlightenment* lays great stress on the use of the Latin term *ludibrium* to describe Rosicrucian activities. A *ludibrium* could mean "a play scene," "a farce," or "a joke." But, as Dr. Yates points out, those who applied the epithet to the Rosicrucians thought of the theater as an influence for good. "The theatricality of the Rosicrucian movement," writes Dr. Yates, ". . . is one of the most fascinating aspects of the whole affair." And later she volunteers one possible interpretation of the Rose Cross *ludibrium* "not as a hoax, but as a dramatic presentation of a profoundly interesting religious and philosophical movement."

The materials of the piece are similar to the case of Gurdjieff, Ouspensky, and the rest. The Rosicrucian manifestos describe how Frater Christian

Rosencreuz traveled to the East in search of knowledge. In the Sly Man's pilgrimage there was material in hand to fashion such a legend. Most important, the Rosicrucians were also called "invisible"—they inhabited an "invisible college," they were an "invisible" brotherhood. Johann Valentin Andreae, a theologian who began by cooperating with the Rosicrucian comedy, eventually turned against the whole *ludibrium* because it had become a "dubious and slippery concern." There were imposters and charlatans in the field, he complained, men claiming to represent the Rosicrucians. When in fact, Andreae implied, there had originally been a definite purpose behind the arrangement of a pious "joke," "with regard to the fashion of the age which seizes avidly on new-fangled notions."

The nature of this purpose must still be very much a matter of opinion, but those who pushed the Rose Cross Brothers on to the European stage were probably interested in a reformation of the world on lines which were at once Protestant, mystical, and scientific. Andreae suggested that the learned world stop blinding itself with mysteries and "learn the way of salvation" not from some occult society "hazy, omniscient only in the eye of its own boastfulness," but from the Christ himself.

And I suspect that this is more than a parallel with the *ludibrium* of the Harmonious Circle. It may be that Gurdjieff himself made the plan, or it may have been suggested by someone else entirely. The play scene is a comedy played in the theater of the world, and the play is for a general purpose which the covert action of the drama may not make clear. It was certainly with "regard to the fashion of the age which seizes avidly on new-fangled notions" that Gurdjieff at one time clothed his teaching in the garb of contemporary occultism. His introductory play-scenes were always similar. First you find out what the inquirer wants and in what he is interested. Then you temper your sales pitch accordingly. On a historical scale, the *ludibrium* or mystery play will serve the function of such an introductory comedy, until the inquirer is thoroughly "entangled."

Then who pushed Gurdjieff on to the stage and began the *ludibrium?* Was it Gurdjieff's own idea, or was he one among many? Who translated material from languages he could not read himself? What sort of people were behind him?

We can only consider possibilities. The least likely is that he was fulfilling a mission devised by some confraternity in Central Asia. Only slightly less probable is the idea that he constructed his System entirely unaided. The more his theoretical teaching is studied, the more it divides itself into two sections: a definitely Oriental part, based largely on Buddhist thought with an admixture of Sufi lore; and a definitely Western part, founded on European occultism as derived from the Gnostics, Neo-Platonists, and Rosicrucians. We know, or at least suspect, that Gurdjieff spent much of his life in Central Asia, and while he must have read widely in contemporary occult literature, it may be doubted if he would have the time or the resources for scholarly research. It is likeliest that he was himself largely responsible for the Oriental side of his teaching: the Buddhist psychology, the theories of movement, and the Eastern aspects of those ideas clearly inspired by Theosophy. It is equally probable that he worked closely with more educated persons who were at home in the scholarly traditions of European occultism. The collaboration of Prince Ukhtomsky alone would confine Gurdjieff's achievement within a more believable compass.

There remains the possibility that the Seekers for Truth existed not as a band of esoteric explorers, but as Gurdjieff's equivalent to the invisible Rosicrucians. However improbable such an organization may sound, it must be insisted that *fin de siècle* Russia could have contained *any* philosophical grouping, including one dedicated to founding a new religion by undercover means. H. P. Blavatsky was a Russian; and there is more than a suggestion of her tactics in Gurdjieff's own. Prince Ukhtomsky's conception of the Theosophical Society as a clandestine organization is also suggestive. It is because of the Russian Revolution that we know of Gurdjieff at all; but the Revolution may also have destroyed evidence of other men engaged in similar activities.

Several of Gurdjieff's followers have alleged that after Essentuki he degenerated. This is often given some mysterious occult significance; but if the observation has any basis in fact, it may simply show that he was handicapped by the loss of his friends. In *Meetings with Remarkable Men* he describes his last interview with the possibly historical "Professor Skridlov" before leaving for the West. If "Skridlov" existed, he was cut off by the Revolution; and Gurdjieff would have been isolated from the moral and material support of any other colleagues he possessed. He had to rely on his own resources, and the *ludibrium* may have been forced on him by circumstances. In Russia he emphasized to Ouspensky that he could not and should not have many pupils; but financial considerations later drove him to revise this dictum. It is not surprising if there seems to be a dilution of quality in the means employed. But it remains possible that Gurdjieff was acting in accordance with some preconceived plan: not as the agent of any powerful occult society, but simply in accordance with what had been discussed among a small group of unusual men, whom he may have encountered at any stage of his unconventional pilgrimage. The Seekers for Truth and the Sarmoun Brotherhood are fraternities like that of the Rosicrucians. And they are strictly invisible.

How then did Gurdjieff become an "esoteric teacher"? It all depends on what that is thought to be. Personal reasons provide a partial answer—the sort of reasons that make a man search for truth at all—and this answer will have to stand until we delve a little further beneath the surface of "what Gurdjieff taught." His vast cosmology was a creation of the times. We will not be wide of the mark if we guess that Gurdjieff put it together himself, although with the help of friends, from what are really the obvious sources; and, of course, as he liked to imply (his head cocked heavenward for signs of supernatural approval) with the Archangel Looisos watching.

2

A Short Space Voyage with the Grand Inquisitor

The distinction between the forms and the content of Gurdjieff's teaching corresponds to that between theory and practice. This fact has been blurred by the ambiguity of the term "the system" which Ouspensky adopted from the private language of Gurdjieff's St. Petersburg group. "The System" might be taken by Ouspensky's followers as referring to the vast combination of cosmological and psychological geography which their teacher had assembled. Or it might be taken as the methodical sequence of his instruction—the "System" of teaching which he followed with his own pupils and had codified from the experience of his time with Gurdjieff. Orage made the distinction clearer by placing the accent on what he called the "Method," and referring to the cosmological or psychological theories as the greater and the lesser "maps." For the Work teacher may instruct his pupils in the outlines of cartography; but—as with all good teachers—the bare facts of his material do not themselves comprise the lesson which he hopes his pupils will learn.

Again we are confronted with the perennial question: what is the Work? The answer lies in the more theatrical side of Gurdjieff's activities, and the perspective of history gives us an advantage over the men and women who were in personal contact with the Master—often unsure whether they were on their heads or their heels, or whether the world itself had turned upside down. Gurdjieff himself was the last person to tell anyone what was going on, and the few explanations he did give often increased the confusion. All that can be done is to question his writings.

Meetings with Remarkable Men may have been heavily edited before its posthumous publication. It was certainly never completed as Gurdjieff originally intended. According to the prospectus printed in *Herald of Coming Good*, it should have consisted of at least three "books"—which would make its projected length similar to that of *Beelzebub's Tales*. At Gurdjieff's death the *Third Series* was left in a fragmentary state. Two chapters alone seem to have been completed, and others exist only in note form. A chapter on "The Four Bodies of Man" which Gurdjieff announced in *Meetings with Remarkable Men* is said to have been destroyed by the author himself. What remains of the *Third Series* is too incomplete to give any real idea of Gurdjieff's intentions for the book. That leaves us with the *First Series, All and Everything: Beelzebub's Tales to his Grandson*.

When *Beelzebub's Tales* was published in the spring of 1950, American reviewers—who had no doubt heard of the underground reputation of THE BOOK—were markedly scathing; and it was left to sympathizers like Gorham Munson to apologize for Beelzebub. Gerald Sykes considered that "Gurdjieff's reputation has been done an irreparable injury by this all but unreadable book." He concluded sourly: "Mark Twain called 'The Book of Mormon,' 'chloroform in print.' We have much better anaesthetics now." The *Saturday Review* thought the style, "even apart from the jargon . . . turbid to a degree that makes it nearly insufferable." There were, this critic said, "a few seeds of truth and wisdom buried in a vast midden of nonsense." British critics were more affable. In *The Spectator* D. S. Savage declared *Beelzebub's Tales* to be "wholly fascinating"; and although in the *New Statesman* Kathleen Raine described the book as "something between *Gulliver's Travels*, somebody's *Outline of Knowledge*, and a paranoiac fantasy," she found it "strangely readable," and concluded that it contained "passages of real wisdom."

According to Nott, the book is an "objective work of art" in Gurdjieff's sense if in no one else's: that is, a work constructed mathematically so as to produce a precise series of effects on its readers. The opportunities which this gives for a species of literary pyramidology scarcely bear thinking about. Orage and Jean Toomer both read and commented on *Beelzebub's Tales*, but Orage's commentary sheds little light on the darkness of the text and claims that "everything has three meanings and seven aspects"— whether or not derived from Gurdjieff himself—simply encourage absurdity. It may be true, as Orage taught, that when Gurdjieff talks about Atlantis, he means the submerged part of man's consciousness with which he is trying to put his pupils in contact; but just as possibly, he had the object of confusing the issue—or possibly Gurdjieff did believe in Atlantis and countless other disreputable theories.

Analysis of *Beelzebub's Tales* leads nowhere. Gurdjieff's versatility as a linguist has been made the excuse for finding a profound significance in the jargon he invented. It may enlighten some readers to be told that "Parktdolg-duty" means "duty" in three languages—therefore "duty-duty-duty"—but if we burrow too deep and discover such clues as delight Baconian cryptographers, we will have fallen into one of the traps. Gurdjieff made use of whatever peculiar etymologies came to hand, with no other consideration than confusion: for example, there is the stellar system called "Salzmanino" which is especially dangerous because it is full of a gas like cyanic acid. Whether Gurdjieff intended any particular dig at Alexander or Jeanne de Salzmann cannot be known; quite possibly he was simply indulging his capricious sense of humor. A reader must beware of categorical statements about *Beelzebub's Tales*. For example, Bennett declares that the name "Karnak," which Gurdjieff gives to Beelzebub's spaceship, is derived from an Armenian word signifying that the body is the prison of the soul—but although this seems quite plausible, and there is in fact an Armenian root which could be bent to give this interpretation, Gurdjieff may just as easily have happened on the name on one of his motor trips through Brittany, the site of the famous prehistoric temple of Carnac.

A story will give point to this argument. While he was writing *Beelzebub's Tales*, Gurdjieff was in Vichy on one of his motor expeditions. He adjourned to a backstreet café with his work. In search of inspiration, he looked up and out of the window. Across the street was a shop, the name of which his companion cannot exactly remember—let us say, for the sake of illustration, Picasso et Duchamp. "Ve-rr-y interesting," said Gurdjieff slowly, and read out the name of the shop. His companion corrected his pronunciation. Gurdjieff ran the two names together, chopped off a syllable and rearranged his word. Then he started to laugh. "Ah, Miss," he chortled, "you read chapter such-and-such and you see I put—very important man, his name will be Dupichampo." Then he began to laugh again. His companion could not see the joke. Well, she asked, perhaps this was a good idea, but what was so funny? "Don't you understand?" said Gurdjieff. "In New York, everyone who read will go to library, try to find name, make translation, everyone will have different interpretation of what *mean* this name!" And he dissolved in laughter all over again.

But if analysis of detail gives no help, the same broadly symbolic interpretation which leads to some understanding of *Meetings with Remarkable Men* can be applied to *Beelzebub's Tales*. Once more Gurdjieff's statements are neither-one-thing-nor-the-other. On the other hand, it is dangerous to state that the characters Beelzebub, Hassein, and Ahoon represent various human faculties and functions or various levels of development. On the other, it is equally wrong to adopt the approach of Boris Mouravieff, who claims that the science fictional form of Gurdjieff's epic was inspired by the literary productions of V. I. Kryshanovsky—a spirit medium who produced popular romances supposed to be dictated by the Earl of Rochester which were much in demand in St. Petersburg in the late nineteenth century. Both attitudes are simplistic—and not simple enough. *Beelzebub's Tales to his Grandson* is about Beelzebub's instructions to his favorite grandson Hassein. "It is not my book," said Gurdjieff, "it is Mr. Beelzebub's," and he advised his pupils to address Beelzebub as "dear grandfather."

The reader, therefore, is to put himself in the position of Hassein, who is taking a trip in a psychological-space ship. There is no point in trying to follow the laborious twists and turns of his instruction; and if *Beelzebub's Tales* were an allegory of "spiritual progress," it would be better to turn straight to *Mount Analogue* or the works of T. S. Eliot. Gurdjieff's Beelzebub instructs directly, chiefly by attacking the absurd habits of life on the planet Earth which he has visited on several occasions. At various stages every one of Gurdjieff's followers might have felt himself singled out for criticism. There are chapters on the insanity of the Russians, the French, the Germans, and a huge chapter on "Beelzebub in America." Gurdjieff's section on "Art" might have been entitled "Bad Art" and is directed against the intellectuals and Bohemians who formed such a large part of his circle; his general assaults on the medical profession and the learned ignorant are also specific denunciations of groups of people with whom he came in contact. All this is in line with Gurdjieff's expressed intention in his book: "Mercilessly, without any compromise whatsoever, to extirpate from the mentation and feeling of man the previous century-rooted views and beliefs about everything existing in the world."

Besides destructive criticism, *Beelzebub's Tales* contains a constructive aspect. In the prospectus which Gurdjieff printed in *Herald of Coming Good*, he refers the task of providing "constructive" material to the second and third series of his writings; but in *Beelzebub's Tales* itself, there are sufficient indications of what he intended. There is, for example, the series of chapters about the great prophet Ashiata Shiemash and the organization he proposes for the salvation of humanity. Ashiata Shiemash is one name from *Beelzebub's Tales* which *can* be directly translated (for what that is worth)—it is a Zoroastrian term signifying the "Eternal Sun." In one aspect Ashiata stands for Gurdjieff himself. He is the son of a poor family, who in his seventeenth year decides to prepare himself for his mission of freeing the world from the illusions under which it lives. He decides—as Gurdjieff himself elsewhere tells us he decided—to make use of the innate faculty of human conscience, the traditional virtues of faith, hope, and love being totally atrophied. The deliberations of the great prophet—like the travels of Beelzebub on Earth—provide something of the material "for a new creation" which Gurdjieff intended to give in *Meetings with Remarkable Men*.

Most importantly, Gurdjieff has a chapter called "The Holy Planet Purgatory," in which he describes the creation of the world and the institution of the laws of cosmic harmony which he expounded to Ouspensky's companions in Russia. Instead of outlining his cosmology clearly, he conceals its details beneath a welter of jargon; for example, the three forces which he had called affirming, denying, and reconciling are styled "Surp-Otheos," "Surp-Skiros," and "Surp-Athanatos." "Must dig dog deeper": yet the dog would have found the same bone. In 1934 Gurdjieff explained his account of the Creation to Toomer who recorded the Master's comment. "Just so I create my world," he said. "But my task more difficult than God's. God have to destroy nothing first."

So what is the role of Gurdjieff's cosmology in the *process*, and did he believe in it himself? There is no doubt that he had made an intensive study of the various occult and religious cosmologies from which he constructed his own, and he most probably did believe—at least as a hypothesis—the laws of the harmonial tradition which he had reconstructed. But this was *his* world—"my world"—and of a piece with the extraordinary atmosphere which he created around himself. His role playing, his hints of possessing strange powers, his conscious posturing and exoticism formed a controlled personal environment which accompanied him wherever he went. Whatever the psychological temperature in Paris, New York, or Chicago, the weather near Gurdjieff was always Gurdjieffian.

He was not above setting the stage to help him achieve his effects. The house outside Moscow which is described in *Glimpses of Truth*, the apartment on the Bolshoia Dimitrovka of which Ouspensky speaks in *In Search of the Miraculous*, the entire Prieuré—but especially the Study House—and at the end his Paris flat, with its glittering decorations and its shutters firmly closed against the city: these were all isolated from the world of everyday—not sensory-deprivation chambers, but association-deprivation chambers where the normal conditioned reflexes of humanity ceased to operate because there was no code of conduct which covered the situation in which the pupil found himself. When, by his contradictory behavior, his concentrated assaults on the self-confidence of would-be followers, and his acute psychological insight, Gurdjieff had managed to destroy most of the conventions which dictated a pupil's responses, he could start his work of creation.

Ouspensky felt that it was impossible to tell a lie in Gurdjieff's Moscow flat. The narrator of *Glimpses of Truth* came from darkness into another world of color and light. The door of the Prieuré was guarded—you had to *ring loudly* to get in—and once *in*, the strange combination of monastery, labor camp, and Mad Hatter's Tea-Party excluded the world beyond the Institute's walls; a world from which Gurdjieff's Citröen arrived, as James Young remarked, like an intruder from reality. Gurdjieff knew all about the practical uses of symbolism. And the function which unaccustomed surroundings performed directly for those who had personal contact with the Master was performed in literary terms by the cosmology of *Beelzebub's Tales*. After destruction—of fixed associations, of vanities, both existing and nonexistent, of the whole frame of reference which constitutes the pupil's picture of the world—something must be put in its place. You cannot show a man that the bridge on which he is standing is built of dreams and fantasies without offering him a rope to cling to. This process of substituting one world picture for another is implied in Ouspensky's title "A New Model of the Universe." Ouspensky had seen the physics of Newton destroyed by those of Einstein, and the apparently solid universe reduced to paradox. He therefore worked out his "new model" while admitting—at least in the beginning—its provisional nature. In the same way Gurdjieff, having destroyed the Newtonian world of inherited conditioning, erected an astonishing Einsteinian universe where nothing was what it seemed, and where relationships of cause and effect were blurred or rearranged in new patterns.

This was "my world," into which the pupil might slip by imperceptible stages until he found himself controlled by a different system of values, able to perceive *new connections*, and to read meaning into previously meaningless operations of the cosmos. *Beelzebub's Tales* cannot provide any real literary sense of the alternative reality which Gurdjieff manufactured, although it contains hints. This function was to be performed by *Meetings with Remarkable Men*. In that book Gurdjieff intended "to acquaint the reader with the material required for a new creation and to prove the soundness and good quality of it." The task of giving literary form to such an alternative reality was as difficult as the problem of expressing in words the preliminary stages of confusion and destruction, and for all its readability, *Meetings with Remarkable Men* is probably even less successful than *Beelzebub's Tales*. The "sense of another reality" which one reviewer attributes to it does exist, chiefly because literary conventions demand some suspension of disbelief. In *Meetings with Remarkable Men* Gurdjieff attempts to use the theme of his search for wisdom to weave around the reader some of the net of "my world." As it turned out, Ouspensky's *In*

Search of the Miraculous has performed this function rather better for large numbers of people.

But how is it done—how is the transition achieved? Gurdjieff explained in *Beelzebub's Tales* and his explanation has already been mentioned when discussing his activities as a professional hypnotist. Significantly, it is contained in two paragraphs which were omitted even from Orage's cyclostyled edition of THE BOOK. They were circulated among the New York groups as a separate fragment. Beelzebub is explaining to Hassein Gurdjieff's new method of hypnotism:

> So, my boy, when the hypnotist, by modifying the tempo of the blood circulation, temporarily suspends the action of the localization of their false consciousness—now the ruling master of their common pres- ence—the sacred data of their genuine consciousness can blend freely during their "waking" state with the entire functioning of their planetary body. If then he rightly assists the crystallization of data evoking in that localization an idea contrary to what has been fixed there, and directs the results of that idea upon the disharmonised part of the planetary body, an accelerated modification of the circulation of the blood in that part can be produced.

Gurdjieff may have intended to convey something by his claims to be able to modify the circulation of the blood; or it may be simply a blind. The point is that he refers to a *new form* of hypnotism which allows him to suspend "false consciousness." He then implants suggestions of a conflicting nature. In other words, he is talking about the process of destroying existing values and providing material for a "new creation"—that is, Gurdjieff's own "new model" of the universe. He admits that this is a form of hypnotism; but hypnotism used to counter the unperceived "hypnotism" of conditioning and conventional wisdom.

At the very beginning of *Beelzebub's Tales* there is a section on the mechanisms which power spaceships. The *Karnak* is a ship of advanced design. Beelzebub and the captain of the ship reminisce about the antiquated vehicles which they knew in their youth. The captain remem- bers how "very complicated and cumbersome" they were, and how their chief use was in transporting about the universe the fuel for their own propulsion. These primitive models were replaced by ships powered according to the "system of Saint Venoma." The principle of this drive was a method of destroying matter and thus creating a vacuum through which the ship could easily pass. There were grave drawbacks, says the captain, chiefly because, although such ships worked well in "atmosphereless spaces," "when nearing some sun or planet it became real torture for the beings directing them, as a great deal of complicated manoeuvring was necessary . . . when the ships were passing near any sun or planet whatsoever, their speed of locomotion had sometimes to be reduced hundreds of times below their usual rate."

It takes some familiarity with Gurdjieff's symbolic methods—and also a certain amount of guesswork—to see that he is referring to earlier methods for disrupting "false consciousness." In talking of planets and suns he probably means distracting influences which could so easily entice away recruits who had entered the "world" of the spaceship. But the system of Saint Venoma was soon superseded, Gurdjieff writes, by that of the Archangel Hariton. The great virtue of this method was that it operated best in conditions of dense matter. The principle Gurdjieff describes is something like the jet—and the point is that this engine makes use of the material obstacles in its path to generate its power. "The ship on which we are now flying belongs to this system," remarks the captain. The *Karnak* represents Gurdjieff's Fourth Way, the Way of the Sly Man. The captain describes its virtues as "simplicity and convenience" and Beelzebub compares it to "perpetual motion." He pronounces what can safely be taken as Gurdjieff's justification for his technique:

It will work perpetually without needing the expenditure of any outside materials.

And since the world without "planets" and hence without atmospheres cannot exist, then it follows that as long as the world exists and in consequence, atmosphere, the cylinder-barrels invented by the great Archangel Hariton will always work.

All you need, he might be saying, to practice this Method is yourself and the challenges of ordinary life. There is no need for the appalling difficulties of trying to maintain an entire society based on theological principles. The closed world of a cult holds fast only when unchallenged by a rival system of values. Neither system bears comparison with the way of the man in the world.

But for all the System's advantages, it is still countering one form of hypnotism with another; and there is no guarantee that the revised world picture has anything to recommend it over the first. It may be that a magical or a religious view of the universe is just as tenable as that of the secondhand car salesman. But it is *no more* tenable. The verdict here depends upon whether one believes that Gurdjieff took his harmonial vision of the universe as a representation of absolute reality. Many of his followers have thought so—and have stuck in the alternative universe he proposed to them. But this is only half the story, one stage in the *process*. It is the error pilloried by the classic Zen story of the man who sees only the pointing finger and not the moon at which it points. In New York, Orage had his own version of this monitory tale which Toomer recorded: "I am a signpost," he said, "I indicate a way. But you do not follow the signpost, you follow the road. You are not to follow me; you are to practice the method I define."

When the pupil has made the psychological-space journey from Newtonian space into Einsteinian space, what comes next?

However we alter the picture of the world which our inheritance has given us—by drugs and by yoga like the young Ouspensky, or by confusion like Gurdjieff and the Masters of Zen—the great temptation is to assume that the new universe is by definition *more real* than the previously limited world one has inhabited. Immediately there are cries of "higher forces"— scarcely ever "different" forces or "other" forces. Our assumptions have been altered, that is all. The poor neophyte discovers that "a mountain is not a mountain"—and sometimes dashes round telling all his friends, in which case he may end up in a padded cell. Man wants to bow down to the lightning, as Gurdjieff came to be only too aware. But if he avoids this trap, he may discover when he returns that the world he has known as rigid is in fact infinitely flexible.

A perception of new orderings may give a peculiar sharpness to old orderings. Old associations may be knocked away, encrustations of spurious meaning vanish. There is a case for considering that a journey out of this world and back is a necessary intellectual adventure, whatever verdict the return may bring; the point of the journey is not to impose upon the pupil an alien vision of the universe, although he will need a "new model" at one particular stage. For after the stages of *destruction* and the *reconstruction* of an alternative world picture, the new vision which has replaced the old must in its turn be destroyed. Its purpose is served once it has shown the pupil that there are other possibilities, not to dictate to him which of those possibilities he should pursue. It may be that he will choose a lifetime of sampling and tasting, with no definite commitment ever made. "I've lived thousands of years," said Gurdjieff to Toomer in 1934. "It is possible to know how to live thousands of years in one life."

Gurdjieff proclaimed that his object in the *Third Series* was to help the reader to form "a veritable, nonfantastic representation . . . of the world existing in reality," and it may be significant that the book remains unfinished. For how could it help an individual to come to this personal conclusions about reality? It could at the most represent

Gurdjieff's own effort. Toomer recorded Orage's terse demonstration of this point in his introductory remarks to one particular group. He asked his audience why they had all assembled.

A: "To hear about a new psychology."
O: "What is the nature of this psychology? Whose is it?"
A: "Gurdjieff's."
O: "No" (the *Method* is Gurdjieff's).

Orage then developed the point that it was one's own individual psychology that was involved.

In an essay called "Scholarship and the Spirit" (1928), which was heavily influenced by Orage, Zona Gale makes much of the chemical term "allotrope." An allotrope of a substance is composed of the same chemical constituents rearranged so as to form a different substance. Zona Gale suggested that men should form "the allotropes of themselves." This implies that the element of chance plays a large part in the process, that the shaking up of the pupil's constituent parts is in reality no more than the rattling of the dice-box. Few of the Work teachers have been foolish enough to deny that they are engaged in an occupation which embodies an element of risk. It does not depend largely on the teacher how the process eventually turns out. Gurdjieff had to expend a great deal of energy to drive some of his closest pupils away; but sooner or later they made the break— and made it for themselves. The pupil himself must escape from the alternative world with which he is presented; and this marks the entrance to a new stage in the process. In the revised edition of his memoir of Orage, Philip Mairet makes some comments which were inspired not only by Orage's break with Gurdjieff, but his own parting from Mitrinović.

Once you are in a school, as in a religion, there is no other truth to live by than what it teaches. In one sense this is even more obligatory in an esoteric school than in an established religious discipline, for here both doctrine and method are dependent, even to the smallest details, upon the master's *ipse dixit*. Thus, if a pupil should be able, after training, to set up an independent group of his own, the new and the old masters will soon disown one another as heretical or untrustworthy; for no pupil must be exposed to the temptation to play off one master's advice against another's. There is elasticity in the discipline, too, but implicit obedience to the master's generally unexpected interventions is all the more burdensome and disturbing because it remains voluntary. A pupil may simply pack up and go, as many did from Gurdjieff: many, perhaps all, were free to come and go upon their business or other occasions. But upon any point that the master decreed essential for the good of the school or his own progress, a pupil was under compulsion by the fact that he had identified his hope of self-realization with the teaching, and the teaching with Gurdjieff. This is the powerful bond which has to be broken, in due course, if the pupil is ever to regain his individuality with a new confidence in life. The rupture can be a grim experience; it is itself an initiatory ordeal.

Although the pupil, when he leaves the Master, may be an allotrope of his former self, it is not chance alone which dictates the nature of this transformation. The nature of Gurdjieff's Fourth Way is that it branches into different roads, and in his teaching Gurdjieff did broadcast material with which his pupils could make their first steps down their different paths. Despite the assertions that the Fourth Way is a way for the householder, to be practiced in ordinary life, we should be aware of assuming that "ordinary life" retains the same significance for those who practice it. The *conditions* of ordinary life are used as a means of transformation, and this must completely alter the way of the man in the world. Gurdjieff told Ouspensky that there was no need to give up anything at the start. The Work begins as a *via gradua*, an easy slope requiring no dramatic renunciations such as attend the monk's vows, no strenuous exercises like those of the fakir, no imaginative or intellectual acrobatics like those of the magician or the yogi. The teachers begin by leading their pupils along a path of extreme reasonableness and ask them to verify everything they are told. But very soon the path gets stormier, and eventually the traveler is faced with a triple fork in the road. Like Thomas the Rhymour under the Eildon Tree, he must sit down and make his decision.

One track is the religious path, the road toward God. Gurdjieff was perpetually irreverent when referring to the Deity—"old Idiot who created such"—and for all its absolutes, his System was agnostic. Once when Ouspensky was asked whether he could give a pupil religious faith, he replied "absolutely not." And yet many of the people who came to Gurdjieff were in search of a God they had lost or never had. So it often happened that Gurdjieff found himself invested with divine attributes by what the anonymous writer in *The Times Literary Supplement* calls so aptly, "Silly men and even sillier women." As this critic remarks, he became for some devotees the "God-substitute, which at least on a conscious level he did not want to be." But for the less susceptible, their religious quest was an aim which Gurdjieff could use, and he helped them on their way. "I have many sons in monasteries," he would rumble; and these monasteries need not all have been built of stone.

The second road is that of the cultist, the pupil who finds a religion in

Gurdjieff's cosmology and a God in the teacher himself. These are the sheep who are content to be eaten: unfortunates who are trapped in the transfer situation and cannot extricate themselves. They have jumped from the frying pan into the fire and will sizzle into cinders. They may be quite happy as cinders but they will have been burned up. New religions are formed by those who have misunderstood, for the religious sheep are useful to the ones who do understand: the Grand Inquisitors . . .

In the second act of T. S. Eliot's *The Cocktail Party*, Sir Henry Harcourt-Reilly puts the problem of the fork in the Fourth Way as that of a straight opposition between the religious quest and a reconciliation with the world. "Neither way is better," he says, "Both ways are necessary. It is also necessary/To make a choice between them." To the character Celia, who asks to be cured "of a craving for something I cannot find/And the shame of never finding it," Sir Henry replies by describing what is in effect the third fork in the way:

> The condition is curable.
> But the form of treatment must be your own choice:
> I cannot choose for you. If that is what you wish,
> I can reconcile you to the human condition,
> The condition to which some who have gone as far as you
> Have succeeded in returning. They may remember
> The vision they had, but they cease to regret it,
> Maintain themselves by the common routine,
> Learn to avoid excessive expectation,
> Become tolerant of themselves and others
> Giving and taking in the usual actions
> What there is to give and take.

Whether the pupil goes on "up and out" or back into the world (but a more flexible world perhaps) or remains fixated on the operation of the Work depends chiefly on the degree of his initial desperation. Those who opt for the religious life are often very desperate people; as Sir Henry says, theirs is a way which requires "the kind of faith which issues from Despair." But after their contact with the Work, they need another sort of discipline than that offered by the Fourth Way.

Although Gurdjieff knew a great deal about both Christian and Buddhist monastic practices, it is doubtful whether he intended his System to be a pathway to mystical experience. One former inmate of the Prieuré told me that he remembered Gurdjieff with "the greatest possible esteem and affection," and that he had found "everything which he had been looking for at the time" during his four years at Fontainebleau. But he emphasized that he had achieved his "peak experiences" under the direction of another Master. Although there are reports of people attaining mystical insights under Gurdjieff's direction, he tended to belittle such occasions, and he was not—so far as we know—that sort of spriritual director.

Again it may be wondered whether this was not in the last analysis the cause of Ouspensky's personal disillusionment—a disillusionment which he passed on to some of his followers. Perhaps it is true psychologically, spiritually, or existentially that there is "something missing" from the System. If the sights of the pupil are fixed on a very lofty goal, Gurdjieff's system may seem incomplete in the sense of spiritually incomplete. Gurdjieff's business was to help people to center on that psychological axis which Jungians call the Self, but it is evident that some of his pupils hoped he could lead them further.

Those who take the way of reconciliation may continue to keep the discipline of self-observation as advocated by Ouspensky—or they may simply plunge joyfully back into the maelstrom from which they had once desperately sought an exit. Gurdjieff could not control—nor did he want to—the precise allotrope which emerged from the period of confusion. His aim, he explained, was to put a man in touch with his real consciousness, which had been overlaid by a complex of mechanisms. As he never tired of repeating, *"The teaching by itself cannot pursue any definite aim. It can only show the best way for men to attain whatever aim they may have."* The way in which it does this is by first forcing its participants to "take serious things seriously," and then confusing the programmed "conscious" mind to a degree at which—so the unwritten theory goes—the subconscious, which for Gurdjieff was the "real consciousness," makes contact with the upper reaches of awareness. What the subconscious contains—unless one decides that we are dealing with a communal unconsciousness or God—has nothing to do with the teacher. Once the pupil has made the necessary contact, he has found, in Aleister Crowley's phrase, his "true Will," his function as a human being.

The man who is reconciled to the world might compare the process with the three stages of the first part of Orage's Method: Self-Observation: when you observe your mechanicality, your contradictions, your obedience to programmed commands. Experiment: when you discover the limits of what is possible within a new context. Participation: reconciliation with the world on a level of greater control. Or, in Timothy Leary's admonition, "drop out, turn on, tune in." In "Portage Potential," Toomer expresses the idea not as part of an esoteric process but as an inevitable human development:

There are three stages—and one must pass through all three of them to complete his cycle. One begins as an ordinary participator. One withdraws—as symbolized by the apprentice who is learning his craft—and develops a certain degree of philosophical knowledge and individuality. One reenters as a superior participator; and at the same time continues and advances the development of himself.

Does the pupil know "who he is" at the end of this elaborate pilgrimage? If a new perception of relativity is all that results, it may be asked whether the game is worth the candle. But it is possible to justify the process simply as an experience—and an extraordinary one. And on a moralistic level, the pupil may not know who he is—but he may have some idea of his correct address.

So the secret is that there is no secret? That the entire operation is a gigantic *ludibrium?* The Man Who Knows does not know—or that he knows the extent of what it is possible to know and aims to educate others in his own disillusionment. . . .

"In the present period of my life," Gurdjieff wrote in 1933, "when declining in years, after having had everything to satiety that life can offer to a human being, and having been thereby fully disillusioned in everything . . ." Gurdjieff's pupils had to follow his own progress through the world of ideas and the spirit. Just as Ouspensky constructed a "system" out of his experience as Gurdjieff's pupil, Gurdjieff could only construct a system out of his own experience. No pupil would reproduce exactly the resolutions, discoveries, and disillusionments which had been Gurdjieff's lot; but he would be steered by Gurdjieff's experience, directed within territory familiar to Gurdjieff—and make his foray into the other world within the context of a universe constructed by Gurdjieff from the debris of his own explorations.

Of course, Gurdjieff's tales of his early sense of mission and his search for knowledge might all have been invented for the benefit of particular audiences—but I do not think so. The facts fit too well together. Gurdjieff would have searched for truth in Christianity, Buddhism, and perhaps also in Islam and Hinduism, as well as in the science and occultism of his day. At the beginning, he informed his pupils, he was "psychopathic." I believe that he meant this seriously. The journey of Hassein on the *Karnak* is a reflection of the progressive disillusionment of Gurdjieff himself.

We can now date the point at which he recognized the extent of his disillusion. This is the time he spent near Yangi Hissar in 1905, after he returned to Central Asia from the Caucasus. At the age of thirty-one, at last realizing that no one and nothing could help him to understand the meaning of existence, Gurdjieff carried out a revision of the premises on which he had based in life. He then set about perfecting a method which might allow his pupils to undergo the disillusioning process at "an accelerated tempo."

To say that Gurdjieff was "fully disillusioned in everything" does not mean that he abandoned all belief in an immemorial tradition of wisdom. But it calls in question the nature of that wisdom. In *Beelzebub's Tales* he declares that the original forms of Christianity and Buddhism have been distorted out of all recognition. It is true that those who talk of "esoteric Buddhism" and "esoteric Christianity" are often the prey of the most elaborate occult fantasies. But Ouspensky regarded Christianity and Buddhism as complementary, and Gurdjieff may well have seen the inner message of both religions as very different from either their public faces or the "esoteric" interpretations of the occultists.

The most interesting pointer to the nature of Gurdjieff's "esoteric Christianity" is to be found in the work of a writer of the preceding generation: Feodor Dostoievsky. The central problem of Dostoievsky's view of Christianity is that of freedom. Gurdjieff also wanted men to be free. I think that it is impossible to doubt that for all his roguery, for all his occasionally exploitive tactics, he was sincere in this hope. It seems probably that he was to some extent inspired by Dostoievsky's *The Brothers Karamazov*, which first appeared in 1880, when Gurdjieff was six. The novel is about three brothers, who represent mind, emotion, and body. Gurdjieff's first attempt to give his ideas literary expression was a film scenario entitled "The Three Brothers," and only when this proved unsuccessful did he turn to *Beelzebub's Tales*. There is no doubt that Gurdjieff's three brothers would also have stood for the three centers of man, and although he claimed that his scenario was inspired by a visit to the cinema, there was certainly some underground connection between his idea and Dostoievsky's novel. The most famous passage in *The Brothers Karamazov* is the poem projected by the intellectual brother Ivan, and known as "The Legend of the Grand Inquisitor." It is here that Dostoievsky poses most cogently the problem of Christianity as a road to freedom.

Gurdjieff may have conceived his mission as being to rescue the gospel of freedom from the well-intentioned perversions of the Grand Inquisitor and his brethren: "God, whose service is perfect freedom." Such an "esoteric" Christianity would know nothing of churches, and its practitioners would form an élite able to tolerate the prospect which repels the rest of mankind. But if from one angle Gurdjieff appears as a follower of Dostoievsky's Christ, from another he seems to be on the side of the Grand Inquisitor. The deceptions, the *ludibrium*, the exasperating, meandering voyage of the *Karnak*, the process of mystification and demystification—Gurdjieff was sometimes playing an Inquisitorial role. If *Beelzebub's Tales* represents a literary version of the *process*, Beelzebub in one sense *is* the Grand Inquisitor, although this role is not voluntarily assumed. Beelzebub is concealing a great deal from his grandson. Denis Saurat comments: "One does not tell children the whole truth, one gives them carefully prepared parts of the truth which one hopes will further the development of their souls." Beelzebub even tells Hassein that it is forbidden from above "to communicate true information" to a human being because this will prevent his from acquiring the knowledge born of experience which alone can free him from illusions.

Gurdjieff may have been consciously following a tradition which was known to sections of the early Church. In fact the book which bears most resemblance to *Beelzebub's Tales* is the *Stromateis* ("Carpetbags," i.e., "Miscellany") of Clement of Alexandria, the saint who with Origen was one of the pillars of Alexandrian Christianity—that eclectic and sophisticated Christianity so frowned upon by orthodox churchmen and which took over so much from the Traditional wisdom of antiquity. The *Stromateis*, Clement declares, "will contain the truth mixed up in the dogmas of philosophy, or rather covered over and hidden as the edible part of the nut in the shell. For in my opinion, it is fitting that the seeds of truth be kept for the husbandmen of faith and no others." A German critic, who disapproves of Clement as "suspiciously Alexandrine," describes the *Stromateis* as "a deliberate thicket, a 'spiritual park' where fruitful and unfruitful trees are planted higgledy-piggledy so that the merely inquisitive and the hypocrite cannot steal the fruit." Clement, he says, is concerned with "truth as an encounter."

Is this not exactly the arrangement and the purpose of *Beelzebub's Tales?* Clement claimed to have inherited a secret tradition derived from the Apostles, and justified the diversionary tactics of the *Stromateis* by the authority of Christ himself. "He did not certainly disclose to the many what did not belong to the many; but to the few to whom he knew that they belonged, who were capable of receiving and being moulded according to them. But secret things are entrusted to speech, not to writing, as is the case with God." "Can I imagine," Margaret Anderson wonders, ". . . anyone so treacherous as to betray that part [of Gurdjieff's knowledge] which can be revealed only by 'word of mouth'?" At several centuries' remove we have the same tradition of an esoteric Christianity and the same tactics.

The central problem of the Grand Inquisitor, as he tells Christ, is that there was a time when he too saw himself as one of the elect. Then it occurred to him that he was ignoring the meek and the humble in favor of the great and the strong who could tolerate freedom. Once he too had stood in the desert, but for all his devotion to the gospel of freedom, he had surrendered to the temptation of temporal power out of compassion for humanity. He joined those whose mission was to feed the sheep.

This happened with Gurdjieff and it happened with most of his followers. It is only in part because of external pressures, because the Inquisitorial mentality must be strong from the first in anyone who sets himself up to teach his fellowmen. Even if the message is freedom—including freedom from his own teaching—*he knows best*. He is one of the elect, the shepherds of humanity. This attitude emerges clearly in the last recorded dream of Maurice Nicoll; the "violence" which he felt that he must overcome arose from a feeling that his efforts to do good to his pupils were not appreciated. Ouspensky believed in an "inner circle" of humanity to which he sought admission. And Middleton Murry actually invoked the Grand Inquisitor by name in his estimate of Orage:

I was always conscious of the existence of a barrier between Orage's mind and my own, which—such was his importance for me—I made many attempts to analyse to my satisfaction. Finally, I came to the conclusion that in Orage there was an obstinate substratum of belief that there was some secret of control over the universe: a key by which one could unlock all the doors, and be a master of Power. There were veritable Masters in Tibet, for instance; or, if the great ones of the earth would adopt Social Credit, the new age would begin: something, in short, of the mentality of the Grand Inquisitor in Dostoevsky's great legend. I happen to belong, by nature, to the other side.

Grand Inquisitors are out of fashion with our age, and today Middleton Murry's point of view is likely to attract many more supporters than he attributes to Orage. In no age can a man who sets himself up to do good to others object to being judged by the severest standards; and any argument which justifies the sometimes unpleasant tactics of Gurdjieff and his followers must be an argument of means being justified by ends. If the inquirer believes that there are no ends, and that only means exist, he may feel he needs to go no further.

3

Of Masters and Men

The reader will ask: why, if the pupils of the Fourth Way are in effect taken for a ride by their teachers, are there not more open denunciations of their real methods? The most obvious reason is that the victims are afraid of looking ridiculous—although as every individual is ridiculous at almost every minute of the day, there is really no reason why such exposure should be feared. A second reason for the victims' silence may be that they have been converted to a belief that the Grand Inquisitors are right; that with the passage of time they have come to value their experience. This argues that a justification can be found for the apparently brutal methods which the Work sometimes used; and that this justification goes beyond a superficial attempt to reform people's personalities. What are the ultimate objectives of the teachers of the Fourth Way?

In the last chapter it was suggested that if the follower of the Fourth Way avoided being trapped in the sheepfold of a new religion, two courses were open to him: that of reconciliation with the world on new terms, or on the road "up and out" toward divinity. Let us now leave aside all considerations of some ascent toward a divine superlative, admitting with Eliot that we cannot know anything of a hypothetical way by which "the human is transhumanised." We must allow the possibility to stand—at the least as a gesture toward the ultimate puzzle of the universe, if not from any personal conviction. But—are the transports of the mystics possibly an extraordinary and intense experience of reconciliation, recorded by extraordinary and intense people? It all depends on what it is to which the individual believes he is reconciling himself; and in certain senses the path toward God and that into the world are identical. As Gurdjieff's dervish appears to be saying in *The Struggle of the Magicians,* belief and unbelief can ultimately be very much the same thing.

And it does not seem—despite all the accumulated divine attributes with which the unconscious minds of their pupils have endowed the teachers of the Work—that there is anything conventionally religious about the ethic of the Fourth Way. Gurdjieff's teaching belongs to the group of disciplines known as "the way of liberation," which may be camouflaged by a religious form for the reasons which will soon become apparent. The object of such disciplines is to engender a right perception of things and to encourage a reconciliation with reality. Such a state entails the recognition that no final explanations will ever be forthcoming from the universe, and that "making the best of things" is not a philosophy of resignation, but the only possible creative attitude to life. Such an attitude of acceptance is in one sense a juvenile insight to market as eternal wisdom; but in another it might be experienced as the salvation of a soul. To the man who seeks a guru the world may well be a dark and terrible place. If he is troubled about the conditions of human existence, the nature of consciousness, whether it is worth living, or a dozen other unimportant questions, he may be infinitely grateful for being brought to an understanding of the accepting attitude to life. And if he is in Ivan Osokin's situation, with the revolver halfway to his temple, it is the mercy of heaven if he happens to meet a magician.

In his *Psychotherapy East and West,* Alan Watts demonstrates that the "liberation" at which Zen Masters or the Hindu gurus are aiming has nothing to do with the sort of gnostic liberation so beloved of occultists. "Liberation" is from the conditioning imposed by social institutions, in particular from the illusion that man possesses an individual ego. The teacher performs his function by trying to make the pupil see that the problems from which he imagines he is suffering are not problems: they are simply the way things are. The teacher's chief weapon is the situation which Gregory Bateson has called the "double-bind," in which a person is placed in a position of apparent paradox, so that his conditioned behavior patterns break down under the strain of contradictory information. Let us say that the *koan* is given, "truth is the sound of one hand clapping"—it is, of course, incapable of any "solution." The aim of the Master is to place the pupil in the state of double bind; his ultimate objective to induce the realization that, in the conclusion of another Zen story, "there is nothing especially to perceive." In other words, the ways of liberation are based on a trick: the teachers pretend to know the answers to their students' questions; but what they are really doing is trying to show that the questions are not questions at all, being based on false premises about the nature of things.

The plan of the Gurdjieff process follows tradition. At any time during the space voyage the pupil may cry "Eureka" and bail out of the ship, for such journeys are of varying duration. Gurdjieff is one of the most confusing masters of liberation because he appears to have used so many different methods. What he was doing was not, as some of his followers have asserted, searching for means to adapt Eastern methods for Western consumption, but adapting the essence of the ways of liberation to different Western milieux. As these changed, Gurdjieff's presentation had to alter. This is because, although the teacher of the way of liberation has strictly speaking nothing to say, he must appear to say something—otherwise no one will listen to him say nothing in his inimitable fashion. . . . He has two basic problems: that of exciting interest and that of asserting his authority. The pupil must be thoroughly entangled if the trick is to work, and the guru must first discover the unconscious premises on which each student bases his life. *The secret that there is no secret. The Man Who Knows does not know*.

In *In Search of the Miraculous* Ouspensky records Gurdjieff talking of the sin of "Black Magic," the sin of "the pretence of doing" as opposed to "real doing." But in a sense, this is what Gurdjieff was doing all the time— he *was* a Black Magician. Eventually the pupil might realize this—and his projections of good and evil would be set in conflict. A "Struggle of the Magicians" would begin in his own mind as he tried to reconcile the "black" and the "white" aspects of Gurdjieff's personality. It was another form of *koan* . . . but at first there was only the occult genius, the master psychologist, or the remarkable teacher of dancing. The guru must be a great authority figure, although his only superiority to his students is that he realizes that the burning questions which torment them are completely unreal. But, for example, if the pupil seems to be hoping for some metaphysical liberation from the condition of being human, the teacher will have to appear as if he himself has transcended the human condition. "It is thus," Alan Watts comments, "that the guru who has a bad temper, or who likes to smoke or drink sake, gives the impression that he indulges in these 'little vices' deliberately."

Another way to put it is as a cosmic allegory: the teacher stands for God. His role is to pose the riddle of life as often as he can from every possible angle. And because the teacher must be God for the pupil, the religious camouflage is the disguise most often adopted by the teachers of the way of liberation.

By centuries of subtle maneuvers, such adepts have often persuaded the societies in which they work that they are in fact the pillars of conventional values. The authority of the Zen Master, the Hindu *sannyasi,* and the Christian priest is backed by all the sanctions of traditional society. In the fragmented societies of the modern West, however, traditional sanctions have lost their meaning. So the guru of the Fourth Way must seem to possess the full social authority of whatever is the milieu in which he operates—quite often the appurtenances of material success. Hence the cachet of a good address in Paris, London, or New York, for certain contemporary practitioners of the Work. I have even heard of one Gurdjieffian guru who demanded the loan of a pupil's Rolls-Royce to reinforce his authority. But material success may have outlived its usefulness as a general catch-all for the Fourth Way, and those in need of what the teachers of liberation have to offer may be more impressed by other sanctions. At the turn of the century it helped to refer darkly to esoteric societies with which the guru was supposedly connected. In the 1970s the ploy was still being used, but today Amerindian sorcerers are more authoritative than Mahatmas from Tibet.

Because of the lack of a commonly accepted code of social values, the Western guru has a much harder task than his Oriental counterpart. It is not only that he must constantly be seeking for fresh means of establishing himself as an authority. He lacks the security of a conventionally accepted framework within which to operate, and therefore of a master-pupil relationship which can help the process toward a speedy conclusion. His activities will appear to be wildly inconsistent as he searches for a method of teaching the many different types who seek him out. Some may respond to the suggestion of hidden powers, others to the implications of material success. Eventually the whole process may become free-form—and perhaps even be sprung unsolicited on its subjects.

This raises an important ethical point. In the more traditional forms of the ways of liberation—and in the West these may be hidden in the form of psychotherapy—the "pupil" or student comes to the guru or therapist either because he is conscious that he has a problem or because he has a general anxiety about the nature of life. What of the pupil who is not conscious that he has a problem at all, but is simply faced with the ethic underlying the system: the illusory ego with which society provides all her children? He shares the fate of any pupil who approaches the Work, whether in a spirit of puzzlement, devotion, or curiosity. What happens to him is never what he expects. In his memoir of Orage, Philip Mairet describes the inevitable disillusion which the "esoteric pupil" will suffer:

Each pupil projects, more or less unconsciously, his own human ideal, the image of what he would like to be, upon the teacher, who must be able to sustain it. In short, the esoteric neophyte, far more than the religious one, is inspired by the hope of attaining a higher state of being through self-knowledge and self-discipline . . . What happens to the esoteric devotee who perseveres is not, however, what he expects: if his initial aspiration has been highly coloured by imaginations of acquiring abilitities he admires or envies in the teacher, the higher knowledge he at last attains may be that this is what he can never do in this life; so that he may end up a simpler, more modest person, perhaps in a lower walk of life than before.

This is the attitude of the former devotee of "esotericism" who has come to see a value in the process through which he has passed. It is a tolerant and resigned attitude—the attitude which accepts the position of victim, and continues to discover meaning in what otherwise might be remembered only as a tragic mixture of folly and deception. But there are many reasons why the disillusioned "esotericist" may never attain this Olympian pinnacle of forgiveness; he may fall along the way, may drop out of the process before it has run its course and become autonomous, may regard the trick as a piece of knavery pure and simple. All these things have happened to pupils of the Fourth Way; and many of the attacks on Gurdjieff and his followers can be explained by this incomprehension.

First come the criticisms which assume that the Work teachers were in fact teaching what they appeared to be teaching: that Gurdjieff was an instructor in "harmonious development," that Ouspensky taught a method of "becoming less mechanical," that Nicoll and Orage were past masters at guiding others to a knowledge of their own machine. Now, to say that these things were not taught by gurus of the Fourth Way would be untrue; Gurdjieff undoubtedly did believe that Western civilization encouraged an imbalanced type of human being, Ouspensky did wish to attain "cosmic consciousness," and a pupil might learn a great deal about his minor failings by impersonal self-observation. Yet the matter of such character training is really among the fringe benefits of the Fourth Way, and the study of personality defects and psychological automatism is not conducted for its own sake, but to impose a discipline and to give the pupil an orientation which may lead to other things. If an outsider—say a reviewer of *In Search of the Miraculous* or a reader of Nicoll's *Commentaries*—takes a flatlander's view of Work doctrine, he must pass a verdict which ignores the gradual unfolding and subsequent destruction of the strange "other-world" which it is the teacher's business to create. Because he has never been involved in the process, he takes Ouspensky's record of Gurdjieff's conversation or Nicoll's weekly exhortations as "what they taught," instead of as a record of the material which they used to build up their alternative frame of reference. The outside critic cannot avoid this pitfall; and it also catches the pupil who begins but does not stay the course.

For example, there was Richard Rees, who became editor of the *Adelphi* after Middleton Murry and remained convinced that "Gurdjieff undertook to teach his pupils how to secrete God-stuff." Or there was D. H. Lawrence, who maintained a tolerant distance from Gurdjieff—but still assumed that the Master meant what he said:

> In the end, if you Gurdjieff yourself to the very end, a dog that barks at you will become a dynamo sufficient to explode your universe. When you are final master of yourself, you are nothing, you can't even wag your tail or bark.

Lawrence could never have been "tricked" by Gurdjieff, because his revolt came too early. But what seemed for him the impossible obstacle— the fundamental unnaturalness of the Gurdjieff Method—is a basic characteristic of the Fourth Way, and one which it shares with the other ways of liberation. The pupil is directed to do something against nature; the ascetic must mortify the flesh which cries out for care and attention; the Zen student contemplates an insoluble paradox; the yogi studies the universe as an interplay of cosmic principles. Then—snap! The absurdity of the activity strikes him and he realizes that he *cannot* subdue the workings of his animal organism, that reality is an insoluble problem and that, to paraphrase Thomas Carlyle's words to the lady who told him that she could "accept the universe," "by God, he'd better."

"Man cannot remember himself," said Gurdjieff—and directed his pupils to try. "Man is mechanical," he said—and at once the neophytes attempted to nurture an infant superhumanity. Their lives became more and more stilted, more and more unnatural, until at last they were faced with the loss of their humanity—even of their lives—altogether. Colin Wilson argues that it is at this point that the Outsider, the religious misfit, may have his moment of illumination. The threat of death animates his sleeping will, and he realizes that "he wants more life, not less." Wilson's examples are Ramakrishna and the Buddha: two extraordinary human beings endowed with the capacity for sainthood. It is perhaps here—at the furthest attenuation of life—that the Fourth Way may lead its followers to the vision of life abundant.

For the others, they have reached the fork in the way, the obstacle which they cannot surmount, the decision that, if they cannot attain whatever ideals they had unconsciously harbored, they must reconcile themselves to the world. But instead of realizing that this is exactly one of the objects of the teacher—did not Gurdjieff call his Institute a "workshop for spoiled automobiles"—the automobile may now realize that its engine is working as well as ever it will and may even backfire in the face of the mechanic who has decoked it. The sensation of having had as much as one can take—and not merely from a personal relationship but from opposing oneself to an implacable universe—may produce a sharp about-face, and if the pupil forgets the state in which he approached the teacher, he may feel quite justified in accusing his former idol of defrauding and deceiving him, of taking his money and wasting his time. Of course, he will be partly right. Imagine the extent of Ouspensky's chagrin when he realized that the man for whom he had sacrificed a promising career and allowed himself to be trapped in Bolshevik Russia was to all intents and purposes a fraud. If the pupil gives himself time to consider, he will realize that his own lunatic unconscious has trapped him, and not his guru. He may become grateful to the man who has shouldered the difficult burden of his projections, and returned him to life alive and kicking; although even Ouspensky had to separate Gurdjieff and the "ideas" before he found it possibile to forgive his teacher. But the newly "awoken" pupil may not give himself time for thought, and the shock of disillusion results in the second largest group of criticisms of Gurdjieff's Method. What such critics are really attacking are their own former selves.

Alan Watts writes about the tricks of liberation:

> The technique will naturally seem to be dishonest. But this is a conscious and deliberate dishonesty to counter an unconscious and otherwise ineradicable self-deception on the homeopathic principle of *similia similibus curantur*—likes are cured by likes. Set a thief to catch a thief. Speaking of mutual recognition between those who are liberated, a Zen Buddhist text says:
> *When two thieves meet they need no introduction:*
> *They recognise each other without question.*

Did the Sly Man not say repeatedly that he might have *stolen* the System?

And this leads to another of the remarkable characteristics of Gurdjieff's Method. If the pupil is to enter the "other world" created by the Master, he must be encouraged to regard his teacher as a great authority figure. Yet, if the teacher of the Gurdjieff Method is doing his job, he will at the same time be planting the seeds of future doubt in the pupil's mind; hence the ambiguous impression which Gurdjieff made on many of those who encountered him. While encouraging the pupil to regard him as a great magician, the Master should be telling him all the time that he is cheating.

There is a good example of Gurdjieff doing just this in Kathryn Hulme's *Undiscovered Country*. He spends considerable time instructing her in breathing exercises—then devotes an equal period to mocking her for doing as she is told. Surely she doesn't really believe that she can extract the substances from the air which are necessary to create immortality? She does, of course, and bravely records the fact in her book.

When the pupil "wakes up" his first reaction may be anger, his second a reluctant acceptance of the situation. This may be followed by a different sort of anger: an overpowering irritation at himself for having been so stupid. Here there is a definite danger that the newly "awoken" person will need some way of exorcising his vindictiveness; that because he has been through the process himself, he will then decide that it is his vocation to put others through it in turn. The guru-game is self-perpetuating, and the motives of Grand Inquisitors are always a little suspect. Although they may believe that they are acting for their quarry's own good, their compassion may well be mixed with an unrecognized wish to see others wriggle where they have wriggled before.

The winnowing of the unconscious which results from the process may be incommunicable in the strict sense—although it could be described. Perhaps only the passage of time will show the victim whether or not the episode has been of value; and the experience of each pupil will undoubtedly be different not only in the obvious external ways, but in the interior psychological results. It is possible to make a ground plan of the process, but there can be no real comparison of notes. It is therefore impossible to judge when the process is "successful," and unfairly easy to say when it has gone wrong.

The cases of suicide which are from time to time linked with the Work do not prove a great deal. The unstable people attracted to "occult" theories include numerous potential suicides. On the other hand, the teacher must be considered responsible for any pupil whom he accepts and he must be aware that he will attract people in dangerous psychological states. The teacher should be able to monitor his pupils with the skill of a psychological technician; he has to know precisely what pressures to apply and when; he must be an exceptionally sensitive person, and he should certainly have undergone lengthy training in the skills needed by a manipulator of the Fourth Way. Little is known about how the Work teachers are trained except the famous adage, "to learn more you must teach," and a rumor recalled by Louis Pauwels that it takes seven years to make a group leader. There is no doubt that the Gurdjieff groups are conscious of their responsibilities. Nonetheless things do go wrong: they went very wrong for Gurdjieff himself on a number of occasions, and they have certainly gone equally wrong for a number of his followers. This is not condemnation; merely a warning that although the Fourth Way may be an enlightening psychological adventure, it is also dangerous.

It is dangerous because, although its practitioners claim that they warn prospective neophytes of the suffering which awaits them, they can never warn them sufficiently. For the Work to work, the pupil must be hit from his blind side; indeed part of the process will be to point out that he *has* a blind side. Gurdjieff himself had an exaggerated disrespect for direct instruction; he was so busy creating confusion and playing his various roles that at times he seems rarely to have explained anything at all. The Work operates by surprise attack, and if this attack is overdone, it may merely shock the pupil into a position of dependence which he or she will never be able to break. There must have been numerous unfortunates temporarily or semi-permanently warped for ordinary life by their experiences in the Work. There should be no psychological snobbery here. *No one* can stand up to an astutely conducted campaign to implant in him the sense of an alternative reality. If the teacher cannot attach the pupil to him, he risks the departure of his charge in a reconditioned but not rehabilitated state. This is equivalent to driving someone mad and renouncing responsibility for it.

The Fourth Way is based on violence; and this is the most serious objection to its methods. Such violence might be justified by the specious counterargument used by some fashionable anarchists: that the tacit "violence" of the prevailing system—in this case an existential situation and the conditioning of social institutions—can only be corrected by violence in its turn. Violence is used to create the "other world"; violence is used to shock the pupil into realizations; it is by violence that he escapes from his imprisonment. If the degree of force necessary is not gauged very accurately, either the process will be ineffective or there is a risk of destroying the pupil altogether.

Mouravieff sums up the possible adverse effects of the Fourth Way when its techniques are wielded by an incompetent or unlucky instructor. "A dissolution of the personality," he writes, "is usually the result. Malaise, moral depression, black pessimism, persecution-mania are the symptoms of this progressive dissolution. In the gravest cases, this can lead to a complete state of imbalance leading to the denial of the Self, which opens the way to suicide." Ouspensky probably felt the truth of this criticism and modified Gurdjieff's methods accordingly. Maurice Nicoll further sugared the pill with a religious topping. But this process of watering down Gurdjieff's strong medicine has produced an apparently inevitable paradox: that although the strongest objections to the Fourth Way turn on its use of violence, efforts to make it more charitable may simply increase the number of "sheep" who become trapped in the alternative world. If we are to admit any value at all in the whole "liberating" process, we must also admit that its most violent versions—although they may result in the greatest tragedies—may also produce the greatest effects.

Such a verdict seems to imply approval of the ethic behind the ways of liberation. But is this merely the quietest, Taoist "way of the straw dogs" which sees the universe as game or theater and counsels detachment from the gaudy show as the only salvation? If we are to believe Alan Watts, liberation is an even more specific state of being, and implies release from the duality of ego and universe. "There is," he writes, "nothing occult or supernatural in this state of consciousness, and yet the traditional methods for attaining it are complex, divergent, obscure, and, for the most part, extremely arduous." The harmoniously developed man, who feels himself in tune with the cosmos, who "goes with the flow," accepts his own nature and that of his environment, is not generally considered as an active creature; not that he is particularly inactive, but that the sound and fury which result from the striving of the ego to impose its patterns on the universe are experienced as irrelevant because they are seen to stem from an identification with an illusory self. As Jacob Needleman comments: "A system of serious ideas helps a man to become still."

Yet it could be maintained that the whole concept of the Man of the Way is itself based on an unperceived illusion, which may have arisen because the majority of people who become interested in the ways of liberation are instinctive world renouncers, driven from a normally active life by temporary setbacks or a desire for a permanently contemplative existence. It is not possible to argue about the sense of "cosmic consciousness," "universe as organism," or "loss of ego." This is a subjective and quite nonmystical experience; and the Work has certainly led people toward such a realization. But whether the experience is in any sense "objective," or what should be a man's relation to it are other questions. Even if a man is able to live out the philosophy of the universe as theater, he must see that innumerable roles are necessary in the theater of the universe. There can be no specific conclusion to the process; as by the end of his instruction the pupil's decisions have become his own, and he no longer inhabits a universal situation. His conscious life is in fact only just beginning, and although the question "what happens next?" cannot be strictly answered, it is the most important question to ask.

Gurdjieff dealt in the mechanics of human illusion. Sometimes he dealt in the general illusions, but the most important part of his work was concerned with those illusions which are individual. He never claimed that he was able to give a pupil knowledge which he or she did not already possess; but said that all he did was to arrange the pupil's knowledge in a new way. An added perspective brings the individual within his own field of observation—but not in any trite sense of knowing whether he walks with a slouch, has a bad temper, or prefers to put on his left sock first in the mornings. Such minor observations may serve as an aid to greater objectivity, but the relativization of self is an existential experience and involves the total organism. As a greater and more comprehensive detachment becomes possible, it is open to the individual to decide how extensive he feels that this should be. How will he take the theatrical universe? On the terms of the mystics, of those who are Puritans in the renunciation of their illusory ego—or in a more Nietzschean way like E. R. Eddison? For Eddison accepts the notion of the universe as theater, and yet finds it quite possible to will an acceptance of the play in progress. He suggests that there may be "no *necessity* for these peculiar and (to us) inconvenient arrangements, but that—for the moment—they are amusing." He explains the fact that "they are far from *amusing* to *us* here and now" as a failure of human faith in any real immortality. But it is possible to adopt his attitude even if we believe that death is absolute.

Watts and the semi-Theosophical writers of the ways of liberation tend toward the Puritan interpretation. They approve of men of the Tao, detached and unassertive; men who recognize the illusory nature of the ego and are content to allow themselves to be "existed in." Yet if the ego is such a harmful human attribute, why was it developed? The answer is that most tasks—among them the most essential tasks of physical survival—demand the sensation of "I" to carry them through. A man who really and in every particular lived out an ego-less philosophy would soon not trouble to feed himself; and societies pervaded by such passive philosophies are the static societies, in whose conditions an attitude of acceptance is the only way to approach an intolerable existence. It has often been remarked that Taoism was developed in a China where life was all but insupportable; where wars and natural disasters were everyday currency, and where a stoical acceptance of these inevitable tragedies was an invaluable aid to survival. The unsettled condition of the contemporary West has seen a flight to the consolations of Oriental wisdom, and there is no doubt that the success of a discipline like that of the Work has come about partly in response to human necessity. It would be a hard man who condemned out of hand all such helpful philosophies. Yet to Western minds they will always have about them something of the effete.

To be able to maintain an attitude of detachment in the face of great personal loss or hardship is a faculty to be envied. But to a man who wants to lead an active life, it will seem to be no more than a useful weapon in his psychological armory, to be brought out on occasion. By all means allow your "ego" to dissolve if it is overwhelmingly assailed by misfortune. But you will waste the very short time at your disposal if you live semi-permanently in a dispersed condition. If you want to make the most out of the play in progress—and for "you" there will be no other play—you should collect about you the shards of some serviceable persona as soon as possible, literally *pull yourself together* and jump back into the ring. You may have learned in the Work that you can play many more roles than you had ever imagined were possible for you—but unless you propose to devote your life to contemplation, you had better get out there and play them. And—whatever the arguments of Watts and the proponents of a "unified field of consciousness"—you do appear to possess an organism which has to be manipulated. From time to time you may decide that, for example, your vision of the world is situated inside you rather than outside, that there is in fact no separation between observer and observed. But unless you are a very unusual person, your prevailing mode of consciousness is liable to maintain the illusion of separation. Even assuming that you could ever be certain that this *was* an illusion and not just another metaphor, you would still have to operate within the convention. *Even an illusion of self creates the reality.*

Let us suppose that we make our bow in the direction of the *anima mundi* and obtain the taste of a "liberated consciousness." What we do with it will be entirely a matter of temperament and vocation. (It might be more accurate to say, what *it* does with *us.*) It is open to the individual player to rejoin the game with renewed zest and vigor. This may also be the Tao, the way "which is not the constant way." If the game he is playing requires a high degree of ego-identification, the individual may even choose to regard the decision to play it as his own. Although the man who chooses "the way of the straw dogs" may be purer, calmer, more "in touch with himself" than the man who chooses to play another game, other games *must* be played, perhaps with great energy, apparent submersion in events, and ultimate futility in the eyes of the philosopher. We are presented with a version of Pascal's "Wager," and the dice are loaded in favor of the man of action. If the philosopher of the Ways is "wrong," the game-player will be "right." But if the philosopher is right, the game-player must be right anyway. He cannot lose.

Much of this history of the Work has concerned pathological material both in Gurdjieff's and in the clinical sense of the term. This is because in order to rid a pupil of his delusions, the teachers of the Fourth Way have first to elicit a full expression of them, then to encourage the pupil to act upon his illusory concept of the world until he discovers his error. And because the teachers have to absorb the projections of successive generations of pupils, their images are inflated beyond all measure. Kathleen Raine has compared the relationship of Ouspensky to Gurdjieff with those of Trotsky to Lenin and Jung to Freud. She remarks that "the spiritual stature, or spiritual pride of these two men, invites ambitious comparison."

To some extent she is correct: both Gurdjieff and Ouspensky sometimes nodded. The guru may occasionally believe in himself. But what Miss Raine is really criticizing are the accumulated projections of Work pupils, which compose the icons of Gurdjieff and the other teachers for posterity. Much of what is visible in the story of the Harmonious Circle is madness or the result of madness; deliberately induced so that it should destroy itself. Much may appear to be madness which is not so in fact; for how can a teacher of the Fourth Way write books about Gurdjieff without reinforcing the legend of the source of his own authority? There are also madnesses which the Work has encouraged despite itself. But all this—and numerous reservations about the methods of the Work—should not be allowed to hide the fact that underneath the apparent lunacy lies a technique of extraordinary interest.

The achievements of Gurdjieff and his followers are large enough to escape devaluation by talk of "Gurdjieff's mission" or "a new age." The Work is a method of higher education which has been of great benefit to large numbers of people. If we consider it as "psychodrama," it has an enormous advantage over all other forms in that for a considerable time the pupil may not suspect that the situations in which he finds himself are manufactured. Far from being inhuman, this is the Work's final justification. It removes the possibility—which invalidates all other forms of psychodrama—that the patient will respond in an artificial manner to situations which he knows are themselves artificial. Because the teacher's knowledge is unknown, his powers infinite, and his manifest nature elicited by his pupil's unconscious, the situations in which a pupil is placed are more real to him than those he encounters day by day. As soon as he begins to suspect the true objective of the process—he is waking up.

The enlightenment offered by the Work can, of course, be as easily obtained in the course of ordinary life. Gurdjieff's objection was that it cannot be obtained quickly enough. The Sly Man takes "a little pill," and saves years of useless agony chasing daydreams. But it is also true that Gurdjieff, as Arnold Keyserling says, "described Hell." We do not all of us live all the time in the nethermost regions. And it cannot really be argued that if someone approaches a teacher of the Fourth Way, he is automatically in need of help: for simply by practicing as an "esoteric teacher," the guru creates the impression that there is something to be learned. As such he is a gigantic irrelevancy, a creator of sleep rather than wakefulness, and the chief enemy of his own function. On the other hand, he might reply that to disabuse a person of the illusion that he can learn from anyone at all was only the next step in a process of awakening which had already proceeded some way in the course of nature.

And what of the biographer, puzzled by the historical glyph and the sense of sacred time? He also has withdrawn his projections. Some time ago we left him posing as a scribe contemplating the mysteries of the Christian Church as interpreted by Origen. In Ptolemy's library at Alexandria he has set down his pen at the end of the last roll of vellum. For a moment he toys with the idea of shuffling the different sheets, chopping them in odd pieces and handing them in a bag to those who would have read his book. There would be a certain faithfulness in that, although little practicality. He sighs and begins to gather up the vellum sheets. He does not want to encourage anyone to enter the Fourth Way; but if a person is set on the encounter, he cannot prevent them. If this is abdication, it is the abdication which is always the only honest answer.

In the corridors of the library at Alexandria it is dark and twilight-colored. Figures hurry along with a padding of sandals, and sometimes the scribe bumps into them. Glancing through a door he sees the stars are out, and beneath them the variety and promise of the night. Suddenly he laughs. As if his own opinions mattered to anyone but himself. Like Pilate in the Christian books he has just been reading, the scribe mentally washes his hands. He steps through the doorway and out of the cloistered gloom.

On through the world outside.

> *The end of mystification*
> *Is not the end of mystery*
> *And the mark of the wise*
> *Is not the search for wisdom:*
> *Here at the junction of illusions*
> *(Spirit and matter)*
> *Rests that self-regarding episode*
> *Called Man.*

Sources

In the preface I briefly explained that I was prevented from naming or acknowledging some of my informants. With the knowledge of the various schisms, personal enmities, and conflicting points of view which have bedeviled the "visible" history of the Work, the reader is in a better position to appreciate that certain people might not want their identities revealed; and that I therefore decided to suppress even the names of those with no objections to being cited, if their part in the story was relatively minor. I have kept a record of the source of all information derived from interviews and personal communications which is unattributed in the text, in case this should be of interest to scholars.

Because there must be so much unpublished material which I have not seen—and which may never be published—the bibliography which follows cannot hope to be complete, and I have therefore been encouraged to be selective.

A: Works of the major figures
Writings of G. I. Gurdjieff
The writings ascribed to Gurdjieff present a number of problems. His method of writing "in committee" in fact makes it difficult to assess his personal responsibility for any particular piece of work; and often—as in the cases of *Glimpses of Truth* and *The Struggle of the Magicians*—the real execution of an idea was left to a pupil. The *Third Series* exists in a number

of forms, all incomplete, but some less so than others. (For example, I have seen two typescript versions, both of which differ considerably from one another, and neither of which includes much material contained in the published version.) There are also several different typescript versions of *Beelzebub's Tales*.

Herald of Coming Good (Paris, 1933).

All and Everything: First Series: Beelzebub's Tales to his Grandson (first edition, London and New York, 1950) revised edition, 3 vols., London and New York, 1974; German translation: *Alle und Alles* (Innsbruck, 1951). French translation: *Du tout et de tout* (Paris, 1956).

Second Series: Meetings with Remarkable Men (London and New York, 1963).

Third Series: Life is Real, only then, when I AM (incomplete: private publication, ·New York, 1975).

Lectures and Talks of Gurdjieff

Views from the Real World (London, 1974). Preface by Jeanne de Salzmann. A better translation of *Glimpses of Truth* than that printed here exists in typescript—probably by Ouspensky.

Les Comptes-Rendus. Unpublished talks and records of answers to questions of Paris groups, March 1943–December 1946. Record of at least a dozen sessions.

Narcotics and Hormones (Cape Town, 1949). Notes by Ouspensky of Gurdjieff's pronouncements on these subjects, some of which do not appear in *In Search of the Miraculous*. Various unpublished talks not included in *Views from the Real World* are preserved in the Toomer Collection in the Library, Fisk University, Nashville, Tennessee.

Gurdjieff Through His Pupils

The Struggle of the Magicians (Cape Town, 1957). The "ballet scenario," inspired by Gurdjieff with the cooperation of pupils in Tiflis and Constantinople. In its printed form, chiefly the literary work of Ouspensky.

Institute for the Harmonious Development of Man: prospectuses for the Tiflis, Constantinople and Fontainebleau Institutes. Extracts from the Tiflis prospectus are printed in *In Search of the Miraculous;* Bennett prints the Constantinople prospectus in *Gurdjieff: Making a New World;* and the Fontainebleau prospectus (largely the work of Ouspensky) exists both in the French form of 1923 and the American translation of 1924. For the former, see the copy in the Warburg Institute, for the latter, the Toomer Collection. Gurdjieff reproduced part of this prospectus in *Herald of Coming Good*.

"L'Art de l'Antique Orient Revivra," in the *Echo des Champs Elysées* no.

37, 1923. (Program of the demonstration of movements at Christmas 1923.) In 1950–51 the Société Janus issued some of the Gurdjieff-de Hartmann music, and more is available privately.

Writings of P. D. Ouspensky

By the time that Ouspensky's *Occult Tales* were published in Petrograd in 1916, he had also published *Kinemodrama* (the original version of *Strange Life of Ivan Osokin*), *The Fourth Dimension*, *Superman* and *What is Yoga?* In 1913 his *The Inner Circle* appeared. For remarks on the incorporation of the last four titles in *A New Model of the Universe*, see Part 2, chapter 11. Ouspensky's works published in English translation are:

The Symbolism of the Tarot (translated by A. L. Pogossky, St. Petersburg, 1913). Later reprinted with alterations in *A New Model of the Universe*.

Tertium Organum (first edition, St. Petersburg, 1912; revised edition, Petrograd, 1916). First English translation by Nicholas Bessaraboff and Claude Bragdon, Rochester, N. Y. 1920; revised by Ouspensky, London, 1923. New and revised translation by Eugenie Kadloubovsky, Cape Town, 1950; abridged edition, Fairfax Hall, Cape Town, 1961.

"Letters from Russia," in the *New Age*, September 4, November 27, December 4, December 11, December 18, December 25, 1919.

A New Model of the Universe (first edition translated by R. R. Merston, London and New York, 1931; second revised edition, London and New York, 1934).

In Search of the Miraculous (New York, 1949; London, 1950).

Strange Life of Ivan Osokin (London, 1947).

The Benevolent Devil (London and New York, 1973). Translation of *Occult Tales* by K. Petroff, Petrograd, 1916, which also includes the short story "The Inventor."

The Psychology of Man's Possible Evolution (first edition, London, 1947; new edition incorporating Ouspensky's "Bibliographical Notes," New York, 1974).

Lectures and Talks of Ouspensky

A Record of some of the Meetings held by P. D. Ouspensky between 1930 and 1947 (Cape Town, 1951).

A Further Record . . . 1928–1945 (Cape Town, 1952).

The two *Records* provided material for three short syntheses, *Memory, extracts from the Sayings and Writings of P. D. Ouspensky about Memory, Self-Remembering and Recurrence* (Cape Town, 1953), *Negative Emotions* (Cape Town, 1953), *Surface Personality* (Cape Town, 1954), and for the comprehensive synthesis edited anonymously by Eugenie Kadloubovsky, *The Fourth Way* (London and New York, 1957.)

Writings of A. R. Orage

This list excludes Orage's writings on political and economic topics. For a survey of these, see the books by Wallace Martin and Philip Mairet in list B below.

Frederick Nietzsche, the Dionysian Spirit of the Age (London and Edinburgh, 1906).

Nietzsche in Outline and Aphorism (London and Edinburgh, 1907).

Consciousness, Animal, Human and Superhuman (London and Benares, 1907).

Articles in *The Theosophical Review:* "The Wise Way" and "Halt! What goes there?," vol. 38; "The Comparative Study of Religions" and "What is man?," vol. 39; these attacked by Dr. Montague Lomax, and the attack countered by Orage in ibid.; "After Ten Years," "Occult Faculty" and "In Defense of Agnosticism," vol. 39; "The New Romanticism," "Theoretical and Real Morality" and "Wanted—Proofs of Reincarnation," vol. 40.

The New Age (London: see especially 1907–21).

Readers and Writers, 1917–1921, "by R. H. C." (London, 1922).

"Unedited opinions," in *The New Republic,* vols. 39, 41, 45.

"An Editor's Progress," four articles originally published in *Commonweal,* 3, and reprinted in the *New Age* in five parts in March–April 1926.

The Art of Reading (New York, 1930).

Psychological Exercises (New York, 1930).

Selected Essays and Critical Writings (edited by Herbert Read and Denis Saurat, London, 1935). Incorporates "On Love," "On Religion," and "Talks with Katherine Mansfield."

The New English Weekly (London: especially 1932).

"My Note-Book," in *The Aryan Path,* August 1933–October 1934.

Essays and Aphorisms (London, 1954).

The Active Mind: Adventures in Awareness (London, 1954).

Orage as Critic (edited by Wallace Martin, London, 1974).

Orage Through his Pupils

Notes of Jean Toomer in the Toomer Collection.

Charles Daly King, *The Oragean Version* (New York, 1951).

C. S. Nott, *Teachings of Gurdjieff* (London, 1961). Contains Orage's commentary on *Beelzebub's Tales.*

Writings of Maurice Nicoll

The "Martin Swayne" novels:

The Bishop and the Lady (London, 1909).

Lord Richard in the Pantry (London, 1911).

The Sporting Instinct (London, 1912).
Cupid goes North (London, 1913).
The Blue Germ (London, 1918).

In Mesopotamia (London, 1917).
Dream Psychology (first edition, London 1917; second edition, London 1920).
"Why is the 'Unconscious' Unconscious?," symposium with Ernest Jones and W. H. R. Rivers, in *British Journal of Psychology*, October 1918.
The New Man (London, 1950).
Living Time (London, 1952).
Psychological Commentaries on the Teaching of G. I. Gurdjieff and P. D. Ouspensky (5 vols., London 1952–6).
The Mark (London, 1954).

Writings of Jean Toomer
Cane (New York, 1923; reprinted 1969 with an introduction by Arna Bontemps).
Essentials (Chicago, 1931).
Portage Potential (unpublished).
From Exile into Being (fragmentary unpublished autobiography, in Toomer Collection).
The Flavour of Man (lecture delivered to a Quaker youth group, Philadelphia, 1949).

The Toomer Papers
Besides Toomer's unpublished writings and his correspondence with Orage, Margaret Naumburg, Mabel Dodge Luhan, Gorham Munson, Waldo Frank and other prominent figures, the Toomer Collection at Fisk University, Nashville, Tennessee, includes Toomer's own notes on his practice of the Gurdjieff Method, fragmentary notes on Gurdjieff, and copies of typescript material circulated among Work groups.

Publications of Rodney Collin
Palms and Patios (London, 1931).
The Theory of Eternal Life (first edition, London, 1950; Spanish edition, Tlalpam, 1951; second English edition, London, 1956).
Hellas (Tlalpam, 1950; London, 1951).
El Pyramide del Fuego (Tlalpam, 1953).
The Christian Mystery (Tlalpam, 1953; English edition, 1954).
The Whirling Ecstasy (Tlalpam, 1954). Translation form Fr. C. Huart's French translation of Aflahi's *Lives of the Gnostics* (Paris, 1944).

The Herald of Harmony (Spanish and English edition, Tlalpam, 1954).

The Theory of Celestial Influence (Spanish edition, Tlalpam, 1952; first English edition, London, 1954).

The Theory of Conscious Harmony (London, 1958). Extracts from the letters of Rodney Collin with a "Biographical Note" and a section on "Cuzco." I have been able to check certain unpublished letters against this edition and found it accurate.

The Mirror of Light, from the notebooks of Rodney Collin (London, 1959). Unreliable selection, including material which the editor admits is probably not by Collin.

Unpublished Writings

"Last Remembrances of a Magician." Memoir of Ouspensky and Rodney Collin's interpretation of the last days at Lyne Place.

"A Programme of Study." Dated "Mexico, 1955."

Writings of J. G. Bennett:

The Crisis in Human Affairs (London, 1948).

What Are We Living For? (London, 1949).

Gurdjieff: the making of a new world (typescript lectures delivered at Denison House, London, in October 1949).

Concerning Subud (London, 1958).

Approaching Subud (New York, 1962).

Christian Mysticism and Subud, (London, 1961).

Witness (first edition, London, 1962; enlarged edition, Kingston on Thames, 1971).

Gurdjieff: a Very Great Enigma (Kingston on Thames, 1963).

Energies: Material Vital, Cosmic (Kingston on Thames, 1964).

A Spiritual Psychology (London, 1964).

Long Pilgrimage (London, 1965).

The Dramatic Universe (4 vols., London, 1956–66).

Gurdjieff: Making a New World (London, 1973).

Various minor publications consisting chiefly of records of Bennett's lectures have since appeared.

B: Select bibliography of other Work literature or literature of a general importance for the history of the Work

The Adelphi (London: see especially 1923–25 and Murry's article of November, 1950).

Anderson, Margaret, *My Thirty Years' War* (New York and London, 1930); *The Fiery Fountains* (London, 1953); *The Unknowable Gurdjieff* (London, 1962); *The Strange Necessity* (New York, 1969).

Antébi, Elizabeth, *Ave Lucifer* (Paris, 1972).

Bechhofer Roberts, Carl, *In Denikin's Russia* (London, 1921); *A Wanderer's Log* (London, 1922); "The Forest Philosophers," in *The Century*, May 1924; *Let's Begin Again* (London, 1940).

Beresford, J. D., "Personal and Impersonal Methods," in *The Aryan Path*, October 1930; "The Discovery of the Self," 3 parts in ibid., March–May 1931; "Automatism," in ibid., November–December 1931; "Will and Wish," in ibid., October 1934; *The Case for Faith-Healing* (London, 1934).

Bland, Rosamund (Rosamund Sharp), *Extracts from Nine Letters written at the beginning of P. D. Ouspensky's London work in 1921* (London, 1952).

Bowyer, E. C. et al., Reports on the Fontainebleau Institute in *The Daily News*, February 15–27, 1923.

Bragdon, Claude, Introduction to 1920 edition of *Tertium Organum; Merely Players* (New York, 1929); *The Secret Springs* (London, 1939).

Butkovsky-Hewitt, Anna, *With Gurdjieff in St. Petersburg and Paris* (London, 1978).

Caruso, Dorothy, *Dorothy Caruso: a personal history* (New York, 1952).

Cohen, J. M., "In the Work" (unpublished radio script, first broadcast January 5, 1966).

Collin-Smith, Joyce, "Beloved Icarus," in *Astrological Journal*, vol. XIII, no. 4, autumn 1971).

Cosgrave, John O'Hara, *The Academy for Souls*, (New York, 1931); *Man: a citizen of the Universe* (New York, 1947).

Daumal, René, *La Grande Beuverie* (Paris, 1939); *Le Mont Analogue* (Paris, 1952), translated by Roger Shattuck as *Mount Analogue* (London, 1959); *Lettres à ses amis* (vol. I, Paris, 1958); *Essaies et notes* (2 vols., Paris, 1972).

The Enneagram (Sherborne, Gloucestershire, March 1975—).

Frank, Waldo, *Our America* (New York, 1919); as "Searchlight," "Mystery in a Sack Suit," in *Times Exposures* (New York, 1926); *The Rediscovery of America* (New York and London, 1929); *Chart for Rough Water* (New York, 1940).

Guide and Index to G. I. Gurdjieff's All and Everything (Toronto, 1973).

Harton, Marjorie von, *A Way of Living* (Kingston on Thames, 1974).

Hartmann, Thomas and Olga de, *Our Life with Mr. Gurdjieff* (New York, 1964).

Hastings, Beatrice, *The Old New Age: Orage and Others* (London, 1936).

Hermès (Paris), special number 1967–68, *La Voie de René Daumal.*

Hoffman, Maud, "Taking the Life Cure in Gurdjieff's School," in *New York Times*, February 10, 1924.

Hulme, Kathryn, *Undiscovered Country* (London, 1967).

Jackson, Holbrook, "A. R. Orage: personal recollections," in *The Windmill* (1948), vol. 3, no. 11.

Kaffian, Adele, "The Last Days of Katherine Mansfield," in *The Adelphi*, October–December 1946.

King, Charles Daly, as 'Robert Courtney' *Beyond Behaviorism* (New York, 1927); *The Psychology of Consciousness* (London, 1932); *The Oragean Version* (New York, 1951); *The States of Human Consciousness* (New York, 1963). Two unpublished MSS., *The Order of Decline*, and *Heritage: a social interpretation of the history of ancient Egypt*, as well as a collection of Daly King's letters, are in the Warburg Institute, University of London. The unpublished works contain numerous references to Daly King's papers contributed to learned journals during the 1940s.

Kenney, Rowland, *Westering* (London, 1939).

Keyserling, Arnold, *Geschichte der Denkstile* (Vienna, 1968); *Klaviatur des Denkens* (Vienna, 1971); *Chakrale Musik* (Vienna, 1972); with Wilhelmine Keyserling, *Das Rosenkreuz* (Innsbruck, 1957).

Koch, Walter, "Gurdjjew der Schwarzmagier," in *Mensch und Schicksal*, nos. 5–6, May/June 1957.

Kohler, Marianne, *À l'Ecole de Sagesse* (Paris, 1961).

Landau, Rom, *God is My Adventure* (London, 1935).

Lea, F. E., *The Life of John Middleton Murry* (London, 1959).

Leblanc, Georgette, *Maeterlink and I* (Translated by Janet Flanner, London, 1932); *La Machine à Courage* (Paris, 1947).

The Little Review (Chicago, New York and Paris, 1914–29; especially final number, May 1929).

Luhan, Mabel Dodge, *Lorenzo in Taos* (London, 1933).

Mairet, Philip, *A. R. Orage, a Memoir* (first edition, London, 1936; revised edition, New York, 1966).

Mansfield, Katherine, *The Letters of Katherine Mansfield* (2 vols., London, 1928); *Katherine Mansfield's Letters to John Middleton Murry, 1913–1922* (London, 1951); *The Journal of Katherine Mansfield* (London, 1954).

Martin, Wallace, *The New Age under Orage* (London, 1967).

"Masierevitch," Constance (writing anonymously), *On the Four Quartets of T. S. Eliot* (London, 1953); *The Mysteries of the Seed* (Mexico, 1954).

Mouravieff, Boris, *Ouspensky, Gurdjieff et les Fragments d'un Enseignement Inconnu* (Geneva, 1956), reprint from *Synthèses*, 138; *Gnosis* (3 vols., Paris, 1961–65).

Murry, John Middleton, *God* (London, 1929); *Between Two Worlds* (London, 1935).

Needleman, Jacob, *The New Religions* (London, 1972).

The New English Weekly, "A. R. Orage Memorial Number," November 15, 1934.

The New Republic (New York: especially 1924–29).

Nott, C. S., *Teachings of Gurdjieff* (London, 1961); *Journey Through this World* (London, 1969).

"Olgivanna" (Lloyd Wright), "The Last Days of Katherine Mansfield," in *The Bookman* (New York), March 1931; *The Struggle Within* (New York, 1955).

Pauwels, Louis, "Quelques mois chez Gurdjieff," in *Nouvelle Revue Française*, December 1, 1953; *Monsieur Gurdjieff* (Paris, 1954), abbreviated translation, *Gurdjieff* (Douglas, Isle of Man, 1964); *Saint Quelqu'un* (Paris 1946), translated by Bernard Miall as *Not into Clean Hands* (London, 1948); *Les voies de petite communication* (Paris, 1949–50).

Peters, Fritz, *Boyhood with Gurdjieff* (London, 1964); *Gurdjieff Remembered* (London, 1965).

Pogson, Beryl, *Maurice Nicoll, a Portrait* (London, 1961). In addition, her Shakespearean studies, *In the East My Pleasure Lies* (London, 1951), *Three Plays by Shakespeare* (London, 1963) and a volume *Royalty of Nature* (n. d.), have been issued. Some *Work Talks* have also been privately printed.

Popoff, Irmis Barrett, *Gurdjieff: his work on myself, with others, for the Work* (New York, 1969).

Random, Michel, *Les Puissances de dedans* (Paris, 1966); *Le Grand Jeu* (2 vols., Paris, 1970).

Rewelliotty, Irène-Carole, *Journal d'une jeune fille* (Paris 1946). Selected extracts translated in Pauwels, *M. Gurdjieff.*

Reyner, J. H., *The Universe of Relationships* (London, 1960); *God Beyond Time* (London, 1965).

Ropp, Robert de, *Drugs and the Mind* (New York, 1957); *The Master Game*, (New York, 1968); *Sex Energy* (New York, 1969).

Saurat, Denis, "Visite à Gurdjieff," in *Nouvelle Revue Française*, November 1933; "A study of Beelzebub's Tales," in Pauwels, *M. Gurdjieff.*

Schaeffer, Pierre, "The Old Man and the Children of the Age," in Pauwels, *Mr. Gurdjieff; Le Gardien de Volcan* (Paris, 1969).

Seabrook, William, *Witchcraft, its Power in the World Today* (London, 1941).

Selver, Paul, *Orage and the New Age Circle* (London, 1959).

Serant, Paul, *Le Meurtre Rituel* (Paris, 1951).

Sharp, Clifford (writing as "C"), "The Forest Philosophers," article in two parts in *The New Statesman*, March 3–17, 1923.

Systematics, the Journal of the Institute for Comparative Study of History, Philosophy and the Sciences (Kingston on Thames, 1963—).

Tracol, Henri, *Georges Ivanovitch Gurdjieff: l'eveil et la pratique de 'rappel-de-soi'* (Paris, 1967).

Travers, P. L., "Gurdjieff," in *Man, Myth and Magic* (London, 1970–72), articles arranged alphabetically.

Walker, Kenneth, *The Intruder* (London, 1936); *Venture with Ideas* (London, 1951); *A study of Gurdjieff's Teaching* (London, 1957); *The Making of Man* (London, 1963).

Welch, William, *What Happened in Between* (New York, 1972).

Young, James, "An Experiment at Fontainebleau," in *The New Adelphi*, September 1927.

Zigrosser, Carl, "Gurdjieff," in *The New Republic*, June 5, 1929; *Mine Own Shall Come to Me* (1971).

C: Sources for particular episodes and selected background reading (works adequately identified in the text are not listed)

Generally on Georgia and Armenia, see D. M. Lang, *A Modern History of Georgia* (London, 1962) and Sirarpie de Nersessian, *The Armenians* (London, 1969). The best guide to the circumstances of Gurdjieff's childhood is James Bryce, *Transcaucasia and Ararat* (fourth edition, London, 1896). Richard G. Hovannisian, *Armenia on the Road to Independence* (Berkeley and Los Angeles, 1967) is a good introduction to Armenian politics of the period; of Edward Ellis Smith, *The Young Stalin* (London, 1968) for Stalin's youthful political involvements. H. V. Hilprecht (ed.) *Explorations in Bible Lands during the Nineteenth Century* (Edinburgh, 1903) and A. Lobanov-Rostovsky, *Russia and Asia* (New York, 1933) are useful introductions to the archeological and imperialistic questions; David Fraser, *The Marches of Hindustan* (Edinburgh and London, 1908) is a near-contemporary account of archeological and scientific exploration in Central Asia. A good idea of the religious chaos prevailing in the Caucasus during the nineteenth century can be gained from F. C. Conbeare's introduction to *The Key of Truth* (Oxford, 1898).

On Dordjieff, Badmaieff, and Ukhtomsky, see W. A. Unkrig, "Aus den letzten Jarhzehnten des Lamaismus in Russland," in *Zeitschrift für Buddhismus und verwandte Gebiete*, vol. VII (1926); Robert A. Rupen, "The Buryat Intelligentsia," in *Far East Quarterly*, vol. 15; P. L. Mehra, "Tibet and Russian Intrigue," in *Journal of the Royal Central Asian Society*, 1958; Alastair Lamb, "Some Notes on Russian Intrigue in Tibet," ibid.; Wilhelm Filchner, *Sturm über Asien* (Berlin, 1924); (English summary in

JRCAS, 1927); *Zakulissnaya politischeskaya rabota Badmayeva* ("Badmaieff's political work behind the scenes"), for translations from which I am indebted to Mrs. Marina Corby; René Füllop-Miller, *Rasputin, the Holy Devil* (London and New York, 1928); Peter Fleming, *Bayonets to Lhasa* (London, 1961); Sir C. A. Bell, *Portrait of the Dalai Lama* (London, 1946); David MacDonald, *Twenty Years in Tibet* (London, 1932), Percival Landon, *Lhasa* (2 vols., London, 1905); Prince Esper Ukhtomsky, *Travels in the East of Nicholas II, Emperor of Russia, 1890–91* (2 vols., London, 1896 and 1900); foreword to the catalogue by Albert Grünwedel of his lamaistic collection, *Mythologie des Buddhismus in Tibet und der Mongolei* (Leipzig, 1900); and H. S. Olcott, *Old Diary Leaves* (Madras, 1895–1935), series 4 and 6.

The exploits of Ushe Narzunoff are recorded in J. Deniker, "La Premiere photographie de Lhasa," in *La Geographie*, vol. IV, no. 10, October 15, 1901–04. (Deniker's further articles in *La Geographie*, July 15, 1901, November 15, 1903, and especially February 15, 1906); Deniker, "New Light on Lhasa, the Forbidden City," in *The Century*, August 1903; "Trois Voyages à Lhasa (1898–1901) par Ovche Narzunoff, Polerin Kalmouk," in *Le Tour du Monde*, vol. 10, new series, 1904. From the British side, see the Foreign Office document, FO 17 1551 / 39, "Alleged Missions Between Russia and Tibet" (in the Public Record Office); and 'Political and Secret' file for 1921 in the India Office Library, L/PS/11 /195 / P146 / 8, which contains a report by Younghusband on Dordjieff and Narzunoff; and the records of the Foreign Department, Government of India, for June 1900 under "Nurzynoff." See also the *Blue Book, Tibet* (London, 1904) for extracts from the Russian press on the Dordjieff Mission; *The Graphic*, August 17, 1901, for photograph of the Mission in St. Petersburg; and Alexandra David-Neel, "Gurdjieff et Dordjieff," in *Nouvelles Litterarires*, April 22, 1954.

On Russian occultism at the turn of the century, see my own *The Occult Establishment* (La Salle, Ill., 1976). For the cultural background, see Nicholas Zernov, *The Russian Religious Renaissance of the Twentieth Century* (London, 1963); Prince D. P. Mirsky, *Contemporary Russian Literature* (London, 1926); N. O. Lossky, *History of Russian Philosophy* (New York, 1951); cf. Camilla Gray, *The Great Experiment* (London, 1962). On Anthroposophy in Russia, see e.g. Nicholas Berdyaev, *Dream and Reality* (London, 1950); on Theosophy, see "Alba," "Theosophy in Russia," in *Theosophy in Scotland*, vol. I (1910–11). See also E. J. Dingwall (ed.) *Abnormal Hypnotic Phenomena*, vol. III (London, 1968). Ottone Penzig was in close contact with Russian Theosophists: see his *Die Theosophie und die Theosophische Gesellschaft* (Berlin, 1914). For "Ozay," see Paul Dukes, *The Unending Quest* (London, 1950).

For conditions in south Russia during the civil war, Bechhofer Roberts,

In Denikin's Russia, is one of the best sources; see also George A. Brinkley, *The Volunteer Army and Allied Intervention in South Russia 1917–1921* (Notre Dame, 1966); Sir Harry Luke, *Cities and Men,* vol. II (London, 1953); and General Harrington's *Report on Russian refugee situation at Constantinople,* December 3, 1920 (PRO file WO 32 / 5726).

On Salzmann, Dalcroze, Hellerau, and the Progressives, see the files of *Jugend,* especially 1907–09; Emile Jaques-Dalcroze, "Rhythm as a Factor in Education" (translated from *Le Rhythme,* December 1909); Frank Martin, Tibor Denes, Alfred Berchtold, Henri Gagnebin, Bernard Reichtel, Claire-Lise Dutoit, Edmond Stadler, *Emile Jaques-Dalcroze* (Neuchatel, 1965); *Cahiers Paul Claudel,* no. 53 (Paris, 1961) and no. 5 (Paris, 1964); Alexander de Salzmann, "Licht, Belichtung und Beleuchtung," in *Der Rhythmus* (Jena), 1912; Darius Milhaud, *Notes Without Music* (translated by D. Evans, edited by Rollo Myers, London, 1952); Edwin Muir, *An Autobiography* (London 1954).

Additional material on Orage can be found in Mary Gawsthorpe, *Up Hill to Holloway* (n.d.); Martin Cumberland, *Set Down in Malice* (London, 1919); Samuel Hynes, *Edwardian Occasions* (London, 1972); David S. Thatcher, *Nietzsche in England, 1890–1914* (Toronto, 1972); *The Leeds Art Club* (program and list of objects in Leeds Public Library); see also Edwin Muir, *An Autobiography* (London, 1954), Willa Muir, *Belonging* (London, 1968), and my own *The Occult Establishment* for Orage and Mitrinović. On Crowley's involvement with the Sullivan-Beresford group, see John Symonds, *The Great Beast* (revised edition, London, 1971); for early psychoanalysis, J. B. Hobman, *David Eder, memoirs of a modern pioneer* (London, 1945). Anthony Alpers, *Katherine Mansfield* (London, 1954), Roland Merlin, *Le Drame secret de Katherine Mansfield* (Paris, 1950), J. Middleton Murry (ed.), *The Scrapbook of Katherine Mansfield* (London, 1939), *The Collected Letters of D. H. Lawrence,* (edited by H. T. Moore, 2 vols., London, 1962), *The Quest for Ramanim* (edited by G. J. Zytaruk, Montreal and London, 1970) provide further information on Murry, Lawrence, Katherine Mansfield and their response to Gurdjieff and Ouspensky. On Ouspensky's first arrival in London, see David Garnett, *The Flowers of the Forest* (London, 1955). John Carswell, *Lives and Letters* (London, 1978) discusses Orage, Beatrice Hastings, Katherine Mansfield and Middleton Murry. For another impression of the Prieuré, see Ian E. Black, *A Friend of France* (London, 1941). On the reaction to *The Adelphi,* see Hugh L. Anson Fausset, *A Modern Prelude* (London, 1933). Levinson's comments are reproduced in Pauwels, *M. Gurdjieff;* for the reception of the dances, see also Fernand Divoire, *Découvertes sur la danse* (Paris, 1924) and Jacques-Emile Blanche, *More Portraits of a Lifetime, 1918–1938* (London, 1939).

For Gurdjieff and Orage in the United Sates, Jean Toomer's correspondence is of primary importance. For the 1924 expedition, see also John Unterecker, *Voyager, a life of Hart Crane* (London, 1971); *The Letters of Hart Crane* (edited by Brom Weber, Berkeley and Los Angeles, 1965); Sue Jenkins Brown, *Robber Rocks* (Middletown, Conn., 1969); Llewelyn Powys, *The Verdict of Bridlegoose* (London, 1927); John Cooper Powys, *Autobiography* (second edition, London, 1967). On the general background to Orage's success in the United States, see Edmund Wilson, "The Literary Consequences of the Crash," in *The Shores of Light* (London, 1953); T. S. Matthews, *Name and Address* (London, 1961); Robert Morse Lovett, *All Our Years* (New York, 1948); Malcolm Cowley, *Exile's Return* (first edition, London, 1935; second edition, London 1967); Charles Forcey, *The Crossroads of Liberalism* (New York, 1961); Frederick J. Hoffmann, *The Twenties* (New York, 1955). On Gurdjieff as a legend of café society, see Elizabeth Sprigge, *Gertrude Stein* (London, 1957); Monk Gibbon, *The Masterpiece and the Man* (London, 1959); Kay Boyle and Robert McAlmon, *On Being Geniuses Together* (revised edition, London 1970). There may also be a portrait of him in R. H. Ward, "Monsieur X: the Fortune Teller," in *A Gallery of Mirrors* (London, 1956). On Taos, see Langston Hughes, *The Big Sea* (London, 1941) and E. W. Tedlock, Jr., "D. H. Lawrence's Annotation of Ouspensky's *Tertium Organum*," in *Texas Studies in Literature and Language*, vol. II, no. 2, Summer 1960. On Jean Toomer, see Robert A. Bone, *The Negro Novel in America* (New Haven, 1958). On Zona Gale, Margery Latimer and Jean Toomer, see August Derleth, *Still, Small Voice* (New York, 1940) and Harold P. Simonson, *Zona Gale* (New Haven, Conn., 1962). For influence of the Work, see Zona Gale, *Preface to a Life* (New York, 1926) and *Portage, Wisconsin and other Essays* (New York, 1928), and Margery Latimer's story "Original Sin," in *Nellie Bloom and Other Stories* (New York, 1929). William Bittner, *The Novels of Waldo Frank* (Philadelphia, 1958), contains biographical details on Frank.

On Orage's return to England, see Hugh Macdiarmid, *The Company I've Kept* (London, 1966); for Nicoll's background, see T. H. Darlow, *William Robertson Nicoll, Life and Letters* (London, 1925), Beryl Pogson prints Nicoll's account of Jung and a ghost in her *Maurice Nicoll*, and Jung's side is given in Fanny Moser (ed.) *Spuk* (Baden bei Zürich, 1950). Further on Nicoll, see David Scott Blackhall, *This House had Windows* (London, 1961). On Mrs. Bernard Shaw's enthusiasm for Ouspensky, see Janet Dunbar, *Mrs. GBS* (London, 1963); for the Frank Lloyd Wrights, see Finis Farr, *Frank Lloyd Wright* (London, 1962) and Robert C. Twombly, "Organic Living: Frank Lloyd Wright . . . and Georgi Gurdjieff . . . ," in *Wisconsin Magazine of History*, Winter 1974–5; on the Daumals, see also Max-Pol Fouchet, *Un jour, je m'en souviens* (Paris, 1968); for an impression of Gurdjieff just before his death, see "Genet" (Janet Flanner), "Letter from Paris," in *The New Yorker*, November 12, 1949.

Among the reviews and scattered critical articles on Gurdjieff, Ouspensky and their followers some supply information not found elsewhere, or provide particular insights into the subject. Some of the most important are: John O'Hara Cosgrave, "Time and Space," in *The Saturday Review of Literature*, July 25, 1931; Kenneth Burke, "In Quest of the Way," in *New Republic*, September 9, 1931; D. S. Savage, "The New Gnosticism," in *The Spectator*, April 28, 1950; Kathleen Raine, "Golden Thigh or Feet of Clay," in *The New Statesman*, June 10, 1950; Rom Landau, "A Modern Esoteric System," in *The Nineteenth Century and After*, July 1950; *Time* review of Kenneth Walker, *Venture with Ideas*, January 28, 1952; Robert Kemp, "Ames en quête," in *Nouvelles Litteraires*, March 18, 1954; Roger Bezault, "Cérémonie d'Execration sur Gurdjieff," in *Les Cahiers de la Pierre-qui-vire*, July 1954; Yahya Abdullah, "New Lamps for Old," in *Hibbert Journal*, October 1956; Rayner Heppenstall, "A Mechanical Prison," in the *New Statesman*, June 8, 1957; Richard Rees, "Monsieur Gurdjieff," in *The Twentieth Century*, November 1958; Manuel Rainord, "Gurdjieff revêlé par lui-meme," in *Critique*, 16:2 (1960); Edwin Seaver, "Solving the Human Enigma," in *The Saturday Review of Literature*, May 18, 1963; "Wisdom through Mystification," in *The Times Literary Supplement*, March 12, 1964. An interesting lecture delivered in New York, March 1, 1961, by Henry Leroy Finch, "The Gurdjieff Perspective Today," remains unpublished. Whitall N. Perry has published two parts of a three-part article on "Gurdjieff in the Light of Tradition," in *Studies in Comparative Religion*, Autumn, 1974 and Winter 1975. The books of Hugh l'Anson Fausset, *Towards Fidelity* (London, 1952), Richard Rees, *A Theory of My Time* (London, 1963) and Max-Pol Fouchet, *Les Appels* (Paris, 1967) present particular points of view. For the popular picture of Gurdjieff brought up to date, see Gilbert Guilleminault and Philippe Bernert, *Les Princes des Années Folles* (Paris, 1970).

Further on Schaeffer and Gurdjieff, see Marc Pierret, *Entretiens avec Pierre Schaeffer* (Paris, 1968). For Salmanov, see Ernst Jünger, *Das Zweite Pariser Tagebuch* (*Werke*, Band 3, *Tagebücher III*, Stuttgart, 1962) for March 30, 1943; on J. M. Hauer, see Walter Szmolyan, *Josef Matthias Hauer* (Vienna, 1965) and Monika Lichtenfeld, *Untersuchungen zur Theorie der Zwöftontechnik bei J. M. Hauer* (Regensburg, 1964).

A typescript account of Rodney Collin's death was circulated by Janet Collin-Smith soon after the events of Cuzco; the fullest biographical account is Joyce Colin-Smith, "Beloved Icarus." Anna Logan (i.e., Janet Collin-Smith), *Answering Gods* (Tlalpam, 1951) and G. Zodec, *Lessons in Religion for a Skeptical World* (Mexco City, 1956) provide additional material for the atmosphere of the Mexican group.

On Hugh Romney, see *East Village Other*, vol. 2, no. 17 and vol. 3, no. 4. For how Gurdjieff's ideas on theater have either influenced or run mysteriously parallel to those of the avant-garde, cf. Jerzy Grotowski, *Towards a Poor Theatre* (London, 1970), and foreword by Peter Brook.

Further reading on sources of and parallels with Gurdjieff's cosmology and philosophy might start with the following books and articles: Christopher Butler, *Number Symbolism* (London, 1970); Albert, Freiherr von Thimus, *Die Harmoniale Symbolik des Altertums* (2 vols., Cologne, 1868 and 1876); Jacques Handschün, "Ein mitterlälterlicher Beitrag zur Lehre der Spharenharmonik," in *Zeitschrift für Musikwissenschaft*, January 1927; F. E. Robbins, "The Tradition of Greek Arithmology," in *Classical Philology*, April 1921; Nichomachus of Gerassa, *Introduction to Arithmetic* (translated by Martin Luther D'Ooge, New York, 1926); Frances Yates, *The French Academies of the Sixteenth Century* (London, 1947); Cesare Vasoli, "Francesco Giorgio Veneto," in *Testi Umanistici su L'Ermetismo* (Rome 1955); P. J. Amman, "The Musical Theory and Philosophy of Robert Fludd," in *Journal of the Warburg and Courtauld Institutes*, 1967; Alain Daniélou, *Introduction to the Study of Musical Scales* (London, 1943) acknowledges the help of Ethel Merston of the Prieuré. On Cabala, see Gerschom Scholem, *Major Trends in Jewish Mysticism* (London, 1955), and *Gnosticism, Merkhaba Mysticism and Talmudic Tradition* (New York, 1960); see also J. L. Blau, *The Christian Interpretation of the Cabala in the Renaissance* (New York, 1944) and François Secret, *Les Kabbalistes Chretiens de la Renaissance* (Paris, 1964). On Lull and the Lullian Art, see J. N. Hillgarth, *Ramon Lull and Lullism in Fourteenth Century France* (Oxford, 1971) and E. W. Platzeck, *Ramon Lull* (2 vols. 1961).

For the belief that Syriac was the language of Christ, see B. F. Westcott, *A General survey of the History of the Canon of the New Testament* (7th ed., London 1896); for Armenian and Assyrian Christianity, see Archdeacon Dowding, *The Armenian Church* (London 1910); F. C. Burkitt, *Early Eastern Christianity* (London 1904); W. A. Wigram, *An Introduction into the History of the Assyrian Church* (London 1910); H. J. W. Drijvers, *Bardaissan of Edessa* (tr. G. E. van Baaren-Pape, Assen, 1966).

On Gnosticism see Hans Jonas, *The Gnostic Religion* (2nd ed., Boston, 1963); R. McL. Wilson, *The Gnostic Problem* (London, 1958); R. M. Grant, *Gnosticism, an Anthology* (London, 1961); on Victorian esoteric Christianity, see further Zernov, *Russian Religious Revival*, and William Kingsland, *The Esoteric Basis of Christianity* (London, 1895); Edward Conze, *Buddhism, Its Essence and Development* (Oxford, 1951) is a superb introduction to Buddhism, and the *Abhidhamma* can largely be read in the translations published by the Pali Text Society; D. T. Suzuki's *The Training of the Zen Buddhist Monk* (Kyoto, 1934) is almost too well known to need mention; cf. the Lama Angarika Govinda, *The Psychological Attitude of Early Buddhist Philosophy* (London, 1961).

On parallels with nineteenth-century occultists, see H. W. Schneider and G. Lawton, *A Prophet and a Pilgrim* (New York, 1942) for Thomas Lake Harris, A. Viatte, *Les Sources occultes du romantisme,* vol. I (Paris, 1928) for Martinès de Pasqually; Israel Regardie, *The Golden Dawn,* vol. IV (River Falls, Wisconsin, 1970) for the Golden Dawn's use of the enneagram; on the chakras see "Arthur Avalon" (Sir John Woodroffe) *The Serpent Power* (3rd ed., Madras, 1931), and the Theosophical version of C. W. Leadbeater, *The Chakras* (Adyar, 1927).

On psychodrama, see Jacob L. Moreno (ed.) *The Sociometry Reader* (Glencoe, Illinois, 1960); cf S. H. Foukes and E. J. Anthony, *Group Psychotherapy* (London, 1957) on the esoteric view of the theater, the essential work is Frances Yates, *Theatre of the World* (London, 1969); cf. also H. B. Hawkins, "All the World's a Stage" in *Shakespeare Quarterly,* 1966, and Jean Jacquot, "Le Theatre du monde" in *Revue de Littérature comparée,* 1957; on the Rosicrucians, see especially Frances Yates, *The Rosicrucian Enlightenment* (London, 1972); and on the ways of liberation, Allan Watts, *Pyschotherapy, East and West* (New York, 1961; London, 1971).

INDEX